BILATERAL STUDIES IN PRIVATE INTERNATIONAL LAW

NINA MOORE GALSTON, Editor

No. 4

AMERICAN-GERMAN PRIVATE INTERNATIONAL LAW

Second Edition
(revised and expanded)

by

ULRICH DROBNIG

Published for the
PARKER SCHOOL OF FOREIGN AND COMPARATIVE LAW
COLUMBIA UNIVERSITY IN THE CITY OF NEW YORK
WILLIS L. M. REESE, Director

by

OCEANA PUBLICATIONS, INC., DOBBS FERRY, NEW YORK
1972

Library of Congress Cataloging in Publication Data

Drobnig, Ulrich.

American-German private international law.

(Bilateral studies in private international law, no. 4)

Rev. and expanded ed. of American-German private law relations cases, 1945–1955, by M. Domke.

Includes bibliographical references.

1. Conflict of laws—Germany (Federal Republic, 1949–) 2. Conflict of laws—U.S. I. Domke, Martin, 1892– American-German private law relations cases, 1945–1955. II. Title. III. Series.

340'.9 79-132281

ISBN 0-379-11418-6

MANUFACTURED IN THE UNITED STATES OF AMERICA

Foreword

An earlier edition of this study was written by Dr. Martin Domke and published in 1956. As indicated by its title, *American-German Private Law Relations Cases 1945–1955*, that monograph was concerned largely with immediately post-War problems. Prior commitments having prevented Dr. Domke from preparing a new edition of his book, which is now out of print, the Parker School was fortunate in persuading Dr. Ulrich Drobnig to undertake the task. The book has been completely revised and considerably expanded and now covers the whole spectrum of American-German legal relations.

Nina Moore Galston, *Editor.*

Preface

This book belies the title of the series in which it appears in two respects. Neither is it truly bilateral nor, on the other hand, is it restricted to Private International Law proper. It offers an exposition of the German rules (with side-glances at those of East Germany) on the Conflict of Laws in the widest sense of the term. Special emphasis is laid on American-German legal relations; in this framework the corresponding American rules are taken into account, without, however, attempting to state them fully. The law is stated as of the end of 1969, and dollar equivalents of German marks are calculated at the official rate of exchange prevailing at that time unless the figures relate to an earlier date, in which case the earlier rate is used.

The author has striven to be realistic and practical. Special efforts have been undertaken to depict truly German judicial practice and to ascertain otherwise the factual implementation of the stated rules. Any additional information will be gratefully appreciated. In the reader's interest some care has been invested in the appendices so as to make the relevant material within and outside the book readily accessible.

I would like to record here my gratitude for the assistance, intellectual and material, liberally granted by the Max-Planck-Institute for Foreign Private and Private International Law in Hamburg, without which this book could not have been written. My colleague *K. Siehr* has accompanied me most effectively through all stages of the work and has contributed parts of chapters 2, 3 and 5 and essentially chapter 4. I have had the benefit of criticism from my colleague Professor *Neuhaus,* who has read most of the manuscript, and from Professor *Lando* (Copenhagen) and Professor *C. Peterson* (University of Colorado Law School), who have kindly commented on chapters 8 and 6, respectively, while Professors *Ulmer* and *Beier* (Munich) have brought to bear their expertise on chapter 12. Mrs. *N. M. Galston* procured liberally American material and undertook the linguistic revision of the manuscript. To all these and many others who provided me with information I owe deep gratitude—but the responsibility for all defects rests on me alone.

Ulrich Drobnig

Hamburg, August 1969

Table of Contents

Chapter I.

LEGAL STATUS OF GERMANY

A brief discussion of the legal status of Germany (and its component parts) is indicated for several reasons: The defeat and occupation have put in issue the legal existence of the German state; the aftermaths of the occupation régime are visible to this day; and the political disintegration of the German territory has created grave new problems. These interrelated phenomena may be brought into proper perspective by a brief survey of some salient post-War events.

I. OCCUPATION OF GERMANY*

The four leading allied governments of the United States, the United Kingdom, the Soviet Union and France in 1945 assumed "supreme authority with respect to Germany," but did not annex the country.[1] In the Potsdam Agreement of August 2, 1945, the Allies placed the eastern parts of Germany under provisional Polish and Soviet control.[2] The rest of the country was divided into four zones of occupation, reserving a special status for Berlin. The United States became responsible for the "American zone" (comprising the three adjacent states of Bavaria, Hesse and

* *Important literature in English*: Bathurst and Simpson, Germany and the North Atlantic Community. A Legal Survey (London 1956); Litchfield et al., Governing Postwar Germany (Ithaca 1953); Mann, Germany's Present Legal Status Revisited, 16 I.C.L.Q. 760–799 (1967) (German version in JZ 1967, 585–591, 617–625); Loewenstein, Law and the Legislative Process in Occupied Germany, 57 Yale L. J. 724–760, 994–1022 (1948); Bathurst, Legislation in the Federal Republic of Germany, 1 I.C.L.Q. 40–53 (1952); Loewenstein, Reconstruction of the Administration of Justice in American-Occupied Germany, 61 Harv. L. Rev. 419–467 (1948); Harvey, Sources of Law in Germany, 11 Modern L. Rev. 196–213 (1948).

Collections of documents: United States, Department of State, Germany 1947–1949, The Story in Documents (publication 3556, 1950); United States (Senate Committee on Foreign Relations), Documents on Germany, 1944–1961 (1961); Die Gesamtverfassung Deutschlands [texts] (1962).

Books in German: Schmoller, G. v./Maier/Tobler, Handbuch des Besatzungsrechts (2 vols. loose-leaf Tübingen 1957); Kaufmann, Erich, Deutschlands Rechtslage unter der Besatzung (1948).

[1] Para. 5 of the preamble to Declaration Regarding Germany of June 5, 1945 (60 Stat. 1949, Documents on Germany, p. 12, Off.Gaz.CCG, supp. no. 1, p. 7).

[2] Protocol of the Potsdam Conference of August 2, 1945, §§ V, IX (b) (2) (Documents on Germany, p. 29, Off.Gaz.CCG, supp. no. 1, p. 13).

Württemberg-Baden in central and southern Germany, and that of Bremen as a port on the North Sea), as well as for the "American sector" of Berlin.[3] Governmental authority in Germany was exercised by the four governments' commanders-in-chief in Germany, acting either jointly as the Allied Control Council in matters affecting Germany as a whole, or individually in their respective zones of occupation.[4] The authority exercised by any individual commander-in-chief was in effect limited to his zone.[5]

The occupation powers, whether acting jointly or individually, constituted in law and in practice the government of Germany. As custodians of the interests of the German nation, their duties in the course of time acquired a fiduciary character. Their acts, whether legislative, administrative or adjudicatory, reflected the duality of their function. These acts cannot uniformly be characterized as acts of the Military Government. Nor has a coherent characterization been evolved for certain types of acts. A few examples may illustrate the doubts and contradictions engendered by the dual function of the occupiers.

A great number of international agreements were concluded by the three Western military governors, not only with foreign powers but also with their respective home countries.[6] This appears to have been an exercise of German authority, and a certain number of these agreements were later on expressly assumed by the Federal Republic of Germany.[7] The same is true of all rights and obligations created by or established through legislative, judicial or administrative action of the occupation powers.[8]

---

[3] Protocol on Zones of Occupation of Sept. 12, 1944, as amended, TIAS no. 3071, 227 UNTS 279, Documents on Germany, 1, 3, 20; Statement on Zones of Occupation of June 5, 1945 (Documents on Germany p. 18; Off.Gaz.CCG, supp. no. 1, p. 11).

[4] Statement on Control Machinery of June 5, 1945, § 1 (Documents on Germany p. 19, Off.Gaz.CCG, supp. no. 1, p. 10). The statement is based on art. 1 of the Agreement on Control Machinery in Germany of Nov. 14, 1944, as amended (TIAS no. 3070, Documents on Germany pp. 5, 10).

[5] Consequently the courts of the U.S. Military Government lacked jurisdiction for crimes perpetrated in Germany outside the American zone (U.S. HICOG v. Grosch, CoA-Rep.XVI 253, 255 (1952); U.S. Mil.Gov. v. Riess, CoA-Rep.VII 141 (1949)) and to entertain a writ for habeas corpus by a person incarcerated in the French zone (Harms v. Donnelly, CoA-Rep.XVI 175 (1952)).

[6] Some details in Bathurst/Simpson 65–67, 82–89. For the bilateral agreements with the U.S., see Treaties B 77–86; for the multilateral conventions in which the U.S. participated, see Treaties M 111, 112, 116–118, 120–125, 129–133.

[7] Convention on the Settlement of Matters Arising out of the War and the Occupation, art. 2 (2) (Treaties M 184) and *see infra* ch. 2 n. 35.

[8] The principle is laid down in ch. 1, art. 2 (1) of the Settlement Convention (preceding note) and elaborated in the treaty. Thus the Marriage Law of the Control Council (Law no. 16 of Feb. 20, 1946) is still in force in West Germany.

In the United States, the Court of Claims denied compensation for damages caused by the currency reform of 1948; the enactment of this legislation by the three Western military governors was deemed an unassailable exercise of sovereign power.[9] On the other hand, American courts have repeatedly applied U.S./U.K. Military Government Law No. 53 imposing exchange restrictions to assignments and disclaimers of succession executed in the American zone.[10] The general criticism leveled at these latter decisions by an English writer[11] appears to be unfounded. It is quite proper that the American courts should take into account foreign asset restrictions prevailing at the place of contracting.[12] This is not to suggest, however, that the practical application of these rules of occupation law in these cases was fully satisfactory. Should not the courts have followed the prevailing German interpretation of Law No. 53 as not applying to disclaimers of succession?[13] And clearly the subsequent validation of the transaction by a competent German authority ought to have been taken into account.[14]

The United States military government established a full-fledged court system.[15] Primarily, these courts had jurisdiction in criminal matters affecting United States personnel and over war crimes, but gradually it was assumed in civil cases also. While the procedure to be followed in both branches was specifically provided for,[16] the courts were to apply not only the law of the occupier but, depending upon the charge, German criminal law as well.[17] The Supreme Court has expressly sanctioned the application of German criminal law to the trial of the wife of an American soldier who killed her

---

[9] Eisner v. United States, 117 F. Supp. 197, 199 (Ct.Cl. 1954). *See also* Aris Gloves, Inc. v. United States, 420 F.2d 1386 (Ct.Cl. 1970) (no compensation for American corporation's East German factory dismantled by Russians after conclusion of Potsdam Agreement.)

[10] Callwood v. Virgin Islands National Bank, 221 F.2d 770, 775 (3d Cir. 1955); Kent Jewelry Corp. v. Kiefer, 119 N.Y.S.2d 242, 248–251 (Sup. Ct. 1952); *In re* Muller's Estate, 199 Misc. 745, 748–749, 104 N.Y.S.2d 133, 136–137 (Sur. Ct. 1951).

[11] MANN 765 n. 22.

[12] *See infra* ch. 9 sub (4) at nn. 64 and 65.

[13] DOMKE 42–43, with references in n. 197.

[14] In the Callwood case (*supra* n. 10), the District Court expressly denied validation (121 F. Supp. 379, 392 (D.V.I. 1954)), while the Court of Appeals, probably through misinterpretation of the license, did not reach the question (p. 776). On this point, MANN's criticism (*supra* n. 11) is justified.

[15] *See* NOBLEMAN, 40 A.J.I.L. 803–811 (1946), and MCCAULEY, 40 A.B.A.J. 1041–1045, 1101–1103 (1954).

[16] Mil. Gov. Ordinances 6, 7, 11 and especially 32 and 33 (Mil. Gov. Gaz. Germany A 73, B 10, C 11, K 44 and K 55).

[17] Mil. Gov. Ordinance 31, art. 7 § 2 (c) (Mil. Gov. Gaz. Germany K 35), U.S. HICOG Law 10, art. 7 § 1 (c) (Off. Gaz. HICOG 643), U.S. HICOG Law 20, art. 6 § 1 (c) (Off. Gaz. HICOG 919).

husband in Germany.[18] The civil consequences of traffic accidents involving American personnel were governed at first by "American common law" as to liability but by German law as to traffic rules and damages.[19] After severe judicial criticism of this chequered deviation from the traditional rule of *lex loci delicti commissi,*[20] German law was declared generally applicable except as otherwise provided.[21] No governing law was prescribed for other civil matters, but German law was applied[22] even as among foreigners.[23] Some one thousand reported cases of the Court of Appeals[24]—cases almost unknown in either country—not only depict vividly the various aspects of the occupation, but are replete with valuable, detailed comparisons between German and American rules of law.

The American occupation courts held the Constitution and statutes of the United States inapplicable, not only to Germans[25] but also to Americans.[26] This statement respecting Americans, however, is probably no longer in accord with contemporary United States constitutional law,[27] and it has never applied to internal relations within the army or the civil service.[28] On the other hand, the exclusion of Germans from rights conferred by American law is confirmed by the standing practice of the United States Supreme Court in refusing to hear petitions for habeas corpus brought on behalf of Germans imprisoned in the American zone.[29]

---

[18] Madsen v. Kinsella, 343 U.S. 341, 361 (1952).

[19] Mil. Gov. Ordinance 6, §§ 19, 20; Mil. Gov. Ordinance 6, § II–3 as enacted by Mil. Gov. Ordinance 18 (Mil. Gov. Gaz. Germany F 7); Schweida v. Nichols, CoA-Rep.IV 147, 153, 161, 162 (1949); Turner v. Dinges, CoA-Rep.VII 90, 92, 94 (1949).

[20] Turner v. Dinges, preceding note.

[21] Mil. Gov. Ordinance 6, § II–3, as amended by Mil. Gov. Ordinance 34, art. II (Mil. Gov. Gaz. Germany L 30); Vollrath v. Ward, CoA-Rep.VI 59, 66 (1950).

[22] *Traffic accident caused by dog of American colonel*: Voth v. McManaway, CoA-Rep. XVII 414, 420 (1953); *assignment of tort claim*: Coen v. Szczes, CoA-Rep. X 376, 379 (1950); *subrogation of insurance carrier to tort claim*: Knoll v. European Exchange System, CoA-Rep. XVII 222, 226 (1953).

[23] *Conclusion of insurance contract between American citizen and Swiss company*: Basinski v. Winterthur, CoA-Rep. XVII 293, 296 (1953).

[24] United States Courts of the Allied High Commission for Germany, Court of Appeals Reports (18 vols. 1949–1954).

[25] U.S. Mil. Gov. v. Flamme, CoA-Rep. III 54, 61 (1949).

[26] *Leading case*: U.S. Mil. Gov. v. Ybarbo, CoA-Rep. I 207, 212, 224, 226–227 (1949); *see also* Bowen v. McCauley, CoA-Rep. XVIII 98, 112–113 (1953); Schaffner v. International Refugee Organization, CoA-Rep. XII 391, 393 (1951).

[27] *See* Reid v. Covert, 354 U.S. 1 (1957), where the Court held the Bill of Rights always binding on the government, whenever it prosecutes an American citizen.

[28] In Casman v. Dulles, 129 F. Supp. 428 (D.D.C. 1955), the court applied the Veterans Preference Act to a Military Government judge desirous of assuming the corresponding position in a HICOG court.

[29] Johnson v. Eisentrager, 339 U.S. 763 (1950), and cases cited at 768 n. 1;

The acts of the Western occupation powers were clearly, and are still (*supra* n. 8), binding on West Germany. However, their legislative or judicial acts were not necessarily accorded the same quality as the corresponding German acts, nor could their legislative acts be affected by German legislation without the consent of the occupiers. The German Federal Constitutional Court during the occupation régime declined to question the constitutionality of legislative or administrative acts of the occupiers,[30] and even today the effects of its judicial review are limited in this area.[31] In the judicial field, the United States High Commissioner accorded to decisions of the American courts in civil matters "the same force and effect as valid judgments rendered by German courts."[32] No express provision was made for decisions in criminal matters, but the German courts generally refused to equate these criminal convictions to those of a German court; consequently they held that an earlier conviction by an occupation court did not create the obstacle of "*ne bis in idem*" and did not justify a severer sentence for recidivism, whether or not the occupation court had applied German criminal law.[33]

This brief survey illustrates the variegated aspects of the authority exercised by the occupation powers in Germany. It also explains the broad variety of reactions to acts of the occupier both in his home country and in the area occupied.

II. PRESENT LEGAL STATUS OF GERMANY

In a discussion of the present status of Germany it is useful to distinguish four aspects: the rights of the Western Allies in West Germany, the special status of West Berlin, the position of East Germany, and the status of the "German Reich."

(1) Rights of the Western Allies in West Germany

Two complex series of conventions and exchanges of notes, the so-called Bonn Treaties of May 26, 1952 and Paris Treaties of October 23, 1954,[34] terminated the occupation régime in West Germany as

---

see also Flick v. Johnson, 174 F.2d 983 (D.C. Cir.), *cert. denied,* 338 U.S. 879 (1949). *See also* 11 WHITEMAN 933–934, 946–947.

[30] *See* BVerfG 24 Apr. 1953, BVerfGE 2, 237, 264; 15 Sept. 1954, BVerfGE 4, 45, 48–49; 11 Oct. 1951, BVerfGE 1, 10, 11.

[31] *See infra* at n. 44.

[32] U.S.-HICOG Law 20 of May 24, 1951, art. 7 (6) (*supra* n. 17).

[33] BGH 21 May 1954, NJW 1954, 1252 with numerous further references; BGH 25 Oct. 1951, NJW 1952, 151; *cf.* U.S. HICOG v. Renz, CoA-Rep. X 588, 591 (1950) and U.S. HICOG v. Migo, CoA-Rep. XIII 178, 180. *See also* OVG Lüneburg 22 Aug. 1951, NJW 1951, 816.

[34] Treaties M 181–186, 207, 208. On these treaties *see* notes by BISHOP, BRIGGS and KUNZ, 49 A.J.I.L. 125, 148, 210 (1955), by KUNZ, 47 A.J.I.L. 106 (1953), and by FENWICK, 46 A.J.I.L. 701–703 (1952).

of May 5, 1955. On the same day the three Western powers established full diplomatic relations with West Germany, expressly confirming their recognition of this country as the only legitimate state and government in Germany.[35] The termination of the occupation régime, however, was not abrupt. Not only was provision made for a smooth transition, but the former occupiers also retained a limited number of political rights. In addition, the status of the military forces and their auxiliaries remaining in the country was regulated.

(a) The three Western Allies, although granting West Germany "the full authority of a sovereign state," reserved for themselves certain essential political rights and responsibilities. These were:

—First, external (political) rights relating to Germany as a whole, including the reunification of the country and a peace settlement[36];

—Second, internal (legal) rights relating to the security of their armed forces in West Germany.[37] The reservation of these latter rights was to lapse with the assurance of effective protection by the German authorities under German legislation. Serious disagreement delayed this legislation until June 1968[38];

—Third, rights and responsibilities with regard to Berlin, to be discussed separately (sub (2)).

(b) The lengthy rules for a smooth transition are laid down in the so-called Settlement Convention.[39] This maintains all legislation

---

[35] Joint Declaration of the U.S., the U.K. and France of Oct. 3, 1954 (pt. V no. 1 of the Final Act of the Nine-Power Conference in London, 31 D.S. Bull. 515, 521 (1954)); Joint Declaration of the same powers of Sept. 19, 1950, 33 D.S. Bull. 530, 559 (1955). *See also* Agreement on the Transfer of Three Paintings to the Federal Republic of Germany for the Weimar Museum of Dec. 9/16, 1966 (Treaties B 206).

Cf. also Zschernig v. Miller, 243 Ore. 567, 574, 412 P.2d 781, 784 (1966), *rev'd on other grounds,* 389 U.S. 429 (1968). Further references *infra* n. 80.

[36] Convention on Relations Between the Three Powers and the Federal Republic of Germany (Treaties M 181), art. 2. The Three Powers are, however, obliged to consult with the Federal Republic, art. 7(4). In exercise of their reserved power, the three Western Allies requested, e.g., that certain legislation of the Allied Control Council be maintained in West Germany (Letters 8a and 8b of May 26, 1952, as confirmed by letter X of Oct. 23, 1954, BGB1. 1955 II 508, 495).

[37] Convention on Relations, art. 5(2), preceding note.

[38] 17th Law to Supplement the Basic Law of June 24, 1968 (BGB1. I 709; *English translation*: 7 Internat'l Leg. Mat. 843–850 (1968)) and Law Restricting the Secrecy of Mail and Telecommunications of Aug. 13, 1968 (BGBl. I 949). *See* Note, Recent Emergency Legislation in West Germany, 82 Harv. L. Rev. 1704–1737 (1969).

See Declaration on Lapse of the Reserved Rights of May 27, 1968 (Treaties M 320).

[39] Convention on the Settlement of Matters Arising out of War and Occupation (Treaties M 184), in Germany popularly (and more properly) called "Transition Convention" (Überleitungsvertrag).

(in the broadest sense of the term) of the occupiers, subject to repeal in all but the reserved areas mentioned above (*see* (a)).[40]

All acquired rights and all obligations derived from legislative, administrative or judicial acts of the occupiers or from their international agreements are expressly recognized, subject, however, to subsequent non-discriminatory changes (ch. 1 art. 2). Chapter 5 provides in detail for the restitution of cultural property taken by Germans in the German-occupied areas; despite initial doubts it is now settled that the provisions of this chapter are not only applicable to the expressly mentioned adhering states, but also to the three Western Allied signatories of the convention and to their citizens.[40a] The next chapter postpones the settlement of reparations to a future peace treaty or other agreements, but West Germany expressly recognizes the validity of all measures relating to German assets outside the country (ch. 6 art. 3). In chapter 9 Germany waives all war claims against the former enemy states, and all claims arising out of the occupation of the country. Chapter 10, finally, provides for the full restoration of all rights and interests in Germany to United Nations nationals and immunity of such nationals from certain post-War fiscal legislation.

Two international tribunals are to supervise the fulfillment of the proprietary obligations embodied in the Settlement Convention. The Supreme Restitution Court, whose seat is in Herford, is to succeed the Allied restitution courts in each former zone of occupation. Each of its three divisions is composed of two justices appointed by the appropriate Western power, two German justices, and one "neutral" justice. The court has final appellate jurisdiction over all German courts in matters of (internal) restitution.[41] The Arbitral Commission on Property, Rights and Interests in Germany, located in Koblenz, on application of the party concerned, was to review certain German administrative or judicial decisions under chapters 5 and 10 of the Settlement Convention. This Commission was composed of three members appointed by the Western Allies, three Germans and three

---

[40] Settlement Convention ch. 1, art. 1. Four German statutes have repealed considerable portions of occupation legislation (BGBl. 1956 I 437 and 446; 1958 I 540; 1960 I 1015). Special rules obtain for the legislation relating to internal restitution of property and compensation of damages caused by political and racial persecution, *see* ch. 1, arts. 9–12, and chs. 2 and 3.

[40a] Scheidt and United States v. Federal Republic of Germany, 8 Decisions of the Arbitral Commission on Property, Rights and Interests in Germany 151 (Plenary Session 26 Mar. 1965), reversing 7 *id.* 203.

[41] Ch. 3, art. 6 and annex to ch. 3 (containing the charter of the court). The court is clearly not an American court, Casman v. Herter, 177 F. Supp. 285 (D.D.C. 1959). The decisions of the three divisions of the court are published separately (and bilingually).

"neutrals."[42] Its decisions were final and binding on the authorities and courts of all member states.[43]

How does the general preservation of occupation law, rights and obligations square with the rule of German law, especially with the supremacy of the constitution? Since the transfer of sovereignty on May 5, 1955, the Federal Constitutional Court, which sits in Karlsruhe, while declaring administrative acts of the occupiers binding if exempt from judicial review prior to 1955,[44] has felt free to review the constitutionality of subsisting occupation laws.[45] If the court finds such a law unconstitutional, it will merely so state and thus compel the legislator to enact a new provision.[46] On the other hand, German judicial decisions affirmed by the presently existing Supreme Restitution Court are not subject to constitutional review, since that court does not exercise German public authority.[47]

(2) Special Status of West Berlin*

Almost from the beginning of the occupation of Germany, Berlin, its former capital, has "enjoyed" a special status. It does so to this day.

The city of Berlin was divided into four sectors, the Allied Kommandatura of Berlin being responsible for matters affecting Berlin as a whole—a true replica of the general occupation régime. The quadripartite military administration virtually came to an end when

---

[42] Ch. 5, art. 7; ch. 10, art. 12; and annex to the Settlement Convention (containing the charter of the Commission). The decisions of the Commission were trilingual. *Cf.* Decisions of the Arbitral Commission on Property, Rights and Interests in Germany, vols. I (1958)–IX (1967).

[43] Settlement Convention, ch. 5, art. 7 (5).

[44] BVerfG 6 Feb. 1962, BVerfGE 14, 1, 7.

[45] BVerfG 21 Mar. 1961 and 16 Feb. 1965, BVerfGE 12, 281 and 18, 353.

[46] BVerfG 20 Mar. 1963, BVerfGE 15, 337, (346–350). This is in derogation of its ordinary powers, *see infra* ch. 2 sub B III (2)(f).

[47] BVerfG 6 Nov. 1956, BVerfGE 6, 15. *See also infra* n. 71.

* *Important literature*: LUSH, The Relationship between Berlin and the Federal Republic of Germany, 14 I.C.L.Q. 742–787 (1965); BATHURST, Legal Aspects of the Berlin Problem, 38 Brit. Y.B. Int'l L. 255–306 (1962); SIMPSON, Berlin: Allied Rights and Responsibilities in the Divided City, 6 I.C.L.Q. 83–102 (1957); METZGER/BISHOP/BAADE/MENDLOWICZ, West-Berlin: The Legal Context (Columbus 1966); PLISCHKE, ELMER, Government and Politics of Contemporary Berlin (The Hague 1963); UNITED STATES (DEPARTMENT OF STATE), Legal Aspects of the Berlin Situation, 40 D.S. Bull. 5–13 (1959), and Documents on Germany, 1944–1961, pp. 367–378; GREEN, L.C., The Status of Berlin (Sydney 1962); MAMPEL, SIEGFRIED, Der Sowjetsektor von Berlin (1963); DRAHT, Die staatsrechtliche Stellung Berlins, AöR 82 (1957) 27–75. *See also brief comments* by WRIGHT, 55 A.J.I.L. 959 (1961); JESSUP, 43 A.J.I.L. 92 (1949) and PAKUSCHER, 1 N.Y.U. J. Int'l L. & Pol. 208–218 (1968); and, further, FINKELNBURG, JuS 1967, 542–544, 1968, 10–14, 58–61; ZANDER, JuS 1968, 161–162; UHLITZ, DÖV 1968, 524–532, especially 527–532.

Documents: FORSCHUNGSINSTITUT DER DEUTSCHEN GESELLSCHAFT FÜR AUSWÄRTIGE POLITIK, Documents on Berlin 1943–1963 (2d ed. Munich 1963); *id.*, Dokumente zur Berlin-Frage 1944–1962 (2d ed. 1962).

the Soviet representatives left the Kommandatura on July 1, 1948, but the three Western powers still cling to the form and to much of the substance of that four-power administration. There is good reason for their attitude. Western presence in and Western access to the city, which lies in the center of East Germany, depend upon a number of Allied agreements.[48] Since it is vital to preserve these Allied rights, the three Western powers are reluctant to relinquish their rights and to permit the full integration of Berlin into West Germany. This conflict of interests has resulted in a peculiar legal situation which has little to do with logic and which is always subject to evolution.

Although the Western powers have continued to insist that the special status of Berlin extends to the whole city, in practice today it is largely limited to West Berlin.[49] This limitation will also be observed in the following discussion.

(a) Both the Bonn and the West Berlin Constitutions proclaim Berlin to be a state (*Land*) of the Federal Republic.[50] However, it is doubtful whether these provisions are fully effective, since the Western powers have attempted to suspend them.[51] One of the direct constitutional consequences is the fact that the representatives of Berlin may sit, but have no voting rights, in the two houses of the West German parliament.[52]

(b) The West German Constitution (Basic Law, *Grundgesetz*, GG) does not apply fully to West Berlin, especially those organizational provisions regulating federal-state relations. The Allies themselves, however, have conceded the validity of those portions of the Basic Law that override conflicting provisions of the Berlin Constitution.[53] The Federal Constitutional Court apparently assumes

---

[48] *Texts* in Documents on Berlin, ch. III, and in Documents on Germany, pp. 41–55, 63–74; *see also infra* n. 75.

[49] On the special status of East Berlin, *see infra* n. 79.

[50] Art. 23 GG; Berlin Constitution of 1950, art. 1 (2) (VOBl. Gross-Berlin 1950 I 433; *English translation*: PLISCHKE, Berlin 94–107).

[51] The views of the Western powers and of Germany differ slightly. The Allies consider Berlin not to be a state of the Federal Republic. *Cf.* Statement of Principles Governing the Relationship Between the Allied Kommandatura and Greater Berlin of May 14, 1949, para. 2; Order (50) 75 of the Allied Kommandatura Berlin of Aug. 29, 1950, approving the Berlin Constitution, para. 2 (b) and (c); Declaration on Berlin of May 5, 1955, para. I. These three documents were reprinted in Documents on Berlin, nos. 66, 77, 106. Letter from the Allied Kommandatura of May 24, 1967, para. 5 (NJW 1967, 1743). The Federal Constitutional Court, on the other hand, counts Berlin as one of the states of the federation, although not with the full rights and obligations of this status. BVerfG 21 May 1957, BVerfGE 7, 1, 7–17; 20 Jan. 1966, BVerfGE 19, 377, 388.

[52] Letter of May 12, 1949, from the three Western Military Governors approving the Basic Law, para. 4, Documents on Berlin, no. 65; art. 144 II GG.

[53] Order (50) 75 of the Allied Kommandatura, *supra* n. 51, para. 2 (c).

that at least the Bill of Rights of the Basic Law is in force in West Berlin.[54]

(c) Since West Berlin may not be "governed" by West Germany,[55] federal legislation does not extend *ipso jure* to the city. Each statute has to be passed by the West Berlin parliament.[56] With the consent of the Allied powers, a practical procedure has been worked out. All federal enactments to be extended to West Berlin are submitted to the Allied Kommandatura, which is deemed to give its consent unless it raises objections within three weeks.[57] Most of the federal statutes that are expressly extended to the *Land* Berlin[58] are implemented by the city parliament within one month after their publication in West Germany.[59] The Berlin legislature has been authorized to use "cover laws" (*Mantelgesetze*) validating federal statutes and making them applicable to Berlin.[60] Ordinances and regulations implementing such laws have to be published by the competent organ of the Berlin city government.[61]

Although most of the federal legislation will thus be adopted in West Berlin, no extensions may be expected in the areas reserved by the Allied powers[62] (*infra* (f)).

(d) A similar procedure has been worked out for the extension to West Berlin of international agreements (in the widest sense of the term) concluded by the Federal Republic. The Allied Kommandatura has permitted Berlin to be included as far as possible within the terms of the Federal Republic's international undertakings and has authorized the city to implement these undertakings in

---

[54] BVerfG 20 Jan. 1966, BVerfGE 19, 377, 388, 389, 392.

[55] Letter of May 12, 1949, *supra* n. 52, para. 4.

[56] Order (50) 75 of the Allied Kommandatura, *supra* n. 51, para. 2 (b) and (c) sent. 3. *See also* Declaration on Berlin, *supra* n. 51, para. IV. Recent analysis by WENGLER, Die Übernahme von Bundesgesetzen für Berlin: Die moderne Demokratie und ihr Recht (Festschrift Leibholz, 1966) II 939–962.

[57] v. MEIBOM, NJW. 1967, 2097; HEIDELMEYER, ZaöRV 28 (1968) 704–730.

[58] The standard "Berlin clause" is a stereotype formula reading, "This statute applies also to the Land Berlin in accordance with §§ 13 and 14 of the Third Transitional Law (Überleitungsgesetz)." *See* the following note. For details, *see* resolution of the Federal Government (Dokumente zur Berlin-Frage no. 136).

[59] Statute on the Status of the "Land" Berlin in the Financial System of the Federation (Third Transitional Law of Jan. 4, 1952, BGBl. I 1 and 115, § 13 I; Berlin Statute of June 12, 1952, GVOBl. Berlin 393, for the adoption of the preceding statute.

[60] Order (51) 56 of the Allied Kommandatura of Oct. 8, 1951, and Letter (52) 19 of Feb. 23, 1952, Documents on Berlin nos. 81, 83. The texts of the adopted statutes are published as appendices to the cover law.

[61] Letter (52) 81 of the Allied Kommandatura of Aug. 28, 1951, Documents on Berlin no. 86; art. II, Berlin statute of June 12, 1952, *supra* n. 59; *see also* § 14 of the federal statute of Jan. 4, 1952, *supra* n. 59.

[62] For a detailed study on the adoption of federal legislation, *see* LUSH 767–770. *See also infra* n. 74.

Berlin.[63] According to a request of the Kommandatura, West Berlin and the Federal Republic have reached an agreement authorizing the latter to represent the former in the conclusion of international treaties.[64] The application of a treaty to West Berlin can be secured only in three ways: first, by an express provision in the text of the treaty extending it to Berlin;[65] second, if the foregoing is impossible, by an express declaration either in the instrument of accession or in a separate statement that the treaty will be applied in Berlin; or, third, in trade and payment agreements, by a declaration that the treaty is applicable to the territory of the DM-West.[66] But the Allied Kommandatura has reserved the right to object, within twenty-one days of notification, to the inclusion of Berlin in any treaty.[67]

If all these conditions are met, the adoption internally of a treaty in West Berlin is effected by virtue of a cover law declaring the relevant federal law adopting the treaty applicable in Berlin. Neither one is republished in West Berlin.[68] The net result corresponds to the position of federal legislation: most, but by no means all, international undertakings of the Federal Republic are valid in West Berlin; no extensions take place in the areas reserved by the Allied powers[69] (*infra* (f)).

(e) In the judicial field, the integration of West Berlin is much closer. The various federal high courts have jurisdiction to hear appeals from the West Berlin courts as from those of any other West German state.[70] However, a remarkable and controversial

---

[63] Declaration of May 21, 1952, regarding inclusion of Berlin in international treaties and undertakings of the Federal Government, paras. 1 (a) (1) and (2), Documents on Berlin no. 84; *German translation*: ZaöRV 27 (1967) 212 n. 347. *See also infra* n. 74.

[64] Exchange of letters of Sept. 16/Dec. 19, 1952, Dokumente zur Berlin-Frage no. 140.

[65] The standard Berlin clause now usually provides that this treaty is also valid for the Land Berlin, unless the West German government makes a contrary declaration to the other contracting party within three months after the coming into force of the treaty. *See* resolution of the Federal Government, para. IV, *supra* n. 58, and ZaöRV 23 (1963) 324.

[66] Declaration of May 21, 1952, para. 1 (a) (3) and (4), *supra* n. 63. Certain East European countries have sometimes refused to accept any of the three forms of the clause with the result of thwarting the conclusion of the treaty.

[67] Declaration of May 21, 1952, para. 1 (c), *supra* n. 63. For a recent instance of a partial objection, *see* ZaöRV 27 (1967) 214.

[68] Berlin Statute on the Promulgation of Laws and Ordinances of Jan. 29, 1953, § 3, GVOBl. Berlin 106.

[69] Several examples are quoted by Lush 775–777. *See also infra* at n. 76.

[70] For the Federal Supreme Court (in ordinary matters), jurisdiction is expressly extended to Berlin in the Berlin Statute of Jan. 9, 1951 (art. 7 nos. 41, 42, GVOBl. Berlin 99), approved by the Kommandatura (Order (51) 10 of Jan. 30, 1951, GVOBl. Berlin 106).

Since East Germany denies the existence of legal relations between Berlin

exception obtains for the Federal Constitutional Court: due to the protest of the Kommandatura, the federal statute establishing this court is not valid in Berlin, and it therefore refuses to review the constitutionality of laws, administrative acts or court decisions emanating from West Berlin sources.[71] Whether or not decisions of the federal high courts in cases originating in Berlin can be reviewed is therefore in doubt. In 1959 the Federal Constitutional Court refused to pass on the constitutionality of such a decision; in 1966 it took a contrary position, but this departure provoked much adverse comment from the Kommandatura as well as from others.[72]

(f) Superimposed upon these more or less close legal links of Berlin with the Federal Republic are the supervening rights of the Allied powers, based to this day on the occupation of Germany. In contrast to West Germany proper, the occupation régime has not been terminated for Berlin. Article 2 of the Convention on Relations between the Three Powers and the Federal Republic of Germany expressly preserves the rights and responsibilities of the Three Powers relating to Berlin.[73] The Declaration on Berlin of May 5, 1955 sets out in general terms that "the Allied authorities retain the right to take, if they deem it necessary, such measures as may be required to fulfill their international obligations, to ensure public order and to maintain the status and security of Berlin and its economy, trade and communications." The Allies assert, however, that they will "normally" exercise powers only in the fields of security of their forces, disarmament and demilitarization, civil aviation and international relations.[74] Federal legislation and international undertakings in these fields are therefore not extended to Berlin. In the areas of restitution, reparations, antitrust law, foreign

---

and the Federal Republic, her state agencies usually do not take appeals from the Berlin courts to any one of the federal high courts.

[71] BVerfG 21 May, 4 and 12 Dec. 1957, BVerfGE 7, at 1, 190 and 192. The same applies, *a fortiori,* for decisions of an Allied court in Berlin, the Supreme Restitution Court for Berlin, BVerfG 6 June 1967, BVerfGE 22, 91.

The rule does not, however, apply to administrative acts by federal authorities sitting in Berlin (e.g., the Federal Cartel Office) or to judicial decisions of West Berlin courts reviewing such acts, BVerfG 11 Oct. 1966, BVerfGE 20, 257, 266–267.

[72] BVerfG 2 Dec. 1959, BVerfGE 10, 229; 20 Jan. 1966, BVerfGE 19, 377. *See* disapproving letter of the Kommandatura of May 24, 1967, NJW 1967, 1742, and notes of Wengler and Beyer, *id.* 1743 and 1791; approving note by Schüssler, NJW 1966, 1067.

[73] Treaties M 181. Art. 6 establishes a duty of the Three Powers to consult the Federal Republic and obligates the latter to co-operate.

[74] But the representation of Berlin in the conclusion of international undertakings and the procedure relating thereto have been sanctioned expressly: Declaration on Berlin (next note), para. III (c) sent. 2 and Order (55) 10 of the Allied Kommandatura of May 14, 1955 on new procedures, para. 2 (Documents on Berlin, no. 107).

interests, displaced persons and admission of refugees, the Allies will intervene only to a limited degree.[75]

Following this summary exposition of the peculiar legal status of West Berlin, it may be pertinent to conclude with a practical observation. The political, legal, economic and social structure of West Berlin is so close to the conditions prevailing in West Germany proper that the average citizen will notice only very slight differences. West Berlin is treated much as if it were an integral part of West Germany. In order to stabilize its economy, moreover, the Federal Republic annually pays considerable subsidies to West Berlin and grants it a number of very important tax concessions. One American court, indeed, has gone so far as to equate West Berlin with West Germany.[76]

(3) **Position of East Germany***

(a) In common parlance, East Germany is that part of Germany that was occupied by the Soviet Union under the supreme authority of the Allied Control Council. (The term therefore does not comprise those Eastern provinces of the German Reich that since the end of the War have been under provisional Polish or Soviet administration, especially Silesia and East Prussia.[77]) On October 7, 1949, with the enactment of a constitution and the organization of a government, the Soviet zone of occupation constituted itself the "German Democratic Republic."[78] Between March 1954 and September 1955, the Soviet Union successively restricted and finally withdrew its powers as an occupier, repealed the occupation law and finally declared East Germany to be a sovereign state. Soviet troops, however, remained in the country, and the Soviet Union

---

[75] Declaration on Berlin of the Allied Kommandatura of May 5, 1955, paras. II, III and V (Documents on Berlin, no. 106, GVOBl. Berlin 1955, 335). As to the Allied prerogative to regulate all air traffic to and from the Berlin air corridors, *see* ch. 12 art. 5 of the Settlement Convention, *supra* n. 39.

[76] In *In re* Kraussman, 130 F. Supp. 926 (D. Conn. 1955), the court refused to extradite an American to the U.S. HICOG on a requisition based on 18 U.S.C.A. § 3185, providing for extradition to an area "occupied by or under the control of the United States."

* *Literature in English*: NETTL, J.P., The Eastern Zone and Soviet Policy in Germany, 1945–1950 (New York 1951); HEIDENHEIMER, A.J., The Governments of Germany (2nd ed. New York 1962).

Literature in German: HACKER, JENS, Die Rechtslage der sowjetischen Besatzungszone Deutschland (Bonn 1964).

[77] In West Germany, these parts of the country are usually called East Germany. (On the German-Polish frontier, *see* SZAZ, A.M., Germany's Eastern Frontiers: The Problem of the Oder-Neisse-Line (Chicago 1960), and the extensive documentation in 3 WHITEMAN 283–392.) The former Soviet zone was until the end of 1969 officially so designated (sowjetisch besetzte Zone or Sowjetzone, abbreviated SBZ) or was called Central Germany (Mitteldeutschland).

[78] GBl. DDR 1949, 1 and 4; 3 PEASLEE, Constitutions of Nations (3d ed. 1968) 344.

recognized, either in law or in fact and to varying degrees, its responsibilities for Germany as a whole and for the traffic of the garrisons of the three Western powers to and from Berlin.

(b) A few words are in order on the position of East Berlin.[79] From 1945 to 1948, it formed an integral part of Greater Berlin under the united régime of the Allied Kommandatura (*see supra* II(2)). The division of the city in the second half of 1948 did not immediately bring about integration of its Eastern sector into East Germany. It is true that the East German Government was established in East Berlin and that the East German currency was introduced there by the currency reform of 1948. In many respects, however, until erection of the Berlin wall on August 13, 1961, East Berlin preserved an existence separate from East Germany, and in some respects this special status has survived to this day.

Certain aspects of this status resemble the relationship between West Berlin and West Germany: Only since 1968 have the deputies from East Berlin had voting rights in the East German Parliament; until that year the East German Constitution was not in force for East Berlin; a great deal of East German legislation still has to be and is enacted separately in East Berlin; West Germans (but not West Berliners) may enter East Berlin without the special permission that is required for entry into East Germany; soldiers in uniform of the three Western powers may enter East Berlin without control; and American, British and French airplanes may fly into East Berlin. On the other hand, the international representation of East Berlin is effected by East Germany, apparently without any special arrangement, and East German international undertakings extend *ipso facto* to East Berlin. On the whole, it may be said that the integration of East Berlin into East Germany is much closer than the relationship between West Berlin and West Germany.

(c) On the international plane the status of East Germany is most decisively affected by the circumstance that the United States and its two Western Allies did not and do not recognize the East German state or government.[80] This non-recognition has many consequences.

---

[79] *Literature*: LUSH 782–786; MAMPEL, SIEGFRIED, Der Sowjetsektor von Berlin (1963); Documents on Berlin 1943–1963; Dokumente zur Berlin-Frage 1944–1962.

[80] Zschernig v. Miller, 243 Ore. 567, 577, 581, 412 P.2d 781, 786, 788 (1966), *rev'd on other grounds*, 389 U.S. 429 (1968); Tripartite Communiqué of Mar. 3, 1966, 54 D.S. Bull. 640 (1966); Tripartite Declaration of June 26, 1964, 52 D.S. Bull. 44 (1964); President Johnson and Secretary of State Rusk on Aug. 1 and 8, 1963, quoted in 58 A.J.I.L. 170, 655 (1964); Letters of Department of State of Feb. 7 and 21, 1964, and of May 23, 1962, quoted in 58 A.J.I.L. 1008, 1006 (1964), 57 *id.* at 410 (1963); Tripartite Communiqué of Sept. 28, 1955, 33 D.S. Bull. 559 (1955); Declaration of the Allied High Commission in West Germany of April 8, 1954 (Documents on Berlin, no. 121; Documents on Germany p. 154); Memorandum of State Department of July 13, 1950, 2 WHITEMAN 795; *see also supra* n. 35.

For instance, East German attempts to revive or to accede to multilateral conventions have been rejected by the United States (*infra* ch. 2 n. 72). East German passports are not recognized in the United States, so that East German citizens have to apply for travel documents to the Allied Travel Board in West Berlin. Whether certifications and authentications of signatures by East German officials are sufficient is doubtful (*see infra* ch. 14 sub V(2)).

Another grave consequence of non-recognition arises in the judicial field. According to a well-recognized American (and English) principle, East German law, as emanating from an unrecognized state, may not be applied by American courts. The exact contours of this principle have not yet been determined, since the courts have only rarely had to apply it in recent years. In view of certain dicta in American cases and in opinions of some of the Law Lords in the English *Zeiss* case, it is probable that the doctrine of non-application will not be pressed to its logical consequences. It has been intimated that exceptions may be made where private rights or routine acts of administration are involved.[81] Since East Germany certainly would not be allowed to bring suit in its own name in an American court and since the status of its government corporations is doubtful, the obvious expedient is to assign its claim to a private party, preferably an American; such an assignment will as a rule be upheld, provided it is a genuine transfer and no expropriation is involved.[82]

West German conflicts law, incidentally, takes quite a different view. It is generally accepted that the law of an unrecognized state or government is applied in the same way as that of a recognized entity. The conflict of laws is thought primarily to protect private interests, and the inhabitants of an unrecognized entity are as much subject to its laws and regulations as the citizens of a recognized state would be.[83] On the basis of this reasoning the West German courts follow in "interzonal" cases the ordinary conflicts rules (with

---

[81] See the opinions of Lords Reid and Wilberforce in Carl-Zeiss-Stiftung v. Rayner & Keeler Ltd. (No. 2), [1967] 1 A.C. 853, 907–908, 954 (H.L.) with references to American cases. *See also* the opinion of the U.S. Court of Appeals in Carl Zeiss Stiftung v. VEB Carl Zeiss Jena, 433 F. 2d 686, 699, 700–701, 703 (2d Cir. 1970).

The Restatement of the Law (Second), Foreign Relations Law of the United States (1965) § 113 would give effect under ordinary conflicts rules to the law of an unrecognized state relating to matters of an essentially private nature (including transfers of property) within the effective control of the unrecognized entity.

[82] Upright v. Mercury Business Machines Co., 13 A.D.2d 36, 213 N.Y.S.2d 417 (1961). The assignee of a trade acceptance given to an East German government-owned corporation in payment for typewriters sold and delivered to the drawee was permitted to sue the drawee-recipient of the goods on the acceptance.

[83] KEGEL, Kommentar no. 99 preceding art. 7 EGBGB with numerous references to cases; NEUHAUS 232.

certain adaptations) and hence are willing to apply East German law, subject, of course, to the reservation of public policy.[84] East German state authorities and public corporations have even been allowed to bring suit in West Germany.[85] A similar recognition, also subject to public policy and to certain exceptions, is accorded to judicial and administrative decisions affecting private rights. It has recently been suggested by an English writer that this West German attitude may also be relevant for English or American courts. In his view the peculiar situation whereby West Germany claims to speak for the whole country entitles foreign courts, acting under their own conflicts rules, to apply East German law whenever West German courts, under interzonal conflicts rules, would in fact apply East German law.[86] The argument is persuasive, but the courts will hardly accept it as long as their general attitude vis-à-vis the law of unrecognized states is sternly negative. They will also be influenced by the difficulties of proving East German law which result from the absence of normal official relations.

(4) **Status of the "German Reich"**

Whether the "German Reich" as a state and a subject of public international law has survived its defeat, the ensuing occupation, and the subsequent division of the country, is a subject of much debate. Legal arguments and political considerations are almost inextricably interwoven. Since the establishment of new and comprehensive governmental organizations in both East and West Germany has complicated the issue, it will be well to distinguish between the period from May 1945 to the fall of 1949, and the period since then.

The Allied powers having assumed "supreme authority" but not sovereignty over Germany (*supra* n. 1), the occupation of the country did not extinguish Germany as a state. Nor, according to the majority view, did the removal of the government and the complete reversal of the political system affect the existence of the state. Only in the Soviet zone were the new régime's identity with or legal succession to the German Reich and its subdivisions, and its

---

[84] BVerfG 25 May 1956, BVerfGE 5, 17; BGH: 21 June 1963, BGHZ 40, 32; 15 Feb. 1961, WM 1961, 390; 14 June 1960, FamRZ 1961, 261; 17 Feb. 1960, IzRspr. 1960–1961 no. 3; 19 Sept. 1957, WM 1957, 1367; and numerous other decisions. *Theoretical justification*: DROBNIG, Jahrbuch für Ostrecht II/2 (1961) 31–55. *Contra in the area of divorce law only*: BGH 28 Mar. 1962, BGHZ 38, 1; 30 Nov. 1960, BGHZ 34, 134. *In the literature*: WENGLER, NJW 1951, 50–53, and RAAPE 154.

[85] *A university*: LG Berlin 29 Apr. 1958, IzRspr. 1958–1959 no. 61; *public trade organizations*: OLG Frankfurt a.M. 1 June 1962, IzRspr. 1962–1963 no. 38; LG Hannover 8 Jan. 1959, *aff'd*, OLG Celle 20 July 1959, IzRspr. 1958–1959 no. 82 A; LG Hamburg 31 Aug. 1961 and 14 June 1957, IzRspr. 1960–1961 nos. 71 and 63. *Impliedly*: BGH 13 July 1959, BGHZ 30, 315.

[86] MANN 793–796.

liability for their obligations, denied.[87] In the West, both in Germany and elsewhere, the overwhelming majority of courts and writers held that the German Reich continued to exist in legal contemplation even though it was temporarily incapable of acting by itself.[88] Few American courts have been confronted with this question.[89] Some nationality cases have dealt with the related issue whether the 1946 elections in the German states of the American zone were political elections in a "foreign state" so that voting in them entailed loss of American citizenship. The only relevant decision of an appellate court answered the question in the affirmative, stating: "Germany at all times remained a political entity—an entity to which men and women could give formal allegiance and in which they could hold citizenship."[90]

The majority view had to reconcile the survival of the German state with the creation, in 1949, of two governmental organizations in East and West Germany, slowly maturing into more or less sovereign states. A confusing variety of theories has been evolved. They can be reduced to three basic types of solution. Some writers think that the former German state was dismembered and dissolved by virtue of the creation of two new German states. Others identify West Germany (and some even East Germany) with the former German state; they regard the other part of the country as a *de facto* political régime that has split off, or as an area dominated by insurgents. While both these views look upon the former German state as having been extinguished, a more sophisticated third theory believes in its survival; in this view, both German states are considered partial régimes within the continually existing, though incapacitated, German state. One of these régimes is thought entitled, if it so

---

[87] *Leading case*: OG 31 Oct. 1951, OGZ 1, 236. Further references in Drobnig, Das Westvermögen reichsdeutscher öffentlicher Rechtsträger mit Sitz in der SBZ, ROW 1963, 95.

[88] Rex v. Bottrill, [1947] 1 K.B. 41 (C.A.); BVerfG 26 Feb. 1954, BVerfGE 3, 288, 319. The most recent collection of authorities is in Mann. *See* the contemporary memorandum of the Legal Adviser to the Department of State (1 Whiteman 332, 2 *id.* 794), a note by v. Laun, K., The Legal Status of Germany, 45 A.J.I.L. 267–285 (1951), and the German books by Kaufmann, Erich, Deutschlands Rechtslage unter der Besatzung (1948) and Stödter, Rolf, Deutschlands Rechtslage (1948), also for further references. Most famous among the dissenters is Kelsen, The Legal Status of Germany According to the Declaration of Berlin, 39 A.J.I.L. 518–526 (1945).

[89] *See* Clark v. Allen, 331 U.S. 503, 514 (1948), where the court met the argument of extinction by referring to the opposing (and the only relevant) view of the State Department. *Cf. also* United States *ex rel.* Kessler v. Watkins, 163 F.2d 140 (2d Cir.), *cert. denied*, 332 U.S. 838 (1947).

[90] Acheson v. Wohlmuth, 196 F.2d 866, 868 (D.C. Cir.), *cert. denied*, 344 U.S. 833 (1952). Two district courts had held otherwise: Brehm v. Acheson, 90 F. Supp. 662 (S.D. Tex. 1950); *In re* Riedner, 94 F. Supp. 289 (E.D. Wis. 1950).

desires, to act as agent for Germany as a whole. Some even suggest that both partial régimes may so act. The two latter theories have found most favor with the courts and writers[91] of West Germany, but neither has clearly prevailed.

---

[91] *More recent German literature, with great numbers of further references*: R. SCHUSTER, Deutschlands staatliche Existenz im Widerstreit politischer und rechtlicher Gesichtspunkte 1945–1963 (Munich 1963); W. FREIHERR VON MARSCHALL VON BIEBERSTEIN, Zum Problem der völkerrechtlichen Anerkennung der beiden deutschen Regierungen (1959); G. SCHEUER, Die Rechtslage des geteilten Deutschland (1960).

The official opinion of the Western Allies appears to be in accord with the first view; *see* the (unpublished) Interpretative Minute to the declaration of Sept. 19, 1950 (*supra* n. 35), as related by BATHURST/SIMPSON 188.

Chapter II.

SOURCES OF LAW

The most specific source for American-German legal relations is the treaty law in force between the two countries, both bilateral and multilateral.[1] It may be useful to sketch briefly the development of these relations and to discuss the most important general issues relating to them, namely, the effect of the two World Wars and of the division of Germany (A). Thereafter, the national sources of German law will be presented (B).

A. AMERICAN-GERMAN TREATY RELATIONS*

I. FROM 1785 UNTIL 1941

The course of American-German treaty relations truly reflects the various changes in the political climate between the two countries. Treaty relations commenced rather early with the conclusion on September 10, 1785 of the Treaty of Amity and Commerce between His Majesty the King of Prussia and the United States of America.[2] This treaty was the fourth treaty of its kind entered into by the United States. Two other commercial treaties with Prussia followed in 1799 and 1828 (Treaties B 2 and 4), and similar treaties were consummated with five other North German states (Treaties B 3, 6, 12–14). Other agreements with German states dealt with the facilitation of emigration, with nationality in connection with emigration and return, with extradition and with consular relations.[3] Among these, the five so-called Bancroft Treaties concerning the nationality of emigrants, concluded in 1868 with most of the German states

---

[1] *See* chronological list in Appendix, subdivided into part B for bilateral treaties and part M for multilateral conventions.

* *General literature*: McINTYRE, Legal Effect of World War II on Treaties of the United States (The Hague 1958); MOSLER/DOEHRING, Die Beendigung des Kriegszustandes mit Deutschland nach dem zweiten Weltkrieg (Beiträge zum ausländischen öffentlichen Recht und Völkerrecht, vol. 37, 1963).

[2] Treaties B 1. The historical and political background of this "epoch-making document" (REEVES, The Prussian-American Treaties, 11 A.J.I.L. 475 (1917)) has been described in detail by F. KAPP, Friedrich der Grosse und die Vereinigten Staaten von Amerika (1871).

[3] *See* Treaties B 7–11; 28–32; 16–23, 25, 36 and 31; 15 and 33.

(Treaties B 29–33), were, and to some degree still are,[3a] of particular relevance.[4]

The foundation of the German Reich in 1871 did not abrogate the existing treaties between the United States and numerous German states,[5] but it did lead to some discussion as to their extension to other states of the German Reich not originally parties to these treaties.[6]

Friendly relations between the two countries deteriorated after the outbreak of World War I and were interrupted by the American declaration of war on April 6, 1917. After commercial relations were resumed on July 14, 1919[7] and the state of war was unilaterally terminated by the Joint Resolution of Congress of July 2, 1921,[8] a Treaty Establishing Friendly Relations was concluded on August 25, 1921.[9] This treaty granted to the United States all the rights and advantages stipulated for its benefit in the Treaty of Versailles;[10] of particular pertinence for our inquiry are those provisions concerning the fate of the earlier agreements.

The multilateral conventions to be applied again between Germany and those of the Allied or Associated Powers which were parties to them were enumerated in articles 282 through 288 of the Treaty of Versailles. The United States and Germany were parties to sixteen of these forty-four conventions.[11] As for bilateral treaties, those which the Allied or Associated Powers wished to revive were to be notified by them to Germany within a fixed period of time.[12] The only American-German treaty thus revived was the Patent Convention of February 23, 1909 (Treaties B 49).[13] The terms of the

---

[3a] Although abrogated since 1917 or 1922. *See infra* p. 60.

[4] *See* United States *ex rel.* Flegenheimer v. Italy, 53 A.J.I.L. 944, 945 (1959) (Italian-U.S. Conciliation Commission 1958). The Commission applied the Bancroft Treaty with Württemberg to the naturalization granted by Württemberg in 1894 to a naturalized American of German stock, who had returned twenty years earlier from the United States.

[5] 5 Hackworth 367–368.

[6] 5 Hackworth 375–376; *see also* quotations by Riesenfeld, Decision of the German Supreme Court on Termination of Treaties of the German States, 720, 722 (1937).

[7] 5 Hackworth 385.

[8] 42 Stat. 105 (1921); Mosler/Doehring 7–8. *See also* preamble to the Treaty of August 25, 1921 (following note).

[9] Treaties B 50; Note, Our Treaties of Peace with the Central Powers, 40 Harv. L. Rev. 752 (1927).

[10] *Cf.* Redmond 3329. The Congress of the United States had refused to ratify the Treaty because of its provisions relating to the League of Nations.

[11] Treaties M 4, 8, 10, 16, 18, 19, 29–32, 35, 39, 51–53 and 56.

[12] Treaty of Versailles, *supra* n. 10, art. 289.

[13] *See* 5 Hackworth 388 and RGBl. 1922 II 132.

Copyright Treaty of January 15, 1892 (Treaties B 41) were unilaterally enacted in Germany in favor of American nationals.[14]

Of all the other treaties between the United States and Germany or the German states, no fewer than thirty-two[15] "are and shall remain abrogated" according to the wording of article 289 (4) of the Treaty of Versailles. However, some American courts have seen fit to restrict the intended abrogation of these bilateral treaties regardless of the circumstances, even in the absence of any notification. One case held that a treaty clause guaranteeing inheritance rights to Germans remained in force even during the War.[16] Two courts invoked treaty provisions concerning harbor duties in favor of German shipping companies for the period between November 1919 and November 1921, that is, after the resumption of trade but before the signing of the Treaty of 1921.[17] And three decisions treated rules of abrogated treaties as applying to the right of inheritance and the admission of aliens during the interval between the lapse of the notification period under the Treaty of 1921 and the coming into force of the Treaty of Commerce of 1923 (Treaties B 55).[18] The notification requirement was evaded by holding the relevant treaty rules to be unaffected by the outbreak of the War and, consequently, not to require revival by notification according to the procedure provided by article 289 of the Treaty of Versailles! This line of decisions was in keeping with the general attitude of the American courts that may be summarized by

---

[14] § 1 sent. 1 of the Statute of May 18, 1922, RGBl. II 129. § 1 sent. 2 expressly declared this protection effective for the time since outbreak of the War. The President of the United States reciprocated by proclaiming on May 25, 1922 (42 Stat. 2271) that the United States was prepared to grant copyright protection to German authors for works first produced or published abroad after August 1, 1914.

[15] Treaties B 3, 4, 7–14, 16, 18, 19, 24–27, 29–33, 37, 38, 39, 41, 42, 44, 45, 47–49. *See also* Note, *supra* n. 9, at 756 n. 33. McIntyre 311 n. 1 enumerates 22 of the treaties.

[16] Goos v. Brocks, 117 Neb. 750, 223 N.W. 13 (1929). The court pointed out that a benefit to the enemy was prevented by the vesting of the assets in the Alien Property Custodian and invoked an inconclusive letter from the State Department.

In the Flegenheimer case, *supra* n. 4, at 950, the Italian-U.S. Conciliation Commission thought, without having to decide, that the Bancroft Treaties with the German states had expired at the outbreak of war.

[17] The Sophie Rickmers, 45 F. 2d 413 (S.D.N.Y. 1930); *cf.* Flensburger Dampfercompagnie v. United States, 59 F. 2d 464 (Ct.Cl.), *cert. denied,* 286 U.S. 562 (1932).

[18] State *ex rel.* Miner v. Reardon, 120 Kan. 614, 245 Pac. 158 (1926); *In re* Meyer's Estate, 107 Cal. App. 2d 799, 238 P. 2d 597 (Dist.Ct.App. 1951); Hempel v. Weedin, 23 F. 2d 949 (W.D. Wash.), *rev'd on other grounds,* 28 F.2d 603 (9th Cir. 1928).

Thus the dicta in Goos v. Brocks, *supra* n. 16, at 15 and in Flensburger Dampfercompagnie, last note, at 471, to the effect that the unnotified bilateral treaties were abrogated by the expiration of the notification period, were not followed.

the formula: Treaty provisions are not abrogated or suspended by war unless they are superseded by express provisions or unless their application would be incompatible with the state of war.[19] The views of the Department of State have vacillated.[20]

The German courts did not pass on the impact of World War I on bilateral American-German treaties. There was less occasion for them to do so; German municipal law, unlike the law of most American states,[20a] does not restrict the right of foreigners to inherit (*see infra* ch. 5 sub II (2)), and German port authorities did not levy discriminatory harbor duties on American shipping companies in the immediate post-War period.[21] Vis-à-vis other enemy states, the German *Reichsgericht* held a commercial treaty and an extradition treaty abrogated by the War.[22] With one exception, the court took the same view with respect to multilateral conventions.[23]

Five years after the end of the War, the Treaty of Friendship, Commerce and Consular Rights with Germany (signed December 8, 1923, in force since October 14, 1925)[24] completed the restoration of normal relations between the two countries. This Treaty consolidated and streamlined the contents of the nineteenth century commercial and consular treaties with the German states and thus

---

[19] *See* Techt v. Hughes, 229 N.Y. 222, 128 N.E. 185 (1920); Society for the Propagation of the Gospel v. New Haven, 21 U.S. (8 Wheat.) 464 (1823). However, in Karnuth v. United States *ex rel.* Albro, 279 U.S. 231 (1929), the Supreme Court held the right of free passage granted by the Jay Treaty with Great Britain of 1794 abrogated by the War of 1812 and not subsequently revived.

[20] The letter from the Department of State cited in Goos v. Brocks, *supra* n. 16, at 15, indicates as ultimate date of termination the expiration of the period of notification. According to a later opinion of the State Department (of June 10, 1936, 5 HACKWORTH 387), all unnotified American-German treaties terminated on April 6, 1917, the date of the U.S. Declaration of War. *See also* MCINTYRE 38–39, 310–319 and Note, *supra* n. 9, at 756 n. 29.

[20a] 1 POWELL, R.B., The Law of Real Property, (rev. ed. 1969), chap. 6.

[21] *See* the finding of the court in Flensburger Dampfercompagnie v. United States, *supra* n. 17, at 465 sub 9.

[22] RG 23 May 1925, RGZ 111 40, 41; RG 23 Aug. 1916, RGSt. 50, 141.

[23] *See* the three decisions of June 27, Nov. 14 and Dec. 15, 1923 concerning the International Convention on Rail Transport, one of which is officially reported (RGZ 107, 282, 283). On the other hand, the Reichsgericht held the Paris Patent Convention valid as part of the municipal law (RG 26 Oct. 1914, RGZ 85, 374, 375), while an appellate court in effect did not apply it (OLG Dresden 31 March 1915, Sächsisches Archiv für Rechtspflege 10 (1915) 244). The Hague Convention on Civil Procedure of 1905 was applied by only one out of twenty decisions; see the count and references by AUBIN, Ist das Haager Zivilprozessabkommen heute in Deutschland anwendbar? DRZ 1948 Beiheft no. 5, pp. 10, 18.

[24] Treaties B 55. *See* the brief note by KUHN, The New Commercial Treaty with Germany, 19 A.J.I.L. 553–555 (1925), and the extensive comment on the most-favored-nation clause by MCCLURE, German-American Commercial Relations, *id.* 689–701.

probably abrogated them at least by implication.[25] The new Treaty also heralded the modern era of American commercial treaties, setting an example which was to be followed by some thirty treaties concluded in the ensuing three decades.[26]

Apart from numerous multilateral conventions to which both the United States and Germany became parties (Treaties M 59–103), some twenty bilateral agreements were concluded between the two World Wars; the most important were those dealing with the Mixed Claims Commission and the payment of debts, with the arbitration and conciliation of political controversies, with extradition and the smuggling of intoxicating liquors and narcotic drugs,[27] and with a number of more technical subjects such as postal communications, aviation, passport and visa fees and customs inspection.[28] In 1935, the Treaty of Commerce of 1923 was amended at German request.[29] No further treaties were concluded thereafter, since in the late thirties political conditions in Germany did not encourage relations going beyond such technical matters.

II. AFTER WORLD WAR II

Friendly relations were again interrupted by the German declaration of war on December 11, 1941.[30] During World War II, the only agreement entered into by the two countries dealt with the exchange of wounded prisoners of war (Treaties B 76). After the German capitulation on May 8, 1945, the Allied Powers controlled Germany absolutely until 1949 and partially until 1955. President Truman proclaimed the cessation of hostilities on December 31, 1946,[31] but the state of war was, at least according to official opinion, not formally

---

[25] *See* dictum in State *ex rel.* Miner v. Reardon, *supra* n. 18, 120 Kan. at 619, 245 Pac. at 161. The older treaties were apparently not invoked later on in American courts for events subsequent to Oct. 14, 1925. An exception is United States v. Hofmann, 24 F. Supp. 847, 850 (S.D.N.Y. 1938), where the court referred to "the practice founded on Article 9 of the German-American Consular Convention of Dec. 11, 1871" (Treaties B 37), although it was actually superseded by art. XXII of the Treaty of 1923 (Treaties B 55).

On the other hand, one court regarded the Treaty of 1923 (designated a "Treaty of Peace"!) as retroactively effective for the period of the War; Vogel v. New York Life Ins. Co., 55 F.2d 205, 209 (5th Cir.), *cert. denied,* 287 U.S. 604 (1932).

[26] *See* WILSON, A Decade of New Commercial Treaties, 50 A.J.I.L. 927, 928 (1956) and McINTYRE 164 n. 3.

[27] Treaties B 51, 61, 62 and 67; 58 and 59; 63, 73; 52, 56 and 57.

[28] *See* Treaties B 54, 60, 66 and 72; 69 and 70; 64 and 68.

[29] Treaties B 55 and 71. *See* the notice of amendment of the German Foreign Office of Nov. 14, 1934, RGBl. 1934 II 1047.

[30] The United States declared war on Germany the same day, 55 Stat. 796 (1941).

[31] 61 Stat. 1048; MOSLER/DOEHRING 20–21.

terminated until the unilateral declaration by the United States in the Joint Resolution of Congress of October 19, 1951.[32]

The four powers occupying Germany apparently never issued general directions concerning the annulment of treaties and conventions of the German Reich.[33] Thus the bilateral treaties for avoidance of double taxation were treated differently by different occupation authorities.[34] On the other hand, the Control Council, and the three Western Military Governments individually, concluded a considerable number of international agreements, mostly of an administrative nature and never published in Germany. Some of them were later expressly assumed by the Federal Republic of Germany.[35]

Several American courts have had to pass on the fate of the Treaty of Commerce of 1923 in controversies arising during the War and before its formal termination. The United States Supreme Court, in the leading case of *Clark* v. *Allen*, affirmed the old "premise that the outbreak of war does not necessarily suspend or abrogate treaty provisions."[36] Of the two important exceptions, namely, incompatibility with the war and supervening municipal regulations, only the latter, in the form of the network consisting of the Trading with the Enemy Act and its complementary rules, played a major rôle. The courts held that the War had no effect upon the right of inheritance guaranteed by article IV of the Treaty[37] or the exemption from taxation for office buildings of the German government as prescribed by

---

[32] 65 Stat 451; 66 Stat. c.3; 46 A.J.I.L. Supp. 12 (1952); MOSLER/DOEHRING 33. *See* Lee v. Madigan, 358 U.S. 228, 230 (1953).

American writers have usually regarded the War as terminated in 1945, *see* references in MOSLER/DOEHRING 26 n. 57.

[33] They had empowered themselves to do so by art. III no. 6 of Proclamation no. 2 of the Control Council of Sept. 20, 1945 (Off.Gaz. CCG no. 1 p. 8); the relevant sections are quoted by MCINTYRE 334. The effect of these provisions was, however, not free from doubt, *see* MCINTYRE 335 and AUBIN, *supra* n. 23.

[34] In the Soviet zone the occupation authorities declared the treaties abrogated (Circular no. 210 of the German Central Finance Administration, Deutsche Finanzwirtschaft 1 (1947) no. 5 p. 41; SPILLER, StuR 8 (1959) 1397, 1407–09). In the Western zones, the treaties were regarded as suspended, but nevertheless relief from double taxation was granted internally, sometimes on condition of reciprocity (KLEIN, StuW 1947 I 186–187, 206–207, 311).

[35] *See* Treaties B 77–86 and M 111, 112, 116–118, 120–125, 129–133 and 146. All these treaties are enumerated in the List of Treaties (BGBl. 1955 II 512–564) enclosed with Letter No. 10a (BGBl. 1955 II 511), confirmed by Letters Nos. 10c and d (BGBl. 1955 II 565–66), exchanged at Bonn in May 1952 on the signing of the Bonn Conventions. These letters were confirmed or amended by Letter No. X of Oct. 23, 1954 (BGBl. 1955 II 497–98), exchanged on Oct. 23, 1954, at the conclusion of the Paris Conventions (Treaties M 207). *See also supra* ch. 1 at n. 7.

[36] Clark v. Allen, 331 U.S. 503, 508 (1947).

[37] Clark v. Allen, last note; Zschernig v. Miller, 243 Ore, 567, 578, 412 P. 2d 781, 787, 415 P. 2d 567 (1966), *rev'd on other grounds*, 389 U.S. 429 (1968); *In re* Knutzen's Estate, 31 Cal. 2d 573, 191 P. 2d 747 (1948); Blank v. Clark, 79 F. Supp. 373 (E.D.Pa. 1948).

article XIX.[38] However, in all these instances the interests of the German parties were represented by the Attorney General of the United States and were thus (presumably) in safe hands. When a German residing in Germany personally sued on a promissory note, the court gave judgment for the American defendant who had invoked against the Treaty of Commerce the overriding prohibition against the bringing of suits by enemy aliens in American courts.[39] The government and especially the State Department seem generally to have shared the view of the courts.[40]

The German courts never passed on the status of these bilateral treaties, either during or after the War. Two wartime decisions, on the other hand, dealt with a multilateral convention to which the United States is a party; in both, the *Reichsgericht* applied the Paris Patent Convention in favor of Dutch firms during the German occupation of the Netherlands, and it did not even mention the possible impact of the War.[41] Post-War decisions rendered by the West German courts will be discussed below.

For the period following the formal division of Germany in 1949, treaty relations have to be considered separately for the two parts of the country.

(1) **Federal Republic of Germany**

From its inception in 1949 until the restoration of full sovereignty in May 1955 (*supra* ch. 1 sub II (1)), West Germany's external relations were to varying but steadily diminishing degrees influenced and supervised by the three Western powers. West German courts frequently passed on the post-War status of various multilateral conventions as against former enemy states. One court held that the Berne Copyright Convention, as part of the municipal law, had been unaffected by the War, invoking an exceptional decision rendered by the *Reichsgericht* early in World War I.[42] Practically to the same

---

[38] Brownell v. San Francisco, 126 Cal. App. 2d 102, 271 P. 2d 974 (Dist. Ct. 1954).

[39] Meier v. Schmidt, 150 Neb. 383, 34 N.W. 2d 400 (1948).

[40] *See* the extensive documentation in McIntyre 52–299 and the two letters reproduced by Rank, Modern War and the Validity of Treaties, 38 Cornell L.Q. 321–355 and 511–540, at 343 and 344 (1953). *See also* the letter quoted in Ränk, Einwirkung des Krieges auf die nichtpolitischen Staatsverträge (Uppsala 1949) 51–52.

On the other hand, the State Department held the provision for the admission of "treaty merchants" in art. I of the Treaty of Commerce defunct in the absence of a specific decision by an appropriate court, *see* statement by Waugh, 29 D.S. Bull. 225 (1953).

[41] RG 29 June 1942, RGZ 169, 240; RG 28 Jan. 1943, RGZ 170, 302.

The appellate court in Berlin invoked the Berne Copyright Convention (to which the U.S. is not a party), stating expressly that it had not been affected by the War, KG 31 July 1942, Ufita 1942, 418, 421.

[42] OLG München 25 Feb. 1952, IPRspr. 1952/53 no. 268, p. 535, invoking RG 26 Oct. 1914, *supra* n. 23; similarly, OLG München 29 Jan. 1959, GRUR/

effect are three decisions of the *Bundesgerichtshof* holding the Paris Patent Convention to have been suspended *de facto* during wartime, but to have become *ipso facto* applicable immediately thereafter.[43] Other conventions on private international law and procedure which were also considered suspended by the War remained inapplicable thereafter until expressly reinstated by the contracting parties.[44] According to an early advisory opinion of the Supreme Tax Court, the bilateral commercial treaties with enemy countries were abrogated entirely.[45]

The view of the West German government was less specific and was concerned only with determining which treaties should be regarded as abrogated by the War. Apart from agreements of a typically political nature, these were deemed to be treaty provisions concerning nationality and consular affairs and bilateral cultural and commercial treaties (except rules relating to establishment and to private rights of citizens). All other treaties and conventions were regarded as unaffected by the War.[46] The Federal Ministry of Finance in May 1952 reinstated three directives dated 1923 and 1924 that had carried out the agreed relief from double taxation on shipping profits of American shipowners.[47]

In order to clarify these doubts on the impact of the War, in general, and on the application to West Germany of the numerous treaties concluded by the German Reich, in particular, the Allied High Commission devised a special procedure.[48] This led to the

---

Ausl. 1960, 75; applied without hesitation by BGH 6 Nov. 1953, BGHZ 11, 135, 138.

43 BGH 18 Dec. 1959, BGHZ 31, 374, 380; 16 Nov. 1954, IPRspr. 1954/55 no. 160; 6 Oct. 1953, IPRspr. 1952/53 no. 242. These cases confirm the earlier practice of the Patent Office in Munich, *see* decision of Oct. 28, 1950, GRUR 1951, 32.

44 *Hague Convention on the Law Applicable to the Conclusion of Marriage*: KG Berlin 28 Oct. 1957, IPRspr. 1956/57 no. 99; LG Essen 4 July 1952, IPRspr. 1952/53 no. 98; *see also* BayObLG 9 Sept. 1960, BayObLGZ 1960, 370, 375.

Geneva Conventions of 1923 and 1927 on arbitration: OLG Hamburg 1 Oct. 1954, IPRspr. 1954/55 no. 187.

As to the *Hague Convention on Civil Procedure*, *see* references by KEGEL, Kommentar n. 15 preceding Art. 7 EGBGB n. 19.

45 OFH 5 April 1946, JIR 1 (1948) 189.

46 RANK, *supra* n. 40, 352–55, whose report is based on information gathered from an official of the German Foreign Ministry (p. 351 n. 125).

On the controversy in the German Parliament concerning the effect of war on the U.S.-German Treaty of Commerce of 1923, *see* the report in ZaöRV 23 (1963) 274. The government thought the Treaty suspended except for certain provisions.

On the views with regard to other bi- and multilateral agreements, *see* ZaöRV 18 (1957/58) 725, ZaöRV 23 (1963) 193, 275, 302 and ZaöRV 24 (1964) 681.

47 See Treaties B 53 and circular of the Federal Ministry of Finances of May 5, 1952, including the text of the three directives in BStBl. 1952 I 286.

48 Directive no. 6 of March 19, 1951 (Off.Gaz. of the Allied High Com-

reinstatement of a great number of pre-War treaties in the territories of the Federal Republic and West Berlin. Three bilateral treaties (the Patent Treaty of 1909, the Friendship Treaty of 1923 and the Extradition Treaty of 1930) were expressly "revived,"[49] the first two without prejudice to their *status quo ante*.[50] The applicability of five of the pre-War bilateral treaties seems to be tacitly assumed,[51] and that of the twelve others tacitly excluded.[52] Nine multilateral conventions to which both the United States and Germany were once parties were declared by West Germany to be again in force;[53] the applicability of the other twenty-six conventions seems to be tacitly assumed.[54]

---

mission p. 846, reproduced also by McINTYRE 336 and by RANK, *supra* n. 40, 350 n. 124). On background and practice under the Directive, *see* PLISCHKE, Reactivation of Prewar German Treaties, 48 A.J.I.L. 245, 253–256 (1954).

[49] Statement regarding agreement concerning re-application of the Patent Convention (Treaties B 49) in 31 D.S. Bull. 881 (1954) and BGBl. 1954 II 13; agreement of 1953 concerning the Treaty of Commerce of 1923 (Treaties B 104); statement regarding agreement concerning re-application of the Extradition Treaty of 1930 (Treaties B 63) after January 1, 1956, in McINTYRE 148 and BGBl. 1956 II 900.

[50] See the final sentence of the statement concerning the Patent Convention of 1909 (Treaties B 49 and preceding note), and art. I sent. 2 of the Agreement of 1953 concerning the Commercial Treaty of 1923 (Treaties B 104). The formula was apparently suggested by the State Department and was also included in the statements regarding the revival of the Extradition Treaty of 1930 (Treaties B 63) and the re-application of certain multilateral conventions (see the letters from the office of the Legal Adviser to the State Department, quoted, respectively, by McINTYRE 148 and by RANK, *supra* n. 40, at 345). In the official German statements concerning the Extradition Treaty and the multilateral conventions the phrase does not appear.

[51] *Copyright Treaty of 1892* (Treaties B 41): A note of the West German government of February 6, 1950, was of the opinion that the Treaty is applicable again. The reply of the American High Commissioner of June 20, 1950, avoids the required answer (on the reasons, *see* PLISCHKE, *supra* n. 48, at 261) and merely states that U.S.-German copyright relations do in fact exist again (BAnz. 1950 no. 144 p. 2, Bl.f.PMZ 54 (1952) 157–58). Nevertheless, the State Department has listed the Treaty as still effective (Treaties in Force as of Jan. 1, 1969, at 84). McINTYRE 337 regards the Treaty as reactivated although abrogated after World War I (at 219)!

Treaty Establishing Friendly Relations of 1921, *Arbitration* and *Conciliation Treaties of 1929* and *Agreement Concerning Parcel Post of 1939* (Treaties B 50, 58, 59 and 72): These four treaties are apparently in force again since they are listed in the above-mentioned official compilation of the Department of State at 86–87. *See also* PLISCHKE, *supra* n. 48, at 258–261.

[52] All pre-War bilateral treaties which are not expressly revived or which despite post-War negotiations for their revival (*see* PLISCHKE, *supra* n. 48, at 260–61) are not contained in the Department of State's compilation (preceding note) must be deemed to be no longer in force, Treaties B 51–54, 56, 57, 61, 64, 67–70. Some of them have been superseded by new agreements, especially Treaties B 53, 57, 68, 69, 70 by Treaties B 112, 118, 95, 126, 154, respectively.

[53] Treaties M 10, 16, 41, 52, 61, 65, 78, 80 and 100.

[54] Treaties M 4, 15, 30, 31, 39, 40, 42–49, 51, 55, 59, 60, 64, 70, 73, 74,

By an interim agreement of June 3, 1953, the provisions of the Treaty of Friendship of 1923 with Germany were revived with minor modifications pending negotiation of a new commercial treaty.[55] A new Treaty of Friendship, Commerce and Navigation was concluded on October 29, 1954, entering into force on July 14, 1956.[56] This Treaty does not make an entirely fresh start: the consular provisions of the Treaty of 1923 are expressly reserved pending conclusion of a new consular convention (art. XXVIII), and the old Treaty of 1923 is expressly abrogated only for the territory of the Federal Republic and West Berlin (arts. XXVI and XXVIII) (*see infra* (2) at n. 76). Moreover, many of the older provisions have been restored, and the European Economic Community, playing an expanding role in German foreign trade policy determination, has provisionally maintained in force the commercial provisions of the 1954 Friendship Treaty.[56a]

Although a formal treaty of peace has not yet been concluded with West Germany, courts in both countries have held that peace as a condition for the accrual of private rights must be deemed to have been restored during the course of the year 1955.[57]

The close political, military, economic and cultural ties of Western Germany to the United States resulted in an extraordinarily high number of agreements in the post-War period. More than 120 new bilateral treaties and agreements have been concluded in the nearly twenty years since the founding of the Federal Republic of Germany —150% more than in the preceding 150 years of American-German legal relations! Most prominent among the subjects dealt with in these treaties are matters of defense;[58] of economic, financial and technical cooperation;[59] of aviation and shipping;[60] and of postal relations and telecommunications.[61]

76–77, 79 and 81 are listed in the official compilation of the State Department (*supra* n. 51), indicating Germany as a party.

[55] Treaties B 104. Art. XIX of the original treaty was supplemented by a new paragraph; art. VI had previously been denounced by the United States. The special occupation régime was expressly reserved. *See* statement by WAUGH before the Senate Committee on Foreign Relations on July 13, 1953, 29 D.S. Bull. 224 (1953).

[56] Treaties B 117. *See also infra* (2).

[56a] Decision of the Council, 13 Oct. 1970, J.O.E.C., 1970 L 231 p. 7.

[57] *In re* Bahrenburg's Will, 208 Misc. 829, 145 N.Y.S. 2d 280 (Sur. Ct. 1955); BGH 15 Nov. 1956, BGHZ 22, 148.

[58] *See* Treaties B 90, 106, 107, 113, 114, 121, 122, 124, 125, 129, 131, 138–144, 146, 149, 150, 153, 155, 157, 159–167, 173, 174, 177, 184, 187, 191, 195, 197, 201, 202, 209.

[59] *See* Treaties B 87–89, 92, 94, 96–101, 105, 109, 110–112, 115, 119, 120, 128, 130, 132, 135, 137, 145, 147, 148, 156, 158, 171, 175, 178, 179, 181, 185, 188, 190, 192, 196, 199, 205, 207, 208.

[60] *See* Treaties B 126, 127, 151, 154, 168, 169, 180, 182, 194.

[61] *See* Treaties B 91, 170, 183, 204.

(2) **German Democratic Republic***

Contrary to the position with respect to municipal law (*supra* ch. 1 at n. 87), prevailing opinion in East Germany maintains that for international law purposes the German Democratic Republic is one of the two successor states to the German Reich. While treaties of the latter are deemed suspended, East Germany claims the option to reinstate them for her own use and at her own discretion.[62] Treaty practice accords with this view. East Germany has declared again in force some sixty of the 129 multilateral conventions concluded by the German Reich.[63] No bilateral treaties have been revived in this fashion; probably they are considered abrogated.[64] Multilateral treaties are applied without regard to reciprocity,[65] the writers generally stating that it is irrelevant whether the other contracting parties

---

* A useful (West German) list of the international agreements concluded by East Germany is given by KAPSA, Zusammenstellung der von der "Deutschen Demokratischen Republik" seit deren Gründung (7. Oktober 1949) abgeschlossenen Verträge und Vereinbarungen (5th ed. Bonn 1967).

62 Memorandum of the government of the GDR of Oct. 17, 1955, Prop. ind. 72 (1956) 21. Undated memorandum, Deutsche Aussenpolitik 4 (1959) 811–812.

AMBERG/HARHAMMER, Zur Wiederanwendung von Konventionen durch die Deutsche Demokratische Republik, Deutsche Aussenpolitik 4 (1959) 764–769; KIRSTEN, Einige Probleme der Staatennachfolge ([East] Berlin 1962) 147; PECK, Die Völkerrechtssubjektivität der Deutschen Demokratischen Republik ([East] Berlin 1960) 202; REINTANZ, Introduction p. 12, *in* Internationales Seerecht I ([East] Berlin 1962); WEPPE, Die Pariser Verbandsübereinkunft und die Mitgliedschaft der Deutschen Demokratischen Republik, EuV 13 (1964) 557–561, 558; LÜBCHEN, NJ 1963, 143, 144; ENDERLEIN/KEMPER/WIEMANN, StuR 9 (1960) 61, 72; WINKLBAUR, *in* Erfinder- und Neuererrecht der Deutschen Demokratischen Republik II (1968) 746; *see also* ZACHAROVA, StuR 13 (1964) 226.

For automatic revival with the end of the War (and apparently without the exercise of the option), NATHAN, Die Universalität der Pariser Verbandsübereinkunft, Neuerer 16 (1967) 237, 239; SEIFFERT, *id.* 1968 B 259; STEINIGER, *in* Der internationale Schutz von Erfindungen im Zeitalter der technischen Revolution (1966) 59.

63 *See* AMBERG/HARHAMMER, last note, at 765; REINTANZ, last note, at 13.

Public notice of the re-application has been given for 44 of the treaties. *See* decree of March 15, 1956, GBl. DDR I 271, relating to four treaties on industrial property (*inter alia,* Treaties M 91); notice of April 16, 1959, GBl. DDR I 505, relating to 39 conventions (*inter alia,* Treaties M 10, 30, 51, 52, 55, 65, 69, 78, 80, 81, 86 and 100); and resolution of April 8, 1965, GBl. DDR I 133, relating to the Hague Convention on Civil Procedure of 1905. The dates for re-application, if indicated, vary from November 1952 to December 1958.

64 The point, even as late as 1965, was said to be controversial among the writers (GLÜCKSMANN, NJ 1965, 686, 691). *For abrogation*: BRANDWEINER, Deutsche Aussenpolitik 1 (1956) 498. *For automatic revival after the end of the War*: KIRSTEN, *supra* n. 62, at 145. *For revival through declaration of re-application with the consent of the other party*: GRAEFRATH, StuR 7 (1958) 12, 27–28; apparently also KAUL, NJ 1965, 760.

65 *See* indications in the advisory opinion of ROLIN and TROLLER, StuR 16 (1967) 1288, 1289.

do or do not recognize East Germany's declaration[66] (*see infra*); however, the right to require reciprocity is often reserved.[67]

In a few instances East Germany has acceded to multilateral conventions of general importance concluded outside the Eastern bloc after World War II.[68] For those countries that do not recognize East Germany, the effect of these accessions will be as doubtful as the effect of the revival declarations discussed below. East Germany herself, however, will be bound irrespective of reciprocity (*see supra*).

The effect of these East German declarations of revival or of accession in the Western countries like the United States[69] who do not recognize East Germany varies and has to be examined in each instance or at least for each country. Some Western states as depositaries of the treaties have delayed or even refused notification of East German declarations to the member states.[70] Moreover, the reaction to notification has varied; some "neutral" countries have accepted the declarations and therefore seem to be bound by them; they have only disavowed any implied recognition of the declarant.[71] The majority of Western contracting parties—among these the Federal Republic of Germany and the United States—have declared generally that they take no notice of East German declarations.[72] This attitude is

---

[66] AMBERG/HARHAMMER, *supra* n. 62, at 768; NATHAN, *supra* n. 63, at 243; ROSE/HASCHKE, Die DDR ist Mitglied des Weltpostvereins, Deutsche Aussenpolitik 4 (1959) 759–763, at 763; BECHER, Neuerer 15 (1966) 570, 572; BIRKLEIN, Der Neuerer 14 (1965) 381; WEPPE, AH/RiA 1965 no. 1 p. 12.

[67] AMBERG/HARHAMMER, BECHER, BIRKLEIN, preceding note; REINTANZ, *supra* n. 62, at 14.

[68] *Inter alia,* Treaties M 152–155 (GBl. DDR 1956 I 917, 1957 I 365); M 39 and 40 (GBl. DDR 1961 II 93); M 244 (GBl. DDR 1965 I 1, 131); M 259 and 260 (GBl. DDR 1966 II 9); M 289 and 315B (GBl. DDR 1970 I 176, 177).

[69] *See supra* ch. 1 at n. 35.

[70] *See* the difficulties in connection with the *Universal Postal Convention* of 1952, described by PECK, *supra* n. 62, at 158–169; ZACHMANN/HASCHKE, Die Stellung der DDR im Weltpostverein, Deutsche Aussenpolitik 3 (1958) 578–582; and ROSE/HASCHKE, *supra* n. 66; as to the *Convention on Submarine Cables* and the *International Telecommunication Convention* of 1947, *see* PECK 169–170 and 171–174; as to the *Convention Concerning Safety of Life at Sea* of 1948, *see* ALEXY, ZaöRV 26 (1966/67) 495, 520 n. 122; and *cf.* general remarks by AMBERG/HARHAMMER, *supra* n. 62, 766–769.

[71] Notably Austria, Sweden, and Switzerland. *See* the summary of reactions concerning the *Paris Patent Union* by the International Bureau, Prop. ind. 83 (1967) 79 and 73 (1957) 4, Bl.f.PMZ 59 (1957) 59; the Swiss note *in* Prop. ind. 72 (1956) 153–154. For the *Berne Copyright Union, see* the diplomatic notes *in* Dr. aut. 69 (1956) 106, 170; 70 (1957) 177; *in German,* GRUR/Ausl. 1956, 480–483.

[72] *West Germany*: As to the *Paris Patent Convention, see* last note and Prop. ind. 72 (1956) 153, Bl.f.PMZ 58 (1956) 215, GRUR/Ausl. 1956, 479; as to the *Berne Copyright Union, see* Dr. aut. 69 (1956) 105–106; as to several *other conventions, see* ALEXY, *supra* n. 70, at 519–520 nn. 121 and 122; *see also id.* at 152.

United States: As to the *Paris Patent Convention, see* last note; for several

confirmed by West German court decisions,[73] and it may be expected that American courts will take the same view.

It appears, therefore, that from the American viewpoint no multilateral convention (except certain humanitarian conventions, *see* n. 72 para. 3) is in effect between the United States and East Germany. On the other hand, the status of some of the pre-War bilateral treaties and in particular the Friendship Treaty of 1923 is not yet fully settled. In *Zschernig* v. *Miller*, the Oregon Supreme Court applied the treaty provision granting national treatment in matters of succession to German heirs residing in East Germany.[74] The court relied heavily on two letters of the State Department declaring that the abrogation of the Treaty of Friendship of 1923 by the Treaty of 1954 with West Germany is restricted to the latter's territory,[75] and this, indeed, is the plain meaning of article XXVI of the Treaty of 1954.[76] In view of the supremacy of the executive in treaty matters, the court felt bound to accept the contention of the State Department that the Treaty of 1923 is still applicable vis-à-vis East Germany irrespective of the latter's willingness or ability to fulfil its treaty obligations. In the United States Supreme Court, which reversed on another ground, Mr. Justice Harlan's concurring opinion expressly endorsed this holding.[77]

---

other treaties, see Opinion of the Legal Adviser to the State Department, August 14, 1963, 58 A.J.I.L. 171, 174 (1964), and ALEXY, *supra*; and *see* the identical notes in DEPARTMENT OF STATE, Treaties in Force on January 1, 1969 (1969), at 263 n. 1, 301 n. 10, 308 n. 1, 315 n. 18, 328 n. 6, 359 n. 4, relating to Treaties M 78, 91, 244, 80, 100, 55, 81, 281, 51 and 30.

But both countries have taken notice of the accession of East Germany to the four *Geneva Conventions on War Victims* of 1949 (Treaties M 152–155), *see* 37 D.S. Bull. 861 (1957) and opinion of the Legal Adviser, *supra*. A similar but more reserved formula has been employed by the United States with regard to the *Nuclear Test Ban Treaty* of 1963 (Treaties M 287) and the *Space Treaty* of 1967, *see* DEPARTMENT OF STATE, *supra* at 345 n. 6 and 319 n. 9.

[73] BGH 18 Dec. 1959, BGHZ 31, 374 (non-recognition of international registration of trademark first registered in East Berlin); Patent Office Munich 10 June 1958, IzRspr. 1958/59 no. 96 (registration of patent in East Berlin does not create priority for subsequent registration in West Germany). For agreement of the legal writers with this view, *see* note by HEFERMEHL, GRUR 1960, 238, and incisive statements by WENGLER, Die Geltung völkerrechtlicher Kollektivabkommen zwischen Bundesrepublik und DDR, NJW 1961, 1–4, and NEUHAUS 216.

[74] Zschernig v. Miller, 243 Ore. 567, 412 P.2d 781 (1966), *rev'd on other grounds*, 389 U.S. 429 (1968).

[75] Quoted in 243 Ore. at 575, 577, 412 P.2d at 785, 786. The State Department on several other occasions had stated that the inheritance provisions of art. IV of the 1923 Treaty "may still be applicable" in favor of residents of East Germany, *see* letters of the Legal Adviser to the Department of State, February 7 and 21, 1964, 58 A.J.I.L. 1008, 1006 (1964).

[76] *See supra* II (1) at n. 56. A certificate of the West German Foreign Office, quoted in 243 Ore. at 575, 412 P.2d at 785, however, bases its contrary opinion on the unitary nature of German citizenship. *See infra* ch. 3 sub A II (1) (b).

[77] Zschernig v. Miller, 389 U.S. 429, 449 (1968).

The result, at least, seems acceptable for the right of inheritance as such (*see infra* ch. 5 sub II (2)).

B. SOURCES OF GERMAN LAW*

The officially recognized sources of German law, as well as their hierarchy, differ profoundly from Anglo-American conceptions. They are impregnated with the peculiar tradition and outlook on law that are characteristic of the European Continent. Orthodox teaching recognizes as sources of law statutes and customary law, but not case law or the writings of jurists. This traditional view is, however, hardly in line with the realities of the day as the following survey of each of these possible fountainheads will show.

I. INTERNATIONAL LAW

(1) **General Rules**

General rules of public international law form part of the federal law and rank before the statutes (art. 25 GG). What rules of international law are general enough to qualify as such, however, is a matter of speculation. The writers give as examples rules like "*pacta sunt servanda,*" the exclusive jurisdiction exercised by each state over its territory, and the absence of (unrestricted) jurisdiction of one state over another.[78] If serious doubts about the existence of a general rule arise in litigation, the court has to certify the question to the Federal Constitutional Court (art. 100 II GG),[79] and its decision has the force of law.[80] Two such decisions, both relating to the immunity of foreign states from suit, have been rendered so far.[81] General rules of international law may, with certain restrictions, be abrogated by international undertakings.[82]

(2) **Treaties**

Treaties and other instruments of international law lack the dignity and rank of the "general rules" discussed above. Treaties whose provisions are directly binding on the citizens are on a par with national

---

* *In English*: 1 COHN 3–55; SZLADITS, Guide to Foreign Legal Materials, French-German-Swiss (New York 1959) 119–176 [excellent, though slightly outdated]; Introduction by BAUR and Preface *in* Bibliography of German Law (Karlsruhe 1964) 8–58, 146–162.

[78] *See* the commentaries on art. 25 GG, e.g., MAUNZ/DÜRIG, Grundgesetz, Kommentar (loose-leaf) no. 20, and MANGOLDT/KLEIN, Das Bonner Grundgesetz (1957 ss.) no. III 3 c. Details are controversial.

[79] Serious doubts of other authorities suffice, even if the court itself has no doubts. BVerfG 14 May 1968, BVerfGE 23, 288, 316–319.

[80] §§ 31 II 1, 13 no. 12 Gesetz über das Bundesverfassungsgericht (BVerfGG) of March 12, 1951, BGBl. III 1104–1. On details of the procedure, *see* §§ 83, 84 BVerfGG.

[81] BVerfG 30 April 1963, BVerfGE 16, 27; 30 Oct. 1962, *id.* 15, 25. *See infra* ch. 14 sub I (1)(a).

[82] BVerfG 7 April 1965, BVerfGE 18, 441, 448–449.

legislation; thus they may be overridden (insofar as their effects within Germany are concerned) by subsequent enactments,[83] although the avowed internationalism of the German Constitution (*see* art. 24 GG) will lead the court to attempt to reconcile a subsequent conflicting statute with a treaty by appropriate construction of the former.[84] In addition, the constitutionality of treaties themselves may be challenged.[85]

The Federal Parliament must approve by statute all treaties regulating the political relations of West Germany or relating to matters within the Parliament's legislative jurisdiction.[86] This "law of approval" is published together with the treaty in part II of the Federal Gazette (*Bundesgesetzblatt*, BGBl.),[87] and this publication is followed usually by a separate notice upon the coming into force of the treaty.

Executive agreements are, under German constitutional law, those international instruments that do not require parliamentary approval by statute.[88] Since the area of parliamentary approval is fixed in the Constitution, as mentioned, the difficulties of distinguishing between these agreements are avoided. Executive agreements bind the citizen only where the executive has been duly empowered to enact a legislative provision.[89] They may be concluded by the Federation

---

83 BVerfG 26 March 1957, BVerfGE 6, 309, 363; MAUNZ/DÜRIG, *supra* n. 78, no. 29 on art. 25 GG; MOSLER, Das Völkerrecht in der Praxis der deutschen Gerichte (Schriftenreihe der Juristischen Studiengesellschaft Karlsruhe no. 32/33, 1957) 27; BERBER, Lehrbuch des Völkerrechts I (1960) 100.

However, in extradition cases, some penal departments both of the Reichsgericht and of the Bundesgerichtshof, invoking a general rule of international law, have repeatedly asserted the precedence of treaty (law) over a subsequent German statute, BGH 3 March 1954, BGHSt 5, 396, 402; RG 2 Sept. 1936 and 18 Jan. 1932, RGSt 70, 304, 305 and 66, 87. The supposed rule has no basis either in general international or in German law, but may perhaps be explained as an attempt at conforming interpretation of the statute (*see* text).

84 In one instance involving the *American-German Friendship Treaty* of 1954, this was done by resort to the age-old adage "lex specialis derogat legi generali", *infra* ch. 6 n. 56. See also TOMUSCHAT, ZaöRV 28 (1968) 75–76 with references. The legislator frequently avoids undesirable results by an express saving clause that preserves the precedence of treaty rules.

85 To be more precise, the Federal Constitutional Court reviews the constitutionality of the statute approving a treaty: BVerfG 21 March 1961, 21 March 1957, 4 May 1955 and 30 July 1952, BVerfGE 12, 281, 288; 6, 290, 294; 4, 157, 162; 1, 396, 410.

86 Art. 59 II 1 GG. The provision is *not* concerned—as its text might suggest—with the delimitation of legislative jurisdiction between federation and states, BVerfG 29 July 1952, BVerfGE 1, 351, 388–390.

87 *See*, e.g., BGBl. 1966 II 97.

88 A thorough study of the theory and practice of these agreements by HÄRLE, Die völkerrechtlichen Verwaltungsabkommen der Bundesrepublik, JIR 12 (1965) 93–139.

89 Absent such authorization, an executive agreement does not affect the rights of a citizen, LG Coburg 6 July 1955, NJW 1955, 1408.

and in certain instances they require the consent of the *Bundesrat*.[90] The publication of these agreements is unfortunately dispersed, incomplete and often tardy. Those of a general interest usually appear in the Federal Bulletin (*Bundesanzeiger*, BAnz.), and others of restricted interest in various specialized official bulletins; the rest remain unpublished.[91]

The states may conclude international treaties in their narrow area of legislative jurisdiction, but only with the consent of the Federal Government. The latter, in turn, has to consult with a state whose special interests are involved in a "federal" treaty.[92]

A collection of all the international undertakings binding on West Germany is lacking. A series published by the Foreign Office comprises at the present time only the multilateral treaties (including executive agreements).[93] The two appendices to this book attempt to list all the relevant multi- and bilateral instruments concluded between the United States and (West) Germany (Treaties M and B), together with their sources.

The German courts are free to pass on the validity or subsistence of a treaty[94] and to interpret it following the canons of construction of international law.[95] For these as for other issues of international law, governmental certificates are unknown. An opinion from the Foreign Office may be requested, but it does not bind the court.[95a]

II. LEGISLATION AND ADMINISTRATIVE RULES

German law is essentially enacted law. Court decisions interpret and sometimes reshape enactments; but they are a primary source of law only in the relatively few uncodified fields. An enactment may take the form of a constitution, a statute, a regulation or another administrative rule.

---

[90] Art. 59 II 2 GG. *See* for details MAUNZ/DÜRIG, *supra* n. 78, nos. 37–42 on art. 59 GG.

[91] Sometimes the line of demarcation between treaties and executive agreements is said to depend on the fact whether or not the instrument is negotiated in the name of the President of the Federal Republic. This different qualification cannot, of course, change the effect of the constitutional provisions regarding parliamentary approval.

[92] *See* art. 32 II, III GG and the "Lindau agreement" of the Federation with the states (reprinted in MAUNZ/DÜRIG, *supra* n. 78, no. 45 on art. 32 GG). Generally LEISSNER, The Foreign Relations of the Member States of the Federal Republic of Germany, 16 U.Toronto L.Rev. 346–360 (1966), and v. MEIBOM, NJW 1968, 1607.

[93] Verträge der Bundesrepublik Deutschland. Serie A: Multilateral Verträge (some 30 vols. plus two loose-leaf vols. with supplements and index).

[94] BVerfG 26 March 1957, BVerfGE 6, 309, 326; MOSLER, *supra* n. 83, at 21–25.

[95] BVerfG 4 May 1955, BVerfGE 4, 157, 168; MOSLER, *supra* n. 83, at 25–27.

[95a] OLG Hamm 5 Nov. 1962, BB 1963, 67, declined to follow an opinion of the U.S. Treasury on the question whether gold dollars were still legal tender.

(1) Constitutions

(a) The Federal Constitution or Basic Law of May 23, 1949[96] is the highest-ranking piece of German legislation. It has precedence over the constitutions of the ten (with Berlin, eleven) federal states and prevails also over all other enactments of the Federation and the federal states (art. 31 GG). Although originally meant to be only a provisional instrument pending adoption of a constitution for the whole of Germany (*see* preamble and art. 146 GG), the Basic Law has now virtually acquired the dignity of a full-fledged constitution. It opens with a Bill of Rights in nineteen articles, supplemented by the due process provisions of articles 101 through 104 GG. Both the text of the rules and their judicial construction favor strongly the individuals protected. While most of the fundamental rights are granted to everybody, including foreign individuals, certain of them are expressly limited to Germans. However, foreign legal entities (as defined *infra* ch. 10 sub I (1)) are generally excluded from the enjoyment of most of these fundamental rights—a very regrettable provision.[97]

The federal legislature consists of two houses, the *Bundestag* and the *Bundesrat*. The former represents the whole West German population, is elected directly and has the greater weight. Like the United States Senate, the latter represents the states of the Federation. Its members, however, are not popularly elected but are delegates from the state governments and vary according to the number of inhabitants of these states.

The "keeper of the Constitution" is the Federal Constitutional Court (*Bundesverfassungsgericht*) whose members are elected by

---

[96] *English translation*: 3 PEASLEE, Constitutions of Nations (3d ed. 1968) 361–398.

Literature in English: KAUPER, The Constitutions of West Germany and the United States: A Comparative Study, 58 Mich. L. Rev. 1091–1184 (1960); LENHOFF, The German (Bonn) Constitution with Comparative Glances at the French and Italian Constitutions, 24 Tul. L. Rev. 1–50 (1949); FRIEDRICH, Rebuilding the German Constitution, 43 Am. Pol. Sci. Rev. 461–482, 704–720 (1949); PLISCHKE, Contemporary Government of Germany (Boston 1962); DAINOW, The Constitutional and Judicial Organization of France and Germany and Some Comparisons of the Civil Law and Common Law Systems, 37 Ind. L. J. 19–27 (1961); DIETZE, Unconstitutional Constitutional Norms? 42 Va. L. Rev. 1–22 (1956); RICH, Civil Liberties in Germany, 65 Pol. Sci. Q. 68–85 (1950). For a broad comparative approach, *see* Studies in Federalism (BOWIE AND FRIEDRICH, eds., Boston and Toronto 1954).

[97] Art. 19 III GG; BVerfG 1 March 1967, BVerfGE 21, 207. NIESSEN, NJW 1968, 1019, maintains that this decision, which concerned a New York company, is contrary to the conventional guarantee of free access to courts. The salient point, however, is a refusal not of access but of a constitutional (substantive) right. Nevertheless, the constitutional due process clauses also benefit foreign legal entities and entitle them to lodge constitutional complaints (*Verfassungsbeschwerde*). *See* BVerfG 8 Nov. 1960, 7 April 1965 and 1 March 1967, BVerfGE 12, 6, 8; 18, 441, 447; 21, 207.

Parliament. It has broad powers in the constitutional field (*see infra* III (2) (f)), and has played an essential rôle in activating the letter and spirit of the Constitution. Thus it declared unconstitutional, between 1951 and 1967, some sixty legislative provisions.

(b) The state constitutions[98] are, in structure and content, similar to the Federal Constitution, but due to the political weight of the Federation, they are of minor importance.

(2) Statutes

A statute (*Gesetz*) can only be passed by a legislature (federal or state) and must be in due form. Apart from the great bulk of statutes, each of which covers only one or a few specific areas, Germany has comprehensive codes, especially of civil, commercial and penal law and procedure.

(a) Legislative jurisdiction is divided between the Federation and the states (arts. 70–76 GG); the former clearly prevails. The Federation has exclusive legislative jurisdiction in eleven areas; these, essentially, are foreign affairs and foreign trade, communications, money, industrial property and copyright (art. 73 GG). In some twenty broad fields it has concurrent competence;[99] it may legislate if necessary to preserve legal or economic unity within the Federation, or if legislation by a state either would be ineffective or would prejudice the interests of other states or of the Federation (art. 72 GG). In the areas of concurrent jurisdiction the states may only legislate if and insofar as the Federation has not acted. In the relatively few areas that remain,[100] the states alone are competent to legislate. In conflicts between federal and state law, the former naturally prevails (art. 31 GG).

Statutes enacted prior to the founding of the Federal Republic continue in force unless they contravene the new Constitution (art. 123 GG). Such former laws generally have become federal law if they fall within the Federation's exclusive or concurrent legislative jurisdiction.

The practical upshot is that all matters of more than regional relevance may be, and in fact usually are, regulated by federal law.

(b) The rules of statutory interpretation are more liberal than in the Anglo-American orbit. There is no desire to protect the unwritten "common law" (*gemeines Recht*) against statutory invasion.

---

[98] On these, *see* NEUMANN, New Constitutions in Germany, 42 Am. Pol. Sci. Rev. 448–468 (1948); LEWIS, New Constitutions in Occupied Germany (Washington 1948).

[99] Art. 74 GG enumerates civil and penal law, courts and procedure, the bar and notaries; social welfare, war damage and restitution; economy, labor and social security; research; agriculture, real property and housing; shipping, fishery, road traffic and railways.

[100] *Essentially,* police, education and culture, local government, water and roads.

Fixed canons of statutory construction do not exist. There is general agreement that three factors have to be taken into account, namely, the literal meaning of the text, the preparatory materials, and the practical result; but the relative weight to be attributed to these three elements is a matter of eternal dispute.[101]

(c) Publication of federal statutes takes place in the Federal Gazette and is obligatory (art. 82 I 1 GG). The Gazette has appeared since 1951 in two separately paged parts, part II comprising mainly international treaties and treaty developments. (The statutes of the German Reich were published in a similar manner.[102]) Citation of the Gazette is to year, part and page (1965 I 643), but the year is often omitted if the date of enactment has been indicated previously and is identical with that of publication.[102a] An official consolidation of presently valid federal law has been published since 1958 as part III of the Federal Gazette (*Sammlung des Bundesrechts*). With the completion of the consolidation most provisions of federal law enacted prior to January 1, 1964, and not reprinted in the consolidation will be ineffective. On the other hand, inclusion in the consolidation will not validate a law otherwise invalid.[103] The consolidation is kept up to date by periodic supplements.[104] There are also many private collections of important federal laws[105] and there is a useful current index of legislation.[106]

Statutes enacted by the states are published in the official gazette of each (usually styled *"Gesetzblatt"* or *"Gesetz- und Verordnungsblatt"*). Most of the states have in recent years produced either official or private consolidations of their existing statutory law.[107]

One journal has since 1950 published all current legislative texts of the Federation and the more important ones of the states.[108]

---

[101] *See, in general,* ENNECCERUS/NIPPERDEY, Allgemeiner Teil des Bürgerlichen Rechts (Lehrbuch des Bürgerlichen Rechts, vol. 1, 15th ed. 1959), § 55; *cf. also* ZWEIGERT/PUTTFARKEN, Statutory Interpretation—Civilian Style, 44 Tul. L. Rev. 704–719 (1970).

[102] They were published in the Reichsgesetzblatt (RGBl.), which, beginning in 1922, was also in two parts.

[102a] E.g., Law of September 17, 1965, BGBl. I 643.

[103] § 3 I 2 and IV of the Law on the Consolidation of Federal Law of July 10, 1958 (BGBl. I 437) and the Law on the Completion of the Consolidation of Federal Law of December 28, 1968 (BGBl. I 1451).

[104] Fundstellennachweis der Sammlung des Bundesrechts und der Bundesgesetzgebung (annually).

[105] The most popular are the two loose-leaf collections of SCHÖNFELDER, Deutsche Gesetze (containing private and penal statutes, including procedure) and of SARTORIUS, Verfassungs- und Verwaltungsgesetze der Bundesrepublik (containing constitutional and administrative law).

[106] SCHLEGELBERGER, Das Recht der Gegenwart (4th ed., loose-leaf).

[107] Titles in Bibliography of German Law 178–181.

[108] Sammelblatt für Rechtsvorschriften des Bundes und der Länder (since 1950).

(3) **Regulations** (*Verordnungen*)

Exceptionally, the executive may enact legal rules binding on the citizens, provided it has been expressly and duly empowered to do so by statute. Article 80 I GG provides that this statute must fix the content, purpose and extent of such an authorization, and that the resulting regulation must refer expressly to the statutory authorization. These regulations create generally applicable law, as indicated by their correct although rarely used designation as "*Rechtsverordnungen*", which distinguishes them from mere rules (*Verwaltungsverordnungen*) (*see infra* (4)).

Federal regulations are published either in the Federal Gazette or in the Federal Bulletin (with a corresponding notice in the Gazette).[109] State regulations are included in the official state gazettes.

(4) **Administrative Rules**

The issuance of internal rules, ordinances, orders, by-laws, and so forth, by administrative bodies does not require statutory authorization. Such rules, which merely regulate the internal administrative process, have not the quality of law and are not binding on the citizen. However, every individual indirectly affected by them is vitally interested in their content.

Almost any high-ranking administration has a bulletin of its own for the publication of its rules. These bulletins are usually styled "*Ministerialblatt*" if issued by a ministry, or "*Amtsblatt*" or "*Mitteilungsblatt*" if emanating from another office. The fifteen ministries of the Federal Government issue eight bulletins.[110] The more important items of general interest are also set forth in the Federal Bulletin which appears daily and which indicates the contents of the federal ministers' special bulletins. However, a systematic compilation comparable to the Code of Federal Regulations is lacking.

(5) **Form of Legal Rules and Citation**

An individual legal provision, whether statutory or administrative, is as a rule designated as a *Paragraph* (§, equivalent to a section). Only rarely are articles used. The subdivisions are called *Absatz* (paragraph, in the English sense, abbreviated "*Abs.* 1" or simply "I")

---

[109] Law of January 30, 1950 (BGBl. 23) § 1. Tariffs for railways, shipping, etc., may be published in the Tarif- und Verkehrsanzeiger der Eisenbahnen or in the Verkehrsblatt—Amtsblatt des Verkehrsministeriums (§ 2).

[110] Eight ministers (foreign affairs, interior, expellees and refugees, housing, all-German problems, affairs of the Bundesrat, family, atomic energy) publish jointly the Gemeinsames Ministerialblatt. In addition, there are the Ministerialblatt des Bundesministers (MBl.) der Finanzen (finances), MBl. für Wirtschaft (economics), MBl. für Ernährung, Landwirtschaft und Forsten (agriculture), MBl. für Verteidigung (defense), Bundesarbeitsblatt (labor), Verkehrsblatt (traffic) and Amtsblatt des Bundesministers für das Post- und Fernmeldewesen (communications).

and *Satz* (sentence). If tersely written, a reference to a particular legal provision may read, for example, "§ 254 II 2 BGB" or "§ 254 II S. 2 BGB," meaning paragraph 2 sentence 2 of § 254 BGB (*Bürgerliches Gesetzbuch,* the Civil Code).

III. JUDICIAL DECISIONS

(1) Rôle of Case Law[111]

The doctrine of stare decisis does not, in general, obtain in Germany. However, a constant practice of the courts (*ständige Rechtsprechung*), especially of one of the federal supreme courts, may qualify as a formal source of law in the guise of customary law. The latter is composed of two elements, namely, long-standing usage plus the conviction of the binding quality of the rule. The requisite conviction of the binding quality of a constant court practice will be present if the majority of the authoritative legal writers approve the practice or acquiesce in it. Substantial agreement between courts and writers constitutes a "prevailing opinion" (*herrschende Meinung*), a factor of considerable moment. But only after a long period of such agreement will a prevailing opinion ripen into a rule of customary law.

The number and importance of these time-honored and essentially judicial rules are considerable. Most general rules of administrative law, for example, are the creation of customary law; so is the whole institution of the chattel mortgage (*Sicherungsübereignung*); and so, too, is the generalization of the codified rules of conflict of laws, originally formulated as narrow unilateral rules but now in many respects grown into customary law.

Even apart from their eventual qualification as customary law, cases are an indispensable and well-recognized indicator of what the courts will decide in the future. Although, in general, neither the higher nor the lower courts are formally bound, decisions of the various German federal supreme courts are highly persuasive. They are regularly cited in briefs, in argument and in court opinions, and a legal adviser who overlooks even a single relevant supreme court case may be liable for negligence. But, however persuasive, decisions are not formally binding. Thus they may be disputed, especially if the legal literature does not agree with the rule enunciated by the highest court. And there are instances in which a federal supreme court, after fifty years and more of constant court practice, has changed its mind, giving in to the critical arguments of legal writers.

---

[111] *See* BAUR, The Place of Court Decisions in a Codified Legal System, 4 Texas Int'l L. F. 340–358 (1968) and DAINOW, *supra* n. 96, at 48–50. The style of a German judicial decision is illustrated and compared by FOLKE SCHMIDT, The Ratio Decidendi (Uppsala 1965) 3–18, 21–27.

There are two recent illustrations of such an about-face in the field of conflict of laws.[112]

In summary, it must be emphasized that the words of any of the codes or other pieces of legislation may be utterly deceptive if taken at face value without ascertaining how they are construed and applied in judicial practice.

(2) **German Court System***

A proper understanding and evaluation of German case law requires some basic information about the complex court system. Justice is administered by six principal categories of courts: "ordinary" courts (*ordentliche Gerichte*) in civil and penal matters, labor courts, social courts (*Sozialgerichte*), administrative courts, tax courts and constitutional courts. In addition, there is a division between federal and state courts. While the Federation and each state (except Berlin) has its own constitutional court, each of the five other categories has only one hierarchy of courts, starting with state courts and ending with a federal supreme court (*Oberstes Bundesgericht*) (art. 95 I GG, as revised by the Act of June 18, 1968, BGBl. I 659). Consequently, state courts apply both state and federal law, while the federal courts, generally speaking, have jurisdiction only in matters of federal law.

Federal law prescribes expressly that all the courts (and other authorities) have to assist each other (art. 35 GG). More specifically, the issuance of a summons, the service of process and the enforcement of a decision must be effected according to the ordinary rules of procedure irrespective of the seat of the court in one or another German state.[113] In view of the wide uniformity of substantive and procedural laws, a refusal to recognize or to enforce a decision from another West German state on the ground of public policy, though conceivable, is not a practical possibility.[114] Thus, in spite of its

---

[112] BGH 14 June 1965, BGHZ 44, 46 (Great Senate in Civil Matters) (concerning appellate review of the assumption of international jurisdiction by the German courts); BGH 22 March 1967, BGHZ 47, 324 (permitting judicial separation of foreign spouses).

* *A brief survey in* DAINOW, *supra* n. 96, at 27–38; *slightly outdated,* HARRIS and SCHWARZ, Comparative Law: Important Contrasts in the Administration of Justice in the United States and Western Germany, 30 Texas L. Rev. 462–486 (1952); *lively descriptions,* ENSOR, Courts & Judges in France, Germany and England (Oxford 1933) ch. III (with appendices) and BEDFORD, The Faces of Justice (New York 1961) 99–213.

[113] § 160 Gerichtsverfassungsgesetz (GVG) of Jan. 27, 1877, BGBl. III 300–2. This provision was declared applicable by § 5 III Sozialgerichtsgesetz (SGG) of Sept. 3, 1953 (BGBl. III 330–1), § 173 Verwaltungsgerichtsordnung (VwGO) of Jan. 21, 1960 (BGBl. III 340–1) and § 155 Finanzgerichtsordnung (FGO) of Oct. 6, 1965 (BGBl. I 1477).

[114] The Federal Supreme Court even held that an arbitral award, if rendered in violation of special price regulations obtaining in Berlin, would violate "general public policy" and therefore could not be declared enforceable, BGH 12 May 1958, BGHZ 27, 249.

federal structure, West Germany is in effect a single jurisdiction.

(a) "Ordinary" courts* competent in civil and penal matters are the *Amtsgerichte* (county courts), the *Landgerichte* (district courts), the *Oberlandesgerichte* (courts of appeals) and the *Bundesgerichtshof* (Federal Supreme Court). The constitution and competence of these courts are established in the Judiciary Act of 1877 (*Gerichtsverfassungsgesetz,* GVG),[115] and their rules of procedure in the Codes of Civil and of Criminal Procedure.[116]

The *Amtsgericht* (AG) decides petty cases and is also a judicial-administrative agency in non-contentious proceedings (*freiwillige Gerichtsbarkeit*); these, among other matters, include the keeping of numerous registers, the supervision of guardianships, the devolution of estates, and the enforcement of court decisions. The *Landgericht* (LG) is both the principal court of first instance and the principal appellate court for cases appealed from the *Amtsgerichte. Landgerichte* are divided into divisions (*Kammern*) for civil, criminal, and (in larger cities) commercial matters, usually sitting with three judges each. The eighteen *Oberlandesgerichte* (OLG) have almost exclusively appellate jurisdiction, exercised over decisions rendered by the *Landgerichte* as courts of first instance. These courts are divided into departments (*Senate*), civil and criminal, each usually sitting with three judges. In criminal matters and in non-contentious proceedings, the *Oberlandesgerichte* are formally bound by published decisions of courts of equal rank and higher courts.[117] If an *Oberlandesgericht* proposes to deviate from such a precedent, it has to

* *Important modern literature in English: A general sophisticated comparison:* VON MEHREN, The Judicial Process in the United States and Germany, *in* Festschrift Rabel (1954) I 67–98. *On civil procedure:* KAPLAN/VON MEHREN/SCHAEFER, Phases of German Civil Procedure, 71 Harv. L. Rev. 1193–1268, 1443–1472 (1958); SHARTEL/WOLFF, Civil Justice in Germany, 42 Mich. L. Rev. 863–908 (1944); SCHOPFLOCHER, Civil Procedure: A Comparative Study of Some Principal Features Under German and American Law, 1940 Wis. L. Rev. 234–264; LIPSTEIN, Doctrine of Precedent in Continental Law, 28 J. Comp. Leg. (3d ser.) 34–44 (1946). *For a lively description of the style of German decisions in civil matters, see* WEYRAUCH, The Art of Drafting Judgments: A Modified German Case Method, 9 J. Leg. Ed. 311–331 (1956). *On non-contentious proceedings, see* NEITZEL, Non-contentious Jurisdiction in Germany, 21 Harv. L. Rev. 476–494 (1907/08) (hardly outdated). *On criminal procedure, see* WOLFF, Criminal Justice in Germany, 42 Mich. L. Rev. 1067–1088, 43 *id.* 155–178 (1944) (slightly outdated).

115 Law of January 27, 1877, as newly enacted by the Law of September 12, 1950, *supra* n. 113.

116 *Code of Civil Procedure* (Zivilprozessordnung, ZPO): Law of January 20, 1877, as newly enacted by the Law of September 12, 1950, BGBl. III 310–4.

Code of Criminal Procedure (Strafprozessordnung, StPO): Law of February 1, 1877, as newly enacted by the Law of September 17, 1965, BGBl. I 1374.

117 Details may be found in §§ 120 III, 121 II GVG, 28 II Gesetz über die Angelegenheiten der freiwilligen Gerichtsbarkeit (FGG) of May 17, 1898 (BGBl. III 315–1), 79 II Grundbuchordnung (GBO) of March 24, 1897 (BGBl. III 315–11), and in a number of special laws.

transfer the file to the Federal Supreme Court by a "motivated" decree—in other words, by a decree containing the reasons for its action. The Supreme Court can decide the case without being bound by its prior decisions.

The Federal Supreme Court in civil and criminal matters is the *Bundesgerichtshof* (BGH) in Karlsruhe (with a detached criminal senate in Berlin). In civil matters, the court reviews the more important decisions of the *Oberlandesgerichte* on points of law only. The principal conditions for appeal in civil matters are either that the subject-matter in dispute exceeds the value of 25,000 DM (= $6,830), or that the *Oberlandesgericht* has granted leave to appeal; such leave may be given only if the legal issue is of general importance, but must be given if the *Oberlandesgericht* has deviated from a decision of the Federal Supreme Court. The court is divided at present into ten civil, five criminal, and a few special departments (including one for antitrust suits), each sitting with a president and four associate judges. An elaborate system ensures uniformity of practice within the court. Two Great Senates, consisting of members of the different departments of the civil and criminal benches, respectively, rule on any issue in which one department proposes to depart from a decision of another department or of the Great Senate. A department may also refer to the Great Senate any question that is of fundamental importance for the development of the law or for the uniformity of judicial practice (*see* § 132 GVG). The same system obtains for the other federal supreme courts.

(b) Jurisdiction in labor matters* is exercised by the *Arbeitsgerichte* (Labor Courts, ArbG), the *Landesarbeitsgerichte* (District Labor Courts, LAG) and the *Bundesarbeitsgericht* (Federal Labor Court, BAG). The constitution and competence of these courts and their rules of procedure are established in the Labor Court Act of 1953.[118] It is to be noted that laymen, representing employees and employers equally, sit on the bench at all three levels.

(c) In social matters (including, in particular, social security and workmen's compensation), justice is administered by the *Sozialgerichte* (Social Courts), *Landessozialgerichte* (District Social Courts) and the *Bundessozialgericht* (Federal Social Court). These have been created and are governed by the Social Court Law of 1953.[119] Like the labor courts these benches also include laymen.

---

* *In English*: COLE, The Role of the Labor Courts in Western Germany, 18 J. Pol. 479–498 (1956); MCPHERSON, Basic Issues in German Labor Court Structure, 5 Lab. L. J. 439–452 (1954). The following are slightly outdated: WUNDERLICH, German Labor Courts (Chapel Hill 1946); BLACHLY/OATMAN, The New Labor Courts in Germany, 9 Sw. Pol. & Soc. Sci. Q. 87–96 (1928); DAVIS, German Labor Courts, 44 Pol. Sci. Q. 397–420 (1929).

[118] Arbeitsgerichtsgesetz (ArbGG) of September 3, 1953, BGBl. III 320–1. §§ 2–5 of the statute define the competence *ratione materiae* of the labor courts.

[119] Sozialgerichtsgesetz (SGG) of September 3, 1953, *supra* n. 113. § 51

(d) Administrative matters* are decided by the *Verwaltungsgerichte* (Administrative Courts, VG), the *Oberverwaltungsgerichte* (Superior Administrative Courts, OVG), and the *Bundesverwaltungsgericht* (Federal Administrative Court, BVerwG). The relevant statute is the Administrative Courts Act of 1960.[120] Paragraph (§) 40 VwGO defines the general competence of the administrative courts as comprising all public-law disputes except those involving constitutional law and those that by statute have been referred to other courts, for example, social and tax courts; moreover, certain public-law matters have been entrusted to the ordinary courts.

(e) The decision of tax disputes is entrusted to the *Finanzgerichte* (Tax Courts, FG) and to the *Bundesfinanzhof* (Federal Tax Court, BFH). These courts and their procedure are governed by the Tax Courts Act of 1965.[121]

Two major disadvantages resulting from the high specialization of all the courts discussed so far are the frequency with which plaintiffs choose the wrong court and the fact that the five federal supreme courts on occasion rule differently on the same issue. A palliative for the first of these troubles is the general possibility of transferring an action, on plaintiff's motion, to a court of another category.[122] As for the uniform application of federal law by the five federal supreme courts, this originally was intended to be preserved by one Supreme Federal Court (art. 95 GG, former version); however, this court has not been established, and in its place a Common Senate of the federal supreme courts, operating on the "Great Senate" system (*supra* (a)), was created in 1968.[122a]

(f) The *Bundesverfassungsgericht* (Federal Constitutional Court) in Karlsruhe is in a class apart.** Its constitution and procedure are

---

SGG defines the competence of the social courts. It comprises essentially all administrative disputes concerning social security.

* *Important literature in English*: BACHOF, German Administrative Law with Special Reference to the Latest Developments in the System of Legal Protection, 2 I.C.L.Q. 368–382 (1953); ULE, German Administrative Jurisdiction, 25 Rev. int. des sciences administratives 173–183 (1959); SCHINDLER, Judicial Review of Administrative Acts in Germany, 2 Brit. J. Admin. L. 113–120 (1956); FELD, The German Administrative Courts, 36 Tul. L. Rev. 495–506 (1962); BACHOF, Special Administrative Tribunals, 25 Rev. int. des sciences administratives 184–192 (1959); PAKUSCHER, Administrative Law in Germany—Citizen v. State, 16 Am. J. Comp. L. 309–331 (1968). UHLMANN/RUPP, German System of Administrative Courts, 31 Ill. L. Rev. 847–878, 1028–1046 (1937) is of historical interest.

[120] Verwaltungsgerichtsordnung (VwGO) of Jan. 21, 1960, *supra* n. 113.

[121] Finanzgerichtsordnung (FGO) of Oct. 6, 1965, *supra* n. 113.

[122] Details may be found in the conforming provisions of §§ 17 GVG, 48 ArbGG, 52 SGG, 41 VwGO and 34 FGO.

[122a] Art. 95 III 1 GG, as revised by the 16th Law Amending the Basic Law of June 18, 1968 (BGBl. I 659) and Law of June 19, 1968 (BGBl. I 661).

** *Important literature in English*: MCWHINNEY, Constitutionalism in Germany and the Federal Constitutional Court (Leyden 1962); LEIBHOLZ, Politics and Law

embodied in articles 93, 94, 99 and 100 GG and in the Law on the Federal Constitutional Court of 1951.[123] The court has jurisdiction in constitutional disputes between the Federation and the states and between the highest organs and bodies of the Federation. It has power to declare certain fundamental rights to be forfeited (art. 18 GG) or to dissolve a political party as unconstitutional as was done in the case of the Communist Party and again of an extreme right-wing party. On request by the federal or a state government or by one-third of the members of the *Bundestag* (*supra* II (1) (a)), the court must settle a dispute as to whether a state law is compatible with a federal law, or whether a state or federal law is compatible with the Federal Constitution. This court alone, to the exclusion of all other courts, may declare a post-1949 statute unconstitutional, may find a state statute irreconcilable with a federal statute, or may hold a rule of general international law to be part of the federal law. Finally and most importantly, the court may hear a "constitutional complaint" (*Verfassungsbeschwerde*) by anybody alleging the infringement of a fundamental or other right guaranteed by the Constitution. These complaints may be brought against any act of a public authority, including a judicial decision. However, the complainant must have exhausted the ordinary judicial remedies. Not infrequently have judicial decisions been overthrown in this way, even including some rendered by the federal supreme courts.

The Federal Constitutional Court succeeded quickly in winning high prestige. It sits in two senates, each of which has eight justices who are elected by the two houses of the Federal Parliament.

(3) **Reporting of Cases**

Germany has neglected the art of reporting cases properly. This is so although—or perhaps because—as a rule any decision terminating an instance must be reduced to writing and is issued as a per curiam opinion, not that of an individual judge. The publication of dissenting opinions or even of the votes of the judges is, except in certain constitutional courts,[124] unknown. The reports of judicial decisions are spread over many publications and are often incomplete, especially with regard to the facts. Research aids for the analysis of case law are underdeveloped.

(Leyden 1965) 271–313; MÜLLER, The Federal Constitutional Court of the Federal Republic of Germany, 6 J. Int'l Comm. Jur. 191–218 (1965); RUPP, Judicial Review in the Federal Republic of Germany, 9 Am. J. Comp. L. 29–47 (1960); *see also* the further note by NAGEL, 3 Am. J. Comp. L. 233–241 (1954).

[123] Bundesverfassungsgerichtsgesetz (BVerfGG) of March 12, 1951, *supra* n. 80.

[124] *See* note by COHN, Dissenting Opinions in German Law, 6 I.C.L.Q. 540–543 (1957). But the admission of dissents has recently been strongly urged, *see* ZWEIGERT, Verhandlungen des 47. Deutschen Juristentages, vol. 1 (1968) part D.

(a) Official (or semi-official) reports exist for the decisions of all the federal supreme courts and of the Federal Constitutional Court.[125] However, these reports are incomplete; not only do they contain none but the most important decisions, but even the cases reported are not always given in full.

The first of these defects has to some degree been remedied by the publication of semi-official reference collections edited for most of the federal supreme courts (except the Federal Social Court) and the Federal Constitutional Court.[126] These collections are arranged systematically according to the law and legal provision involved. Often only the official syllabus is reproduced. But these collections are also incomplete since many cases are not deemed worthy even of a syllabus.

Official reports of a highly selective nature are also published by the Supreme Court in civil and penal matters for the *Land* Bavaria[127] and by the various state appellate courts in administrative matters.[128]

(b) The majority of case reports are private. Commercial publishers print selected cases of both high and low courts, some of which are officially reported and some of which are not. The most important source for these current reports is the legal journals,[129] but, in addition, there are a small number of periodicals or private collections devoted almost exclusively to the publication of cases. These sources tend to give the full text of the opinion and usually a comprehensive exposition of the facts. Also worth mentioning are: for commercial cases, "*Wertpapiermitteilungen*" (WM); for tort and insurance cases, "*Versicherungsrecht*" (VersR); for international conflict of laws, "*Die deutsche Rechtsprechung auf dem Gebiet des internationalen Privatrechts*" (IPRspr.); for interzonal conflict of laws, "*Sammlung der deutschen Entscheidungen zum interzonalen Privatrecht*" (IzRspr.);

---

125 The abbreviations for the reports are derived from the usual abbreviation for the court: BGHZ and BGHSt (cases of the BGH in civil (Z) and criminal (St) matters), BAG, BSGE, BVerwGE, BFH and BVerfGE.

126 LINDENMAIER/MÖHRING, Nachschlagewerk des Bundesgerichtshofs (LM) (Munich 1950——, loose-leaf); HUECK/NIPPERDEY/DIETZ, Nachschlagewerk des Bundesarbeitsgerichts, Arbeitsrechtliche Praxis (AP) (Munich 1954——, loose-leaf); BUCHHOLZ, Sammel- und Nachschlagewerk der Rechtsprechung des Bundesverwaltungsgerichts(Berlin 1957——, loose-leaf); BECK'sches Nachschlagewerk der Entscheidungen des Bundesfinanzhofs (BFH-N) (Munich 1966——); Nachschlagewerk Bundesverfassungsgericht (Munich 1968——, loose-leaf).

127 BayObLGZ and BayObLGSt, decisions of the Bayerisches Oberstes Landesgericht in civil and in criminal matters. The special functions of this court, an intermediary between the three Bavarian appellate courts and the Federal Supreme Court, cannot be elaborated here.

128 *See* the enumeration of the titles in SZLADITS 230, and in the Bibliography of German Law 186 *et seq.*

129 Useful surveys of the great number of German legal periodicals now existing or formerly published may be found in SZLADITS 239–244 and 262–292 (*passim*) and in the Bibliography of German Law 190–202.

and for important cases in civil matters generally, as decided by the courts of appeals, "*Entscheidungen der Oberlandesgerichte in Zivilsachen*" (OLGZ).

There is no equivalent of Shepard's citator. The deficiency is partly compensated for by the habit of publishing final decisions only, unless the contrary is expressly indicated. There is no means, however, for tracing subsequent references to a final decision.

Cases are cited usually by indicating the court (in abbreviated form) and its seat; if unreported, the date of the decision[130] and the file number are mentioned, or else the report (or reports) by volume or year and page, sometimes with the date of the decision, is given.

IV. LEGAL SCHOLARSHIP*

Scholarship always has had a very important influence on the shaping of German law. A "governing opinion in court practice and among legal writers" is of highest authority, second only to an unambiguous legislative enactment. Writers are quoted almost as frequently in judicial opinions, especially in those of the higher courts, as are cases. An explanation for this phenomenon resides in the fact that legal writers, in general, do not merely reflect or explain court practice, but offer their own views in criticism or support of such practice.

The most distinctively German species of legal writing is the commentary. It is keyed to the individual provisions of a statute and explains in detail its legislative history, factual background, judicial construction and literary treatment. These remarks are usually numbered separately for each provision. Accordingly, citations refer to the number of this note ("annotation [*Anmerkung*, Anm.] 4 on § 30 BGB") rather than to the page. Of the commentaries for the great codes, the most popular appear annually in new editions, enhanced with the most recent harvest of cases and articles.[131] There are also commentaries for the more important statutes.

As for monographs, these run into the thousands, and articles by legal writers are legion. A highly useful selection of books is given in the *Bibliography of German Law*. An index to legal periodicals has existed only since 1965 and so far without any consolidation of the monthly supplements.[132]

A peculiarly German method of bringing scholarship to bear on the decision of a case is submission by an attorney to the court of the opinion of a scholar of repute. Such opinions are resorted to

---

[130] The order of date in German is day, month, year.

* Critical comment by COHN, German Legal Science Today, 2 I.C.L.Q. 169–191 (1953).

[131] PALANDT, Bürgerliches Gesetzbuch.

[132] Karlsruher Juristische Bibliographie (Munich 1965).

frequently in difficult matters, often by attorneys for both parties. Even the court itself, if it has to apply foreign law, may request an opinion from a German authority (*see infra* ch. 14 sub II (5)). The courts pay due regard to such opinions, and sometimes even discuss them in their decisions. The filing of opinions as *amicus curiae,* on the other hand, is not known in Germany.

V. EAST GERMANY*

The sources of law recognized in East Germany differ profoundly from those in the West. The most outstanding features are, on the one hand, the unitary character of the state and the consequent lack of a pronounced separation of powers and, on the other hand, the preponderant and all-pervading influence of the governing political party, the Socialist Unity Party. Both formal legal texts and court decisions play only limited rôles.

(1) International Law

The generally recognized rules of international law "that serve the peace and the peaceful cooperation of the peoples" are, according to articles 8 I 1 and 91 of the Constitution of 1968, binding upon state authority and upon every citizen. In practice, however, these are never invoked. Treaties have to be confirmed by Parliament, provided they touch upon laws passed by the legislature; the same is true for the denunciation of such treaties (art. 51). An order of the State Council regulates the internal method of conclusion of international agreements.[133]

(2) Legislation

(a) The Constitution of 1949,[134] which had become obsolete in many respects, due to later drastic changes in all political, social and economic conditions, was replaced by a new Constitution in 1968.[135] Since 1952 East Germany has been a strongly centralized state. With the evaporation (without formal abolition) of the five former states, their functions have been absorbed by the central state. Prior state

---

* A useful periodical publication in English with articles and selected pieces of major legislation is Law and Legislation (since 1959); *see also* MARKOVITS, Civil Law in East Germany, 78 Yale L.J. 1–51 (1968).

[133] Order (*Erlass*) of the State Council of Jan. 30, 1961, GBl. DDR I 5. *See* the compilation of treaties by KAPSA, *supra* A II (2) asterisked note.

[134] *English translation*: 3 PEASLEE, *supra* n. 96, at 334–356. *See,* briefly, PLISCHKE, *supra* n. 96, at 181–211.

[135] GBl. DDR 1968 I 199. *English translation*: The Constitution of the Socialist State of the German Nation (Dresden 1968). *See* the acute analysis by BOTHE, The 1968 Constitution of East Germany, 17 Am. J. Comp. L. 268–291 (1969).

legislation continues to exist, unless subsequently overridden or abrogated, as local law within restricted areas.

More than twenty articles of the Constitution establish the individual and collective rights of individuals. While they contain democratic and socialist ideas, their enforcement is entrusted almost exclusively to the legislature and the executive. Only in the field of family law have the courts directly enforced one of the fundamental rights, namely, that proclaiming the equality of men and women.

The head of the state since 1960 has been a collective, the State Council. Its president, Walther Ulbricht, is also First Secretary of the dominant Socialist Unity Party. The functions of the State Council are extremely wide. It represents Parliament when not in session, its resolutions have the binding force of law, and it controls and directs all state authorities. The council of ministers serves merely as its agent in directing the executive. Administrative or constitutional courts as fetters upon state power do not exist. The review of the constitutionality of laws is monopolized by the State Council (arts. 65 (2), 89 (3) of the Constitution) but seems never to have been invoked!

(b) A strict hierarchy of legal sources is lacking. Many administrative authorities are expressly bound to follow the resolutions of the dominant party, and judicial decisions must also conform to them. Only relatively few laws are enacted as statutes by Parliament. The great bulk of the law consists of regulations, decrees and orders issued by the executive. Legislation is published in the Official Gazette,[136] the first slim part containing the statutes, the second the more important decrees and orders, and the third the less important. There are periodic indexes of existing legislation.[137] Pre-1949 legislation, unless superseded or abrogated, continues to apply, especially the big codes for civil and commercial law, both substantive and procedural. The interpretation, of course, has often changed. It is typical that neither pre-War nor contemporary (West) German decisions or writers are cited by courts or scholars. A family code was enacted in 1965,[138] and a new penal code and code of criminal procedure in 1968.[139] New codes of substantive civil law and procedural law are in preparation and may be expected in the near future.

(3) **Judicial Decisions**

The court system,* in contrast to the too-complicated West German

---

[136] Gesetzblatt der Deutschen Demokratischen Republik, GBl. DDR.

[137] Gesetzes-Generalregister (1961); Das geltende Recht (2 parts), 1963, 1967, 1969.

[138] Law of December 20, 1965, GBl. DDR 1966 I 1.

[139] The two codes (and three supplementary statutes) date from Jan. 12, 1968 (GBl. DDR I 1 and 49).

* *See*, for revealing comments in English, from the Eastern side, BENJAMIN, The System of Law Courts in the German Democratic Republic, 1960 L. &

structure, is overly simple.[140] Only ordinary courts exist for civil, labor and criminal matters. Each of the 215 regions (*Kreise*) has a Regional Court (*Kreisgericht*), competent as a general court of first instance, with a special chamber for labor matters. Appeals, based on both law and fact, lie only to the District Courts (*Bezirksgerichte*), of which there is one in each of the fourteen districts; this court has a special department for labor matters. The public prosecutor may ask for the annulment of any decision of a *Kreisgericht* within a year after it becomes final. The President of the court may call up cases which he deems to be of particular importance from the *Kreisgerichte* of his district for decision by his court. The Supreme Court (*Oberstes Gericht*) in Berlin hears appeals from the *Bezirksgerichte* in the relatively few cases decided by those courts at first instance. The court rules on applications by the Attorney General and the President of the court to quash final decisions of the lower courts; such applications are rarely refused. In politically important criminal cases the Supreme Court acts as court of first and last instance. One of its main functions is the direction and control of adjudications by the lower courts; this task is performed in a variety of ways, for example, by work parties which inspect the files, by discussions with the judges, and by the issuance of binding resolutions and guidelines (*Richtlinien*) on important issues.

Controversies among the many legally separate units of the state economy are settled by so-called "contract courts" (*Vertragsgerichte*), corresponding in function and method to the East European state arbitral tribunals. These are administrative bodies specially charged with the settlement of disputes arising from the more or less planned contracts for the exchange of values within the state economy.

The reporting of East German case law is either official or semi-official and is highly selective. Only the Supreme Court publishes an official report, appearing in three series for civil, criminal and labor matters, respectively.[141] The main source for opinions of the lower courts is the bi-weekly journal "*Neue Justiz,*" edited by the Supreme Court.

Leg. no. 1 pp. 5–23, and *id.*, The Election of the Judges in 1960 and the Further Development of the Administration of Justice in the German Democratic Republic, 1961 L. & Leg. no. 1 pp. 5–21; Toeplitz, The Functions of the Courts of the German Democratic Republic on the Basis of the State Council Decree, 1963 L. & Leg. no. 1 pp. 19–27. *From Western authors*: Rosenthal, The Powers of the Judiciary in East Germany, 4 J. Int'l Comm. Jur. 134–149 (1962), and Kirchheimer, The Administration of Justice and the Concept of Legality in East Germany, 68 Yale L. J. 705–749 (1959).

140 The relevant statute is the Judiciary Act of April 17, 1963 (GBl. DDR I 45).

141 Entscheidungen des Obersten Gerichts der Deutschen Demokratischen Republik in Zivilsachen (OGZ), in Strafsachen (OGSt) and in Arbeitsrechtssachen (OGA).

(4) Legal Scholarship

Academic writing in East Germany is scarce, often highly ideological and of little influence upon the courts.[142] This literature is included in the *Bibliography of German Law*.

---

[142] The acid account of East German legal science given in 1952 by COHN, *supra* IV asterisked note, at 171–178, is largely still correct.

Chapter III.

GENERAL POINTS OF CONTACT

The two criteria most widely applied to determine the personal law of an individual are his nationality and his domicile or residence. His legitimacy, his duty to pay taxes, his claim to social security benefits, his liability to military draft—all these and innumerable other rights and obligations hinge as a rule on the general point of contact. For legal entities there are similar criteria; more specifically, what is looked to is the place of incorporation, the seat, or the center of administration or of doing business (ch. 10 sub I (1)(a)).

A. NATIONALITY OF INDIVIDUALS*

Nationality was originally applied, and should properly be understood to apply, to individuals only; it is in this technical sense that the relevant statutes, the most important source of law in this area, have been drafted in both countries. Relatively speaking, nationality is of greater importance in Germany than in the United States. This is especially true of the German conflicts rules relating to personal status; these, unlike the American rules, look in principle to a person's nationality rather than to his domicile.

I. LAW GOVERNING

Apart from a minor rule on proof[1] and the obscure article 278 of the Treaty of Versailles,[1a] there are no treaty provisions presently in force between the United States and Germany relating to questions

* Nationality statutes of the United States, Germany and other nations and treaties concerning nationality are compiled in a volume of the United Nations Legislative Series entitled Laws Concerning Nationality (1954, with 1959 Supplement).

[1] Art. XXV (6) of the U.S.-German Treaty of Friendship of 1954 (Treaties B 117). *See infra* II 6.

[1a] This article became effective between Germany and the United States by the Treaty Restoring Friendly Relations of 1921 (Treaties B 50). Its different interpretations by the United States and Germany culminated in the Rupprecht case in the late thirties. *Cf.* Foreign Relations 1938, vol. II 464–479; 3 Hackworth 398–403. By virtue of this unsettled controversy, art. 278 in effect plays no rôle in American-German relations.

of nationality.[2] This gives free play to the well-settled principle of international law that each state determines under its own law who are its nationals. Other states generally have to respect this determination;[3] it is recognized and applied in both the United States and Germany.[4] Thus German courts decide questions of American nationality according to American law[5] and American courts settle

---

[2] The Bancroft Treaties of 1868 (Treaties B 28–32), dealing with the nationality of emigrants, were abrogated in 1917 or 1922 (*supra* ch. 2 sub A I). As to these Treaties, *cf.* WEIL, La nationalité dans les rapports de l'Allemagne avec les Etats-Unis et les traités Bancroft, Clunet 44 (1917) 424; THIESING, Dual Allegiance in the German Law of Nationality and American Citizenship, 27 Yale L.J. 494–504 (1918). The draft of a Treaty Between the United States of America and Germany Relating to Nationality and Military Obligations (*cf.* Foreign Relations 1938, vol. II, 466–468) did not become law.

[3] MAKAROV, Allgemeine Lehren des Staatsangehörigkeitsrechts (2d ed. 1962) 191; 1 RABEL 146; PARRY, The Duty to Recognize Foreign Nationality Laws, ZaöRV 19 (1958) 337.

Under another principle of international law, American courts have declined to recognize German collective naturalizations with respect to citizens who had left their countries before the German annexations and who did not elect to become German nationals. United States *ex rel.* Schwarzkopf v. Uhl, 137 F.2d 898, 902 (2d Cir. 1943); United States *ex rel.* D'Esquiva v. Uhl, 137 F.2d 903 (2d Cir. 1943); United States *ex rel.* Reichel v. Carusi, 157 F.2d 732 (3d Cir. 1946), *cert. denied,* 330 U.S. 842 (1947); United States *ex rel.* Zeller v. Watkins, 167 F.2d 279 (2d Cir. 1948); BORCHARD, Collective Naturalization after Conquest—Its Inapplicability to Non-Residents, 37 A.J.I.L. 634 (1943); MAKAROV, Die Behandlung der deutschen Sammeleinbürgerungen 1938–1945 in der ausländischen Rechtsprechung, ZaöRV 18 (1957/58) 329. For German post-War treatment of these collective naturalizations, *cf.* MAKAROV, Zur Behandlung von deutschen Zwangseinbürgerungen 1938 bis 1945, JZ 1952, 403; SCHMIDT, HORST-ALEX, Staatsangehörigkeitswechsel bei Staatensukzessionen (thesis Munich 1966) 24–28. But in United States *ex rel.* Schwarzkopf v. Uhl, *supra* at 903, the court recognized, although subsidiarily, the German regulation of Nov. 25, 1941, RGBl. I 722, forcibly expatriating all German Jews residing abroad. *Cf.* MAKAROV, Die deutschen Ausbürgerungen 1933–1945 im internationalen Rechtsverkehr, *in* Festschrift Raape (1948) 257. *Cf. also infra* (5)(a).

[4] United States v. Wong Kim Ark, 169 U.S. 649, 668 (1898); 2 HYDE, International Law (2d ed. 1947) 1066; HARVARD LAW SCHOOL, Research in International Law, Draft convention on the law of nationality, art. 2, 23 A.J.I.L. (Spec. Supp. 1929) 13.

Germany: BVerfG 28 May 1952, BVerfGE 1, 322, 328–29; BGH 12 July 1963, WM 1964, 97, 98; 4 Oct. 1951, BGHZ 3, 178; KG Berlin 14 June 1954, IPRspr. 1954/55 no. 104; OLG Hamm 1 July 1955, NJW 1955, 1724; KEGEL, IPR 155.

This principle of international law was also applied by the American-German Mixed Claims Commission established pursuant to the Agreement of Aug. 10, 1922 (Treaties B 51), by deciding American nationality according to the municipal law of the United States, e.g., United States *ex rel.* Coughlin v. Germany, M.C.C. 513; United States *ex rel.* Williams v. Germany, M.C.C. 221, 19 A.J.I.L. 806 (1925); United States *ex rel.* Richards v. Germany, M.C.C. 637, 20 A.J.I.L. 599 (1926).

[5] RG 4 Mar. 1915, JW 1915, 583; 21 Nov. 1929, RGZ 126, 353; BayObLG 6 Nov. 1967, BayObLGZ 1967, 418, 422; KG Berlin 14 Sept. 1936, JW 1937,

issues concerning German nationality according to German law.[6]

II. GERMAN NATIONALITY*

(1) General Remarks

(a) *Sources.*—The basic German rules of nationality are amazingly simple as contrasted with the intricate American legislation on the subject. Legislation on German nationality (as distinct from that of the various German states[7]), started with the statute enacted on June 1, 1870 by the North German Union and extended, in 1870 and 1871, to all the states of the German Empire.[8] Some forty years later the Act of 1870 was replaced by the *Reichs- und Staatsangehörigkeitsgesetz* (Nationality Act, RuStAG) of July 22, 1913 (BGBl. III 100–1) which, although amended,[8a] is still in force in West Germany.

However, repercussions of the many and violent political upheavals undergone since the golden days prior to 1914 are reflected in numerous special enactments and international agreements: First, there were the treaties terminating World War I. Then, between

---

238; 10 Mar. 1933, IPRspr. 1933 no. 53; 3 July 1933, IPRspr. 1933 no. 96; OLG Karlsruhe 13 June 1933, IPRspr. 1933 no. 95; LG Kassel 10 Dec. 1952, NJW 1953, 307; LG München II 16 Oct. 1953, IPRspr. 1952/53 no. 304 a; LG Tübingen 25 July 1934, JW 1934, 2802; AG Heidenheim/Brenz 17 Nov. 1953, IPRspr. 1952/53 no. 230.

6 United States *ex rel.* Schwarzkopf v. Uhl, *supra* note 3 at 902–903; Zander v. Clark, 80 F. Supp. 453, 454 (D.D.C. 1948), *vacated on another ground sub nom.* McGrath v. Zander, 177 F.2d 649 (D.C. Cir. 1949); United States *ex rel.* Steinvorth v. Watkins, 159 F.2d 50, 51 (2d Cir. 1947); Rueff v. Brownell, 116 F. Supp. 298, 303 (D.N.J. 1953); Bauer v. Watkins, 171 F.2d 492 (2d Cir. 1948); *In re* Zietz' Estate, 201 Misc. 580, 585, 105 N.Y.S.2d 876, 880 (Sur. Ct. 1951), *aff'd*, 279 App. Div. 903, 111 N.Y.S.2d 751, 280 App. Div. 919, 115 N.Y.S.2d 923 (1952).

* MAKAROV, Deutsches Staatsangehörigkeitsrecht. Kommentar (1966); LICHTER, Die Staatsangehörigkeit nach deutschem und ausländischem Recht (2d ed. 1955); LICHTER/HOFFMANN, Staatsangehörigkeitsrecht (3d ed. 1966); SCHÄTZEL, Das deutsche Staatsangehörigkeitsrecht (2d ed. 1958); MASSFELLER, Deutsches Staatsangehörigkeitsrecht (2d ed. 1955, Supps. 1957 and 1958); FLOURNOY, Observations on the New German Law of Nationality, 8 A.J.I.L. 477 (1914).

7 For the situation before 1870, *cf.* MAKAROV, Kommentar 17–19. State citizenship as contrasted with national citizenship was abolished by the Regulation of Feb. 5, 1934, RGBl. I 85. According to art. 73 no. 2 GG, the Federation has exclusive legislative jurisdiction over national citizenship. State citizenship may be regulated both by the Federation and the states (art. 74 no. 8 GG). *Cf.* MAKAROV, Kommentar 235–40. Although some of the state constitutions, notably that of Bavaria, provide for state citizenship, neither the Federation nor the states have enacted specific legislation so far.

8 Gesetz über die Erwerbung und den Verlust der Bundes- und Staatsangehörigkeit, BGBl. 1870, 355. For the extension, *cf.* CAHN, Das Reichsgesetz über die Erwerbung und den Verlust der Reichs- und Staatsangehörigkeit vom 1. Juni 1870 (3d ed. 1908) 17 note 1.

8a BGBl. III 102–1. For an English translation, *cf. supra,* asterisked note preceding note 1.

1933 and 1945, a large number of special statutes and ordinances dealt mainly with facilitation of naturalization, with collective naturalization in consequence of territorial expansion, and with expatriation of thousands of political enemies, especially Jewish citizens living or emigrating abroad.[9] After World War II, all these measures of the Nazi period were reconsidered and most of them rectified. Those expatriated were either considered never to have lost their German nationality or at least to be entitled to renaturalization (*infra* (5)(a) and (2)(a)(iv)); in order to preclude such events in the future, the Constitution in strong terms prohibits denaturalization against one's will (art. 16 I GG). Other post-War statutes dealt with the problems arising from collective naturalization. But the end of the War also created grave new problems, particularly as to the nationality and the status of those millions of German stock who had to leave their homes abroad and who settled in Germany (*infra* sub (d)).

The new constitutional régimes created in 1949 in the East and West with their emphasis, *inter alia,* on the legal equality of men and women,[10] affected the old Act of 1913 in several respects. The latest step in the evolution of German nationality law has been the promulgation of a separate Nationality Act by East Germany (GDR); it deserves special consideration in the framework of the German East-West problem.

(b) *East-West Problem.*—Prior to February 1967 the Nationality Act of 1913, although amended and supplemented in both East and West, was still the common source of nationality law in both parts of the country.[11] On February 20, 1967, the German Democratic Republic (GDR) replaced the Act of 1913 by a fundamentally new statute, the *Staatsbürgerschaftsgesetz* (StbG).[12] Of particular importance for East-West relations are its rules conferring GDR citizenship on German nationals. Paragraph 1 (a) of the Act claims as a GDR citizen every German national who had German nationality at the founding of the GDR (October 7, 1949) and was domiciled or permanently resident there at that time or thereafter. Paragraph 1 (b) confers citizenship upon those German nationals domiciled or residing permanently outside the GDR who have not acquired another nationality since October 7, 1949 and who by virtue of

---

[9] Garner, Recent German Nationality Legislation, 30 A.J.I.L. 96 (1936); Feist, Development of German Law on Nationality, 186 L.T. 122 (1938); Makarov, *supra* n. 3, JZ 1952, 403; Makarov, *supra* n. 3, Festschrift Raape 257.

[10] *Cf.* Memorandum of Oct. 5, 1953 by the permanent observer of the Federal Republic of Germany to the United Nations on the changes made in the Nationality Act of July 22, 1913, by art. 3 II of the Basic Law concerning married women, in Laws Concerning Nationality 186–87.

[11] The two versions of the RuStAG are reprinted in Makarov, Kommentar 31–36.

[12] GBl. DDR 1967 I 3. *Cf.* short note in 16 I.C.L.Q. 1165 (1967).

registration with a competent authority are listed as GDR citizens. The other more traditional rules on acquisition and loss of nationality will be discussed in the proper context.

This GDR citizenship is not recognized by the Federal Republic of Germany, which assumes that there is only one German nationality.[13] States like the United States which do not recognize East Germany will share this view.[14] The practical consequences of the West German position are important and manifold: Naturalizations effected by East German authorities before the enactment of the 1967 statute were held to confer "the" German nationality unless West German public policy intervened.[15] Moreover, according to settled practice, West German consular and diplomatic authorities grant diplomatic protection to German nationals domiciled in Eastern Germany if they apply for it.[16]

(c) *German National and "German."*—Of great importance is the distinction, initiated by article 116 I GG, between a German national and a "German" (*Deutscher*). The latter term, within the meaning of the Basic Law, unless otherwise provided by statute includes not only a German national but also any person who, as a refugee or expellee of German stock (or as his spouse or descendant), has been admitted to the territory of the German Reich as it existed on December 31, 1937. The status of "Germans" who are not German nationals is considered below (*infra* (5)(b)).

(2) **Acquisition of Nationality**

German nationality may be acquired by birth, by legitimation, and by naturalization.

(a) *Birth.*—German nationality law, based on the principle of

---

[13] MAKAROV, Kommentar 21–26, with further references. Therefore, Germans moving from East to West Germany (if that is physically possible) are regarded automatically in West Germany as German nationals. On the other hand, the rights conferred and obligations imposed on German nationals by treaties with West Germany are implicitly, if not expressly, restricted to German nationals residing in West Germany or otherwise (by possession of a passport, etc.) connected with it, *see* MAKAROV, Kommentar 25–6. *Cf. also supra* ch. 2 sub A II(1).

[14] This seems to be the general American attitude with respect to nationality laws of unrecognized governments. Kolundjija v. Hanna Ore Mining Co., 155 Minn. 176, 180, 193 N.W. 163, 165 (1923); Murarka v. Bachrack Bros., Inc., 215 F.2d 547, 552 (2d Cir. 1954); 2 WHITEMAN 655; 1 O'CONNELL, International Law (1965) 195.

[15] BGH 23 Feb. 1954, BGHSt 5, 317 (extradition granted since naturalization asserted on basis of issuance in East Germany of identity card noting German nationality of bearer was in conflict with essential formalities of naturalization in West Germany). *In accord,* SCHÄTZEL 109.

[16] *Cf.* note of the West German Government to the Government of the Soviet Union of Sept. 5, 1956, ZaöRV 18 (1957/58) 713–15, and SCHÄTZEL 109; *see also* WENGLER, Deutschland als Rechtsbegriff, *in* Festschrift Nawiasky (1956) 61.

ius sanguinis and not on that of *ius soli*, attaches primary importance to descent and not to place of birth. Descent from the father is decisive, in the first instance: the legitimate[17] child of a German father acquires German nationality by birth (§ 4 I 1 RuStAG). In this case nationality of the mother is irrelevant as is residence of the parents in Germany.

In the absence of a German legitimate father a German mother may in certain circumstances confer her nationality upon her child: *First*, she may confer it upon a legitimate child if the latter would otherwise be stateless (§ 4 I 2 RuStAG).[18] This recent innovation, which seeks to prevent statelessness, will apply, for example, to a legitimate child born in Germany or elsewhere outside the United States to a father who is a citizen of the United States but who has not complied with the requirements of residence in the United States, and to a German mother; since the child will not acquire American citizenship from his father,[19] he would be stateless in the absence of this special rule making him a German. *Second*, the illegitimate[20] child of a German mother acquires German nationality at birth (§ 4 I 1 RuStAG), again irrespective of his place of birth and of whether his mother has resided in Germany.[21]

East Germany follows essentially the same pattern: A child, legitimate or illegitimate, acquires East German nationality at birth if either of his parents is an East German national (§ 5 StbG). Further, birth in East Germany confers this nationality provided the child has not acquired another nationality at birth (§ 6 I StbG).

(b) *Legitimation.*—If the German father of an illegitimate child validly legitimates his child according to German substantive law,[22] the child becomes a German national at the same time (§ 5 RuStAG). In contrast to the American rule, this acquisition of nationality has no retroactive effect to the time of the child's birth.

(c) *Naturalization.*—In Germany, as a country of emigration rather than of immigration, naturalization both in fact and in law plays a

---

[17] The law governing the legitimacy of the child is determined by the German conflicts law, *i.e.*, by art. 18 EGBGB; *cf.* MAKAROV, Kommentar 43; SCHÄTZEL, no. 3 b on § 4 RuStAG; LICHTER, no. 2 on § 4 RuStAG. *See infra* ch. 4 sub B I. Generally, on these preliminary questions, *see* MAKAROV, Die privatrechtlichen Vorfragen im Staatsangehörigkeitsrecht, ZfRV 3 (1962) 147; *id.*, Allgemeine Lehren (*supra* n. 3) 239–290.

[18] As amended by art. 1 of the West German Act of Dec. 19, 1963, BGBl. I 982. According to art. 2 of this Act of 1963 the new § 4 I 2 RuStAG is given retroactive effect back to Apr. 1, 1953, unless the child exercises his right to disclaim German nationality within one year after the Act enters into effect.

[19] I.N.A. § 301 (a) (4) or (7), 8 U.S.C. § 1401 (a) (4) or (7) (1964 ed.).

[20] *Cf. supra* n. 17, MAKAROV, Kommentar 51.

[21] *Cf. with* I.N.A. § 309 (c), 8 U.S.C. § 1409 (c) (1964 ed.).

[22] The legitimation must be valid according to German law. Art. 22 I EGBGB (*cf. infra* ch. 4 sub B I(2)(a)).

considerably less important rôle than in the United States.[23] The restraint exercised by German administrative practice in granting naturalization reflects favorably on the status so acquired; it is treated as fully on a par with that acquired in any other way. In particular, a naturalized German is not liable to loss of German nationality for reasons other than those obtaining generally for any German national.[24] Nationality is granted by the various state governments, whose decision may be reviewed by the courts (*infra* (7)). The substantive prerequisites for naturalization differentiate among four classes of persons: unqualified aliens, foreign spouses of Germans, qualified aliens (with an actionable claim for naturalization), and former Germans.

(i) *Unqualified aliens.*—For aliens who do not qualify under the following subsections ((ii) or (iii)), the German Nationality Act (§ 8 RuStAG) requires compliance with five conditions. The applicant must: reside in Germany[25]; be *sui juris* according to his present national law or according to German law, or if he is a minor the application must be filed by his legal representative or with the latter's consent; be of good repute; own a dwelling or lodging; and be able to support himself and his family.

These rather vague notions have been implemented by administrative rules (*Richtlinien*). Under the most important of these, naturalization will be granted normally only after ten years of continuous residence in Germany and generally it will be refused if it would result in dual nationality.[26] The other rules dealing with matters such as linguistic requirements are substantially similar to their American counterparts. The grant of naturalization, however, lies in the discretion of the competent authorities.

German naturalization extends to those children for whom the naturalized person acts as legal representative by virtue of parental

---

[23] In 1963, when the population was 57 million inhabitants, 17,799 persons were naturalized in West Germany and West Berlin. 5,797 of these persons had no actionable claim to be naturalized (*cf.* Statistisches Bundesamt Wiesbaden, Fachserie A: Bevölkerung und Kultur, Reihe 1: Bevölkerungsstand und -entwicklung: V Staatsangehörigkeit 1962 und 1963 p. 13 (Stuttgart and Mainz 1965)). In the same year in the United States, with a population of 190 million inhabitants, 124,178 persons were naturalized (U.S. BUREAU OF THE CENSUS, Statistical Abstract of the United States 1964 (85th ed.) 101 no. 130).

[24] Due to the American-German case, Schneider v. Rusk, 377 U.S. 163 (1964), the main difference between American citizenship by birth and by naturalization has vanished.

[25] The naturalization authorities may disregard the residence requirement; this is generally provided by the Regulation of January 20, 1942, BGBl. III 102–4, and especially for ethnic Germans by § 9 I Gesetz zur Regelung von Fragen der Staatsangehörigkeit (1st StARegG), BGBl. III 102–5.

[26] *Cf.*, e.g., Circular of the Minister of the Interior of Nordrhein-Westfalen of May 15, 1964, notes 8.2 and 2.3 to § 8 RuStAG, StAZ 1964, 189, and MAKAROV, Kommentar 183 and 181.

authority (§ 16 II RuStAG).[27] Extension of the husband's naturalization to his wife will be discussed later (*infra* (4)(c)).

It may also be mentioned that special conditions obtain for naturalization of a foreigner employed by the Federal Government who has his official residence abroad.[28]

(ii) *Foreign spouse of a German.*—Between 1957 and 1969 the foreign wife of a German husband could under certain conditions acquire her husband's German nationality by declaration (*infra* (4)(a)). This preferential treatment of a foreign wife was replaced on January 1, 1970 by a general rule for any foreign spouse of a German. The new provision (§ 9 I RuStAG[28a]) refers, in the first place, to the general conditions for the naturalization of an unqualified alien (*supra* (i)). If these general conditions are fulfilled, the authorities are directed to exercise their discretion in favor of naturalizing the foreign spouse, provided two additional requisites are present: *First,* the foreign spouse must lose his (or her) prior nationality by virtue of the marriage itself or by virtue of the application for, or the grant of, naturalization; if not, he must resign it. *Second,* the authorities must be satisfied that the foreign spouse is integrated into the German way of life; a resolution of Parliament expresses the assumption that the administrative authorities will, as a rule, require no more than five years for this latter purpose.[28b] However, the application may still be refused if it conflicts with weighty interests of the Federal Republic, especially its external or internal security or international relations. Naturalization under these special conditions may even be applied for within one year after the dissolution of the marriage through death or divorce, provided the foreign spouse has custody of a child of the marriage who is already a German (§ 9 II RuStAG).

(iii) *Qualified aliens.*—There are three groups of aliens who, although not former German nationals, may have an actionable claim for naturalization: "Germans" within the meaning of article 116 I GG (*supra* (1)(c)), according to § 6 of the first *Staatsangehörigkeitsregelungsgesetz* (1st StARegG, *supra* n. 25); persons of German stock who are not "Germans" according to article 116 I GG, and their spouses (1st StARegG §§ 8, 9 II); and aliens permanently residing in Germany who were excluded on racial grounds from certain collective naturalization measures (1st StARegG § 11).

(iv) *Former German nationals.*—Like United States law (I.N.A.

---

[27] *See* Rueff v. Brownell, *supra* n. 6. On certain problems in this connection *cf.* Makarov, Kommentar 92–94.

[28] § 34 RuStAG, as modified by the Act of May 15, 1935, BGBl. III 102–3.

[28a] Inserted by Act of Sept. 8, 1969, BGBl. I 1581, which also abrogated § 3 no. 3 RuStAG.

[28b] BAnz. 1969 no. 111 p. 8.

§ 324, 8 U.S.C. § 1435 (1964 ed.)), German law facilitates the naturalization of former nationals and their children (§ 13 RuStAG).[29] Apart from the peculiar German-Austrian aspects of nationality,[30] there are two classes of former German nationals who have an actionable claim for naturalization: *first,* those who between January 30, 1933 and May 8, 1945, by Nazi legislation invalidated *ex tunc* (*infra* (5)(a)), were deprived of their German nationality for political, racial or religious reasons, but thereafter lost it validly under the rules of the RuSt AG (*infra* (3)(a)–(c) and (4)), and their descendants (art. 116 II 1 GG), are regarded as never having lost their German nationality if they take up their domicile in Germany after May 8, 1945 without expressing a contrary intent (art. 116 II 2 GG, *infra* (3)(d)); *second* are those who in consequence of Nazi measures of persecution acquired a foreign nationality before February 26, 1955, and thereby lost their German nationality (1st StARegG § 12 I, as modified by art. III of the 3d StARegG, BGBl. III no. 102–7). Descendants of these latter persons might claim naturalization until December 31, 1970 (1st StARegG § 12 II, as introduced by 3d StARegG, art. III).

(v) *East Germany.*—East Germany has only a single provision relating to naturalization. Not only does it leave everything to the discretion of the authorities (§ 7 StbG), but it provides that naturalization may be revoked within five years if the applicant misstated the facts on his application or if he proves to be unworthy (§ 12 StbG).

(3) Loss of Nationality

According to article 16 GG nobody may be deprived of his German nationality. Any exception must be decreed on the basis of a statute, and no one may be deprived against his will if he is rendered stateless thereby. This constitutional rule reflects the reaction against the arbitrary denaturalization of thousands of German Jews who emigrated after 1933 and who were deprived of all diplomatic protection abroad. The consequences of these denaturalizations are discussed below (*infra* (d)).

The Nationality Act in its present version prescribes only three bases for loss of nationality: release on application, acquisition of a foreign nationality, and legitimation of an illegitimate child by a foreigner.

(a) *Release.*—Every German *sui juris*[31] must, upon application,

---

[29] § 13 RuStAG has been criticized by American writers because the applicant need not reside in Germany. *See* Comment, The German Imperial and State Citizenship Law, 9 A.J.I.L. 939 (1915); THIESING, *supra* n. 2, at 492.

[30] *Cf.* Zweites Gesetz zur Regelung von Fragen der Staatsangehörigkeit (2d StARegG) of May 17, 1956, BGBl. III 102–6.

[31] The release of minors must in certain cases be approved by the competent German court. § 19 RuStAG.

be released from German nationality provided he is not an official or subject to military service (§ 22 RuStAG). This release, which does not extend to the applicant's wife and minor children, becomes effective upon issuance of an instrument of release (§ 23 RuStAG). If one year thereafter the released person still maintains his domicile or permanent residence in Germany, the release is deemed to be inoperative (§ 24 RuStAG).

(b) *Acquisition of foreign nationality.*—A German citizen who has neither domicile nor permanent residence in Germany loses his German nationality if he acquires a foreign nationality (§ 25 I RuStAG) upon his own or his legal representative's[32] application. No expatriation will occur if he obtains the prior written consent of the competent German authorities to retention of his German citizenship (§ 25 II RuStAG). However, this consent is discretionary and in order to avoid double nationality it is seldom given;[33] according to administrative practice,[34] it is given only in those cases where the two are not incompatible. Since an application to retain German nationality would be incompatible with the oath of allegiance required for American naturalization,[35] the German authorities refuse their consent to retention of German nationality by German residents of the United States.[36]

(c) *Legitimation.*—If, according to German private international law (art. 22 EGBGB and *infra* ch. 4 sub B I (2)–(4)), a German

---

[32] Here as well, § 19 RuStAG must be observed. *Cf.* preceding note.

[33] VG Hamburg 7 Sept. 1961, StAZ 1963, 219; MAKAROV, Kommentar 138.

[34] MAKAROV, Kommentar 136, 138–39.

[35] I.N.A. § 316, 8 U.S.C. § 1427 (1964 ed.) does not require the petitioner for naturalization to abandon his foreign nationality. Whether retention of his German citizenship upon his application will amount to a violation of his oath of renunciation and allegiance (I.N.A. § 337, 8 U.S.C. § 1448 (1964 ed.)) has apparently never been decided by the American courts. However, the merely theoretical (*see* following note) possibility of retaining German nationality aroused critical comment abroad (*cf.* GUSTAV SCHWARTZ, Das Recht der Staatsangehörigkeit in Deutschland und im Ausland seit 1914 (1925) 153–54) and in the United States. For the latter, *see* MARSHAL, Dual Allegiance and Section 25 of the German Nationality Law of July 22, 1913, 3 Int'l L. Notes 79 (1918); THIESING, *supra* n. 2, at 479; HILL, Dual Citizenship in the German Imperial and State Citizenship Law, 12 A.J.I.L. 356 (1918); Comment, *supra* n. 29, at 940; FLOURNOY at 480–81; MATTERN, Paragraph 25 of the New German Citizenship Law, 204 North Am. Rev. 856–68 (1916); *cf.* the severe criticism of JOHN WIGMORE, Domicile, Double Allegiance and World Citizenship, 21 Ill. L. Rev. 761, 766 (1927), and the correspondence between him and ERNST FREUND, disagreeing, 22 Ill. L. Rev. 174, 429 and 433 (1927). Even a court, expressly pointing to § 25 RuStAG, advised great caution in the naturalization of German citizens. *In re* Haas, 242 Fed. 739 (W.D.N.Y. 1917). But this case seems to have been a solitary decision. *Cf. also In re* Zietz' Estate, *supra* n. 6.

[36] To date, administrative practice has seen no case in which a petitioner for American naturalization has been allowed to retain his German nationality. This practice is based upon the interpretation of this provision, correctly pointed out by THIESING, *supra* n. 2, at 488–92.

illegitimate child is validly legitimated by a foreigner, the child will lose its German nationality (§ 17 no. 5 RuStAG) unless it will become stateless thereby. This latter restriction has been in effect since May 24, 1949 (art. 16 I 2 GG).

If the American father of an illegitimate child marries the German mother, the child will lose its German nationality (*supra* (2)(a)) in the two following cases: where the child is born in the United States, since it retains its American citizenship acquired by INA § 301 (a)(1) and thus does not become stateless by legitimation; or where the child is born outside the United States and it acquires American citizenship by legitimation because the legitimation takes place while the child is under twenty-one years of age and the legitimating father has been physically present in the United States for not less than ten years (INA § 309 (a), § 301 (a)(7)).

(d) *Deprivation of German nationality between 1933 and 1945.*—After 1933 naturalizations granted between November 9, 1918 and January 30, 1933 could be revoked if deemed to be inconsistent with National Socialist policy. German nationality could be cancelled if the conduct of a German national residing abroad violated his duty of loyalty to Germany and injured German prestige.[37] In 1941 all Jews residing abroad or thereafter taking up residence abroad were deprived of their German nationality.[38]

After World War II these statutes were abolished[39] and invalidated *ex tunc* by the Federal Constitutional Court because of their political, racial, or religious discrimination.[39a] The nationality of these persecuted persons will be dealt with later (*infra* (5)(a)).

(e) *East Germany.*—It is characteristic of East German rules that while release may not be claimed as of right, expatriation is admitted. A citizen may be released only if his domicile is or will be transferred abroad with permission of the authorities, if he has or intends to acquire foreign nationality, and if there are no reasons operating against his release (§ 10 StbG). The discretion of the authorities is practically unfettered. By contrast, a citizen living outside East Germany may be expatriated if he has grossly violated his duties as a citizen (§ 13 StbG).

(4) Married Women

The Nationality Act of 1913 followed traditional paternalistic lines by striving to confer upon a wife the nationality of her husband. Thus an alien woman upon marrying a German citizen automatically

---

[37] Act of July 14, 1933, RGBl. I 480. *Cf.* SANDIFER, A Comparative Study of Laws Relating to Nationality at Birth and to Loss of Nationality, 29 A.J.I.L. 248, 276 (1935).

[38] Regulation of Nov. 25, 1941, RGBl. I 722.

[39] MASSFELLER 103; MAKAROV, Kommentar 201.

[39a] BVerfG 14 Feb. 1968, BVerfGE 23, 98.

acquired German nationality (§ 6 RuStAG, original version),[40] while a German woman through marriage to an alien lost her German nationality (§ 17 no. 6 RuStAG). Naturalization of a foreigner also extended by law to his wife (§ 16 II RuStAG). These rules, however, contravened the post-War constitutional principle of equality of man and woman established in article 3 II GG, and they were either abrogated after a provisional period of four years on March 31, 1953 (*see* art. 117 I GG),[41] or replaced.

The present situation is as follows:

(a) Between August 24, 1957 and December 31, 1969,[42] an alien wife marrying a German obtained her German husband's nationality at once if immediately after the marriage ceremony she deposited with the German marriage registrar (*Standesbeamter*) a declaration of intention to become a German national (§ 6 II RuStAG). Absent such a declaration she could, but without retroactive effect to the time of the marriage, claim naturalization as long as the marriage subsisted and the husband was a German national (§ 6 I 1 RuStAG). The claim even survived a marriage dissolved by death or by final divorce decree (without fault of the wife) if the former wife filed her application during the succeeding year (§ 6 I 2 RuStAG). The registrar was obliged to inform the alien wife of these two opportunities to acquire German nationality.[42a]

These rules were recently modified because they were thought to favor foreign wives unduly and because they were abused by certain women. Since January 1, 1970, the foreign spouse of a German may acquire German nationality only under the general rules, subject, however, to certain special conditions (*see supra* (2)(e)(ii)).

(b) Since April 1, 1953, a German woman, like an American woman, no longer loses her nationality upon marriage to an alien when she acquires her husband's nationality by operation of law.[43]

---

[40] This led to dual nationality where an American woman married a German. Acheson v. Wohlmuth, 196 F.2d 866 (D.C. Cir.), *cert. denied*, 344 U.S. 833 (1952); Brehm v. Acheson, 90 F. Supp. 662 (S.D. Tex. 1950); Zander v. Clark, *supra* n. 6.

[41] BVerfG 10 July 1958, BVerfGE 8, 81, 87. A brief summary of the former law is given by EDER, Effects of Marriage on the Nationality of Women, *in* Proceedings, Third International Congress of Comparative Law, London, 1950, sec. II-B.

[42] § 6 RuStAG, as modified by art. I of the Act of Aug. 19, 1957, BGBl. III 102–7. Art. II of this Act provides that women who married German nationals between Apr. 1, 1953 and Aug. 23, 1957 had claims to be naturalized retroactively to the date of marriage.

[42a] § 179 DA.

[43] MAKAROV, Kommentar 217. The same rule applied between May 24, 1949 and Mar. 31, 1953 to a German wife who during this period married an alien without acquiring her husband's nationality by marriage. *See* MAKAROV, Kommentar 226–31.

(c) Also since April 1, 1953, as in the United States, German naturalization of a foreign husband no longer extends to his wife. She has to apply separately for naturalization.[44]

According to these recent innovations an American woman who marries a German no longer automatically acquires German nationality while retaining her American citizenship. This source of dual nationality fortunately has been eliminated since an American woman who acquires German nationality by declaration or by application for naturalization will lose her American citizenship by force of INA § 349 (a)(1).[45]

In East Germany marriage has no effect whatsoever on the nationality of the wife, whether German or alien.

(5) **Refugees**

Persecution, oppression and wars have forced millions to leave their homes and to settle in unfamiliar surroundings and even in foreign countries. These movements have caused grave social and legal problems, one of which is the need to find a substitute for the refugee's original nationality, since the latter, typically, no longer serves as a meaningful contact for diplomatic and legal protection. With respect to American-German relations, four different groups of refugees must be distinguished: (a) German refugees from Germany; (b) German refugees, and refugees and expellees of German stock, in Germany; (c) German refugees from East Germany to West Germany; and (d) international refugees.

(a) *German refugees from Germany*.—Between 1933 and 1945 thousands of German citizens left Germany in order to escape tyranny or persecution.[46] Many of them were deprived of their German nationality by special German enactments because they were Jews, opponents of fascism, or both (*see supra* (3)(d)). These denationalizations were much discussed in Great Britain and the United States where a great number of Germans took refuge.[47] The

---

[44] However, in practice the naturalization authorities encourage the naturalization of all members of a family. *Cf., e.g.*, Circular, *supra* n. 26, note 2.2 to § 8 RuStAG.

[45] Although the declaration provided for in § 6 II RuStAG was not called an application for naturalization to be granted immediately, this declaration, in substance, amounts to acquisition of German nationality by a deliberate and voluntary act and therefore should be treated as naturalization within I.N.A. § 349(a)(1), 8 U.S.C. § 1481(a)(1) (1964 ed.).

[46] It is estimated that between 1933 and 1939 about 280,000 German Jews and about 40,000 other Germans fled from Germany. *Cf.* 3 Staatslexikon, 6th ed. 1959, col. 352.

[47] KAUFFMANN, Denationalization and Expropriation. The German Law Depriving Jewish Emigrants of Nationality and Property, and its Effects, 92 L.J. 93 (1942); ABEL, Denationalization, 6 Mod. L. Rev. 57 (1942); *id.*, Effect of the German Denationalization Decree of November 25th, 1941, 8 Mod. L. Rev. 77 (1945); KEMPNER, Who is Expatriated by Hitler: An Evidence Problem in Administrative Law, 90 U. Pa. L. Rev. 824 (1942).

expatriating effect of the German regulation of November 25, 1941 (*supra* n. 38) was, although subsidiarily, recognized in *United States ex rel. Schwarzkopf* v. *Uhl*;[48] but the status of these refugees became doubtful when the Allied Military Government on September 18, 1944, issued Abrogation Law No. 1[49] revoking, *inter alia*, this denationalization regulation.[50] The West German Constitution provides in article 116 II 1 that those Germans who between January 30, 1933, and May 8, 1945, were expatriated for political, racial, or religious reasons, and their descendants, are to be naturalized upon application. They are considered never to have lost their German nationality if they have taken up their domicile in Germany after May 8, 1945, and have not expressed a contrary intent (art. 116 II 2 GG). For example, an expatriated German who had been naturalized in the United States was held not to have expressed such an intent, his naturalization having taken place in 1946 before the effective date of the Basic Law. In addition, the fact that he subsequently designated himself before the German authorities as a United States citizen was deemed innocuous absent a showing that he thereby intended to renounce his German nationality.[51] Although it was agreed in post-War Germany that the denationalization enactments violated both international and domestic law,[52] article 116 II 1 GG was interpreted as not setting them aside retroactively.[52a] It was not thought appropriate to re-impose German nationality on those many persons who were unwilling to have any further connection with their former home country. A recent decision of the Federal Constitutional Court, however, has changed that theory completely by invalidating the regulation of November 25, 1941, *ex tunc*.[52b] Article 116 II GG is now interpreted as dealing only with persecuted persons still alive on May 8, 1945. Although Germans, they will not be treated as such unless they invoke their German nationality either by taking up their domicile in Germany (without expressing a reservation) or by applying for naturalization. If, after the ineffective expatriation, they lost their German

---

[48] *Supra* n. 3, at 903.

[49] Mil.Gov.Gazette, Germany, Sixth Army Group Area of Control, no. 1, pp. 11–12. The Regulation issued under Abrogation Law No. 1 listed the German Regulation of Nov. 25, 1941: Mil.Gov.Gazette, Germany, U.S. Zone, Eastern Military District, no. 3, July 14, 1945, p. 44. *Cf.* following note, at 377 nn. 15 and 16.

[50] SALWIN, Uncertain Nationality Status of German Refugees, 30 Minn. L. Rev. 372 (1946).

[51] BVerfG 10 July 1958, BVerfGE 8, 81, 87. For details concerning art. 116 II GG, *see* MAKAROV, Kommentar 251–260; MAUNZ/DÜRIG, Grundgesetz, vol. 2 (loose-leaf 1968) nos. 27–29 on art. 116 GG.

[52] BGH 11 June 1958, BGHZ 27, 375, 377; BVerwG 19 Nov. 1954, BVerwGE 1, 234, 236; MAUNZ/DÜRIG, last note, no. 27 on art. 116 GG.

[52a] Last note and MAKAROV, Kommentar 254.

[52b] BVerfG, *supra* n. 39a.

nationality under the ordinary rules of the RuStAG, as by naturalization in a foreign country, they may reacquire German nationality by invoking it according to article 116 II GG (*supra* II (2)(d)(iv)). On the other hand, those persons who died before May 8, 1945, have to be treated as never having lost their German nationality unless they expressed a contrary intention; this, however, will not be lightly assumed.[52c]

(b) *German refugees, and refugees and expellees of German stock, in Germany.*—During and after World War II more than seven million Germans left their homes in the eastern parts of Germany which are now under Polish or Soviet control, and about five million people of German stock (*deutsche Volkszugehörige* or *Volksdeutsche*) were forced to leave their homes, mainly in Eastern Europe.[53] This migration continues, although on a small scale, to this day. Up to 1964 more than 75% of these twelve million refugees had finally settled in the Federal Republic of Germany.[54]

With respect to the German refugees, no special problems arise since they are German nationals. As to the refugees and expellees of German stock,[55] article 116 I GG provides that they and their spouses and descendants are "Germans" if they have been admitted to the territory of the German Reich as it existed on December 31, 1937 (*supra* (1)(c)). These provisions in effect equate the post-War refugees and expellees of German stock to German nationals, without any regard to their original nationality. Even a person of dual nationality expelled from one of the countries of which he is a national has been considered a "German."[56] While the equation was originally limited to political rights and duties, it was later extended to all issues of German private and procedural law turning on the nationality of persons.[57] This extension is particularly important for German conflicts law.

Although already treated in most respects as German nationals, the "Germans" within article 116 I GG have an actionable claim for naturalization (*supra* (2)(d)(iii)).

[52c] The Federal Constitutional Court did not decide with respect to those persons who died after May 8, 1945, but before the coming into force of the GG on May 24, 1949. They too should be treated as Germans unless they have shown a contrary intent.

[53] The figures are taken from 3 Staatslexikon, *supra* n. 46, col. 356.

[54] Statistisches Jahrbuch für die Bundesrepublik Deutschland 1967, 45.

[55] The terms "expellee" (Vertriebener) and "person of German stock" (deutscher Volkszugehöriger) are defined in §§ 1 and 6 Bundesvertriebenengesetz, BGBl. III 240–1. As to a former American of German stock treated as a German within art. 116 GG, *cf.* OLG Stuttgart 15 Aug. 1963, DÖV 1964, 165.

[56] BVerwG 24 Feb. 1966, BVerwGE 23, 272.

[57] Art. 9 II no. 5 of the Family Law Amendment Act of Aug. 11, 1961, BGBl. I 1221.

(c) *German refugees from East Germany and East Berlin to West Germany.*—Between 1946 and 1961 about five million persons moved from East Germany and East Berlin to West Germany.[58] Many of these have been recognized as so-called Soviet-Zone refugees (*Sowjetzonenflüchtlinge*)[59] for purposes of West German social legislation, but this status is irrelevant for conflicts law. They too are treated as German citizens because they are either German nationals or "Germans" within article 116 I GG (*supra* (1) (c)). Conflicts between East and West German family or succession law which may arise out of this migration are determined on the basis of domicile or habitual residence.

(d) *International refugees.*—The status of the refugees and displaced persons qualifying under the United Nations Convention of 1951 will be dealt with later (*infra* B) because, for these persons, nationality has been replaced by domicile or residence as the general point of contact. If refugees do not qualify under this Convention, their personal status will be determined according to the law of their nationality or, if they are stateless, according to that of their domicile.

(6) **Multiple Nationality**

Multiple nationality, a frequent phenomenon today, is caused by the hitherto unknown international mobility of persons. The conflicting basic principles governing acquisition of nationality easily produce double nationality. Thus, by the interplay of the American *ius soli* and of the German *ius sanguinis,* all legitimate children of German fathers and all illegitimate children of German mothers, if born in the United States, are dual nationals (*supra* (2)(a)).[60] However, marriage of an American woman to a German, as we have seen, no longer results in dual nationality of the woman.

There is no West German statutory rule regulating conflicts arising from dual nationality.[61] A German national who has another citizenship also will in most respects be treated as a German.[62] If neither

---

[58] Statistisches Jahrbuch, *supra* n. 54, 1966, 46.

[59] This term is defined by § 3 Bundesvertriebenengesetz, *supra* n. 55.

[60] *Cf.* Gensheimer v. Dulles, 117 F. Supp. 836 (D.N.J. 1954). Another case of dual nationality occurred where an American girl married a German before Mar. 31, 1953. *Cf. supra* (4), especially n. 40. *See,* further, n. 27. Generally, on the different causes of dual nationality, *see* ORFIELD, The Legal Effect of Dual Nationality, 17 Geo. Wash. L. Rev. 427 (1949).

[61] There is, in particular, no provision like I.N.A. § 350, 8 U.S.C. § 1482 (1964 ed.), according to which a dual national is, under certain circumstances, divested of his American nationality.

[62] This is the common practice of the courts: RG 25 Jan. 1916, RGSt 49, 373, 374; 19 Mar. 1936, RGZ 150, 374, 376, 382; BGH 4 Oct. 1951, BGHZ 3, 178, 180; BFH 20 Sept. 1951, IPRspr. 1950/51 no. 111; OLG Hamm 1 July 1955, NJW 1955, 1724, 1725. *See also* § 140 II DA, and, expressly, § 3 I of the East German StbG. Even in the case of multiple nationality, many conflicts scholars favor for conflicts law the principle of effective nationality:

of his nationalities is German, he will be treated as a national of the country where he is domiciled.[63]

(7) **Procedural Questions**

In Germany matters of nationality are primarily dealt with by administrative agencies. It is they who issue certificates of citizenship (*Staatsangehörigkeitsausweise*) and certificates of residence (*Heimatscheine*), decide applications for naturalization, and determine whether German nationality has been lost. All these decisions can be challenged before the administrative courts.[64]

An American-German treaty provision declares a valid passport or certain other identity documents to be sufficient evidence of the bearer's German or United States nationality.[65]

B. DOMICILE AND RESIDENCE

The domicile of a natural person plays only a limited rôle in German conflicts law for private law matters, especially issues of status, succession and the like. It serves merely as a substitute if nationality, the primary point of contact (*infra* chs. 4 and 5), fails because the person involved has no effective nationality. The personal law of a stateless person is the law of his habitual residence or, if even this is lacking, of his simple residence (art. 29 EGBGB). The personal law of a recognized refugee is, according to article 12 I of the Convention on Refugees (Treaties M 308), the law of his domicile or, subsidiarily, of his residence. Virtually the same result is achieved for refugees of German stock who have taken refuge in West

---

KEGEL, IPR 156; NEUHAUS 143; FERID, Zur kollisionsrechtlichen Behandlung von Inländern mit zugleich ausländischer Staatsangehörigkeit, RabelsZ 23 (1958) 498, 508. In Miyuki Okihara v. Clark, 71 F. Supp. 319, 322 (D. Hawaii 1947), a Japanese-American woman was treated as an enemy under the Trading with the Enemy Act. *Contra,* Zander v. Clark, *supra* n. 6, at 454 (German-American woman). For the American practice, *cf.* BAR-YAACOV, Dual Nationality (London 1961) 46–7, 64–5, 146–7; 3 HACKWORTH 352–377; RODE, Dual Nationals and the Doctrine of Dominant Nationality, 53 A.J.I.L. 139 (1959); ORFIELD, *supra* n. 60, at 428–432. The principle of election was applied by the umpire of the U.S.-German Mixed Claims Commission with regard to a British-American citizen, United States *ex rel.* Mackenzie v. Germany, M.C.C. 628.

[63] RG 24 Jan. 1908, FJG A II 1 no. 98 (p. 448); DPA 16 Nov. 1953, IPRspr. 1952/53 no. 313. *See* § 140 IV i DA. German scholars prefer the principle of effective nationality in this situation, too, *supra* n. 62; it is taken into account subsidiarily by § 140 IV 2 DA, where there is no domicile or residence in either national state.

[64] BVerwG 27 Feb. 1957, BVerwGE 4, 298; 30 Sept. 1958, BVerwGE 7, 237; *contra,* HANS SCHNEIDER, Die Ablehnung eines Einbürgerungsantrages vor den Verwaltungsgerichten, ZaöRV 19 (1958) 449–63. For further details, *cf.* MAKAROV, Kommentar 77–79.

[65] U.S.-German Treaty of Friendship (Treaties B 117) art. XXV (6) with Protocol no. 22.

Germany, by equating a "German" to a German citizen (*supra* A II (5)(b)). Nevertheless, even though domicile and residence are, generally speaking, of limited importance in German conflicts rules, the converse is true, curiously enough, in the practice of American-German legal relations. This is primarily due to the fact that through the liberal German admission of renvoi (art. 27 EGBGB and *infra* chs. 4 and 5), American conflicts rules in matters of personal status and succession, largely dominated as they are by the law of the domicile, are imported into German conflicts law. Therefore German courts frequently apply the American notion of domicile (*infra* (2)(b)). It must also be emphasized that German conflicts rules, outside the private-law area proper, often use domicile or residence as the decisive point of contact.

(1) Basic German Notions

German law provides three concepts to denote the varying degrees of relationship between person and place: *Wohnsitz* (domicile), *gewöhnlicher Aufenthalt* (habitual residence), and *einfacher Aufenthalt* (simple residence or mere presence). Only the first is defined by legislative rules.

(a) According to § 7 I BGB, domicile is the place where a person establishes himself permanently. Clearest proof of an establishment is the renting of living quarters. But it has to be accompanied by an *animus manendi,* in other words, the valid intention (of a legally competent person, *see* § 8 BGB) to make this place, not only temporarily, his abode. Accordingly, a domicile is not given up until a person terminates his establishment with the valid intention no longer to regard the place as his abode (§ 7 III BGB). No longer does a wife necessarily share her husband's domicile, but a legitimate minor child still has the domicile of his parents, and an illegitimate one that of his mother. If only one of the parents of a legitimate child has custody, the child is domiciled with that parent only (*see* § 11 BGB). Probably because of its lesser legal relevance, the German notion of domicile does not know those Anglo-American doctrines that are meant to insure the continuity and the unity of domicile. Thus a person may have several domiciles (§ 7 II BGB), or he may have no domicile at all.

(b) Habitual residence might be defined as domicile without *animus manendi.* Most important, minor children may have a habitual residence separate from that of their parents. Likewise, soldiers and students who stay for a certain time in one place are habitually resident there.

(c) A simple residence or mere presence needs no explanation.

This brief exposition of the basic German rules has shown that the American and German notions of domicile differ. It is therefore necessary to inquire what law is determinative in cases of conflict.

(2) **Law Governing Domicile and Residence**

(a) *Basic rule.*—When the terms "domicile" and "habitual residence" occur in German legal rules, they have to be interpreted according to German law unless the context clearly demands the contrary (*infra* (b)). This is the basic rule; it applies whether the place in question is in Germany[66] or abroad,[67] and irrespective of the nationality or the present residence of the person involved.[68] Thus, as a basis for their jurisdiction, German courts have applied their own law to determine the habitual residence of American soldiers (and their wives) stationed in Germany[69] and of an American student studying in Heidelberg.[70]

(b) *Exceptions.*—However, there are at least three situations in which German courts have looked to American rather than German law to determine domicile:

First, they have done so in order to determine the "national" law of Americans. The federal structure of the American legal system has usually been understood by German courts and has led them to conclude that in matters of personal status and of succession a reference by a German conflicts rule to an American's "national law"

---

[66] BayObLG 31 May 1966, BayObLGZ 1966, 203, 205–6; KG Berlin 16 Feb. 1961, FamRZ 1961, 383 (domicile of a child for purposes of venue and jurisdiction. The contrary decision (RG 12 Jan. 1939, RGZ 159, 167) is not followed); BGH 19 Mar. 1958, BGHZ 27, 47, 48; LG Ansbach 24 July 1963, IPRspr. 1962/63 no. 182; LG München II 16 Oct. 1953, IPRspr. 1952/53 no. 304 a (habitual residence for purposes of venue and jurisdiction); LG Düsseldorf 10 Dec. 1958, IPRspr. 1958/59 no. 174 (domicile in Germany for purposes of security for costs); erroneously, OLG Köln 30 Nov. 1956, IPRspr. 1956/57 no. 180.

[67] BGH 29 Nov. 1961, IPRspr. 1960/61 no. 190; 17 Jan. 1962, IPRspr. 1962/63 no. 53 (time for appeal). Whether this rule also applies if the existence of a domicile abroad has to be ascertained for jurisdictional purposes has not been settled. The better and more modern view is to apply German law in this case also: RG 5 Apr. 1921, RGZ 102, 82, 84; KG Berlin 16 Feb. 1961, *supra* n. 66, at 384; BayObLG 31 May 1966, *supra* n. 66, at 205; SERICK, ZZP 68 (1955) 278–301. Preliminary questions that may arise, especially in determining the domicile of dependents, remain subject to the law applicable thereto; BayObLG, *supra,* applied the German rules on the domicile of a child, but submitted the preliminary question of his legitimacy to American law, as required by art. 22 EGBGB.

The courts at one time applied foreign local law if a foreign domicile was at issue: RG 19 Nov. 1894, RGZ 34, 392, 399; 25 Oct. 1883, Gruchot 28, 889, 890; KG Berlin 31 Mar. 1941, DR 1941, 1855; 2 May 1938, JW 1938, 2843; 4 Jan. 1937, JW 1937, 821.

[68] BayObLG 31 May 1966 and KG Berlin 16 Feb. 1961, *supra* n. 66; BGH 17 Jan. 1962 and 29 Nov. 1961, *supra* n. 67.

[69] E.g., OLG Koblenz 24 May 1960, NJW 1960, 2193; LG Augsburg 6 Feb. and 17 Oct. 1963, IPRspr. 1962/63 nos. 180a and b; LG Kaiserslautern 13 June 1961, IPRspr. 1960/61 no. 183; SCHWENK, Scheidung amerikanischer Ehen durch deutsche Gerichte, NJW 1955, 1707–1709, 1708.

For residence as the basis of jurisdiction, *see infra* ch. 14 (2) (a).

[70] OLG Karlsruhe 15 May 1963, IPRspr. 1962/63 no. 181.

is meaningless. Further specification is required, and there is unanimity that the relevant additional factor is the domicile[71] (or the *last* domicile[72]) of the American citizen in one of the states, to be determined according to "American" law.[73] There is less unanimity on the method of arriving at this result. The reasoning most consonant with German legal thinking would be to invoke a uniform (or concurrent) American conflicts rule based on the first sentence of section 1 of Amendment XIV to the Federal Constitution by virtue of which citizenship in an individual state of the Federation is created through residence in this state.[74] Some writers would prefer to apply a specialized German conflicts rule, pointing to the habitual or simple residence within the United States, and subsidiarily to the *last* habitual or simple residence there.[75]

Second, domicile is also determined by American standards in connection with renvoi. While the German conflicts rules on matters of personal status and succession refer to a person's national law, the legislator has directed that a renvoi (or reference over) from the foreign legal system has to be recognized (art. 27 EGBGB). Thus for American citizens living outside the United States, the "American" law's conflicts principle of domicile becomes relevant (*infra* chs. 4 and 5). It is generally recognized that the notion of domicile in these American conflicts rules must be interpreted according to American law, and that this is usually internal state law.[76]

Third, American rules on domicile become relevant in connection with German divorce jurisdiction over Americans. The jurisdiction of the German courts over foreign spouses depends upon ultimate recognition of the resulting decree in the foreign husband's home country (§ 606 b no. 1 ZPO, *infra* ch. 4 sub A V (1)(b)). Since "American" recognition rules usually require that at least one of the spouses must have been domiciled in the state of the rendering court, the necessary domicile has to be determined under American

---

[71] E.g., BGH 4 Mar. 1960, FamRZ 1960, 229; BayObLG 31 May 1966, *supra* n. 66, at 207; 29 Dec. 1959, IPRspr. 1958/59 no. 211; 7 Feb. 1958, BayObLGZ 1958, 34, 38; KG Berlin 24 June 1937, JW 1937, 2527, 2528; LG München II 16 Oct. 1953, *supra* n. 66; RAAPE 149–50.

[72] BGH 19 Mar. 1958, BGHZ 27, 47, 49 (impliedly); OLG Karlsruhe, *supra* n. 70; LG Heidelberg 10 Dec. 1964, IPRspr. 1964/65 no. 234; LG Kaiserslautern, *supra* n. 69. However, 1 RABEL 144–46 has pointed out that the reasoning, although not the result, of this rule is not correct.

[73] Expressly, BayObLG 31 May 1966, *supra* n. 71; LG Heidelberg, *supra* n. 72.

[74] BGH 4 Mar. 1960 and KG Berlin 24 June 1937, *supra* n. 71; LG München II 16 Oct. 1953, *supra* n. 66.

[75] KEGEL, IPR 138–9. *See also* NUSSBAUM, Deutsches internationales Privatrecht (1932) 109; LEWALD, Das deutsche internationale Privatrecht (1931) 13; 1 EHRENZWEIG 134.

[76] BayObLG 7 Feb. 1958, *supra* n. 71, at 39; 9 July 1965, BayObLGZ 1965, 245, 249; LG München II 30 Nov. 1955, IPRspr. 1954/55 no. 215.

law. At present, this is generally understood to mean American internal law.[77]

In applying "American" law, the most frequent but still controversial issue has been whether American soldiers stationed in Germany have become domiciled there.[78] Almost as frequent has been the necessity for determination of the domicile of dependent persons such as children[79] and (according to an old-fashioned view) wives.[80]

---

[77] BGH 19 Mar. 1958, BGHZ 27, 47, 51 (as found by the lower court); RG 21 Nov. 1929, JW 1930, 1309; LG Stuttgart 17 Dec. 1968, NJW 1969, 384; LG Mannheim 24 Apr. 1964, IPRspr. 1964/65 no. 230; LG Kaiserslautern, *supra* n. 69; LG Hamburg 19 June 1957, IPRspr. 1956/57 no. 113; *see also* cases *infra* n. 80. *See also* 1 RABEL 442; SCHWENK, *supra* n. 69. On the lone dissenting case, LG München II 16 Oct. 1953, *supra* n. 66, *see infra* ch. 4 sub A V (1)(b) n. 141.

[78] *In the negative*: BayObLG 6 Feb. 1962, BayObLGZ 1962, 39, 41; LG Mannheim 4 July 1961, IPRspr. 1960/61 no. 184, *aff'd*, OLG Karlsruhe 15 May 1963, IPRspr. 1962/63 no. 181; LG Mannheim 24 Apr. 1964, preceding note; LG Augsburg 6 Feb. and 17 Oct. 1963, *supra* n. 69; LG Wiesbaden 26 Mar. 1957, IPRspr. 1956/57 no. 115; SCHWENK, *supra* n. 69, to the effect that as a rule there is no domicile there.

In the affirmative: OLG Koblenz 24 May 1960, and LG Kaiserslautern 13 June 1961, *supra* n. 69; LG Stuttgart 17 Dec. 1968, *supra* n. 77; LG Wiesbaden 30 Oct. 1958, IPRspr. 1958/59 no. 185.

[79] *See* BayObLG 9 July 1965, *supra* n. 76, at 251–3, and 6 Feb. 1962, preceding note; OLG Bamberg 2 Oct. 1963, IPRspr. 1962/63 no. 109.

[80] BayObLG 9 July 1965, *supra* n. 76, at 251; OLG Bamberg 2 Oct. 1963, preceding note; OLG Hamburg 30 Jan. 1957, IPRspr. 1956/57 no. 114; LG Wiesbaden 26 Mar. 1957, *supra* n. 78; LG München II 30 Nov. 1955, *supra* n. 76, and 16 Oct. 1953, *supra* n. 66.

Chapter IV.

FAMILY LAW AND PERSONAL STATUS*

There are no treaty relations between the United States and Germany in matters of family law, and hence all issues in this field are governed by the general conflict of laws rules of the two countries. Although German family law has been radically altered by the constitutional postulate of equality of the sexes (art. 3 II GG),[1] by legislation implementing this principle,[2] and by a recent statute on the legal status of illegitimate children,[2a] the private international law aspects, according to court practice[3] and to most legal writers,[4] have not been directly affected. The basic rules laid down in articles 13 through 23 EGBGB are therefore still binding. As for East Germany, 1965 saw the enactment, together with the new *Familiengesetzbuch*,[5] of separate conflicts rules for family law.[6]

A. HUSBAND AND WIFE

I. ENGAGEMENT TO MARRY

The really important question in both American and German law is whether the breach of a promise to marry gives rise to an action

---

* 1 Cohn 221–256; Beitzke, Familienrecht (15th ed. 1970); Dölle, Familienrecht (2 vols. 1964–65); Gernhuber, Lehrbuch des Familienrechts (1964); Henrich, Familienrecht (1970); Hoffman/Stephan, Ehegesetz (2d ed. 1968).

[1] Mosheim, The Legal Effects of Equal Marital Rights for Women in Germany, 2 I.C.L.Q. 430–442 (1953).

[2] Gesetz über die Gleichberechtigung von Mann und Frau auf dem Gebiet des bürgerlichen Rechts (Gleichberechtigungsgesetz) of June 18, 1957, BGBl. I 609. *Cf.* Leyser, Comment, 7 Am. J. Comp. L. 276–287 (1958).

[2a] Gesetz über die rechtliche Stellung der nichtehelichen Kinder of Aug. 19, 1969, BGBl. I 1243; Bohndorf, The New Illegitimacy Law in Germany, 19 I.C.L.Q. 299–308 (1970).

[3] BGH 18 Jan. 1954, NJW 1954, 837; 17 Oct. 1956, NJW 1957, 100; BayObLG 16 Jan. 1959, BayObLGZ 1959, 8; and further decisions quoted by Kegel, Kommentar, note 2 at p. 717.

[4] Kegel, IPR 259; Raape 43; further references by Kegel, Kommentar, note 2 at p. 717.

[5] Familiengesetzbuch der Deutschen Demokratischen Republik (FamGB) of Dec. 20, 1965, GBl. DDR 1966 I 1.

[6] Einführungsgesetz zum Familiengesetzbuch der Deutschen Demokratischen Republik (EGFamGB) of Dec. 20, 1965, GBl. DDR 1966 I 19.

for damages. German domestic law[7] answers this affirmatively but confines the damages to the expenses actually incurred in expectation of the marriage, to damage for loss of virginity, and to restitution of gifts[8] (§§ 1298–1301 BGB). These rules differ substantially from those of most of the American states, and actual conflicts have already occurred.

A German court will award damages if the engagement is valid[9] and if the defendant under his *lex patriae* is liable for damages,[10] irrespective of whether this liability is qualified, as in Germany, as contractual, or whether it is deemed a tort.[11] A renvoi by a foreign *lex patriae* will be accepted.[12] This means that the liability of an American party will be determined by his American *lex domicilii* unless there is a renvoi or a transmission. If the American is domiciled in a common law state, a German court may be asked to award general damages exceeding the amount recoverable under German law. Although no German court decision appears to have been

---

[7] For a short account of German law *cf.* WEIDENBAUM, Breach of Promise to Marry in Private International Law, 14 N.Y.U. L. Rev. 451, 454–456 (1937); BROCKELBANK, The Nature of the Promise to Marry—A Study in Comparative Law, 41 Ill. L. Rev. 1, 17–18 (1946); 1 COHN 222–223.

[8] The restitution of gifts is to be decided by the defendant's *lex patriae*: FRANKENSTEIN, Internationales Privatrecht III (1934) 46; *contra*: RAAPE 278 (plaintiff's *lex patriae*).

[9] Validity is determined for each party by his national law (analogous to art. 13 I EGBGB, *see infra* II (1) (a)): BGH 21 Nov. 1958, BGHZ 28, 375, 376; KG Berlin 7 Feb. 1938, JW 1938, 1715; OLG Köln 4 Dec. 1925, Recht 1926 Rspr. no. 454; *accord*: KEGEL, Kommentar, no. 14 preceding art. 13 EGBGB; RAAPE 274.

[10] BGH, *supra* n. 9; KG Berlin: 7 Feb. 1938, JW 1938, 1715; 23 Feb. 1933, IPRspr. 1934 no. 41; 2 May 1932, IPRspr. 1932 no. 66; OLG Köln, *supra* n. 9; *accord*: LUTHER, Ersatz immaterieller Schäden bei Verlöbnisbruch im internationalen Privatrecht und in Auslandsrechten, FamRZ 1959, 475, 477; WOLFF 185; *contra,* that is, granting the abovementioned action only if the personal laws of the parties bind the defendant and entitle the plaintiff to an action: OLG München 13 Mar. 1929, IPRspr. 1929 no. 69; LG Hamburg 5 Nov. 1954, NJW 1955, 548; *accord*: KEGEL, Kommentar, no. 16 preceding art. 13 EGBGB, and others mentioned there at n. 6. *Cf.* RAAPE 278 and GAMILLSCHEG, Das Verlöbnis im deutschen internationalen Privatrecht, RabelsZ 32 (1968) 473, 486, for the *lex domicilii* of the innocent party in certain cases.

[11] GAMILLSCHEG, *supra* n. 10, at 481–484; KEGEL, Kommentar, no. 17 preceding art. 13 EGBGB, for certain cases only; *infra* ch. 7 at n. 31. The proper law of torts (*infra* ch. 7 sub (1)) governs only those claims which under German standards would not be qualified as breaches of contract but as belonging to general tort law. *Contra*: KEGEL; OLG Frankfurt/M. 5 July 1923, IPRspr. 1930 no. 62 (applying the *lex loci delicti commissi* because the conduct of the defendant, although constituting a breach of contract under German standards, was regarded as a general tort by the *lex loci*).

[12] In accordance with the general rule (art. 27 EGBGB), BGH, *supra* n. 9, at 376; KEGEL, Kommentar, no. 18 preceding art. 13 EGBGB; RAAPE 274; but not with respect to a characterization different from German law: GAMILLSCHEG, *supra* n. 10, at 481–482.

reported, it is doubtful whether the court would do so rather than limit the measure of damages according to German standards; an award of general damages would be tantamount to a prohibited constraint to marry and would therefore violate German public policy.[13] The conclusion is equally doubtful where an American defendant is domiciled in a state which has abolished "heartbalm" actions. In 1939 a German court refused to award damages to a German fiancée in accordance with the law of New York, the domicile of the defendant.[14] It is not clear whether a German court would follow this decision today under all circumstances; in 1958 the Federal Supreme Court, vigorously criticized by scholars,[15] held that the application of a foreign statute to deny damages to a German fiancée for the loss of her virginity violates German public policy.[16]

II. MARRIAGE*

In German conflicts law the rules controlling the substantive and the formal requirements of marriage differ.

(1) Substantive Requirements

The substantive requirements are determined separately for each party by the law of his own nationality (art. 13 I and II EGBGB).[16a] This means that there is no valid marriage unless all the requirements for a valid marriage under both personal laws are fulfilled.[16b]

(a) Whether a German party is allowed to marry is decided according to German law (art. 13 I 1 EGBGB), that is, according to the Marriage Law (*Ehegesetz*, EheG).[17]

(b) Whether an alien is allowed to marry in Germany depends upon his own national law (art. 13 I 2 EGBGB), or if he is stateless upon the law of his habitual residence or his abode (art. 29 EGBGB). However, a renvoi by his personal law in the form either of a reference back to the German *lex fori* or of reference over to another foreign law will be complied with according to the general rule

---

[13] BGH, *supra* n. 9, at 379 (obiter); NUSSBAUM, Deutsches internationales Privatrecht (1932) 131; WOLFF 185; *contra*: FRANKENSTEIN, *supra* n. 8, at III 46. A similar situation arises between the American states: *cf.* cases cited by EHRENZWEIG, A Treatise on the Conflict of Laws (1962) 376 n. 9.

[14] KG Berlin 11 Jan. 1939, DR 1939, 1012.

[15] DÖLLE, JZ 1959, 489, 490–492; KEGEL, IPR 261; LÜDERITZ, NJW 1959, 1032–1033; LUTHER, *supra* n. 10, at 477–478; modestly, GAMILLSCHEG, *supra* n. 10, at 485–486.

[16] BGH, *supra* n. 9.

* G.O.W. MUELLER, International Choice of Law to Determine the Validity of Marriage, 2 Howard L.J. 21, *passim* (1956).

[16a] MUELLER 42–43.

[16b] *Cf.* StAZ 1962, 288, where no marriage was held to exist because it was null and void according to Oregon law, even though valid under German law.

[17] BGBl. III 404–1; COHN no. 482.

already referred to (art. 27 EGBGB).[18] Therefore, with respect to United States citizens,[19] the German courts and authorities will check the law of their present or last domicile in the United States[20] as their national law. If that law does not refer to German law (as the *lex domicilii* of the spouses or the place of celebration of the marriage), the requirements for marriage are determined by the domestic law of the American's domiciliary state.[21] Thus the German authorities will apply American restraints upon marriage unless these violate German public policy (art. 30 EGBGB).[22]

In some reported cases, however, the German courts have found that the American's domiciliary state applies the *lex domicilii*[23] or the *lex loci celebrationis*.[24] The capacity to marry in Germany of an American domiciled there is consequently determined finally by German domestic law. This renvoi by American law to German law includes all the German substantive requirements for marriage. It implies that the *Vormundschaftsrichter* has jurisdiction to grant a dispensation from these requirements.[25]

In order to make strict compliance with the relevant foreign law feasible for the normal marriage registrar, a special procedure has been devised: An alien who wishes to be married in Germany

---

[18] LG Hamburg 16 Oct. 1958, StAZ 1960, 99, 100; KEGEL, Kommentar, no. 92 on art. 13 EGBGB; RAAPE 69–70.

[19] Since 1955 the following also applies to U.S. soldiers in Germany, *infra* n. 35.

[20] *Supra* ch. 3 sub B (2) (b). In favor of the present or last habitual or simple residence in the United States: BÖRNER, Personalstatut und Ehefähigkeit von Angehörigen der U.S.A., StAZ 1956, 43, 44–45. § 148 I DA only refers to the state the law of which determines the law applicable, but does not specify exactly which state it is.

[21] *Cf. supra* n. 20. § 176 I DA points out that all American jurisdictions except Minn., Nev., S.C., V.I. and Wash. require a medical certificate. U.S. soldiers always have to supply a special marriage permit issued by a military civil-affairs office: BACHMANN, StAZ 1955, 189, 191; *cf.* also the conclusion of the Bavarian Minister of Interior of July 3, 1968, on § 166 IV DA, StAZ 1968, 283, 286 sub no. 4.

[22] Up to now no American impediment to marriage has been declared against public policy by German courts. A permanent restraint of remarriage (KEGEL, Kommentar, no. 94 on art. 17 EGBGB) or a prohibition based on difference of race (WOLFF 190; BACHMANN, StAZ 1955, 189, 191) would be disregarded in Germany. *Cf.* KG Berlin 16 Feb. 1909, OLG 19, 106.

[23] OLG Dresden 15 Jan. 1912, OLG 26, 211, with reference to the "American private international law."

[24] OLG Karlsruhe 3 Oct. 1968, StAZ 1969, 71; LG Tübingen 25 July 1934, JW 1934, 2802, with reference to the "competent American conflicts law." WOLFF 190.

[25] KEIDEL, Freiwillige Gerichtsbarkeit, 9th ed. 1967, no. 13a on § 56 FGG (capacity to marry); no. 8 on § 44a (impediment of affinity); no. 11 on § 44b (prohibition of remarriage). If a male alien is a minor and his personal law does not refer back to German law as to emancipation, German courts have no jurisdiction to emancipate the minor (*infra* sub C (1) (c)) and therefore cannot give a dispensation under § 1 II EheG.

generally has to supply a certificate of ability to marry (*Ehefähigkeitszeugnis,* § 10 I EheG). (Strangely enough this is required even if his personal law refers back to German law.[26]) This is a document in which the competent authorities of the alien's home country certify that his personal law does not prohibit the marriage.[27] As American authorities do not issue such certificates,[28] an American citizen must apply to the registrar for a dispensation.[29] The president of the competent German court of appeals will grant such a dispensation provided the law applicable according to article 13 I EGBGB permits the marriage;[30] his refusal to do so is subject to review by the ordinary courts.[31]

(2) Formal Requirements

It is necessary to distinguish between marriages celebrated in Germany and those celebrated abroad.

(a) Marriages celebrated in Germany must comply with German domestic law as to formalities even if both parties are foreigners (art. 13 III EGBGB). As an exception to this severely criticized provision,[32] a marriage between parties neither of whom is a German national may, according to § 15a I EheG, be concluded before a person duly empowered by the government of a country of which either party is a national, according to the form prescribed by the law of that country.[33] However, as American Foreign Service officers are

---

[26] § 166 III 1 DA; *cf.* OLG Karlsruhe, *supra* n. 24; MASSFELLER/HOFFMANN, Personenstandsgesetz, Kommentar (1963) no. 15 on § 10 EheG (preceding §§ 3*ff.* PStG); HOFFMANN/STEPHAN, no. 8 on § 10 EheG. This surprising attitude is partly to be explained by the difficulties in deciding whether there is a renvoi or not. By requiring a certificate and checking the person's national law this vexatious question may be avoided. When a renvoi, however, is beyond any doubt, the requirement makes no sense.

[27] *Cf.* as to this requirement 1 RABEL 307–308; MARQUARDT, Le certificat de capacité matrimoniale en droit comparé (Paris 1965).

[28] As to American states: 1 RABEL 308 n. 180; 2 HACKWORTH 356–358; MARQUARDT, last note, at 65; as to consular officers, *cf.* 22 C.F.R. § 52.5 (1967).

[29] § 170 I 1 DA in connection with § 166 IV DA. § 171 II DA enumerates the documents to be joined with the application. In OLG Karlsruhe, *supra* n. 24, dispensation was granted to an American. That, according to the law of Texas, he was not allowed to marry within 12 months after his Texas divorce, was no obstacle because the court held that this restraint of remarriage under Texas law does not nullify a subsequent marriage before expiration of that period and therefore a German marriage will be recognized in the United States.

[30] BEYER, StAZ 1957, 29, 34–36; DÖLLE I 152; HOFFMANN/STEPHAN, nos. 28–33 on § 10 EheG; NEUMAYER, RabelsZ 20 (1955) 66, 72.

[31] §§ 23–30 Einführungsgesetz zum Gerichtsverfassungsgesetz (EGGVG) of Jan. 27, 1877, RGBl. 77; version in force: BGBl. III 300–1; BGH 12 Feb. 1964, BGHZ 41, 136, 138–139; KG Berlin 14 Sept. 1961, NJW 1961, 2209.

[32] KEGEL, Kommentar, no. 54 on art. 13 EGBGB; Vorschläge und Gutachten zur Reform des deutschen internationalen Eherechts (1962) pp. 10–12.

[33] § 15a EheG has a broad field of application in those cases where, e.g., the Greek and Spanish governments have authorized priests in Germany to celebrate

not authorized to celebrate marriages[34] and as special exemptions for members of the United States Army in Germany expired in 1955,[35] a civil ceremony before the registrar (§ 13 I EheG) is now the only form of marriage for Americans in Germany.

According to German law a marriage is concluded by a declaration by the contracting parties made in person and in the presence of each other before the registrar that they wish to marry (§ 13 I EheG). This means that marriages by proxy or *inter absentes* by mail, and marriages solemnized by ministers of religious denominations or societies[36] or by captains of German vessels, do not constitute valid marriages under German domestic law. They are void *ex nunc* and *ex tunc*, respectively.[37]

(b) The formal validity of a marriage performed outside Germany is determined either by the *lex causae* (art. 11 I 1 EGBGB), which means by the personal law of both parties governing the substantive validity of the marriage (art. 13 I EGBGB), or by the *lex loci celebrationis* (art. 11 I 2 EGBGB). Because of the latter alternative, common law marriages,[38] marriages celebrated by American ministers[39] or by registrars,[40] marriages by proxy[41] or *inter absentes* by mail[42]—all are

---

marriages. A marriage of Americans concluded in Germany before an authorized British military chaplain is absolutely void ab initio: StAZ 1968, 202.

[34] 22 U.S.C. § 1172 (1964 ed.); 22 C.F.R. § 52.1 (1969); PARRY, A Conflicts Myth: The American "Consular" Marriage, 67 Harv. L. Rev. 1186–1212 (1954); 1 RABEL 257. Today the marriage of Loring v. Thorndike, 87 Mass. (5 Allen) 257 (1862) solemnized by the U.S. consul in Frankfort on the Main would be void ab initio in Germany. It may be valid according to American state law: *cf.* Gen.Stat. Conn. § 46–6 (1965 Supp.); Ann. Laws of Mass. c. 207 § 43 (1969).

[35] 1 RABEL 261 n. 182; BACHMANN, StAZ 1955, 189–197.

[36] Generally it is a regulatory violation if a minister celebrates the religious ceremony before the civil marriage has been performed by the registrar: § 67 PStG. In Kaltman v. Kaltman, N.Y.L.J. Jan. 7, 1966, p. 14, col. 6 (Sup.Ct.) a ceremonial marriage performed in Germany was correctly held void ab initio.

[37] The marriage by proxy is void ex nunc (voidable) according to § 17 EheG: DÖLLE I 212; HOFFMANN/STEPHAN, no. 13 on § 13 EheG; the absence of a registrar causes a marriage to be absolutely void ab initio (*Nichtehe*): DÖLLE I 255–257; HOFFMANN/STEPHAN, no. 55 on § 11 EheG. *Cf. infra* V (4).

[38] RG 26 Oct. 1932, RGZ 138, 214; RG 1 May 1902, JW 1902, 361; LG Hamburg 6 July 1934, StAZ 1934, 442; LG Tübingen 25 July 1934, JW 1934, 2802; *cf.* also AG Mainz 9 Dec. 1955, IPRspr. 1954/55 no. 83; KEGEL, Kommentar, no. 48 on art. 13 EGBGB; 1 RABEL 241 n. 92.

[39] LG Nürnberg-Fürth 3 June 1953, IPRspr. 1952/53 no. 101.

[40] OLG Hamburg 15 Nov. 1926, HansGZ 1927 B 4. Although the marriage had been performed by a registrar as in German law the case had to be decided according to the *lex loci celebrationis* because the personal law of the Greek party as *lex causae* did not allow a civil marriage.

[41] KEGEL, Kommentar, no. 50 on art. 13 EGBGB with further references.

[42] LG Hamburg, *supra* n. 38: The general German conflicts rule was stated correctly but applied wrongly to the facts as the offer was accepted in Germany, the domestic law of which neither as *lex causae* nor as *lex loci celebrationis* allows a marriage *inter absentes* (supra (2) (a)). *Cf.* BERGMANN, Note in StAZ 1934, 442; KEGEL, Kommentar, no. 49 on art. 13 EGBGB.

recognized as valid in Germany even if these forms are not recognized by the law governing the substantive validity of the marriage. The same would be true of marriages performed by captains of American vessels where this is authorized by American law.[43] German foreign service officers in the United States are not authorized by German law to solemnize marriages.[44]

(3) **Law of East Germany**

The law of East Germany, although amended in 1965, is in its truly private law aspects very similiar to that of West Germany. Paragraph 15 I 1 EGFamGB, like article 13 I EGBGB, applies the spouses' national law to the substantive requirements for marriage. According to § 15 I 2 EGFamGB, an East German desiring to marry a noncitizen of the GDR has to obtain a permit issued by the public authorities. In view of the political conditions usually attached to such a permit, it is doubtful whether this requirement can be complied with outside East Germany. The form of marriage is to be determined, as in article 11 I 2 EGBGB, according to the *lex loci celebrationis* (§ 15 II EGFamGB). If the marriage is celebrated outside the GDR it suffices to observe the formal requirements of the home country of only one of the parties (§ 15 III EGFamGB).[45]

III. PERSONAL EFFECTS OF MARRIAGE*

Marriage may affect the spouses' personal relations in many respects: among others, it may change the wife's name, obligate the husband to support his wife, or create interspousal immunity. In German conflicts law one set of rules determines the law governing all of these problems. These rules will therefore be discussed first in general, after which their impact on the most important personal effects of marriage will be illustrated.

(1) **German Conflicts Rules in General**

(a) *Law governing.*—The conflicts rules relating to the personal effects of marriage are only partially codified. The law is well settled for spouses with a common personal law (*infra* (i)), but not otherwise (*infra* (ii)). However the rules are detailed and have two

---

[43] KEGEL, Kommentar, no. 51 on art. 13 EGBGB. *Cf.* 2 HACKWORTH 371–374.

[44] They have not been empowered by the Federal Chancellor according to § 1 of the Law of May 4, 1870, BGBl. 599; present version in MASSFELLER/HOFFMANN, supra n. 26, part I no. 11; StAZ 1965, 290 and 1968, 8.

[45] *Cf.* art. 11 I 1 EGBGB (both parties), *supra* (2)(b); Das Familienrecht der DDR. Lehrkommentar (1967) 355–358.

* DÖLLE, Die persönlichen Rechtsverhältnisse zwischen Ehegatten im deutschen internationalen Privatrecht, RabelsZ 16 (1951) 360–386; *id.*, Persönliche Rechtsbeziehungen der Ehegatten: Deutsches Recht, *in*: Das internationale Familienrecht Deutschlands und Frankreichs (1955) 63–91 (*in French in*: Le droit international privé de la famille en France et en Allemagne (1954) 50–77).

features in common: *First,* in keeping with the general approach of German law, personal law is generally determined by one's nationality. *Second,* it is the nationality possessed at the time in question which is relevant. This means that the personal effects of the marriage may change during its course whenever one or both spouses change nationality.[46]

(i) *Spouses with a common personal law.*—According to article 14 I EGBGB the personal effects of the marriage of German spouses are governed by German law even if their domicile is abroad. Alien spouses with the same personal law are treated in the same manner, their domicile being ignored. This is unanimous court practice and writers' opinion.[47] As a result, the personal incidents of a marriage between two American citizens will ultimately be determined by the law of their common American domicile,[48] or, if there is a renvoi (*infra* (b) (2)), according to the law referred to by the conflicts rules of that domicile.

(ii) *Spouses with different personal laws.*—Four different solutions have been applied or proposed for the situation where the spouses have different personal laws, not one of which is prescribed by any written rule. For the purpose of legislative reform, it has been proposed that the spouses' present or last common domiciliary law, should govern.[49] Application of the last common national law is expressly provided in article 14 II EGBGB for one case only: if the husband has lost his German nationality but the wife has retained hers, German law continues to govern the spouses' personal rights and obligations. This provision has been extended by some courts and writers to all cases where the spouses once had a common personal law.[50] According to a third solution, the spouses have mutual rights

---

[46] DÖLLE, RabelsZ 16 (1951) 360, 361; KEGEL, Kommentar, no. 7 on art. 14 EGBGB; RAAPE 324; 1 RABEL 326. Exceptions to this rule are discussed *infra* sub (a) (2) and at n. 81.

[47] *Spouses with a common national law*: BayObLG 24 Mar. 1966, FamRZ 1966, 354, and decisions cited by KEGEL, Kommentar, note 1 at p. 753; *stateless spouses with the same habitual residence or abode*: BayObLG 20 Apr. 1955, StAZ 1955, 260; DÖLLE, *supra* n. 46, at 366–7; *spouses one of whom resides as a stateless person in the other's country*: BayObLG 12 Oct. 1956, BayObLGZ 1956, 345. As to *spouses of multiple nationality,* the general principles (*supra* ch. 3 sub A II (6)) apply: KEGEL, Kommentar, no. 42 on art. 14 EGBGB. *Literature*: DÖLLE, *supra* n. 46, at 361; KEGEL, IPR 277; PALANDT/LAUTERBACH, nos. 1 and 2 on art. 14 EGBGB.

[48] LG Detmold 2 Aug. 1930, IPRspr. 1930 no. 152 at p. 253.

[49] Vorschläge und Gutachten zur Reform des deutschen internationalen Eherechts (1962) p. 2 sub § A nos. 3 and 4, RabelsZ 25 (1960) 340. This rule is at present supposed to violate the principle of nationality (*supra* sub (1) (a)): KEGEL, IPR 278.

[50] KG Berlin 25 Sept. 1958, FamRZ 1958, 464 (interlocal case); OLG Kiel 24 Jan. 1931, IPRspr. 1931 no. 64 (nonconflicts case); AG Berlin-Zehlendorf 15 Mar. 1961, NJW 1961, 1728; KEGEL, Kommentar, no. 5 on art. 14 EGBGB;

and obligations only insofar as their personal laws agree on a certain issue. This rule of cumulation of two different personal laws has been applied and favored especially in recent years as the best solution, within the framework of the principle of nationality, to obey the constitutional postulate of equality between husband and wife (art. 3 II GG, *supra* at nn. 1–4).[51] The rule has been applied in two reported American-German cases, but both of them were non-conflict cases;[52] in the first case the American wife had to share her German husband's domicile according to the laws both of New Jersey and of Germany;[53] in the second, the German wife had no claim against her American husband for support or advance payment for the cost of a lawsuit, either under American or German law.[54] If there had been a true conflict, the suit in both cases should have been dismissed under this third rule. Prevailing court practice and the majority of legal writers, finally, apply the husband's national law.[55] This rule, too, was invoked in a non-conflicts case dealing with a German wife's name after her American husband's change of name.[56]

Hence no firm answer can be given at the present time to the question as to how the German courts will handle true conflicts cases involving spouses with different personal laws.

(b) *General choice of law problems*

(i) *Characterization of "personal effects."*—It must be emphasized that the rules laid down above (sub (a)) pertain to the personal effects of marriage only, in other words, to legal consequences other than those which relate to property. The following matters, according to German law as the *lex fori,* have been characterized as the personal effects of marriage: the wife's domicile,[57] name[58] and capacity;[59] interspousal immunity;[60] rights to decide any differences between the

---

WOLFF 197; *contra*: RG 19 June 1913, WarnRspr. 6 (1913) 521; OLG Stuttgart 24 Sept. 1932, JW 1933, 2072 (obiter); LG Göttingen 15 Dec. 1948, MDR 1949, 356, 357; RAAPE 325.

51 OLG Düsseldorf 9 Aug. 1967, FamRZ 1967, 626, 628; and decisions cited by KEGEL, Kommentar, note 8 at p. 754; KEGEL, IPR 278; PALANDT/LAUTERBACH, no. 2a on art. 14 EGBGB.

52 As to the term, *cf.* EHRENZWEIG 86–8.

53 OLG Braunschweig 19 Jan. 1913, OLG 26, 232.

54 LG Fulda 21 June 1960, IPRspr. 1960/61 no. 94.

55 AG Bielefeld 29 Aug. 1961, StAZ 1962, 253; and decisions cited by KEGEL, Kommentar, note 7 at p. 754; RAAPE 323–24; WOLFF 197–98.

56 OLG Frankfurt/M. 18 Apr. 1967, FamRZ 1967, 481.

57 KG Berlin *supra* n. 50; OLG Braunschweig, *supra* n. 53; DÖLLE, *supra* n. 46, 375; KEGEL, IPR 280; RAAPE 325; 1 RABEL 333–335; Bekanntmachung des Bayerischen Staatsministers des Innern of March 18, 1968, concerning the execution of the Federal Law on Passports, StAZ 1968, 224, 225; *contra*: OLG Hamburg 8 May 1907, OLG 15, 99, 100. *Cf. supra* ch. 3 sub B (1).

58 *Infra* sub (2) (b).

59 *Infra* sub (2) (c).

60 *Infra* sub (2) (e).

spouses and to control the conduct of the other party;[61] the duty to live together and the right to sue for restitution of conjugal rights;[62] the wife's right and duty to render services,[63] including her agency power;[64] the duty to support one another[65] and to make advance payments for the costs of a lawsuit;[66] the wife's lien on the husband's property;[67] the prohibition of certain contracts between the spouses[68] or between the wife and third parties;[69] the presumptions of ownership;[70] and the declaration of death as a prerequisite for a new marriage.[71]

(ii) *Renvoi.*—It is a view unanimously held today that a renvoi or a transmission by a foreign law which is declared applicable by a German conflicts rule must be taken into account.[72] The omission of

---

[61] OLG Dresden 14 Jan. 1914, LZ 1914 col. 1581; DÖLLE, *supra* n. 46, 372–373; KEGEL, Kommentar, no. 15 on art. 14 EGBGB; 1 RABEL 332.

[62] RG 15 Apr. 1935, RGZ 147, 385, 388; LG Berlin 6 Mar. 1961, IPRspr. 1960/61 no. 182; and older cases cited by KEGEL, Kommentar, note 3 at p. 756; DÖLLE, *supra* n. 46, 370–372; 1 RABEL 332 n. 50.

[63] KEGEL, Kommentar, no. 16 on art. 16 EGBGB; RAAPE 325; 1 RABEL 332.

[64] *Infra* sub (2) (d).

[65] *Infra* sub (2) (f).

[66] OLG Düsseldorf 9 May 1961, NJW 1961, 1583; 19 Aug. 1965, FamRZ 1965, 616; OLG München 15 May 1953, MDR 1953, 490; KEGEL, IPR 280; PALANDT/LAUTERBACH, no. 4e on art. 14 EGBGB. If the foreign law cannot be ascertained quickly, the *lex fori* will be applied: OLG Düsseldorf 19 Aug. 1965, *supra* and *cf. infra* n. 92.

That this question was once characterized as one of marital property was mainly due to the fact that before the enactment of the Gleichberechtigungsgesetz, *supra* n. 2, the duty to make these advance payments was dealt with in the marital property law of the BGB. *Cf.* KEGEL, Kommentar, no. 22 on art. 14 EGBGB.

[67] *Cf.* DÖLLE, *supra* n. 46, at 384–85; KEGEL, Kommentar, no. 27 on art. 14 EGBGB; 1 RABEL 352. The *lex rei sitae* must agree to the creation of a lien (*infra* ch. 6 sub I (1)).

[68] KG Berlin 20 Mar. 1939, DR 1939, 938, with note by REU; DÖLLE, *supra* n. 46, at 383; KEGEL, IPR 280–81; PALANDT/LAUTERBACH, no. 4 g on art. 14 EGBGB; 1 RABEL 345–48. As to the influence of art. 7 III EGBGB, *see infra* C (1) (b). The prohibition of companies between spouses may be a question of marital property: RG 11 Apr. 1940, RGZ 163, 367, 375–77.

[69] DÖLLE, *supra* n. 46, at 383–84; KEGEL, Kommentar, no. 34 on art. 14 EGBGB; RAAPE 328; 1 RABEL 341–42. As parties to a contract concluded in Germany will be protected by art. 7 III 1 EGBGB (*infra* C (1) (b)), the German courts will come to the solution reached in Milliken v. Pratt, 125 Mass. 374 (1878).

[70] *Infra* IV (2) (e) (ii).

[71] LG Göttingen, *supra* n. 50, *aff'd,* OLG Celle 11 Feb. 1949, MDR 1949, 357 with Note by BEITZKE; LG Göttingen 29 Oct. 1949, IPRspr. 1945/49 no. 6; AG Bielefeld, *supra* n. 55; *see, generally, infra* C (5).

[72] RG 15 Feb. 1906, RGZ 62, 400, 404; BayObLG 20 Mar. 1953, BayObLGZ 1953, 102, 105; OLG Kiel, *supra* n. 50; *contra*: KG Berlin, *infra* n. 76, without reasonable arguments because it would have been nonsense to mention art. 14 EGBGB in art. 27 as a unilateral rule pointing to German law. *See* KEGEL, Kommentar, no. 40 on art. 14 EGBGB; PALANDT/LAUTERBACH, no. 1 on art. 14 EGBGB; RAAPE 324; WOLFF 198.

article 14 EGBGB in the general renvoi provision of article 27 EGBGB is innocuous.[73] This means that German law governs if American state law refers back either to the German *lex fori*[74] or to the German situs of real property.[75]

(iii) *Preliminary question: does a marriage exist?*—Courts and scholars agree that the preliminary question whether there is a marriage at all is to be decided according to articles 11 and 13 EGBGB (*supra* II) and to the rules about divorce and annulment (*infra* V). It is irrelevant whether or not a marriage bond exists according to the law governing the personal incidents of the marriage.[76]

(2) **Personal Effects of Marriage: Specific Aspects**

(a) *Wife's name.*—Unlike American law, German statutes regulate in great detail the law of a person's surname.[77] According to German conflicts rules the personal law generally governs all issues relating to the name (*infra* C (2)), but whether marriage affects a wife's name is to be determined by the law governing the personal incidents of the marriage.[78] This latter law also decides whether a husband's change of name extends to his wife. Accordingly it was held in one case that an American husband's change of name, effected by an American court decree, extended to his wife who was a *de facto* stateless person residing with him.[79] Moreover, although a wife does not acquire her husband's surname by marriage, she may use it in her daily life, even when signing documents, provided the law governing the personal incidents of the marriage permits such a practice.[80]

Since the law governing the personal effects of marriage is mutable (*supra* at n. 46), a change of the spouses' personal law should alter their name if their new personal law differs in this respect from their

---

73 The omission is explained by the simple fact that art. 14 EGBGB expressly refers only to German spouses.

74 If, for example, an American court applies the *lex fori* to the husband's duty to support his wife, a German court will apply German law (as *lex fori* rather than the parties' personal law).

75 This may happen if the spouses' personal law determines the personal effects of marriage with respect to real property, e.g., the wife's capacity to sell land, according to the *lex rei sitae*.

76 KG Berlin 27 May 1927, JW 1928, 73; LG Detmold, *supra* n. 48; LG Düsseldorf 20 June 1952, MDR 1952, 623; KEGEL, Kommentar, nos. 38 and 39 on art. 14 EGBGB.

77 As to the wife's name, *cf.* 1 COHN no. 505.

78 BGH 12 July 1965, BGHZ 44, 121, 124; and cases cited by KEGEL, Kommentar, note 2 at p. 760; KEGEL, IPR 280; PALANDT/LAUTERBACH, no. 4 c on art. 14 EGBGB; RAAPE 325–26; *contra*: WENGLER, NJW 1963, 593 and 2230; FICKER *in* Festschrift Nipperdey I 297, 308, applying the wife's personal law only.

79 OLG Frankfurt/M., *supra* n. 56.

80 BayObLG 8 June 1965, BayObLGZ 1965, 221, 225–26; OLG Frankfurt/M. 3 Dec. 1964, FamRZ 1965, 45; 22 Aug. 1963, NJW 1963, 2231. Therefore the wife of an American may use her husband's name in Germany: Runderlass des Ministeriums der Justiz für Hessen, Jan. 30, 1968, StAZ 1968, 129, 132.

former law. Yet it has been decided that once a name is fixed it can be changed only by governmental authority or by a change of status but not by a mere change of personal law.[81] Whether a former wife may use her husband's name after a divorce is to be determined under article 17 EGBGB (*infra* V (2) (c)).

(b) *Wife's capacity.*—Generally capacity is governed by one's personal law (*infra* C (1)). This is true where a wife acquires by marriage full capacity under her personal law;[82] any disabilities, however, except those with respect to marital property,[83] are determined by the law applicable according to article 14 EGBGB and its collateral rules.[84] Moreover, such a limitation upon a German wife's capacity might be held to be against public policy.[85] Finally, despite any disabilities which may exist under foreign law, the general rule of article 7 III EGBGB (*infra* C (1) (b)) protecting transactions concluded in Germany is applicable by analogy.[86]

(c) *Wife's agency power.*—For the same reason there is an important exception to the general rule that the wife's power to obligate her husband—be her agency statutory, implied, or by necessity—is governed by the law applicable according to article 14 EGBGB and its companion rules.[87] According to article 16 II EGBGB the general provision granting a broad statutory agency power to the wife, § 1357 BGB,[88] is applicable to a foreign wife domiciled in Germany if more favorable to third parties than the otherwise applicable foreign rule.[89] Article 16 II EGBGB makes it unnecessary to look to the foreign spouses' personal law or to its conflicts rules.

---

[81] BayObLG 26 Jan. 1968, BayObLGZ 1968, 7, 12–14.

[82] KEGEL, Kommentar, no. 28 on art. 14 EGBGB; PALANDT/LAUTERBACH, no. 2 on art. 7 EGBGB.

[83] They are determined according to the law governing the marital property (*infra* IV): KEGEL, Kommentar, no. 31 on art. 14 EGBGB.

[84] *Cf.* RG 10 Jan. 1918, RGZ 91, 403, 407–8; OLG Dresden 28 June 1926, IPRspr. 1926/27 no. 78; DÖLLE, *supra* n. 46, at 376–77; KEGEL, Kommentar, no. 29 on art. 14 EGBGB; PALANDT/LAUTERBACH, no. 4 h on art. 14 EGBGB; 1 RABEL 335–6.

[85] KEGEL, Kommentar, no. 29 on art. 14 EGBGB.

[86] LEWALD, Das deutsche internationale Privatrecht (1931) 95; KEGEL, Kommentar, no. 30 on art. 14 EGBGB; RAAPE 327; *cf.* 1 RABEL 342 at n. 90.

[87] *General rule*: KG Berlin 5 Apr. 1906, RJA 7 (1906) 162, 164; OLG Stuttgart, *supra* n. 50; DÖLLE, *supra* n. 46, at 377–79; KEGEL, Kommentar, no. 16 on art. 14 EGBGB; PALANDT/LAUTERBACH, no. 4 d on art. 14 EGBGB; 1 RABEL 342–45.

[88] 1 COHN no. 512; 1 RABEL 342; MÜLLER-FREIENFELS, 16 I.C.L.Q. 409, 426 (1967).

[89] 1 RABEL 344. Whether the husband is allowed to divest his wife of authority is to be decided by the rules stated above at n. 87, even if the scope of the wife's power in Germany is determined by § 1357 BGB: KG Berlin, *supra* n. 87. The divestiture must be filed with the marital property register (*infra* IV (2) (b) (ii)).

(d) *Interspousal immunity.*—Any reduction in the spouses' liability to each other is governed by article 14 EGBGB,[90] and this would be true even if all liability for negligence were excluded. It is quite unlikely that a German court would hold the American rules on interspousal immunity to be contrary to German public policy.

(e) *Support.*—Article 14 EGBGB and its corollary rules govern the question whether one spouse must support the other during a subsisting marriage, even if they are separated[91] or engaged in a divorce proceeding. In the latter case, the court may by provisional decree order payments.[92] Article 14 EGBGB and its supplementary rules also apply when the issue of support arises as an incidental question, especially in tort cases.[93] A contract between the spouses concerning their support is subject to the same rules,[94] but support after divorce is determined by the law governing divorce (*infra* V (2) (c)).

Although the general rules on recognition and enforcement of foreign judgments (*infra* ch. 14) apply to foreign support decrees, problems have arisen with respect to American support orders. An agreement and order for support issued by the Domestic Relations Court of New York was not recognized in Germany because of a lack of reciprocity between Germany and New York,[94a] since the New York courts before recognizing a foreign support decree will investigate whether the decree has been obtained by fraud; because the German courts do not check this point, recognition was declined. It is doubtful whether this reasoning is correct since a fraudulently obtained foreign order for support might not be recognized in Germany because in violation of German public policy (*infra* ch. 14 sub

[90] Kegel, Kommentar, no. 17 on art. 14 EGBGB; Staudinger/Raape p. 283 with further references.

[91] RG, *supra* n. 50; *supra* n. 72, at 404; and cases cited by Kegel, Kommentar, note 8 at p. 757, *cf. also* two German-American cases: LG Detmold, *supra* n. 48; LG Fulda, *supra* n. 54. *See* Dölle, *supra* n. 46, at 380–81; Kegel, IPR 279–80; Palandt/Lauterbach, no. 4 e on art. 14 EGBGB; 1 Rabel 349–50.

German substantive law: Kilian, Matrimonial Maintenance in Germany, *in* Parental Custody and Matrimonial Maintenance. A Symposium (London 1966) 223–225.

During separation: LG Köln 28 June 1950. IPRspr. 1950/51 no. 71; AG Mannheim 17 Mar. 1954, IPRspr. 1954/55 no. 85; AG Regensburg 26 June 1951, IPRspr. 1952/53 no. 112.

[92] KG Berlin 9 Mar. 1931, IPRspr. 1931 no. 66; 19 Dec. 1932, IPRspr. 1932 no. 88; OLG München, *supra* n. 66; Dölle, *supra* n. 46, at 381; Kegel, Kommentar, no. 18 on art. 14 EGBGB; Palandt/Lauterbach, no. 4 e on art. 14 EGBGB; 1 Rabel 351. The *lex fori* will be applied in exceptional cases where foreign law cannot be ascertained quickly: KG Berlin, *supra*.

[93] OLG Celle 21 July 1966, MDR 1967, 126, to the effect that under German torts law only those relatives who had a claim for support against the deceased have an action for wrongful death; the question of support for an American family was answered by reference to their domiciliary law (California law). *Cf. also infra* ch. 7 sub (2) (c) (ii).

[94] LG Berlin 3 Apr. 1950, RabelsZ 17 (1952) 130 with Note by Neumayer.

[94a] KG Berlin 22 Oct. 1963, IPRspr. 1962/63 no. 196, *aff'g* LG Berlin 6 Nov. 1961, IPRspr. 1960/61 no. 192.

II (8)); it is arguable that the New York investigation into fraud should not be considered a lack of reciprocity. Nevertheless, the recognition of American support orders in Germany has been severely hampered by this decision.

IV. MARITAL PROPERTY*

Like the German rule covering the personal effects of marriage (*supra* III), all matters of marital property are generally governed by a single law (*infra* (1) (a)). Although this rule in nearly all respects differs from its American counterparts, many German-American conflicts in this field are avoided by resort to renvoi (*infra* (1) (b) (ii)) and by several exceptions which limit considerably the actual scope (*infra* (2)) of the general German rule.

(1) German Conflicts Rules in General

(a) *Law governing.*—Marital property questions are generally governed by the husband's national law at the time of marriage. This rule is stated in article 15 EGBGB for German husbands and for aliens domiciled in Germany, but the courts have extended it to all other foreigners.[95] The wife's nationality is completely irrelevant in this regard, and no case has questioned this rule in the light of the constitutionally postulated equality of the sexes.[96] As distinct from the rule governing the personal effects of marriage (*supra* III (1) (a)), the law prescribed by article 15 EGBGB is immutable.[97] Consequently, a husband's change of nationality during coverture does not affect the spouses' property relations.[98] This means that the marital

---

* FERID, Vermögensrechtliche Wirkungen der Ehe: Deutsches Recht, *in* Das internationale Familienrecht Deutschlands und Frankreichs (1955) 114–144 (*in French*: Le droit international privé de la famille en France et en Allemagne (1954) 96–125); REITHMANN, Das Ehegüterrecht im deutschen Internationalen Privatrecht, *in* Les Régimes Matrimoniaux et les Successions en Droit International Privé (Brussels 1963) 227–242 (*French translation*: 319–334).

[95] BGH 5 Feb. 1954, FamRZ 1954, 110; BayObLG 6 Oct. 1954, BayObLGZ 1954, 225, 234 *et seq.*; KG Berlin 10 Dec. 1934, IPRspr. 1934 no. 45 at p. 97.

[96] *Cf.* dicta of the BayObLG, 15 Feb. 1963, BayObLGZ 1963, 45, 49; 28 Mar. 1961, BayObLGZ 1961, 123, 126; 17 Mar. 1959, BayObLGZ 1959, 89, 98. Thus the general conflicts rule on marital property is firmly established, in contrast to the uncertainty with respect to art. 14 EGBGB regulating the personal effects of marriage (*supra* III (1) (a)).

[97] It has been proposed that the immutability be abolished and the conflicts rules for the personal effects of marriage and for marital property thus harmonized. *Cf.* Vorschläge, *supra* n. 49, 2 and 90–2. A special statute has converted the matrimonial régime of all refugees of German nationality or with the status of a German (*see supra* ch. 3 sub A II (1) (c)) living in West Germany under a foreign statutory régime, to that of West Germany. Law of Aug. 4, 1969, BGBl. I 1067.

[98] Immutability does not mean that the marital property régime will not be affected by subsequent amendments to the substantive law applicable according to the German conflicts rule. In general, German law points to that law which

property relations of United States citizens will be decided under German law if the husband was German at the time of his marriage;[99] it means also that problems of adjustment will arise, especially in succession cases, since under German conflicts law the decedent's last national law governs questions of succession (*infra* (2)(c)).

(b) *General choice of law problems*

(i) *Characterization.*—Because of the above-mentioned difference between articles 14 and 15 EGBGB the delimitation between these provisions is very important. The various personal effects of marriage have been enumerated (*supra* III (1)(b)(i)). This list, especially the presumption of ownership, shows that not all property questions are classified as matters of marital property; the only ones so classified are those that deal specifically with the creation, regulation, or dissolution of a special marital property régime.[100] Accordingly the following matters are deemed to pertain to marital property: certain disabilities of a spouse with regard to certain property;[101] the liability of one of them for certain debts of the other;[102] marriage settlements;[103] and the dissolution of the marital property régime by death, divorce, or separation.[104]

(ii) *Renvoi.*—A renvoi or transmission from the husband's national law will be accepted by the German courts (art. 27 EGBGB). In American-German relations this is particularly important for real property (*infra* (2)(a)) and for marriage settlements (*infra* (2)(b)).

(iii) *Preliminary question: does a marriage exist?*—This preliminary question is answered, as it is for the personal effects of marriage (*supra* III (1)(b)(iii)), by applying the special conflicts rules of articles 11 and 13 EGBGB.[105]

---

was the national law of the husband at the time of the marriage, but in its present form, so that this law itself may decide whether subsequent changes affect prior marriages. BayObLG 17 Mar. 1959, *supra* n. 96, at 101; OLG Stuttgart 4 Dec. 1957, NJW 1958, 1972, 1973; 1 RABEL 380. For the exceptional "petrification" of the substantive law in cases involving refugees, *cf.* KEGEL, Kommentar, no. 40 on art. 15 EGBGB.

There are exceptions to the principle of immutability with respect to marriage settlements. *See infra* (2) (b) (ii) at n. 113.

[99] *Cf.* BayObLG 31 Mar. 1966, BayObLGZ 1966, 115, 122–126; OLG Celle 10 Sept. 1959, IPRspr. 1958/59 no. 148.

[100] OLG Celle, *supra* n. 99, at p. 495; KEGEL, Kommentar, no. 6 on art. 15 EGBGB.

[101] KG Berlin 20 June 1930, IPRspr. 1930 no. 70, at p. 155; KEGEL, Kommentar, no. 6 on art. 14 EGBGB at note 16.

[102] OLG Breslau 11 Nov. 1929, JW 1930, 1880; 31 Oct. 1929, JW 1930, 1011 and 1881.

[103] *Infra* sub (2) (b).

[104] BayObLG: 9 Sept. 1960, BayObLGZ 1960, 370, 375; 20 Mar. 1953, BayObLGZ 1953, 102, 105; OLG Stuttgart, *supra* n. 98; OLG Hamm 28 Feb. 1968, FamRZ 1968, 321.

[105] KEGEL, Kommentar, no. 36 on art. 15 EGBGB.

(2) **Scope of the General Conflicts Rule**

(a) *Marital property and the lex situs.*—The general conflicts rule on matters of marital property (*supra* (1) (a)) applies to personal as well as real property. Yet the *lex situs* has a threefold impact on this rule:

(i) As the German courts are required to accept a renvoi (*supra* (1) (b) (ii)), they will apply the *lex situs* if referred to by the husband's national law in marital property questions. Therefore the German courts have applied German substantive law to German realty because the "national" law of the American husband refers such matters of marital property to the *lex situs*;[106]

(ii) Article 28 EGBGB achieves the same result, but by a direct route. The "normal" conflicts rule on matrimonial property does not apply to certain property located outside the jurisdiction if the law of the situs provides "special" rules for this property. Special conflicts rules for specified types of property are "special" rules within the meaning of article 28 EGBGB.[107] Under this approach a German court will, because of the separate treatment of real property in American conflicts law, apply American law to American real property even though the husband is a German;[108]

(iii) The *lex rei sitae* determines the kinds of property interests and the modes of their creation, transfer, modification, and termination (*infra* ch. 6 at nn. 4 and 5). If the law governing marital property produces effects either completely unknown to the *lex situs* or requiring some additional act of the parties, then the latter prevails. However, the spouses are under obligation to perform whatever acts are necessary under the *lex rei sitae* to bring about these effects.[109]

(b) *Marriage settlements.*—

(i) Generally speaking, the husband's national law at the time of marriage also governs marriage settlements irrespective of whether they are concluded before or after the ceremony.[110] There is no free choice of law as in general contracts law (*infra* ch. 8 at n. 1).[111]

---

[106] KG Berlin: 2 Aug. 1934, IPRspr. 1934 no. 44; 20 June 1930, *supra* n. 101; OLG Colmar 24 Aug. 1911, RheinZ 4 (1912) 295. *Contra*, but without mentioning the renvoi question: LG Saargemünd 24 Nov. 1903, ElsLothJZ 29 (1904) 79.

[107] BGH 5 Apr. 1968, BGHZ 50, 63, 68–70; BayObLG 27 Oct. 1959, BayObLGZ 1959, 390, 398. *Accord*: STAUDINGER/RAAPE 336–38, 767 *et seq.*; PALANDT/LAUTERBACH, no. 3 on art. 15 EGBGB, no. 4 on art. 28 EGBGB; *contra*: KEGEL, Kommentar, no. 38 on art. 15 EGBGB, no. 11 on art. 28 EGBGB.

[108] 1 RABEL 367–68; RAAPE 334.

[109] LG München I 30 Apr. 1963, WM 1963, 1355, 1356; OLG Dresden 1 Dec. 1896, AnnSächsOLG 18 (1897) 513, 515; 1 RABEL 360–62; KEGEL, Kommentar, no. 7 on art. 15 EGBGB.

[110] KG Berlin 15 Feb. 1932, IPRspr. 1932 no. 70 at p. 146. This is the unanimous opinion; *cf.* KEGEL, Kommentar, no. 16 on art. 15 EGBGB.

[111] OLG Stuttgart, *supra* n. 98; KG Berlin, *supra* n. 110.

Apart from the impact of the *lex situs* (*supra* (a)), there are certain other exceptions to this rule.

(ii) Foreign spouses domiciled in Germany may enter into a marriage settlement even if the husband's national law does not permit it (art. 15 II EGBGB).[112] They may agree, as Germans can, upon a German or foreign marital property system or upon individually-designed provisions.[113] But if the spouses reside in Germany when the marriage settlement is entered into, they are not allowed to incorporate a foreign régime merely by reference to the foreign rule without expressly stating the contents of that rule (§ 1409 I BGB).[114] All settlements by foreigners residing in Germany, like all those of Germans wherever residing, must be filed with the matrimonial property registrar in order to be effective against innocent third parties with whom the spouses have contracted (art. 16 I EGBGB, § 1412 BGB).[115]

(iii) The capacity of the parties to conclude a marriage settlement is to be decided under the personal law of each (art. 7 I EGBGB).[116] If this law, as in some American states, refers to the law of the place of contracting,[117] the German courts will accept this renvoi or transmission.

(iv) The marriage agreement is valid as to form if it complies with the requirements either of the law governing matters of marital property or with the *lex loci actus* (art. 11 I EGBGB).

(c) *Marital property and succession.*—If the law governing marital property questions does not coincide with the law governing succession, it may be difficult to decide how to classify a provision disposing of certain property. Recently two German court decisions characterized California Probate Code § 201.5 as a rule of succession.[118] Since the emphasis is on the inheritance rights of surviving spouses, the whole matter will be discussed later (*infra* ch. 5 sub III (4) (c)).

(d) *Marital property and divorce.*—The dissolution of a marital property régime by divorce is also governed by article 15 EGBGB.[119]

---

[112] The same is true if the husband acquires German nationality during coverture (art. 15 II EGBGB). *Cf.* 1 RABEL 386–87.

[113] BayObLG 9 Sept. 1960, *supra* n. 104; KG Berlin 23 June 1932, JFG 10 (1933) 186; OLG Düsseldorf 25 Apr. 1952, IPRspr. 1952/53 no. 116.

[114] If one party at the time of marriage or at the time of conclusion of a postnuptial settlement resides abroad, a reference to the marital property law of this place of residence is valid (§ 1409 II BGB).

[115] OLG Breslau 11 Nov. 1929, *supra* n. 102; 1 COHN no. 516; 1 RABEL 400.

[116] KEGEL, Kommentar, no. 30 on art. 15 EGBGB.

[117] KG Berlin 7 June 1929, IPRspr. 1929 no. 88 at p. 125; KEGEL, Kommentar, no. 24 on art. 7 EGBGB.

[118] BayObLG and OLG Celle, *supra* n. 99.

[119] OLG Stuttgart, *supra* n. 98; *cf. also* BayObLG 20 Mar. 1953, *supra* n. 104; OLG Hamburg 30 Nov. 1928, HRR 1929 no. 583.

It is not settled whether support agreements concluded by the spouses before or at the time of divorce fall under article 15 EGBGB, under the law governing the effects of divorce,[120] or under both of these laws.[121] As such a support agreement generally will be incorporated in any arrangements dissolving the marital property or, at the least, will have close links with marital property questions, it is probably the better view to apply article 15 EGBGB exclusively to the whole arrangement.[122]

(e) *Protection of the public in Germany against unknown foreign rules on marital property.*—For practical reasons, German law does not follow the principle of nationality to its logical end, but makes certain concessions to the German law of the domicile or place of contracting. In order to protect parties contracting in Germany with German domiciliaries whose marital property relations are governed by foreign law, several provisions equate these relations to those of German internal law:[123]

(i) As already mentioned, foreign spouses domiciled in Germany have to enter their marriage settlement or their foreign statutory marital régime (art. 16 I EGBGB) in the matrimonial register if the settlement or régime is to be effective as against creditors in Germany (*supra* (2) (b) (ii));

(ii) Paragraph 1362 I BGB creates a presumption in favor of a creditor of either spouse to the effect that movables in the possession of either or both spouses belong to the debtor.[124] This presumption, already classified as a personal incident of marriage (*supra* III at n. 69), also applies against foreign spouses domiciled in Germany unless the foreign law governing their personal relations is even more favorable to third parties (art. 16 II EGBGB);

(iii) Under German rules of community property a spouse's debt incurred in an independent business enterprise cannot be enforced against the community property in any case. A spouse who does not manage the community property alone needs either the other's assent

---

[120] KG Berlin 25 Sept. 1933, IPRspr. 1933 no. 32 at p. 70; 30 Mar. 1931, *id.* 1931 no. 70.

[121] KG Berlin, *supra* no. 110, at 146, applies art. 15 EGBGB with respect to the period preceding a final divorce, and the law governing divorce for support following the divorce.

[122] KEGEL, Kommentar, no. 14 on art. 15 EGBGB.

[123] *German internal property law*: 1 COHN 236–41; WEBER, The Property Rights of Spouses Under German Law, 78 S. Afr. L. J. 209–13 (1961); KAHN-FREUND, Matrimonial Property—Some Recent Developments, 22 Mod. L. Rev. 241, 253–57 (1959); LEYSER, "Equality of the Spouses" Under the New German Law, 7 Am. J. Comp. L. 276–87 (1958).

Prior German law: PURCELL, 34 Tex. L. Rev. 1065–81 (1956); MASSFELLER, *in* Matrimonial Property Law (FRIEDMANN ed., London 1955) 369–409; KAHN-FREUND, 2 I.C.L.Q. 611–14 (1953); MOSHEIM, *id.* at 432–39; HAHLO, 54 S. Afr. L. J. 298–309 (1937).

[124] 1 COHN no. 513.

to individual transactions or his general assent to the conduct of the independent business enterprise (§§ 1431, 1456 BGB).[125] Such a general assent may be given expressly or will be assumed if a spouse knows of the other's business and does not file a protest against it in the matrimonial property register. These German provisions will apply to a spouse's independent business enterprise in Germany, whether or not the applicable foreign community property law protects innocent third parties in the same way. But, here again, foreign rules providing better protection prevail (art. 16 II EGBGB).

V. DIVORCE AND ANNULMENT

Contrary to Anglo-American concepts, German international family law distinguishes between jurisdiction in divorce proceedings and the law applicable to the divorce. This means that where the German courts have jurisdiction, they do not automatically apply their *lex fori* to a divorce. For this reason, jurisdiction of the German courts will be discussed first, then the law governing divorce; the German rules of recognition of foreign divorce decrees will follow; and, finally, the law of annulment will be dealt with as a whole.

(1) Divorce Jurisdiction of German Courts

According to the present version of §§ 606 and 606b ZPO,[126] the German courts[127] have divorce jurisdiction in two cases: (a) if at least one of the spouses is a German national, this jurisdiction is exclusive;[128] (b) there may also be jurisdiction if neither of them is a German national, under certain circumstances. Members of the United States Armed Forces are no longer exempt from this jurisdiction.[128a]

---

[125] A similar rule gives § 11 a Gewerbeordnung, BGBl. III 7100–1. *Cf.* KEGEL, Kommentar, nos. 24–26 on art. 16 EGBGB.

[126] These provisions were changed in 1941 (RGBl. 1941 I 654, 657 *et seq.*) and again in 1957 by the GleichberG (*supra* n. 2). The present version, however, has remained substantially the same since 1941.

[127] The Landgerichte (*supra* ch. 2 sub III (2)) are competent at first instance, so that the parties must be represented by attorneys.

[128] *Cf.* § 40 II ZPO which prohibits agreements altering the competence (Gerichtsstand) of the German courts in non-proprietary matters or in derogation of an exclusive competence. This provision, at least in respect to the second alternative, is also applied as between German and foreign courts: BGH 13 Dec. 1967, NJW 1968, 356; RIEZLER 307–09; STEIN/JONAS/SCHÖNKE/POHLE, no. II 3 on § 40 ZPO.

June 1946, SJZ 1946, 67.

[128a] Art. VIII (9) NATO Status of Forces Agreement (Treaties M 173) and *infra* n. 142. Formerly the German courts had no jurisdiction: OLG Stuttgart 1

(a) *At least one of the spouses a German.*—Jurisdiction of the German courts in this case derives from § 606 ZPO.[129] It does not matter whether the German spouse is a dual national,[130] where the spouses reside,[131] or whether a resulting German divorce decree will be recognized abroad. This means, for example, that a German wife, who no longer loses her German nationality by marriage,[132] may sue her foreign husband or may be sued by him for divorce in a German court.[133] This jurisdiction of the German courts without any requirement of domicile or at least of residence may seem strange to Americans. However, it is one of the more important implications of the German principle of nationality: A German always has access to a German court for the determination of his marital status which, according to the German conflicts rule, is governed by the law of his nationality (*infra* sub (2)).

(b) *Foreign spouses.*—A German court may divorce spouses neither of whom is a German national only if at least one of them has his habitual residence (*gewöhnlicher Aufenthalt*) in Germany and if either of two additional prerequisites is fulfilled: *first,* if a German divorce decree will be recognized by the husband's *lex patriae,*[134] or *second,* if one of the spouses is stateless[135] (§ 606b no. 1 ZPO). The first alternative is the more important. It is in line with the German

---

[129] This becomes clear only by contrasting § 606 ZPO with § 606b ZPO, dealing with the second case, *i.e.,* where neither is a German national. § 606 ZPO on its face determines competence for all kinds of actions concerning marital status.

[130] BGH 4 Oct. 1951, BGHZ 3, 178, 180–81; STEIN/JONAS/SCHÖNKE/POHLE, no. II on § 606b ZPO; WIECZOREK, no. E I b 3 on § 606 ZPO.

[131] This is clarified by § 606 III ZPO which provides that the Landgericht Berlin will hear the case if the spouses have never had their usual matrimonial residence in Germany and if neither spouse now has a usual residence in Germany, with the result that no other German court has competence according to § 606 I or II ZPO. German decrees rendered under § 606 ZPO, even though the parties were domiciled in the United States, were recognized in the United States if both parties were represented in the German courts, in Oettgen v. Oettgen, 196 Misc. 937, 94 N.Y.S.2d 168 (Sup. Ct. 1949); Martens v. Martens, 260 App. Div. 30, 20 N.Y.S.2d 206, *rev'd on another ground,* 284 N.Y. 363, 31 N.E.2d 489 (1940).

[132] *Supra* ch. 3 sub A II (4).

[133] OLG Hamburg 30 Jan. 1957, IPRspr. 1956/57 no. 114; LG München II 30 Nov. 1955, MDR 1956, 236. In both cases American husbands sued their German wives.

[134] This provision has been held constitutional under art. 3 II GG (equality of husband and wife), expressly by LG Wiesbaden 26 Mar. 1957, IPRspr. 1956/57 no. 115, at p. 367, and implicitly by BGH 19 Mar. 1958, BGHZ 27, 47.

[135] This alternative is important for all cases where by marriage a wife lost her nationality and did not acquire that of her husband (*cf. supra* ch. 3 sub A II (4)). *Cf.* pre-1953 cases of German-born wives of American husbands: LG Kassel 10 Dec. 1952, NJW 1953, 307; LG Regensburg 6 Feb. 1952, IPRspr. 1952/53 no. 159; LG Traunstein 9 Aug. 1949, IPRspr. 1952/53 no. 158. In neither of the latter two cases was the wife's nationality mentioned; from the courts' reasoning, however, it must be concluded that both wives were stateless.

conflicts rule under which the divorce of foreign spouses is governed by the husband's *lex patriae* (art. 17 I EGBGB, *infra* (2)), and it is designed to prevent a limping divorce valid in Germany but invalid under the applicable law. Whether either spouse has his habitual residence in Germany is decided by German law (*supra* ch. 3 sub B (2) (a)).[136] Whether a German divorce decree will be recognized by the husband's *lex patriae* naturally has to be ascertained from this law. The German courts have always held that a German divorce decree will be recognized in the United States provided one of the two following conditions is fulfilled:[137] *first,* if at least one of the spouses has his bona fide domicile in Germany at the time of the decree and if due process has been granted to the defendant;[138] or, *second,* if, even though neither party was domiciled in Germany, the defendant did not question the court's jurisdiction, so that he will be estopped to question it in an American court.[139] These two principles are unanimously supported by German literature.[140] The vexatious question of domicile has not always been decided, as it should be, according to American state law. Some courts have applied German law on the ground that an American court, when asked to recognize

---

[136] BGH, *supra* n. 134, at p. 48.

[137] Neither condition was fulfilled in LG Augsburg 6 Feb. 1963, IPRspr. 1962/63 no. 180a; LG Mannheim 4 July 1961, IPRspr. 1960/61 no. 184.

[138] BGH, *supra* n. 134, at 49–51; OLG Karlsruhe 15 May 1963, IPRspr. 1962/63 no. 181; OLG Koblenz 24 May 1960, NJW 1960, 2193; LG Ansbach 24 July 1963, IPRspr. 1962/63 no. 182; LG Kaiserslautern 13 June 1961, IPRspr. 1960/61 no. 183; LG Wiesbaden 30 Oct. 1958, IPRspr. 1958/59 no. 185; 26 Mar. 1957, *supra* n. 134; LG Hamburg 19 June 1957, IPRspr. 1956/57 no. 113; LG Heidelberg 3 Dec. 1954, FamRZ 1955, 74; LG Stuttgart 17 Dec. 1968, NJW 1969, 384; LG Würzburg 30 Nov. 1954, IPRspr. 1954/55 no. 97; LG München II 16 Oct. 1953, IPRspr. 1952/53 no. 304a.

Before the first amendment to § 606 ZPO in 1941 (*supra* n. 126) the German courts were allowed to divorce aliens only if they had jurisdiction under the husband's national law. *See* RG 2 June 1932, RGZ 136, 361; 21 Nov. 1929, RGZ 126, 353; OLG Frankfurt 20 June 1910, FrankfRundsch. 45 (1911) 44; LG Berlin III 24 Apr. 1928, JW 1928, 3128; LG München 1 July 1921, JW 1921, 1471.

[139] OLG Karlsruhe 15 May 1963, preceding note; OLG Koblenz 24 May 1960, preceding note; LG Augsburg 17 Oct. 1963, IPRspr. 1962/63 no. 180b; LG Ansbach 24 July 1963, preceding note. *Cf.* Oettgen v. Oettgen and Martens v. Martens, *supra* n. 131.

[140] GRASMANN, Die Anerkennung ausländischer Scheidungsurteile in den USA als Voraussetzung der deutschen Zuständigkeit, FamRZ 1964, 345, 349–52; GRÄBER, Die Scheidung der Ehe von USA-Bürgern, die sich in Deutschland befinden, FamRZ 1963, 493–95; DEUTSCH, Die Anerkennung ausländischer Urteile in den Staaten der USA, ZZP 71 (1958) 321–39; SCHWENK, Scheidung amerikanischer Ehen durch deutsche Gerichte, NJW 1955, 1707–09, NJW 1956, 660; LENHOFF, Die Anerkennung und Vollstreckung ausländischer Urteile in den USA, RabelsZ 19 (1954) 201–41. *Cf. also* PETERSON, Die Anerkennung und Vollstreckung ausländischer Urteile in den Vereinigten Staaten von Amerika, RabelsZ 33 (1969) 543–63.

a German divorce decree, will apply the German *lex fori* to this question.[141] Most courts, however, have applied American state law, holding that an American court will ascertain under its *lex fori* whether there was a domicile in Germany and therefore whether the German court had jurisdiction.[142]

(c) *Provisional orders during divorce suit.*—If a German court has divorce jurisdiction, it may upon request also settle certain urgent incidents of marital discord by a provisional order (*einstweilige Anordnung*). These incidents include separation of the spouses, mutual support and advance payments for costs, custody of the minor children of the marriage but not their legal representation, support of the children by their parents, and use of household effects and furniture (§ 627 I ZPO). All these orders, except that relating to custody, become inoperative as soon as the divorce becomes *res judicata*.[143] Final adjudication of these matters is, as a rule, not entrusted to the divorce courts but to different courts.[144] The only exception relates to the statutory claim for support that one spouse may have against the other; this claim may be settled provisionally by an order of the divorce court accompanying the divorce decree (§ 627b ZPO). Although it has never been questioned that the German courts have jurisdiction in these incidental matters, it is not settled what law governs. The courts are inclined to apply the *lex fori* because the question is procedural.[145] The better view seems to be that incidental matters are governed by their regular *lex causae*[146] and that the German *lex fori* will be applied only in those urgent cases

---

[141] LG München II 16 Oct. 1953, *supra* n. 138, at p. 614, referring to RG 2 June 1932, *supra* n. 138, at p. 363. In the second case and under the former version of § 606 ZPO, *supra* n. 138, this sort of renvoi made sense as the American divorce courts also apply their own forum's notion of domicile.

[142] *Supra* n. 138. Whether the courts have applied American state law correctly is another question. In several cases they assumed that American soldiers stationed in Germany were also domiciled in Germany: OLG Koblenz 24 May 1960, LG Kaiserslautern 13 June 1961, LG Stuttgart 17 Dec. 1968, and LG Wiesbaden 30 Oct. 1958, all *supra* n. 138. The better view seems to have been chosen by the LG Mannheim 4 July 1961, *supra* n. 137, which held to the contrary. *Cf. also* ch. 3 sub B (2) (b) at nn. 78–80.

[143] STEIN/JONAS/SCHÖNKE/POHLE, no. IV 1 on § 627 ZPO.

[144] These will usually be the Amtsgerichte, *supra* ch. 2 sub B III (2) (a), under § 23 no. 2 e GVG and § 35 FGG.

[145] OLG Hamburg 26 Feb. 1968, MDR 1968, 670; OLG München 7 Mar. 1960, NJW 1960, 1771; OLG Karlsruhe 22 Apr. 1957, FamRZ 1957, 271; OLG Stuttgart 14 June 1956, NJW 1956, 1404; OLG Hamm 22 Sept. 1932, JW 1932, 3824; OLG Köln 14 Dec. 1928, IPRspr. 1929 no. 77.

[146] OLG Düsseldorf 9 May 1961, NJW 1961, 1583; 25 Apr. 1952, IPRspr. 1952/53 no. 116; OLG Köln 23 Apr. 1956, FamRZ 1956, 235; OLG München 23 Jan. 1954, NJW 1955, 227; 15 May 1953, MDR 1953, 490; KG Berlin 25 May 1936, JW 1936, 3577; 11 Jan. 1932, IPRspr. 1932 no. 90; OLG Karlsruhe 2 Apr. 1930, IPRspr. 1930 no. 145; STEIN/JONAS/SCHÖNKE/POHLE, no. VIII on § 627 ZPO; M. WOLFF 210 n. 18.

in which an immediate decision has to be made and the regular *lex causae* and its contents cannot be ascertained quickly.[147]

(d) *Lis pendens.*—The general principles apply to *lis pendens* (*infra* ch. 14 sub II (7)), in other words, the German courts will abstain if a divorce suit between the same parties has been brought before a foreign court prior to the institution of the proceeding in Germany and if the foreign decision will be recognized in Germany. But there are some court decisions to the contrary which reason that a pending foreign suit can only be taken into consideration if a formal recognition proceeding (*infra* (3)(a)) is unnecessary.[147a] This reasoning is not convincing, however, since the administrative agencies which handle such matters apply the same legal rules as the courts.

(2) Law Governing Divorce

(a) *General rule.*—According to article 17 I EGBGB, a divorce is governed by the husband's *lex patriae* at the time the action is brought.[148] Although the wife's nationality is generally irrelevant, a German wife's action for divorce is always governed by German law (art. 17 III EGBGB).[149] The preliminary question whether a valid marriage was entered into is answered under articles 11 and 13 EGBGB (*supra* II).[150]

The reign of the husband's national law over the grounds for divorce is qualified by two exceptions. The more important is stated in article 17 IV EGBGB, providing that a divorce based upon foreign law may be granted by a German court only if the facts proved also constitute a ground for divorce under the German *lex fori.*[150a] Because of this public policy provision it will be useless to plead, for example, the recently enacted New York provision that "confinement of the defendant in prison for a period of three or more consecutive years after the marriage of plaintiff and defendant" is a ground for divorce.[151] Under the German marriage law a long-term confinement

---

[147] OLG Düsseldorf 19 Aug. 1965, FamRZ 1965, 616; KG Berlin 25 May 1936, preceding note; 22 Oct. 1931, IPRspr. 1931 no. 67.

[147a] KG Berlin 2 Feb. 1960, IPRspr. 1960/61 no. 198; LG Berlin 22 Feb. 1960, *id.* no. 199; *cf. also* LG Stuttgart 25 Apr. 1963, IPRspr. 1962/63 no. 197 (obiter dictum).

[148] This provision was expressly held constitutional under art. 3 II GG (equality of husband and wife): BGH 18 Jan. 1954, NJW 1954, 837.

[149] The importance of this provision has increased since a German wife no longer loses her nationality by marrying a foreigner (*supra* ch. 3 sub A II (4)).

[150] KEGEL, Kommentar, no. 2 on art. 17 EGBGB. Whether the marriage has already been dissolved abroad depends upon the recognition of the foreign divorce decree (*infra* (3)).

[150a] For German substantive law, *cf.* 1 COHN 227–34; FRICKE, Divorce in German Law, 8 Am. J. Comp. L. 508–15 (1959).

[151] New York Domestic Relations Law § 170 (3) (McKinney 1964 and 1967 Supp.), version of L. 1968, c. 700 of the Laws of New York (2 McKinney's 1968

in prison and even a separation for more than three years give rise to no cause of action.[152] The second qualification of the general conflicts rule is much more specific: If the husband has changed his nationality, the action may be based on facts occurring before the change, provided these facts constitute a ground for divorce or separation under both his former and his present *lex patriae* (art. 17 II EGBGB).

(b) *Renvoi.*—Under article 27 EGBGB the German courts recognize a renvoi by the husband's *lex patriae* to German law. Whether there is such a renvoi, however, is often not easily decided. With respect to the United States, courts[153] and writers[153a] for more than fifty years have accepted a so-called "hidden" renvoi from American law if the husband was domiciled (by American standards) in Germany at the time of filing of the divorce suit; this position is based on the argument that American courts like other common-law tribunals apply the *lex fori* in divorce suits and certain other proceedings relating to personal status. As their jurisdiction is normally based upon a person's domicile in the forum state, the courts in fact apply the *lex domicilii.*[154] Thus American law by its jurisdictional provisions tacitly refers back to the *lex domicilii* as the governing law. On the basis of this hidden renvoi, a German court which has jurisdiction under the American jurisdictional rule applies the *lex domicilii* which, in this case, is identical with the German *lex fori.*

This reasoning has been correctly criticized in the United States

---

Session Laws of New York (1968) 1473); *cf also* LG Heidelberg 3 Dec. 1954, *supra* n. 138.

[152] BGH 23 Nov. 1962, BGHZ 38, 266, 268–69; HOFFMANN/STEPHAN, n. 21 on § 48 EheG.

[153] RG 2 June 1932, *supra* n. 138; KG Berlin 14 Sept. 1936, JW 1937, 238; OLG Frankfurt/M. 20 June 1910, *supra* n. 138; OLG Hamburg 30 Jan. 1957, *supra* n. 133; OLG Karlsruhe 15 May 1963, *supra* n. 138; OLG Koblenz 24 May 1960, *supra* n. 138; OLG Stuttgart 4 Dec. 1930, JW 1932, 601; LG Ansbach 24 July 1963, *supra* n. 138; LG Berlin III 24 Apr. 1928, *supra* n. 138; LG Hamburg 19 June 1957, *supra* n. 138; LG Kaiserslautern 13 June 1961, *supra* n. 138; LG Kassel 10 Dec. 1952, *supra* n. 135; LG München II 30 Nov. 1955, *supra* n. 133; 16 Oct. 1953, *supra* n. 138; LG München 1 July 1921, *supra* n. 138; LG Stuttgart 17 Dec. 1968, *supra* n. 138; LG Wiesbaden 30 Oct. 1958, *supra* n. 138; 26 Mar. 1957, *supra* n. 134; LG Würzburg 30 Nov. 1954, *supra* n. 138; *contra*: LG Regensburg 6 Feb. 1952 and LG Traunstein 9 Aug. 1949, *supra* n. 135, applying the substantive law of Georgia and Florida, respectively; *uncertain*: LG Heidelberg 3 Dec. 1954, *supra* n. 138.

[153a] HANISCH, Die "versteckte" Rückverweisung im internationalen Familienrecht, NJW 1966, 2085–92; KEGEL, Kommentar, no. 105 on art. 17 EGBGB; NEUHAUS § 37; NIEMEYER, Das internationale Privatrecht des Bürgerlichen Gesetzbuchs (1901) 151–52; *cf.* 1 RABEL 481–82.

[154] *Cf.* GOODRICH/SCOLES, Handbook of the Conflict of Laws (4th ed. 1964) § 128.

as well as in Germany,[155] yet the German practice is sound. By their pragmatic approach and by using the general German tools of conflict avoidance, the courts escape the absurdity of applying American law in cases over which American courts do not claim jurisdiction and therefore would not apply their own law.[156]

The weakness of the hidden renvoi argument appears whenever the German courts, lacking jurisdiction under American law, nevertheless assume jurisdiction to divorce American spouses on the ground that the defendant will be estopped to question the decree and that therefore it will be recognized in the United States (*supra* n. 139). In these cases, too, the German courts apply German divorce law under the pretext of an American hidden renvoi.[157]

(c) *Domain of the law governing divorce.*—A divorce not only dissolves the marriage but also may affect all the other relations between the spouses as well as those between them and their children. Of these various incidents of divorce only a few are governed by the law applicable under article 17 EGBGB, such as the name of the wife[158] and the support duties between the divorced spouses.[159] Most of the other effects of divorce, the division of marital property,[160] the rights of inheritance,[161] and the relation between parent and child,[162] are decided under the rules which normally govern these issues irrespective of divorce.

Some of the collateral effects of divorce may vary if one of the spouses has been found to be solely or preponderantly guilty of

---

155 EHRENZWEIG § 72; WENGLER, Zur Adoption deutscher Kinder durch amerikanische Staatsangehörige, NJW 1959, 127, 129; BEITZKE, Note, NJW 1960, 248, 249; MELCHIOR, Die Grundlagen des deutschen internationalen Privatrechts (1932) 215. *See infra* text at n. 157.

156 NEUHAUS 194; WOLFF 207; FRANKENSTEIN III, *supra* n. 8, at 424 n. 28; EHRENZWEIG 404 n. 48.

157 *Supra* n. 139; especially LG Augsburg 17 Oct. 1963, *supra* n. 139, at 401.

158 OLG Celle 1 Sept. 1966, StAZ 1968, 23; KG Berlin 27 June 1941, JFG 22, 381; 17 Dec. 1926, StAZ 1927, 82; 13 Oct. 1916, OLG 33, 343; LG Berlin II 20 May 1927, StAZ 1927, 195; KEGEL, Kommentar, no. 91 on art. 17 EGBGB.

159 OLG Hamburg 4 Apr. 1918, OLG 38, 251; KG Berlin: 30 May 1938, JW 1938, 2750; 21 Dec. 1935, JW 1936, 2466, 2467; 16 Feb. 1909, OLG 19, 106; AG Altona 19 Mar. 1926, JW 1926, 1357; KEGEL, Kommentar, no. 90 on art. 17 EGBGB.

160 BayObLG 20 Mar. 1953, BayObLGZ 1953, 102; OLG Stuttgart 4 Dec. 1957, NJW 1958, 1972; KG Berlin 31 Jan. 1938, JW 1938, 1244; KEGEL, Kommentar, no. 95 on art. 17 EGBGB.

161 KEGEL, Kommentar, no. 95 on art. 17 EGBGB, and *infra* ch. 5.

162 KG Berlin 21 Feb. 1966, OLGZ 1966, 321, 324–25; OLG Hamm 21 Aug. 1964, FamRZ 1965, 92; *cf. also* RG 25 Jan. 1940, RGZ 162, 329, 332; BayObLG: 21 Mar. 1952, BayObLGZ 1952, 74; 13 Mar. 1912, BayObLGZ 13, 136; KG Berlin 3 May 1935, JW 1935, 2750; OLG Saarbrücken 14 July 1965, NJW 1966, 308. In these cases, however, the law governing the relation between parent and child was identical with that governing divorce. KEGEL, Kommentar, no. 95 on art. 17 EGBGB.

violation of the matrimonial duties.[163] If according to the law governing the divorce guilt of one of the spouses is important for the determination of collateral effects, the divorce decree must expressly recite the existence of guilt (*Schuldspruch*).[164]

(3) Recognition of Foreign Divorce Decrees

This section will deal only with divorce decrees rendered by courts. So-called private divorce, allowed by certain legal systems, will not be discussed because it plays almost no rôle in American-German relations.[164a]

(a) *Recognition procedure.*—In order to avoid divergent pronouncements by German courts and other authorities regarding the effects of foreign divorce decrees in Germany, such decrees as a rule require formal recognition. The procedure is laid down in article 7 § 1 of the Act Modifying the Family Law (*Familienrechtsänderungsgesetz,* FamRÄndG) of 1961.[165] Competence to issue a formal decree of recognition rests, in the first instance, with one of the twelve *Landesjustizverwaltungen,* the ministries of justice or equivalent administrative agencies of the states dealing with the administration of justice. The party seeking recognition applies to the *Landesjustizverwaltung* of the German *Land* where one of the spouses has his habitual residence or, if neither resides in Germany, where a new marriage will be celebrated or, as the last resort, to that of Berlin (art. 7 § 1 II FamRÄndG). The decision of the *Landesjustizverwaltung* may be contested by the applicant or by either spouse in the competent *Oberlandesgericht* (art. 7 § 1 IV-VI FamRÄndG). It is also possible to apply for a "negative" decision declaring that a foreign divorce cannot be recognized in Germany. The administrative decision or, if contested, the adjudication are final and binding *erga omnes* (art. 7 § 1 VIII FamRÄndG).

One single class of foreign divorces is exempt from this formal procedure of recognition. These are decrees from the nation to which both spouses belonged at the time of the divorce, and which therefore do not conflict with any exclusive German jurisdiction (*infra* (b)). Hence American divorce decrees will be exempt only if the spouses were American citizens and were domiciled in the American forum

---

[163] *Cf.* §§ 56, 58, 73 EheG and § 1671 BGB; 1 Cohn nos. 504–09.

[164] *Cf.* Kegel, Kommentar, nos. 55–61 on art. 17 EGBGB. According to art. 17 III EGBGB the alien respondent to a German wife's suit may ask that his wife be declared guilty if such declaration is well founded under German law.

[164a] For a discussion of the complicated rules dealing with "private divorces," *cf.* Kleinrahm/Partikel, Die Anerkennung ausländischer Entscheidungen in Ehesachen (2d ed. 1970) 145–167. *Cf. also* OLG Düsseldorf 15 Apr. 1966, FamRZ 1968, 87 concerning a Jewish bill of divorce mailed in Germany and received in New York.

[165] BGBl. 1961 I 1221.

state.[166] While in this area conflicting German decisions are possible,[167] the risk is minimal.

It should be stressed that the administrative declaration and the judicial determination of recognition follow an identical set of substantive rules.

(b) *Substantive rules of recognition.*—The substantive rules governing recognition of foreign divorce decrees are, in principle, identical with those governing the recognition of foreign judgments in general as laid down in § 328 ZPO (*infra* ch. 14 sub II (8)). Additional rules, designed specifically for foreign divorces, are contained in § 606a ZPO and in article 7 § 1 I 2 FamRÄndG, abolishing the requirement of reciprocity.[167a]

Recognition of foreign divorce decrees is subject to four major conditions: jurisdiction of the divorce court, due process, compliance with the German conflicts rule, and observance of German public policy.

(i) *Jurisdiction.*—Paragraph 328 I no. 1 ZPO excludes recognition "if the courts of the state to which the foreign [judgment] court belongs have no jurisdiction according to German law." The rules on the jurisdiction of German divorce courts have already been discussed (*supra* (1)). Applying them in this connection leads to recognition of the jurisdiction of a foreign divorce court in two situations: *first,* if at least one of the spouses is a national of the forum state, regardless of residence (*supra* (1)(a)); *second,* if neither spouse is a citizen of the forum state but at least one of them has his usual residence there, provided at least one of them is stateless or provided the divorce decree will be recognized by the husband's *lex patriae* (*supra* (1)(b)). These two rules operate as long as no German national is involved.

If, however, one of the spouses is a German national, again regardless of residence, the above rules come into conflict with the claim of exclusive German jurisdiction (§ 606 ZPO and *supra* (1)(a)) which would exclude foreign jurisdiction entirely. The German legislature realized that this rule would seriously hamper international legal relations and would lead to limping divorces; therefore it provided in

---

[166] GRÄBER, Die Scheidung der Ehe von USA-Bürgern, die sich in Deutschland befinden, FamRZ 1963, 493, 495; KLEINRAHM/PARTIKEL, *supra* n. 164a, at 103 n. 20. *Cf. also* KG Berlin 14 Oct. 1932, JW 1932, 3822.

[167] NEUHAUS, FamRZ 1957, 394; *contra*: LG Lübeck 7 Oct. 1956, FamRZ 1957, 223; RAAPE, Die Anerkennung eines ausländischen Ehenichtigkeitsurteils mit besonderer Berücksichtigung des § 24 der 4.DVO EheG, MDR 1949, 586; KLEINRAHM/PARTIKEL, *supra* n. 164a, at 94.

[167a] Due to the alterations mentioned in n. 126 and to the enactment of § 606a ZPO (*infra* (i)), the survey of German law by VREELAND, Validity of Foreign Divorces (1938) 274–82, is outdated. Even STEEFEL's contribution on the recognition of Mexican divorces in Germany does not cover recent German legislation and case law: 1 Int'l Lawyer 106–09 (1967).

§ 606a ZPO for four instances, mostly with substantial foreign connections, where German exclusive jurisdiction will not bar the recognition of foreign divorce decrees: where the original defendant was a foreign national (no. 1) or had his habitual residence outside Germany (no. 2, 1st case); or where the spouses' last common habitual residence was outside Germany (no. 2, 2d case); or where the original defendant is the party applying for recognition of the foreign decree (no. 3). The exact meaning of § 606a ZPO is controversial. According to the restrictive interpretation prevailing today,[168] the rule is merely negative; it dispenses with the exclusivity claimed for German jurisdiction by § 606 where one of the parties is a German, but it does not prescribe positive jurisdictional requirements for recognition of a foreign divorce. These requirements must be sought elsewhere, namely, in §§ 606 and 606b ZPO (*supra*). Without attempting to furnish a complete theoretical and practical guide through this labyrinth of rule and exception, it is still possible to point out certain results:

A foreign court lacks jurisdiction over German spouses whose habitual residence is in Germany. None of the exceptions of § 606a ZPO applies, no. 3 being interpreted narrowly. Therefore a Mexican or Nevada divorce of such a couple will not be recognized even if neither party objected to the court's assumption of jurisdiction. Under German law the parties to a divorce suit are not free to choose the forum they want and they are not precluded from raising the jurisdictional issue although it was not litigated in the foreign court.[169]

Jurisdiction exists over German spouses whose habitual residence is in the forum state (§ 606a no. 2, 2d case, § 606b no. 1 ZPO). Therefore the Illinois divorce of a German couple residing in Illinois has been recognized,[170] and the jurisdiction of a New York court which dissolved the marriage of Germans residing in New York was not questioned.[171]

There is no jurisdiction over German spouses whose habitual residence, although outside Germany, is also outside the forum state. None of the exceptions of § 606a ZPO applies, no. 3 being interpreted narrowly. A German court refused to recognize the Mexican divorce

---

168 KG Berlin 30 Jan. 1964, FamRZ 1964, 262. *Cf.* NEUHAUS, Die internationale Zuständigkeit in Ehesachen nach dem Gleichberechtigungsgesetz, FamRZ 1958, 13–14; *id.*, Die Anerkennung sowjetzonaler und ausländischer Scheidungsurteile, FamRZ 1964, 18, 20–22; G. LORENZ, Die internationale Zuständigkeit als Voraussetzung für die Anerkennung ausländischer Eheurteile in Deutschland, FamRZ 1966, 465–79; BEITZKE, Die deutsche internationale Zuständigkeit in Familienrechtssachen, FamRZ 1967, 592, 598; STEIN/JONAS/SCHÖNKE/POHLE (19th ed.) no. I on § 606a ZPO. *Contra*: BAUMBACH/LAUTERBACH, no. 2 Bd on § 606a ZPO.

169 § 40 II ZPO and *supra* n. 128.

170 KG Berlin 3 May 1935, *supra* n. 162.

171 KG Berlin 16 Feb. 1909, *supra* n. 159.

of a German couple residing in New York even though the defendant wife was represented in Mexico and hence the decree would be recognized in New York, and even though it was the wife who asked for recognition in Germany.[172] The fact that the party applying for recognition is not estopped to question the court's jurisdiction was pointed out above. Another German court refused to recognize an ex parte Nevada divorce granted to a German wife whose husband resided in New York.[173]

Where the spouses are German and only one has his habitual residence in the foreign forum state, the forum has jurisdiction if it is the defendant who resides in the forum state (§ 606a no. 2, 1st case, 606b no. 1 ZPO), but it has no jurisdiction if the plaintiff is the resident. Therefore a German court refused to recognize an Illinois ex parte divorce procured by a German wife who had left her husband in Germany.[174]

In the case of a German husband and an alien wife, the forum has jurisdiction if the wife is the defendant and the forum is her national state (§ 606a no. 1, § 606 ZPO) or a third state where one or both of the spouses have their usual residence (§ 606a no. 2). The forum also has jurisdiction if the wife sues her husband in one of the courts mentioned above and the husband applies for recognition of the divorce (§ 606a no. 3, § 606 or § 606b no. 1 ZPO, respectively).

If the nationalities are reversed, the husband being an alien and the wife a German, the forum has jurisdiction if one of the exceptions under § 606a ZPO exists and the foreign jurisdiction is recognized by the law applicable under the German conflicts rule (art. 17 EGBGB, *infra* (6) sub (b) and (c)). According to this principle German courts and authorities have recognized divorce decrees procured by a German wife against her American husband in an American state other than the husband's domicile.[175]

In the case of alien spouses, the courts of the common home country have jurisdiction and their decrees do not even require a formal declaration of recognition. Courts outside their common home country have jurisdiction if the law governing the divorce under article 17 I EGBGB recognizes the divorce decree; this rule permits German courts and other authorities to disregard German prerequisites for recognition of foreign divorce decrees in order to avoid

---

[172] OLG Düsseldorf 30 Dec. 1965, FamRZ 1966, 200.

[173] KG Berlin 14 Oct. 1932, *supra* n. 166.

[174] OLG Hamburg 27 May 1914, OLG 29, 181. Such a divorce, however, was recognized in New York in Berweger v. Berweger, N.Y.L.J. June 4, 1954, p. 7 col. 7 (Sup. Ct.). The decree will be recognized in Germany if it is the original defendant who applies for recognition (§ 606a no. 3 ZPO, *supra* (i)), BGH 28 June 1961, LM § 606a ZPO no. 1.

[175] *Cf.* BayObLG 7 June 1967, BayObLGZ 1967, 218; OLG Bremen 8 Feb. 1966, OLGZ 1966, 373.

limping divorces;[176] on this basis Mexican "quickie" divorces of American citizens have been recognized where these decrees were valid in the American domiciliary states.[177] If German law applies by virtue of renvoi (*supra* (2)(b)), the courts of the husband's or wife's national state (§ 606 ZPO) or of the state where one or both reside, have jurisdiction (§ 606b no. 1 ZPO). Jurisdiction is lacking in other cases.

(ii) *Due process.*—According to § 328 I no. 2 ZPO, a judgment against a German defendant who was not represented in court will not be recognized unless he was personally served either in the forum state or in Germany by German judicial assistance (*infra* ch. 14 II (3)(b)). For foreigners a similar result is assured by the requirement that German public policy must be complied with (§ 328 I no. 4 ZPO, *infra* (iv)).[178]

(iii) *Compliance with German conflicts rule.*—According to § 328 I no. 3 ZPO, a foreign divorce decree will not be recognized in Germany if the foreign court failed to comply with article 17 EGBGB (*supra* (2)(a)) to the detriment of a German party. This does not mean that the divorce court must have applied the German conflicts rule; it means merely that the divorce decree must not be based on facts which would not constitute a ground for divorce under German law (*supra* (2)(a)), and that it must not produce effects which are alien to German law.[179] Under this rule a New York decree which prohibited remarriage by a German defendant was denied recognition.[180]

(iv) *German public policy.*—Paragraph 328 I no. 4 ZPO generally declines recognition of foreign judgments if they are against German public policy (*guten Sitten*) or in conflict with German legislation.[181] Where divorce is concerned, this would be the case if, for example, the parties were divorced merely because one of them had tired of the marriage. It must be added, however, that in divorce cases the

---

[176] NEUHAUS, FamRZ 1964, 18, 22; JONAS, Notes, JW 1934, 2555, and JW 1936, 283; FRANKENSTEIN, *supra* n. 8, I (1926) 347.

[177] OLG München 2 Apr. 1964, FamRZ 1964, 442; 25 Feb. 1963, NJW 1963, 1158 (recognition in both cases); OLG Hamburg 1 Oct. 1935, JW 1935, 3488; LG Detmold 2 Aug. 1930, IPRspr. 1930 no. 152 (no recognition of an ex parte divorce); RAAPE 314. OLG Düsseldorf 25 Sept. 1967, JMBlNRW 1968, 199 seems to depart from this line of decisions because it does not ask whether the Mexican divorce would be recognized in the United States.

[178] BAUMBAUCH/LAUTERBACH, no. 5 B on § 328 ZPO; WIECZOREK, no. E IV b 2 on § 328 ZPO.

[179] STEIN/JONAS/SCHÖNKE/POHLE (18th ed.), no. VI 3 on § 328 ZPO; KLEINRAHM/PARTIKEL, *supra* n. 164a, at 114–121.

[180] KG Berlin 16 Feb. 1909, *supra* n. 159.

[181] OLG Hamburg 1 Oct. 1935, *supra* n. 177, refused to recognize an ex parte divorce against a wife residing in Germany who had once been a German and later reacquired German nationality, although the decree was recognized by the law of her American husband's domicile, New Jersey.

general provision of § 328 I no. 4 ZPO does not play an important rôle. German parties are protected by § 328 I no. 3 ZPO, discussed above, while German public policy rarely intervenes with respect to aliens because in most cases German recognition depends upon the validity of the decree under the husband's personal law and it is seldom that the parties' connection with Germany is close enough to warrant disregarding the foreign decree.[182]

(c) *Extent of recognition.*—Recognition of foreign divorce decrees relates primarily to the dissolution of the marital union. However, under German substantive law it is also relevant to certain incidents of divorce and to the application of certain other rules that one of the spouses has been found guilty of violating his marital duties (*supra* (2) (c)). Hence these findings by a foreign divorce court have been recognized in Germany.[183] Recognition also extends to a decision as to costs.[184]

Often the divorce decree is accompanied by orders of support, of custody and the like. Insofar as these collateral orders presuppose a valid divorce, they will not be recognized if the divorce decree is invalid in Germany.[185] As for other orders, they need not be formally recognized,[186] but they must comply with the general rules for recognition of foreign judgments (*infra* ch. 14 sub II (8)).[187] Provisional orders (*supra* (1) (c)) will be dealt with in the same way.[188]

(d) *East German divorce decrees* are not treated as foreign decisions. Normally they will be recognized in West Germany without formality (*supra* (3) (a)). However, West German courts under certain circumstances may decline recognition.[189]

(4) Annulment

According to German substantive law a marriage may be non-existent (if not celebrated before the registrar, *supra* II (2) (a)), null

---

182 LG Dresden 16 Oct. 1935, JW 1935, 3493 (recognition of a foreign default judgment divorcing aliens although such a decree could never be rendered by a German court).

183 BSG 16 May 1968, Bundesversorgnungsblatt 1968, 140 (with respect to public pension claims); KG Berlin 3 May 1935, *supra* n. 162, at 84 (with respect to a custody order).

184 RG 5 Jan. 1925, RGZ 109, 383, 387.

185 KG Berlin 16 Feb. 1909, *supra* n. 159.

186 E.g., an American order that the German wife of an American husband must resume her maiden name: OLG Celle 1 Sept. 1966, *supra* n. 158.

187 OLG Celle 1 Sept. 1966, *supra* n. 158; *cf.* KG Berlin 3 May 1935, *supra* n. 170.

188 OLG Hamburg 20 Dec. 1907, OLG 18, 392; BAUMBACH/LAUTERBACH, no. 1 B on § 328 ZPO.

189 *Cf.* BGH 30 Nov. 1960, BGHZ 34, 134; FamRZ 1961, 208. For details, *see* DROBNIG, Anerkennung und Rechtswirkungen sowjetzonaler Ehescheidungen, FamRZ 1961, 341.

and void, or voidable.[190] For conflicts purposes these different forms of nullity are treated alike and therefore they will be discussed together.

(a) Jurisdiction of the German courts to annul a marriage is the same as divorce jurisdiction (*supra* (1)).[191] In addition, these courts may annul a marriage between foreign spouses if the wife was German at the time of marriage and either she or the public prosecutor requests the annulment (§ 606b no. 2 ZPO).

(b) Whether a marriage is non-existent, null and void, or voidable is to be determined by the laws governing validity according to article 13 EGBGB (*supra* II (1) and (2)).[192]

(c) The principles governing recognition of foreign annulment decrees are the same as those for divorce decrees (*supra* (3))[193]: They must be formally recognized, and the jurisdiction of the foreign courts tested in the same manner (*supra* (3) (b) (i), with the addition of § 606b no. 2 ZPO (*supra* (a)). If one of the parties is German, the foreign decree must comply with article 13 I and III EGBGB, the German conflicts rule concerning celebration of marriage (§ 328 I no. 3 ZPO, *supra* (3) (b) (iii)).

(5) **Law of East Germany**

(a) According to § 3 *Familienverfahrensordnung* (FamVerfO) of 1966,[194] the courts of East Germany have exclusive jurisdiction in divorce and annulment cases if at least one of the spouses is a citizen of the GDR or has his residence there.

(b) According to § 17 I 1 EGFamGB the divorce is governed by the spouses' common national law at the time when suit is commenced. A renvoi will be accepted by the East German courts (§ 22). If the parties are nationals of different states, the law of the GDR applies (§ 17 I 2 EGFamGB), and it governs also if the wife lost her German nationality by marriage before the adoption of the principle of equality of husband and wife (§ 17 II EGFamGB). If the foreign law which is applicable under § 17 I 1 EGFamGB prohibits divorce completely or makes it difficult to obtain, the law of the GDR will also apply (§ 17 III EGFamGB).

(c) Foreign divorce and annulment decrees, in general, must be formally recognized by the East German Ministry of Justice (§ 26 I 1 EGFamGB). Such a formal recognition is not necessary in two cases: *first,* if the spouses were citizens of the forum state at the time

---

[190] 1 Cohn nos. 487–93.

[191] In Roth v. Roth, 104 Ill. 35 (1882), *error dismissed sub nom.* Roth v. Ehman, 107 U.S. 319 (1882), a German annulment decree with respect to spouses domiciled in Germany was recognized in Illinois.

[192] OLG Dresden 15 Jan. 1912, OLG 26, 211; LG Tübingen 25 July 1934, JW 1934, 2802; Kegel, Kommentar, nos. 72–85 on art. 13 EGBGB.

[193] Raape, *supra* n. 167, at 586–90; Kleinrahm/Partikel, *supra* n. 164a at 76–77.

[194] GBl. DDR 1966 II 171.

of the foreign decision (§ 26 III EGFamGB); *second*, with respect to decrees of the courts of West Germany and West Berlin, unless the East German Ministry of Justice, upon application, decides that the prerequisites for recognition have not been fulfilled (§ 26 I 2 EGFamGB). Since § 328 ZPO no longer applies to family law (§ 48 III no. 1 FamVerfO), the only provision establishing substantive requirements for recognition is § 26 II EGFamGB; according to this provision, decrees of foreign courts even where they lack jurisdiction under the law of the GDR will be recognized if one of the parties resides in the GDR and applies for recognition.

(d) East Germany applies the same principle of jurisdiction and recognition to annulment as it does to divorce (*supra* (a) and (c)): According to § 17 IV EGFamGB, whether a marriage may be annulled is decided under the law governing the marriage (*supra* II (3)).

B. PARENT AND CHILD

German family law still distinguishes between legitimate and illegitimate children.[194a] This basic distinction is also reflected in the conflicts rules affecting children. Hence we deal first with the law governing the various modes of acquiring (*a priori* or *a posteriori*) the status of legitimacy (I 1–4), before discussing the relations of legitimate (I 5) and illegitimate children (II).

I. LEGITIMACY*

(1) Birth to a Married Woman

(a) *General conflicts rule.*—According to article 18 I EGBGB the legitimacy of a child must be decided under German law where the mother's husband was a German at the time of the child's birth (or, where he died before that time, if he was a German at his death). From this unilateral provision a general conflicts rule has developed: the legitimacy of a child born to a married woman is governed by her husband's national law at the time of the child's birth.[195] If the marriage has been dissolved through divorce or

---

[194a] The recent statute of Aug. 19, 1969 on the legal status of illegitimate children (*supra* n. 2a) to a large extent approximates their status to that of legitimate children but still distinguishes between legitimate and what are now called "non-legitimate" ("nichteheliche" instead of "uneheliche") children.

* Ficker, Eheliche Kindschaft: Deutsches Recht, *in* Das internationale Familienrecht Deutschlands und Frankreichs (1955) 257–71 (*in French*: Le droit international privé de la famille en France et en Allemagne (1954) 218–31); Kilian, Parental Custody in Germany, *in* Parental Custody and Matrimonial Maintenance. A Symposium (London 1966) 97–101.

[195] BGH 22 Jan 1965, BGHZ 43, 213, 218; BayObLG 4 Jan. 1966, BayObLGZ 1966, 1, 5; 8 Oct. 1963, BayObLGZ 1963, 265, 268; 9 Aug. 1963, BayObLGZ 1963, 214; OLG Bamberg 2 Oct. 1963, IPRspr. 1962/63 no. 109; Kegel, Kommentar, no. 11 on art. 18 EGBGB.

death of the husband, the significant date is that of dissolution. As the law governing legitimacy is immutably tied to the husband's national law on that date, a subsequent change of his nationality is irrelevant.[196] According to these principles the legitimacy of the child of an American husband and a German wife has been decided under the husband's American domiciliary law.[197]

(b) *Renvoi and preliminary question.*—A renvoi from the husband's national law will be accepted by the German courts.[198] Of greater importance is the preliminary question concerning the law governing the validity of the mother's marriage. Must it, too, be answered by the husband's national law as the law governing the child's legitimacy (*supra* (a)), or is it subject to the general principles governing the validity of marriage (*supra* A II (1) and (2))? The Federal Supreme Court has finally chosen the second alternative: the validity of the marriage of the child's mother is determined according to articles 11 and 13 EGBGB.[199] Marriages celebrated in Germany therefore must comply *inter alia* with German formal requirements (*supra* A II (2)) even if the marriage is formally valid under the spouses' personal law. The offspring of a marriage which is formally void under German law is illegitimate, unless treated as legitimate[200] in an exceptional case.

(c) *Declaration of illegitimacy.* — German family law, like American law, presumes that a child conceived in wedlock is legitimate (§§ 1591, 1592 BGB).[201] But in contrast to American law this presumption can be rebutted only in a special court proceeding culminating in a conclusive declaration that the child is illegitimate

---

[196] OLG Freiburg 14 Dec. 1951, JZ 1952, 481; KEGEL, Kommentar, no. 12 on art. 18 EGBGB.

[197] OLG Bamberg 2 Oct. 1963, IPRspr. 1962/63 no. 109; LG Hamburg 30 Sept. 1968, StAZ 1970, 23; AG Stolberg 18 Feb. 1965, IPRspr. 1964/65 no. 116.

[198] LG Nürnberg-Fürth 20 June 1960, StAZ 1961, 134; KEGEL, Kommentar, no. 38 on art. 18 EGBGB.

One American-German case (LG Hamburg, preceding note) illustrates a "split" renvoi and its consequences. The law of New York, the domicile of the American husband, referred to the law of the parents' domicile at the time of the child's birth. As the parents had then been living apart for three years, the German mother being domiciled in Germany, the court applied New York law to the child's relation to the husband, under which it was held to be illegitimate, and German law to its relation to the mother, under which it was held to be legitimate. Thus "split" renvoi may lead to a limping status.

[199] BGH 22 Jan. 1965, and BayObLG 4 Jan. 1966, *supra* n. 195.

[200] LG Hamburg 27 Feb. 1954, StAZ 1956, 115, where, however, the child was afterwards legitimated by his parents' marriage, valid under German law; KEGEL, Kommentar, no. 5 on art. 18 EGBGB; *contra*: WENGLER, Note to BGH 22 Jan. 1965, *supra* n. 195, JZ 1965, 534, 536–37. If the marriage is voidable and finally dissolved, the laws applicable under art. 13 I EGBGB (*supra* A II (1)) govern the legitimacy of the offspring: KEGEL, IPR 307. However, such children may be treated as legitimate in exceptional cases. *See infra* n. 312.

[201] 1 COHN no. 524.

(§§ 1593–1600 BGB). This declaration is res judicata not only *inter partes* but also *inter omnes* (§ 640 h ZPO as revised in 1969); until the court so declares, the child's legitimacy cannot be questioned (§ 1593 BGB).[202]

Whether and how the presumption of legitimacy may be rebutted is also governed by the husband's national law at the time of the child's birth (*supra* (a)).[203] Exceptionally, however, article 18 II EGBGB extends the reign of German law to the case where only the mother is German. The legislature wanted to make sure that in all cases where a German parent was involved the presumption of legitimacy might be rebutted according to German law.[204] An action seeking a court declaration of illegitimacy normally must be filed by the father against the child.[205] A German court has jurisdiction if at least one of the parties has his residence in Germany or is a German, or if the mother is a German.[206]

(d) *Special problems of American law.* — The law of most American states permits a rebuttal of the presumption of legitimacy whenever the question is at issue and requires no formal declaration of illegitimacy following a special proceeding. If in a case governed by American law the father brings an action in Germany, it will be regarded as an action asking for a simple judicial declaration that he is not the child's father.[207] As such a declaratory judgment is conclusive only between the parties, a corresponding correction of the civil register will be refused.[208]

(e) *Recognition of foreign decisions.*—Foreign decisions as to the child's legitimacy, especially foreign judicial declarations of illegitimacy, will be recognized under the general conditions of § 328 ZPO (*infra* ch. 14 sub II (8)(a)). But it must be emphasized that there will be no recognition of a foreign decision if article 18

---

202 1 Cohn no. 525.

203 RG 12 Jan. 1939, RGZ 159, 167, 170; OLG Hamm 30 June 1964, FamRZ 1965, 90; 27 Oct. 1952, IPRspr. 1952/53 no. 178; OLG Freiburg/Br. 14 Dec. 1951, *supra* n. 196; KG Berlin 28 Feb. 1931, JW 1932, 2296; Kegel, Kommentar, no. 7 on art. 18 EGBGB. So long as the child's illegitimacy has not been asserted, the child will be held legitimate. *Cf.* OLG Bamberg 2 Oct. 1963, *supra* n. 195, dealing with the law of New Jersey.

204 For details, *cf.* Kegel, Kommentar, nos. 14–20 on art. 18 EGBGB.

205 The public prosecutor can no longer apply for such a declaration.

206 § 640a, as revised in 1969, in connection with §§ 13–16 ZPO; LG München I 9 July 1952, IPRspr. 1952/53 no. 180.

207 LG Ulm 18 Dec. 1959, IPRspr. 1958/59 no. 126. But in a noncontentious proceeding such a declaration cannot be made: AG Stolberg 18 Feb. 1965, *supra* n. 197.

208 *English law*: OLG Hamm 30 June 1964, *supra* n. 203, *rev'g* AG Bielefeld 22 Apr. 1963, FamRZ 1963, 458. *Contra*: Sonnenberger, Die Ehelichkeitsanfechtung bei amerikanischer Staatsangehörigkeit der Beteiligten, FamRZ 1964, 238, 240–242, advocating a decree working res judicata inter omnes. This suggestion is untenable because the courts are unable to bestow such force on their decrees.

EGBGB has been disregarded to the disadvantage of a German party (§ 328 I no. 3 ZPO).

(2) **Subsequent Marriage of the Parents**

(a) *General conflicts rule.*—According to article 22 I EGBGB the legitimation of an illegitimate antenuptial child is governed by German law if the father is German at the time of legitimation. This rule has been extended into the unanimously supported general principle that legitimation by subsequent marriage is governed by the father's national law at the time of marriage.[209] (The special consents required for German children (art. 22 II EGBGB) were until the recent statutory change inapplicable where the children were not German.[210]) Applying this principle, the illegitimate child of an American father domiciled in Michigan and of a German mother was held by a German court to have been legitimated according to Michigan law by his parents' subsequent marriage in Germany.[211]

(b) *Renvoi, preliminary question, and public policy.*—A renvoi or a transmission by the law applicable under the general principle of article 22 I EGBGB has been accepted by the German courts. An Argentine father domiciled in Florida married a German mother who had had a child by him born in Germany. Argentine law was looked to to determine whether the child had been legitimated by his parents' marriage, and as the Argentine conflicts rule referred to the law of the father's domicile, the legitimation was submitted to the law of Florida.[212]

Whether the marriage of the child's parents is valid will be

---

[209] BGH 17 Sept. 1968, BGHZ 50, 370, 372; BayObLG 31 May 1966, BayObLGZ 1966, 203; 18 July 1958, *id.* 1958, 204; KG Berlin 9 Dec. 1957, NJW 1958, 635; 21 Nov. 1930, StAZ 1931, 51; OLG Frankfurt/M. 29 Jan. 1959, FamRZ 1960, 77; SCHWENN, Legitimation: Deutsches Recht *in* Das internationale Familienrecht Deutschlands und Frankreichs (1955) 361–75 (*in French*: Le droit international privé de la famille en France et en Allemagne (1954) 308–20); KEGEL, Kommentar, no. 2 on art. 22 EGBGB; RAAPE 377; PALANDT/LAUTERBACH, no. 2 on art. 22 EGBGB. This is true even if the child is legitimate under his father's personal law through birth in lawful wedlock: LG Hamburg 27 Feb. 1954, *supra* n. 200.

[210] This was due to the fact that under the former § 1719 BGB, legitimation by subsequent marriage was effected by the marriage alone. *Cf.* 1 COHN no. 544 (a). Under the new § 1719 (in connection with § 1600 a), an acknowledgment of the child by the husband or a judicial declaration of paternity is an additional requirement (*cf. infra* II (2) (a) and (b)). As the German child must give his consent to the acknowledgment (§ 1600 c I BGB, *infra* II (2) (a)), absence of this consent will invalidate the legitimation unless the husband has been declared by court order to be the father.

[211] BayObLG 31 May 1966, *supra* n. 209. *Cf. also* OLG Stuttgart 24 Sept. 1965, DAVorm. 1966, 93, concerning a legitimation under the law of Tennessee.

[212] KG Berlin 5 Feb. 1932, StAZ 1932, 162; 21 Nov. 1930, StAZ 1931, 51. *Cf. also* LG Wiesbaden 10 Oct. 1932, JW 1933, 193. *See also* AG Hamburg

decided under the general rules of articles 11 and 13 EGBGB governing the validity of marriage (*supra* A II (1) and (2)).[213] Thus in the Michigan case mentioned above (*supra* (a)) the validity of the German marriage was upheld under German law because the wife was German and the American husband's domiciliary law referred back to German law as the law of the place of celebration (*supra* A II (1)(b)).[214]

German public policy has been invoked several times against foreign rules on the subject, for example, rules legitimating children not the offspring of the man marrying their mother;[215] rules making no provision for legitimation;[216] and, most importantly, rules prohibiting the legitimation of adulterine bastards. In the Michigan case already mentioned, the child was the result of an adulterous union, but the applicable Michigan law did not prohibit his legitimation.[217] The German courts have vacillated as to the Dutch[218] but upheld the English prohibition.[219] Recently the Federal Supreme Court held that the Italian prohibition was against German public policy with respect to a family living in Germany.[220] It may be added that the fact that the foreign law required, in addition to marriage of the parents, acknowledgment of the child by one or both of them was not regarded as contrary to German public policy under the pre-1969 version of the German Civil Code which required nothing but the marriage.[221]

---

15 July 1966, StAZ 1967, 301, where a Liberian father married the German mother of his child in New Jersey, the domicile of the father.

[213] OLG Hamm 10 Nov. 1958, FamRZ 1959, 28; 18 Sept. 1954, StAZ 1956, 62; LG Braunschweig 22 Oct. 1947, IPRspr. 1945–49 no. 78; LG Hamburg 3 July 1961, StAZ 1962, 250, *contra*. LG Köln 20 Feb. 1953, MDR 1953, 489, applying the father's national law as governing under art. 22 I EGBGB.

[214] BayObLG 31 May 1966, *supra* n. 209, at 208.

[215] KG Berlin 9 Dec. 1957, *supra* n. 209; OLG Karlsruhe 31 Dec. 1964, FamRZ 1965, 624; LG Freiburg/Br. 9 May 1955, JZ 1956, 253.

[216] OLG Hamm 10 Nov. 1958, *supra* n. 213.

[217] BayObLG 31 May 1966, *supra* n. 209, at 209; AG Mettmann 28 Feb. 1956, IPRspr. 1956/57 no. 123.

[218] *Violation of German public policy*: LG Frankfurt/M. 12 July 1955, NJW 1955, 1959; 6 Dec. 1953, StAZ 1954, 156; LG Karlsruhe 15 May 1952, IPRspr. 1952/53 no. 195 a. *Contra*: AG Bingen 24 July 1952, IPRspr. 1952/53 no. 195; AG Worms 19 Nov. 1955, DAVorm. 1955/56, 328, because neither parents nor child were domiciled in Germany. Even though there were strong contacts with Germany, the Dutch statute was upheld in OLG Frankfurt/M. 28 Feb. 1956, NJW 1956, 672; LG Kleve 18 Oct. 1962, StAZ 1963, 191; AG Bielefeld 24 Oct. 1962, StAZ 1963, 304.

[219] OLG Celle 13 July 1954, NJW 1954, 1891, *aff'g* LG Hannover 18 May 1954, StAZ 1955, 289; AG Hamburg-Altona 28 Feb. 1958, IPRspr. 1960/61 no. 114.

[220] BGH 17 Sept. 1968, *supra* n. 109, at 375–78.

[221] BayObLG 18 July 1958, *supra* n. 209; KG Berlin 29 Nov. 1929, StAZ 1930, 101; OLG Hamm 13 Feb. 1948, StAZ 1948, 37. As to the present 1969 version, *cf. supra* n. 210.

(c) *Jurisdiction of German courts.*—According to the earlier German local law, legitimation by subsequent marriage needed no court action. For purposes of civil registration, however, the *Amtsgericht* (county court) in a non-contentious proceeding had to make a declaration concerning the legitimation and to order correction of the civil register (former § 31 I PStG). In derogation of the general rules of German international jurisdiction in non-contentious proceedings (*infra* ch. 14 sub I (2) (d)), the German courts asserted jurisdiction to make this declaration if the child was or had to be registered in the German civil register or if the father or the child was German (former § 31 PstG).[222] Whether the German courts were allowed to do more than this, if, for example, the applicable foreign law required acknowledgment of the child by the parents or a special court decree, was less clear; whereas civil registrars recorded such acknowledgments,[223] the courts sometimes hesitated to render decrees of legitimation on the ground that these decrees would be invalid under the applicable law.[224]

According to the newly enacted German law, the civil registrar must always be authorized by court decree to correct the civil register where a legitimation has taken place under foreign law (§ 31 II PStG, as revised in 1969). Since the present law also requires additional acts of acknowledgment or filiation orders to validate a legitimation by subsequent marriage, the German courts and registrars will probably be less hesitant to act in such cases in the future.

(d) *Recognition of foreign decisions.*—Since in many countries legitimation by subsequent marriage is effected by operation of law without court action, recognition of foreign decisions of legitimation is seldom at issue. However, § 328 I no. 3 ZPO might prevent recognition if article 22 EGBGB has been disregarded to the disadvantage of a German. In view of the very simple rule of the earlier German substantive law, to the effect that only subsequent marriage is required for legitimation (*supra* n. 210), this was not likely to occur.[225] In the future, however, article 22 II EGBGB

---

[222] BayObLG 31 May 1966, *supra* n. 209; KG Berlin 9 Dec. 1957, *supra* n. 209; OLG Frankfurt/M. 13 Feb. 1958, NJW 1958, 636; OLG Hamm 10 Nov. 1958, *supra* n. 213; 2 May 1949, DRpfl. 1949, 414; OLG Stuttgart 24 Sept. 1965, *supra* n. 211.

[223] OLG Hamm, 13 Feb. 1948, *supra* n. 221; OLG Nürnberg 8 May 1950, SJZ 1950, 909; LG München 9 May 1949, IPRspr. 1945/49 no. 27; *cf. also* §§ 29, 29a and 29b PStG; KEGEL, Kommentar, no. 27 on art. 22 EGBGB.

[224] *Declining jurisdiction*: LG Stuttgart 8 June 1956, IPRspr. 1956/57 no. 122; LG Bonn 23 Jan. 1952, IPRspr. 1952/53 no. 197; AG Leonberg 5 Oct. 1955, IPRspr. 1954/55 no. 112.

Asserting jurisdiction: OLG Nürnberg 8 May 1950, *supra* n. 223; LG Bonn 11 Mar. 1954, IPRspr. 1954/55 no. 111.

[225] LG Freiburg/Br. 26 July 1965, FamRZ 1965, 622 (recognition of a

will play an important rôle in any case where the German child has not consented to acknowledgment by the husband.

(3) **Court Decree**

(a) *General conflicts rule.*—A court decree of legitimation, as distinct from one merely declaring that legitimation has been effected by subsequent marriage (*supra* (2) (c) and (d)), is governed by the same general conflicts principle as the legitimation by subsequent marriage (*supra* (2) (a)), in other words, by the father's national law at the time of legitimation (*cf.* art. 22 I EGBGB).[226] Here the exception of article 22 II EGBGB is also pertinent. According to this provision the legitimation of a German child will not be granted upon application of his alien father unless the consents required by German local law have been furnished; under that law the child and, if it is a minor, its mother have to agree to the legitimation (§ 1726 BGB).[227] If the child applies for legitimation, his surviving parent must consent (§ 1740 b I BGB, as revised in 1969).

(b) *Jurisdiction of German courts.*—A German county court has jurisdiction to render a decree of legitimation if the applicant, either father or child, irrespective of his nationality, is domiciled or resident in Germany at the time of his application. It also has jurisdiction if the applicant, although resident abroad, is German.[228]

(c) *Recognition of foreign decisions.*—A foreign court decree of legitimation will be recognized in Germany if the foreign court had jurisdiction under German standards (*supra* (b)), if the decree complies with the law designated by article 22 EGBGB, and if, in the case of legitimation of a German child, the consents required by German law were given.[229]

(4) **Governmental Act and Recognition**

(a) *Legitimation by governmental act.*—As German law does not provide for this form of legitimation, only the recognition of a foreign act may become an issue. There is only a single German precedent dealing with a Czech governmental act,[230] but it will probably be followed in the future; this case held that a govern-

---

French decree proclaiming the legitimation of a German child by the marriage of his mother to a Frenchman who was not the child's father.) *Cf. also supra* n. 215.

226 RAAPE 390.

227 1 COHN no. 544.

228 *Cf.* § 43 a FGG, as revised in 1969; KEGEL, Kommentar, no. 32 on art. 22 EGBGB.

229 *Cf.* BayObLG 8 June 1921, BayObLGZ 21 (1921) 266, 269; KEGEL, Kommentar, no. 32 on art. 22 EGBGB. *See generally infra* ch. 14 sub II (8) (a).

230 BayObLG 8 June 1921, preceding note.

mental legitimation would be recognized if enacted by the father's national state upon compliance with article 22 II EGBGB dealing with consent requirements for a German child.

(b) *Legitimation by acknowledgment.*—German domestic law also contains no provision for legitimation by mere acknowledgment, yet a German registrar will record an act of acknowledgment by a foreign father if his national law regards it as valid (§ 29 PStG, § 377 (1) and (5) DA). If this acknowledgment pertains to a German child, however, the consent requirements of article 22 II EGBGB have been held applicable[231]; therefore a foreign act of acknowledgment has been disregarded in Germany because it was not approved by the child or his guardian.[232]

(5) **Incidents of Legitimacy**

(a) *General conflicts rules.*—According to article 19 EGBGB the relationship between a legitimate child and his parents is governed by German law if his father—or, after his father's death, his mother—is German. German law is also controlling if the father or mother has lost his or her German nationality but the child has retained his (art. 19 sent. 2 EGBGB).[233] This latter provision has been regarded as an exception to the general conflicts rule that the father's national law governs the relationship between a legitimate child and his parents.[234] It must be emphasized that the law governing the relations between parent and child is mutable (in contrast to the issue of legitimacy, *supra* (1) (a)). It is the father's national law at the time when the issue arises which is decisive. If the father changes his nationality, the law governing future questions of this nature will change also.[235]

The following case may illustrate the general conflicts rules. The German wife of an American husband who had served in the United States Army in Germany declined to follow him to New Jersey when he was discharged. Long after their separation she gave birth to a child which she entrusted to the defendants as prospective adoptive parents. The wife later changed her mind and filed a custody suit

---

[231] MASSFELLER, Das gesamte Familienrecht, 2d ed., vol. 2 (1965) 214; *contra*: KEGEL, Kommentar, no. 10 on art. 22 EGBGB, applying art. 19 EGBGB (*infra* (5)(a)).

[232] LG Koblenz 16 Dec. 1958, DAVorm. 1958/59, 342.

[233] OLG Hamm 1 July 1955, NJW 1955, 1724.

[234] RG 3 Dec. 1942, RGZ 170, 198, 199; 28 Mar. 1931, JW 1932, 588; 23 May 1927, WarnRspr. 1927 no. 121; 29 Dec. 1910, JW 1911, 208; BayObLG 3 Nov. 1967, FamRZ 1968, 269; 17 May 1963, BayObLGZ 1963, 123; 6 Feb. 1962, *id.* 1962, 39; KG Berlin 28 Oct. 1954, IPRspr. 1954/55 no. 102; KEGEL, Kommentar, no. 1 on art. 19 EGBGB.

[235] AG Berlin-Lichterfelde 9 June 1934, StAZ 1934, 362; KEGEL, Kommentar, nos. 5 and 6 on art. 19 EGBGB.

against the defendants. The German court[236] held: *first,* the preliminary question as to legitimacy should be answered affirmatively by applying the law of New Jersey as directed by article 18 I EGBGB;[237] *second,* a parent's right to claim a legitimate child from other persons is an incident of the relation between parent and child[238] and therefore the governing law must be determined by article 19 EGBGB; *third,* article 19 EGBGB in this instance refers to American law, here, to the law of New Jersey, but the latter by a "hidden" renvoi refers back to German law as the child's domiciliary law. German law was therefore applicable.[239]

(b) *Custody.*—All matters of custody are governed by the rule of article 19 EGBGB: a parent's right and duty to take care of the child;[240] his statutory agency;[241] his right to claim the child from a third person or a parent who has been deprived of custody;[242] and the latter's right to visit the child.[243] There are four other matters also which have frequently occupied the courts:

(i) According to § 1666 BGB guardianship courts (*Vormundschaftsgerichte*)[244] are required to take appropriate steps to safeguard a child's welfare against abuse of parental power, neglect, or immoral behavior on the part of a parent.[245] The German courts have held that they have jurisdiction to apply this provision in favor of all children residing in Germany, even if under the rule of article 19 EGBGB foreign law would ordinarily govern the relationship between parent and child.[246] Whether the courts may act where the parents

---

[236] OLG Bamberg 2 Oct. 1963, *supra* n. 195. A similar case was decided by LG Stuttgart 12 Nov. 1953, RabelsZ 19 (1954) 153, where the court, according to the law of New York, dismissed an action of the American husband against his stateless wife in Germany.

[237] KEGEL, Kommentar, no. 49 on art. 19 EGBGB. If the question of a valid legitimation or adoption is at issue, it has to be answered under art. 22 EGBGB (*supra* (2)(a) and *infra* III (2)).

[238] RG 25 Jan. 1940, RGZ 162, 329; 23 May 1927, *supra* n. 234; OLG Köln 4 June 1954, FamRZ 1955, 113; LG Stuttgart 12 Nov. 1953, *supra* n. 236. *Cf.* KEGEL, Kommentar, no. 16 on art. 19 EGBGB.

[239] RG 29 Dec. 1910, *supra* n. 234; BayObLG 17 May 1963 and 6 Feb. 1962, *supra* n. 234; KEGEL, Kommentar, no. 50 on art. 19 EGBGB.

[240] KEGEL, Kommentar, no. 16 on art. 19 EGBGB.

[241] *Ibid.*

[242] *Supra* n. 238.

[243] BayObLG 3 Nov. 1967, *supra* n. 234; KG Berlin 12 Jan. 1934, JW 1934, 699; LG Wiesbaden 2 Mar. 1965, FamRZ 1965, 284; *cf. also* RG 29 Dec. 1910, *supra* n. 234.

[244] The guardianship courts are sections of the county courts (*supra* ch. 2 sub B III (2)), acting usually in non-contentious proceedings.

[245] *Cf.* 1 COHN no. 536; KILIAN 98–9.

[246] BGH 22 May 1963, BGHZ 40, 1; BayObLG 23 July 1959, IPRspr. 1962/63 no. 101; 16 Oct. 1926, BayObLGZ 25 (1926) 369; 22 Apr. 1922, BayOLGZ 22 (1922/23) 69; OLG Hamm 12 Nov. 1964, FamRZ 1965, 89. *Cf. also* KG Berlin 5 Apr. 1906, KGJ 32 A 23.

are not at fault but the child's welfare is endangered by external forces will be discussed below ((5) (b)), as this is not a matter of private relations beween parent and child;

(ii) Mention has already been made (A V (1) (c)) of the fact that German divorce courts may issue provisional orders under § 627 ZPO in order to settle temporarily questions which have arisen between the spouses themselves or between them and their children. The care of the child may also be regulated in this way although the courts disagree as to whether this case is controlled by the *lex fori* or the law applicable under the rule of article 19 EGBGB;[247]

(iii) The most important problem is the award of custody after the divorce of the parents. If a provisional order under § 627 ZPO (*supra* sub (ii)) has been issued, it will remain in force until changed by the guardianship court (§ 627a ZPO). Under what conditions a German guardianship court has international jurisdiction to regulate parental power has long been disputed.[248] In recent times there has been a strong judicial tendency to claim German jurisdiction if the courts have competence under §§ 43 or 36 FGG.[249] This means that the German courts have jurisdiction if the child is domiciled or at least resident in Germany (§ 43 I, § 36 I FGG)[250] or if the child is a German (§ 43 I, § 36 II FGG). In the latter case the *Amtsgericht* Schöneberg (in West Berlin) has competence if the child has neither domicile nor residence in Germany. In other words—and this is similar to the law of New York[251]—the domicile or residence of the parents is irrelevant; it does not confer jurisdiction[252] even if the child shares their German domicile but does not actually reside in Germany,[253] and it does not exclude jurisdiction if the parents are abroad but the child resides in Germany.[254] In contrast to American law, the existence of jurisdiction does not entail application of the law of

---

247 BayObLG 8 June 1962, IPRspr. 1962/63 no. 103 (divorce of an American husband); KG Berlin 11 Jan. 1932, IPRspr. 1932 no. 90; OLG München 7 Mar. 1960, NJW 1960, 1771; *cf. also* the cases cited in nn. 145–147.

248 For a detailed analysis, *cf.* BayObLG 16 Jan. 1959, BayObLGZ 1959, 8.

249 BayObLG 16 Jan. 1959, preceding note, and KG Berlin 27 June 1963, FamRZ 1963, 576, overruling their prior practice which held that a German court must have personal jurisdiction over the parents and the child. OLG Hamm 21 Aug. 1964, FamRZ 1965, 92; OLG Saarbrücken 14 July 1965, FamRZ 1966, 42.

250 *Cf.* BayObLG 16 Jan. 1959, *supra* n. 248, where the mother and the child only were domiciled in Germany.

251 The New York Supreme Court in Matter of Hillers, N.Y.L.J. 18 Oct. 1954, p. 12 col. 1, held that New York courts have no custody jurisdiction with respect to a child who lives with his mother in Germany.

252 Whether the parents'—especially the father's—German nationality alone will confer jurisdiction upon the German courts, has apparently not been decided.

253 KG Berlin 27 June 1963, *supra* n. 249.

254 BayObLG 21 Mar. 1952, BayObLGZ 1952, 74, overruled by BayObLG 16 Jan. 1959, *supra* n. 248, at p. 21.

the forum. As in the case of divorce (*supra* A V), jurisdiction and applicable law are treated separately. A German guardianship court will determine a matter of custody according to the law indicated by article 19 EGBGB[255] unless that law violates German public policy.[256] A renvoi from the foreign law will be accepted. Thus the national law of an American father has been held to refer back to the child's or the parents' German domiciliary law and therefore German local law has been applied to regulate the custody of children after their parents' divorce;[257]

(iv) The German courts will recognize foreign custody decrees if these comply with German prerequisites for recognition. If the custody decree is part of a foreign divorce decree, § 328 ZPO applies (no formal recognition being necessary under art. 7 § 1 FamRÄndG, *see supra* A V (3) (a)). The foreign custody decree will not be recognized if (a) the foreign court lacked jurisdiction according to German standards, or (b) due process was not observed, or (c) German public policy, which insists primarily on safeguarding the child, was violated, or (d) reciprocity would not be accorded in a case where a German court would also have jurisdiction (§ 328 I no. 5, II ZPO).[258] The same conditions, except the last one, will also prevent recognition of a custody decree not contained in a divorce decree but rendered by a judge in a non-contentious proceeding or by some other authority.[259]

The recognition of a foreign custody decree does not preclude a German court from altering or amending it if under the law applicable according to article 19 EGBGB such a decision is justified. Thus, while it recognized an Illinois custody decree rendered between parties who were all Germans, one court amended the decree according to German local law.[260]

(c) *Property rights.*—Also governed by the rule of article 19 EGBGB are the rights of the parents in the property of their minor child, their responsibility for it, and their statutory agency for the

---

255 KG Berlin 28 Oct. 1954, *supra* n. 234 (Italian law); KG Berlin 10 Feb. 1933, IPRspr. 1933 no. 47 (Polish law); OLG Hamm 19 May 1949, IPRspr. 1945–49 no. 24 (Swiss law).

256 KG Berlin 6 Nov. 1967, FamRZ 1968, 92 (Iraqi law); OLG Düsseldorf 14 Nov. 1961, IPRspr. 1960/61 no. 113 (Egyptian law). Both cases held it contrary to public policy that Islamic law excludes the mother from custody over her child beyond a certain age.

257 BayObLG 6 Feb. 1962, *supra.* n. 234; 13 Mar. 1912, BayObLGZ 13 (1913) 136; IPG 1965/66 no. 30 (Hamburg) at pp. 320–22.

258 KG Berlin 3 May 1935, StAZ 1935, 413; KEGEL, Kommentar, no. 46 on art. 19 EGBGB.

259 DÖLLE, Über einige Kernprobleme des internationalen Rechts der freiwilligen Gerichtsbarkeit, RabelsZ 27 (1962) 201, 235.

260 KG Berlin 3 May 1935, *supra* n. 258.

child in this respect.[261] The father's national law also determines which parent after divorce is to be responsible for the care of the child's property. A hidden renvoi from American law will be accepted.[262]

With respect to property, however, article 19 EGBGB is modified by article 28 EGBGB, to the effect that property located elsewhere is subject to "special rules" of the law of its situs, if any exist. Let us take the following illustration: German parents are by law guardians of their child's property and as such they have to administer his estate and may, under certain circumstances, use the profits for their own maintenance; under article 19 EGBGB these German parents may claim the same rights in real property located in the United States; but if the conflicts rule of the American situs would apply to the same questions not the father's national law but the *lex rei sitae,* then the German courts would yield to the American conflicts rule.

As to the power of American parents to deal with property of their children situated in Germany, several older German decisions held that, since American parents have no power under their own law to administer and control their children's property outside the United States, a German court should appoint a curator (*Pfleger, infra* C (1) (d)) to act on the children's behalf.[263] If one American parent has been appointed as guardian of his children's property by an American court, his authority has been regarded as restricted, under American law, to the state of appointment; in these cases, too, a curator has been appointed in Germany.[264]

The law governing mutual rights of inheritance between legitimate children and their parents is not determined by article 19 EGBGB, but by the conflicts rules governing succession (*infra* ch. 5).[265]

(d) *Support and maintenance.*—The parents' duty to support their children[266] as well as their right to maintenance from them[267] are governed generally by the rule of article 19 EGBGB, which also

---

[261] RG 3 Dec. 1942 and 28 Mar. 1931, *supra* n. 234; AG Berlin-Lichterfelde 9 June 1934, *supra* n. 235; KEGEL, Kommentar, no. 17 on art. 19 EGBGB.

[262] IPG 1965–66 no. 30 (Hamburg) at pp. 322–23; *cf. also supra* (5) (b).

[263] KG Berlin 8 Dec. 1902, NiemeyersZ 13 (1903) 153; LG Posen 2 Jan. 1903, Juristische Monatsschrift für Posen, West- und Ostpreussen und Pommern VI (1903) 4; AG Tauberbischofsheim 14 June 1910, Bad.Rspr. 12 (1910) 189.

[264] KG Berlin 23 July 1902, OLG 5, 100; OLG Darmstadt 14 Oct. 1910, OLG 24, 50.

[265] KEGEL, Kommentar, no. 11 preceding art. 24 EGBGB.

[266] OLG Hamm 7 Sept. 1959, JMBl. NRW 1959, 269; LG Düsseldorf 27 Nov. 1953, 269; LG Düsseldorf 27 Nov. 1953, ZBlJugR 1954, 115; LG Frankfurt/M. 29 Oct. 1931, JW 1932, 2307; LG Berlin II 5 Nov. 1929, KGBl. 1930, 77.

[267] LG München I 5 June 1929, IPRspr. 1930 no. 77.

applies if the parents' marriage has been dissolved.[268] Accordingly the duty of an American father to support his children has been decided under the law of California in a German wrongful death action.[269] If, however, the child has his habitual residence in Germany or in another country which is a party to the Hague Convention on the Law Applicable to Obligations to Support Minor Children of October 10, 1956,[269a] the law of that country governs the parents' duty to support. As this Convention does not require reciprocity it is also applied to nationals of a country, like the United States of America, which is not a party.[269b]

Jurisdiction in support actions is subject to the general rules (*infra* ch. 14 sub I (2)). However, there is one special feature: even if the defendant does not reside in Germany, an action may be brought at the plaintiff's domicile or residence in Germany (§ 23 a ZPO). Recognition abroad of the resulting decree will depend upon the circumstances. The mutual recognition and enforcement of support orders is still largely *terra incognita.* It goes without saying that the American courts will not recognize German support decrees if the general requirements for recognition of foreign judgments are not met (*infra* ch. 14 sub II (8) (b)). The peculiar difficulty with support decrees is the usual American refusal to recognize foreign judgments that are not "final," in other words, that are still subject to modification by the rendering court. Under German law, such modifications may be made only prospectively and only if circumstances have changed substantially; arrears cannot be modified whether or not they have been reduced to judgment (§ 323 ZPO). If the American courts apply the same standards to the recognition of German support orders as to those of their sister states,[270] these German judgments should be recognized at least as to outstanding arrears. This does not mean that an American court will never recognize a judgment for future alimony or support; in some states, for example, California, foreign support or alimony decrees, although not final under the law of the rendering court, are recognized as

---

[268] AG Ellwangen/Jagst 7 Nov. 1949, IPRspr. 1945–49 no. 25; Zweigert, Unterhaltspflicht zwischen Verwandten: Deutsches Recht, *in*: Das internationale Familienrecht, *supra* n. 209, 438–455, 440 (*in French*: Le droit, *supra* n. 209, at 369–85).

[269] OLG Celle 21 July 1966, VersR 1967, 164; *cf. infra* ch. 7 at n. 38.

[269a] BGBl. 1961 II 1013; 1962 II 16; *translation*: 5 Am. J. Comp. L. 656 (1956). As of the end of 1968, the following had also ratified the Convention: Austria, France, Italy, Luxembourg, the Netherlands and Switzerland.

[269b] Dierk Müller, NJW 1967, 141; Scheucher, ZfRV 4 (1963) 82, 83; de Winter, Ned. T. Int. R. 4 (1957) 133, 152.

[270] *Cf.* especially the rules under Barber v. Barber, 323 U.S. 77 (1944), Sistare v. Sistare, 218 U.S. 1 (1910), and Lynde v. Lynde, 181 U.S. 183 (1901).

modifiable decrees so that either party may apply for such modification as could be made by the rendering court.[271]

This sketch of the American rules will suffice to indicate when a German court will find that the requisite reciprocity exists (§ 328 I no. 5 ZPO, *see infra* ch. 14 sub II (8) (a) and (b)). In one case, a New York support order was (erroneously) refused recognition under the general rules.[272] A recent German decision, by contrast, correctly recognized a New York support order with regard to arrears of alimony, although these are subject to modification under New York Domestic Relations Law § 244.[273] Foreign support orders, even if recognized, may be modified by the German courts in light of new circumstances, if and when the law governing the support duty so permits.[274]

(e) *Miscellaneous incidents.*—Tort immunity between parents and their legitimate children,[275] the name of the latter[276] and their domicile,[277] are all governed by the rule of article 19 EGBGB. If, however, the question of the child's domicile arises incidentally to the determination of German jurisdiction, German law must be applied as the *lex fori.*[278] The German courts have sometimes failed to do so,[279] although harmlessly because a minor child shares his parents' domicile under German law and the concept of "*Wohnsitz*" in many instances is identical with the American concept of "domicile" (*supra* ch. 3 sub B).

(6) Law of East Germany

According to § 18 EGFamGB filiation and declaration of illegitimacy are governed by the law of the state whose nationality the child has acquired at birth. The relationship between parent and

---

271 Worthley v. Worthley, 44 Cal. 2d 465, 283 P. 2d 19 (1955).

272 KG Berlin 22 Oct. 1963, *supra* n. 94a.

273 LG Hamburg 29 Aug. 1968—13 O 256/56, unreported.

274 STEIN/JONAS/SCHÖNKE/POHLE, no. II 5 on § 323 ZPO; LG Hamburg 29 Aug. 1968, preceding note, which erroneously declined to modify retroactively outstanding arrears of alimony because the German law of civil procedure prohibits such retroactive modification.

275 KEGEL, Kommentar, no. 44 on art. 12 EGBGB. On the general problem of intra-family tort liability *cf.* BINDER, Zur Auflockerung des Deliktsstatuts, RabelsZ 20 (1955) 401, 485–87; *cf. also infra* ch. 7 n. 31.

276 AG Bielefeld 26 Feb. 1964, StAZ 1964, 222 (a child of a German father and an American mother was not allowed to have his mother's surname as a middle name because under German law a child takes his father's name only); KEGEL, Kommentar, no. 26 on art. 19 EGBGB; FICKER 264.

277 KG Berlin 14 June 1954, IPRspr. 1954/55 no. 104; KEGEL and FICKER, preceding note.

278 BGH 29 Nov. 1961, RzW 1962, 182; KG Berlin 16 Feb. 1961, FamRZ 1961, 383; and *infra* ch. 14 sub I (2) (a).

279 E.g., BayObLG 31 May 1966, *supra* n. 209.

child will be adjudicated under the child's national law at the time when the issue arises (§ 19 EGFamGB). A renvoi to German law will be accepted (§ 22 EGFamGB). If the child is stateless, the law of his habitual residence is invoked (§ 23 I EGFamGB).

II. RELATIONS OF ILLEGITIMATE CHILDREN*

Children who do not meet the requirements discussed above (sub I) are deemed illegitimate. Their relations with their mother and their father, respectively, are subject to different rules.

(1) Relations with the Mother

Relations with the mother are governed by German law if the mother is German (art. 20 sent. 1 EGBGB), or if, while she has lost her German nationality, the child has remained German (art. 20 sent. 2 EGBGB). The courts and legal writers have derived from these statutory provisions the general principle that the mother's national law governs her relations with her illegitimate child,[280] whose nationality is irrelevant in all cases but one (art. 20 sent. 2 EGBGB).[281] Application of the mother's law means that the governing law changes if the mother changes her nationality.[282] A renvoi or transmission from a foreign law will be accepted by a German court.[283]

All questions concerning the child's relationship to his mother are submitted to the mother's national law. Generally speaking, these questions are the same as those covered by article 19 EGBGB with respect to legitimate children (*supra* I (5)(b) (c)).[284] Thus article 20 EGBGB applies to the mother's custody of the child's person and property;[285] to the mutual support duties between mother and child;[286] and to the child's assumption of the mother's name. Accordingly the name of a German mother's illegitimate child was subject to German law even though both had formerly resided in California

---

* WENGLER, Uneheliche Kindschaft: Deutsches Recht, *in* Das internationale Familienrecht Deutschlands und Frankreichs (1955) 315–334 (*in French*: Le droit international privé de la famille en France et en Allemagne (1954) 269–286).

[280] BayObLG 2 Oct. 1953, BayObLGZ 1953, 323; OLG Karlsruhe 26 Nov. 1926, JFG 4, 67; LG Frankenthal 11 July 1955, MDR 1955, 676; AG Bielefeld 23 June 1961, StAZ 1962, 102; KEGEL, Kommentar, nos. 1 and 2 on art. 20 EGBGB; RAAPE 358; PALANDT/LAUTERBACH, no. 2 on art. 20 EGBGB.

[281] OLG Karlsruhe, preceding note; KEGEL, Kommentar, no. 3 on art. 20 EGBGB.

[282] *Cf.* OLG Karlsruhe, *supra* n. 280; KEGEL, Kommentar, no. 4 on art. 20 EGBGB.

[283] KEGEL, Kommentar, no. 20 on art. 20 EGBGB.

[284] *Cf.* KEGEL, Kommentar, nos. 9–14 on art. 20 EGBGB.

[285] LG Frankenthal, *supra* n. 280; AG Hamburg-Altona 26 Mar. 1968, DAVorm. 1968, 427.

[286] KEGEL, Kommentar, no. 13 on art. 20 EGBGB.

where the child had been known by his father's name;[287] on the other hand, it was recognized by a German court that an American mother of an illegitimate child was allowed under Florida law to bestow on her child the name of her deceased husband.[288] It is not settled what law determines whether the husband himself is permitted to give his name to his wife's illegitimate child,[289] but the better and prevailing view seems to be that the mother's national law governs this question also.[290]

The German law of guardianship with respect to illegitimate children has been changed three times in recent years. This must be borne in mind in examining German case law. Since July 1, 1970, the mother is the guardian of her illegitimate child (§ 1705 BGB). In certain situations, for example, in maintenance suits (*cf.* § 1706 BGB), she will be assisted by an official curator (§ 1709 BGB).[291] These provisions of German local law apply only if German law is applicable under the conflicts rule of article 20 EGBGB. Before 1970 an illegitimate child was subject automatically to official guardianship provided, *inter alia,* the mother or, according to an earlier version of the statute, the child was German.[292] As the nationality of an illegitimate child depends upon his mother's nationality and the mother's nationality is the connecting factor under article 20 EGBGB, the recent changes in the German local law have not seriously affected the conflicts rules. Therefore what has been said with respect to official guardianship will also be true of official curatorship: it does not terminate upon the child's emigration to the United States[293] and, absent other provisions, it can be terminated only by German court order.[294]

---

[287] *Cf.* Hasta 1968, 58.

[288] AG Bielefeld, *supra* n. 280.

[289] On former § 1706 BGB, *cf.* 1 Cohn no. 539 as to the so-called "Einbenennung," and Breidenbach, Kann eine Einbenennung nach § 1706 BGB rechtswirksam durch ein Gericht der USA verfügt werden? StAZ 1962, 111–112. *Cf.* § 1618 BGB, as revised in 1969, introducing minor changes in the German local law.

[290] RG 23 Nov. 1927, RGZ 119, 44; AG Duisburg 1 Oct. 1958, DAVorm. 1958/59, 231; AG Memmingen 9 Dec. 1960, StAZ 1961, 289; AG München 18 Feb. 1963, StAZ 1963, 303; *contra*: KG Berlin 3 July 1925, OLG 46, 183, applying the child's national law. *Cf.* Kegel, Kommentar, no. 16 on art. 20 EGBGB, with further references in note 28.

[291] These innovations are due to the statute of 1969 on the legal status of illegitimate children, *supra* n. 2a. *See,* generally, on curators, *infra* C(1)(d).

[292] *Cf.* § 40 Gesetz über Jugendwohlfahrt of Aug. 11, 1961, BGBl. I 1206; *cf.* 1 Cohn no. 552; former § 35 JWG; BayObLG 11 Feb. 1959, BayObLGZ 1959, 47; LG Hagen 24 May 1956, MDR 1956, 553.

[293] LG Bielefeld 3 Aug. 1955, DAVorm. 1955/56, 333; LG Nürnberg 2 July 1956, DAVorm. 1956/57, 155.

[294] Riedel, Jugendwohlfahrtsgesetz (3d ed. 1963) no. 9 on § 45 JWG. Other grounds of termination may be the child's coming of age: §§ 1918, 1705, 2 BGB.

As for matters of procedure, what are applied are essentially the same principles as those discussed above with respect to legitimate children.[295]

(2) **Relations with the Father**

The recently enacted German statute on the legal status of illegitimate children[295a] seems to have approximated the German local law to that of most of the American states. Whereas the earlier version of the BGB recognized a claim against the father of an illegitimate child without requiring any prior acknowledgment or paternity proceeding, the new version of the code provides generally that the relation between the father and his illegitimate child can only be asserted if the father has acknowledged the child in a public document or if paternity has been established by a court order (§ 1600a BGB).

These innovations in the local law also influence the conflicts rules. Too much reliance must not be placed on the following statements, however, because decisions on the precise points are still lacking and the writers have not yet evolved a common opinion.

(a) *Acknowledgment.*—There is no special conflicts provision in German law for determination of the law applicable to the acknowledgment of an illegitimate child. The acknowledgment prescribed by the superseded version of § 1718 BGB has been treated under article 21 or article 20 EGBGB (*infra* (c) and (d)). This is also true of acknowledgments governed by foreign law even though these have often had a substantial influence on the legal relations between the father and his illegitimate child.[295b] Because the impact on the child's status is substantial it has been suggested by scholars and sometimes held by courts that these foreign acknowledgments should be equated to legitimation or adoption and therefore subject to article 22 EGBGB.[295c] The main reason for this suggestion was the notion that a substantial change of the child's status should not be made without the consents of the child or his relatives required by German law for certain legitimations and for adoption. According to article 22 II EGBGB these requirements must be complied with in conflicts cases also if the child is German, but this would not be the case if article 20 were to be applied and if the acknowledger were a foreigner whose personal law did not refer back to German law.

As the new type of acknowledgment under the amended provision

---

[295] LG Frankenthal, *supra* n. 280; AG Hamburg-Altona, *supra* n. 285; KEGEL, Kommentar, no. 18 on art. 20 EGBGB.

[295a] *Cf. supra* nn. 2a and 194a.

[295b] AG Bayreuth 5 Mar. 1962, StAZ 1963, 11; *cf. also* LG Freiburg/Br. 26 July 1965, FamRZ 1965, 624.

[295c] KEGEL, Kommentar, no. 12 on art. 22 EGBGB; FRANK, FamRZ 1969, 626, 628 *et seq.*; LG Koblenz 16 Dec. 1958, DAVorm. 1958/59, 342.

requires the child's consent (§ 1600 c I BGB) and, again in contrast to the old type, establishes paternity for all matters between father and child, it should be brought under the rule of article 22 I EGBGB. Consequently, the substance and effect of the acknowledgment are governed generally by the father's national law at the time of acting unless this law refers to German law or to the law of a third jurisdiction. An exception to this general rule will be discussed later (sub (c)). If the child is German his consent is required to make the acknowledgment valid (art. 22 II EGBGB). Since acknowledgment and consent are formal acts each is formally valid according to article 11 I EGBGB if it complies either with the law governing it under article 22 EGBGB or with the law of the place of acting.

An acknowledgment governed by German local law may be contested in a special court proceeding by the father, by the mother or by the child himself (§ 1600 g I BGB). As in the case of a declaration of illegitimacy (*supra* B I (1) (c) at n. 206), the German courts normally have jurisdiction if at least one of the parties has his habitual residence in Germany or is a German, or if the mother is German (§ 640 a ZPO).

The same principles apply to the recognition of foreign acknowledgments and consents as those indicated below (III (4)) for foreign adoptions and consents.

(b) *Paternity proceedings.*—The other method of establishing paternity under German local law is to institute a paternity proceeding (§§ 1600 n and o BGB, as revised in 1969). The German courts have jurisdiction if either the putative father or the child has at least his habitual residence in Germany or if one of them is German (§ 641 a I ZPO, as revised in 1969). Even if the German courts have jurisdiction, this does not imply the automatic application of German substantive law. Whether or not the defendant is the child's father is determined, in general, by the defendant's national law under the principle of articles 19 and 20 EGBGB (*infra* (d)) unless there is a renvoi or transmission. A German judgment establishing paternity becomes res judicata in Germany even against a person who has not been a party to the proceeding (641 k ZPO, as revised in 1969).

The decision of a foreign court in a paternity proceeding will be recognized under the regular requirements of § 328 ZPO (*infra* ch. 14 sub II (8)). However, in derogation of these general rules, § 641 a II ZPO, as revised in 1969, provides a special rule for the jurisdiction of the foreign court (§ 328 I no. 1 ZPO): the defendant or the child must have had at least his habitual residence in the foreign country, or both of them must have been its nationals.

(c) *Support.*—The relevant statutory conflicts rule provides that the mother's national law at the time of the child's birth governs the father's duty to support his illegitimate child and to compensate the mother for the costs of pregnancy, delivery and maintenance (art. 21 first part EGBGB).[296] Accordingly a suit for support against the American father of an illegitimate child born to a German mother will be governed by German law.[297] This means that the American must have acknowledged the child (*supra* (a)) or must have been declared to be the father in a paternity proceeding (*supra* (b)) because—as already mentioned above (before (a))—one of these acts is generally the prerequisite for such a claim. In exceptional and urgent cases, however, support for the child may be ordered temporarily by the court even if one of the two basic prerequisites is not satisfied (§ 1615 o BGB, §§ 641 d—641 g ZPO, as revised in 1969; *cf.* also *infra* ch. 14 sub II (6)).

For all other purposes, too, the questions whether the defendant is the child's father[297a] and whether the father's acknowledgment is needed, is valid, or affects the duty of support,[297b] will be answered by article 21 EGBGB. As that article employs an immutable point of contact, it is irrelevant if the mother changes her nationality after having given birth to the child.[298] The parties are not allowed to choose the applicable law.[299] If the child has his habitual residence in Germany or in any other member state of the Hague Convention on the Law Applicable to Obligations to Support Minor Children, the law of that state applies (*supra* at nn. 269a and 269b). Unlike article 21 EGBGB, the Hague Convention (*supra* n. 269a) uses a mutable point of contact (art. 1 II).

If support is claimed by the child of an alien mother, three additional rules have to be observed:

First, the mother's national law will be applied only if there is no renvoi to German law.[300] With respect to the United States it

---

[296] BayVerfGH 13 Mar. 1956, BayGVBl. 1956, 78; *cf. also* the cases cited by KEGEL, Kommentar, note 8 art. 21 EGBGB.

[297] LG Bayreuth 26 Jan. 1961, DAVorm. 1961, 110; LG München 24 Sept. 1962, FamRZ 1962, 486.

[297a] AG Hamburg-Blankenese 5 June 1953, IPRspr. 1952/53 no. 226; AG Landsberg 28 Sept. 1950, IPRspr. 1952/53 no. 202; KEGEL, Kommentar, no. 20 on art. 21 EGBGB.

[297b] LG Frankfurt/M. 17 Aug. 1932, JW 1933, 191; KEGEL, Kommentar, no. 14 on art. 21 EGBGB.

[298] LG Berlin 21 Mar. 1968, DAVorm. 1968, 214; LG Nürnberg-Fürth 24 Mar. 1966, FamRZ 1967, 163.

[299] *Cf.* NEUHAUS 169–171; *contra*: AG Nürnberg 27 July 1950, IPRspr. 1952/53 no. 212.

[300] Although art. 21 EGBGB is not mentioned in art. 27 EGBGB (admitting renvoi), courts and literature observe a renvoi of the law to which art. 21 EGBGB refers: LG Flensburg 17 Dec. 1952, MDR 1953, 298; LG München I 14 June 1962, DAVorm. 1962, 298; LG Wiesbaden 22 March 1957, FamRZ 1957, 384; KEGEL, Kommentar, no. 52 on art. 21 EGBGB; *partially contra*: RAAPE 362, 363.

has been held that the American courts apply their *lex fori* and therefore by a hidden renvoi refer back to German law;[301]

Second, if the defendant is a German, his obligations are limited to those duties which German law imposes on him.[302] Before the recent statutory change in the law of illegitimacy,[302a] this limitation restricted the father's support duties severely: The father's statutory duty to support his illegitimate child came to an end as soon as the child reached eighteen years of age (former § 1708 I 1 BGB).[303] Moreover, the amount of money to be paid was to be computed with reference to the mother's standard of living (former § 1708 I 1 BGB); this implied that a German father's duty to support an illegitimate child living with its mother in the United States was to be computed according to American living standards without regard to the fact that he would have had to pay less if the child lived in Germany.[304] Finally, a German father in a suit for support could not be precluded from rebutting the statutory presumption that a person who had had intercourse with the mother during the period of conception was the father of the child (former § 1717 I 1 BGB);[305] unless he had recognized his illegitimate child (§ former § 1718 BGB), he could always try to prove that others had had intercourse with her during the same period; if the presumption was thus rebutted, the child was required to prove, perhaps by scientific investigations, that the defendant was his father.[306] Under the

---

[301] AG Stuttgart I 22 Oct. 1930, JW 1931, 157; *accord on other grounds*: Frankenstein, Note, JW 1931, 157, 158; *contra*: Seeger, WürttZ 73 (1931) 257–62; LG Nürnberg-Fürth, *supra* n. 298, with a fact pattern identical to that of AG Stuttgart I, *supra,* does not even mention the possibility of an open or hidden renvoi from New York law but applies the latter. This may be due either to the fact that the father had recognized the child before the Commissioner of Deeds of New York and obligated himself to pay support, or to the fact that the main issue was whether the support agreement was valid under art. 21 second part EGBGB. *Cf. infra* text at n. 304.

[302] Art. 21 second part EGBGB has been restrictively interpreted so as to apply to German fathers only: LG Münster 10 June 1959, IPRspr. 1958/59 no. 136; LG Bartenstein 18 Nov. 1929, IPRspr. 1930 no. 263; Kegel, Kommentar, nos. 7–9 on art. 21 EGBGB.

[302a] *Supra* n. 2a.

[303] *Cf.*, on former § 1708 BGB: LG Nürnberg 11 June 1930, NiemeyersZ 43 (1930/31) 412. If the father agreed to payments beyond the statutory limit, he cannot plead art. 21 second part EGBGB: LG Berlin I 19 May 1930, IPRspr. 1931 no. 86. If the amount under the foreign law is low and the duty to pay continues longer than under German law but the whole amount to be paid does not exceed that due under German law, art. 21 second part EGBGB cannot be invoked: AG Bielefeld 5 July 1929, IPRspr. 1930 no. 80; Kegel, Kommentar, nos. 12 and 13 on art. 21 EGBGB.

[304] LG Berlin and LG Nürnberg-Fürth, *supra* n. 298.

[305] For German substantive law, see 1 Cohn no. 541.

[306] LG Bielefeld 11 Aug. 1954, DAVorm. 1954/55, 181; LG Düsseldorf 24 Oct. 1952, MDR 1953, 236; LG Schweidnitz 14 Mar. 1929, JW 1929, 1603; Kegel, Kommentar, no. 14 on art. 21 EGBGB.

amended code, the father's support duties do not terminate at a fixed date (*see* § 1615 a BGB), the amount of support is computed with reference to the father's standard of living (§ 1615 c BGB), and the exception of the former § 1717 I 1 BGB has been abrogated.[307] The only important limitation which a German father may plead (under art. 21 second part EGBGB) today is the principle mentioned above that a German must generally have acknowledged the child or must have been declared the father in a paternity proceeding before the child can make any claim against him.[308] This limitation, however, is not peremptory because it can always be dispensed with, at least by a filiation order;

Third, if the father's own national law imposes on him support duties which exceed those computed under that of the mother (art. 21 EGBGB), the father's law will be applied by the German courts under the rule stated below (sub (d)).[308a] Consequently, the duty of German fathers to support their illegitimate children will in the future usually be governed by German law which, as a result of the recent changes, will often be more favorable to these children than the mother's foreign national law applicable according to article 21 EGBGB.

(d) *Other questions.*—All other questions concerning the illegitimate child and his father, such as rights to custody or visitation (*supra* I (5) (b), (c), (e)) or anticipated payment in lieu of a substituted claim to inherit,[308b] are governed by the father's national law at the time the question arises.[309] This rule has been developed by analogy from articles 19 and 20 EGBGB (*supra* I (5) (a), II (1)).[310] The question of paternity with respect to these matters (as distinguished from support duties of the father, or from a suit to establish conclusively

---

[307] *Cf. supra* at n. 2a.

[308] Up to now this problem has not arisen under art. 21 second part EGBGB because this second part applies to German fathers only (*cf. supra* n. 302) so that similar limitations of foreign jurisdictions became important only under art. 21 first part EGBGB. These limitations of foreign law were held to be valid restrictions: LG Düsseldorf 25 June 1954, MDR 1954, 615; LG Hirschberg 30 June 1929, IPRspr. 1929 no. 86. There are, however, some doubts whether this is also true if they are peremptory ones: KEGEL, Kommentar, nos. 18 and 58 on art. 21 EGBGB; LEWALD no. 202.

[308a] *Cf.* as to this problem KEGEL, Kommentar, nos. 17–19 on art. 21 EGBGB.

[308b] Such an anticipated claim has been introduced in German law by recent legislation: *cf.* § 1934 d BGB and *infra* ch. 5 n. 42a. By such a claim an illegitimate child between 21 and 27 years of age will be provided with sufficient means to start his own profession.

[309] BayObLG, *supra* n. 280; OLG Bremen 27 Dec. 1963, FamRZ 1964, 219; OLG Düsseldorf 1 Mar. 1957, FamRZ 1957, 182; OLG Stuttgart 13 May 1965, FamRZ 1965, 522; KEGEL, Kommentar, nos. 16, 17, 36 on art. 21 EGBGB.

[310] OLG Düsseldorf, preceding note; KEGEL, Kommentar, no. 17 on art. 21 EGBGB.

the child's descent or non-descent from a certain man) must be decided under the national law of the putative father.[311] If that national law, for example, the law of Arizona, treats legitimate and illegitimate children alike, this position will be recognized in Germany under the same rule.[312]

(3) **Enforcement of Support Duties**

(a) Since 1945 few problems of American-German legal relations have been more urgent than the enforcement of support duties against American fathers of illegitimate children born in Germany. This is due to at least three major factors: *First,* after World War II thousands of illegitimate children (between 1945 and 1951 approximately 94,000[313]) were born to German women who had had relations with soldiers of the occupying forces. *Second,* until 1955 the German courts had no jurisdiction over these soldiers and therefore could not enforce support claims against them.[314] This situation aroused considerable anger against the Allied Powers. It explains a German judgment which invoked the laws of civilized nations, the English Bill of Rights, the American Declaration of Independence and the French *Déclaration des droits de l'homme et du citoyen,* and by way of retaliation flatly refused to decide a support suit brought by an American woman against the German father of her illegitimate child;[315] the decision was reversed on the ground that a court not empowered to do so by the government cannot resort to retaliation (art. 31 EGBGB),[316] but it illustrates the common sentiment against the denial of justice resulting from the restrictions on German jurisdiction. *Third,* since 1955, foreign soldiers have been subject to German civil jurisdiction[317] and the United States Army since 1963 has afforded assistance with respect to support claims of German subjects against American soldiers.[318] To this extent, at

---

311 *Supra* n. 309; KEGEL, Kommentar, no. 21 on art. 21 EGBGB.

312 KEGEL, IPR 327; *id.,* Kommentar, no. 16 on art. 21 EGBGB.

313 LUISE FRANKENSTEIN, Soldatenkinder (1954) 5; for comment, *see* Das Problem der Besatzungskinder, NachrD 1952, 101, 102.

314 Law no. 13 of the Allied High Commission for Germany of Nov. 25, 1949, art. 2 (Off.Gaz.HICOG 1949, 54); Law no. 6 of the Office of the U.S. High Commissioner for Germany of Aug. 11, 1950, art. 3 (2) (Off.Gaz.HICOG 1950, 526); as amended by Law no. 25 of the same office of Aug. 17, 1951 (Off.Gaz.HICOG 1952, 1139) and by Law no. 33 of June 13,1952 (Off.Gaz.HICOG 1952, 1759).

315 AG Nürnberg 28 Aug. 1953, JZ 1954, 159.

316 LG Nürnberg-Fürth 24 June 1954, IPRspr. 1954/55 no. 3.

317 Forces Convention (Treaties M 182) art. 9; Settlement Convention (Treaties M 184) art. 3 (3) (II).

318 *Cf.* Understanding of Aug. 3, 1959 relating to maintenance claims for illegitimate children of members of foreign forces stationed in the Federal Republic of Germany (Treaties B 166).

least, the situation improved. However, the real difficulties now emerged. While the various American states have adopted the Uniform Reciprocal Enforcement of Support Act,[319] and Germany has ratified the United Nations Convention on the Recovery Abroad of Maintenance of June 20, 1956[320] and the Hague Convention on Recognition and Enforcement of Decisions Concerning Obligations to Support Minor Children of April 15, 1958,[321] the two countries are not both parties to any treaty dealing with support duties, except for the NATO-Status of Forces Treaty mentioned below (*infra* (b)). Their different policies with regard to support of illegitimate children therefore clash head-on. In Germany it has been unquestioned at least since 1900 that a man has a legal, not only a moral, obligation to support his illegitimate child.[322/23] Recent legislation has reinforced this obligation.[324] The German law is noteworthy in two respects: (i) suit may be brought in Germany even if only the plaintiff resides there (§ 23 a ZPO) and (ii) the defendant's wages may be garnished without the usual restrictions (§ 850 d ZPO). For these reasons, and because of the general obligation of residents of Germany to register, the enforcement of support duties does not encounter serious problems in Germany except in conflicts cases, especially in American-German relations.

(b) German courts have jurisdiction if the defendant is domiciled (§ 13 ZPO) or, under the circumstances of §§ 16, 20 ZPO, at least resident in Germany. If he has neither domicile nor residence in Germany, suit may be brought if the plaintiff is domiciled or resident in Germany (§ 23 a ZPO). The *Amtsgerichte* (*supra* ch. 2 sub B III (2)) at the defendant's or the plaintiff's domicile or residence have exclusive competence to hear the case (§ 23a no. 2 GVG). If an American soldier stationed in Germany is sued, the special provisions of the NATO-Status of Forces Agreement (Treaties M 174) and of the supplementary Agreement of 1959 (Treaties M 250) must be observed. Here it need only be noted that German jurisdiction with respect to support claims[325] does not terminate if the soldier

---

[319] In one or another of its versions (1952, 1958 or 1968) it is in force in all the states: Handbook of the National Conference on Uniform State Laws (1968) 345 n. 6. Only Michigan has by legislation extended its application to foreign countries: Mich. Stat. Ann. § 25.225 (3) (1) (1969 cum. supp.).

[320] *Cf.* CONTINI, 3 Am. J. Comp. L. 543–51 (1954); BGBl. 1959 II 149–63.

[321] *Cf.* 5 Am. J. Comp. L. 650, 658 (1956); Conférence de la Haye de Droit International Privé. Actes de la Huitième Session, 3 au 24 octobre 1956 (1957) 351–55; BGBl. 1961 II 1005.

[322/23] 1 COHN nos. 541–43.

[324] *See supra* n. 2a and text at n. 307. For the former situation, *see supra* text at nn. 303–306 and 1 COHN no. 541.

[325] AG Frankfurt/M. 29 July 1957, DAVorm. 1958/59, 110; Report of the German Foreign Office of Dec. 6, 1965, on support claims of German illegitimate children against members of the foreign forces stationed in Germany;

leaves the country while a support suit is pending.[326] It is also recognized that an American soldier may acknowledge his child before a German registrar.[327]

(c) German support decrees will be enforced in Germany according to German domestic law unless treaty rules provide otherwise, as they do with respect to soldiers of the NATO forces stationed in Germany.[328] Enforcement of German support decrees is seriously hampered by the fact that an American soldier's pay cannot be garnished.[329]

No special rules apply to the recognition and enforcement of foreign support decrees.[330] With respect to the general rules (*infra* ch. 14 sub II (8) (a)), it may be emphasized that foreign decrees against German fathers will not be enforced if they impose heavier duties than those which would be due under German law (*supra* (2) (c)).[331] No German court seems to have dealt with the problem of reciprocity (§ 328 I no. 5 ZPO and *infra* ch. 14 sub II (8) (b)) in a case of support of an illegitimate child, but the same rule will apply as to other support orders (*supra* I (5) (d)).[332]

(d) Up to now no case seems to have been reported of a German support order which has been recognized in the United States.[333] Therefore two German courts refused to allow a suit *in forma pauperis* against an American father on the ground that a German decision would be of no use in an American proceeding.[334] However, another court stated (correctly) that the German plaintiffs could bring an action on the German support decree in the United States.[335]

Deutscher Bundestag, 5. Wahlperiode, Drucksache V/106, Foreign Office file V F – 81.53/14; and Report of Mr. Hauser (MP.) of Feb. 11, 1966 on this subject, *id.* Drucksache V/297; and Orders of various state ministries of interior affairs *in* StAZ 1955, 231, 282, 283; *cf. also* Notes, DAVorm. 1967, 98; NachrD. 1955, 361 *et seq.*; *id.* 1957, 79–81.

[326] LG Bayreuth 26 Jan. 1961, DAVorm. 1961, 110.

[327] Report of the German Foreign Office and Orders and Notes, *supra* n. 325. The same will be true of the newly enacted requirement of acknowledgment (*supra* sub (a)) or of a similar act under foreign law.

[328] Supplementary Agreement of 1959 (Treaties M 250) art. 34 (3); *cf.* DAVorm. 1959/60, 202 *et seq.*, for American-German diplomatic discussions concerning improvement of the present situation.

[329] *Cf.* the pertinent U.S. Army Regulations mentioned in the Understanding, *supra* n. 318.

[330] *Cf.* KEGEL, Kommentar, nos. 44–50 on art. 21 EGBGB.

[331] AG Ettlingen 9 Aug. 1956, FamRZ 1957, 385; KEGEL, Kommentar, no. 45 on art. 21 EGBGB.

[332] KG Berlin 22 Oct. 1963, *supra* nn. 94a and 272; LG Hamburg, *supra* n. 273.

[333] *In re* Neidnig's Estate, 108 N.Y. Supp. 478 (App. Div. 1908) (German recognition of paternity accompanied by support agreement held to be "quasi criminal" in nature and hence not recognized).

[334] LG München I 24 Sept. 1962, FamRZ 1962, 486; LG Tübingen 19 Oct. 1964, IPRspr. 1964/65 no. 253.

[335] LG Kassel 6 July 1966, DAVorm. 1966, 250.

Nevertheless, the prospects of such a suit are discouraging. American federal courts have declined jurisdiction because such suits concern the status of parent and child,[336] and New York has closed its courts unless at least the mother resides in the United States.[337] On the other hand, a New York court assumed jurisdiction in a paternity proceeding filed by a German mother residing in New York against another New York resident who allegedly was the father of her illegitimate child born and still residing in Germany.[338] Only two other cases were found in which German plaintiffs were successful. The Municipal Court of Philadelphia ordered a former American soldier, who had pleaded guilty under § 732 of the Pennsylvania Penal Code,[339] to make monthly payments to his illegitimate child living with its mother in Germany;[340] and in a California case the child's mother was successful because, in order to file a suit against the child's father, she went to the United States, became resident there and entrusted the case to an attorney who was appointed guardian *ad litem* for the child left in Germany.[341] Generally speaking, the German courts, lawyers, state governments, and public agencies, the German Consulate General in New York, and even the German *Bundestag* (the Federal Parliament) complain about the difficulty of enforcing support duties against American fathers[342] and deem their residents fortunate where they can procure payments from American social security or workmen's compensation funds.[343]

(4) Law of East Germany

As East Germany in 1965 abolished the distinction between legitimate and illegitimate children,[344] there are no special conflicts rules for the latter. The general rules (*supra* I (6)) apply to all children.

---

[336] Buechold v. Ortiz, 401 F.2d 371 (9th Cir. 1968); Brandtscheit v. Britton, 239 F. Supp. 652 (N.D. Cal. 1965), with some reservations if access to state courts is factually precluded.

[337] Feyler v. Mortimer, 299 N.Y. 309, 87 N.E.2d 273 (1949); *cf.* 57 A.L.R.2d 689, 695 (1958).

[338] Duerr v. Wittmann, 5 A.D.2d 326, 171 N.Y.S.2d 444 (1958).

[339] 18 Purdon's Pa. Stat. Ann. § 4732 (1963).

[340] Schmidt, F., Unterhaltsansprüche deutscher unehelicher Kinder in USA, NJW 1959, 1310–11. The same case is discussed in DAVorm. 1959/60, 168.

[341] *Cf.* Note, DAVorm. 1962, 112.

[342] LG München I, *supra* n. 334; AG Nürnberg, *supra* n. 315; Schwenk, Die Pflicht zum Unterhalt unehelicher Kinder seitens Angehöriger der amerikanischen Streitkräfte, NJW 1953, 1776–78; Ladermann, SchlHA 1959, 286–91; Borchard, ZBlJugR 1969, 259–63; Orders of state governments, *supra* n. 325; Notes, DAVorm. 1955/56, 183, 328; 1959/60, 168, 202; 1961, 30, 71, 266; 1968, 216; Memorandum of the German Consulate General in New York concerning the enforcement of support claims in the United States and Canada, RdJug. 1958, 269, DAVorm. 1957/58, 51; Report, *supra* n. 325.

[343] DAVorm. 1955/56, 208; 1959/60, 200; 1966, 34, 258; *claims as to insurance*: StAZ 1962, 274–75, 308; DAVorm. 1953/54, 62.

[344] §§ 42–78 FamGB, *supra* n. 5.

III. ADOPTION*

(1) West German Domestic Law

American-German adoptions have been frequent since the end of World War II. It has been estimated that from 1955 to 1967 at least 18,000 German children were adopted by United States citizens.[345] The American-German conflicts problems in this field cannot be understood without some preliminary remarks on the German domestic law of adoption.

Under German law adoption is a contract between the adoptee and the adopter (§ 1741 BGB). This contract requires consent of the adopted child's parents (§ 1747 BGB) and that of the adopter's spouse (§ 1746 BGB) and, finally, approval of the guardianship court (*Vormundschaftsgericht*) (§ 1754 BGB). If the adoptee is less than fourteen years of age his guardian must act for him, and if although older he is still minor, his guardian's consent is needed for the child's contract (§ 1751 BGB); in both cases the specific permission of the court is also necessary (§ 1751 BGB),[346] that is, in addition to the court approval of the contract as a whole.

(2) Law Governing

If the adopter is German at the time of the adoption the transaction will be governed by German law (art. 22 I EGBGB). This provision has been expanded into a general rule that the national law of the adopter at the time of the adoption governs.[347] Hence a common adoption by spouses of different nationalities is subject to two different laws,[348] unless there is a renvoi or transmission to a commonly applicable law. The adoptee's nationality and domicile, in general, are irrelevant. In two cases, however, they become important:

First, article 22 II EGBGB protects German children by providing

---

* KRUSCH, Adoption: Deutsches Recht, *in* Das internationale Familienrecht Deutschlands und Frankreichs (1955) 406–423 (*in French*: Le droit international privé de la famille en France et en Allemagne (1954) 342–358); DE NOVA, Adoption in Comparative Private International Law, *in* Recueil des Cours 104 (1961 III) 69, 105–106; LÖHNING, Adoption under English and German Law, 3 Int'l L.Q. 267–278 (1950).

[345] Letter of Mar. 12, 1969, of the Deutsches Institut für Vormundschaftswesen to the author. *Cf. also* DAVorm. 1969, 93, and Statistisches Bundesamt Wiesbaden, Fachserie K: Öffentliche Sozialleistungen. Reihe 2: Öffentliche Jugendhilfe 1967, p. 26.

[346] 1 COHN 248 *et seq.*

[347] BGH 4 Mar. 1960, FamRZ 1960, 229, 230; BayObLG 19 Apr. 1962, BayObLGZ 1962, 151, 159; 22 Mar. 1957, *id.* 1957, 118, 123; 25 July 1956, *id.* 1956, 285, 287; KG Berlin 13 July 1959, NJW 1960, 248, 250; KEGEL, Kommentar, nos. 1 and 34 on art. 22 EGBGB.

[348] *Cf.* e.g., BayObLG 19 Apr. 1962, preceding note; KG Berlin 10 Mar. 1933, IPRspr. 1933 no. 53 a.

that the adoption of a German child by a foreigner is invalid unless the child and those persons who must consent under German law agree to the adoption;[349]

Second, the child's domicile has been important in several American-German cases. According to the general nationality rule mentioned above, American law governs the adoption by American foster parents of a child living in Germany. Since, however, a renvoi must be accepted even in an adoption case,[350] the German courts have had to examine American conflicts rules. They have found that American courts apply their *lex fori,* which, however, is identical with the domiciliary law of at least one of the parties because only a court at the domicile of one of the parties has jurisdiction in an adoption case. The German courts have therefore frequently assumed a "hidden" American renvoi to German local law if the child to be adopted was domiciled in Germany.[351]

(3) **German Jurisdiction**

The question of German jurisdiction arises primarily in connection with the final approval of an adoption contract required under German law (*supra* sub (1)). The statute provides directly only for the competence of the court at the domicile or residence of the adopter in Germany (§ 66 I FGG). If the adopter is a German but lacks a domicile or residence in Germany, the *Amtsgericht* Schöneberg (in West Berlin) has jurisdiction (§ 66 II FGG).[352] The courts have held that these rules of competence also confer international jurisdiction.[353] Thus the German court may approve an adoption

---

[349] Up to now the courts have declined to extend this provision to foreign children: RG 11 July 1929, RGZ 125, 265; KG Berlin 7 June 1929, IPRspr. 1929 no. 88; *contra*: KEGEL, Kommentar, no. 15 on art. 22 EGBGB.

[350] BGH, *supra* n. 347; BayObLG 19 Apr. 1962 and 22 Mar. 1957, *supra* n. 347; KEGEL, Kommentar, nos. 48, 49 on art. 22 EGBGB.

[351] BayObLG 29 Dec. 1959, IPRspr. 1958/59 no. 211; 22 Mar. 1957, *supra* n. 347; KG Berlin, *supra* n. 347; LG Berlin 15 Aug. 1957, DAVorm. 1958/59, 108; LG Darmstadt 8 Oct. 1951, IPRspr. 1950/51 no. 154; LG Mannheim 7 Mar. 1958, StAZ 1958, 292; LG Schweinfurt 3 June 1957, IPRspr. 1956/57 no. 139; AG Heidenheim/Brenz 24 May 1955, IPRspr. 1954/55 no. 126; *accord*: RAAPE 398–400; GÜNDISCH, FamRZ 1961, 352–58; JAYME, 21 U. Fla. L. Rev. 290, 294 (1969); *contra*: BEITZKE, NJW 1960, 248, 249; WENGLER, NJW 1959, 127–130. Whether there will be a "hidden" renvoi to the law of the domicile or residence of the child depends upon the American state law indicated by art. 22 I EGBGB; *cf.* AG Mainz 21 Oct. 1966, StAZ 1967, 243, and JAYME, *supra,* 294 at n. 27.

[352] Whether § 66 II FGG gives exclusive jurisdiction to the German courts has not been finally settled. The better view seems to be that §§ 66 II FGG does not preclude foreign courts from acting on behalf of Germans: BayObLG 18 Dec. 1968, BayObLGZ 1968, 331, 333; KEGEL, Kommentar, no. 37 on art. 22 EGBGB; *contra*: KG Berlin 8 Oct. 1937, JW 1937, 2975; RAAPE 397.

[353] BayObLG 19 Apr. 1962, 22 Mar. 1957, 25 July 1956, *supra* n. 347; KG Berlin 10 Mar. 1933, *supra* n. 348; LG Darmstadt 8 Oct. 1951, *supra* n. 351; AG Heidenheim 24 May 1955, *supra* n. 351.

contract even though the adopter has been in Germany only one day in order to conclude the contract.[354] This objectionable practice, however, is not firmly established. One court declined jurisdiction on the ground that a court of the United States where the parties (an American husband, his German wife, and her child by her first marriage) went immediately after conclusion of the adoption contract was a more convenient forum.[355]

Some difficulties have arisen where the German courts have been called upon to apply foreign law requiring consideration of policy and of the child's welfare as a condition of approval of an adoption. Under German law such questions have to be answered by the guardianship court when consenting to the child's contract (§ 1751 BGB, *supra* (1)) and by the Youth Office (§ 48 JWG), but not by the approving court. Before World War II German courts declined to consider such questions under the applicable foreign law.[356] Recently, however, there has been a welcome change in their attitude and a tendency to apply American law, if necessary, as their American counterparts would do.[357] In view of the "hidden" renvoi of American to German law (*supra* (2)(b)), however, the issue will not often arise.

(4) **Recognition of Foreign Adoptions**

Foreign adoptions, whether by contract, court order, or decision of some other competent authority, will be recognized in Germany if they are valid under the adopter's national law[358] and if the German protective provisions for a German child (*supra* (2) (a)) have been observed.[359]

There have been several instances in American-German relations where the absence of the guardian's consent has been at issue, because the adoption was granted by an American court. In these cases the foreign adoption has been held to be invalid until such time as the necessary consents, which may subsequently be furnished in Germany, have been obtained.[360] In a recent decision, however,

---

[354] BayObLG 29 Dec. 1959, *supra* n. 351; LG Saarbrücken 4 Feb. 1955, IPRspr. 1954/55 no. 205; AG Heidenheim/Brenz, *supra* n. 351.

[355] KG Berlin 4 June 1959, IPRspr. 1958/59 no. 209.

[356] KG Berlin 10 Mar. 1933, *supra* n. 348; 15 Jan. 1932, DJZ 1932, 683; 30 June 1922, OLG 42, 188; LG Berlin II 14 July 1933, StAZ 1934, 59; *contra*: Rabel, RabelsZ 6 (1932) 310–324; Beitzke, FamRZ 1967, 592, 605.

[357] LG Schweinfurt 19 Feb. 1957, IPRspr. 1956/57 no. 138; *cf. also* LG Saarbrücken, *supra* n. 354.

[358] BayObLG 19 Nov. 1964, FamRZ 1965, 95; OLG München 16 Oct. 1959, IPRspr. 1958/59 no. 141.

[359] BGH, *supra* n. 347; OLG Celle 29 July 1964, FamRZ 1964, 578; 14 Apr. 1954, JZ 1954, 702; KG Berlin 11 Jan. 1962, StAZ 1963, 124.

[360] BGH, *supra* n. 347; BayObLG 25 July 1956, *supra* n. 347, at 291–93; OLG Hamm 9 June 1959, StAZ 1960, 98; OLG Karlsruhe 29 Aug. 1956, FamRZ 1957, 224; LG Augsburg 3 May 1967, StAZ 1967, 299; AG Rottweil 7 Nov. 1957, IPRspr. 1956/57 no. 136 c. *But compare* OLG Celle 20 Jan. 1969, *infra* n. 361a.

an American adoption decree was recognized even though the consent of the child's German guardian and the court approval necessary under German law were both missing;[361] the court held that the Minnesota adoption procedure was equivalent to that of Germany. Whether this decision will be followed is not clear, however, as the result can also be justified by the fact that the formerly German adopting mother and the German child became American citizens and lost their German nationality subsequent to the adoption.[361a] If followed, the number of limping adoptions would be diminished, but until this practice has been confirmed, competent German authorities will continue to make sure that all the German requirements are fulfilled before a child leaves Germany to live with his foster parents abroad.[362] They will also make sure that a German child will be given to proper persons who will be supervised by welfare organizations until an adoption decree has been issued.[363]

(5) **Effects of Adoption**

Under German conflicts law the effects of adoption are determined by the same law as the validity of the adoption (*supra* (2)).[364] For support claims, however, the law of the child's habitual residence governs if the above-mentioned requirements of the Hague Support Convention are met (*supra* nn. 269a and 269b). Accordingly it has been recognized on several occasions that an American court order has validly conferred the American adopter's name upon his adoptee.[365] Whether, however, the rule of article 22 I EGBGB also governs the child's inheritance rights with respect to his adopter is disputed. The prevailing view seems to be that the rule of article 22 I EGBGB decides whether an adoptive child and his adopter are in the same position as a legitimate child and his natural parent, whereas the conflicts rule governing decedents' estates (*infra* ch. 5 sub II (3) (a)) determines the shares of the respective persons.[366]

---

[361] BayObLG 18 Dec. 1968, *supra* n. 352.

[361a] OLG Celle 20 Jan. 1969, NJW 1969, 993, refusing to recognize an Australian adoption order although the adoption had subsequently been approved by a German court. The court held that a foreign adoption by court order differs so substantially from a German adoption that it cannot be validated by subsequent German court action. This assertion is not convincing.

[362] AG Heidenheim/Brenz 21 Oct. 1955, DAVorm. 1955/56, 267.

[363] *Cf.* Circular of the Minister of Labor of Northrhine-Westphalia: DAVorm. 1962, 51.

[364] KEGEL, Kommentar, nos. 42–44 on art. 22 EGBGB.

[365] BGH, *supra* n. 347; OLG Celle 23 Sept. 1960, StAZ 1961, 81; OLG Karlsruhe, *supra* n. 360; LG Schweinfurt, *supra* 351. Circulars of the Ministers of the Interior of Baden-Württemberg and of Lower Saxony, StAZ 1966, 41 and 1961, 78.

[366] KEGEL, Kommentar, no. 44 on art. 22 EGBGB; KRUSCH 415–16.

(6) **Law of East Germany**

Under the new East German Code of Family Law (*supra* n. 5), the adoption of a child is decreed by an administrative agency upon request of the adopter (§ 68 I FamGB). The conflicts provisions on adoption have also been adjusted to the radical changes in the substantive law (Introductory Law, *supra* n. 6). According to § 20 EGFamGB the adoption itself, its effects, and its cancellation are all governed by the adopter's national law at the time of the adoption or cancellation. If spouses at least one of whom is an East German citizen adopt a child, only the law of East Germany applies (§ 20 I 2 EGFamGB).[367] On the other hand, the adoption of an East German citizen by a foreigner is invalid unless the competent authority in East Germany has approved it and consents have been obtained from those persons whose consent is necessary under East German substantive law;[368] but it may well be doubted whether the requirements of official approval will be respected in other countries since it is obviously designed to prevent emigration.

C. OTHER MATTERS OF PERSONAL STATUS

(1) **Capacity**

(a) *Basic rule.*—As capacity and legal personality of companies and other organizations will be dealt with separately (*infra* ch. 10 sub I (2) (a)), the present discussion will be limited to capacity of natural persons. Under the general rule of article 7 I EGBGB, a person's national law determines whether he is capable of entering into legal transactions.

(b) *Exceptions.*—There are three major exceptions to the basic rule:

(i) According to the express provision of article 27 EGBGB a renvoi from the national law must be accepted. If therefore the law of the American state (either expressly or under the rule of validation) looks to the law of the place of contracting, the capacity of an American who enters into a contract in Germany will be determined under German domestic law;[369]

(ii) A foreigner who has capacity under his national law retains it even if he acquires German nationality and his new German national law would otherwise limit or incapacitate him (art. 7 II EGBGB). Therefore an eighteen-year-old American capable under Georgia law

---

[367] WIEMANN, Das internationale Familienrecht des Einführungsgesetzes zum Familiengesetzbuch, Staat und Recht 1966, 398, 405.

[368] Consent of the following persons is necessary: the parents, the child if older than fourteen years, the father of a child born out of wedlock if he is awarded custody of the child, and other legal representatives (§ 69 I FamGB). The parents' consent may be substituted (§ 70 FamGB).

[369] *Cf. supra* A II (1) (b) with respect to capacity to marry.

was held still capable upon becoming a German although under German law he would not have attained full capacity until the age of twenty-one;[370]

(iii) In order to protect business transactions concluded in Germany, article 7 III 1 EGBGB provides that a foreigner, although wholly or partially incapable under his national law, will nevertheless be held capable to enter into these transactions if he would have such capacity under German domestic law.[371] It is uncertain whether this protective rule applies in favor of all those with whom he contracts or merely those in good faith, and also whether it is strictly limited to transactions entered into in Germany.[372] The better view seems to be that article 7 III 1 EGBGB states a general principle and that therefore its operation should be unlimited,[373] but there is no authority as yet for extension of the rule to extra-German transactions. According to article 7 III 2 EGBGB this protective rule does not apply to transactions in the field of domestic relations or decedents' estates or to certain transactions with respect to foreign real estate.

(c) *Emancipation.*—Normally only the national law and tribunals have jurisdiction to emancipate a child before he acquires full legal capacity. If, however, there is a renvoi from that law to German law, the German courts will exercise jurisdiction to emancipate a minor alien.[374]

(d) *Guardianship.*

(i) *In general.*—That Germany claims jurisdiction to put a German where necessary under the control of a guardian, thereby depriving him wholly or partially of his capacity, is in line with the general rule that a person's national law is competent to determine his capacity.[375] In article 8 EGBGB, however, the jurisdiction of the German courts to deprive persons of their capacity is extended to foreign persons domiciled or at least resident in Germany; this rule also empowers the courts to apply German law to these aliens. Nevertheless the courts will exercise their power with caution and will endeavor to reconcile their decision with the person's national law if possible.[376]

---

370 1 COHN 75.

371 *Cf. supra* A III (2) (b) with respect to the wife's capacity to contract.

372 *Cf.* KEGEL, Kommentar, nos. 15–17 on art. 7 EGBGB, with further references.

373 KEGEL, Kommentar, preceding note. Such a provision, with one exception, has been enacted for the capacity to draw certain negotiable instruments (art. 91 II WG and Art. 60 II ScheckG, *cf. infra* ch. 8 sub V at n. 166).

374 *Cf. supra* A II (1) (b) at n. 25.

375 This rule is based on art. 7 I EGBGB (*supra* (1) (a)): KEGEL, Kommentar, no. 10 on art. 8 EGBGB. According to § 648 II ZPO there is always a German court with competence in this regard.

376 KEGEL, Kommentar, no. 8 on art. 8 EGBGB.

(ii) *Appointment of a guardian.*—Whether a guardian or curator will be appointed for an alien by a German court is determined under a separate rule. Article 23 I EGBGB provides for such an appointment only if the alien is entitled to care under his national law and it has not been provided in his own country, or if he is entitled to such care under German law;[377] unless a guardian or curator has been appointed, a German guardianship court may merely prescribe provisional measures.[378] If a German court has jurisdiction to act on behalf of an alien, it will apply his national law.[379] However, German law governs if there is a renvoi[380] or if the alien has been put under the control of a guardian under article 8 EGBGB (*supra* (i)) or if provisional measures under article 23 II have been taken.[381]

(iii) *Examples.*

As already indicated (*supra* B I (5) (c)) the German courts have held that American parents as guardians of their children's property are not deemed empowered by their American appointment to represent their children with respect to property situated abroad. Therefore the German courts will appoint curators of such real or personal property located in Germany.[382]

A curator may also be appointed for an absent person, as was done in the case of a former German citizen who had gone to the United States and whose whereabouts were unknown.[383] If, however, the absentee has acquired American citizenship, the German decree will not be recognized in the United States.[384]

If necessary, and especially if the child's national law does not provide for his representation in court, a German court may appoint a guardian *ad litem* for him.[385]

Parents may be deprived of their parental power if they neglect their children (*supra* B I (5) (b) (i)). But apart from this, children may be placed under educational supervision under the Youth Welfare

---

[377] BayObLG 6 Nov. 1929, BayObLGZ 29 (1930) 436.

[378] For German domestic law, *cf.* 1 COHN 250–55.

[379] KEGEL, Vormundschaft über Minderjährige: Deutsches Recht, *in* Das internationale Familienrecht Deutschlands und Frankreichs (1955) 472–79, 492–98, at 474 (*in French*: Le droit international privé de la famille en France et en Allemagne (1954) 398–406, 415–22 at 401).

[380] KEGEL, preceding note, at 477 and 404, respectively.

[381] KEGEL, *supra* n. 379, at 475 and 401–402 respectively.

[382] KG Berlin 23 July and 8 Dec. 1902, NiemeyersZ 12 (1903) 468 and 13 (1903) 153; OLG Colmar 2 Oct. 1911, ElsLothZ 37 (1912) 85; OLG Darmstadt 14 Oct. 1910, NiemeyersZ 20 (1910) 543; OLG Jena 8 May 1907, *id.* 18 (1908) 180; OLG Stuttgart 10 Dec. 1915, DR 1916 no. 261; LG Posen 2 Jan. 1903, *supra* n. 263; AG Gera, no date, NiemeyersZ 14 (1904) 399; AG Tauberbischofsheim, *supra* n. 263. *Cf. also* KEGEL, Kommentar, no. 24 on art. 23 EGBGB.

[383] OLG Karlsruhe 28 Dec. 1901, NiemeyersZ 12 (1903) 123; KEGEL, Kommentar, nos. 49 and 50 on art. 23 EGBGB.

[384] Mayer v. Garvan, 278 Fed. 27, 32 (1st Cir. 1922).

[385] BayObLG 31 May 1966, BayObLGZ 1966, 203, 210–211.

Act;[386] as this sort of protection is deemed to be a matter of public law, it is ordered whenever necessary irrespective of the children's or their parents' nationality.[387]

(iv) *Recognition of foreign order.*—According to the principle that a country has the duty to care for its own nationals, a German court will recognize a foreign act affecting a national of the acting state.[388] It will, therefore, terminate a guardianship if the ward has been declared *sui juris* in his own country.[389] On the other hand, since German law controls the personal status of Germans, an American adoption order has been held not to terminate a German official guardianship over German illegitimate children (*supra* B II (1));[390] the German guardian's consent would be required either to validate the adoption in Germany or to terminate the guardianship (*supra* B III (4)). Nevertheless, even where the ward is a German, a foreign guardianship will be recognized if the ward resides habitually in the foreign country, if the foreign decision does not violate German public policy, and if the same decision with similar effects could have been rendered by a German court;[391] in this case no ancillary guardian need be appointed in Germany since a German guardianship may be transmitted to a foreign authority if the ward settles abroad (§ 47 FGG).

(2) Name

Firm names and the protection of trade names will be discussed later (*infra* ch. 10 sub II(4) and ch. 12 sub V). A natural person's name is governed by his national law.[392] This general rule, however, is subject to so many exceptions that it has little significance. As has been pointed out, the wife's name during coverture and thereafter is governed by her husband's national law (*supra* A III (2)(a) and A V (2) (c)); and the child's name is governed by the national law of his legitimate father (*supra* B I (5)(e)), his illegitimate mother (*supra* B II (1)), or his adoptive parent (*supra* B III (5)). Thus nothing remains of the general rule except for the determination or change of a name without a change of personal status,[393] and the

---

[386] *Cf.* 1 Cohn no. 560.

[387] RG 22 May 1933, WarnRspr. 25 (1933) 252; BayObLG 24 Aug. 1953, BayObLGZ 1953, 289; 13 Oct. 1950, NJW 1951, 275; KG Berlin 12 July 1929, IPRspr. 1929 no. 91.

[388] *Cf.* Kegel, Kommentar, nos. 1, 13–21 on art. 23 EGBGB.

[389] *Cf.* the case reported by Berndorff *in* DJZ 1905, 405.

[390] AG Heidenheim/Brenz 20 Oct. 1955, DAVorm. 1955/56, 267. This case was decided under the former JWG; *cf. supra* n. 292.

[391] BGH 7 Dec. 1955, BGHZ 19, 240.

[392] Kegel, Kommentar, no. 1 appendix to art. 7 EGBGB.

[393] *Cf.* Gesetz über die Änderung von Familiennamen und Vornamen, as revised Aug. 29, 1961, BGBl. I 1621. Therefore a change of name effected by a German in the United States was not recognized: OVG Münster 21 June 1966, StAZ 1967, 214, *aff'd,* BVerwG 8 Nov. 1968, BVerwGE 31, 28, 29.

protection of the name.[394] It has been held, for example, that a change of name will be recognized in Germany if valid under the bearer's national law.[395]

(3) **Foreign Academic Degrees**

Without official permission of the competent governmental authority Germans are not allowed to display an academic degree from a foreign institution of higher learning (*Hochschule*).[396] The same is true of foreigners unless they are in Germany exclusively on an official mission or are present temporarily only and without intent to do business; in the latter two exceptional cases it is sufficient if the holder is entitled to the degree under the law of his own country.[397] One who violates these restrictions may be prosecuted, as may one who falsely claims to be the holder of a German or foreign academic degree.[398]

The official permission mentioned above may be sought from the cultural department of a state government. It will be granted only upon careful examination of the academic standing of the foreign institution. There is a (not unjustified) distrust of certain American "degree factories." The Federal Administrative Court declined, for example, to recognize the degree of "doctor of philosophy in political science" awarded by McKinley-Roosevelt Incorporated of Chicago to a student by correspondence.[399] If the foreign institution complies with the standard of an academic institution of higher learning, permission will be granted for the foreign degree to be used in its original form in the foreign language with a German translation in brackets; it need not be the equivalent of a corresponding German

---

[394] KEGEL, Kommentar, no. 2 appendix to art. 7 EGBGB.

[395] *Cf.* OLG Frankfurt, *supra* n. 56, with respect to changes of name effected as part of the American naturalization of Germans: StAZ 1960, 136, and 1968, 116; LG Berlin II 18 Sept. 1930, StAZ 1931, 132. A first name validly acquired during the residence of a naturalized Hungarian immigrant in the United States is retained on subsequent removal of the domicile to Germany: LG München I 19 Aug. 1965, IPRspr. 1964/65 no. 18.

[396] *Cf.* § 2 of the Gesetz über die Führung akademischer Grade of June 7, 1939, RGBl. I 985, BGBl. III 221–1 and 221–1–1; Resolution of Mar. 28, 1968, of the State Ministers of Culture, BAnz. 1968 no. 99 p. 4, concerning the uniform application of this statute by the state governments. This statute has been held constitutional although the standards of permission are rather sweeping: BVerwG 23 June 1967, BVerwGE 27, 222. *Contra*: BayObLG 1 Aug. 1967, NJW 1968, 2123, which therefore held that it was no criminal offense to hold the American degree "doctor of optometry" (Dr. P., Optometrist) without governmental permission. Similarly, for the pre-statutory period, *see* OLG Karlsruhe 4 Nov. 1901, NiemeyersZ 12 (1903) 470, concerning the American degree "doctor of dental surgery."

[397] § 3 Gesetz, preceding note.

[398] § 5, Gesetz, *supra* n. 396.

[399] BVerwG, *supra* n. 396.

degree.[400] Permission granted by one of the German states will be valid throughout the Federal Republic.[401]

(4) **Military Service**

Since article VI of the American-German Friendship Treaty of 1923 (Treaties B 55) was abrogated on June 2, 1954 (Treaties B 103), military service is now governed exclusively by domestic law.[401a]

Whereas male aliens "admitted for permanent residence" are liable for military service under the United States Military Selective Service Act of 1967[402] and German immigrants have therefore been inducted into the Armed Forces,[403] German law pursues a less stringent course. According to § 2 I *Wehrpflichtgesetz*,[404] aliens are liable to military service in Germany only if their native country imposes such an obligation upon Germans and if the German authorities have issued a regulation ordering their military service in the German armed forces. Up to now no such regulation has been issued and hence United States citizens may not be inducted into the German army. Multinational individuals, however, are subject to German military service if one of their nationalities is German. In these and other cases, the period of active service in a foreign army is subtracted from the training period required under German law if the foreign service resulted from a statutory obligation or the German Minister of Defense agreed to this foreign service.[405]

In view of the liberal provisions of German law, the harsh rules of the American Military Selective Service Acts have aroused German sentiment on behalf of German non-immigrants inducted into the United States army while employed in the United States.[406] These cases have now been settled,[407] and it is also clear that Germans residing in the United States will be relieved from service in the American army if they have already performed their training

---

[400] Resolution of Mar. 28, 1968, *supra* n. 396, sub II (4).

[401] Art. I of the Treaty between the German states, GVBl. Hamburg 1960 I, 428.

[401a] The draft of a Treaty Between the United States of America and Germany Relating to Nationality and Military Obligations (Foreign Relations 1938, vol. II, 466–68), designed to prevent a second Rupprecht case, did not become effective. *Cf.* Foreign Relations 1938, vol. II, 464–79; 3 HACKWORTH 398–403.

[402] 50 App. U.S.C. § 454 (1964 ed., Supp. III).

[403] *Cf.* United States v. Lacher, 299 F.2d 919 (9th Cir. 1962); Leonhard v. Eley, 151 F.2d 409 (10th Cir. 1945). *Cf. also* Petition of Zumsteg, 122 F. Supp. 670 (S.D.N.Y. 1954), where a German was held not to have lost his right to apply for naturalization although he had refused to serve in the United States army.

[404] Military Service Act, version of May 14, 1965, BGBl. I 391, BGBl. III 50–1.

[405] § 8 II 2 Wehrpflichtgesetz, preceding note.

[406] *Cf.* debate in the German Bundestag of Sept. 15, 1966, BAnz. 1966 no. 175, p. 4; KNUTH, Wehrpflicht deutscher Staatsangehöriger in den US-Streitkräften, Neue Zeitschrift für Wehrrecht 10 (1968) 14–16.

[407] KNUTH, preceding note, at p. 15 n. 8.

in the German forces for eighteen months.[408] Despite these improvements the German government has been urged to discuss the problems of military service with the United States government with a view to concluding a new treaty on the subject or at least to compelling the American immigration agencies to make clear to immigrants before they enter the United States and assume residence there what their military obligation will be.[409]

(5) **Declaration of Death**

There is no general presumption of death of missing persons in German law. Such a presumption can only be established by a judicial declaration of death.[410]

(a) *Jurisdiction of German courts.*—Under the German Law on Missing Persons (*Verschollenheitsgesetz*) and certain supplementary rules,[411] the German courts have jurisdiction to issue a declaration of death in six major cases:

(i) the missing person was a German when last heard of (§ 12 I VerschG);

(ii) the missing person was formerly a German but lost his German nationality without acquiring another; in this case the German courts will assume jurisdiction if there is some legitimate need for a German declaration of death (§ 12 IV VerschG);

(iii) the missing person, even if he was an alien, and provided certain other conditions are fulfilled, disappeared during World War II (art. 2 § 1 IV VerschÄndG);

(iv) the last national law of the missing person refers back to German law and confers jurisdiction upon the German courts;[412]

(v) although the missing person was an alien, he may be declared dead with respect to his German legal relations and his German property (§ 12 II VerschG);

(vi) although the missing person was an alien or a stateless person, he may be declared dead on application of his spouse if the spouse is domiciled in Germany and is a German national or a refugee of German stock (*supra* ch. 3 sub A II (5)(b)), or if the spouse was a German until her marriage (§ 12 III VerschG).

(b) *Law governing.*—According to § 12 I *Verschollenheitsgesetz* a missing person whose last known nationality was German may be

---

[408] New York Times, Sept. 16, 1966, according to KNUTH, *supra* n. 406, at p. 57 n. 77.

[409] KNUTH, *supra* n. 406, at pp. 60–62. On German efforts to prevent induction of Germans into the United States army for service in Vietnam, *cf.* ZaöRV 29 (1969) 112, 114.

[410] 1 COHN no. 110.

[411] BGBl. 1951 I 63, version of the supplementary statute (VerschÄndG) of Jan. 15, 1951, BGBl. I 59.

[412] KEGEL, IPR 196.

declared dead under German law. This unilateral rule has been broadened into a general rule to the effect that a missing person's last known national law governs his declaration of death.[413] This latter rule, however, has several exceptions: A renvoi from the missing person's foreign national law will be accepted by the German courts; and in the two cases mentioned above (sub (a)(iii) and (v)), the German courts are ordered by statute to apply German domestic law to the declaration of death of the alien.[414]

(c) *Recognition of foreign declarations of death.*—The general rules of § 328 ZPO apply to foreign declarations of death (*infra* ch. 14 sub II (8)(a)). This means that a declaration of death rendered by a court of the country of the missing person's last nationality creates a presumption of death under German law.[415] A foreign declaration concerning a German national will not be recognized, however, even as a rebuttable presumption of death.[416] It is not settled whether the jurisdiction of the courts at the missing person's last domicile or habitual residence should also be recognized,[417] but there is much to be said for adoption of the holding of an American court that judicial findings at the missing person's last domicile furnish a presumption of death, not conclusive but sufficient to justify a domestic finding of death where there is no contradictory evidence.[418]

(6) Law of East Germany

Articles 7 and 8 EGBGB are still valid in East Germany so that the same rules apply to capacity as in the Federal Republic (*supra* sub (1)(a)–(c)(i)).

Whether a guardian or curator may be appointed or discharged will be decided under the national law of the ward (§ 21 I EGFamGB). However, a provisional guardianship or curatorship may be decreed under East German law even on behalf of a foreigner if he needs protection and is domiciled or resident in the country (§ 21 II EGFamGB). The relation between the guardian or curator and his ward is governed by the law of the appointing state (§ 21 III EGFamGB).

---

413 KEGEL, IPR 194–95.

414 For the effect of the latter declarations, *cf.* BRINTZINGER, JZ 1963, 536.

415 EGON ARNOLD, Verschollenheitsrecht (1951) 147–48; KEGEL, IPR 194. If such a declaration conflicts as to the time of death with a subsequent German declaration, the foreign decree prevails: BGH 8 Jan. 1965, BGHZ 43, 80.

416 BGH 29 Apr. 1959, BGHZ 30, 140.

417 KEGEL, IPR 195.

418 *In re* Kuehnert's Estate, 147 N.Y.S.2d 713, 715 (Sur. Ct. 1955); *In re* Bellmer's Estate, 144 Misc. 462, 258 N.Y. Supp. 964, 965 (Sur. Ct. 1932); DOMKE 27–29.

On recognition in the United States of German declarations of death, *see infra* ch. 5 sub II (1).

As essentially the same statute still applies in East and West Germany, the principles stated above (sub (5)) with respect to declarations of death are valid in East Germany, too, except in the case of a disappearance during World War II (sub (a)(iii)).

Chapter V.

SUCCESSION*

American-German relations in the field of succession have increased considerably in both frequency and complexity during the last thirty years. There are several reasons: *First,* the Nazi persecution of the Jews led some American states to enact alien inheritance statutes to prevent the transfer of American assets to Germany where they could be taken by the Nazi government;[1] the impact of these statutes and the operation of the Trading with the Enemy Act kept American officials and courts busy long after the close of hostilities in World War II. *Second,* in the aftermath of the Nazi crimes, the German probate courts were called upon in numerous cases to determine the heirs of former Germans who had died abroad so that compensation could be distributed properly and restitution claims adjudicated. *Third,* while these two sources of difficulty have largely disappeared, another still survives, namely, the fundamental difference between the domestic decedents' estates laws of the two countries. Hence it may be useful to glance briefly at the German domestic law before embarking upon American-German conflicts problems of descent, distribution, and estate taxation.

I. SIGNIFICANT FEATURES OF GERMAN DECEDENTS' ESTATE LAW

(1) Universal Succession

The most striking contrasts follow from the German principle of "universal succession" (§ 1922 BGB)[2] by which, for the benefit of the heirs and creditors of the deceased, the entire estate, meaning all

---

* Breslauer, The Private International Law of Succession in England, America and Germany (1937); Emmerich, Estate Practice in the United States and in Europe. A Report to the Conference of the International Bar Association of July 1950 (The Hague 1950); Beecher, Wills and Estates Under German Law (Berlin/Frankfurt 1958); Knur/van Randenborgh/Dumoulin/Pinckernelle, Das Erbrecht im deutschen Internationalen Privatrecht, *in* Les Régimes Matrimoniaux et les Successions en Droit International Privé (Brussels 1963) 243–300 (*French translation*: 335–96); Ferid/Firsching, Internationales Erbrecht (4 vols. loose-leaf); Firsching, Deutsch-amerikanische Erbfälle (1965).

[1] Opton, Legacies to Foreign Residents and the New Amendment to Section 269, Surrogate's Court Act, N.Y.L.J. Sept. 21, 1939, p. 728 col. 1. The further destiny of this and similar provisions is summarized in the Note, 1967 U. Ill. L. F. 141.

[2] 1 Cohn no. 572.

the assets and liabilities, immediately upon his death vests in and passes to the heirs. This has important consequences:

No personal representative is needed to administer the estate. It is the heir who collects the assets, pays the creditors and carries out the last will of the deceased. If the deceased has provided by will for an executor (*Testamentsvollstrecker*) (§§ 2197–2199 BGB),[3] this executor administers the estate according to his orders and to the provisions of the BGB (§§ 2203–2224); ownership of the estate does not vest in the executor, however.

Several heirs form a special community with respect to the estate (§ 2032 BGB).[4] Like the partners in a private partnership, they are joint owners of all assets. If one or more of them want to liquidate this community, each item in the estate must be distributed and transferred to an heir as the exclusive owner, or the assets must be sold and the proceeds divided.

To the heirs' ownership of the assets of the estate corresponds their liability for all the obligations of the deceased and of the estate (§ 1967 I BGB).[5] Not only must the estate's assets answer for these obligations but also the heirs' other property, unless they abstain from commingling the assets with it and apply for administration of the estate by a court-appointed administrator (*Nachlassverwalter,* §§ 1975–2017 BGB).

(2) Uniform Treatment of Property

German succession law does not distinguish between movables and immovables. All property, except homesteads[6] and certain farms,[7] is treated alike.

(3) Testamentary Dispositions

A testator may dispose of his property not only by a last will which he may revoke at any time (§ 2253 BGB), but also by a common reciprocal will together with his spouse,[8] or by a contract of inheritance.[9] The distinctive feature of the last two modes of disposition is that the common reciprocal will becomes binding on one spouse upon the death of the other (§ 2271 II BGB), and the contract of inheritance immediately upon execution (§ 2290 BGB). If a testator by will or by contract of inheritance excludes his spouse, parents, or descendants from the succession, these persons may claim

---

[3] *Id.* at 280–82.

[4] *Id.* at 268–70.

[5] *Id.* at 264–67; RHEINSTEIN, European Methods for the Liquidation of the Debts of Deceased Persons, 20 Iowa L. Rev. 431, 449–58 (1935).

[6] *Cf.* LANGE, Lehrbuch des Erbrechts (1962) 718–19.

[7] *Cf. id.* at 712–18.

[8] 1 COHN no. 622.

[9] *Id.* at 284–85.

a compulsory portion (*Pflichtteil*). This is a money claim against the heirs amounting to one-half of the share to which they would be entitled on intestate succession (§ 2303 BGB).[10] Dispositions by will or contract of inheritance may be in favor of heirs, legatees or mere beneficiaries of so-called burdens (*Auflagen*). There is no testamentary trust in German law. Heirs may be full heirs or only provisional or reversionary heirs.[11] If a testator wants to dispose of his estate in favor of two or more persons successively, the first person to be favored is called a provisional heir (*Vorerbe*) because the estate will pass to the reversionary heir (*Nacherbe*, § 2100 BGB) at the moment determined by the testator (§§ 2100–2146 BGB). In order to protect the interest of the reversionary heir, the provisional heir is restricted in his power to dispose of the estate (§§ 2112–2115 BGB), unless the testator has freed him from certain of these restrictions; he is then called an exempted provisional heir (*befreiter Vorerbe*, § 2136 BGB). A legatee (*Vermächtnisnehmer*) has a mere claim against the heirs (§ 1939, §§ 2147–2191 BGB);[12] no title in the estate vests in him. The beneficiary of a burden has a mere expectancy;[13] the burden may be enforced in the first instance by the heirs (§§ 2192–2196 BGB).

II. DESCENT

(1) Proof of Death

Before any issue of succession can arise, the death of the decedent must be duly proved, and the death of a beneficiary may also be in issue. The best means of proof would seem to be the certificate of a civil registrar (*Standesamt*).[14] A judicial declaration of death by a German court creates a presumption of death under German law (*supra* ch. 1 sub C (5)). Such decrees have been recognized as rebuttable evidence of death by New York courts, irrespective of the nationality or domicile of the missing person.[15] In Germany the writers disagree as to whether presumptions of death are governed by the personal law of the missing person or by the law governing the succession.[16] The first opinion would seem to be more consistent with the idea of submitting matters of personal status to one legal system.

---

[10] *Id.* at 282–84.

[11] *Id.* at 270–72.

[12] *Id.* no. 576.

[13] *Id.* no. 579.

[14] *See* e.g., State Land Board v. Gennies, 204 Ore. 443, 446, 283 P.2d 655, 656 (1955).

[15] *In re* Kuehnert's Estate, 147 N.Y.S.2d 713, 715 (Sur. Ct. 1955); *In re* Rosenbergers' Estates, 131 N.Y.S.2d 59, 66 (Sur. Ct. 1954); *In re* Bellmer's Estate, 144 Misc. 462, 463, 258 N.Y. Supp. 964, 965 (Sur. Ct. 1932); Estate of Edelmuth, N.Y.L.J. Apr. 1, 1949, p. 1178 col. 2 (Sur. Ct.).

[16] *For personal law, see* Kegel, Kommentar nos. 6 and 10 preceding art. 24 EGBGB; *for law of succession, see* Raape 438–39 and M. Wolff 97–98.

The tragic fate of the Jews persecuted during World War II frequently created difficult problems of proving death without a judicial declaration of death. American courts have often taken judicial notice of the conditions prevailing in Germany before and during the War and have therefore held the general presumption of continued existence to be rebutted.[17]

(2) **National Treatment**

Since the coming into force on July 14, 1956, of the United States-German Treaty of Friendship of 1954 (Treaties B 117), national treatment with respect to the acquisition of property of all kinds by testate or intestate succession is accorded to nationals and companies of either party within the territories of the other (art. IX (3) sent. 1). "Should they because of their alienage be ineligible to continue to own any such property, they shall be allowed a period of at least five years in which to dispose of it" (art. IX (3) sent. 2). It has been asserted that this latter rule applies only to immovables in the United States that have been left to a German beneficiary.[17a] However, it is unambiguous and would seem applicable as well to the converse situation (*infra* ch. 6 at n. 47). No American court appears to have subjected an estate opened after July 14, 1956, in favor of a German to inheritance restrictions incompatible with the Treaty.[18]

With respect to estates accrued before that date, national treatment had already been granted by article IV of the old American-German Friendship Treaty of 1923 (Treaties B 55), which *Clark v. Allen*[19] had held unaffected by World War II (*supra* ch. 2 sub A II at n. 37). *Clark v. Allen* also decided, although incorrectly, that article IV restricts reciprocal national treatment to immovables.[20] Therefore American courts had to apply state benefit and reciprocity statutes to a succession to personal property and thus had to consider the German domestic law of succession. Questions as to benefits have been answered differently for West and East Germany. It has been held that German heirs residing in West Germany receive the benefit of shares transmitted to them.[21] But the courts have been reluctant to transfer the proceeds of an American estate to East Germany because of the

---

[17] *Expressly, In re* Estate of Strauch, N.Y.L.J. Apr. 2, 1953, p. 1090 col. 6 (Sur. Ct.); *see also* Matter of Schreiber, N.Y.L.J. Apr. 30, 1952, p. 1732 col. 6 (Sur. Ct.).

[17a] Apparently to this effect, *see* SIEHR, RabelsZ 33 (1969) 294 n. 25.

[18] The cases referred to *infra* nn. 21 and 23 were decided under the old American-German Friendship Treaty of 1923.

[19] 331 U.S. 503, 508–14 (1947).

[20] 331 U.S. at 514–16. As to this interpretation, *cf.* MEEKISON, Treaty Provisions for Inheritance of Personal Property, 44 A.J.I.L. 313, 318–20 (1950), and *also* Mr. Justice Harlan in Zschernig v. Miller *infra* n. 24.

[21] *In re* Niggol's Estate, 202 Misc. 290, 292, 115 N.Y.S.2d 557, 559 (Sur. Ct. 1952); Matter of Strasser, N.Y.L.J. Aug. 31, 1955, p. 8 col. 6 (Sur. Ct.).

lack of evidence that the heir will receive the benefit of the property.[22] In reciprocity cases, on the other hand, no distinction has been drawn between East and West Germany, as most cases have concerned estates accrued during World War II or shortly thereafter. American courts have vacillated as to whether Germany at that time granted reciprocity to American heirs.[23] In view of the new Friendship Treaty of 1954 and the decision in *Zschernig v. Miller*,[24] it seems inappropriate to review these American cases which have been dealt with in masterful fashion by Domke in the first edition of this study[25] and which to a great extent seem to be merely of historical interest for American-German relations. As, however, the Friendship Treaty of 1954 is not applied by American courts to East Germans[26] and as the exact meaning of *Zschernig v. Miller* has not yet been settled,[27] two remarks on West and East German domestic law may be useful.

The German Civil Code (BGB) and its conflicts rules (EGBGB) do not discriminate against alien heirs; more especially, they do not require reciprocity or refuse succession rights or the transmission of assets unless the heirs will get the benefit of the estate.[28] The BGB does not even mention the word "alien"[29] and the EGBGB and its supplementary rules look to the deceased's nationality primarily because succession is governed by his last national law (*infra* (3)).

---

22 *In re* Waessel's Will, 27 Misc.2d 694, 210 N.Y.S.2d 647 (Sur. Ct. 1960); *In re* Nezold's Will, 1 Misc.2d 611, 148 N.Y.S.2d 197 (Sur. Ct. 1956); Matter of Groth, N.Y.L.J. June 24, 1955, p. 8 col. 3 (Sur. Ct.); Matter of Strasser, N.Y.L.J. Dec. 4, 1953, p. 1334 col. 3 (Sur. Ct.), but distribution after heir moved to West Germany, *id.*, N.Y.L.J. Aug. 31, 1955, p. 8 col. 6 (Sur. Ct.); Matter of Hildebrand, N.Y.L.J. July 2, 1952, p. 16 col. 5 (Sur. Ct.); Matter of Niedorf, N.Y.L.J. Aug. 7, 1952, p. 214 col. 6 (Sur. Ct); Estate of Zoch, N.Y.L.J. June 17, 1952, p. 2396 col. 3 (Sur. Ct.); *In re* Perlinsky's Estate, 202 Misc. 351, 115 N.Y.S.2d 549 (Sur. Ct. 1952), and *In re* Mark's Estate, 115 N.Y.S.2d 174 (Sur. Ct. 1952) (both cases concerning East Berlin); *In re* Miller's Will, 115 N.Y.S.2d 255 (Sur. Ct. 1952); *In re* Thomae's Estate, 199 Misc. 940, 105 N.Y.S.2d 844 (Sur. Ct. 1951).

23 *Reciprocity granted*: Estate of Schneider, 140 Cal.App.2d 710, 296 P.2d 45 (Dist. Ct. App.), *app. dismissed sub nom.* Seibert v. Brownell, 352 U.S. 938 (1956); *reciprocity denied*: Clostermann v. Schmidt, 215 Ore. 55, 332 P.2d 1036 (1958). For older cases, *cf.* DOMKE 14–19.

24 389 U.S. 429 (1968). *Cf.* ZaöRV 28 (1968) 594; GRAEFRATH, NJ 1969, 200–03.

25 DOMKE 11–25.

26 Zschernig v. Miller, 243 Ore. 567, 590–91, 412 P.2d 781, 792–93 (1966), *rev'd on other grounds*, *supra* n. 24. However, art. IV of the 1923 Friendship Treaty was applied in favor of East Germans, but restricted to American real property, in *In re* Estate of Kraemer, 81 Cal. Rptr. 287 (Dist. Ct. App. 1969).

27 *Cf. In re* Estate of Leikind, 22 N.Y.2d 346, 239 N.E.2d 550, 292 N.Y.S.2d 681 (1968); *In re* Estate of Kish, 52 N.J. 454, 246 A.2d 1 (1968).

28 KG Berlin 5 May 1938, JW 1938, 2477, 2478.

29 If a person dies abroad, according to §§ 1944 III and 1954 III BGB longer periods of time are provided for a disclaimer (*cf.* 1 COHN no. 583) and its refutation.

There is only one collateral provision which favors German heirs: it provides special rules for their succession claims under German domestic law against the estate of an alien whose last domicile, in the German sense (*supra* ch. 3 sub B (2)(a)), is Germany (art. 25 sent. 2 EGBGB). This rule, which will almost never apply to American-German relations (*infra* (3)(a)(ii)), by favoring Germans discriminates only indirectly against foreign heirs. No direct retorsion against foreign states and their citizens is applied. Although article 31 EGBGB empowers the German government to make use of retaliatory measures, the German government up to now has never taken such steps.[30]

What has been said of the BGB and the EGBGB is true for both parts of Germany because the relevant provisions are still in force in the East. To this extent no difference exists between them. No American case could be found denying succession rights to Germans on the ground that either East Germany[31] or West Germany[32] fails to grant reciprocity to American heirs. Whether East German foreign exchange restrictions[33] will affect the application of American benefit and reciprocity statutes, or whether these statutes are abrogated by *Zschernig v. Miller* or have become irrelevant in view of the Friendship Treaty of 1954, are open questions. American courts have in recent times held correctly that these statutes do not justify retention in the United States of American assets instead of their transfer to East German heirs.[34]

(3) Intestate Succession

Only two German conflicts rules deal directly with matters of succession. They do not differentiate, except on minor points, between intestate and testamentary succession or between succession, administration, and distribution. The special rules that have been developed on these latter points will be discussed later. (For testamentary succession, *see infra* (4); for administration and distribution, *infra* III.)

---

[30] KEGEL, Kommentar no. 6 on art. 31 EGBGB.

[31] The cases cited *supra* n. 23 deal with the question of reciprocity at certain periods when Germany had not yet been divided into two parts.

[32] *In re* Fahs' Estate, 33 Misc.2d 796, 226 N.Y.S.2d 230 (Sur. Ct. 1962).

[33] *Cf.* the statutes collected by H.-G. GRIMM, Devisen- und innerdeutscher Zahlungsverkehr (1961).

[34] *For Pennsylvania, see* Brendler Estate, 14 Fiduciary Rep. 177 (Pa. Orphans' Ct. 1964); Lange Estate, 7 Fiduciary Rep. 257 (Pa. Orphans' Ct. 1957); *cf. also* Liebelt Estate, 13 Fiduciary Rep. 63 (Pa. Orphans' Ct. 1962). *For New York, see* Estate of Becher, N.Y.L.J. Nov. 6, 1969, p. 15 col. 4 (Sur. Ct.); *but cf. also* earlier cases cited *supra* n. 22. *Contra*, on the basis of the newly enacted subd. 1(a) of § 2218 of the N.Y. Surrogate's Court Procedure Act: Estate of Hinz, N.Y.L.J. Mar. 10, 1969, p. 17 col. 2 (Sur. Ct.).

(a) *Law governing.*—The basic German conflicts rule on succession has not been spelt out by the legislator. Article 24 I EGBGB provides that the succession of a German, even if domiciled abroad, is governed by German law. Another provision submits the succession of a foreigner domiciled in Germany to the decedent's national law at the time of his death (art. 25 sent. 1 EGBGB). From these two special rules the following general principle has been derived: succession is governed by the national law of the decedent at the time of his death.[35] Therefore the estate of a German who has died domiciled in the United States is submitted in Germany to German law, while in the United States, of course, the law of the decedent's domiciliary state is applied.[35a] If the decedent was stateless or, as a refugee, regarded as stateless, the law of his last habitual residence or, if none, of his last residence is decisive.[36] However, the import of the basic rule is modified by a number of exceptions which open the door, directly or indirectly, to the law of the decedent's domicile and the *lex situs.*

The most important, although indirect, concession to the law of the decedent's domicile results from the broad admission of renvoi in Germany. Under article 27 EGBGB, as it is generally understood today, any renvoi or transmission from the decedent's national law to his domiciliary law is accepted in Germany.[37] Thus succession to the personal property of American citizens who have died domiciled in Germany has been submitted to German law, by virtue of the "American" domiciliary principle.[38] In accordance with general rules (*supra* ch. 3 sub B (2)(b) nn. 76 and 73), the decedent's domicile is determined according to "American" law, in other words, the law of his last domicile in the United States.[39] In these cases, German law governs the succession to all the personal property in the estate, wherever situated. (On the delimitation between personal and real property, *see infra* (3).)

---

[35] BGH 2 May 1966, BGHZ 45, 351; 21 Dec. 1955, BGHZ 19, 315, 316; RG 8 Nov. 1917, RGZ 91, 139, 140–41; BayObLG 3 Jan. 1967, BayObLGZ 1967, 1, 3; KEGEL, Kommentar no. 3 preceding art. 24 EGBGB, with further references.

On the treatment of a decedent with several nationalities, *see supra* ch. 3 sub A II (6) at nn. 62, 63.

[35a] Two decisions: *In re* Dankerl's Estate, 16 Misc.2d 751, 752, 185 N.Y.S.2d 475, 476 and 16 Misc.2d 834, 835, 185 N.Y.S.2d 477, 479 (Sur. Ct. 1959), *aff'd,* 12 A.D.2d 678, 207 N.Y.S.2d 514 (1960).

[36] Art. 29 EGBGB for stateless persons, and art. 12 I of the Convention on Refugees (Treaties M 308).

[37] KEGEL, Kommentar nos. 74–76 preceding art. 24 EGBGB, with references.

[38] *See,* e.g., BGH 15 Apr. 1959, WM 1959, 662, 663; BayObLG 7 Feb. 1958, BayObLGZ 1958, 34, 38–39; *see also* RG 23 Oct. 1911, JW 1912, 22; KEGEL, Kommentar no. 76 preceding art. 24 EGBGB; FIRSCHING 28–29.

[39] BGH 15 Apr. 1959 and BayObLG 7 Feb. 1958, *supra* n. 38.

A direct though obscure concession to the law of the decedent's domicile is contained in article 24 II EGBGB. If a German has died domiciled abroad, his heirs may invoke his domiciliary law as far as limitation of liability for his debts is concerned. This rule does not seem to play any rôle in practice. Each heir of a German who has died domiciled in Chicago might therefore invoke in Germany the Illinois rules of administration in order to limit his own liability (*infra* III (4)(g)). If no administration under American law takes place in Germany, it will be necessary to adapt the Illinois rules to German circumstances; it would be appropriate to hold that the heir's liability is limited to the estate as prescribed by German law where an administration is taking place under German law (§ 1975 BGB).

More important for American-German relations is the third concession to the domiciliary law. If a foreigner dies domiciled in Germany, a German may, as an exception to the general rule, raise inheritance claims under German law, unless the decedent's national law in a corresponding case would submit the estate of a German exclusively to German law (art. 25 sent. 2 EGBGB). This is an odd "*privilegium Germanicum*," designed as a retaliatory measure against foreign legal systems like the American system, based on the domiciliary rule. Indeed, the succession of a German domiciled in one of the states of the United States is submitted to the law of his domicile. Therefore the condition for the application of the rule is fulfilled in the case of American citizens who die domiciled in Germany.[40] In accordance with the general rules on the subject (*supra* ch. 3 sub B (2)(a)), domicile is determined here according to German law.[41] The most important inheritance claim covered by article 25 sentence 2 EGBGB is the claim to a compulsory share; but disputes between co-heirs or between the heirs and an executor concerning the distribution of the estate also qualify.[42] In the future, the inheritance claim of an illegitimate child against his father and the latter's relatives may play some rôle.[42a] The courts have expressly refused to extend the provision to situations where a foreign

---

[40] BGH 15 Apr. 1959 and RG 23 Oct. 1911, both *supra* n. 38; OLG Hamburg 15 June 1906, NiemeyersZ 18 (1908) 146. *But see infra* n. 44.

[41] BGH 3 May 1961, FamRZ 1961, 364; 15 Apr. 1959, *supra* n. 38; 21 Dec. 1955, *supra* n. 35.

[42] *See* cases cited *supra* nn. 40 and 41.

[42a] § 1934 a BGB, introduced by Law of Aug. 19, 1969, BGBl. I 1243, has accorded an illegitimate child a "substituted" claim to inherit from his father and the latter's relatives. The anticipated claim to which the child may be entitled under certain circumstances according to § 1934 d BGB before his father's death is clearly a claim inter vivos although it terminates the substituted claim to inherit, *see supra* ch. 4 sub B II (2) (d).

decedent has died domiciled abroad.[43] It should be pointed out in conclusion that for American-German relations the retaliatory function of article 25 sentence 2 EGBGB is restricted to cases where an American decedent is domiciled in Germany according to German, but not according to American, law.[44] In the latter case German law is already applicable by virtue of the domiciliary renvoi from American law (*see supra*).

Under still another exception to the nationality principle, the *lex rei sitae* may be taken into account, again both directly and indirectly. An indirect reference to the situs by way of renvoi is by far the most important instance. Article 27 EGBGB is understood by prevailing opinion in Germany as controlling any reference back or over, by the conflicts rules of the decedent's national law, to the *lex situs* of real property located outside the decedent's own country.[45] Since "American" conflicts rules refer the devolution of real property to the *lex rei sitae,* constant court practice has applied German law to the succession to German real property left by an American citizen.[46] The qualification of "real property" is left to the foreign conflicts rule pronouncing the renvoi.[47] But if this rule refers the classification to the foreign *lex situs,* as American law does, the reference back is also followed.[48] German courts have thus been confronted with the task of differentiating between movable and immovable property—a task for which they are ill equipped since neither German internal law nor German conflicts rules employ this distinction. Claims for restitution of immovable property have been classified as immovable.[49] A share in a community of heirs or in a company whose assets consist essentially of immovables will also be

---

[43] BGH 15 Apr. 1959, *supra* n. 38, at 662–63; KG Berlin 24 June 1937, JW 1937, 2527, 2528 (obiter dictum).

[44] None of the American-German cases that have invoked art. 25 sent. 2 EGBGB, *supra* n. 40, qualifies under this analysis because the courts did not find an American renvoi to the German *lex domicilii* of the decedent.

[45] *See,* generally, KEGEL, Kommentar nos. 76 and 77 preceding art. 24 EGBGB.

[46] *See, inter alia,* BGH 20 Mar. 1967, FamRZ 1967, 473, 474 (bound by the findings of the inferior court); 5 June 1957, BGHZ 24, 352, 355; OLG Frankfurt 29 Dec. 1962, IPRspr. 1962/63 no. 146; KG Berlin 24 June 1937, *supra* n. 43; OLG Dresden 6 May 1930, IPRspr. 1931 no. 95; KEGEL, Kommentar no. 76 preceding art. 24 EGBGB, with references in n. 15; RAAPE 414. An occasional deviation (as in BGH 26 Oct. 1967, BGHZ 49, 1, 2) is due to overlooking the American conflicts rule.

[47] RG 5 July 1934, RGZ 145, 85, 86–87; KEGEL, Kommentar no. 75 preceding art. 24 EGBGB.

[48] BGH 5 June 1957 and OLG Frankfurt 29 Dec. 1962, *supra* n. 46.

[49] OLG Frankfurt 2 July 1953, NJW 1954, 111; OLG Köln 3 Dec. 1954, NJW 1955, 755; LG München 23 May 1958, IPRspr. 1958/59 no. 144; BGH 5 June 1957, *supra* n. 46, at 361 (doubtful).

treated as immovable.[50] But if the estate of such a community or company is comprised of movables as well as immovables, the shares will be classified as movable.[51] The main reason understandably is that Germany, ignoring as it does the categories of "movable" and "immovable," refuses to countenance this distinction and the resulting diversity of legal régimes for assets located in Germany itself.[52] Claims for compensation in money are regarded, of course, as movable.[53]

A direct avenue to the *lex situs* is opened by article 28 EGBGB. This provision permits "special rules" of the *lex rei sitae* respecting certain objects to supersede the provisions that would be applicable under ordinary conflicts rules, thus realistically legalizing from the standpoint of German law a practice which will in fact be followed by the situs. To what extent this rule differs from an outright reference to the *lex rei sitae* obviously depends upon the meaning of the term "special rules." This notion is generally held to cover at least those provisions excepting from the ordinary rules of succession a certain class of objects, such as immovables; examples are primogeniture and other feudal rules or, in the former British zone, certain special provisions for the inheritance of farms.[54] But only special rules of substantive law count, not those of procedure.[55] Article 28 EGBGB is also extended to conflicts rules such as American rules that subject succession to immovables to the law of the situs, whatever system of law may govern the succession to the movables belonging to the estate.[56] Those writers who oppose this latter extension[57] overlook the underlying policy, namely, to harmonize German law with the more effective legal rules of the *lex situs.* For American-German relations article 28 EGBGB has importance for American immovables of German decedents by insuring the application of the law of the situs; it does not affect immovables of American decedents,

---

[50] LG Kassel 25 Sept. 1958, IPRspr. 1958/59 no. 146; *cf.* BGH 5 June 1957, *supra* n. 46, at 363 (obiter). *Contra*: RAAPE 417–18.

[51] BGH 5 June 1957, *supra* n. 46, at 363–69.

[52] *See,* notably, BGH 5 June 1957, *supra* n. 46, at 368–69; RAAPE 416–17.

[53] BayObLG 31 Mar. 1966, BayObLGZ 1966, 115, 116; OLG Hamm 21 July 1954, NJW 1954, 1731; IPG 1965/66 no. 51.

[54] BGH 14 July 1965, LM no. 1 on art. 28 EGBGB; RG 5 July 1934, RGZ 145, 85, 87; 2 Oct. 1930, IPRspr. 1930 no. 88; OLG Köln 1 Dec. 1954, IPRspr. 1954/55 no. 133; KG Berlin 10 Apr. 1941, DR 1941, 1611.

[55] Thus the special procedural rules concerning the "alien" certificate of inheritance to be issued in case of successions not governed by German law (*infra* III (3) (b) (ii)) do not qualify under art. 28 EGBGB and therefore do not make applicable the German substantive law of succession, OLG Neustadt 25 May 1951, JZ 1951, 644.

[56] BGH 5 Apr. 1968, BGHZ 50, 63, 64–69; 2 May 1966, BGHZ 45, 351, 352; BayObLG 27 Oct. 1959, BayObLGZ 1959, 390, 398, 399.

[57] Notably KEGEL, Kommentar no. 80 preceding art. 24 and no. 10 on art. 28 EGBGB.

since the American reference to the *lex rei sitae* and its acceptance by German law (*see supra*) covers all possible situations which might arise under that article.

An implied reservation of the *lex rei sitae* is contained in the general conflicts rule of property law which submits the creation of a real right to its own law, thus barring any foreign property rights which might otherwise spring from the law governing the succession.[58] In consequence a testamentary trust, whether created in a will governed by "American" or by German law, will not in Germany have the property effects of Anglo-American law,[59] even though the testator's intentions must be carried out as far as possible through resort to analogous institutions.

If we summarize the basic rule of the decedent's national law and the more important concessions to the law of the domicile and that of the situs, the following complicated picture of the succession to an American decedent emerges. The German courts will apply (in conformity with American concepts unless otherwise stated):

(i) if the American decedent was domiciled in one of the states of the United States, this state's law to personal property (the basic rule);

(ii) if the American decedent was domiciled outside the United States, the law of his domicile to his personal property (the basic rule plus art. 27 EGBGB);

(iii) to immovables (here, according to the law of the situs) of the American decedent, the *lex rei sitae* (the basic rule plus art. 27 EGBGB);

(iv) exceptionally, if the American decedent was domiciled (according to German, but not American, law) in Germany, German law to the succession claims of a German (art. 25 sent. 2 EGBGB).

If, on the other hand, the decedent was a German, the German courts will apply German law to his property of every kind regardless of his domicile (art. 24 I EGBGB), subject to one exception: they will apply "American" law to his immovables in the United States (art. 28 EGBGB).

(b) *Issues governed.*—On principle, all issues of descent and distribution are subject to the law governing the succession (*supra* (a)). More particularly, one may point to questions such as (i) what assets of the decedent fall into the estate (*infra* III (4)(d)), and (ii) whether a foreign public legal entity has the general capacity to receive property. The American courts, without entertaining any doubts, have upheld the validity of bequests (obviously made by immigrants

---

[58] RG 2 Oct. 1930, *supra* n. 54, and BayObLG 13 Jan. 1961, BayObLGZ 1961, 4, 19–20 (creation and effects of a testamentary usufruct). *Cf.* KEGEL, Kommentar no. 277 preceding art. 7 EGBGB.

[59] FERID/FIRSCHING, US Grundzüge no. 62 f.

of German extraction) to German charitable organizations and to municipalities,[60] and German law certainly would take the same position. But any restrictions upon a legal entity's capacity to receive as heir or by bequest established by the law governing that entity (*infra* ch. 10 sub I (1)) have to be taken into account.[61] A special problem is presented by corporate foundations (*Stiftungen*) instituted by the testator himself. If the official approval requisite for the creation of a German corporate foundation as a legal entity is not granted until after the founder's death, the foundation is still considered as having been created, for the purpose of taking bequests, before the founder's decease (§ 84 BGB). Thus a German court has held valid the bequest by an American domiciled in the United States of his German immovables to a German foundation created by his last will; this conclusion was based on German law, which governed by virtue of a renvoi to the German situs.[62] The same result would have been reached if American law had governed the succession.[63] Paragraph 84 BGB has also been applied, correctly, in a case where a German testatrix appointed as her heir a foundation that was to be, and in fact had been, organized in Israel after her death.[64]

The law of the succession also governs (iii) the heirs in intestate succession,[65] (iv) most aspects of last wills and contracts of inheritance, except those for which special conflicts rules have been established (*infra* (4)); (v) unworthiness to inherit;[66] and (vi) a contractual[67] or unilateral disclaimer by the heir. German heirs or beneficiaries of estates governed by "American" law have not infrequently resorted, in order to prevent vesting in the Alien Property Custodian, to the

---

[60] Brownell v. Fidelity Union Trust Co., 119 F. Supp. 755 (D.N.J. 1954); Matter of Walter, N.Y.L.J. June 3, 1954, p. 1876 col. 1 (Sur. Ct.); *see also In re* Ollesheimer's Estate, 205 Misc. 62, 126 N.Y.S.2d 477 (Sur. Ct. 1953); Matter of Heubach, N.Y.L.J. Sept. 2, 1954, p. 8 col. 5 (Sur. Ct.).

[61] KEGEL, Kommentar no. 9 preceding art. 24 EGBGB.

[62] OLG Dresden 6 May 1930, IPRspr. 1931 no. 95, p. 183 *et seq.*

[63] *In re* Groedel's Estate, 23 Misc.2d 1046, 198 N.Y.S.2d 843 (Sur. Ct. 1960), *aff'd,* 22 A.D.2d 852, 254 N.Y.S.2d 81 (1964); *see also,* in the same matter, 23 Misc.2d 1056, 203 N.Y.S.2d 587 (Sur. Ct. 1960).

[64] BayObLG 17 Mar. 1965, BayObLGZ 1965, 77, 85–86.

[65] *See* KEGEL, Kommentar no. 11 preceding art. 24 EGBGB. A German court held that the statutory share to which the surviving spouse is entitled according to § 83 subd. 4 of the New York Decedent Estate Law makes the spouse an heir, KG Berlin 7 Feb. 1969, RzW 1969, 341. Another court regarded California Probate Code § 201.5, excluding descendants in favor of the surviving spouse, as a rule of descent (and not of marital property) and held it compatible with German public policy, OLG Celle 10 Sept. 1959, IPRspr. 1958/59 no. 148.

[66] OLG Düsseldorf 6 Feb. 1963, NJW 1963, 2227, 2230.

[67] Contractual disclaimer (Erbverzichtsvertrag) LG München II 5 June 1967, IPRspr. 1966/67 no. 20, IPG 1965/66 no. 68.

unilateral disclaimer or renunciation admitted by German law (*Ausschlagung*) but unknown for intestate succession in most American jurisdictions. Such a declaration should be interpreted according to German law as the law the declarant obviously had in mind,[68] and under which he is deemed never to have become an heir (§ 1953 BGB). The effects, on the other hand, must be ascertained by the law governing the succession. Understandably enough, the interpretation of the "American" law on this point, with which German writers have seldom had to deal, is unsettled. The majority attributes to a disclaimer the same effects it would have in Germany since a beneficiary may release his claims against the administrator.[69] Firsching opposes this conclusion and regards a disclaimer as at most a contractual transfer of a position acquired by succession.[70] It is probably necessary to draw distinctions: Firsching's solution fits if the beneficiary acquires the estate immediately and directly on the decedent's death; if, however, an administration takes place, the prevailing opinion appears justified, since the administrator performs precisely one of the functions which the waiver, within the different framework of the German law, is designed to achieve.

Finally, the law of succession controls (vii) the mutual relations between the heirs or beneficiaries of the estate,[71] and also the relations between these persons and any administrator or executor (*see infra* III (4)); (viii) prerequisites and effects of a transfer of the estate or a share in it;[72] and (ix) all aspects of probate, administration and distribution (*see infra* III).

Two points deserve special mention, namely, split estates and preliminary questions. The acceptance of a foreign renvoi to the law of the situs, or application of the special rules obtaining there (*supra* (a) at n. 45), may result in a multiplicity of legal systems governing the succession. Thus, whether viewed from the standpoint of the United States or of Germany, the personal property, wherever situated, of a decedent domiciled in Iowa is subject to Iowa law, while his German and English immovables are governed by German and English law, respectively. In German law, each of the three segments of this estate must be regarded, in principle, as a separate unit. Thus German law is applied to all aspects of the succession relating to the German real estate as if the decedent were a German national: the heirs and beneficiaries of an intestate succession, the permissible contents of a last will, probate, administration and

---

[68] RFH 5 July 1929, IPRspr. 1929 no. 94.

[69] WENGLER, JR 1955, 41, 43; KÜHLEWEIN, NJW 1963, 142; IPG 1965/66 no. 51; *see also* references by FERID/FIRSCHING, US Grundzüge 40/174 n. 1.

[70] FERID/FIRSCHING, US Grundzüge no. 60d (p. 40/174).

[71] KEGEL, Kommentar no. 18 preceding art. 24 EGBGB.

[72] OLG Schleswig 19 Dec. 1961, IPRspr. 1960/61 no. 22 (Canadian estate); LG Berlin 28 Apr. 1961, *id.* no. 144.

distribution.[73] As far as personal property located in Germany is concerned, all the above issues are subject to Iowa law. In spite of this strict separation of the segments of the estate, the factual interdependence of its several parts cannot be negated completely. Thus a German court, in determining the formal validity of an American citizen's last will relating to his German immovables, was required to determine whether the formal invalidity of the will according to New Jersey law was relevant in Germany; it correctly applied the German rule on partial nullity of a last will and concluded that this testator would have willed in the same way if he had known of the defect under New Jersey law.[74] Another case is even more illuminating: An Oklahoma resident died after making a bequest to his brother. When the heirs were sued by the brother in Germany, where an immovable of the decedent's estate was situated, the heirs invoked a final probate decree of an Oklahoma District Court in which the brother had failed to file his claim. The German court rightly held that each segment of the estate was severally liable for its debts and the German part of the estate was unaffected by the Oklahoma decree.[75]

Preliminary questions, such as the continued existence of a marital union between the decedent and one claiming to be his widow, or the legitimacy of children, are not subject to the substantive law governing the succession. How the proper law of such preliminary questions has to be determined, however, is somewhat doubtful. According to the better view such special issues should be solved according to those rules which would be applied by the courts of the legal system which governs the succession. Therefore the law governing a preliminary question must be ascertained by looking to the conflicts rule not of the forum but of the law governing the succession.[76] According to another view, probably still prevailing, a preliminary question should be decided in the same way as it would be decided by a court of the forum if presented as the main

---

[73] *See*, e.g., BGH 5 Apr. 1968, BGHZ 50, 63, 69–70; 5 June 1957, BGHZ 24, 352, 355; KG Berlin 2 July 1962, IPRspr. 1962/63 no. 144; OLG Köln 3 Dec. 1954, NJW 1955, 755; OLG Karlsruhe 21 Jan. 1930, IPRspr. 1930 no. 89.

[74] OLG Dresden 6 May 1930, *supra* n. 62; *in accord*: OLG Köln 8 Aug. 1960, IPRspr. 1964/65 no. 72.

[75] LG Kassel 25 Sept. 1958, *supra* n. 50.

[76] *Legitimacy of children*: KG Berlin 18 Jan. 1960, IPRspr. 1960/61 no. 137; OLG Hamm 14 Sept. 1957, IPRspr. 1956/57 no. 148 b; OLG Karlsruhe 20 Mar. 1931, IPRspr. 1931 no. 96; LG Wiesbaden 5 Oct. 1957, IPRspr. 1956/57 no. 145.

Validity of marriage: LG Wiesbaden, preceding paragraph; LG Berlin 3 Apr. 1950, IPRspr. 1950/51 no. 69; IPG 1965/66 no. 14 (p. 144).

Validity of adoption: BayObLG 13 Jan. 1961, BayObLGZ 1961, 4, 17.

See, generally, RAAPE 434–435; NEUHAUS 238; FERID/FIRSCHING I Einführung no. 28.

issue; this view prefers consistency of decisions in the forum to harmony with the courts of the legal system governing the succession; it ascertains the applicable law by looking to the conflicts rules of the forum.[77]

(4) Wills*

Wills and the German contract of inheritance are, in principle, subject to the law governing the succession. However, certain special rules intervene due to the fact that a will expresses the testator's intentions and is thus a legal act which comes into being before the testator's death.

(a) *Classification as a will.*—It is not always clear whether an instrument signed or a disposition made by the testator is a last will or a disposition *inter vivos*. The German courts usually classify acts according to the German *lex fori.*[78] An act held to be a gift which will become effective at the donor's death (*Schenkung von Todes wegen*) is subject to the law governing the succession.[79]

(b) *Form.*—Germany ratified the Hague Convention of 1961 on the conflict of laws relating to the form of testamentary dispositions, to take effect from January 1, 1966.[80] The rules of the Convention apply to all cases in which the testator has died since that date (art. 8) irrespective of his nationality or of the law applicable under the Convention (art. 6). The Convention is a new conflicts norm of general application and thus for some time to come Germany will apply two different sets of rules in this field: the new conventional rules for testators dying after January 1, 1966 and the old national rules for testators dying prior to that date. The conventional rules will also be applied to successions of "Americans"[81] even though the United States is not a party to the Convention.

(i) *The Hague Convention.*—The Convention deals with the formalities of testamentary dispositions, including revocations (art. 2) and joint or mutual wills (art. 4), but excluding contracts of

---

[77] BGH 5 Apr. 1968, BGHZ 50, 63, 70; *see also* BayObLG 31 Mar. 1966, BayObLGZ 1966, 115, 121–122; KEGEL, Kommentar no. 11 preceding art. 24 EGBGB.

* LIBRARY OF CONGRESS (Law Library, Foreign Law Section), Form and Effect of a Public Will Under German Law (1954).

[78] *Expressly*: BFH 20 Sept. 1951, IPRspr. 1950/51 no. 111; *see also* LG Berlin 3 Apr. 1950, *supra* n. 76. *But see* BGH 15 Apr. 1959, WM 1959, 662, 663 (New York savings-bank trust classified according to New York law as act *inter vivos*).

KEGEL, Kommentar no. 52 preceding art. 24 EGBGB prefers the national law of the donor at the time of the gift.

[79] BGH, *supra* n. 78, at 662; BFH, *supra* n. 78.

[80] BGBl. 1965 II 1145, 510 UNTS 175.

[81] BayObLG 6 Nov. 1967, BayObLGZ 1967, 418, 424.

inheritance. Article 5 extends coverage to special formal rules based upon the age, nationality or other personal qualities of the testator or the witnesses.[82] These formal rules apply even to testamentary dispositions that German law does not view as relating to succession, such as nomination of a guardian (art. 12).

Article 1 contains the central conflicts rules. Its first paragraph offers the testator a choice of no fewer than seven legal systems to govern the formalities of his last will. These are the internal law[83]:

(*a*) of the place where the testator made it, or
(*b*) of a nationality possessed by the testator, either at the time when he made the disposition, or at the time of his death, or
(*c*) of a place in which the testator had his domicile either at the time when he made the disposition, or at the time of his death, or
(*d*) of the place in which the testator had his habitual residence either at the time when he made the disposition, or at the time of his death, or
(*e*) so far as immovables are concerned, of the place where they are situated.

Contrary to the general rule in Germany, the determination of domicile in this context is governed by the law of the place in question (art. 1 (3); *see supra* ch. 3 sub B (2)(a)). In the case of a "non-unified" system, like the United States, the applicable law, in the absence of interregional conflicts rules, is to be determined "by the most real connexion which the testator had with any one of the various laws within that system" (art. 1(2)). It is to be expected that this formula will yield the same results that have hitherto been reached by referring to the domicile (or the last domicile) of an American citizen in the United States (*see supra* ch. 3 sub B (2)(b)).

A revocation is formally valid if the revocation itself complies with article 1, or if it complies with one of the laws which according to article 1 governs the will revoked (art. 2).

Finally, article 3 reserves national conflicts rules that validate the form of a last will, on the basis of any other legal system. Germany, however, has no such rules (*see infra* (ii)).

(ii) *German national conflicts rules.*—In the absence of a special rule on the formal validity of last wills, the general provision on formalities of legal acts of article 11 EGBGB applies. It offers only two choices: compliance with the forms either of the law governing

---

[82] Thus the appointment of a witnessing lawyer as executor that would be invalid under German law has been held valid under the applicable "American" law, BayObLG *supra* n. 81, at 428. *See also infra* n. 88.

[83] This provision excludes a renvoi from a foreign law, e.g., by the "American" law of an American citizen to that of his last domicile in Germany, BayObLG, *supra* n. 81, at 425–28.

the underlying relationship, meaning the law of the succession (sent. 1), or of the law of the place of making (sent. 2). Neither requires much comment.

The conflicts rule governing succession (including the exceptions to that rule through renvoi and so forth), has been dealt with elsewhere (*supra* (3)(a)). It is to be noted that it is the law of the testator's nationality at the time of his death and not the law at the time of execution of the will which is relevant (arts. 24 I and 25 sent. 1 EGBGB). The hardship caused by this aspect of the rule is mitigated by a special provision (art. 24 III 1 EGBGB) which looks to the national law of a foreign testator at the time of making (or revoking) a last will, provided the testator subsequently acquires German nationality. Thus the will of a New York resident made according to New York law remains valid in form even if the testator later becomes a naturalized German. In addition, compliance with the formal rules of German law, as the law governing the succession, may suffice;[84] this latter rule has frequently (and correctly) been extended to other instances of a testator's change of nationality.[85]

As for the place of making, compliance with the local form suffices (art. 11 sent. 2 EGBGB). This is so even if the testator later changes his nationality, making his national law at the time of making the will applicable under article 24 III 2 EGBGB. The local form remains available, even if the law governing the succession, like the common law, disregards it.[86] If the law governing under either of these two sub-rules is violated, the consequences have to be derived from that particular law.[87]

It is not always easy to separate form from substance. Even the Hague Convention has solved only a few cases, leaving other questions open. On principle, the German courts look to the German *lex fori* for classification, but they do not ignore the peculiarities of foreign law. Thus the prohibition of benefits for the notary drawing a testament has been classified as an issue of form.[88] Classification of the widespread prohibition of joint wills is more difficult. Here it

---

[84] But this is very controversial. For exclusion of the law governing the succession, BayObLG 22 Feb. 1963, BayObLGZ 1963, 52; KEGEL, Kommentar no. 35 preceding art. 24 EGBGB; RAAPE 429–30.

[85] BayObLG 22 Feb. 1963, *supra* n. 84, at 56–57; 13 Dec. 1960, BayObLGZ 1960, 478, 484–85; KG Berlin 10 Oct. 1960, IPRspr. 1960/61 no. 140; *see also infra* n. 96.

Contra: OLG Dresden 6 May 1930, IPRspr. 1931 no. 95 (last will of German, later naturalized in the United States, complying with German but not New Jersey formalities, held invalid); RAAPE 430.

[86] BGH 12 Jan. 1967, NJW 1967, 1177; for standing court practice, *see* KEGEL, Kommentar no. 35 preceding art. 24 EGBGB, with references in n. 14. *Contra*: RAAPE 424; FERID/FIRSCHING, US Grundzüge no. 62.

[87] *See* BFH 20 Sept. 1951, *supra* n. 78; KEGEL, Kommentar no. 27 on art. 11 EGBGB.

[88] LG Zweibrücken 11 Nov. 1954, NJW 1955, 1800; *see also supra* n. 82.

may be helpful to distinguish two questions: Is the prohibition merely directed against testation by two persons in one document? This is an issue of form. But if the prohibition is directed primarily against the mutual interdependence and irrevocability of the dispositions, it pertains to substance and is therefore subject to the law governing the succession.[89]

(iii) *Probate.*—Since there is no probate proceeding in German law, a probate decree of an "American" domiciliary court is not a prerequisite to German recognition of the validity of a will governed by "American law."[90] In a doubtful case,[91] however, it may be advisable for a German court to request such a decree.[92]

(c) *Substance.*—Two aspects should be distinguished: the determination of the law governing and the ascertainment of the issues governed.

(i) In principle, the law controlling substantive validity is the law which would govern an intestate succession (*supra* (3)(a)). This basic rule is limited in only a few respects.

Dölle has suggested that the testator should be free to choose the law to apply to his succession.[93] This thesis appears acceptable if the testator's autonomy is restricted to the laws of his domicile and his nationality (or of one of his several nationalities or domiciles), but it has not yet been accepted by present-day decisions in Germany.[94] Only to the extent that a foreign law governing a succession permits it will the testator's choice be recognized.[95]

Certain aspects of the substantive validity of wills and contracts of inheritance are, like formalities (*supra* (b)(ii)), submitted to a testator's foreign national law at the time of making his will if he subsequently becomes a German (art. 24 III 1 EGBGB). The German courts have extended this rule liberally to all cases where a testator has changed his personal law,[96] and they subsume several issues under "substantive validity," such as the admissibility of certain species of last will or of

---

[89] NEUHAUS/GÜNDISCH, Gemeinschaftliche Testamente amerikanischer Erblasser, RabelsZ 21 (1956) 550–74, 563–64; *see also* BayObLG 13 Dec. 1957, BayObLGZ 1957, 376, 381–82.

[90] FERID/FIRSCHING, US Gründzüge no. 63b.

[91] LG Nürnberg-Fürth 29 Dec. 1962, IPRspr. 1962/63 no. 148; FERID/FIRSCHING, *supra* n. 90.

[92] FERID/FIRSCHING, *supra* n. 90.

[93] DÖLLE, Die Rechtswahl im internationalen Erbrecht, RabelsZ 30 (1966) 205–40; *see also* the notice of a discussion, RabelsZ 31 (1967) 337–40.

[94] *Expressly contra*: OLG Frankfurt 22 Sept. 1965, IPRspr. 1966/67 no. 168a, *rev'd on another ground*, BGH 19 June 1967, *id.* no. 168b; LG Berlin 3 Apr. 1950, IPRspr. 1950/51 no. 69; *see also* KG Berlin 11 July 1911, KGJ 41, 62, 64.

[95] LG Bochum 21 May 1959, IPRspr. 1958/59 no. 147, *aff'd on second appeal*, BGH 2 May 1966, BGHZ 45, 351.

[96] BayObLG 13 Dec. 1960, BayObLGZ 1960, 478, 486–488; 13 Jan. 1961, BayObLGZ 1961, 4, 13; AG Bremen 8 June 1967, IPRspr. 1966/67 no. 179; KEGEL, Kommentar no. 41 preceding art. 24 EGBGB. *See references to*

a contract of inheritance, and their binding effect.[97] Article 24 III 1 EGBGB mentions specifically the testator's capacity to make a will. This capacity is preserved even if a foreigner is naturalized in Germany and he is a minor under German law.[98] Thus he retains his capacity to make a will as a German although one born a German could not do so.

(ii) The coverage of the law governing the succession extends to all those aspects of wills and contracts of inheritance that have not specifically been mentioned heretofore. Thus the admissible types of will, such as a joint or reciprocal will, and the possibility of concluding a contract of inheritance, depend upon the law governing the succession.[99] This law also controls the substantive provisions of the will, such as the possibility of appointing a provisional and a reversionary heir (*Vorerbe* and *Nacherbe*),[100] the prohibition against instituting certain persons as heirs,[101] and the possibility of instituting an executor (*Testamentsvollstrecker*) and of restricting thereby the rights of the beneficiary.[102] The law governing the succession also determines whether the parties to a contract of inheritance or joint (or mutual or reciprocal) will are bound by its contents;[103] if the law of an American jurisdiction applies, a contract between the testators declaring their joint or mutual will to be irrevocable is required,[104]

---

contrary opinion, *id.* n. 31 and IPG 1965/66 no. 60 p. 691 with n. 4. *See also supra* n. 85.

[97] *See* preceding note. *Contra*: OLG Neustadt 29 Feb. 1952, IPRspr. 1952/53, no. 234, although reaching the same result with the help of a renvoi from the law governing the succession to the common national law of the testators at the time of making their will.

[98] Details are controversial, *see* KEGEL, Kommentar no. 30–34 preceding art. 7 EGBGB. This rule corresponds to art. 7 II EGBGB on the general capacity of a person, *see supra* ch. 4 sub C(1)(b)(ii).

[99] BayObLG 13 Dec. 1957, *supra* n. 89, at 385–86; OLG Düsseldorf 26 Aug. 1963, IPRspr. 1962/63 no. 151; KG Berlin 10 Apr. 1941, DR 1941, 1611, 1612; LG Berlin 3 Apr. 1950, *supra* n. 94. This law also determines whether conversion into two separate wills is possible, LG Nürnberg-Fürth 29 Dec. 1962, IPRspr. 1962/63 no. 148. If, however, according to German law the prohibition of a joint or a reciprocal will is considered a question of form, the will may be valid under the law at the place of making, *see supra* (b)(ii).

[100] OLG Celle 3 Dec. 1956, FamRZ 1957, 273. The interest of a provisional heir with unrestricted powers under German law has been characterized as a legal life estate with power of invasion, *In re* Hirschmann's Estate, 124 N.Y.S.2d 801, 804 (Sur. Ct. 1953); followed for tax purposes in two decisions in Hirschmann v. United States, 202 F.Supp. 722 and 725 (S.D.N.Y. 1962); followed in Estate of Zietz, 34 T.C. 351 (1960).

[101] LG Frankenthal 17 Apr. 1962, IPRspr. 1962/63 no. 143.

[102] LG München 23 May 1958, IPRspr. 1958/59 no. 144; OLG Frankfurt 25 Sept. 1958, *id.* no. 145. For details, *see infra* III (4) (e).

[103] OLG Hamm 18 Dec. 1963, NJW 1964, 553, 555; OLG Düsseldorf 6 Feb. 1963, NJW 1963, 2227, 2229.

[104] *See* BayObLG 6 Nov. 1967, BayObLGZ 1967, 418, 429, applying alternatively German, Kentucky and New York law.

but the American courts have been quite liberal in implying such a contract if the testator was of German origin and had concluded a contract of inheritance or a joint will, either in Germany or in the United States.[105]

Revocation of a will or contract of inheritance is again subject to the law governing the succession.[106]

German law in effect limits a testator's freedom considerably by providing forced shares for his spouse, his descendants and his parents (§ 2303 BGB). All issues relating to forced shares (or comparable provisions, such as exemptions for the benefit of the family, widow's allowances, and so on) are also subject to the law governing the succession.[107] The *Reichsgericht* held that German public policy was not violated by the application of New York rules on succession which at the time of the case made no provision for shares for near relatives.[108] In a later case, a New York court applied the statutory right of election (§ 18 of the New York Decedent Estate Law) to the German-domiciled widow of a German-domiciled testator, apparently without noticing the conflicts issue.[109]

Last, but not least, the construction of a will or contract of inheritance is subject to the law governing the succession.[110] Two difficulties have to be overcome. No special problems arise if a will has to be construed within the framework and for the purposes of the law governing the succession. But great difficulties are bound to arise if the construction has to be made under one law while the testator, inadvisedly, has drawn his will under another law; this may occur due to a subsequent change of nationality or domicile, or because the laws governing the succession are split, or because the foreign will has to be classified for the application of the forum's procedural or fiscal laws. We shall discuss one of the more important issues that have arisen in Germany in attempts to "translate" American wills into German law. For purposes of taxation or the issue of a certificate of inheritance in Germany the central question has been whether or not an American beneficiary qualifies as heir (*supra* I (5)). This question will be discussed here without considering

---

[105] Estate of Detterbeck, N.Y.L.J. Jan. 8, 1964 p. 15 col. 3 (Sur. Ct.) (contract of inheritance by American testatrix during visit to Germany); Rich v. Mottek, 11 N.Y.2d 90, 181 N.E.2d 445, 226 N.Y.S.2d 428 (1962) (joint reciprocal will executed five years after immigration from Germany).

[106] OLG Neustadt 29 Feb. 1952, *supra* n. 97; LG Bochum 21 May 1959, *supra* n. 95.

[107] *See* e.g., KG Berlin 2 July 1962, IPRspr. 1962/63 no. 144; OLG Düsseldorf 26 Aug. 1963, *id.* no. 151; BayObLG 13 Jan. 1961, BayObLGZ 1961, 4, 16–17.

[108] RG 23 Oct. 1911, JW 1912, 22; *see also* IPG 1965–66 no. 67, pp. 786–88.

[109] *In re* Herter's Estate, 193 Misc. 602, 83 N.Y.S.2d 36 (Sur. Ct.), *aff'd* 274 App. Div. 979, 84 N.Y.S.2d 913 (1948), *aff'd*, 300 N.Y. 532, 89 N.E.2d 252 (1949).

[110] KEGEL, Kommentar no. 47 preceding art. 24 EGBGB.

the relevance of an executor or trustee (as to which *see infra* III (4)(e)). If an American-domiciled testator devises an estate which includes German realty in fractions to various persons, the latter may be regarded with respect to the German immovables as co-heirs.[111] The same conclusion is warranted if an American-domiciled testator makes a number of specific legacies and bequeaths the rest of his estate to his spouse as residuary legatee; the spouse in this case must be regarded as sole heir.[112] If the estate (or fractions of it) is divided into successive present and future estates between two (or more) persons, it appears appropriate to designate the holder of the life estate as the provisional heir (*Vorerbe*) and the holder of the future estate as reversionary heir (*Nacherbe*).[113] All of these rough rules are, of course, subject to the peculiar circumstances of each case. If one dares to draw a general conclusion from the treatment of the foregoing typical situations, it is this: For the "translation" into the concepts of German law the formal classification of a bequest or the location of title to an estate are irrelevant; an heir is, as a rule, any person who obtains substantially the whole estate or an undivided fraction of it, as distinguished from individual items of property.

Rules against perpetuities and comparable provisions in Germany (*cf.* §§ 2044 II, 2109, 2162, 2210 BGB) should also be determined by the law governing the succession. Foreign rules imposing no time limitation at all upon a provisional estate or a longer limitation than the normal German 30-year term should not be regarded as contravening German public policy, even for property situated in Germany. In the United States, however, a testamentary trust seems to be immune to the "American" rules against perpetuities only if the law applicable to the succession is foreign and the trust is to be executed abroad. In addition, the applicable foreign law must not oppose the carrying out of the trust.[114]

III. PROBATE AND ADMINISTRATION

(1) Treaty Provisions

(a) *Sources and scope of application.*—Articles XVII through XXVIII of the American-German Friendship Treaty of 1923 (Treaties

[111] Ferid/Firsching, US Grundzüge no. 62b, and unreported case cited.

[112] Ferid/Firsching, *supra* n. 111; Gottheiner, RabelsZ 21 (1956) 67–70; Mueller, RabelsZ 7 (1933), 808–49, 817.

[113] Ferid/Firsching, *supra* n. 111, nos. 62 d–e; Gottheiner, Anpassungs- und Umdeutungsprobleme bei deutsch-englischen Erbrechtsfällen (thesis Tübingen 1955) 156–58. *See also* the reverse classification, *In re* Hirschmann's Estate, *supra* n. 100.

[114] Stieglitz v. Attorney-General, 91 Misc. 139, 154 N.Y. Supp. 137 (Sup. Ct. 1915) (testatrix domiciled in Germany and trust to be carried out there held valid).

B 55), as amended by article II of the Agreement of June 3, 1953 (Treaties B 104), have been maintained expressly for the time being by article XXVIII sentence 2 of the Friendship Treaty of 1954 (Treaties B 117). However, the territorial scope of the 1923 consular articles is restricted "to the same extent as that provided in art. XXVI of the present Treaty," in other words, to West Germany. The American and the German governments disagree as to the power of West German consuls with respect to East German citizens. In decedent estate cases in particular the issue has arisen whether West German consuls may under the Treaty of 1954 receive assets of American estates for transmission to East German heirs and thereby prevent their deposit under the American "iron curtain" statutes (*supra* sub II (2)).[115] The West German government, at least before the enactment of the East German nationality statute of 1967 (*supra* ch. 3 sub A II (1)(b)), thought that the Treaty of 1954 applied to residents of East Germany.[116] The United States government, however, has taken the view that "consuls of the Federal Republic [of Germany] are not authorized to act on behalf of German nationals residing in Eastern Germany,"[117] although the conventional property guaranties of the American-German Friendship Treaty of 1923 are deemed to be still in force between the United States and East Germany.[118] While the American view is formally correct under the above-cited treaty provision (*see supra* ch. 2 n. 76), it overlooks the great need for protection of the interests of East German residents. In view of the lack of any official relations between East Germany and the United States, the latter should admit in the interest of the individuals affected the protective functions of the West German consuls, to the extent that the latter have been asked for protection by residents of East Germany (*see supra* ch. 3 n. 16).

(b) *Treaty rights and the most-favored-nation clause.*—Under the Friendship Treaty of 1923 the receiving state grants certain rights to consuls of the other high contracting party. With respect to matters of succession these rights pertain to information about

---

[115] *Cf.* Zschernig v. Miller, 243 Ore. 567, 589, 412 P.2d 781, 792–93 (1966), *rev'd on other grounds*, 389 U.S. 429 (1968).

[116] *Cf.* the Foreign Office certificate of the Federal Republic of Germany of Sept. 30, 1963, quoted in Zschernig v. Miller, 243 Ore. at 575, 412 P.2d at 785. *Cf. also* ch. 3 sub A II (1) (b) at n. 16.

[117] Letter released by the Office of the Legal Adviser, Department of State, May 23, 1962, 57 AJIL 403, 410 (1963), affirmatively quoted in Zschernig v. Miller, 243 Ore. at 590, 412 P.2d at 793. *Cf. also* the letter of Feb. 13, 1964 from Ely Maurer, Assistant Legal Adviser for European Affairs of the United States Department of State to Attorney General of Oregon Robert Y. Thornton, quoted in Zschernig v. Miller, 243 Ore. at 577, 412 P.2d at 785, with reference to art. XXVI (1) of the Treaty of 1954.

[118] Zschernig v. Miller, 389 U.S. at 440 (per Mr. Justice Harlan); *see also supra* n. 26.

certain cases of death (art. XXIV (1)), to safekeeping and administration of estates (art. XXIV (2)), and to receipt and transmission of distributive shares (art. XXV). These treaty rights will be discussed later (*infra* (4)(b), (f)(i) and (v)). The same will be true of the most-favored-nation clause of article XVII (2) sentence 1 of the Friendship Treaty of 1923 (*infra* (4)(f)(i) and (v)).

(2) **German Probate Jurisdiction**

As has already been pointed out (*supra* II (4)(b)(iii)), German domestic law does not know a specific probate procedure. Therefore when the term "probate" is used for German law it must be taken in a general sense denoting all those matters relating to succession and handled by courts in non-contentious proceedings.

(a) *General principle.*—Apart from individual cases, German law does not state when German probate courts have international jurisdiction. Due to this lack of statutory regulation, the courts and legal scholars in a cautious approach to this problem have developed the unanimously supported general principle that the German probate courts have jurisdiction whenever German substantive law must be applied to a succession case,[119] in accordance with German conflicts rules.

Since under German conflicts law succession is generally governed by the decedent's national law (*supra* II (3)(a)(i)), provided there is no renvoi to the *lex domicilii* (*supra* II (3)(a)(ii)) or to the *lex situs* (*supra* II (3)(a)(iii)), the German probate courts always have jurisdiction if:

(i) a German national dies in Germany or abroad, except as to property subject to special treatment by the *lex situs* (art. 28 EGBGB, *supra* II (3)(a)(iii)); or

(ii) an alien is domiciled in Germany, insofar as his national law refers back to German law as the law of his last domicile (*supra* II (3)(a)(ii)); or

(iii) an alien dies seized of German real estate, and his national law subjects this property to the *lex situs* (*supra* II (3)(a) (iii)); or, finally,

(iv) German law under article 25 sentence 2 EGBGB applies irrespective of the deceased's personal law (*supra* II (3)(a)(ii)).

Under this general principle, which has been stated correctly by an American court,[120] German probate courts have assumed jurisdiction

---

[119] BayObLG 7 Feb. 1958, BayObLGZ 1958, 34, 37; 19 Dec. 1919, BayObLGZ 19, 373, 375; KG Berlin 11 July 1911, KGJ 41, 62, 67; KEGEL, Kommentar no. 54 preceding art. 24 EGBGB; NEUHAUS 242, 246–47; RAAPE 444–47; BRESLAUER 203–06.

[120] *In re* Zietz's Estate, 201 Misc. 580, 583–84, 105 N.Y.S.2d 876, 879 (Sur. Ct. 1951), *aff'd*, 279 App. Div. 903, 111 N.Y.S.2d 751 (1952), 280 App. Div. 919, 115 N.Y.S.2d 923 (1952).

over the estates of United States citizens who have either died domiciled in Germany[121] or left German real property.[122]

This general principle has long been regarded as exclusive, so that the German probate courts have declined jurisdiction where an estate is governed by foreign law. They have therefore refused to appoint an executor,[123] to accept a disclaimer of inheritance (*Erbausschlagung*),[124] and to order the partition of the estate between several heirs of a deceased alien.[125] Sometimes the reluctance of the German courts may have been unwarranted,[126] but in general it has been correct. Just as the American courts have declined primary jurisdiction with regard to the movable estate of an alien, have referred the probate of a will to the domiciliary state, and claimed ancillary jurisdiction only over the local estate,[127] so have the German courts, generally speaking, refused to interfere with a decedent's national courts which are expected, under German conflicts rules, to apply their domestic law as *lex hereditatis* and therefore to claim primary jurisdiction in matters of succession. Like the American ancillary administration there are, however, exceptions with regard to foreign estates in Germany.

(b) *Exceptions.*—Courts and writers have admitted a number of exceptions to the general principle. These exceptions may be rationalized as follows: Even if German law does not govern a succession, the German courts may exercise jurisdiction either if the law of primary jurisdiction will recognize the German decision[128] or, as in American ancillary proceedings, if the matter to be regulated is so closely connected with Germany that a refusal of jurisdiction would seriously hamper the devolution of property situated in Germany[129] or would amount to a denial of justice.[130]

German jurisdiction has therefore by way of exception been claimed for the following purposes:

(i) securing and protecting an estate which has not yet been

---

[121] BayObLG 6 Nov. 1967, BayObLGZ 1967, 418; 7 Feb. 1958, BayObLGZ 1958, 34.

[122] BGH 26 Oct. 1967, BGHZ 49, 1; KG Berlin 24 June 1937, JW 1937, 2527; LG München 23 May 1958, IPRspr. 1958/59 no. 144.

[123] OLG Neustadt 25 May 1951, JZ 1951, 644, 645, with disapproving Note by NEUHAUS.

[124] LG Mannheim 3 Dec. 1927, IPRspr. 1928 no. 57.

[125] OLG Köln 30 Nov. 1905, RheinArch. 102 I (1906) 155, 158–159.

[126] *Cf.* Notes by NEUHAUS, JZ 1951, 646, and DROBNIG, JZ 1959, 318.

[127] *Cf.*, e.g., New York Surrogate's Court Procedure Act § 206; Callwood v. Virgin Islands National Bank, 221 F.2d 770 (3d Cir. 1955); *In re* Regensburger's Estate, 126 N.Y.S.2d 849 (Sur. Ct. 1953); *In re* Zietz's Estate, *supra* n. 120 (all are American-German cases).

[128] DÖLLE, Über einige Kernprobleme des internationalen Rechts der freiwilligen Gerichtsbarkeit, RabelsZ 27 (1962) 201, 234; NEUHAUS 245 (Zuständigkeits-Rückverweisung).

[129] DÖLLE, *supra* n. 128, at 234–35.

[130] BayObLG 2 Dec. 1965, BayObLGZ 1965, 423, 431.

accepted by the heir, or where the heir is unknown or it is uncertain whether the estate has already been accepted (§ 1960 I BGB).[131] In these cases the probate court may deposit the assets, draw up an inventory, and appoint a curator for the heir (§ 1960 II BGB);

(ii) appointing a curator for an heir where this is a prerequisite to the bringing of a court action by a creditor against the heir (§ 1961 BGB);[132]

(iii) opening a will after the testator's death (§ 2260 BGB)[133] or enforcing the delivery of a will located somewhere in Germany to the probate court (§ 2259 BGB);[134]

(iv) receiving the declaration of the heir that he will accept[135] or disclaim the inheritance (§ 1945 BGB);[136]

(v) appointing an executor (§ 2200 BGB);[137]

(vi) issuing a certificate of executorship to an executor (§ 2368 BGB, *infra* (4));[138]

(vii) issuing a certificate of inheritance (§ 2369 BGB, *infra* (3)). As certificates of inheritance are of special importance in Germany and have been the subject of several American decisions, they will be dealt with separately.

(3) Certificate of Inheritance

Because there are already several publications in English on the German certificate of inheritance (*Erbschein*),[139] the significance of this document will not be discussed in detail but merely summarized briefly.

(a) *German domestic law.*—The German certificate of inheritance is issued, upon application, to the heirs in whom, as we have seen, the estate vests upon the decedent's death (*supra* I (1)). It is

---

[131] KG Berlin 29 Dec. 1902, KGJ 25 A 241, 243 (obiter); KEGEL, Kommentar no. 59 preceding art. 24 EGBGB.

[132] KG Berlin 8 Feb. 1934, JW 1934, 909; 8 Dec. 1921, KGJ 53, 77, 79; OLG Hamburg 14 Dec. 1959, NJW 1960, 1207; OLG München 23 July 1937, JFG 16, 98, 104; LG Berlin 26 May 1961, IPRspr. 1960/61 no. 147; LG Wiesbaden 1 Feb. 1933, IPRspr. 1933 no. 59; AG Dresden 9 Nov. 1932, IPRspr. 1933 no. 58. *Obiter dicta*: BGH 26 Oct 1967, BGHZ 49, 1, 2–3; BayObLG 22 Feb. 1963, BayObLGZ 1963, 52, 54.

[133] BayObLG 19 Dec. 1919, BayObLGZ 19, 373, 376; LG Lübeck 25 Mar. 1958, IPRspr. 1958/59 no. 202; LG Bonn 22 July 1954, IPRspr. 1954/55 no. 209; LG München I 5 Sept. 1912, BayZ 1912, 405.

[134] KG Berlin 3 June 1908, KGJ 36 A 85.

[135] BayObLG 2 Dec. 1965, BayObLGZ 1965, 423, 429.

[136] *Cf.* IPG 1965–66 no. 51 (München) at 524–528.

[137] NEUHAUS, *supra* n. 126.

[138] The (international) jurisdiction in this case is based on § 2369 I BGB which, according to § 2368 III BGB, applies also to certificates of executorship. *Cf.* BayObLG 10 Nov. 1965, BayObLGZ 1965, 376, 382.

[139] BEECHER 33–34; BRESLAUER 206–209, 231–233; 1 COHN 288–290; EMMERICH 11; SCHUSTER, The Principles of German Civil Law (1907) 637–638.

designed to certify and legitimate those persons who have title to, and power to deal with, the estate (§§ 2353–2370 BGB). Therefore persons such as debtors of the decedent or buyers who deal in good faith with the persons identified by a certificate of inheritance receive statutory protection (§§ 2366, 2367 BGB). Because of this protective function of the certificate of inheritance it is nearly impossible to act as an heir in Germany without it, although it is merely declaratory in nature and may be revoked if incorrect (*infra* (b)). There are even statutes requiring that heirship be evidenced by such a certificate.[140]

(b) *German conflicts law.—*

(i) The German probate courts have jurisdiction to issue certificates of inheritance in two cases: where the succession is governed by German law (§ 2353 BGB),[141] and where property of an estate governed by foreign law is situated in Germany (§ 2369 I BGB).[142] Apart from movables and immovables located in Germany, all property for which a register is provided in Germany and claims as to which the German courts have jurisdiction (*infra* ch. 14 sub I (2)(a)) are deemed to be situated in Germany (§ 2369 II BGB). Accordingly, mortgages on German land,[143] claims against debtors residing in Germany,[144] and restitution and reparation claims against the German government,[145] have been held to be located in Germany and certificates of inheritance have been issued even where the succession was not governed by German law and the applicable foreign law did not know such a certificate.[146]

Different types of certificate of inheritance are issued in the two different situations mentioned above: the "domestic" certificate (*Eigenrechtserbschein*), which is issued if the succession is governed

---

[140] *Cf.* § 35 GBO for registration of title to real property: KG Berlin 15 Jan. 1953, JR 1954, 186. Certificates of inheritance were also important in matters of restitution and compensation for Nazi persecutions although the competent authorities could not insist on the production of certificates: OLG München 13 Mar. 1967, WM 1967, 812, 814.

[141] BayObLG 6 Nov. 1967, BayObLGZ 1967, 418, 433; 26 May 1961, *id.* 1961, 176, 181; KG Berlin 24 June 1937, JW 1937, 2527, 2529; OLG Dresden 15 Jan. 1929, JFG 6, 123, 124; LG Berlin 14 July 1941, DFG 1942, 61–62.

[142] BayObLG 13 Jan. 1961, BayObLGZ 1961, 4, 8; KG Berlin 22 Nov. 1962, IPRspr. 1962/63 no. 223; 18 Jan. 1960, IPRspr. 1960/61 no. 137; OLG Düsseldorf 24 July 1957, JMBl.NRW 1957, 202, 203; OLG Hamm 17 May 1957, *id.* 1957, 161.

[143] KG Berlin 18 May 1908, KGJ 36 A 109, 110; AG München 29 Dec. 1927, BlIntPr. 1928, 187.

[144] OLG Colmar 30 Dec. 1912, RJA 12, 210, 211.

[145] OLG Bamberg 22 Mar. 1951, JZ 1951, 510–11; OLG Düsseldorf 24 July 1957, and OLG Hamm 17 May 1957, *supra* n. 142; OLG München 13 Mar. 1967, WM 1967, 812, 813.

[146] RG 3 June 1940, HRR 1940 no. 1289; BayObLG 13 Jan. 1961, BayObLGZ 1961, 4, 15; OLG Dresden 20 Dec. 1906, OLG 14, 153, 154.

by German law,[147] and the "alien" certificate (*Fremdrechtserbschein*, § 2369 BGB).[148]

(ii) A certificate of inheritance is issued only upon application of those persons who assure the probate court of their legal interest (§ 85 FGG). These are not only the heirs but also creditors, who may, for example, want to sue the heirs upon a debt of the deceased.[149]

The formalities of the application and of the issuance of certificates are, of course, governed by German law as the *lex fori*.[150] This means that the applicant must provide detailed evidence of the time of death, the relation between the heir and the deceased, further possible heirs, the existence of a last will, and pending suits concerning the applicant's right of inheritance (§ 2354 BGB). If testate succession is alleged, the last will has to be presented (§ 2355 BGB). Most of these facts must be proved by public documents or, if they cannot be procured without great difficulty, by other evidence (§ 2356 I BGB).[151] The probate court may issue a certificate of inheritance only if it is convinced that the facts supporting the application have been established (§ 2359 BGB). For this reason it is required to procure further pertinent evidence *ex officio* (§ 2358 I BGB, *infra* ch. 14 sub II (4)(e))—that is, on its own initiative—and to refuse to grant the application if the evidence does not support it. German courts have held that if the German form is unknown abroad at the heirs' residence, compliance with other appropriate formalities is sufficient.[152] They have taken appropriate steps to discover any wills of the testator[153] and to ascertain the contents of lost wills.[154] A copy of a testament has been declared sufficient proof of the original document.[155] These examples demonstrate that the German

---

[147] *Cf.* the specimen of a domestic certificate of inheritance in BEECHER 34; 1 COHN 288; FIRSCHING, Handbuch der amtsgerichtlichen Praxis, vol. 6: Nachlassrecht (2d ed. 1960) 160–62.

[148] *Cf.* specimen in FIRSCHING, *supra* n. 147, at 162–64; and IPG 1965–66 no. 51 (München) at p. 530.

[149] OLG Dresden 25 Oct. 1932, JFG 10, 81; KEIDEL, Freiwillige Gerichtsbarkeit (9th ed. 1967) nos. 2 and 4 on § 85 FGG.

[150] BayObLG 13 Jan. 1961, BayObLGZ 1961, 4, 11–12; KG Berlin 30 Sept. 1926, JW 1927, 2316, 2317; 18 May 1908, KGJ 36 A 109, 111; OLG Hamm 18 Dec. 1963, NJW 1964, 553, 554; OLG Dresden 20 Dec. 1906, OLG 14, 153.

[151] *Cf.* the forms of application in BRESLAUER 319–323; FIRSCHING, *supra* n. 147, at 141–44.

[152] LG Berlin 27 Apr. 1951, IPRspr. 1950/51 no. 113: certification of signature (Beglaubigung) by a notary in Israel instead of the applicant's affidavit (eidesstattliche Versicherung) required by § 2356 II 1 BGB. The same will be true for certifications of American notaries.

[153] LG Berlin 31 Jan. 1966, IPRspr. 1966/67 no. 170.

[154] OLG Neustadt 29 Feb. 1952, IPRspr. 1952/53 no. 234, at 458.

[155] BayObLG 13 Jan. 1961, BayObLGZ 1961, 4, 9. In a succession case governed by New York law a New York admission to probate evidenced the validity of a New York testament: OLG München 13 Mar. 1967, WM 1967, 812, 815.

courts do not require irrefutable evidence to prove inheritance rights. This is, of course, in part due to the fact that the issuance of a certificate of inheritance is not a final adjudication of inheritance rights or of the validity of a will.

The same general attitude is taken where the recognition of foreign certificates of inheritance or similar documents is at issue. In most cases they have not been recognized as binding upon the German probate judge because they were private or public documents not binding even in the country of their origin.[156] It is also evident that foreign certificates cannot preclude independent German inquiries if a succession is governed by German law. Therefore an American certificate of heirship was not recognized for the purpose of the devolution of the German real estate of an American decedent.[157] Yet such letters or certificates do furnish prima facie evidence.[158] The situation is different only in those rare cases where, in the state whose law according to German conflicts law governs the succession, questions of inheritance have been finally adjudicated. As German conflicts law looks to the deceased's last national law as the *lex hereditatis* (*supra* II (3)(a)(i)), the German probate courts will consider themselves bound by an American probate decree rendered at the American decedent's last domicile and finally settling a dispute concerning a will.[159] The same is true as to letters granted abroad to personal representatives (*infra* (4)(e)(iii)). In addition, foreign final decrees of distribution should be recognized as binding, again on the condition that they are rendered by the state having primary jurisdiction in probate matters under German conflicts law.

(iii) The contents of an "alien" certificate of inheritance (*supra* (i)) is governed by both German law and the foreign law governing the succession. German law dictates the general contents and the purposes of the certificate:[160] it indicates the names of the heirs and their respective shares[161] and any restrictions upon their power of

---

[156] KG Berlin 18 Jan. 1960, IPRspr. 1960/61 no. 137, at 444, *aff'g* LG Berlin 12 Oct. 1959, IPRspr. 1958/59 no. 149 at 498–99; OLG Neustadt 29 Feb. 1952, IPRspr. 1952/53 no. 234, at 457 (all cases dealing with a Dutch "certificaat van erfrecht"); for an Austrian "Einantwortungsurkunde," *cf.* KG Berlin 1 July 1954, JR 1954, 464; 15 Jan. 1953, JR 1954, 186; LG München I 28 Nov. 1952, WM 1953, 37. *Cf. also* BayObLG 10 Nov. 1965, BayObLGZ 1965, 376, 383 (Spanish certificate).

[157] KG Berlin 24 June 1937, JW 1937, 2527, 2528.

[158] AG Bremen 22 Nov. 1951, IPRspr. 1950/51 no. 17, at 38; *cf. also* OLG München 13 Mar. 1967, *supra* n. 155.

[159] FERID/FIRSCHING, US Grundzüge no. 63b, p. 40/217 at no. 4.

[160] BayObLG 13 Jan. 1961, BayObLGZ 1961, 4, 9.

[161] If a certificate of inheritance mentions all heirs and their respective shares (*cf.* specimen in BEECHER 34 and 1 COHN 288) it is called "common certificate of heirship" (gemeinschaftlicher Erbschein, § 2357 BGB). Each heir, however, may

disposition (*infra* (4)(e)(i) and (iii)). The applicable foreign law, on the other hand, decides which persons are heirs, their respective shares, and any further restrictions upon their powers. The general difficulties of "translating" foreign interests into German concepts have already been shown (*supra* II (4)(c)(ii)), and these difficulties are increased by the peculiarities of the German certificate of inheritance. Apart from personal representatives (*infra* (b)), it names only heirs.[162] Therefore the German courts have to decide which interests amount to heirship under German law. Examples of interests which have failed to qualify are that of a widow who has a statutory usufruct over the estate under French law[163] and that of a personal representative under Anglo-American law,[164] whereas residuary legatees and distributees[165] and a widow with her allowance under Anglo-American law[166] have been recognized as full or partial heirs under German law.

Because of its legitimating function (*supra* (3)(a)), a certificate of inheritance has to contain every restriction imposed upon the heirs immediately at the time of the decedent's death. Therefore a certificate must state that an executor has been designated by the testator (§ 2364 BGB) so that third parties may gather from the document that it is the executor, and not the heirs, who is entitled to dispose of the estate. This provision has produced difficult questions in American-German relations because it has not always been clear whether American testamentary trustees and administrators should, like executors, be mentioned in the certificate of inheritance as persons restricting the heirs' power to dispose of the estate. The presently prevailing German practice is to permit an American executor, trustee or administrator to apply for a certificate of executor-

---

apply for a partial certificate (Teilerbschein, § 2353 BGB), which mentions only his name and his share (specimen in FIRSCHING, *supra* n. 147, at 161).

162 FERID/FIRSCHING, US Grundzüge no. 63a, at 40/215; *contra*: KEGEL, IPR 369; GOTTHEINER, RabelsZ 21 (1956) 36, 67–72.

163 BayObLG 27 Feb. 1959, IPRspr. 1960/61 no. 135; LG Frankenthal 21 Dec. 1961, *id* no. 150, at 498; *accord as to Italian law*: BayObLG 13 Jan. 1961, BayObLGZ 1961, 4, 20–21; *accord as to Belgian law*: OLG Hamm 21 July 1954, NJW 1954, 1731, 1733; *contra*: IPG 1965–66 no. 52 (Köln) at 557; no. 53 (Köln) at 573; *cf. also* IPG 1965–66 no. 47 (Hamburg) at 505 (Roumanian law); no. 48 (Hamburg) at 510 (Polish law).

164 OLG Frankfurt 25 Sept. 1958, IPRspr. 1958/59 no. 145, at 487; LG München 23 May 1958, *id.* no. 144; LG Nürnberg/Fürth 29 Dec. 1962, IPRspr. 1962/63 no. 148; IPG 1965–66 no. 61 (Hamburg) at 709; KEGEL, IPR 368; RAAPE 452; SCHWENN, NJW 1952, 1113, 1115; WENGLER, JR 1955, 41.

165 IPG 1965–66 no. 51 (München) at 530; no. 66 (Kiel) at 775; no. 67 (Köln) at 793–94; FIRSCHING, DNotZ 1960, 640, 642; *supra* preceding note.

166 KG Berlin 7 Feb. 1969, RzW 1969, 341; LG Berlin 30 June 1965, IPRspr. 1964/65 no. 170; LG Düsseldorf 2 Dec. 1960, JZ 1961, 745 with affirming Note by HENRICH; IPG 1965–66 no. 67 (Köln) at 782–83, 793; FERID/FIRSCHING, US Grundzüge no. 63a.

ship (*Testamentsvollstreckerzeugnis,* § 2368 BGB, *infra* (4)(e) and (f)) and therefore each must be mentioned in a certificate of inheritance.[167]

As has been shown above (II (3)(a)), an estate dispersed in several countries may be subject to different laws governing the local assets. A certificate of inheritance has to take account of this localization. Because the whole estate of a German decedent wherever situated is usually governed by German law exclusively, normally no local restrictions are indicated in the certificate of inheritance issued to his heirs. If, however, article 28 EGBGB regarding "special rules" (*supra* II (3)(a)) applies as, for example, where a German decedent leaves American real property, German domestic law does not govern this estate and the German courts do not claim jurisdiction (*supra* (2)(a)), and therefore the certificate of inheritance must indicate that it does not cover the real property located in the United States.[168]

If German law, by virtue of a renvoi from the decedent's personal law, governs the succession (*supra* II (3)(a)), a domestic certificate of inheritance is issued to the heirs. If this renvoi is total, meaning that it subjects all the property of the estate to German law, the certificate is the equivalent of that issued upon the death of a German. If, however, the renvoi is restricted to particular assets or types of assets, the certificate must mention these restrictions, and hence a certificate issued upon the death of a United States citizen domiciled in Germany and seized of both German and foreign real estate will be limited to the personal property wherever situated and to the realty located in Germany.[169]

If the succession is governed by foreign law, the German courts issue certificates only for the local assets (so-called "alien" certificates of inheritance, § 2369 BGB).[170] What assets are deemed to be situated in Germany is clarified by § 2369 II BGB (*supra* (3)(b)(i)).

As a warning against the risks that may arise in the application of foreign law, it is German court practice to mention in a certificate of inheritance the fact that a foreign law governs the succession.[171]

---

[167] *Executor*: IPG 1965–66 no. 67 (Köln) at 796; KEGEL, IPR 368; RAAPE 452; *trustee*: IPG 1965–66 no. 66 (Kiel) at 775; *administrator*: IPG 1965–66 no. 61 (Hamburg) at 709; KEGEL, IPR 368; *contra*: FERID/FIRSCHING, US Grundzüge no. 63a at p. 40/214; WENGLER, JR 1955, 41–42.

[168] *Cf.* BayObLG 27 Oct. 1959, BayObLGZ 1959, 390, 399–400; STAUDINGER/FIRSCHING V/2 (1960) no. 80 on § 2353 BGB at p. 1885.

[169] OLG Köln 3 Dec. 1954, NJW 1955, 755; IPG 1965–66 no. 61 (Hamburg) at 708; KEGEL, Kommentar, no. 67 preceding art. 24 EGBGB.

[170] *Cf.* KG Berlin 21 Aug. 1950, JR 1951, 762; IPG 1965–66 no. 51 (München) at 530; KG Berlin 2 July 1962, IPRspr. 1962/63 no. 144 (domestic and alien certificates of inheritance may be joined in one document); STAUDINGER/FIRSCHING V/2 (1960) no. 5 on § 2369 BGB; FIRSCHING, *supra* n. 147, at 163 (sub F VI 138) (specimen).

[171] BayObLG 13 Jan. 1961, BayObLGZ 1961, 4, 22; 26 May 1961, *id.* 176,

The adaptation of the foreign interests in the estate to German concepts, therefore, need not be carried to an extreme.

(iv) The fact that the German courts issue certificates of inheritance implies jurisdiction to cancel them if incorrect.[172] This brings into focus another peculiarity of these German certificates. Normally they are not res judicata because they are not issued following a formal proceeding where all interested parties have an opportunity to be heard. So a certificate may turn out to be incorrect because another will has been discovered or a missing heir has appeared or the law has been misapplied. Moreover the recent decision of the Federal Constitutional Court on the nationality of political refugees from Germany[173] (*supra* ch. 3 at n. 39a) may vitiate many certificates of inheritance issued to former German nationals because the courts have applied foreign rather than German succession law. In all these cases the certificate has to be revoked *ex officio* (§ 2361 BGB) and a new one substituted upon application.[174] On the other hand, innocent third parties who have transacted business with the heirs named in an incorrect certificate will be protected (§§ 2366, 2367 BGB), and final adjudications of the rights of different persons to inherit will be upheld (§§ 95 III 3, 79 II BVerfGG).[175]

(c) *German certificates of inheritance abroad.*—Because German certificates of inheritance are not final adjudications, they should not be recognized abroad as conclusive. American courts have therefore properly attributed merely prima facie value to these documents when deciding the order of succession under German law,[176] or who is the proper person to designate an American ancillary administrator.[177] But it should also be remembered that the probative force of the German certificate of inheritance is restricted to persons in good faith (*supra* (a)). Under German law an innocent foreigner, such as an American bank, is protected if it pays to the person who, according to a German certificate, is entitled to receive payments directly as heir of the estate. Whether the foreign creditor is validly

---

182–83; OLG Düsseldorf 6 Feb. 1963, NJW 1963, 2227, 2230; IPG 1965–66 no. 51 (München) at 530; KEGEL, IPR 368; FERID/FIRSCHING, US Grundzüge no. 63a.

[172] LG Berlin 31 Jan. 1966, *supra* n. 153; AG München 29 Dec. 1927, BlIntPr. 1928, 187, 188.

[173] BVerfG 14 Feb. 1968, BVerfGE 23, 98.

[174] DIERK MÜLLER, RabelsZ 32 (1968) 676, 684; *cf.* older cases: OLG Hamm 18 Dec. 1963, NJW 1964, 553, 554; AG München 29 Dec. 1927, *supra* n. 172.

[175] The general impact of a final adjudication of inheritance claims on a certificate of inheritance is set out in STAUDINGER/FIRSCHING V/2 (1960) nos. 8–11 on § 2360 BGB.

[176] Vogel v. New York Life Ins. Co., 55 F.2d 205, 209 (5th Cir.), *cert. denied,* 287 U.S. 604 (1932); *cf. also In re* Fahs' Estate, 33 Misc.2d 796, 797, 226 N.Y.S.2d 230, 232 (Sur. Ct. 1962).

[177] *In re* Regensburger's Estate, *supra* note 127, at 851.

discharged under his own law depends upon that law's recognition of the legitimating force of the German certificate. Recognition will probably be refused in the United States if a German dies domiciled there since a different law governs succession to movables according to the conflicts rules of the two countries: in Germany the German national law, and in the United States the "American" domiciliary law.[178]

(4) **Administration**

(a) *German domestic law.*—German law has no institution like the Anglo-American administration of estates. Although it is true that a testator may provide for an executor (*Testamentsvollstrecker*) and that the estate may be administered for the creditors by an administrator (*Nachlassverwalter*) or a trustee in bankruptcy (*Konkursverwalter*) (*supra* I (1)), neither domiciliary nor ancillary administration is compulsory under German law. It is entirely up to the heirs and creditors of the estate to protect their own interests by appropriate means (*infra* (f) and (g)). This has to be kept in mind where problems of adaptation of American law to German concepts (especially *infra* (e) and (f)) are in issue.

(b) *Treaty provisions as to information and safekeeping.*—According to article XXIV (1) of the Friendship Treaty of 1923 the High Contracting Parties are obliged in certain cases to inform the nearest consular officer of the death of a national of the sending country. It is the domestic law of the parties which takes care that this duty to notify will be fulfilled.[179] In Germany civil registrars are obliged to give such information and furnish a certificate of death to the competent foreign consul even if the deceased leaves known heirs or executors in Germany.[180] This obligation insures that American consulates will be informed if any American dies in Germany.

If a national of either state dies intestate in the territory of the other, "the consular officer of the State of which the deceased was a national and within whose district the deceased made his home at the time of death, shall, so far as the laws of the country permit and pending the appointment of an administrator and until letters of administration have been granted, be deemed qualified to take charge of the property left by the decedent for the preservation and protection of the same" (art. XXIV (2) sent. 1 Treaty of 1923). This provision does not alter the domestic law of the parties. German

---

[178] *In re* Dankerl's Estate, 16 Misc.2d 751, 185 N.Y.S.2d 475 (Sur. Ct. 1959), *aff'd*, 12 A.D.2d 678, 207 N.Y.S.2d 514 (1960).

[179] As to American state law, *cf.* BOYD, Constitutional, Treaty, and Statutory Requirements of Probate Notice to Consuls and Aliens, 47 Iowa L. Rev. 29, 52–65 (1961).

[180] §§ 113 (1) no. 3, 117 DA (1968), formerly § 304 DA (1958).

consuls, who are empowered by German law to take care of German estates in foreign countries,[181] must comply with America state law. United States consuls, authorized by detailed American provisions,[182] must look at German law to ascertain whether they are qualified for provisional safekeeping. This will be the case if the heirs are unknown or if the creditors want to sue unknown heirs, and the probate court has to appoint a curator (*Nachlasspfleger*) or take other appropriate measures for protection of the estate (§§ 1960, 1961 BGB). Under these circumstances the German courts have jurisdiction irrespective of any foreign law governing the succession (*supra* (2)(b)) but they will abstain from exercising it if the foreign consul decides to assume the responsibility for the estate.[183]

(c) *German conflicts law in general.*—With respect to jurisdiction the same general principles apply as for testamentary succession (*supra* (2)(a)): the German courts have jurisdiction if German law governs the estate. Nearly all matters of administration are governed by the *lex hereditatis* (*supra* II (3)(a)); these include the scope of the estate,[184] the obligations to be paid out of the estate,[185] the status of personal representatives,[186] the liability for the decedent's debts,[187] and the relations among the heirs.[188] The German courts have issued domestic certificates of executorship to executors[189] and have enforced a partition among several heirs[190] where German law governed. On the other hand, they have declined, where foreign law controlled, to

---

181 § 18 KonsG., BGBl. III 27–1; *English translation*: 1 FELLER/HUDSON, A Collection of the Diplomatic and Consular Laws and Regulations of Various Countries (1933) 550–54. The old general service instructions are reprinted in English translation in 1 FELLER/HUDSON, *supra,* at 554–60.

182 22 U.S.C. §§ 1175–1179 (1964 ed.); 22 C.F.R. §§ 71.1–72.55 (1969).

183 KG Berlin 29 Dec. 1902, KGJ 25 A 241, 243; PINCKERNELLE *in* KNUR/VAN RANDENBORGH/DUMOULIN/PINCKERNELLE 289 and 384; BRAND/KLEEFF, Nachlasssachen in der gerichtlichen Praxis (2d ed. 1961) 570.

184 KEGEL, Kommentar, no. 7 preceding art. 24 EGBGB; *infra* (d).

185 OLG Celle 21 July 1966, VersR 1967, 164, 165; KEGEL, Kommentar, no. 21 preceding art. 24 EGBGB; *infra* (g).

186 BGH 3 Oct. 1962, NJW 1963, 46, 47; 25 May 1955, IPRspr. 1954/55 no. 135, at 392; RG 25 Jan. 1888, HansGZ 1888 Hbl. 174; BayObLG 10 Nov. 1965, BayObLGZ 1965, 376, 382, 386.

187 BGH 5 Feb. 1954, IPRspr. 1954/55 no. 197, at 558; 26 Mar. 1953, BGHZ 9, 151, 154 (obiter); BayObLG 2 Dec. 1965, BayObLGZ 1965, 423, 437; *infra* (g).

188 BGH 10 June 1968, WM 1968, 1170, 1171; 29 Jan. 1964, WM 1964, 348, 349; RG 5 Nov. 1928, JW 1929, 434; RFH 5 July 1929, LZ 1930, 60; OLG Nürnberg 20 Oct. 1964, AWD 1965, 93; LG Frankenthal 21 Dec. 1961, RzW 1962, 277; *infra* (5).

189 KG Berlin 13 May 1912, KGJ 42, 141; LG Wiesbaden 18 Jan. 1960, IPRspr. 1960/61 no. 138 at 447; *cf. also* LG Frankfurt/M. 25 Oct. 1935, JW 1936, 1154; *infra* (e).

190 LG Koblenz 17 July 1958, JZ 1959, 316, 317.

appoint[191] or to discharge[192] an executor, to appoint an administrator (*Nachlassverwalter*),[193] to dissolve a community of heirs by partition,[194] or to take care of foreign real estate.[195] Some of these decisions failed to take into account the fact that the German courts could properly claim jurisdiction if the foreign state would recognize German court action,[196] and that they should exercise jurisdiction if their refusal to do so would amount to a denial of justice[197] (*supra* (2)(b)). As will be shown later, the modern German tendency is to display less reluctance to take jurisdiction, and to strive to decide cases on substantive grounds by paying heed to the directions of the foreign governing law and adapting foreign concepts to domestic procedure.[198]

(d) *Estate and matrimonial property.*—The *lex hereditatis* (*supra* II (3)(a)) not only governs the distribution of the estate, but at the same time decides what assets are part of it[199] and what claims may be brought against it. The second question has been answered several times, especially with regard to funeral expenses,[200] whereas the first has been dealt with in connection with savings-bank trusts and marital property.

In two cases the Federal Supreme Court had to determine whether a savings-bank account, which was a Totten trust created by the decedent with an American bank in favor of third parties, was part of the decedent's estate.[201] The court did not question the general principle that it is the *lex hereditatis* which decides the composition of an estate, but under German law as *lex fori* it qualified these savings-bank trusts as donations *inter vivos* governed by American state law which governed the relations between the deceased as settlor and the bank as trustee.[202] Therefore the trusts were not

---

[191] OLG Neustadt 25 May 1951, JZ 1951, 644, 645, with disapproving Note by NEUHAUS.

[192] KG Berlin 11 July 1911, KGJ 41, 62, 67–68.

[193] LG Schwerin 6 May 1902, NiemeyersZ 13 (1903) 174, 176, *aff'd*, OLG Rostock 16 Dec. 1902, *id.* 177.

[194] OLG Köln 30 Nov. 1905, RheinArch. 102 I (1906) 155, 158–159; *cf. also* AG Stuttgart 10 Jan. 1913, WürttZ 55 (1913) 204–205.

[195] BayObLG 27 Oct. 1959, BayObLGZ 1959, 390, 398; OLG Dresden 7 Feb. 1914, KGJ 47, 238, 239.

[196] NEUHAUS, JZ 1951, 646.

[197] BayObLG 2 Dec. 1965, BayObLGZ 1965, 423, 429–431.

[198] BayObLG, preceding note; IPG 1965–66 no. 46 (München) at 494.

[199] BGH 15 Apr. 1959, WM 1959, 662, 663 (obiter); KEGEL, Kommentar, no. 7 preceding art. 7 EGBGB.

[200] OLG Celle 21 July 1966, VersR 1967, 164, 165; OLG Colmar 13 July 1914, ElsLothZ 40 (1915) 355–356; *cf. also* BGH 19 Feb. 1960, DAR 1960, 179. KEGEL, Kommentar, no. 21 preceding art. 24 EGBGB.

[201] BGH 10 June 1968, WM 1968, 1170; 15 Apr. 1959, *supra* n. 199; *cf. also* BGH 29 Jan. 1964, WM 1964, 348.

[202] BGH: 10 June 1968, *supra* n. 201, at 1172; 15 Apr. 1959, *supra* n. 199, at 662.

part of the estate. There are, however, grave doubts about this qualification. Closer analysis reveals that such Totten trusts should be considered as donations *mortis causa* and hence as part of the estate,[203] and therefore the two decisions are not persuasive on this point, although they can be justified on other grounds.[204]

The demarcation between the law governing succession and the law governing marital property is one of the most difficult problems in German conflicts law. Succession is governed by the decedent's last national law (*supra* II (3)(a)), while marital property questions are immutably governed by the husband's national law at the time of marriage (*supra* ch. 4 sub A IV (1)(a)). Two examples may illustrate the problems arising from this divergence and also the possible solutions.

German spouses who emigrate to the United States, settle in California, and become United States citizens still live, according to German conflicts law and at least as to their movable property, under German marital property law. In the United States, however, their movable estate is governed by their California domiciliary law. This situation could cause serious injustice if the German marital law failed to provide for the surviving spouse and if the California decedents' law also neglected him on the ground that California's marital property law normally affords sufficient protection to spouses. In order to escape this preposterous result, the German courts have qualified § 201.5 of the California Probate Code as a rule of succession and by this means have reached the same result as a California probate court would reach.[205]

The new statutory marital property régime introduced in Germany in 1957 is dissolved and liquidated on the death of one spouse by increasing the surviving spouse's statutory share by adding one-quarter of the estate (§ 1371 I BGB).[206] It has been held that this increase will be effectuated only if the spouses have lived under the statutory régime of the "community of surplus" (§§ 1363–1390 BGB).[207] It is still controversial whether the increase of the surviving spouse's statutory share depends upon the application of German

---

203 Knauer, Note to BGH 15 Apr. 1959, *supra* n. 199, RabelsZ 25 (1960) 318, 332.

204 In BGH 15 Apr. 1959, *supra* n. 199, the *lex hereditatis* was identical with the *lex contractus;* in BGH 10 June 1968, *supra* n. 201, the duty to adjust advancements was affirmed so that the same result was reached as if the trust formed part of the estate.

205 OLG Celle 10 Sept. 1959, RzW 1960, 235; *cf. also* BayObLG 31 Mar. 1966, BayObLGZ 1966, 115, 124; Erlanger, RzW 1958, 206, and *id.* 1959, 55; Ettisch, RzW 1958, 381.

206 1 Cohn no. 518; Leyser, 7 Am.J.Comp.L. 276, 284–286 (1958).

207 BayObLG 28 Mar. 1961, BayObLGZ 1961, 123, 132; OLG Frankfurt 7 Nov. 1961, IPRspr. 1960/61 no. 101b, at 350.

succession law.[208] Be this as it may, the net result for American spouses who have German real property may be summarized as follows: As there is a renvoi to the German *lex situs* from American marital property law (*supra* ch. 4 sub A IV (2)(a)(i)) as well as from American succession law (*supra* II (3)(a)), the surviving spouse under both German marital property and German succession law will get one-half as his statutory share of the German real estate, if there are also surviving children (§§ 1931, 1371 I BGB).

If conflicts between marital property law and the law of succession cannot be harmonized by interpretation of a will[209] or by qualification,[210] the whole matter of property claims of the surviving spouse should be subjected to a functional approach under the *lex hereditatis*.[211]

(e) *Executors, trustees and certificate of executorship.*—German domestic law, too, provides for an executor (*Testamentsvollstrecker, supra* I (1)). He has to carry out the testator's last will (§ 2203 BGB) and to see to the division of the estate between the heirs and thereby the dissolution of their community (§ 2204 BGB). He is not obliged to pay the creditors, but they may sue him (§ 2213 BGB), as he in turn may sue the debtors of the estate (§ 2212 BGB). The heir is not entitled to dispose of the estate. The executor alone can administer it. In order to certify to his position as executor a letter of executorship (*Testamentsvollstreckerzeugnis*) will be issued to him by the probate court upon application (§ 2368 BGB). This certificate, like American letters testamentary, has the same function as the certificate of inheritance (*supra* (3)). It furnishes prima facie proof of the executor's power to dispose of the estate, bring actions, and receive payments due to the estate. Third parties will be protected if they rely in good faith on a letter of executorship (§§ 2368 III, 2366, 2367 BGB).[212] It must also be stated in the certificate of inheritance that an executor has been appointed so that the heir will not be deemed authorized to dispose of the estate (*supra* (3)(b)(iii)).

According to German conflicts law the *lex hereditatis* governs all issues concerning an executor and his duties and powers except procedural questions.[213] It is this law which decides whether he has

---

[208] *Cf.* Eike von Hippel, RabelsZ 32 (1968) 348–351; IPG 1965–66 no. 56 (Köln) at 626–628.

[209] LG Augsburg 18 Mar. 1957, IPRspr. 1956/57 no. 144.

[210] RG 16 Mar. 1938, JW 1938, 1718; cases *supra* n. 205.

[211] Neuhaus 82.

[212] Beecher 36; Breslauer 206–209; 1 Cohn 289; *generally on German executors*: Beecher 34–36; 1 Cohn 280–282; Wormser/Burchard, Administration of German Decedents' Estates, 83 U.Pa.L.Rev. 37, 40–45 (1934).

[213] *Supra* n. 186.

been validly appointed,[214] whether the testator may substitute another law as governing law,[215] whether the executor or the heir alone or one with the consent of the other may dispose of the estate,[216] whether he may sue debtors in the German courts,[217] and whether his successor qualifies to succeed him.[218] Under the general principle of jurisdiction in matters of succession (*supra* (2)(a)), the German courts assume international jurisdiction if German substantive law is the *lex hereditatis.* In these cases a domestic certificate of executorship will be issued to the executor.[219] On the other hand, if a foreign law applies, the courts have shown reluctance to appoint or discharge executors[220] even though the foreign authority would have approved of the German exercise of jurisdiction, which therefore should have occurred under the exceptional rule mentioned above (*supra* (2)(b) at n. 128).[221] By express statutory provision, however, it is made clear that the German probate courts must issue an "alien" certificate of executorship (§§ 2368 III 1, 2369 BGB, *beschränktes Testamentsvollstreckerzeugnis*) which, like the alien certificate of inheritance (*supra* (3)(b)(iii) at n. 168), is expressly restricted to property located in Germany (§§ 2368 III, 2369 I BGB)[222] and indicates the law governing the administration.[223] As executors, like heirs, need certificates for most of their activities in Germany,[224] these will be issued whether or not they are known to the *lex hereditatis.*[225] The application for and issuance of a certificate of executorship as matters of procedure are of course governed by the German *lex fori*[226] (*see supra* (3)(b)(ii) at n. 150).

Besides the need for a certificate of executorship as evidence, German law as the *lex fori* poses no restrictions on foreign executors;

---

214 LG München 23 May 1958, IPRspr. 1958/59 no. 144 at 479; BayObLG 10 Nov. 1965, BayObLGZ 1965, 376, 387 (obiter).

215 KG Berlin 11 July 1911, KGJ 41, 62, 64.

216 BGH 29 Jan. 1964, WM 1964, 348, 349; 3 Oct. 1962, NJW 1963, 46, 47.

217 OLG Hamburg 14 Dec. 1955, IPRspr. 1954/55 no. 63 at 185; 1 Oct. 1887, HansGZ 1887 Hbl. 289, *aff'd,* RG 25 Jan. 1888, HansGZ 1888 Hbl. 174; OLG Tübingen 8 Jan. 1953, RzW 1953, 335.

218 OLG Dresden 22 Oct. 1919, JW 1920, 661.

219 *Supra* n. 189. Specimen of such a certificate in BEECHER 36; FIRSCHING, *supra* n. 147, at 192 sub F VI 165.

220 *Supra* n. 191 and n. 192.

221 NEUHAUS, *supra* n. 196.

222 *Cf.* LG München 23 May 1958, *supra* n. 214, at 482; IPG 1965–66 no. 58 (Köln) at 678 (specimen of an alien certificate of executorship).

223 LG München 23 May 1958, IPRspr. 1958/59 no. 144 at 482; KG Berlin 18 May 1908, KGJ 36 A 109, 113; IPG 1965–66 no. 58 (Köln) at 678; no. 67 (Köln) at 794; KEGEL, IPR 369; RAAPE 452.

224 LG Frankfurt/M. 25 Oct. 1935, JW 1936, 1154, 1155.

225 BayObLG 10 Nov. 1965, BayObLGZ 1965, 376, 388–389.

226 BayObLG 10 Nov. 1965, *supra* n. 225, at 382–383, 386; KG Berlin 18 May 1908, *supra* n. 223, at 113; LG München 23 May 1958, IPRspr. 1958/59 no. 144 at 482.

more particularly, it does not deny to them standing to sue. This liberality, in contrast to American law (*infra* (5)), is to be explained by the fact that German succession law does not require probate courts *ex officio* to protect local creditors of the estate (*supra* (a)) and hence there is no need to supervise a foreign executor and therefore to require the additional appointment of a local administrator.

American executors have, without exception, been recognized by the German courts as personal representatives with power to act even respecting an estate located in Germany.[227] If German domestic law applies by renvoi, they are regarded as entitled to apply for a domestic certificate of executorship which, of course, like the corresponding domestic certificate of inheritance (*supra* (3)(b)(iii)), is limited to the property to be distributed according to German domestic law.[228] If foreign law applies, an alien certificate of executorship will be issued to the American executors, expressly limited to property located in Germany.[229] The only controversial point is whether the certificate should mention the fact that it is American state law which governs the administration. In practice this indication is usually given because the power of an American executor under American law is thought to extend to German movable property if, as in Germany, the *lex situs* does not require an ancillary administration to satisfy local creditors first.[230] Therefore New York letters testamentary have been held sufficient evidence to prove a New York executor's right to receive a certificate of executorship in Germany.[231]

An American executor, by way of exception, was refused recognition in Germany as personal representative where he was, at the same time, the sole heir.[232] In this case the executor was recognized as heir only, and a certificate of inheritance without restrictions as to administration was issued to him. The reason for this result is the German system of distribution without supervised administration for

---

[227] OLG Frankfurt 25 Sept. 1958, IPRspr. 1958/59 no. 145 at 487; OLG Tübingen 8 Jan. 1953, RzW 1953, 335; LG München 23 May 1958, IPRspr. 1958/59 no. 144 at 481; *cf. also* LG Nürnberg/Fürth 29 Dec. 1962, IPRspr. 1962/63 no. 148; IPG 1965–66 no. 62 (München) at 725–726; no. 66 (Kiel) at 770, 775; *English executors*: *cf.* BGH 17 Oct. 1968, WM 1969, 72, 73; 19 June 1967, IPRspr. 1966/67 no. 168b, *aff'g* OLG Frankfurt/M. 22 Sept. 1965, *id.* no. 168a; OLG Dresden 22 Oct. 1919, JW 1920, 661; OLG Hamburg 14 Dec. 1955 and 1 Oct. 1887, *supra* n. 217; Klingenstein v. Maier, Recueil IV (1925) 6, 9.

[228] *Cf. supra* n. 219.

[229] *Cf. supra* n. 222.

[230] LG München 23 May 1958, IPRspr. 1958/59 no. 144 at 482; KEGEL, IPR 369; RAAPE 452; *contra*: STAUDINGER/FIRSCHING V/2 (1960) no. 34 on § 2368 BGB at 1954.

[231] LG München 23 May 1958, *supra* n. 230, at 481.

[232] OLG München 13 Mar. 1967, WM 1967, 812, 815.

the protection of creditors and certain types of beneficiaries; it would make no sense if the sole heir (or heirs as a group) were permitted only to exercise the powers of an executor. Since the German courts do not supervise an executor acting under a foreign *lex hereditatis* and do not enforce his obligations, the position of an heir-executor under American law is equivalent to that of an heir in Germany unrestricted by administration. This, however, is only true if the executor is the sole heir or all the heirs are also executors. If an executor gets only a small portion of the estate as beneficiary or residuary legatee, he will be recognized as executor and, if he qualifies as an heir under the German concept, he will be mentioned as heir in a certificate of inheritance, but an heir who is restricted by the existence of an executorship.[233]

An American trustee has been recognized in Germany as a so-called "long-term" executor (*Dauertestamentsvollstrecker*, § 2209 BGB) if under American law he administers the estate.[234] As such, he is entitled to a certificate of executorship.[235] Whether he must also be mentioned as provisional heir (*Vorerbe*) or as absolute heir (*Vollerbe*) in the certificate of inheritance, or is to be regarded as a legatee (*Vermächtnisnehmer*) only, is another question. The answer requires a careful interpretation of the will itself.[236]

That German executors receive different treatment in the United States from the treatment accorded to American executors in Germany can be easily explained by the different procedures for liquidation of decedents' estates. The differences, however, are not serious and do not create difficult problems. Although foreign executors normally cannot sue local debtors of the estate in the United States, they can do so if there are no local creditors or beneficiaries whose interests might be violated by the unsupervised collection of assets by an executor not appointed by the local probate court.[237] Apart from these exceptional circumstances, executors appointed in Germany are held entitled to appointment by American courts as ancillary administrators c.t.a. or, if they lack capacity as non-resident aliens, are permitted to designate a qualified person of their choice as ancillary administrator of the American estate.[238]

---

233 OLG Frankfurt 22 Sept. 1965 and BGH 19 June 1967, both *supra* n. 227.

234 OLG Frankfurt 29 Dec. 1962, IPRspr. 1962/63 no. 146; 25 Sept. 1958, IPRspr. 1958/59 no. 145 at 487; LG Wiesbaden 18 Jan. 1960, IPRspr. 1960/61 no. 138; IPG 1965–66 no. 66 (Kiel) at 774–75; *cf. also* OLG Frankfurt 22 Sept. 1965, and BGH 17 Oct. 1968 and 19 June 1967, all *supra* n. 227.

235 OLG Frankfurt 29 Dec. 1962 and 25 Sept. 1958, and LG Wiesbaden 18 Jan. 1960, all *supra* n. 234; *contra*: FIRSCHING 143.

236 *Cf.* cases *supra* n. 234 and FIRSCHING 139–44; FERID/FIRSCHING, US Grundzüge no. 63b at p. 40/218.

237 Callwood v. Virgin Islands National Bank, *supra* n. 127, at 778.

238 Vogel v. New York Life Ins. Co., *supra* n. 176, at 208–09; *In re* Zietz's Estate, 198 Misc. 77, 21, 96 N.Y.S.2d 442, 445 (Sur. Ct. 1950); *In re* Schrader's

(f) *Administration by administrators.*—Under article XXIV (2) sentence 2 of the Friendship Treaty of 1923 the consular officer qualified to preserve and protect his countrymen's estates according to sentence 1 "shall have the right to be appointed as administrator within the discretion of a tribunal or other agency controlling the administration of estates provided the laws of the place where the estate is administered so permit." In the United States this provision of the Treaty of 1923 and similar treaty provisions have given rise to the question whether a foreign consul has an actionable right to be appointed administrator of his countrymen's estate upon his application.[239] This question has been correctly answered in the negative because article XXIV (2) sentence 2 of the Treaty of 1923 expressly subjects the consul's eligibility for appointment as administrator to the court's discretion and the permission of the *lex rei sitae.*[240] Even the most-favored-nation clause (art. XVII (2) sent. 1) failed to support the consul's "right" to be appointed administrator[241] because no treaty of the United States could be shown to grant such an actionable right to a foreign consul.[242] In Germany, article XXIV (2) sentence 2 seems to have played no rôle whatsoever, which can easily be explained by the fact that German domestic law does not require administration of decedents' estates (*supra* I (1)).

The position of American administrators in German law is subject to general principles: the *lex hereditatis* decides whether and under what circumstances an administrator is needed and what his powers are. The German courts, in principle, do not claim jurisdiction unless German law applies (*supra* (4)(c)). As a result, they take no notice of the existence of the American administration of a succession governed by German law because, as we have seen, German domestic law does not know administration of the Anglo-American type (*supra* (4)(a)). If the American administration is ancillary, their reluctance can, in addition, be explained by the territorially limited nature of such a proceeding. But the German courts will also refuse to recognize the domiciliary administrator of a German national and will issue a domestic certificate of inheritance to the heirs who qualify under German succession law. Where, on the other hand, American law applies and also governs all matters of administration

---

Estate, 196 Misc. 400, 402, 92 N.Y.S.2d 160, 161 (Sur. Ct. 1949); *In re* Warburg's Estate, 129 Misc. 832, 834, 223 N.Y. Supp. 780, 782 (Sur. Ct. 1927); *cf. also* Horn v. Vasen, 263 App. Div. 669, 34 N.Y.2d 265 (1942).

[239] *Cf.* Boyd, Consular Functions in Connection with Decedents' Estates, 47 Iowa L. Rev. 823, 840–42 (1962).

[240] Schneider v. Hawkins, 179 Md. 21, 25, 16 A.2d 861, 864 (1940); *but cf.* Seaboard Trust Co. v. Topken, 130 N.J.E. 46, 51, 20 A.2d 709, 712 (1941).

[241] Schneider v. Hawkins, *supra* n. 240, 179 Md. at 26–29, 16 A.2d at 864–65.

[242] *Cf.* Boyd, *supra* n. 239, at 840–42.

except mere procedural questions, there has been considerable uncertainty about the recognition in Germany of the American domiciliary administrator as personal representative. It has been argued that the powers of an American domiciliary administrator are restricted to the property located in the state of his appointment,[243] but practice, however, seems to recognize American domiciliary administrators as having extra-territorial powers under American law and to grant certificates of executorship to them even if they are aliens.[244] These certificates are issued with the same restrictions as those issued to executors (*supra* (e)): they are confined to property located in Germany and they mention that the administration is governed by the law of the American state where the decedent was last domiciled.[245] The certificate of inheritance indicates that the powers of the heirs are limited by the American administration.[246] The argument that in order to protect local creditors[247] foreign administrators should not be recognized in Germany is unjustified; it rests mainly on certain shortcomings of German succession law.

(g) *Liability for decedent's debts.*—Although this question is generally governed by the *lex hereditatis,* too,[248] article 24 II EGBGB provides that the heirs may also take advantage of the law of the deceased's last foreign domicile.[249] This provision is a reasonable exception to Germany's general rule that the decedent's last national law governs the succession (*supra* II (3)(a)(ii)), and is of special importance for American-German relations. According to article 24 II EGBGB, the heirs of a German national who dies domiciled in the United States may oppose a creditor's claim on the ground it is barred by the American final decree of distribution. This, however, does not deprive the creditor of a claim with respect to German real property because this would not be included in the American probate proceeding.[250]

If a succession is subject to foreign law, intervention by the

---

243 FIRSCHING 107; *id.*, DNotZ 1960, 640, 643; FERID/FIRSCHING, US Grundzüge no. 55d.

244 Opinion no. 131/58 of July 25, 1958, of the Max-Planck Institute of Foreign and Private International Law in Hamburg and standing practice of the Institute; GOTTHEINER, RabelsZ 21 (1956) 36, 69 at n. 125; *accord*: KEGEL, IPR 369; *contra*: FIRSCHING 130; PINCKERNELLE *in* KNUR/VAN RANDENBORGH/DUMOULIN/PINCKERNELLE 286 and 381; RAAPE 453; SCHWENN, NJW 1952, 1113, 1116.

245 Opinion no. 131/58, *supra* n. 244. *Cf. also supra* nn. 222 and 223.

246 IPG 1965–66 no. 51 (München) at 530; GOTTHEINER, *supra* n. 244, at 70; KEGEL, IPR 368; *cf. also* PINCKERNELLE *in* KNUR/VAN RANDENBORGH/DUMOULIN/PINCKERNELLE 286 and 381; *contra*: FERID/FIRSCHING, US Grundzüge no. 63a.

247 STAUDINGER/FIRSCHING V/2 (1960) no. 34 on § 2368 BGB at 1953, with reference to AG München, VI 8416/59, and DNotZ 1960, 643.

248 *Supra* n. 187; KEGEL, Kommentar, no. 21 preceding art. 24 EGBGB.

249 OLG Hamburg 8 Mar. 1911, OLG 24, 59, 60–61.

250 LG Kassel 25 Sept. 1958, IPRspr. 1958/59 no. 146.

German courts is restricted. They may, according to the exceptions mentioned above (*supra* (2)(b)), take steps to protect the estate[251] or appoint a curator for an heir in order that a creditor may sue for his claim against the estate.[252] They may also establish an inventory of an estate so that the heirs of an Italian decedent, for example, may limit their liability according to Italian law.[253] The German probate courts, however, seem never to have assumed jurisdiction to administer a foreign estate exclusively in favor of local creditors before handing the residue over to a foreign personal representative. But it does not seem out of the question that a German court might order an administration (*Nachlassverwaltung*, § 1981 BGB) or open a bankruptcy proceeding (*Nachlasskonkurs*, §§ 214, 238 KO, *infra* ch. 14 sub IV) if the factual prerequisites for such steps under German law were met.[254] The procedure in such a liquidation of the German estate would be governed, like all procedural questions, by the German *lex fori*.

If there is no basis for such an extreme step to be taken against a bankrupt estate, the German courts are, apart from the above-mentioned exceptions, not entitled to act in favor of local heirs. Therefore they cannot refuse to recognize an American domiciliary administrator with the argument that he will collect the local estate and transfer it abroad without first satisfying local creditors. An heir of a foreign decedent has the same right. The creditors have to protect their own interests. This can be done quickly by an "injunction of attachment" (*infra* ch. 14 sub II (6)), which may be brought if the foreign heir or his personal representative is about to transfer the local assets or their proceeds abroad without having first satisfied local creditors. In this case no further reason need be pleaded to justify the application for this injunction (§ 917 II ZPO). The mere fact, however, that there is a foreign heir of a local estate which is insufficient to satisfy all the local creditors does not entitle a creditor to attach the local assets.[255]

(5) Distribution and Plurality of Heirs

Several heirs under German domestic law form a special community (§ 2032 BGB, *supra* I (1)). This relation between several heirs, like similar communities under foreign laws, is also governed by the *lex hereditatis*.[256] Therefore this law decides the structure of

---

[251] *Supra* n. 131.

[252] *Supra* n. 132.

[253] *Supra* n. 197.

[254] KEGEL, Kommentar, no. 55 preceding art. 24 EGBGB; *contra*: PINCKERNELLE *in* KNUR/VAN RANDENBORGH/DUMOULIN/PINCKERNELLE 295 and 390–91 at n. 1, with further references.

[255] LG Stuttgart 12 Sept. 1956, headnote in IPRspr. 1956/57 no. 208.

[256] *Supra* n. 188.

the community,[257] the rights of its members, the grounds for dissolution, and the reciprocal claims of the heirs to adjust advancements made by the deceased.[258]

With respect to jurisdiction no special problems exist. The German courts have assumed jurisdiction to dissolve a community of heirs where German law governed the succession[259] and have declined to act where foreign law applied,[260] although the foreign jurisdiction would not have opposed German court action.[261]

According to article XXV of the Friendship Treaty of 1923 a "consular officer of either High Contracting Party may on behalf of his non-resident countrymen receipt for their distributive shares derived from estates in process of probate or accruing under the provisions of so-called Workmen's Compensation Laws or other like statutes provided he remit any funds so received through the appropriate agencies of his Government to the proper distributees, and provided further that he furnish to the authority or agency making distribution through him reasonable evidence of such remission." In Germany this provision seems to have raised no problems. In the United States, however, either this or the identical provision in another treaty has been litigated several times. Where consuls have invoked their right to receive payment despite the existence of the so-called "benefit" or "Iron Curtain" statutes, the United States courts seem unanimously to have held that such a treaty provision entitles a consul to receipt only if he can furnish evidence convincing to the probate court that the beneficiary will get the full benefit of his distributive share transmitted by the consul.[262] With respect to West Germany, of course, the benefit statutes are no longer applied (*supra* II (2)), and because of the most-favored-nation clause (Friendship Treaty of 1923 art. XVII (2) sent. 1) perhaps should not be applied.[263] Whether the same will be true as to East Germany depends mainly on the American attitude towards West German consular functions with regard to East German residents (*supra* (1)(a)).

---

[257] LG Frankenthal 21 Dec. 1961, RzW 1962, 277, *aff'd*, OLG Neustadt 6 Mar. 1962, RzW 1962, 374.

[258] BGH 10 June 1968, WM 1968, 1170, 1171–72.

[259] LG Koblenz 17 July 1958, JZ 1959, 316, 317.

[260] OLG Köln 30 Nov. 1905, RheinArch. 102 I (1906) 155, 158–59.

[261] *Cf.* Drobnig, JZ 1959, 317, 318.

[262] *In re* Weidberg's Estate, 172 Misc. 524, 529–30, 15 N.Y.S.2d 252, 257–58 (Sur. Ct. 1939); *cf.* Boyd, Invalidity of State Statutes Governing the Share of Nonresident Aliens in Decedents' Estates, 51 Geo. L. J. 470, 500–09 (1963); *id.*, The Administration in the United States of Alien Connected Decedents' Estates, 2 Int'l Lawyer 601, 644–49 (1968). In Zschernig v. Miller, *supra* n. 115, however, the Supreme Court of Oregon did not apply the Oregon benefit provision, as violating the treaty guaranty of inheritance rights (243 Ore. at 584, 412 P.2d at 790).

[263] *Cf.* Mentula *v.* State Land Board, 244 Ore. 229, 417 P.2d 581 (1966).

The only German conflicts provision on distribution of foreign assets is article 26 EGBGB, which seeks to make sure that German public authorities who are asked to transfer foreign assets to distributees in Germany may do so without obstruction by third parties. Especially in American-German relations is such an obstruction possible if a German national dies domiciled in the United States.[264] In this case the American courts will distribute the personal estate according to American state law, while the German courts under the principle of nationality will look to German domestic law. Because of this divergence the heirs under American law may be different from those entitled to distributive shares under German law. Article 26 EGBGB meets this problem by providing that those persons who are heirs or legatees under German law cannot prohibit the transfer of foreign assets by the German public authorities to those persons who are distributees under the applicable foreign law; the German heir is restricted to claims which he may raise against the foreign heirs.

IV. ESTATE AND INHERITANCE TAXES

A few words on estate and inheritance taxes may be appropriate not only because of the dominant influence of tax considerations on estate planning, but also because the taxation of estates governed by foreign law meets with the same difficulties as does the application of foreign succession law. Therefore the following remarks are devoted to the difficult problem of tax classification of foreign estates and individual interests in estates. They will not deal with problems of taxation proper (*see infra* ch. 16).

(1) American Estates in Germany*

In conformity with the various approaches seen in succession law (*supra* I), the United States federal authorities tax the estate as a whole (estate tax), while in Germany (as in most American states) what is taxed is the share of each beneficiary (inheritance tax).[265] Within the general framework of successions (and other liberalities), private law (including the German conflicts rules, *supra* II) determines what is the exact nature of the acquisition and who is the beneficiary. The German tax authorities therefore have to ascertain under American law, where applicable, the effects of intestate and testate succession, and then have to ascertain their closest equivalents in

---

[264] *Cf. In re* Dankerl's Estate, *supra* n. 178.

* The most recent article is KILLIUS, German Inheritance and Income Taxation of U.S. Estates, 24 Tax L. Rev. 127–58 (1968). Outdated in many respects is MUELLER, RabelsZ 7 (1933) 808–49.

[265] § 15 I Erbschaftsteuergesetz (ErbStG, BGBl. 1959 I 187).

German succession law for the imposition of German inheritance taxation.[266]

German law imposes a tax on the "acquirer" (*Erwerber*), that is, the heir or legatee, at the time of acquisition, usually the death of the decedent. However, if acquisition is subject to a condition precedent, the tax does not fall due until the condition has been fulfilled. And the reversionary heir (*Nacherbe*) is not taxable until he acquires the estate from the provisional heir.[267] How are the beneficiaries of American testamentary trusts to be treated under these rules? The answer obviously depends upon the terms of the last will.

If a trustee is appointed for the management of the testamentary trust, with or without power to distribute the income to one or several persons during a certain period, and only thereafter to distribute the corpus of the trust, the beneficiaries of the corpus will not be taxed as "acquirers" of the estate at the time of the decedent's death; their acquisition is regarded as subject to a condition precedent under German law.[268] The same is true if the beneficiaries of income and corpus are identical, but the trustee has unlimited discretion as to whether and when payments will be made to them.[269] An even stronger case is that of a trustee who is free to distribute the income and later the corpus of the trust to one of a certain number of persons;[270] the taxable acquisition does not take place until a (provisional or final) decree of distribution has been rendered[271] or the trustee has actually paid[272] or has ascertained the residuary legatees.[273]

Where, on the other hand, one who is merely an executor or an administrator has been appointed to wind up the estate, a German beneficiary has been taxed as an heir from the date of the decedent's death even though he received a first (partial) payment only four years later.[274]

It may be said in conclusion that a beneficiary will not be taxed in Germany upon his share until he acquires a presently enforceable claim to income or corpus from the estate.[275] And a transfer of the

---

[266] BFH 31 May 1961, BStBl. 1961 III 312, 314; RFH 24 Sept. 1935, RFH 38, 225, 231–32; 10 Feb. 1931, JW 1931, 1401.

[267] §§ 15 I, 14 I no. 1 a) and h) ErbStG.

[268] BFH 15 May 1964, BFH 79, 481, 485; RFH 24 Sept. 1935, RFH 38, 225, 232–38.

[269] BFH 31 May 1961, BStBl. 1961 III 312, 313.

[270] BFH 20 Dec. 1957, BFH 66, 204 (English law).

[271] BFH 15 May 1964, BFH 79, 481, 487; 31 May 1961, BStBl. 1961 III 312, 314.

[272] BFH 20 Dec. 1957, *supra* n. 270.

[273] BFH 31 May 1961, *supra* n. 269.

[274] RFH 12 May 1938, RFH 44, 23; 2 Dec. 1930, IPRspr. 1931 no. 98. These two decisions seem to be at some variance with the trust cases *supra* nn. 268–72.

[275] KILLIUS 136.

estate to a trustee, executor or administrator has correctly been held tax-free, since these persons do not acquire the estate for their own benefit.[276] Nor is an income beneficiary for life taxable as "acquirer" of an estate.[277]

(2) German Estates in the United States

In two instances at least the United States courts have had to classify, for tax purposes, a German provisional heirship. They have held correctly that the provisional heir (*Vorerbe*) does not acquire a fee simple, but merely a life estate where his interest is limited to his life-time. On his death, the reversionary heir (*Nacherbe*) acquires the fee simple directly from the decedent, not from the provisional heir.[278]

---

[276] BFH 20 Dec. 1957, *supra* n. 270.
[277] RFH 24 Sept. 1935, RFH 38, 225, 238–39.
[278] *See* cases cited *supra* n. 100.

Chapter VI.

PROPERTY AND EXPROPRIATION*

The private and the public international law aspects of property are more closely intertwined than most Continentals like to admit. They are accustomed to regard these two branches of law as quite distinct and independent, separated by the alleged deep gulf between private and public law in general. The following discussion will merge the two aspects in order to give a full view of the whole matter. I shall deal first with the conflicts rules relating to property, then with the conventional guarantees of American property rights in Germany, thereafter with the effects of foreign expropriations in Germany, and finally very briefly with jurisdiction.

I. CONFLICTS RULES RELATING TO PROPERTY

(1) Basic Rule

The basic conflicts rule for property rights refers in Germany, as in the United States, to the *lex rei sitae*. Property rights[1] are governed by the law of the situs at the relevant time. This rule of customary law[2] is supported almost unanimously by courts and writers,[3] apart from certain special situations. The *lex rei sitae* governs the creation, transfer and loss of property rights and their incidents,[4] with respect to chattels as well as to immovables.[5] The

---

* On German substantive law, *see* 1 COHN 170–220; SCHAPS/ABRAHAM, Das deutsche Seerecht (4 vols., 3rd ed., 1959–1967).

[1] Claim of American mortgagee for share in proceeds (deposited in Germany) from public sale of German realty held to be not property right subject to *lex rei sitae*, KG Berlin 20 June 1930, IPRspr. 1930 no. 70.

[2] BGH 20 Sept. 1967, WM 1967, 1198; 20 Mar. 1963, BGHZ 39, 173, 174.

[3] KEGEL, Kommentar, no. 269 preceding art. 7 EGBGB; RAAPE 586–93; NEUHAUS 168; WOLFF 172–73.

[4] BGH 20 Sept. 1967, WM 1967, 1198; 15 Nov. 1961, WM 1962, 185; 4 Feb. 1960, NJW 1960, 774. Rights of finder of dollar notes aboard German ship leaving New York harbor governed by New York/New Jersey common law, OLG Hamburg 14 May 1904, SeuffArch. 60, 143.

[5] *Movables*: *see* the cases cited *supra* n. 4.

Immovables: art. IX para. 1 (b) of the American-German Treaty of Friendship of 1954 (Treaties B 117) fixes even this conflicts rule! The proprietary effects of the appointment of a receiver (in the English sense) by an English mortgagee of German realty are determined by German law, OLG Hamburg 8 Dec. 1931, IPRspr. 1933 no. 29.

On the distinction between real and personal, movable and immovable property, *see supra* ch. 5 sub. II(3)(a)(iii).

only exceptions are found in the areas of matrimonial property, succession and corporation law, where certain transfers follow peculiar rules.[5a] Moreover, unlike the Anglo-American position, capacity to hold or to convey land or chattels is subject to the personal law of the parties rather than the *lex situs*.[6]

A renvoi (that is, a reference "back" or "over") from a foreign *lex situs* will generally be accepted.[7]

(2) **Change of Situs**

If property has been moved from one jurisdiction to another, its situs is determined with reference to the significant time. The law normally applicable is the law of the situs of the movable when the act occurred which allegedly created a new right.[8] Thus, the bona fide purchase of machinery from a non-owner, and the resulting claim of the true owner against the seller for unjust enrichment, are governed by the law of the situs of the machinery at the time of sale.[9]

While full effect will be given to the law of the earlier situs for all legal consequences arising before the change of location, the law of the new situs governs all later acts,[10] and also the fate of expectancies that had not fully matured under the prior law, such as the effect of interruption of a period of acquisitive prescription.[11] Clearly, a reservation of title will be treated differently from a mere expectancy.[12]

A more difficult question is what effect should be given by the new law to rights properly created under the old law. Specifically, how does German law incorporate into its domestic system property rights created abroad? The "translation" is easy where the foreign

---

[5a] *See supra* ch. 4 sub A IV(2)(a) and ch. 5 sub II(3)(a)(iii), as well as *infra* ch. 10 sub I(2)(c).

[6] *Cf.* KG Berlin 20 June 1930, *supra* n. 1, on the capacity of an American married woman with regard to claims for proceeds from the sale of German realty. *See further supra* ch. 4 sub C(1).

[7] Kegel, Kommentar, no. 290 preceding art. 7 EGBGB; Raape 588. Judicial authority is slim; *see* RG 8 Feb. 1910, VII 208/09, cited by Lewald, Das deutsche internationale Privatrecht (1931) 172; LG Kiel 18 Dec. 1959, IPRspr. 1958/59 no. 54.

[8] BGH 20 Mar. 1963, BGHZ 39, 173, 174; RG 14 Dec. 1922, IV 409/21, extract cited by Lewald, *supra* n. 7, at 177–78; OLG Hamburg 2 June 1965, RabelsZ 32 (1968) 535; Kegel, Kommentar, no. 278 preceding art. 7 EGBGB; Raape 587.

[9] BGH 4 Feb. 1960, NJW 1960, 774.

[10] LG Frankfurt/M. 9 July 1958, IPRspr. 1958/59 no. 110.

[11] Kegel, Kommentar, no. 278 preceding art. 7 EGBGB, with references in n. 2.

[12] Impliedly, BGH 2 Feb. 1966, BGHZ 45, 95; *contra*: OLG Hamburg 2 June 1965, *supra* n. 8; Mertens, Eigentumsvorbehalt und sonstige Sicherungsmittel des Verkäufers im ausländischen Recht (1964) 15.

right finds an approximate equivalent in Germany. Full ownership creates no difficulty, and the courts have also been able to equate a foreign reservation of title with a German conditional sale.[13] The German Federal Supreme Court has even given effect to a French chattel mortgage although German law has no close equivalent and although no new notice of the security interest was given after the chattel's removal to Germany.[14] In view of the extremely liberal domestic rules on non-possessory security interests, registration as a rule not being required, foreign security interests can be incorporated with ease into German law. More particularly, the broad security interest created by article 9 of the American Uniform Commercial Code (UCC) will encounter no legal difficulties; all that will be necessary is a relabeling of the interest and distribution of its components among the fragmented German classes of security interests.[15] On the other hand, a foreign security interest requiring possession by the creditor will be held invalid in Germany without such possession.[16]

The foregoing discussion presupposes the unlimited reign of the *lex rei sitae* rule, whereby a change of situs implies a change of governing law. Certain German decisions, however, are authority for a limited exception to that rule. In the last twenty years three higher courts have applied German property law to transactions that took place while the chattels, although earmarked for removal to Germany, were still abroad.[17] These and some additional cases[18] are based largely on the parties' choice of German law. While such a choice is usually declared irrelevant in international property law,[19] these cases can be approved without necessarily relying on

---

[13] *Italian*: BGH 2 Feb. 1966, BGHZ 45, 95; LG Frankfurt/M., *supra* n. 10. For *English* reservation of right of disposal, *see* OLG Hamburg 2 June 1965, *supra* n. 8.

[14] BGH 20 Mar. 1963, BGHZ 39, 173.

[15] The pre-UCC conditional sale is the equivalent of the German Eigentumsvorbehalt, the chattel mortgage of the Sicherungsübereignung, and the assignment of the Sicherungsabtretung, none of which requires registration! An English lien has been held not to be the equivalent of a German conditional sale, but at most a pledge, requiring possession by the creditor, LG München 24 July 1957, IPRspr. 1956/57 no. 97.

[16] LG München, *supra* n. 15.

[17] BGH 2 Feb. 1966, BGHZ 45, 95; OGH Köln 7 July 1949, OGHZ 2, 226, 229; OLG Hamburg 25 Oct. 1961, IPRspr. 1960/61 no. 72. *See also* OLG Hamburg 2 June 1965, *supra* n. 8, reaching the same result by declaring a foreign conditional sale a mere expectancy maturing only in Germany; *see supra* n. 12.

[18] KG Berlin 26 Nov. 1954, IPRspr. 1954/55 no. 28, *aff'd on other grounds*, BGH 14 Dec. 1955, BGHZ 19, 258; BayObLG 3 Jan. 1934, IPRspr. 1934 no. 24 (obiter dictum).

[19] *See* the monograph by PRIVAT, Der Einfluss der Rechtswahl auf die rechtsgeschäftliche Mobiliarübereignung im Internationalen Privatrecht (1964), with references. *Contra*: only MEYER/LADEWIG, AWD 1963, 261–263; *see also*

the doctrine of party autonomy. The parties have a justified interest in the creation of property rights in a chattel that is about to be removed to another jurisdiction in accordance with the latter's rules. But, at the same time, the rights of third parties arising while the chattel is still abroad must be safeguarded according to the then local law.[20] The similarity of this rule with UCC § 9–103(3) sentence 2 is obvious.

(3) **Special Chattels**

Specific rules have been developed for certain peculiar chattels, namely, instruments, goods in transit, ships and airplanes:

(i) For instruments (or, to use the terminology of the UCC, investment securities, documents of title and commercial paper), German conflicts law has developed a uniform, though bipartite, rule. *First,* whether the paper constitutes such an instrument and whether, consequently, a transfer of the paper affects the underlying right embodied in the instrument, is determined by the law governing that right.[21] Whether, for example, a delivery in Germany of United States Government bonds transfers all rights to the transferee depends upon "American" law as the law governing the underlying loan.[22] Whether a bill of lading represents the merchandise depends upon the law governing the latter, in other words, the *lex rei sitae* of the goods[23] (but *see infra* (ii)). *Second,* if we are dealing with an instrument representing or incorporating the underlying right, then a transfer of the paper must comply with the law of its location, the *lex cartae sitae*.[24] This latter part of the rule concerning instruments is in essence the recognition of a renvoi from the law governing the underlying right.

(ii) The treatment of goods in transit is doctrinally highly controversial, but appears to cause few difficulties in practice. Suffice it to say that the modern trend in Germany prefers the law of the place of destination.[25]

(iii) Disputes concerning rights in ships are not infrequent and

---

ERMAN/ARNDT, Handkommentar zum Bürgerlichen Gesetzbuch (4th ed. 1967), no. 5 in appendix 2 to art. 12 EGBGB.

[20] Details in DROBNIG, Eigentumsvorbehalte bei Importlieferungen nach Deutschland, RabelsZ 32 (1968) 450–72.

[21] KEGEL, Kommentar, no. 272 preceding art. 7 EGBGB; WOLFF 183. *See also infra* n. 24.

[22] RG 5 Nov. 1932, IPRspr. 1933 no. 20.

[23] RG 8 Dec. 1927, RGZ 119, 215, 216; KEGEL, *supra* n. 21; RAAPE 594–95.

[24] RG 10 Mar. 1934, IPRspr. 1934 no. 11 (transfer of bearer shares); LG Stuttgart 22 June 1955, IPRspr. 1954/55 no. 59a (bona fide acquisition of bearer bonds). *Too general*: RG 13 Sept. 1935, HRR 1935 no. 1608 (transfer of shares situated in Germany between two Americans in the U.S.).

[25] MARKIANOS, Die res in transitu im deutschen internationalen Privatrecht, RabelsZ 23 (1958) 21–43, 43, with references. He can invoke an obiter dictum of an older decision of the Reichsgericht, extract in LEWALD, *supra* n. 7, at 191.

often raise difficult conflicts problems. Statutes expressly provide that ownership of a ship entered in a German ship register is governed by German law.[26] In spite of its general wording the provision does not exclude recognition of loss of ownership either through public sale abroad or probably also through other foreign acts of a public nature.[27] A corresponding rule will probably apply *mutatis mutandis* to questions of ownership of ships registered in foreign ports.[28] Corresponding non-statutory rules would seem to apply to mortgages of German and foreign ships.[29] Of greater practical importance than the ownership and mortgage of ships, however, are questions relating to maritime liens. It is unsettled what legal system governs their creation, but liens for deliveries and repairs to German ships in foreign ports have consistently been determined by the law of the foreign port.[30] However, the courts will recognize a choice of law by the parties, or at least a choice of German law.[31] A lien for damage to the cargo should logically comply with the law governing the contract of affreightment,[32] while liens for claims of the crew and of their social security carriers are, and should be, determined by the proper law of these legal relations, usually the law of the ship's flag.[33] By thus referring the creation of a maritime lien to the law of the claim to be secured, the German cases appear to be in accord with the American cases. The effects in Germany of maritime liens governed by foreign law depend upon the procedures by which they are enforced. If there are no other competing rights *in rem*, the real effects of the lien will as a

[26] Statute on Rights in Registered Ships (Schiffsrechtegesetz) of 15 Nov. 1940 (BGBl. III 403–4), § 1 II.

[27] *See* BGH 6 July 1961, BGHZ 35, 267; SCHAPS/ABRAHAM I 362, no. 3 on SchRG § 1.

[28] SCHAPS/ABRAHAM I 363, no. 5 on SchRG § 1; RAAPE 621 and KEGEL, Kommentar, no. 288 preceding art. 7 EGBGB, would alternatively take into account the *lex situs* of the ship.

[29] SCHAPS/ABRAHAM I 408–414, no. 113–120 on SchRG § 8; RAAPE 622–624. On the extinction of ship mortgages by public sale abroad, of German ships, *see* LC Aurich 13 Feb. 1967, IPRspr. 1966/67 no. 45; RG 15 May 1930, IPRspr. 1930 no. 50. On the recognition of foreign ship mortgages, *see* RG 9 Feb. 1900, RGZ 45, 276.

[30] RG 20 Jan. 1913, Gruchot 57, 1037; RG 5 Feb. 1913, RGZ 81, 283; OLG Stettin 29 Sept. 1931, IPRspr. 1932 no. 55; OLG Hamburg 22 Mar. 1933, IPRspr. 1933 no. 28; LG Bremen 2 Apr. 1959 and 10 May 1961, IPRspr. 1960/61 nos. 43 and 50 (American ports); LG Hamburg 3 Apr. 1963, IPRspr. 1962/63 no. 50; LG Hamburg 7 Jan. 1965, IPRspr. 1964/65 no. 64 (American port). These decisions are usually based on a combination of *lex rei sitae* and *lex contractus*.

[31] RG 20 Jan. 1913 and LG Hamburg 7 Jan. 1965, *supra* n. 30; LG Hamburg 18 Mar. 1964, IPRspr. 1964/65 no. 61; SCHAPS/ABRAHAM II 1285, no. 33 on § 754 HGB.

[32] PRÜSSMANN, Seehandelsrecht (1968), no. II 3 c preceding § 754 HGB.

[33] For social security claims, *impliedly*: BGH 6 July 1961, *supra* n. 27; *see* HAUDEK, JW 1932, 2635 and PRÜSSMANN, *supra* n. 32, at no. II 3 d preceding § 754 HGB. *Contra*: SCHAPS/ABRAHAM II 1286, no. 36 on § 754 HGB.

rule be fully protected.[34] If, however, a ship, whether foreign or domestic, is on public sale, the priority of the various rights will usually be determined by the German *lex fori*[35] unless the competing rights are all governed by the same foreign legal system.[36] Protection of a foreign maritime lien by the German *lex fori* presupposes the essential equivalence of that lien to a German lien,[37] and such equivalence has been expressly recognized in the case of an American maritime lien.[38] The extinction of German maritime liens on a German ship sold by auction abroad is submitted *mutatis mutandis* to the foreign *lex fori* and is therefore recognized in Germany.[39]

(iv) Ownership and other real rights in aircraft are subject to the uniform rules established by the Geneva Convention of 1948 to which both Germany and the United States are parties.[40]

(4) **Form**

According to article 11 II EGBGB, the formalities of creating or disposing of any right in property are governed exclusively by the *lex causae* which, under the basic rule (*supra* (1)), is the law of the situs. The creation, modification, transfer or termination of rights in German land is thus subject to German formalities. German real property law as a rule requires two steps, namely, consent of the parties and registration.[41] A special form for this agreement (*Auflassung*) of the parties, which is distinguishable from the contract creating an obligation to transfer property (*infra*), is prescribed in only a few cases, especially for the transfer of title to land (§ 925 BGB). German practice and the prevailing doctrine, based on tradition rather than reason, do not permit the substitution of a foreign notary for a German notary, even where they have equivalent status.[42]

---

[34] *See* OLG Stettin 29 Sept. 1931 and LG Bremen 2 Apr. 1959, *supra* n. 30.

[35] RG 20 Jan. and 5 Feb. 1913, and LG Bremen 10 May 1961, all *supra* n. 30; SCHAPS/ABRAHAM II 1287, no. 39 on § 754 HGB. *Contra*: LG Hamburg 3 Apr. 1963, *supra* n. 30.

[36] SCHAPS/ABRAHAM II 1287, no. 40 on § 754 HGB.

[37] RG 20 Jan. and 5 Feb. 1913, and LG Bremen 10 May 1961, all *supra* n. 30; LG Hamburg 18 Apr. 1962, IPRspr. 1962/63 no. 48.

[38] LG Bremen 10 May 1961, *supra* n. 30.

[39] BGH 6 July 1961, *supra* n. 27. But the court permits a claim for unjust enrichment based on German law, if the proceeds have been distributed abroad among "German" claims in disregard of the rank established by German law; *see also* RG 15 May 1930, *supra* n. 29.

[40] Treaties M 141. *See also* the German Law of Feb. 26, 1959 on rights in aircraft (BGBl. 1959 I 57, and III 403–9), §§ 103–106, and the Law on Forced Sale and Administration of Mar. 24, 1897 (BGBl. III 310–14), §§ 171h–171n.

[41] On the German system of land registration, *see* 1 COHN 186–200, 303–07; SCHUSTER, The Principles of German Civil Law (1907) 377–84; *cf. also* DOWSON/SHEPPARD, Land Registration (2d ed. London 1956) 187–90.

[42] LG Berlin 28 Apr. 1961, IPRspr. 1960/61 no. 144 (American notary public); AG Mainz 3 Jan. 1955 (unreported, digested by MANN, NJW 1955, 1178–1179); RIEDEL, DNotZ 1955, 521–26; SAAGE, *id.* 1953, 587; WEBER, NJW

However, a German consul is equated to a notary (§ 16 I 2, IV KonsG) so that title to German land may be transferred by a document drawn abroad by a German consul.

The preceding rules, while governing transfers of land, do not apply to the underlying contractual transaction, for example, the contract to sell land. The substance and form of such a contract follow the general rules on contracts (*infra* ch. 8 sub B). Although a contract to sell land requires notarial form in Germany (§ 313 BGB), such a contract, even if relating to German land, may be concluded informally if the *lex loci actus* (art. 11 I 2 EGBGB) so permits.[43]

In those exceptional cases in which chattels are not governed by the *lex rei sitae* (*supra* (2) and (3)), the latter's formal requirements are replaced by those of the law governing the underlying transaction.[44]

II. CONVENTIONAL GUARANTEES FOR AMERICAN PROPERTY[*]

The American-German Treaty of Friendship of 1954 (Treaties B 117) contains two sets of conventional rules, mutually guaranteeing the acquisition and holding of property as well as protection against its taking. These rules conform to the general American treaty practice after World War II.[44a]

(1) **Acquisition and Holding of Property**

Article IX of the Treaty grants reciprocal rights to acquire, hold, and dispose of rights in real and personal property.

For rights in real property (except leases) only a conflicts rule is laid down (*supra* n. 5). Almost no provision is made for removal of the existing national obstacles against the acquisition or holding of land by foreigners.[45] However, article XIX (3) of the Friendship

---

1955, 1784–86; KEGEL, Kommentar, no. 25 on art. 11 EGBGB; RAAPE 215, 627. *Contra*: MANN, *supra*; WOLFF 130.

43 RG 16 May 1928, RGZ 121, 154, 156; RG 20 Nov. 1930, JW 1931, 572, 574; KEGEL, Kommentar, no. 12 on art. 11 EGBGB with further references in n. 8.

44 BGH 2 Feb. 1966, BGHZ 45, 95 (reservation of title to chattels to be removed to Germany, although formally ineffective in Italy, held effective under German law).

* WILSON 95–125, and 45 A.J.I.L. 83–107 (1951); BENTON, The Protection of Property Rights in Commercial Treaties of the United States, ZaöRV 25 (1965) 50–75; CONNELL, United States Protection of Private Foreign Investment through Treaties of Friendship, Commerce and Navigation, ArchVR 9 (1961/62) 256–77, 302–17.

44a *See* the comparative charts by CONNELL 302–17.

45 The widely differing restrictions on alien ownership in land in the United States are described in detail by 1 POWELL/ROHAN, The Law of Real Property (1969 ed.) §§ 101–109. *Brief summary*: WILSON 135–139, and 48 A.J.I.L. 363–65 (1954). The comparative chart by CONNELL 305 demonstrates the widely different standards employed in United States treaties for the holding of real property.

Treaty of 1923 (Treaties B 55), as added by article II of the provisional agreement of 1953 (Treaties B 104), permits the Governments of the two countries to own and occupy immovables for governmental purposes and to obtain any permission required under local law. But beyond this narrow exception, Americans may neither invoke in Germany the better treatment accorded to certain other treaty aliens nor claim the rights accorded to German nationals.[46] Restrictions on the acquisition of real property by foreigners are traditionally within the legislative jurisdiction of the German states (art. 88 EGBGB) and therefore vary widely, even within a particular state.[47] Only two specific kinds of acquisition, namely, by succession or under judicial sale, are privileged under the first sentence of article IX (3) of the Treaty of 1954. The second sentence would limit this privilege to a period of five years if the aliens are ineligible "because of their alienage . . . to continue to own any such property." However, it may be argued that the German restrictions (*supra* n. 47) relate to acquisition only and do not prohibit continued ownership, so that the time limitation does not apply. As far as leases and other forms of occupation and utilization for all permitted gainful activities are concerned, Americans enjoy national treatment (art. IX (1)(a)), and when it comes to disposing of property, real as well as personal, Americans enjoy national and most-favored-nation treatment (art. IX (4)).

The régime for the acquisition and holding of personal property

---

[46] ARNOLD/HILL/KERN 5.

[47] (1) *Approval of acquisition is necessary for foreign legal entities in*:

(a) *Baden-Württemberg*: in the former parts of *Baden*, for gratuitous acquisitions with value over $1,250 (§ 1 II Stiftungsgesetz of July 19, 1918, bad.GVBl. 254); in the former parts of *Württemberg*, for acquisition of agricultural property with value over $2,500 by legal entities without gainful purposes (art. 128 AGBGB of Dec. 29, 1931, RegBl. 545); in the former parts of *Hohenzollern, see infra* (c);

(b) *Bavaria*: for acquisition of any immovables by legal entities with religious, benevolent or educational purposes (art. 10 AGBGB, BayBS III 89);

(c) *Berlin*: (i) any gratuitous acquisition with a value over $1,250; (ii) the acquisition of any immovable, and (iii) the acquisition and exploitation of mining property and rights (art. 6 § 1 and art. 7 § 2 AGBGB, preuss.GS 1898, 177, and §§ 1 and 3 Prussian statute of June 23, 1909, preuss.GS 619);

(d) *Hessen*: only in the former *Prussian* parts, the special provision relating to mining property, *see supra* (c)(iii);

(e) *Niedersachsen*: *see supra* (c). However, the special provision on mining property, *supra* (c)(iii), is restricted to the former *Prussian* parts;

(f) *Nordrhein-Westfalen*: *see supra* (c)(i);

(g) *Rheinland-Pfalz*: in the former *Hessen* parts, *supra* (c)(i) and (ii), arts. 12 and 15 hess.AGBGB, as revised by Law of Aug. 10, 1922 (RegBl. 240); in the former *Prussian* parts, *see supra* (c); in the former *Bavarian* parts, *see supra* (b);

(h) *Saarland*: for the former *Prussian* parts, *see supra* (c); for the former *Bavarian* parts, *see supra* (b);

(i) *Schleswig-Holstein*: *see supra* (c)(i) and (ii).

(2) *No restrictions of any kind*: *Bremen* and *Hamburg*.

is, as usual, much more liberal. National and most-favored-nation treatment is granted for both tangibles and intangibles. Only alien ownership of materials endangering the public safety or of interests in certain enterprises of a public nature (communications, air or water transport, taking and administering trusts, banking with deposits, and the exploitation of land and natural resources)[48] may be restricted (art. IX (2)). In these cases acquisition by succession or under judicial sale is again privileged (last paragraph). Other restrictions imposed by local law, for example, upon acquisitions by foreign legal entities,[49] are inapplicable in the light of the conventional rule.

(2) **Protection against Taking of Property**

Article V of the Treaty of Friendship of 1954 (Treaties B 117) spells out the broad protection accorded mutually to the property rights and interests of nationals of one country by the other country. Indicative of the scope and importance of this guarantee is the solemn general clause of paragraph 1: "Property of nationals and companies of either Party shall receive the most constant protection and security within the territories of the other Party." Molestation, entry and search of buildings and premises shall be made only according to law and with careful regard for the convenience of the occupants and their business (art. V (2)). Moreover, any discrimination or unreasonable measures against the rights to or interests in enterprises, capital, skills, arts or technology are prohibited (para. 3).

Of greatest importance are the provisions of paragraphs 4 and 5 of article V relating to expropriation,[50] including the transfer of enterprises into public ownership and their placement under public control. Expropriation as such of property is permitted only for the public benefit, upon compliance with due process of law,[51] and against the payment of just compensation. The compensation has to be full ("representing the equivalent of the property taken"),[52] effective[53] and speedy. (The last point means that by the time of

---

[48] On such restrictions in Germany, *see infra* ch. 11 sub II(2)(b).

[49] Such restrictions are reserved by art. 86 EGBGB (as amended by the Law of Mar. 5, 1953, BGBl. I 33, part 2 art. 2 para. 1) to state legislation, which has made wide use of it.

[50] On German law, *see* SCHUBERT, Compensation under the New German Legislation on Expropriation, 9 Am. J. Comp. L. 84–94 (1960).

[51] The German text, "die Möglichkeit, den Rechtsweg zu beschreiten," is broader than the English. Since the latter corresponds to frequently employed clauses in American commercial treaties (*see* CONNELL 307), it appears to have been the original version and should prevail. To the same effect, *see* SCHWENK 199.

[52] BGH 19 Dec. 1957, BGHZ 26, 200, 202 held that this formula of the Treaty meant full compensation; *accord*: BGH 30 Nov. 1959, IPRspr. 1958/59 no. 34; *cf*. BENTON 62 and CONNELL 269.

[53] The words "effectively realizable" probably include a guarantee for with-

taking at the latest, adequate provision must have been made for the determination and payment of compensation.) Even an indirect interest in property entitles the holder to the conventional protection.[54] As far as the amount of compensation is concerned, the precise rule of the Treaty itself is important since general German legislation merely grants reasonable compensation,[55] and hence the rule of the Treaty prevails.[56] Apart from the standards spelled out by the Treaty, national and most-favored-nation treatment is accorded (para. 5). For certain forms of taking of enterprises, namely, transfer to public ownership or establishment of public control, the Treaty requires national and most-favored-nation treatment, provided nationals of the other Party have a "substantial interest" in the enterprise (para. 5 sent. 2).

(3) **Pre-War and Wartime Expropriations***

For the redress of expropriations and any other discriminatory treatment to which foreign property had been subjected in Germany or by Germans in the German-occupied territories, elaborate rules were inserted in the so-called Settlement Convention of 1954 (Treaties M 184). Although the volume of claims under these rules was tremendous and the task has not yet been fully completed, this temporary problem is no longer of special consequence for American-German relations.

(4) **American Property in East Germany****

The status of American and other foreign property in East Germany differs depending upon the date of its creation.

All property owned by Americans in East Germany prior to May 9, 1945 has been under compulsory state administration since the

---

drawal of the compensation as foreign exchange, WILSON 121; *but see* BENTON 61–2, 71, 72.

[54] Protocol to the Treaty, no. 5. Americans with such indirect interest do not thereby become entitled to payment to themselves, but may merely claim conventional protection to be granted to the owner, ARNOLD/HILL/KERN 3.

[55] *See* art. 14 III GG and SCHUBERT, *supra* n. 50.

[56] BGH 19 Dec. 1957, BGHZ 26, 200. The court indicated at p. 202 that the Treaty not only prevails over earlier German legislation (*see supra* ch. 2 at n. 84), but also, as being more specific in regulating the expropriation of Americans, over subsequent legislation.

* *See,* on "internal" restitution, KARASIK, Problems of Compensation and Restitution in Germany and Austria, 16 Law & Contemp. Problems 448–68 (1951). Texts of the restitution laws for the American zone and for Berlin are reprinted in 42 A.J.I.L. (1948) Supplement 11–45 and 44 A.J.I.L. (1950) Supplement 40–67.

** GENTZMANN, Zur Rechtslage des in der SBZ und in Ost-Berlin befindlichen Vermögens von Ausländern, ROW 1959, 101–04; Die Enteignungen in der sowjetischen Besatzungszone und die Verwaltung des Vermögens von nicht in der Sowjetzone ansässigen Personen (edited by the West German Ministry for All-German Questions, 3rd ed., Bonn/Berlin 1962) 75–80.

end of the War. First based on orders of the Soviet occupation authorities, a regulation "on the Administration and Protection of Foreign Property" was issued in 1951 by the East German authorities.[57] It applies to property owned by foreigners in whole or in part or property directly under their control (in the case of companies incorporated under German law, if at least one-half of the shares is held by foreigners). Foreign owners are expressly enjoined from disposing of their rights[58] (Regulation § 5 III). The disposition of administered assets by their administrators is also, as a rule, forbidden unless necessary for their regular administration (Regulation § 4, Implementing Regulation § 10). An enterprise or part of an enterprise is regarded as an independent statutory legal entity (Implementing Regulation § 5) and is also treated as such by the courts of West Germany.[59] Profits are paid into a collective account, from which the costs of administration and prohibitive taxes[60] are withdrawn so that no substantial benefits will be left for the foreign owners. Western owners receive, in practice, only unresponsive replies to inquiries concerning the status of their property.[61] The effect in West Germany of this administration is disputed. The courts tend to equate it with expropriation, thus denying extraterritorial effect as to rights already in existence on May 8, 1945, but granting such effect as to rights created thereafter.[62] In the view of the author, the asserted conservatory and protective function of the administration should be taken at face value and therefore no extraterritorial effect should be given even to newly created rights over the objection of the foreign owner.[63]

Property acquired by Americans subsequent to May 9, 1945 is subject to the East German Foreign Exchange Law of 1956.[64] This

---

[57] Regulation of Sept. 6, 1951, and first Implementing Order of Aug. 11, 1952, GBl.DDR 1951, 839 and 1952, 745. American protests against this delegation of responsibility by the Soviet government were of no avail; *see* exchange of notes, 28 D.S.Bull. 218–19 (1953).

[58] Regulation § 5 III. Thus they may not elect new board members nor transfer the registered office of the corporation to West Germany; contrary acts are void, OG 20 Dec. 1963, OGZ 10, 51.

[59] BGH 18 Dec. 1959, GRUR 1960, 372, 374 ("Kodak" enterprise in East Berlin); *see also* BGH 23 Jan. 1963, GRUR 1963, 473 (same enterprise). This is in keeping with the general rules concerning the application of East German law by West German courts, *see supra* ch. 1 at n. 85.

[60] SPILLER, Souveränität und Steuerrecht, StuR 1959, 1397–1410, 1402–03.

[61] Die Enteignungen 77.

[62] *See* the litigation concerning an old and a new trademark of the Kodak enterprise in East Berlin, *supra* n. 59.

[63] *See* DROBNIG, Note, NJW 1963, 1543–44; SAMSON, Note, BB 1963, 1080–81.

[64] Law of Feb. 8, 1956 (Devisengesetz, GBl.DDR 1956 I 321), with eight Implementing Orders of Mar. 22, 1956. These and other texts are reprinted in a handy collection by H.-G. GRIMM, Devisen- und innerdeutscher Zahlungsverkehr ((East) Berlin 1961).

Law does not institute a compulsory state administration, but leaves the selection of a private administrator to the owner. The administrator also has the power to dispose of the property, but he may exercise it only with prior approval of a state authority.

III. EFFECTS OF FOREIGN EXPROPRIATION

The wave of post-War nationalizations in Eastern Europe and especially in East Germany has provided the West German courts with an unusually rich experience in considering the effects of foreign expropriation. A very brief survey of the most important principles evolved in these cases must suffice for our purposes.

(1) Extraterritorial Effects

The first and most frequently applied principle, uniformly endorsed by the courts and writers, is that foreign expropriations, with or without compensation, do not affect assets located in West Germany at the time of their purported taking.[65] This doctrine is usually designated as the principle of "territoriality" (*Territorialitätsgrundsatz*)[66] and ties in with the *lex rei sitae* conflicts rule for property. It is easily applied to tangible property. The many attempts, for purposes of expropriation, to "localize" intangibles (especially monetary claims at the debtor's domicile or seat[67]) have been riddled by exceptions.[68] Modern writers suggest a more realistic approach, recognizing that a chose in action may be enforced not only at the debtor's domicile but wherever his property can be found. A claim for payment of money has therefore as many sites as there are countries where it may be pursued. The territoriality of an expropriation means only that its legal effects are limited to the territory of the expropriating jurisdiction, while the claim remains unaffected abroad.[69] The cases have clearly moved in this direction.[70] Similarly,

---

[65] E.g., BGH 29 Nov. 1965, WM 1966, 221, 222; BAG 28 Oct. 1958, IPRspr. 1958/59 no. 29; BGH 11 July 1957, BGHZ 25, 134, 140, 150; BGH 11 July 1957, BGHZ 25, 127, 129. *See further* some 35 cases of the BGH in LM on art. 7 EGBGB (Enteignung). *See also* KEGEL, Kommentar, no. 406, 426 preceding art. 7 EGBGB; RAAPE 659; NEUHAUS 120; WOLFF 67, 176–77.

[66] *See* NEUHAUS 117–23 on the many meanings of this ambiguous concept.

[67] E.g., BGH 30 June 1961, WM 1961, 1044; 25 Feb. 1960, BGHZ 32, 97, 99; 11 July 1957, BGHZ 25, 134, 139.

[68] E.g., BGH 25 Feb. 1960, BGHZ 32, 97, 100; 12 Nov. 1959, BGHZ 31, 168, 172; 21 Feb. 1958, IzRspr. 1958/59 no. 145; BAG 28 Oct. 1958, IPRspr. 1958/59 no. 29; ORG Berlin 3 Feb. 1960, ORGE Berlin 14, 78, 82–84.

[69] Especially KEGEL, Kommentar, nos. 405–07, 427–31 preceding art. 7 EGBGB; *id.*, Probleme des internationalen Enteignungs- und Währungsrechts (1956) 16–36; WENGLER, Die Belegenheit von Rechten: Festschrift der Juristischen Fakultät der Freien Universität Berlin zum 41. Deutschen Juristentag in Berlin (1955) 285–352, 301–08, 334–47.

[70] *See* the examples given in n. 68. The risk of double payment has been mitigated by a special doctrine.

the effects of the expropriation of a company or of corporate shares have been strictly limited. A legal entity expropriated and/or extinguished in the foreign country of its incorporation or its seat continues to exist in Germany, provided there are any assets there.[71] The survival of the entity in Germany is independent of its continuation or extinction in the home country. In the latter case, the "old" entity is deemed to have split, the two parts not being identical despite their partial identity with the "old" entity. This doctrine also prevails if all or the major part of the shares of a company are expropriated by the home country.[72] The same principles apply vis-à-vis East Germany.[73]

(2) **Local Effects**

A corollary to the refusal to grant any extraterritorial effect with respect to assets beyond the borders of the confiscator is the recognition, at least de facto, of the expropriation with regard to assets within the confines of the expropriating state. However, this rule, although probably prevailing, is by no means without exception or free from doubt. As long as the confiscated asset remains inside the borders of the confiscating state, the fact of the expropriation will usually be taken into account in West Germany.[74] More important, although in practice rare, is the removal of confiscated goods from the expropriating country. With respect to expropriations in East Germany, the West German courts have been evenly divided as to whether or not the expropriated owner may claim his property from somebody whose title derives from the confiscation. The conflicting cases can be reconciled by distinguishing between them according to the person of the defendant. Where the defendant was a unit of the Eastern state economy that, directly or indirectly, received the confiscated property, the owner's title has been protected.[75] Where the defendant was a private party who purchased

---

[71] E.g., BGH 29 Nov. 1965, WM 1966, 221; 21 Jan. 1965, BGHZ 43, 51, 55–56; 6 Oct. 1960, BGHZ 33, 195, 197–98; 5 May 1960, BGHZ 32, 256, 259; 11 July 1957, BGHZ 25, 134, 143–44; *see further* KEGEL, Kommentar, nos. 446–50 preceding art. 7 EGBGB; RAAPE 670–674. A brief summary in English by MANN, The Confiscation of Corporations, Corporate Rights and Corporate Assets and the Conflict of Laws, 11 I.C.L.Q. 471–502, 483–84 (1962).

[72] E.g., BGH 23 Jan. 1961, WM 1961, 347; 6 Oct. 1960, BGHZ 33, 195, 198; 5 May 1960, BGHZ 32, 256, 259–264; 11 July 1957, BGHZ 25, 134, 144–8; *see* KEGEL, Kommentar, nos. 442–44 preceding art. 7 EGBGB; RAAPE 683–92. English summary in MANN, *supra* n. 71, at 489–90, 493–94.

[73] E.g., BGH 12 Oct. 1962, GRUR 1963, 263; 7 Mar. 1961, GRUR 1961, 420; 30 Jan. 1956, BGHZ 20, 4; 20 May 1955, IzRspr. 1958/59 no. 56; RAAPE 670–674. *See also* Carl Zeiss Stiftung v. V.E.B. Carl Zeiss, Jena, 293 F. Supp. 892, 915 (S.D.N.Y. 1968), 433 F.2d 686, 703 (2d Cir. 1970).

[74] *See* the analysis of West German interzonal cases by DROBNIG, Extraterritoriale Reflexwirkungen ostzonaler Enteignungen, RabelsZ 18 (1953) 659–89.

[75] OLG Nürnberg 19 Sept. 1949, NJW 1950, 228; LG Berlin 16 June 1952,

the goods from a state enterprise, the claim of ownership has failed.[76] This distinction makes good sense.

The Czechoslovakian and Polish post-War expropriations of German property have been held discriminatory and therefore ineffective as to property, especially household goods, brought into Germany.[77] In a commercial setting, an appellate court has rightly denied a claim of ownership of tobacco grown on Dutch plaintiffs' Indonesian plantations after confiscation of the plantations;[78] in this case, the court investigated extensively the conformity of the confiscation with public international law.

(3) **Adjudication of Claims**

The foregoing discussion demonstrates that the German courts feel free to pass on the validity of foreign confiscations of property within the confines of the expropriating state. They do not feel restrained by anything comparable to the American act of state doctrine. But they have been restrained by certain enactments respecting the wartime and post-War measures taken against German property. First, Allied High Commission Law No. 63 of August 31, 1951[79] (maintained in force by the Settlement Convention of 1954[80]) withdrew generally from German jurisdiction all claims arising from the confiscation of German property located outside Germany.[81] The German courts have determined the situs of such assets according to German conflicts rules[82] insofar as the statute itself did not contain an express rule.[83] The Settlement Convention (chap. VI art. 3)

IzRspr. 1945/53 no. 6; *see also* a special case, OLG Oldenburg 14 July 1961, IzRspr. 1960/61 no. 131.

[76] OLG Nürnberg 10 July 1953, IzRspr. 1945/53 no. 9; OLG Hamburg 8 May 1951, JZ 1951, 444; LG Mannheim 12 Oct. 1950, IzRspr. 1945/53 no. 7; *see also* a special case, BGH 17 Feb. 1960, IzRspr. 1960/61 no. 3.

[77] LG Kassel 20 July 1948, RabelsZ 15 (1949) 138; AG Waiblingen 21 June 1948, *id.* 139; AG Dingolfing 7 Dec. 1948, *id.* 141; AG Berchtesgaden 18 July 1951, IPRspr. 1954/55 no. 6. *Contra*: LG Hildesheim 18 Nov. 1947, RabelsZ 15 (1949) 137. *See,* on these cases, GRAUE, 3 Am.J.Comp.L. 93–95 (1954).

In 1951, the Western occupation powers intervened by excluding the jurisdiction of German courts in matters concerning the confiscation of German property abroad, *see infra* n. 80.

[78] OLG Bremen 21 Aug. 1959, IPRspr. 1958/59 no. 7 A (appendix) (defendant was a German agent for the selling of Indonesian tobacco). *See,* on this case, DOMKE, 54 A.J.I.L. 305–323 and BAADE, *id.* 801–835.

[79] Off. Gaz. HICOG p. 1107.

[80] Treaties M 184, chap. VI art. 2.

[81] *See,* e.g., OLG München 14 June 1951, IPRspr. 1950/51 no. 5 relating to Czech confiscated household goods brought to Germany (*cf. supra* n. 77), *rev'd* after enactment of Law No. 63 by BGH 29 Jan. 1953, BGHZ 8, 378.

[82] *See,* e.g., BGH 5 May 1960, BGHZ 32, 256, 265; 14 Jan. 1959, WM 1959, 199; 24 Mar. 1955, BGHZ 17, 74, 78; 7 June 1955, BHGZ 18, 1, 8–9; OLG Celle 22 Dec. 1959, NJW 1960, 1350.

[83] *See* art. 1 (2) (a, b) concerning securities issued by German issuers. The

excluded additional confiscations from German jurisdiction by adding to "German external assets" the words: "or other property, seized for the purpose of reparation or restitution. . . ." This formula included German-owned assets located within Germany, provided they had been effectively seized by the occupation powers or otherwise.[84] Both the effectiveness of such a seizure and the location of the property in Germany are determined on the basis of German law.[85] Thus any claim or plea putting in issue the validity or effect of measures taken under the Trading with the Enemy Act against German-owned assets located in the United States is excluded from cognizance by the German courts.[86]

IV. JURISDICTION

German procedural law has special jurisdictional rules for two classes of actions relating to property. *First,* § 24 ZPO establishes the jurisdiction of the court of the situs of an immovable. This court has exclusive jurisdiction in actions relating to ownership or possession of an immovable or real charges on it. Personal claims secured by charges and certain other personal claims against the owner or possessor of real property may be brought in the same forum (§§ 25, 26 ZPO). *Second,* and of far greater importance for the international jurisdiction of the German courts, is the remarkable forum created by § 23 ZPO, whereby if a non-resident has an asset in Germany, which may even be a cause of action against a debtor domiciled in Germany (§ 23 sent. 2 ZPO), the court at the situs has jurisdiction over any action of a proprietary nature against the non-resident. The value of the asset or its relation to the claim is irrelevant. The ensuing judgment is *in personam* and, from the viewpoint of German law, not limited to the value of the German asset. (For details *see infra* ch. 14 sub I (2)(a).)

---

confiscation of such securities by the United States was therefore without effect in Germany, OLG Hamburg 16 June 1953, WM 1953, 530; LG Mainz 26 Oct. 1956, WM 1957, 38.

[84] *Leading cases*: BGH 11 July 1957, BGHZ 25, 127, 131–134, and BGHZ 25, 134, 140–143; *see further* BGH 5 May 1960, BGHZ 32, 256, 264; OLG Hamburg 25 June 1959, WM 1959, 1100.

[85] BGH 11 July 1957, *supra* n. 84; 23 Jan. 1961, WM 1961, 347; OLG Celle 22 Dec. 1959, NJW 1960, 1350; OLG Hamburg 25 June 1959, *supra* n. 84; OLG Köln 18 Feb. 1959, WM 1961, 183.

[86] A pair of decisions illustrates the meaning of the rule. Jurisdiction is lacking for a declaratory judgment to determine the foreign plaintiff's title to certain values against the German defendant, BGH 11 Apr. 1960, BGHZ 32, 170. But there is jurisdiction for a similar suit between two German parties, BGH 11 Apr. 1960, BGHZ 32, 173.

Chapter VII.

TORTS*

This chapter deals only with "ordinary" torts, including maritime collisions. Business torts, especially unfair competition and the infringement of copyright, patents and trademarks, are reserved for separate treatment (*infra* ch. 12).

(1) **Law Governing**

(a) *Basic rule.*—A tort (*unerlaubte Handlung*, literally, a wrongful or unlawful act) is governed in principle by the *lex loci delicti commissi.* This inveterate rule is implicit in article 12 EGBGB, which protects a German tortfeasor from certain consequences of a tort committed abroad (*infra* (b)(i)). The rule, moreover, is confirmed by the uniform opinion of the courts and writers.[1] The "revolution" that has raged about the American conflicts rules for torts has been noted in Europe[2] but has had no effect there. This may be due in part to the flexible handling, at least in Germany, of incidental questions (*infra* (2)(c)) and to certain exceptions from the basic rule (*infra* (b)).

The place of wrong may in fact be several places, the place of the illegal or risky conduct and the place of the harm to the protected interests. The conduct, either action or omission to act, may itself occur in more than one place, provided each contributing factor goes beyond a mere preparatory act[3]; for example, if a German

* The most recent broad discussion of the German conflict of laws regarding torts is BEITZKE, Les obligations délictuelles en droit international privé, 115 Recueil des Cours 63–145 (1965/II). On the German substantive law of torts, *see,* especially, 1 COHN 151–60, and, further, KRAUSE, The Right to Privacy in Germany, 1965 Duke L. J. 481–530; LEHMAN, The Right of Privacy in Germany, 1 N.Y.U. J. Int'l L. & Pol. 106–27 (1968); TURCK, Contribution Between Tortfeasors in American and German Law, 41 Tul. L. Rev. 1–32 (1966): Note, Tort Liability for Negligent Operation of a Motor Vehicle in Germany and the United States, 1960 Duke L. J. 579–612, 581–99.

[1] References in all commentaries on art. 12 EGBGB, especially KEGEL, Kommentar.

[2] *See,* in particular, KEGEL, The Crisis of Conflict of Laws, 112 Recueil des Cours 92–268, 97–236 (1964). *See,* further, DE NOVA, Le concezioni statunitensi dei conflitti di leggi viste da un continentale (Valladolid 1964); HEINI, Neuere Strömungen im amerikanischen Internationalen Privatrecht, 19 Schweizerisches Jahrbuch für internationales Recht 31–70 (1964); *id.,* Eine neue Methode im Internationalen Privatrecht? 86 Zeitschrift für Schweizerisches Recht 265–81 (1967).

[3] *See,* for details, KEGEL, Kommentar, nos. 2–13 on art. 12 EGBGB.

firm sends written instructions to a foreign attorney to seek to restrain a competitor from unfair dealings, the firm acts both at its own place of business and at the attorney's office abroad.[4] The place of harm (*Erfolgsort*) is only the place where the protected interests are affected; it is immaterial where the damage becomes apparent.[5]

Since this flexibility results frequently in a plurality of places of wrong, what law governs where they are in different jurisdictions? Of greatest importance is a diversity between the place or places of conduct and the place or places of harm. For several decades German case law has looked in this situation to the law most favorable to the victim of the tort.[6] The Federal Supreme Court has recently clarified this rule: a court must itself make the election *ex officio*, even if the victim relies only on one law, unless his choice is unequivocal and exclusive.[7] The same rule is applied if the several places of conduct are in different jurisdictions.[8] By contrast, if there is a plurality of places of harm, the law of each governs the tort to the extent of the particular harm occurring there; it is applied either exclusively or alternatively with the law of the foreign place or places of conduct, but not alternatively with the law of other places of harm.[9]

(b) *Special rules for Germans.*—The only existing German statutory rules in this field create an exception to the general principle of the *lex loci delicti commissi* in favor of German law for torts committed abroad. The legislator on the one hand protects a German tortfeasor and on the other hand envisages the special situation where both parties are Germans.

(i) Where the tortfeasor (or other person liable for a tort) is a German, he is protected by article 12 EGBGB, which provides: "By reason of an unlawful act committed in a foreign country, no greater claims can be enforced against a German than those created by German law." This unilateral privilege is restricted to German nationals[10] and to organizations subject to German law.[11] A court

---

[4] BGH 13 July 1954, BGHZ 14, 286, 291. *Cf.* RG 16 May 1925, Recht 1925 no. 1274.

[5] KEGEL, Kommentar, no. 15 on art. 12 EGBGB.

[6] BGH 23 June 1964, WM 1964, 947, 949; OLG Saarbrücken 22 Oct. 1957, NJW 1958, 752; 5 Mar. 1963, IPRspr. 1962/63 no. 38; RG 12 Nov. 1932, RGZ 138, 243, 246 (on this case, *see also infra* n. 51).

[7] BGH 23 June 1964, *supra* n. 6. Against the idea of "choice" by the victim, *see* KEGEL, Kommentar, no. 46 on art. 12 EGBGB.

[8] BGH 23 June 1964, *supra* n. 6; KEGEL, Kommentar, no. 13 on art. 12 EGBGB.

[9] *See* BGH 2 Oct. 1956, BGHZ 22, 1, 17–18; OLG Hamburg 11 June 1897, HansGZ 1898 Beibl. no. 146; KEGEL, Kommentar, no. 46 on art. 12 EGBGB.

[10] Excluded are stateless persons and refugees who are not "Germans" (*supra* ch. 3 sub A II (1) (c)). *See* KEGEL, Kommentar, no. 59 on art. 12 EGBGB.

[11] Implicitly, e.g., RG 8 July 1930, RGZ 129, 385 (German subsidiary of American corporation); BGH 12 Dec. 1957, VersR 1958, 109 (limited partnership).

must apply it *ex officio.* However, it must look beyond the law of torts and examine the claim in the light of other possible German categories, especially unjust enrichment, breach of contract, conduct of another's affairs (*negotiorum gestio* or *Geschäftsführung ohne Auftrag*) or even maintenance.[12] This broad interpretation of the comparable standard under German law is the only means of mitigating the undesirable effects of article 12 EGBGB,[13] particularly the application of the brief German statute of limitations of three years for torts (§ 852 BGB).[14] Nevertheless, the required examination is sometimes difficult, especially in cases of labor accidents because of the complicated interplay of tort law and social security rules,[14a] and the requirement has met with much criticism in Germany.[15]

(ii) If both the tortfeasor and the injured person are Germans, German law alone is to govern the tort. This rule was enacted by a Regulation of December 7, 1942[16] in view of the existing wartime conditions, but it is still held to be in force.[17] The rule is supported by a line of older cases[18] and by modern doctrinal views seeking a certain flexibility in the principle of *lex loci delicti.* The circle of Germans is to be defined in the same way as for purposes of article 12 EGBGB (*supra* nn. 10, 11). However, it has been urged that the application of the rule should be restricted to Germans ordinarily residing in Germany.[19] It is the common residence of the parties rather

---

See also § 1 II of the Regulation of Dec. 7, 1942, *infra* n. 16. For details, *see also infra* ch. 10 sub I (1).

[12] RG 29 Sept. 1927, RGZ 118, 141, 143–44; LG Regensburg 10 Sept. 1954, IPRspr. 1954/55 no. 120; KEGEL, Kommentar, no. 55 on art. 12 EGBGB.

[13] Some further points are discussed by M. WOLFF 167.

[14] RG 29 Sept. 1927, *supra* n. 12, at 142–43; BGH 12 Dec. 1957, *supra* n. 11. There are many cases to this effect.

[14a] A fine example of the complexities which may arise is BAG 30 Oct. 1963, BAG 15, 79.

[15] *See* RAAPE 572; M. WOLFF 166; LEWALD, Das deutsche internationale Privatrecht (1931) 269.

[16] RGBl. 1942 I 706. § 1 I 1 reads in translation: "Claims for extracontractual damages based on an act or omission of a German national committed abroad are governed by German law, insofar as a German national has been damaged." Official and semi-official comments can be found in DJZ 1943, 20–21 and 36–38.

[17] Especially BGH 2 Feb. 1961, BGHZ 34, 222, 223–26. *See*, further, BGH 15 Nov. 1961, WM 1962, 185, 186; BGH 9 June 1967, VersR 1967, 882, 883.

[18] In particular, for collisions of German ships outside German coastal waters, *see infra* (3) (b), and for unfair competition between Germans abroad, *see infra* ch. 12 sub VI (2). *But see* RG 14 June 1915, LZ 1915, 1443 (Austrian law applied to automobile accident in Austria between Germans domiciled in Germany); RG 30 May 1919, RGZ 96, 96, 98.

[19] To this effect, *see also* KEGEL, Kommentar, no. 24 on art. 12 EGBGB; RAAPE 574; PRÖLSS, Internationalrechtliche Aspekte der Kraftfahr-Haftpflichtversicherung (Karlsruhe 1957) 23–24; *see also* BINDER, Zur Auflockerung des Deliktsstatuts, RabelsZ 20 (1955) 401–99, 411. However, the intention of the legislator was to the contrary. *See* DJZ 1943, 20 and 36–37.

than their common nationality which justifies the application of the law of their home country to a tort claim. Nevertheless, the law of the foreign place of accident cannot be completely disregarded, especially its traffic rules; these will have to be taken into account in determining, under German law, the illegality of the tortious act or the fault of the parties.[20]

I would advocate with Kegel the generalization of these rules: Wherever committed, torts between residents of the same foreign jurisdiction should be judged by their common law.[21] However, the courts have not yet followed suit,[22] and it may be difficult to persuade them against the convenience of applying their own law.

(c) *Choice of law by the parties.*—In recent years the courts have come increasingly to permit the parties to a tort to determine by agreement the law governing their mutual claims.[23] Such an agreement may be express[24] or tacit.[25] If, as is usually the case, it relates to a traffic accident or maritime collision that has occurred abroad, it will generally be interpreted as not precluding the application of the local traffic rules.[26] But the parties may have intended the application of the chosen law to all the conditions as well as the effects of the tort,[27] and their choice does not in practice and should not depend upon the approval of the otherwise applicable *lex loci delicti commissi.*[28]

---

[20] *See* DJZ 1943, 38; PRÖLSS, *supra* n. 19, at 24.

[21] KEGEL, Kommentar, no. 28 on art. 12 EGBGB; *see also* BINDER, *supra* n. 19, at 480–99; NEUHAUS, RabelsZ 16 (1951) 654–55.

[22] *See*, e.g., OLG Stuttgart 12 Nov. 1959, VersR 1960, 722 (collision in Germany of two cars owned and driven by American soldiers). *See also infra* nn. 49, 50.

[23] The nationality and residence of the parties are irrelevant. Not only is an agreement between two German parties on the application of German law admissible (in this case the Regulation of 1942, *supra* (b) (ii), itself makes German law applicable), but also such an agreement with a foreigner (*see* OLG Köln 16 Dec. 1953, IPRspr. 1954/55 no. 35) or between two foreigners.

[24] OLG Hamburg 6 Apr. 1961, VersR 1961, 822; *see also* BGH 10 June 1960, VersR 1960, 907; and *see* the cases cited *infra* nn. 25, 26.

[25] OLG Köln 16 Dec. 1953, IPRspr. 1954/55 no. 35 (the parties had invoked, as to the consequences of a collision in the Netherlands, only German law and had consented to its application by the court). *See*, on the very liberal practice of German courts in finding an agreement of the parties to the litigation that German law be applied to contractual disputes, *infra* ch. 8 sub II(2)(a), (3)(a), (4).

[26] BGH 26 Nov. 1964, BGHZ 42, 385, 388–89. Conversely, the pleading of the foreign traffic rules does not preclude a finding that the parties tacitly intended to submit all other aspects of the tort to the *lex fori*, OLG Köln 16 Dec. 1953, IPRspr. 1954/55 no. 35.

[27] Such a tacit intent has been deduced by a court from the fact that the foreign traffic rules and those of the chosen law were identical in substance, BGH 26 Nov. 1964, BGHZ 42, 385, 388.

[28] *See* the cases cited *supra* n. 24. Even KEGEL, Kommentar, no. 37 on art. 12 EGBGB admits this in effect, although he calls it a restricted ("materiellrechtliche") reference by the parties (on this, *see infra* ch. 8 sub II(1) at n. 16a).

(2) **Issues Governed**

(a) For the application of the rules relating to the choice of the governing law, the concept of tort is given a wide meaning. For example, it includes liability for risk, especially in connection with automobile accidents,[29] and liability for the acts of other persons.[30] On the other hand, wrongs committed between persons who are already connected by statutory or contractual relations, such as spouses, parents and children, or master and servant, ought to be kept outside the purview of the German conflicts rule for torts; such wrongs should be governed by the law applicable to the underlying relationship, including its tort rules.[31]

(b) The law governing a tort decides whether a tort has actually been committed and what consequences flow from it.[32] More particularly, it determines: liability for the acts of dangerous things and other persons (*supra* nn. 29, 30), causation and proof of fault,[33] the remedies available,[34] the amount of the damages,[35] and the limitation of actions.[36]

(c) So-called incidental questions are excluded from the operation of the law governing the tort to the extent that German private international law provides special conflicts rules for them. Two illustrations may suffice:

---

[29] Standing practice of the courts; explicitly, BGH 21 Dec. 1956, BGHZ 23, 65, 67; OLG Celle 21 July 1966, VersR 1967, 164.

[30] BGH 29 Jan. 1959, BGHZ 29, 237, 239 (shipowner for acts of crew); 11 July 1957, WM 1957, 1047, 1051 (master for agents, servants); OLG Saarbrücken 6 June 1956, VersR 1957, 145 (insurer of tortfeasor); OLG Celle 12 July 1965, NJW 1966, 302 (mother for child); *see* BGH 14 Feb. 1952, BGHZ 5, 138 (civil liability of state).

[31] The point is very controversial. It is important for certain claims that may be based both on family law and tort law, especially maintenance of illegitimate children and damages for breach of a promise to marry. *See*, e.g., LG Regensburg 10 Sept. 1954, IPRspr. 1954/55 no. 120; *supra* ch. 4 sub A III (2) (d); NEUHAUS 99; M. WOLFF 58, 165–66; RAAPE 575. Similar to the view here advocated are KEGEL, Kommentar, no. 17 preceding art. 13 and no. 34 on art. 21 EGBGB, and BEITZKE 107–10. *See also supra* ch. 4 sub A I.

[32] KEGEL, Kommentar, nos. 40, 44, and 45 on art. 12 EGBGB, with references.

[33] OGH Köln 1 June 1950, OGHZ 4, 194, 200–04; OLG München 6 Feb. 1932, IPRspr. 1932 no. 42 (German law).

[34] RG 28 Jan. 1939, Seuff.Arch. 93 no. 90 (action to restrain interference and right to publish the court decree); OLG Freiburg 18 Jan. 1951, GRUR 1952, 524. Both cases applied German law.

[35] *Damages for pain and suffering*: LG Bayreuth 5 July 1950, IPRspr. 1950/51 no. 23; *interest on damages*: OLG München 6 Feb. 1932, *supra* n. 33. Damages are calculated on the basis of the price obtaining at the place of impact or, if damaged goods were in transit, at the place of destination, BGH 14 Feb. 1952, BGHZ 5, 138, 143. But in an exceptional case, an American girl living with her parents in Germany, badly injured in a traffic accident there, was held entitled to a costly transplant operation in the United States, BGH 23 Sept. 1969, VersR 1969, 1040.

[36] BGH 12 Dec. 1957, VersR 1958, 109; RG 8 July 1930, RGZ 129, 385, 388.

(i) A German mother is sued for the damages caused by her nineteen-year-old son in a traffic accident in Yugoslavia. Whether the mother is liable for her son's act is determined by Yugoslav law, which admits the liability of a parent for his minor children if he has violated his duty of parental control. Whether the son is a minor (as he is under German law but not under Yugoslav law) is according to article 7 EGBGB a question for the son's national law;[37]

(ii) An American citizen dies in an automobile collision in Germany. His widow and his children, American citizens domiciled in California, sue the tortfeasor for maintenance. Whether the tortfeasor is liable to third persons and to which persons depend upon German law as the law of the place of wrong. German law (§ 844 II BGB) imposes liability vis-à-vis those third persons who had a statutory claim for maintenance against the victim. Whether the American widow and children had such claims is determined, according to the conflicts rules of articles 14 and 19 EGBGB (*supra* ch. 4 sub A III (2)(e) and B I (5)(d)), by California law.[38]

The wide respect given to the proper law of all incidental issues complicates the solution of international tort cases. But at the same time it serves to diminish the rôle of the *lex loci delicti commissi* as an absolute principle.

(d) The transfer of a tort claim also falls outside the domain of the law governing the tort. More and more are tort victims compensated primarily by private insurance or social security carriers or by the state, which in turn may recover from the tortfeasor (or any third person responsible for him). The vehicle for such recovery is the victim's tort claim, to which those paying are either subrogated by operation of law or which is assigned to them by the victim.

The German conflicts rules relating to legal subrogation are not yet settled. Most courts look to the law governing the relation between the victim and the person who pays him.[39] The legal writers have pleaded one or another combination of this law with the law governing the tort claim, in order to protect the debtor.[40] The

---

[37] OLG Celle 12 July 1965, *supra* n. 30. On art. 7 EGBGB, *see supra* ch. 4 sub C (1).

[38] OLG Celle 21 July 1966, *supra* n. 29; *accord*: BGH 22 Sept. 1967, VersR 1967, 1154; *see also* BGH 9 Nov. 1965, VersR 1966, 283; 14 June 1960, FamRZ 1961, 261 (claim of husband for loss of wife's services).

[39] *Law governing insurance contract*: OLG Hamburg 6 Dec. 1966, VersR 1967, 1205; 1 July 1957, IPRspr. 1956/57 no. 50; 5 Mar. 1957, *id.* no. 50a; OLG Bremen 30 June 1966, VersR 1967, 576; OLG Schleswig 21 Dec. 1950, VersR 1951, 66; *law of social security carrier*: OLG Celle 21 July 1966, *supra* n. 29 (implicitly, American law).

[40] Advocating combination with rules protecting the debtor are M. WOLFF 152; LEWALD, *supra* n. 15, at 276–78; BEMELMANS, Das Statut der cessio legis, der action directe und der action oblique, RabelsZ 29 (1965), 511–44. Advocating "admission" of the subrogation are RAAPE 507–11 and KEGEL, IPR 247–48.

Federal Supreme Court has considered the issue but has not yet decided it.[41] It is submitted that the judicial practice respecting legal subrogation must be recognized,[41a] provided rules which protect the debtor are observed. Failing this, the person who has paid may demand the assignment of the tort claim by the victim.[42]

Conventional subrogation, the assignment of the tort claim by the victim, is governed by the law governing the tort.[43]

(3) Maritime Torts

Torts committed on board ship or collisions between ships are subject to the general rules set forth above ((1) and (2)). However, a few peculiarities have to be noted.

(a) Torts occurring on board ship are subject to the law of the vessel's location; if it is in port or in coastal waters, the coastal state's law governs (except between persons domiciled elsewhere but in the same jurisdiction); if it is on the high seas, the law of the home port (which is usually identical with the law of thc flag) applies.[44]

(b) The uniform rules on collisions laid down in the Brussels Convention of 1910 do not apply in American-German relations since the United States is not a party. The uncodified rules of German conflicts law therefore come fully into play. Collisions in ports or coastal waters are subject to the coastal state's law, irrespective of the ships' flags.[45] This law governs all aspects of the tort, including limitation of liability by the ship-owner.[46] Only if both ships fly the German flag is German law applied, and this is by virtue of the Regulation of 1942[47]; in this case, not only the claims of the ship-owners but also those of the cargo against the ship are submitted to German law as being accessory to the former.[48] The German

---

41 BGH 26 Apr. 1966, VersR 1966, 662 (subrogation of the French fisc recognized!); *see also* OLG Düsseldorf 23 Nov. 1961, VersR 1962, 536.

41a A German court has concluded that the subrogation of the United States government provided by P.L. 87–693 of Sept. 25, 1962 has to be recognized in Germany, but that the amount of damages is to be calculated by German standards, OLG Stuttgart 14 Jan. 1970, VersR 1970, 526 (appeal lodged), overruling LG Stuttgart 24 Mar. 1969, VersR 1969, 958.

42 KEGEL, IPR 248 (a so-called adaptation); RAAPE 508.

43 OLG Hamburg 6 Dec. 1966, VersR 1967, 1205. This is in accord with the general rule; *see infra* ch. 8 sub III (6).

44 OLG Hamburg 15 Oct. 1935, HansRGZ 1935 B 584 (tiger aboard German boat injures member of crew).

45 BGH 29 Jan. 1959, BGHZ 29, 237; 27 June 1957, VersR 1957, 515; 6 Nov. 1951, BGHZ 3, 321.

46 BGH 29 Jan. 1959, *supra* n. 45, at 241–44; 6 July 1961, VersR 1961, 785, 787; OLG Hamburg 8 July 1958, VersR 1958, 841. However, a German ship-owner is not liable beyond the provisions of German law, art. 12 EGBGB, *supra* (1) (b) (i).

47 *Supra* sub (1) (b) (ii) at n. 16; BGH 2 Feb. 1961, BGHZ 34, 222.

48 BGH 2 Feb. 1961, BGHZ 34, 227.

courts have not yet extended this rule to the comparable situation of two ships of the same foreign flag colliding in German waters.[49] A collision on the high seas is subject to the law of the common flag, even if it is a foreign flag.[50] The really difficult case of a collision between ships of different flags is hopelessly controversial. The former *Reichsgericht* had good reason to apply to this situation the general principle developed in German international tort law for cases in which the places of acting and of impact are located in different countries: the plaintiff may choose the law more favorable to him.[51]

(4) Tort Liability of Public Authorities and Officials As Against Americans

The German law on the tort liability of officials and public authorities is peculiarly complex.[51a] It reflects a long process of historical development, many traits of which are preserved to this day. A rationally streamlined codification of this important branch of the law is missing. One of the more accidental remnants of the past is a bundle of provisions excluding foreigners from the assertion of tort claims against public authorities in certain areas. In order to appreciate the reach of these exclusionary rules, a few words about public tort liability in non-conflicts cases are necessary.[52]

In the framework of special statutes establishing liability without fault for inherently dangerous activities (involving automobiles, aircraft, railways, electricity, gas, atomic energy), the state as the owner of such objects and a public official as the driver or another servant of the state are liable on the same footing as private individuals. In this area no exclusionary rules exist. However, recovery is usually limited to maximum amounts or to certain kinds of damages. Additional recovery has to be based on proof of fault under one of the following categories.

Ordinary principles of tort liability govern the so-called "proprietary" (*fiskalische*) functions of the public authorities, which are involved where the authorities are clearly engaged in a commercial

---

[49] OGH Köln 1 June 1950, OGHZ 4, 194, 197; RG 30 May 1888, RGZ 21, 136, 140.

[50] RG 18 Nov. 1901, RGZ 49, 182, 187.

[51] RG 12 Nov. 1932, RGZ 138, 243, 246. It is possible to distinguish this case on the ground that defendant only had been at fault.

[51a] On the immunity of foreign officials from tort liability, *see infra* ch. 14 sub I (1).

[52] *Useful descriptions in English*: HINK, German Law of Governmental Tort Liability, 18 Rutgers L. Rev. 1069–1150 (1964); POCK, Systems of Public Responsibility in Switzerland, Germany and Austria, 1966 U. Ill. L. F. 1023–59; BRABAND, Liability in Tort of the Government and its Employees, 33 N.Y.U. L. Rev. 18–49, 22–48 (1958); *see also* Comment, Sovereign Responsibility and the Doctrine of Sacrifice, 24 U. Chi. L. Rev. 513–33, 514–17 (1957).

activity (as buyer or seller or entrepreneur). Here the general rules of the Civil Code apply (*see* §§ 89, 31, 831 BGB), rules that do not distinguish as to the nationality of a claimant.

The intentional or negligent breach of a public duty owed by an official toward a third person originally fixed liability on the official under certain conditions (§ 839 BGB). It embraced a wide circle of official activities. However, it was changed profoundly by article 34 GG which provides that this liability, in principle, is now assumed exclusively by the public authority employing the official. It is also subject to certain quite diverse restrictions established by federal and state law, among which are rules discriminating against foreign claimants (*see infra*).

In the area of governmental functions, case law has even more recently created a second broad category of liability, namely, for encroachment on protected interests. Compensation may be claimed only from the public authorities and does not depend on proof of the breach of an official duty or of fault on the part of the official. Therefore this liability for "sacrifices and quasi-expropriatory invasions" is becoming more and more popular. It may be asserted side by side with liability for breach of an official duty. It would seem that foreign claimants are treated in this area on a par with nationals.[53]

Thus it appears that only the rules on liability for breach of an official duty differentiate between national and foreign claimants. The details follow: The German states were empowered by article 77 of the Introductory Law to the Civil Code to regulate the assumption of an official's primary liability by the public authority. Such provisions were in fact enacted by the various states, but they have by now largely become obsolete because of the general rule of assumption of liability contained in article 34 GG. Only the exclusions provided by the state statutes are still held to be valid.[54] The restrictions against foreigners are of three types[55]:

(i) Liability is completely excluded, unless an official declaration of reciprocity has been published respecting the claimant's country. This is the solution of the Reich statute of 1910, now valid for federal officials, and of the Prussian statute of 1909.[56] No notice of

[53] FROWEIN, Staatshaftung gegenüber Ausländern, JZ 1964, 358–62 and 409–13, 411, advocates an analogous application of the exclusionary rules enacted for breach of an official duty. Such extension is unwarranted.

[54] BGH 13 July 1961, IPRspr. 1960/61 no. 240; 1 Oct. 1956, IPRspr. 1956/57 no. 45; 10 May 1954, BGHZ 13, 241, 242.

[55] Detailed survey in FROWEIN, *supra* n. 53, at 360–61. Texts reprinted in DELIUS, Die Beamtenhaftpflichtgesetze des Reiches und der Länder (4th ed., Berlin/Leipzig 1929) 32–80 (slightly outdated).

[56] *Federation*: § 7 of Statute of May 22, 1910, RGBl. 798.

Former Prussian parts of *Baden-Württemberg, Hessen, Rheinland-Pfalz, Saarland,* whole of *Schleswig-Holstein* and *West Berlin*: § 7 of the Prussian Statute of Aug. 1, 1910, GS 691.

reciprocity concerning the United States or its component states has been published so far, and the deficiency cannot be supplied by proof of actual reciprocity;[57]

(ii) One *Land* adopted a closely similar solution, except that the existence of reciprocity need not be declared officially;[58]

(iii) The "South German" solution leaves it to the discretion of the public authority to refuse damages to a foreign citizen, unless the latter proves reciprocity.[59] It suffices that the foreign state or its public authorities assume merely a secondary liability vis-à-vis a German if the official himself cannot satisfy the claim.[60]

Another, quite sensible variation has recently been introduced in East Germany. Aliens habitually residing in the country are equated to Germans. For aliens residing abroad (including West Germans living in West Germany), reciprocity is required but may be waived in individual cases.[60a]

Only Hamburg has no restrictions against foreign claimants.

Treaty clauses assuring to certain foreigners national treatment for the legal and judicial protection of their persons and property as well as free access to courts have no bearing upon reciprocity,[61] and hence the provisions in articles V and VI of the American-German Treaty of Friendship (Treaties B 117) are of no avail to American claimants. A change of the claimant's nationality or an assignment of the tort claim[62] are also immaterial. Whether reciprocity in fact exists between Germany and the United States relating to public liability is very difficult to answer in view of the great diversity

---

Bremen: § 5 of Statute of Mar. 19, 1921, GBl. 101.

Niedersachsen and *Nordrhein-Westfalen*: same result on the basis of various provisions.

[57] BGH 1 Oct. 1956, IPRspr. 1956/57 no. 45; 13 July 1957, *id.* no. 225; 10 May 1954, BGHZ 13, 241, 243.

[58] Non-Prussian parts of *Hessen* and former Hessian parts of *Rheinland-Pfalz*: art. 80 Hess. AGBGB (GVBl. II 230–1).

[59] The moment when the public authority refuses liability because of lack of reciprocity is decisive; a subsequent change of circumstance is irrelevant, BGH 13 July 1961, *supra* n. 54. Whether this applies also to statutes of the type described under (i) is controversial: *see* RG 15 Apr. 1930, RGZ 128, 238, 240–41; BGH 2 Feb. 1966, WM 1966, 185, 188.

[60] *Baden-Württemberg* (except former Prussian parts): art. 188 II AGBGB Württemberg, as reenacted 1931 (Reg.Bl. 545) and art. 4 IV AGBGB Baden, as reenacted 1925 (GVBl. 281).

Bavaria and former Bavarian parts of *Rheinland-Pfalz* and *Saarland*: art. 60 II AGBGB Bavaria (BaysBS III 89).

[60a] Gesetz zur Regelung der Staatshaftung of May 12, 1969 (GBl. DDR I 34) § 10 (2) and (3).

[61] BGH 2 Feb. 1966, WM 1966, 185, 187–188; BGH 10 May 1954, BGHZ 13, 241, 243; RG 17 Sept. 1935, RGZ 149, 83, 85–88.

[62] RG 24 Sept. 1935, JW 1936, 383 (change of nationality); BGH 1 Oct. 1956, IPRspr. 1956/57 no. 45 (German heirs of foreign claimant); RG 25 Sept. 1925, RGZ 111, 294 (assignment by German claimant to foreigner).

within the American law, which appears on the whole to be more restrictive than German law.[63] If reciprocity, insofar as it is relevant, does not exist, then American claimants are relegated to the personal liability of the acting official,[64] for what it is worth.

(5) Jurisdiction

Claims arising from a tort committed in Germany may be pursued in a court at the place of wrong (§ 32 ZPO). The numerous cases defining the place of wrong for this purpose[65] may also be utilized to determine the place of acting or of impact for purposes of conflict of laws, and vice versa. Under the theory that a maritime collision on the high seas involving a German vessel is also a tort committed aboard the German ship and therefore on German territory (*supra* at nn. 44, 51), it may be argued that the home port of the German ship is constructively the place of wrong.

---

[63] *See*, in particular, MAX-PLANCK-INSTITUT FÜR AUSLÄNDISCHES ÖFFENTLICHES RECHT UND VÖLKERRECHT, Haftung des Staates für rechtswidriges Verhalten seiner Organe (Köln and Berlin 1967), especially pp. 756, 761, 769, 771, 774.

[64] BGH 13 July 1961, IPRspr. 1960/61 no. 240; RG 15 Apr. 1930, RGZ 128, 238, 240. In the literature, this exceptional personal liability has been attacked on various grounds, see FROWEIN, *supra* n. 53, at 409–413; WIESE, DVB 1964, 571–576.

* *See* the commentaries on § 32 ZPO.

Chapter VIII.

CONTRACTS*

International business transactions, in the widest sense of the term, are generally of a contractual nature. Hence the most important single class of conflicts cases involves contracts—although the law courts nowadays may have only a small share in their settlement. However, in Germany as in the United States, the practical significance of international contracts is in inverse ratio to the stability and certainty of the relevant legal rules. There are three apparent causes: the scarcity of legislative or conventional conflicts rules, the oscillations of court practice and legal writing, and the infinite variety of contractual arrangements.

This chapter will: survey the basic rules (I), discuss in detail the rules that determine the law governing contracts (II), describe the scope of the proper law (III), deal with the special rules relating to the authority of an agent (IV) and to certain negotiable instruments (V), speak of the prohibitory rules of public law (VI), and, finally, survey briefly the law of East Germany (VII).

I. SURVEY OF THE BASIC RULES

Germany has not adopted the Hague Convention on the Law Governing International Sales of 1955 and will probably never do so. Nor has it enacted any other conflicts rule governing contracts in general, and only a few exceptional rules for specific types of contract. The law in this area more than in any other is thus entirely decisional, with the appropriate academic gloss.

The almost undisputed basic conflicts rule for contracts is four-tiered: The prime factor is an express choice of law by the parties. Absent an express choice, an implied (or tacit) choice is taken into account. Where even this is lacking, there will be a balancing of the interests at stake. And, finally, as a sort of emergency exit, the law of the place (or places) of performance is resorted to. This unique four-step rule is firmly settled in contemporary court practice[1] and

---

* Reithmann, The Proper Law of Contract: German Doctrine and Practice, 1 CILSA 84–99 (1968). *Recent German monographs*: Kreuzer, Das internationale Privatrecht des Warenkaufs in der deutschen Rechtsprechung (Arbeiten zur Rechtsvergleichung no. 21, 1964); Reithmann, Internationales Vertragsrecht (1963).

[1] BGH 9 June 1960, WM 1960, 938; 14 Feb. 1958, NJW 1958, 750; 10 Jan. 1958, IPRspr. 1958/59 no. 37; 17 Dec. 1957, IPRspr. 1956/57 no. 23 d; 11 July

is also espoused by the majority of writers.[2] Unfortunately, however, its acceptance does not insure uniformity of results.

An analysis of present-day court practice will be preceded by a brief sketch of the evolution of the present rule.[3] The starting point was Savigny in the middle of the last century; under his dominating influence priority was assigned to the *lex loci solutionis*, based originally on the presumed intention of the parties.[4] By the beginning of the twentieth century the courts had recognized one decisive drawback, namely, the fact that a bilateral contract might have more than one statutory place of performance under the potentially governing legal systems. In consequence, the doctrine of presumed choice of law by the parties began to find favor; the courts inquired into their presumed intention (*hypothetischer Parteiwille*), asking what system of law they would have chosen if they had thought about the issue.[5] Fifty years later it was admitted that this inquiry into the hypothetical intention of the parties was in reality a judicial balancing of the objective interests at stake;[6] however, this rephrasing of the parties' "hypothetical choice of law," although commonly accepted, has not yet been fully carried into effect with respect to individual contracts. Moreover, this doctrine has had to yield priority to another test that has become firmly established in practice and in legal writing in the past forty years, namely, party autonomy. Not only do express choice of law clauses play an increasing role in the drafting of international contracts, but the respect accorded to them has overshadowed the more or less fictional "tacit" choice of law by the parties. This brief historical sketch not only depicts a fascinating doctrinal evolution, but is indispensable to a proper understanding and evaluation of the contemporary four-step rule.

II. THE LAW GOVERNING CONTRACTS

(1) First Step: Express Choice of Law

An express agreement of the parties on the law applicable to their contract enjoys absolute priority.[7] Choice of law clauses are

---

1957, WM 1957, 1047; 22 Nov. 1955, BGHZ 19, 110, 111; 14 Apr. 1953, BGHZ 9, 221, 222.

[2] Kegel, Kommentar, nos. 180, 185, and 204 preceding art. 7 EGBGB, with further references; Raape 455–88; Wolff 136–46; Reithmann 1–21.

[3] *See*, in particular, the well-documented study by Kreuzer.

[4] *See*, e.g., ROHG 28 June 1878, ROHGE 24, 168, 181–82; ROHG 9 Dec. 1874, ROHGE 15, 209, 212 (export sale of ale from Bremen to New Orleans).

[5] *Leading case*: RG 4 Apr. 1908, RGZ 68, 203, 205–08. *Less enthusiastic*: RG 4 Feb. 1913, RGZ 81, 273, 274–275. *See also* RG 17 June 1939, RGZ 161, 296, 298, and 20 Mar. 1936, RGZ 151, 193, 199.

[6] *Leading case*: BGH 1 Feb. 1952, NJW 1952, 540.

[7] *See* the cases *supra* n. 1.

increasingly resorted to in practice, especially in the widely used "printed conditions": Bills of lading and charter-parties[8]; forwarding,[9] insurance[10] and banking[11] conditions; the printed rules of the German Foreign Office for the employment of German local labor abroad;[12] the model contracts for the employment of the more than a million foreign workers in Germany[12a] and the contract relating to construction work for the American forces in Germany[12b]—all of these contain express choice of law clauses. They are still rather exceptional in other contracts.

The parties are free to choose any system of law for their contract.[13] The courts have repeatedly sanctioned the choice of English law by German parties to sales contracts relating to international commodities where arbitration in London has been agreed upon.[14] The selection of a "neutral" law by parties from two different countries is justified

---

[8] *See* cl. M 4 sent. 2 of the bill of lading form, reprinted by SCHLEGELBERGER/LIESECKE, Kommentar zum Seehandelsrecht (2d ed. 1964) no. 20 on § 643 HGB.

[9] § 65 (B) of the obligatory General Conditions of German Forwarding Agents: "The legal relations between the forwarding agent and his principal or his successors in title are governed by German law." *See* comment *in* KRIEN/HAY, Die Allgemeinen Deutschen Spediteurbedingungen (ADSp) (1959) 461.

[10] *See,* e.g., § 126 sent. 1 of the (generally applied) General Rules on Marine Insurance of 1919: "All relations and differences arising out of the contract of insurance are governed by German law."

[11] *See,* e.g., no. 26 sentences 1 and 2 of the General Conditions of Private Banks of 1955: "The office where the books of account are kept is the place of performance for both parties. All legal relations between the customer and the bank are governed by the law of the place of performance, even for litigation pending abroad." *See* brief comment in SCHÜTZ, Bankgeschäftliches Formularbuch (17th ed. 1966) 34.

[12] § 15 of the Rules (1956 version) contained an express reference to German law. The Rules presently in force (1967 version) merely declare applicable the relevant provisions of the Civil Code and of certain other German enactments (§ 24), a clear case for a tacit choice of German law, reinforced by the agreed forum in Bonn (§ 25), *see infra* nn. 45, 47. I am informed that contracts with foreign local labor are usually concluded on the basis of the foreign local law.

[12a] § 8 sent. 1 of the officially agreed-upon model contracts for Greek, Moroccan, Portuguese, Spanish, Turkish and Yugoslav labor, respectively, and § 7 sent. 1 of the Italian contract, BAnz. 1961 nos. 25 and 219; 1964 no. 104; 1965 no. 63; BArbBl. 1962, 960 and 1963, 602; BGBl. 1969 II 1112.

[12b] Dollar Construction Contract 1956, cl. 152 (MBl. BMF 1956, 899) declares American law applicable.

[13] The influence of prohibitory rules will be discussed *infra* VI.

[14] OLG Hamburg 2 June 1965, IPRspr. 1964–65 no. 46; OLG Rostock 22 Feb. 1909, SeuffArch. 65, 1. *Cf.* two cases decided during World War I where a London arbitration clause between two Germans was held inoperative during the War and therefore also the choice of English law: RG 29 June 1915, JW 1915, 995, 996; 8 June 1918, RGZ 93, 166, 167. *See,* further, Private Arbitration Hamburg 2 Oct. 1930, IPRspr. 1930 no. 56 (charter-party between Germans). *See also* OLG Hamburg 3 Sept. 1954, IPRspr. 1954/55 no. 179; BGH 29 Nov. 1961, LM no. 4 on art. 11 EGBGB.

even in the absence of any other connection with that law.[15] In no case has a contractual choice of law been avoided because of the absence of a legitimate interest. The parties' choice of law is also widely respected as to subject-matter. It is generally recognized today that the law chosen prevails even over compulsory rules of the *lex fori* or of the "otherwise applicable law," at least over those of a "private law" nature.[16] On the other hand, the parties may agree that the provisions of the law selected by them are to govern only to the extent that the rules of the otherwise applicable law are permissive, so that the latter's compulsory rules are preserved.[16a] The parties may, if they so desire, submit certain aspects only of their contract to the law selected by them; the rest of the contract is then governed by the otherwise applicable law.[17] Or they may choose different laws for the different parts of their agreement.[18] It is also permissible to make a choice subject to conditions.[19] Thus an alternative clause naming the law of the "defendant's" domicile would clearly be valid.[20] The choice of the governing law may be made after conclusion of the contract and even after litigation arises.[21] It may be made indirectly, for example, by reference to

---

[15] KEGEL, Kommentar, no. 172 preceding art. 7 EGBGB.

[16] BGH 30 Jan. 1961, NJW 1961, 1061 (German commercial agent's claim for compensation for efforts (Ausgleichanspruch), although compulsory under German internal law, may be derogated from by choice of Dutch principal's law); LG Ravensburg 3 Feb. 1966, IV O 602/63 (application of Dutch rather than German rules on instalment sales against German purchaser); the divergent decision of RG 28 Mar. 1931, JW 1932, 591, may be explained by the absence of any protective rules of Dutch law at that time. *See* KEGEL, Kommentar, nos. 168–70 preceding art. 7 EGBGB; RAAPE 466; NEUHAUS 173–74; REITHMANN 96–116.

[16a] German doctrine has termed such a limited choice of law by the parties as "materiellrechtliche Verweisung," as to which *see* KEGEL, Kommentar, no. 168 preceding art. 7 EGBGB.

[17] E.g., clauses in a bill of lading for shipments from United States ports referring to the Harter Act: OLG Hamburg 5 July 1907, HansGZ 1907 H 244; 7 July 1905, *id.* 1905 H 227; *see also* 12 Feb. 1936, HansRGZ 1936 B 243. Reference in a contract of insurance to a Dutch standard insurance policy and the underlying rules of the Dutch commercial code, OLG Düsseldorf 10 Jan. 1929, IPRspr. 1929 no. 48. *See also* OLG Köln 29 Oct. 1958, IPRspr. 1958/59 no. 42.

[18] RG 28 May 1936, JW 1936, 2058 (dollar-bonds issued by German debtor in the United States subject to New York law, while rights of bondholders as to security submitted to German law); BGH 28 Nov. 1963, BGHZ 40, 320, 323.

[19] The usual paramount clauses in bills of lading are valid, *see, e.g.*, OLG Hamburg 11 May 1967, VersR 1967, 1173 (Swedish law unless Dutch law compulsorily claims application); *see also* OLG Hamburg 12 Feb. 1936, HansRGZ 1936 B 243.

[20] *Cf.* OLG Bremen 16 Nov. 1967, Hansa 1968, 326 (choice between Finnish and German laws and jurisdiction).

[21] The attorneys for both parties expressly declare German law to be applicable, BGH 4 Feb. 1963, WM 1963, 456; OLG Hamburg: 12 May 1961, IPRspr. 1960/61 no. 51, and 13 Dec. 1962, IPRspr. 1962/63 no. 23. *See also infra* n. 24.

another contract[22] or to printed business conditions containing a choice of law clause.[23]

(2) **Second Step: Tacit Choice of Law**

In the absence of an express choice of law by the parties, their implied intention must be ascertained. The province of a "tacit" as distinguished from a "hypothetical" choice of law (*infra* (3)) is unclear in practice. Even after the objective reinterpretation of the subrule (*supra* I), the courts have tended to confuse the two approaches, although procedural demands at least would seem to command their unequivocal separation. However, juxtaposition with the next succeeding step, the weighing of the objective interests at stake, makes it clear that tacit choice emphasizes the individual, subjective traits of a contract or of contractual demeanor.

In determining the law tacitly chosen, German practice treats two circumstances as almost conclusive: the reliance on one law during litigation, and the choice of a forum.

(a) *Reliance on one law during litigation.*—Probably the most popular species of implied choice of law is the reliance by both parties on one system of law once litigation has arisen. It is popular with attorneys as well as courts since it leads almost inevitably to the application of German law.[24] The details, however, especially the degree of reliance necessary and its effect, are not quite certain.

There is no question of degree of reliance if both parties rely on German law at every stage of the court proceeding.[25] If, on the other hand, one party, having first proceeded on the basis of German law, later discovers and invokes foreign law, the outcome depends upon the stage of the proceeding; the plea is unacceptable if not raised until the second appeal.[26] By contrast, it would seem to be

---

[22] *See infra* n. 33.

[23] A choice of law clause incorporated in a charter party may be made applicable to the bill of lading by the usual reference in the latter to the former, BGH 5 Dec. 1966, WM 1967, 141; RG 24 Nov. 1928, RGZ 122, 316, 319.

Reference was made to printed conditions in BGH 11 Feb. 1953, BGHZ 9, 34, 37; OLG Hamm 6 June 1957, IPRspr. 1956/57 no. 27 (loan to American businessman from German bank); BAG 10 May 1962, BAG 13, 121.

[24] *Exceptions*: OLG Stuttgart 30 Nov. 1960, IPRspr. 1960/61 no. 213 (New York law applied to suit between New York residents for legal advice relating to restitution claim in Germany); BGH 17 Jan. 1966, WM 1966, 140, 141 (French law); OLG Saarbrücken 11 Jan. 1966, IPRspr. 1966/67 no. 53, *aff'd*, BGH 20 Sept. 1967, VIII ZR 43/66.

[25] *See*, e.g., BGH 23 Nov. 1964, WM 1965, 102; 21 May 1964, WM 1964, 768, 769; 24 June 1958, WM 1958, 1136, 1137; 17 Dec. 1957, IPRspr. 1956/57 no. 23d; OLG Hamburg 25 Oct. 1961, IPRspr. 1960/61 no. 72. An express declaration of the attorneys about the applicable law falls under the head of an express choice of law, *supra* n. 21.

[26] BGH 17 Jan. 1966, WM 1966, 140, 141; 7 Mar. 1962, NJW 1962, 1005; 21 Oct. 1960, VersR 1961, 52.

precluded prematurely if raised in the court of first instance, even though the "trial" has begun.[27]

The effect of reliance on a particular system of law is less clear. Is the implication as to the parties' choice of law conclusive or not? Court practice is not yet settled on this point. Many cases are based exclusively on the parties' reliance in the court proceeding,[28] while others refer to additional circumstances like those taken into account in determining the "center of gravity."[29] There are two cases which declare the parties' reliance on German law entirely irrelevant,[30] but prevailing opinion probably views it as a strong though not conclusive indication of their choice of law.[31] It is merely a logical extension of this opinion to assume, as some cases do, that the parties' reliance on one law constitutes not an implicit choice of law but merely the decisive element in the determination of the "center of gravity."[32] There is little practical difference. Reliance on German law during litigation prevails even over a prior express clause providing for the application of another law;[33] this is an instance of subsequent change of the selected law.[34]

(b) *Stipulation of forum or arbitration.*—According to longstanding court practice the contractual stipulation of the court that is to assume jurisdiction in controversies between the parties implies choice of the *lex fori.*[35] Apparently there is no post-War decision to the contrary. If some cases rely exclusively on the jurisdictional

---

[27] LG Lübeck 21 May 1957, IPRspr. 1960/61 no. 42; but the result may be justified on other grounds.

[28] *See,* e.g., BGH 23 Nov. 1964, 21 May 1964 and 24 June 1958, *supra* n. 25.

[29] *See,* e.g., BGH 17 Dec. 1957; OLG Hamburg 25 Oct. 1961, *supra* n. 25.

[30] BGH 13 July 1959, WM 1959, 1110 (parties' references to German law based on an error); *cf.* OLG Celle 29 Nov. 1961, IPRspr. 1960/61 no. 35; *see also* RG 20 Mar. 1936, RGZ 151, 193, 199–200. Foreign law was applied in all these cases.

[31] BGH 21 Oct. 1960, VersR 1961, 52; 6 May 1955, WM 1955, 1588; OLG Bremen 19 Apr. 1960, IPRspr. 1960/61 no. 46; OLG Neustadt 25 Nov. 1955, IPRspr. 1954/55 no. 14.

[32] BGH 7 Mar. 1962, NJW 1962, 1005; KG Berlin 18 Dec. 1962, WM 1963, 629, 630, *aff'd in this respect,* BGH 21 June 1965, WM 1965, 766; OLG Neustadt, *supra* n. 31; LG Frankfurt 18 Oct. 1963, IPRspr. 1962/63 no. 32.

[33] OLG Hamburg 21 Oct. 1965, VersR 1965, 1209, 1210; 24 Sept. 1940, HansRGZ 1940 B 356; *see also* BGH 2 Feb. 1961, WM 1961, 320.

[34] Some courts emphasize the retroactive effect of the parties' reliance even though they have not made a prior express choice of law, OLG Saarbrücken 13 Oct. 1965, OLGZ 1966 no. 61; OLG Hamburg 13 Dec. 1962, IPRspr. 1962/63 no. 23. This is a truism since reliance without retroactive effect would make little sense in these cases.

[35] BGH 15 Mar. 1962, IPRspr. 1962/63 no. 41; 30 Jan. 1961, NJW 1961, 1061, 1062; OGH Köln 4 May 1950, OGHZ 4, 138, 144; OLG Frankfurt 21 Mar. 1961, IPRspr. 1960/61 no. 33; OLG Düsseldorf 15 Jan. 1959, IPRspr. 1958/59 no. 48; LG Frankfurt 10 Jan. 1964, AWD 1964, 90.

clause[36] while others enumerate additional factors,[37] this is a difference in style rather than substance. The rule makes sense if the stipulated forum is in Germany, as it usually is. Otherwise, the proper course would be to apply the foreign *lex fori,* including its conflict of laws rules, which are binding on the foreign court.[38]

If the parties agree that the plaintiff may elect between two or more fora, whether any choice of law is implied is doubtful. The *Reichsgericht* strongly opposed it,[39] while the *Bundesgerichtshof* seems to have accepted it.[40] This latter solution, although logically not persuasive, seems to be in accord with the thinking in commercial circles in Germany today. While it may not afford an answer before litigation, it certainly does after a court has been seized.

An arbitration clause has been held to raise an even stronger presumption that the parties intend to refer their contract to the law obtaining at the seat of the arbitral proceeding.[41] This presumption applies at least to institutional arbitrations (except those of the International Chamber of Commerce[42]), which usually (at least in Germany, Great Britain, and the United States[43]) apply the substantive law of their seat. The *Reichsgericht* held correctly that the implication collapses if the arbitration clause is ineffective; the *Bundesgerichtshof* has disagreed in one case.[44]

(c) *Other factors.*—The designation of a single place of performance had, and to some extent still has, a relatively high indicative value. Historically, it derived from the primary rôle of the law at the place of performance (*supra* I). Its present value stems from the fact that under German procedural law the court at the place of performance has jurisdiction in contract matters (§ 29 ZPO), so that the agreed single place of performance, if located in Germany, is tantamount to a stipulation of German jurisdiction (on this, *see supra* (b)).[45] Nevertheless, the importance of this circumstance has notably

---

[36] OGH Köln, and OLG and LG Frankfurt, *supra* n. 35.

[37] BGH and OLG Düsseldorf, *supra* n. 35.

[38] *Contra*: OLG Düsseldorf, *supra* n. 35.

[39] RG 12 Mar. 1928, JW 1928, 1196.

[40] BGH 3 July 1959, IPRspr. 1958/59 no. 53; *also, impliedly,* OLG Frankfurt 21 Mar. 1961, *supra* n. 35.

[41] BGH 5 Dec. 1966, WM 1967, 141; 1 July 1964, WM 1964, 1023; BAG 30 May 1963, IPRspr. 1962/63 no. 51; OLG Düsseldorf 12 Jan. 1961, IPRspr. 1960/61 no. 219; OLG Hamburg 29 Oct. 1958, IPRspr. 1958/59 no. 43.

[42] OLG Stuttgart 23 May 1960, IPRspr. 1960/61 no. 25; *see also* OLG Düsseldorf 4 Aug. 1961, GRUR/Ausl. 1962, 256.

[43] *See* DOMKE, The Law and Practice of Commercial Arbitration (1968) 257–58, with references (notwithstanding the assertion to the contrary at p. 257 para. 1).

[44] *See* RG, *supra* n. 14. *Contra*: BGH 5 Dec. 1966, *supra* n. 41.

[45] *See,* e.g., RG 5 July 1935, RGZ 148, 42, 43. But the rule has also been applied to the stipulation of a *foreign* place of performance: RG 29 Oct. 1938,

decreased since World War II, and the Federal Supreme Court has in one case lightly brushed it aside.[46]

Other circumstances have little weight. An express reference to the provisions of a particular system of law,[47] or the utilization of forms or expressions similarly inspired,[48] come into play only subsidiarily,[49] and even then they are not necessarily decisive. The place of contracting has no importance in this connection.

Whether the parties have manifested a tacit intention is a mixed question of fact and law. On the second appeal the Federal Supreme Court is permitted to examine only whether the lower courts have correctly weighed individual factors in finding an implied intention.[50]

(3) **Third Step: Balancing of Interests**

Absent an express or implied choice of law by the parties, it is the court which determines the law applicable to an international contract. This third and most important step in choosing the law governing a contract is generally designated in Germany as the search for the "hypothetical intention of the parties"—a misnomer adopted fairly recently. Earlier, the *Reichsgericht*, for a period of thirty years, did in fact inquire what law the parties would probably

---

RGZ 159, 33, 44–45; 5 July 1935, RGZ 148, 42, 43; BayObLG 3 Jan. 1934, IPRspr. 1934 no. 24.

[46] BGH 25 Nov. 1957, BGHZ 26, 91 (place of performance in Switzerland). The court expressly overruled a contrary holding, LG Karlsruhe 21 Jan. 1955, IPRspr. 1956/57 no. 28a. *See*, however, OLG München 15 July 1954, IPRspr. 1954/55 no. 18 (place of performance in Germany).

[47] KEGEL, Kommentar, no. 182 preceding art. 7 EGBGB, and *supra* n. 12. However, the cases on which KEGEL relies (n. 34), do not support his conclusion. And there are almost as many holdings to the contrary, *see* BGH 13 July 1959, WM 1959, 1110; OLG Hamburg 7 July 1905 and 5 July 1907; and OLG Düsseldorf 10 Jan. 1929; all *supra* n. 17.

[48] *Printed form*: OLG Hamburg 21 Feb. 1930, IPRspr. 1930 no. 46 (marine insurance). Whether charter parties drafted in English and referring to English rules (like the Gencon) implied a choice of English law was controversial; in the *affirmative*, RG 4 Nov. 1933, JW 1934, 835; 24 Nov. 1928, RGZ 122, 316, 318–19; OLG Hamburg 13 Feb. 1934, IPRspr. 1934 no. 38; *contra*: RG 3 Nov. 1937, SeuffArch. 92, 122, 124; Arbitration Hamburg, IPRspr. 1931 no. 41, and OLG Hamburg 28 Sept. 1954, IPRspr. 1954/55 no. 34 b, *aff'd*, BGH 17 Apr. 1956, IPRspr. 1956/57 no. 55. The question has become moot for contracts of affreightment because of the widespread use of express choice of law clauses.

Expressions: Reference to salary and leave claims according to a collective agreement, BAG 7 July 1960, IPRspr. 1960/61 no. 26; *see also* BAG 4 Aug. 1960, IPRspr. 1960/61 no. 27.

[49] OLG Hamburg 29 Oct. 1958, IPRspr. 1958/59 no. 43, and Arbitration Hamburg 22 July 1937, HansRGZ 1937 B 371 (stipulation of arbitration prevails over implication drawn from use of printed forms based on a specific legal system).

[50] *See*, e.g., BGH 1 July 1964, WM 1964, 1023, 1024; 9 June 1960, WM 1960, 938, 939.

have chosen if they had dealt, reasonably, with the question.[51] This subjective formula, although preserved by some contemporary writers,[52] was replaced after World War II by an objective approach. The Federal Supreme Court has held consistently that the "so-called hypothetical intention" does not purport to determine the hypothetical subjective intentions of the parties, but is directed rather to a reasonable balancing of interests on a purely objective basis.[53]

What does this "objective" formula mean in practice? An analysis of the post-War decisions shows that the courts have succeeded with respect to some but not all types of contracts, applying tests similar in certain respects to the catalogue proposed for the Restatement (Second) of the Law of Conflict of Laws, §§ 189–197.[53a] A review of the case law will demonstrate the results, and perhaps also the reasons for the failures.

(a) *Sales contracts.*—German writers have frequently suggested that sales contracts should be subjected to the law of the seller's business residence because his performance is much more complicated and therefore more "characteristic" than the buyer's.[54] However, the courts have refused to adopt this simple rule on the ground that the seller's performance does not "clearly" take precedence.[55] The real motive may lie in the fact that most of the disputes before German courts arise from import sales so that the seller's law is foreign law. A combination of the following factors is often thought to justify the application of German law to import sales: the buyer's business residence, the German destination of the goods, and the further fact that the negotiations have been carried on by the foreign seller's German representative.[56] Sometimes the buyer's German

---

[51] Starting with RG 4 Apr. 1908, RGZ 68, 203, 205, and continuing to 17 June 1939, RGZ 161, 296, 298.

[52] KEGEL, Kommentar, no. 185 preceding art. 7 EGBGB; NEUHAUS 176–79; GAMILLSCHEG, AcP 157 (1958/59) 303, 324–41; *see also* RAAPE 474, corrected at p. 476.

[53] BGH 28 Oct. 1965, BGHZ 44, 183, 186; 19 Oct. 1960, WM 1960, 1360, 1361; 9 June 1960, WM 1960, 938, 939; 10 Jan. 1958, IPRspr. 1958/59 no. 37; 22 Nov. 1955, BGHZ 19, 110, 112–13; 14 Apr. 1953, BGHZ 9, 221, 223.

[53a] Proposed Official Draft No. 2 (1968).

[54] KEGEL, Kommentar, no. 201 preceding art. 7 EGBGB; NEUHAUS 124; KREUZER 98; GAMILLSCHEG, *supra* n. 52, at 333.

[55] BGH 9 June 1960; 10 Jan. 1958, *supra* n. 53; OLG Stuttgart 23 May 1960, IPRspr. 1960/61 no. 25; *see* RG 4 Feb. 1913, RGZ 81, 273, 275. *See,* however, BGH 7 May 1969, WM 1969, 772 (Belgian law applied where Belgium was seller's business residence, place of contracting and of payment, and place where goods were located and were handed over).

[56] BGH 9 Dec. 1964, BGHZ 43, 21, 25; OLG Frankfurt 25 Nov. 1960, IPRspr. 1960/61 no. 31, *rev'd on other grounds,* BGH 20 June 1962, WM 1962, 1036.

residence alone, as the place of performance of payment of the purchase price,[57] and even the mere existence of German public law rules establishing minimum quality standards, have been held decisive.[58] In an export sale, contract clauses providing for delivery "F.O.B. Hamburg" and "payment against documents" have been held sufficient contacts with Germany.[59] German law, on the other hand, is not applied to international sales when the merchandise is not to be brought to Germany,[60] or to sales deemed purely "foreign."[61] As can be seen, the courts seem unfortunately to follow but one maxim, namely, to apply German law at any cost.

There is one type of sale for which a uniform solution, inspired by the characteristics of the contract, has been evolved. This is the sales contract relating to an immovable.[62]

Finally, solution of the not infrequent case in which no one interest clearly prevails is relegated to the place-of-performance device (*infra* (4)).

(b) *License contracts.*—The German courts apply a uniform criterion to all kinds of license contracts, whether relating to patents, publications or films. The law applied is that of the licensee's business residence,[63] and it so happens that this is usually German law.[64]

(c) *Contracts for work, service or labor.*—Different treatment is accorded the different contracts in this miscellaneous group. It has been held, for example, that the contract of an American shipyard for repairs to a foreign vessel is governed by American law,[65] and

---

[57] OLG Hamburg 5 Aug. 1958, NJW 1958, 1919; *cf.* OLG Hamburg 30 May 1963, IPRspr. 1962/63 no. 28 (foreign seller's residence agreed to as place of performance for payment); *see also* BGH 26 June 1968, VersR 1968, 995 (Dutch hull insurer doing business in Germany bought spare parts from American seller; German law applied since contract was concluded in Germany and payment was to be made there).

[58] BGH 19 Oct. 1960, *supra* n. 53.

[59] OLG Stuttgart 23 May 1960, *supra* n. 55.

[60] OLG Hamburg 30 May 1963, *supra* n. 57.

[61] BGH 9 June 1960, *supra* n. 53 (sale between two American parties residing in the United States).

[62] Application of the *lex rei sitae*: KG Berlin 20 May 1961, IPRspr. 1960/61 no. 58; LG Hamburg 18 Jan. 1952, IPRspr. 1952/53 no. 27.

[63] *Patents*: OLG Düsseldorf 4 Aug. 1961, GRUR/Aus. 1962, 256; LG Stuttgart 14 Mar. 1957, IPRspr. 1956/57 no. 29; *see also* LG Hamburg 7 July 1967, IPRspr. 1966/67 no. 192.

Publications: BGH 19 Dec. 1958, GRUR 1959, 331; 22 Nov. 1955, BGHZ 19, 110, 113; *see also* 29 Mar. 1960, GRUR 1960, 447; OLG München 25 Feb. 1952, GRUR 1953, 302.

Films: BGH 3 July 1959, IPRspr. 1958/59 no. 53; 20 Mar. 1956, WM 1956, 1265.

[64] *See*, however, LG Stuttgart 14 Mar. 1957, *supra* n. 63.

[65] LG Bremen 2 Apr. 1959, IPRspr. 1960/61 no. 43.

this accords with general opinion.[66] As for the relations between commission agent and principal, these have for a long time been submitted to the law of the agent's business residence.[67] The contract for a broker's services, if intimately connected with it, may follow the law governing the contract mediated;[68] in other cases, it will follow the law of the broker's business residence.[69] A mercantile agency is usually governed by the law of the agent's business residence; this place is considered the center of gravity of the agent's activities, which are more important than those of his principal.[70] Under special circumstances, however, the courts sometimes apply the latter's law, as where the principal is a German who has contracted on the basis of a printed form which he uses in his relations with agents the world over and where the agent also has close relations with Germany.[71] In one case, American law was applied to the relations between an American principal temporarily residing in Germany and a Canadian agent engaged in selling American foodstuffs to American military bases in Spain.[72] The law governing other agency relations is less certain. An agent engaged by a foreign principal to administer German real property will normally be subject to the *lex rei sitae*.[73] The prosecution in Germany of a claim for restitution and damages by an agent residing in the country of the foreign principal was correctly submitted by one court to the law of the parties' common residence, but another court applied German law.[74]

Labor contracts are as a rule governed by the law of the place where the services are performed. This holds true for foreigners working for German firms mostly in Germany[75] as well as for Germans

---

[66] LG München 24 July 1957, WM 1957, 1378; KEGEL, Kommentar, no. 193 preceding art. 7 EGBGB.

[67] BGH 23 Nov. 1964, WM 1965, 126, 127; OLG Frankfurt 17 Jan. 1967, WM 1967, 219; *see also* OLG Saarbrücken 3 Aug. 1966, IPRspr. 1966/67 no. 55a. *See* RG 21 Nov. 1910, JW 1911, 148 (American law applied to sales commission by American agent for German firm). For details, *see* STOLL, Kollisionsrechtliche Fragen beim Kommissionsgeschäft, RabelsZ 24 (1959) 601–38.

[68] BGH 17 Apr. 1956, IPRspr. 1956/57 no. 55.

[69] BGH 19 Nov. 1962, IPRspr. 1962/63 no. 22.

[70] BGH 15 Mar. 1962, IPRspr. 1962/63 no. 41; OLG München 8 Mar. 1956, IPRspr. 1956/57 no. 46; LG Frankfurt 6 Dec. 1963, IPRspr. 1962/63 no. 43; LG Wuppertal 2 Oct. 1962, IPRspr. 1962/63 no. 42.

[71] LG Hamburg 29 Jan. 1965, IPRspr. 1964/65 no. 42.

[72] LG Frankfurt 3 July 1964, IPRspr. 1964/65 no. 39.

[73] BGH 16 Oct. 1958, WM 1959, 354; 5 Feb. 1954, IPRspr. 1954/55 no. 197.

[74] OLG Düsseldorf 8 Jan. 1959, IPRspr. 1958/59 no. 46; LG München I 19 Dec. 1960, IPRspr. 1960/61 no. 214. *See also infra* n. 84.

[75] BAG 27 Aug. 1964, AP no. 9 on Internat. Privatrecht, Arbeitsrecht; 20 July 1961, IPRspr. 1960/61 no. 34 (American actress playing in German film); 4 Aug. 1960, IPRspr. 1960/61 no. 27. *Contra*: LAG Frankfurt 14 Mar. 1951, IPRspr. 1950/51 no. 20.

engaged by foreign employers for services in Germany.[76] A seaman working on a vessel flying the German flag is by statute subjected to German labor law,[77] and the law of the flag is by analogy applied to a seaman aboard a foreign vessel.[78] The contract between a German and a Delaware company for services to be performed in the United States has been held to be governed by Delaware law.[79] By contrast, if German enterprises engage Germans for services to be rendered abroad, the courts tend to submit these relations to German law,[80] and foreign law is applied if labor is to be performed by foreigners in Germany for a firm of their home country.[81] Special conflicts may arise between American and German labor law since the latter has a considerably greater number of protective provisions. In one case, an American occupation court in Germany applied a German statute protecting motherhood in labor relations to a contract governed by German law.[82] A pension plan will usually be submitted to the same law that governs the underlying labor contract.[83] The requirement of an employment permit for work to be performed by a foreigner in Germany will be dealt with later (*see infra* ch. 11 sub II (1)(a)).

The authority of an agent to represent his principal is governed by separate rules (*infra* IV).

(d) *Contracts for legal advice.*—Contracts for the services of an attorney are usually subject to the law at the attorney's professional residence.[84] The status of those former German attorneys who after emigration were admitted to practice in their new home and then after the War were readmitted to practice in Germany is unsettled.

---

[76] BAG 9 and 13 May 1959, BAG 7, 357, 359–360 and 7, 362, 364; LAG München 16 May 1950, IPRspr. 1950/51 no. 21.

[77] Under § 1 Seemannsgesetz of July 26, 1957, (BGBl. II 713) the provisions of the Law are enacted for all vessels flying the German flag. *See* BAG 30 May 1963, IPRspr. 1962/63 no. 51.

[78] OLG Bremen 9 Feb. 1960, IPRspr. 1960/61 no. 45.

[79] RAG 20 July 1935, JW 1935, 3665.

[80] BAG 21 Sept. 1966, NJW 1967, 414; *see also* BAG 10 May 1962, BAG 13, 121, 124; 7 July 1960, IPRspr. 1960/61 no. 26; *contra*: LAG Düsseldorf 12 July 1956, IPRspr. 1956/57 no. 26 (in effect overruled by BAG 10 May 1962).

[81] BAG 20 July 1967, AP no. 10 on Internat. Privatrecht, Arbeitsrecht (American technician working in Germany for New York company may not invoke German protective provisions on dismissal).

[82] American AHC-Court Frankfurt 17 Apr. 1953, IPRspr. 1952/53 no. 30.

[83] BAG 18 Dec. 1967, AP no. 11 on Internat. Privatrecht, Arbeitsrecht (German local labor of New York company).

[84] BGH 24 Jan. 1957, IPRspr. 1956/57 no. 4; 15 Nov. 1956, IPRspr. 1960/61 no. 1 (American attorney); OLG Köln 19 Jan. 1960, NJW 1960, 1301; OLG München 20 Feb. 1958, IPRspr. 1960/61 no. 208 (American attorney); KG Berlin 12 July 1958, IPRspr. 1958/59 no. 40; LG Berlin 15 Dec. 1959, IPRspr. 1958/59 no. 8; *see* RG 20 Mar. 1936, RGZ 151, 193, 199.

The respected appellate court in West Berlin has twice held that contracts relating to services to be rendered to American clients in Germany are governed by German law; another court has disagreed.[85] In line with the first two decisions is a case of the Federal Supreme Court on a reverse set of facts: an American attorney residing in the American zone of Germany had been admitted by the American authorities to practice according to American law, and his services relating to an occupation matter were held to be subject to "American" law.[86] And a lower court has held, correctly, that an agreement between two German-born immigrants residing in New York, by which one was to enforce the reparation claims of the other in Germany as well as the United States, should be subject to the law of New York.[86a]

The most important practical issue determined by the law governing legal services is the amount of the attorney's fees. The methods used in the two countries for the fixing of these fees differ considerably. German attorneys are regulated by an elaborate statute with a table of fees based on the value of the issue in controversy, irrespective of the amount of work performed.[87] While lower fees, as a rule, may not be agreed upon, an agreement for higher fees must be in writing and separate from the power of attorney or a printed form.[88]

An agreement for a contingent fee or a "*quota litis*," although no longer prohibited by statute, contravenes the Attorneys' Code of Ethics.[89] In view of the high number of applications for restitution or compensation brought after the War by persons residing outside Germany and often represented by foreign counsel who agreed to take the case for a *quota litis*, it is not surprising that some of the clients invoked the German prohibition of this agreement. Since the contract with the foreign attorney was not subject to German law, the only way in which the latter could come into play was by claiming a contravention of German public policy (art. 30 EGBGB). The attitude of the German courts in this respect is not uniform and

[85] KG Berlin 19 May 1960 and 21 Apr. 1961, IPRspr. 1960/61 no. 211 a, b; *see also* BGH 31 Mar. 1969, Rpfl. 1969, 239; LG Düsseldorf 28 Nov. 1963, IPRspr. 1962/63 no. 209; *contra*: OLG München 20 Feb. 1958, *supra* n. 84.

[86] BGH 28 Oct. 1965, NJW 1966, 296, 297; *see also* KG Berlin 11 July 1959, IPRspr. 1962/63 no. 202.

[86a] LG München I 11 Feb. 1965, IPRspr. 1964/65 no. 43.

[87] Bundesgebührenordnung für Rechtsanwälte (BRAGebO) of July 26, 1957, BGBl. I 907, BGBl. III 368–1.

[88] § 40 of the Attorneys' Code of Ethics (Grundsätze des anwaltlichen Standesrechts), issued by the Federal Chamber of Attorneys in May 1963 on statutory authority, reprinted by KALSBACH, Bundesrechtsanwaltsordnung, 1960, 340; § 3 I BRAGebO.

[89] § 41 of the Code of Ethics, *supra* n. 88.

seems to be influenced by the circumstances of each case. The Federal Supreme Court has not invoked article 30 EGBGB against quotas of 1.5% and 1% for the recovery of relatively high sums.[90] In a smaller case it has reduced a quota of 35% to 20%.[91] Other courts have limited the quota to 10% of the amount recovered.[92] A forecast of the courts' future attitude in this particular field is difficult,[93] but it appears that the courts are becoming somewhat more liberal.[93a]

(e) *Contracts for carriage of goods.*—Separate rules have developed for land and for maritime transportation. The courts tend to apply the law of the carrier's business residence to land carriage,[94] and similarly a client's relations with a forwarding agent are usually submitted to the law of the latter's residence.[95] Contracts for ocean carriage of goods are usually governed by the law of the flag;[96] however, problems connected with unloading are subject to the law of the port of discharge,[97] and the rights of the holders of a bill of lading are determined by the law of the port of destination.[98]

(f) *Financial contracts.*—A loan contract is often subjected by the courts to the law of the debtor's domicile on the ground that this is usually the place of performance of his obligation to repay.[99] It would seem indeed that the debtor's domicile is normally the center of gravity of a loan. The earlier inclination to depart from this rule where the loan was contracted between compatriots living in a

---

[90] BGH 15 Nov. 1956, IPRspr. 1956/57 no. 3, 1960/61 no. 1; 24 Jan. 1957, IPRspr. 1956/57 no. 4 (partial amount only of the agreed 7.5%).

[91] BGH 28 Oct. 1965, BGHZ 44, 183; *see also* OLG München 20 Feb. 1958, IPRspr. 1960 no. 208.

[92] KG Berlin 12 July 1958, IPRspr. 1958/59 no. 40; LG Berlin 15 Dec. 1959, *id.* no. 8. Partial recovery of less than 10% was held not objectionable, KG Berlin 11 July 1959, *supra* n. 86.

[93] *See* the authoritative comment on §§ 40, 41 of the "Richtlinien" by KALSBACH, *supra* n. 88, at 326–41.

[93a] *25% for an American attorney*: KG Berlin 19 Nov. 1962, IPRspr. 1962/63 no. 206; *15%*: LG Düsseldorf 28 Mar. 1962, *id.* no. 205a; *12%*: LG Hildesheim 18 Jan. 1962, *id.* no. 203.

[94] BGH 30 Apr. 1959, IPRspr. 1958/59 no. 75. If the contract is made with a foreign branch, the law at its seat controls, OLG Hamburg 13 Dec. 1953, IPRspr. 1952/53 no. 21.

[95] OLG Saarbrücken 22 July 1953, IPRspr. 1952/53 no. 39; OLG Freiburg 26 Oct. 1950, IPRspr. 1950/51 no. 22; LG Aschaffenburg 7 July 1953, IPRspr. 1952/53 no. 38.

[96] BGH 20 Mar. 1956, WM 1956, 792; RG 28 May 1936, HansRGZ 1936 B 475, 476 (obiter); LG Berlin 15 Nov. 1956, IPRspr. 1956/57 no. 56. *Contra*: KEGEL, Kommentar, no. 196 preceding art. 7 EGBGB; *see also* SCHAPS/ABRAHAM, Das deutsche Seerecht (3d ed. 1962) II 279–82.

[97] BGH 14 Apr. 1953, BGHZ 9, 221, 223–24.

[98] This is constant practice, *see* BGH 26 Sept. 1957, BGHZ 25, 250, 254; 20 Mar. 1956, *supra* n. 96; 20 May 1952, BGHZ 6, 127, 134.

[99] BGH 18 Feb. 1965, BGHZ 43, 164, 166; 25 Nov. 1957, BGHZ 26, 91 (this case must be criticized on another ground, *see supra* n. 46); RG 18 Nov. 1937, RGZ 156, 158, 160; 5 Oct. 1936, RGZ 152, 213, 215.

foreign country has fortunately receded today,[100] but loans by German banks are expressly submitted to German law (*supra* n. 11). Similar considerations apply to security transactions: the guarantor's domicile usually will be the center of gravity.[101] But there may be circumstances which vary the situation: if a foreign bank agrees to pay and to deposit the amount of the collateral in Germany, it is correct to apply German law.[102] Of the many suretyship contracts entered into by American companies in favor of their German subsidiaries, apparently only one has been litigated; in view of the close connection with the secured obligation, the court applied the German law agreed upon for the secured loan.[103]

For insurance contracts, the complexity of the insurer's performance and the size of its enterprise combine to justify application of the law of the insurer's residence.[104] However, if the contract is concluded with the German representative of a foreign company and is to be performed in Germany, German law applies.[105]

The same principle demands submission of a German citizen's savings account with a New York bank to New York law, especially if this has clearly been envisaged by the parties' agreeing upon an "in trust for" (or "Totten trust") account.[105a]

(g) *Gratuitous transfers.*—These are considered contracts in German law. Since the emphasis is on the donor's obligation, the law of his residence should be decisive.[106]

The foregoing examples demonstrate the more important results of a balancing of interests. It may be expected that the courts will follow them in the future provided the typical facts are similar. If, however, relevant individual traits differ, the balancing process will

---

[100] *Foreigners living in Germany*: BGH 9 Nov. 1960, IPRspr. 1960/61 no. 29; KG Berlin 16 Aug. 1956, NJW 1957, 347.

Germans living abroad: OLG Karlsruhe 15 Dec. 1965; WM 1966, 1312, 1314; *contra*: LG Tübingen 16 Feb. 1966, IPRspr. 1966/67 no. 22.

[101] LG Aschaffenburg 7 July 1953, *supra* n. 95, at 145–46; *see also* OLG Hamburg 25 Nov. 1959, IPRspr. 1958/59 no. 61.

[102] LG Frankfurt 16 Oct. 1962, NJW 1963, 450.

[103] KG Berlin 6 June 1957, IPRspr. 1956/57 no. 27.

[104] OLG Hamburg 1 July 1957, IPRspr. 1956/57 no. 50; 5 Mar. 1957, *id.* no. 50a; 24 Apr. 1956, *id.* no. 55a (although there were ten insurers from four countries, since nine were from France or French-influenced countries, French law was applied).

[105] BGH 11 Feb. 1953, BGHZ 9, 35, 41; 24 Mar. 1955, BGHZ 17, 74, 76–77; RG 5 July 1935, RGZ 148, 42, 43; *see* OLG Karlsruhe 12 Nov. 1959, VersR 1960, 722 (insurance contract between American soldier stationed in Germany and American insurance company doing business in Germany held governed by German law). This conclusion is reinforced by the jurisdiction of the German court at the foreign insurer's German branch office (§ 21 ZPO), which is compulsory (§ 109 VAG); *see also supra* II (2) (b).

[105a] BGH 10 June 1968, WM 1968, 1170, 1172.

[106] OLG Frankfurt 24 June 1964, IPRspr. 1964/65 no. 37; RAAPE 481–82.

lead to different results. The balancing of interests, incidentally, is a mixed question of fact and law. On the second appeal the Federal Supreme Court may only examine whether the lower courts have correctly evaluated all the relevant factors.[107]

(4) **Fourth Step: Statutory Places of Performance**

Although a balancing of interests should always result in discovery of the proper law, the German courts use a fourth-ranking criterion in their search for the law governing contracts, namely, the statutory places of performance.[108] It is used almost exclusively for sales contracts.[109] The courts keep this emergency exit open despite strong objections from the legal writers[110] by asserting that in international sales the seller's performance does not clearly outweigh that of the buyer (*supra* (3)(a)). The true reason is the preference of the courts for their own law, already alluded to, which leads in most instances, directly or indirectly, to the *lex fori*.[111]

(a) An unfortunate aspect of the place-of-performance approach is the diversity of this concept in the different legal systems. The German courts meet it by applying the German test contained in § 269 BGB.[112] If the foreign law applicable under this test itself employs the place-of-performance concept, the foreign characterization is then applied,[113] and this may result in a renvoi to German internal law.[113a]

---

[107] *See* BGH 28 Oct. 1965, BGHZ 44, 183, 186; 15 Mar. 1962, IPRspr. 1962/63 no. 41; 19 Oct. 1960, WM 1960, 1360, 1362. But the court itself lacks a clear conception, the seventh division emphasizing the legal aspect, thus advocating full review (BGH 28 Oct. 1965, *supra*), the eighth stressing the factual aspect, thus excluding (BGH 9 Dec. 1964, WM 1965, 82) or at least limiting (BGH 19 Oct. 1960, *supra*) review. In fact, however, the formula mentioned in the text is generally followed. *See also supra* n. 50 on the review of a finding of tacit intention.

[108] An agreed place of performance, especially if valid for both parties, will express a tacit choice of law by the parties, *supra* nn. 45, 46.

[109] Of ten reported post-War cases, only one is not a sales, but a service, case, OLG Frankfurt 27 Oct. 1966, NJW 1967, 501.

[110] RAAPE 483–86; NEUHAUS 85, 189; SANDROCK, Zur ergänzenden Vertragsauslegung im materiellen und internationalen Schuldvertragsrecht (1966) 204–14; GAMILLSCHEG, *supra* n. 52, at 321.

[111] Only in three out of ten reported post-War international sales cases governed by the place of performance was foreign law eventually applied; one of these cases was a purely intra-United States sale.

[112] BGH 9 June 1960, WM 1960, 938, 939; 10 Jan. 1958, IPRspr. 1958/59 no. 37, at 147; 23 Mar. 1955, WM 1955, 765; KEGEL, Kommentar, no. 206 preceding art. 7 EGBGB, with further references.

Under § 269 BGB the place of performance is fixed, unless something else is agreed or results from the circumstances, by the debtor's (business) residence at the time of contracting.

[113] OLG Frankfurt, *supra* n. 109, at 503; RAAPE 46–47, 486.

[113a] *See* OLG Frankfurt, *supra* n. 109.

(b) The chief practical disadvantage of the place-of-performance doctrine is the necessity to split the law governing the contract into two or more segments depending upon the number of places where the parties have to perform. Not only is it difficult to allocate the rights and obligations of the parties to one or another legal system, but grave difficulties can be expected to arise from their interdependence. However, the courts have managed to avoid subjecting one contract to two or more systems of law by proper allocation of one party's rights and the other party's corresponding duties to the same law. Thus the obligation of the seller as to the quality of the goods sold is governed by the law of his business residence.[114] The buyer's obligation to pay the purchase price, and the running of the statute of limitations affecting it, is governed by the law of his business residence;[115] but this obligation is thought to include all the buyer's rights (and corresponding obligations, especially the notice of rejection) based upon defects,[116] including a claim for reimbursement after payment of the price.[117]

While the evil consequences of splitting the governing law can thus be avoided in the sales area, there is no similar solution in many other areas of general contract law, like formation[118] and validity of the contract.

(c) The artificial nature of the place-of-performance device is well illustrated by the fact that the courts regularly look for a renvoi from a foreign place of performance. Almost always, at least in export sales, they succeed in finding such a renvoi, which means German law is ultimately applicable.[119]

(5) **Renvoi**

The rôle that renvoi (which is widely accepted in matters of status and inheritance) should play in German international contract law is controversial. The courts and writers are unanimous only in regarding a choice of law by the parties, express or tacit, as referring

---

[114] BGH 23 Mar. 1955, WM 1955, 765, 766.

[115] BGH 9 June 1960, *supra* n. 11 (sale of chocolate by seller in Chicago to buyer in New Orleans; Louisiana law applied); BGH 23 Mar. 1955, *supra* n. 114; BGH 26 June 1963, WM 1963, 844, 845 (sale "cash against documents," refusal to pay on presentation of documents).

[116] BGH 14 Feb. 1958, NJW 1958, 750; 19 Oct. 1960, WM 1960, 1360, 1361 (obiter); OLG Celle 29 Nov. 1961, IPRspr. 1960/61 no. 35; OLG Nürnberg 13 Jan. 1959, IPRspr. 1958/59 no. 47; LG Bielefeld 12 July 1963, IPRspr. 1962/63 no. 31 (sale of machinery by American seller).

[117] BGH 14 Feb. 1958, *supra* n. 116; OLG Stuttgart 23 May 1960, IPRspr. 1960/61 no. 25.

[118] In BGH 9 Dec. 1964, BGHZ 43, 21, the appellate court had not been able, by balancing of interests, to find one single law for a sales contract and, therefore, took refuge in splitting. The BGH had to find one law governing the question whether a contract had come into existence.

[119] *See supra* n. 111 and n. 113a and *infra* (5).

to the substantive rules of the law chosen, thus excluding renvoi.[120] If the governing law is selected by balancing the interests involved, the courts also refuse to accept a renvoi, although on the erroneous ground that here again the (hypothetical!) intention of the parties is involved.[121] A better justification for this correct result would seem to be the fact that the balancing of interests leads to the application of the law best suited to the individual contract. It would run counter to the very nature of this approach to accept, merely because it is prescribed by a foreign system of law, a different outcome of the balancing process or even a mechanical rule looking to a fixed place.[121a]

Where, on the other hand, the applicable law has been found with the help of the place-of-performance rule, the situation is quite different. Here the Federal Supreme Court has repeatedly accepted a renvoi to German law from the law of the foreign place of performance.[122] In a case involving an American contract it has even declared relevant a possible transmission from Louisiana law as the law of the buyer's place of performance to Illinois law, the law of the seller's domicile.[123] The court has justified its position by stressing both the emergency nature of the place-of-performance rule, and the resulting application of German law as being a frequent and welcome consequence of the acceptance of renvoi.[124] Another advantage is the restoration of the unity of the applicable law in place of diversity. German doctrine is divided on the subject,[125] for good reasons. The whole question would become moot if the courts would abandon the unnecessary place-of-performance test, but as long as they preserve it, renvoi in many cases avoids its undesirable results.

A renvoi from the law of the foreign place of performance may also result from an express rule of that law[126] or even from its different construction of the concept of "place of performance."[127]

---

[120] KEGEL, Kommentar, no. 218 preceding art. 7 EGBGB, with references in n. 94.

[121] BGH 14 Feb. 1958, NJW 1958, 750, 751.

[121a] *Similarly,* KLAUS MÜLLER, Zum Problem der Gesamtverweisung, *in* Rechtsvergleichung und Rechtsvereinheitlichung (1967) 191–212, 206–07.

[122] BGH 14 Feb. 1958, *supra* n. 121 (Italy, renvoi found); 10 Jan. 1958, IPRspr. 1958/59 no. 37 (England, renvoi found); *see also* OLG Stuttgart 23 May 1960, IPRspr. 1960/61 no. 25 (Sweden, no renvoi found); OLG Frankfurt 27 Oct. 1966, NJW 1967, 501 (Switzerland, renvoi found).

[123] BGH 9 June 1960, WM 1960, 938.

[124] BGH 14 Feb. 1958, *supra* n. 121.

[125] *For* renvoi in these cases: KEGEL, Kommentar, no. 218 preceding art. 7 EGBGB; WOLFF 78, 143; GRAUE, AWD 1968, 121–31, 129. *Contra*: RAAPE 70–71, 488 (*but see* 486); KREUZER 290–95; HARTWIEG, Der Renvoi im deutschen Internationalen Vertragsrecht (1967) 150–52.

[126] *See, especially,* BGH 14 Feb. 1958, *supra* n. 121.

[127] OLG Frankfurt, *supra* n. 113a.

III. SCOPE OF THE PROPER LAW

The law governing an international contract as a rule determines all questions connected with the contract, such as its formation, validity, interpretation, performance, discharge, and the limitation of actions with respect to it. Outside the scope of this law are questions of capacity of the parties and authority of agents (*infra* IV); special rules obtain for formalities. A brief discussion of each of these topics is in order. (As to capacity, *see supra* ch. 4 sub C (1).)

(1) **Formation**[128]

Controversies relating to the effective formation of a contract are resolved in practice by the law that would govern the contract if effectively concluded.[129] It is unsettled whether the legal qualification of certain behavior (such as silence rather than a letter of acceptance) must not also take into account the law of the offeree's business residence.[130] This appears clearly necessary. Other difficulties will arise if the law governing the contract is split because there are two places of performance (*supra* II (4)).[131] Claims for damages arising from the conduct of negotiations are qualified by the German courts, following German substantive law, as contractual rather than tort claims; they are therefore subject to the law governing the contract.[132]

(2) **Formal Validity**

The formal validity of an international contract is governed primarily by the proper law. This follows from the general rule of article 11 I 1 EGBGB which applies even if the governing law has

---

[128] A brief comparative paper dealing with the substantive and conflicts aspects of conclusion is DREISS/v.BORRIES, Das Zustandekommen von Distanzverträgen Deutschland-U.S.A., JuS 1968, 54 60.

[129] BGH 11 July 1957, WM 1957, 1047, 1048; OLG Stuttgart 23 May 1960, IPRspr. 1960/61 no. 25; RG 3 Feb. 1933, IPRspr. 1933 no. 10 (negotiations in Paris between American and German businessmen); LAG Frankfurt 14 Mar. 1951, IPRspr. 1950/51 no. 20 (conclusion of contract denied on basis of "American" law).

[130] Details are very controversial among writers; *see*, e.g., KEGEL, Kommentar, nos. 144–45 preceding art. 7 EGBGB; *see also* LG Hamburg 28 Dec. 1954, IPRspr. 1954/55 no. 164; OLG München 15 July 1954, IPRspr. 1954/55 no. 18; BGH 29 Feb. 1968, WM 1968, 689, 690.

[131] The BGH once sought a special unitary system covering only conclusion, BGH 9 Dec. 1964, BGHZ 43, 21, 23–25. Writers differ; *see*, e.g., RAAPE 496–98 and WOLFF 125.

[132] OLG München 15 July 1954, IPRspr. 1954/55 no. 18; OLG Hamburg 2 June 1965, IPRspr. 1964/65 no. 46; KEGEL, Kommentar, no. 142 preceding art. 7 EGBGB. *Contra*: LAG Frankfurt 14 Mar. 1951, IPRspr. 1950/51 no. 20.

been chosen by the parties.[133] However, compliance with the formal requirements of the law of the place of contracting always suffices (art. 11 I 2). Questions of form arise in only a few types of international contracts.[134] It is not settled whether foreign rules excluding actionability in certain cases, like the Anglo-American statutes of frauds, are to be treated as formal requirements.[135]

(3) Substantive Validity

Questions of substantive validity are subject exclusively to the proper law. It is this law which determines under which conditions a defect of consent, such as mistake or fraud, is present and what effect it has.[136] Whether a New York accountant's contract for legal services to be rendered partly in Germany to a New York resident constituted forbidden "legal practice," was correctly examined under New York law.[137] The relevance of public-law prohibitory rules will be dealt with later (*infra* VI). Whether consideration, that peculiarity of the common law, should be treated as a substantive or a formal requirement, has been debated by the writers.[138]

(4) Interpretation and Performance

The interpretation of an international contract is subject to the canons of construction established by the law governing the contract,[139] and this is also true of all questions of proper or improper performance, especially requisites and consequences.[140] In contracts for the maritime carriage of goods, the governing law also determines all issues from creation through termination of the contract, especially such matters as the contractual limitation of liability, the rights of

---

133 *See* BGH 29 Nov. 1961, JZ 1963, 167.

134 As to the form of contracts for the sale of German immovables, *see supra* ch. 6 n. 43.

135 A decision of the BGH, 29 Nov. 1961, JZ 1963, 167, 168, treats them impliedly as a formal requirement. *See, however,* BGH 30 July 1954, JZ 1955, 702 (French law), where a similar rule was qualified as procedural and therefore governed by the *lex fori.* For formal qualification, *see* KG Berlin 25 Oct. 1927, JW 1929, 448, and most German writers; *see* KEGEL, Kommentar, no. 22 on art. 11 EGBGB with n. 6.

136 OLG München 15 July 1954, *supra* n. 132; OLG Frankfurt 24 June 1964, IPRspr. 1964/65 no. 37.

137 OLG Stuttgart 30 Nov. 1960, IPRspr. 1960/61 no. 213.

138 For substantive qualification, *see* KEGEL, Kommentar, no. 20 on art. 11 EGBGB; *see also* OLG München 13 Apr. 1929, IPRspr. 1929 no. 49. For formal qualification, *see* RAAPE 224–225 and NEUHAUS 92.

139 BGH 19 June 1961, WM 1961, 999; 19 Mar. 1959, WM 1959, 816.

140 BGH 19 June 1961, *supra* n. 139; 11 Feb. 1953, BGHZ 9, 34, 37; KG Berlin 20 May 1961, IPRspr. 1960/61 no. 58. On the determination of these questions in case a contract is governed by the legal systems of its two places of performance, *see supra* II (4).

the holder of a bill of lading, and its indorsement and transfer.[141] Also questions of discharge are submitted to the proper law provided it has been selected expressly or tacitly by the parties; in other cases, discharge is governed by the law of the port of discharge.[142]

(5) Limitation of Actions

In Germany as in most Continental countries the limitation of actions has been entirely divorced from procedure and integrated into substantive law. Consequently the German courts regard all problems of this nature as subject to the proper law of the contract.[143] This is particularly relevant if a contract is subject to "American" or English law. In 1882 the *Reichsgericht* in an unfortunate case held a claim governed by Tennessee law to be imprescriptible; the claim fell outside the German rules because these were not part of the *lex causae,* and the court refused to apply the American rules as being procedural.[144] Today it is well-settled practice that the Anglo-American limitation of actions is within the scope of the law governing the contract.[145] A renvoi to the German *lex fori* will be refused.[146]

According to § 209 BGB, the bringing of an action interrupts the running of the period of limitation. A lawsuit in a foreign court will have the same effect provided the resulting decision can be recognized in Germany. This doctrine is firmly entrenched,[147] but it should be confined to cases where the limitation itself is governed by German law, or any other law recognizing the same rule.[148] To the extent that American decisions are not recognized in Germany (*infra* ch. 14 sub II (8)) and therefore do not toll a German statute of limitations,

---

[141] BGH 19 Mar. 1959, *supra* n. 139; LG Berlin 15 Nov. 1956, IPRspr. 1956/57 no. 50.

[142] BGH 5 Dec. 1966, WM 1967, 141, 142; 14 Apr. 1953, BGHZ 9, 221, 223–34.

[143] *See, e.g.,* BGH 10 Jan. and 14 Feb. 1958, IPRspr. 1958/59 no. 37 and NJW 1958, 750.

[144] RG 23 Jan. 1882, RGZ 7, 21; *see also* RG 18 May 1889, RGZ 24, 282, 392–93.

[145] *Expressly,* BGH 9 June 1960, WM 1960, 938, 939; RG 6 July 1934, RGZ 145, 121, 126–31; LG Bremen 10 May 1961, IPRspr. 1960/61 no. 50. *See also* RG 21 Nov. 1910, JW 1911, 148; 8 May 1880, RGZ 2, 13.

[146] *Expressly,* LG Bremen, *supra* n. 145. For renvoi, *see* Kegel, Die Grenze von Qualifikation und Renvoi im internationalen Verjährungsrecht (1962), *especially* 37–43.

[147] RG 8 July 1930, RGZ 129, 385, 389; 18 Sept. 1925, JW 1926, 374; OLG Breslau 19 Dec. 1938, JW 1939, 344.

[148] If suit is brought in the country whose law governs the claim and that law deems the statute tolled upon commencement of a lawsuit, this effect should be recognized in other countries, too, even if the court decision as such cannot be recognized. *See* OLG Breslau, *supra* n. 147; *infra* ch. 14 sub II (8) (c).

this may be a legitimate ground for permitting a second suit in Germany.[149]

(6) Assignment and Set-off

The contractual transfer of contractual and other claims follows the law governing the claim assigned. The law governing the transaction underlying the assignment is immaterial.[150]

Set-off, like the limitation of actions (*supra* (5)), is regarded as substantive rather than procedural. It is invariably subjected to the proper law of the claim against which the set-off is sought.[151]

IV. AUTHORITY OF AGENT[152]

In German conflicts law the power of an agent to represent his principal is not necessarily subject to the law controlling the relations between principal and agent (*supra* II (3)(c)). This is consistent with the German substantive law of agency, which distinguishes between the bilateral principal-agent contract and the authority of the agent, which is deemed to affect third persons primarily. The law governing a power of attorney is also treated as not necessarily coincident with the proper law of a contract concluded by the agent with a third person.

(1) Law Governing

Statutory powers of attorney (for example, those of parents for their children, of a guardian for his ward, of an executor or administrator, or of the officers of a company) are subject to the law governing the underlying relationship.[153] A different rule has developed for contractual powers of attorney. As a general proposition, such a power is subject to the law of the territory where it is put to use. This formula, with modifications for certain typical circumstances,

---

[149] *See* Sperry Rand Corp. v. Sunbeam Corp., 285 F.2d 542, 546 (7th Cir. 1960).

[150] *Constant practice*, e.g., BGH 7 Dec. 1961, WM 1962, 263, 265; 28 Oct. 1957, WM 1957, 1574, 1575; LG Aschaffenburg 7 July 1953, *supra* n. 95, at 140–41.

[151] BGH 22 Nov. 1962, BGHZ 38, 254, 256; OLG Frankfurt 27 Oct. 1966, NJW 1967, 501, 502; LG Aschaffenburg, *supra* n. 95. Birk, AWD 1969, 14, would follow the procedural qualification of the *lex causae*; if Anglo-American law governs the set-off, it would be admissible only in a judicial proceeding; this deviation from the generally admitted substantive qualification of the German *lex fori* appears unwarranted. On the special problem arising if the two claims are expressed in different currencies, *see infra* ch. 9 sub (2) (c).

[152] *Especially* v. Caemmerer, Die Vollmacht für schuldrechtliche Geschäfte im deutschen Internationalen Privatrecht, RabelsZ 24 (1959) 201–21, and the underlying reports, at 326–41.

[153] *See supra* ch. 4 sub B I (5) (a) and (c), II (1) and III (5), and C (1) (d); ch. 5 sub III (4); *infra* ch. 10 sub I (2) (b).

is designed to protect both the interests of third parties and those of the principal.

If a professional agent exercises his business or profession from a permanent location, the law of the place of his establishment governs.[154] Thus the authority of German-based agents of American enterprises is determined under German law,[155] and the German lawyer's power of attorney to represent foreign clients before a German court is governed by German law.[156]

A corresponding rule has been applied to powers of attorney in private affairs, such as the distribution of the German assets of a decedent's estate by the American heirs, or the acquisition and administration of a German immovable for an American citizen.[157] As for an agent's power to dispose of immovables, this is controlled by the *lex rei sitae.*[158]

The form of a power of attorney is governed primarily by the law governing the power itself, according to article 11 I 1 EGBGB. However, this rule is modified by sentence 2 which states that compliance with the law of the place of acting suffices. For the most frequent case, namely, that of a power to dispose of a German immovable, the place of acting is determined according to German rules. Under § 167 BGB a power of attorney is created by a declaration of the principal directed towards the agent or a third party. The courts have correctly emphasized the place where the power is issued rather than the place where the document is received by the agent or the third party, and consequently a power which complies with the formal rules of the place of issue is valid in Germany.[159] It must be observed, however, that in order to dispose of German immovables or rights in such immovables it is necessary to obtain at least a notarial certification of the principal's signature (§§ 29–31 GBO).

(2) **Issues Governed**

The law governing a power of attorney determines all questions concerning its creation, substantive validity, scope, and termination.

Whether a person has acted as agent for another or in his own name has to be decided according to the rules governing the contract

---

154 BGH 9 Dec. 1964, BGHZ 43, 21, 26; 29 Nov. 1961, JZ 1963, 167; 13 July 1954, NJW 1954, 1561; OLG Hamburg 26 June 1959, IPRspr. 1958/59 no. 52.

155 RG 14 Oct. 1931, RGZ 134, 67, 69; 3 Apr. 1902, RGZ 51, 147, 149.

156 BGH 5 Feb. 1958, WM 1958, 557, 558.

157 RG 14 Nov. 1907, Recht 1908 no. 93; 31 May 1943, DR 1943, 1066.

158 RG 31 May 1943, *supra* n. 157; LG Berlin 5 Oct. 1932, IPRspr. 1932 no. 63; KG Berlin 14 Dec. 1933, IPRspr. 1933 no. 9.

159 KG Berlin 8 Jan. 1931, IPRspr. 1931 no. 21 (issue in California); OLG Nürnberg 11 Dec. 1928, IPRspr. 1929 no. 26.

between them.[160] However, the creation of an agent's authority is submitted to the law of the place where it is exercised. More particularly, this law decides whether in the absence of actual authority the principal has created or has permitted the creation of apparent authority,[161] and it passes also on the substantive validity of a power of attorney, if any,[162] and the scope of the authority. Thus a power of attorney issued in the United States in the English language for use in Germany has been interpreted according to German law and thus given a much wider meaning than that intended by its authors.[163] Similarly, the effect of the abuse of a power of attorney is subject to the law governing the authority.[164] The same holds true of its termination, as, for example, by death of the principal.[165]

V. BILLS OF EXCHANGE AND CHEQUES

In the narrow field of commercial instruments, meaning bills of exchange, including promissory notes, and cheques, German conflicts law has adopted statutory rules derived from the Geneva Conventions of 1930/1931. Fragmentary though they are, they apply not only to convention countries, but generally to all international commercial instruments. They reflect the older German theory which emphasized the place of performance.

Capacity to sign bills, notes or cheques is governed by the law of the signer's nationality, including its conflict of laws rules. However, even though a person lacks capacity under his national law he may nevertheless, in general, act validly if he has capacity according to the law at the place of signature.[166]

The form of the promise in a commercial instrument is determined as a rule by the law of the place of signature. For cheques it is sufficient to observe the formalities at the place of payment. Apart from another minor exception (obtaining only between nationals of the forum), the rule of relative validation is important: if a declaration is formally invalid by the law of the place of signature, but is formally valid by the law of the place where a subsequent declaration

---

160 OLG Hamburg 2 June 1965, IPRspr. 1964/65 no. 46.

161 BGH 9 Dec. 1964, BGHZ 43, 21, 27; 23 Oct. 1963, BGHZ 40, 197, 203; OLG Hamm 6 June 1957, IPRspr. 1956/57 no. 27.

162 Unlimited irrevocable power of attorney held void under German law, LG Berlin 5 Oct. 1932, IPRspr. 1933 no. 63.

163 RG 31 May 1943, *supra* n. 157; *see also* BGH 29 Nov. 1961, JZ 1963, 167.

164 *See* RG 14 Oct. 1931, RGZ 134, 67, 69, 71; 31 May 1943, *supra* n. 163.

165 BGH 5 Feb. 1958, WM 1958, 557, 559.

166 Art. 91 Wechselgesetz (WG, BGBl. III 4133–1); art. 60 Scheckgesetz (ScheckG, BGBl. III 4132–1). These rules are in accord with the general provision on capacity to contract in art. 7 EGBGB, *see supra* ch. 4 sub C (1).

is signed, the validity of the latter is not affected by the invalidity of the former.[167]

The effect of a declaration in a commercial instrument is generally also subject to the law of the place where it is signed.[168] The law of the place of payment, however, determines who may be designated as drawee of a cheque and what is the effect of the declarations of the issuer of a promissory note or the drawee of a bill of exchange.[169] Questions relating to payment and to loss of the instrument are also regulated by the law of the place of payment, and this law governs certain other aspects of cheques, among these the necessity of protest.[170] Generally speaking, the form and time limits for protest are governed by the law of the place where protest is necessary,[171] and the time limit for the exercise of recourse by the law of the place of issue.[172]

VI. PROHIBITORY RULES (OF PUBLIC LAW)

The "normal" private-law conflicts rules heretofore considered do not automatically embrace the prohibitory rules of public law, German or foreign, contained in the proper law of the contract. In this respect there is an important distinction between German and foreign rules.

(1) German Rules

The German courts apply German prohibitory rules of public law to all appropriate contracts, irrespective of the private law governing the contract. Thus German provisions relating to foreign exchange, import and export restrictions, labor, taxation, and so forth, limit all transactions whatever their private law régime.[173] In a few instances the legislature has specified expressly the international scope of an enactment, as, for example, dealing with restrictive trade practices[174] or future contracts on an exchange.[175]

(2) Foreign Rules

No fixed rules have yet been devised by the German courts for the application of foreign prohibitory provisions, but the modern German writers have developed quite definite ideas in this area. On the

---

167 Art. 92 WG; art. 62 ScheckG.

168 Art. 93 II WG; art. 63 ScheckG.

169 Art. 61 ScheckG; art. 93 I WG.

170 Arts. 96, 98 WG; art. 65 ScheckG.

171 Art. 97 WG; art. 66 ScheckG.

172 Art. 94 WG; art. 64 ScheckG.

173 Details in REITHMANN 23–41.

174 *Infra* ch. 13 n. 4.

175 § 61 Börsengesetz of 1896, as revised in 1908 (BGBl. III no. 4110–1), extends to certain transactions concluded or to be performed abroad the rules of the preceding §§ 52 through 60. *See* KG Berlin 18 Dec. 1962, WM 1963, 629, *rev'd*, BGH 21 June 1965, WM 1965, 766 (forward contract on London Bullion Market invalid for the German party).

whole, this branch of conflicts law is very much in flux, with the sole exception of foreign exchange law (*infra* ch. 9 sub (4)).

One potential barrier is German public policy (art. 30 EGBGB): if a foreign prohibitory rule is directed specifically against German interests, it will not be applied in Germany.[176] Another is the non-application of public regulations clearly serving only the interests of a foreign state, such as tax rules[177] or trading prohibitions directed generally against foreigners.[178] Absent such immediate threats to German interests or exclusive promotion of foreign interests, the application of foreign prohibitory rules is uncertain. Contracts for the sale or insurance of merchandise to be smuggled into a foreign country are generally held void because of their corrupting effect.[179] In 1960 and 1962, the Federal Supreme Court also voided both a sales and an insurance contract relating to merchandise to be re-exported into Eastern bloc countries in violation of the American export control regulations. The decisions were motivated by the political interest of the Western nations in containing the war potential of the East European powers.[180]

Generally speaking, the close harmony of their political and economic standards creates a favorable German climate for a sympathetic treatment of American prohibitory rules. Thus it is not unlikely that the German courts may even apply the private-law sanctions of American antitrust legislation under certain conditions.[181] But even if the courts refuse to apply foreign prohibitory rules *qua lex,* they do not hesitate to pay regard to their de facto effects. A statutory prohibition against performance may thus be treated as a valid ground of impossibility that may or may not excuse the debtor.[182] This results in employment of the same criterion as that employed with relation to East German exchange restrictions (*infra* ch. 9 sub (4)).

---

[176] E.g., a Trading with the Enemy Act; RG 28 June 1918, RGZ 93, 182, 183; KEGEL, Kommentar, no. 227 n. 107 preceding art. 7 EGBGB.

[177] OLG Hamburg 25 Nov. 1959, IPRspr. 1958/59 no. 61, at 242; OLG Hamm 27 Apr. 1912, OLG 25, 333; KG Berlin 19 Nov. 1908, OLGE 20, 91; KEGEL, IPR 388; for details, *see* MANN, Öffentlich-rechtliche Ansprüche im internationalen Rechtsverkehr, RabelsZ 21 (1956) 1–20.

[178] *Trading prohibitions*: RG 24 June 1927, JW 1927, 2288; *see,* however, BAG 26 Sept. 1963, AP no. 1 on § 74a HGB.

Foreign prohibitions against doing business if insurance contracts are subject to German law: KG Berlin 8 Feb. 1930, IPRspr. 1930 no. 16, *aff'd,* RG 1 Oct. 1930, RGZ 130, 47; KG Berlin 19 Dec. 1928, IPRspr. 1929 no. 12; 10 Oct. 1928, IPRspr. 1928 no. 21.

[179] LG Berlin 2 Nov. 1928, IPRspr. 1929 no. 13 (alcohol to be smuggled into the United States); for further references, *see* REITHMANN 84–85.

[180] BGH 21 Dec. 1960, BGHZ 34, 169, 177; 24 May 1962, NJW 1962, 1436.

[181] *Infra* ch. 13 sub (2).

[182] *See* BGH 11 July 1963, NJW 1963, 1971; RG 28 June 1918, RGZ 93, 182, 184.

VII. EAST GERMAN LAW

East Germany to a large extent follows the unwritten conflicts rules of contract described above. Authority, however, is slim since the ordinary courts are in practice precluded from passing on foreign trade disputes; exclusive jurisdiction in these matters resides with the Arbitral Tribunal of the Chamber for Foreign Commerce in East Berlin (*infra* ch. 14 sub III (5)), whose decisions are rarely published. No treatise on conflicts law exists. A choice of law by the parties is expressly recognized by paragraph 27 (1) of the rules of the Arbitration Tribunal.[183] A tacit choice of East German law is inferred from a clause conferring jurisdiction on the Arbitration Tribunal.[184] If both are lacking, the law of the business residence of the seller or of the grantor of a license governs the contract.[185]

---

[183] Arbitration Rules of July 3, 1957, *infra* ch. 14 n. 328a.

[184] Practice of the Tribunal, as related by FELLHAUER, AH 1962 no. 7, appendix RiA pp. 1–6, 6.

[185] WIEMANN/KEMPER, AH 1962 no. 7, appendix RiA pp. 7–12, 10; *id.*, AH 1961 no. 3, appendix RiA pp. 1–4, 3–4; FEIGE/SEIFFERT, Internationale Lizenzen ([East] Berlin 1965) 154.

Chapter IX.

CURRENCY AND FOREIGN EXCHANGE*

Due to the fluctuations of currencies and increasing governmental intervention, the discussion of monetary questions has become quite involved in recent times. There is no general consensus, not only as to the answers, but even as to the basic issues in this field. The following brief exposition of the German conflicts rules will employ a pragmatic approach, discussing *seriatim*: (1) the currency in which an obligation arises, (2) foreign money as the money of payment, (3) devaluation and depreciation of currencies, and, finally, (4) foreign exchange regulations.

(1) In What Currency Does an Obligation Arise?

Whether a monetary obligation arises in German or in foreign currency has considerable importance. But it must be pointed out that the generally accepted distinction between money of account (*Schuldwährung*) and money of payment (*Zahlungswährung*) is also basic for German law.[1] It might be logical for the law governing an obligation (*lex causae*) to determine the money of account.[2] However, questions of conflicts law rarely arise in this connection. The *Reichsgericht* did inquire in one case whether a currency option was valid under the Austrian law governing the loan,[3] and, indeed, the interpretation of currency clauses and their validity are subject to the law governing the contract.[4] Whether a prohibition contained in that law against agreement on a foreign money of account must be respected by the member states of the International Monetary

---

* The standard books on the German and the international law of money are: MANN, The Legal Aspect of Money (Oxford, 2d ed. 1953) (*German version*, brought up to date: Das Recht des Geldes, Frankfurt/Berlin 1960); NUSSBAUM, Money in the Law, National and International (New York 1950), and *id.*, Das Geld in Theorie und Praxis des deutschen und ausländischen Rechts (Tübingen 1925). *See also* DOMKE 31–50; KAHN, Depreciation of Currency under German Law and German Conflict of Laws, 14 J. Comp. Leg., 3d series, 66–67 (1932).

[1] *See, especially,* § 244 BGB and the discussion *infra* (2) (b) at n. 38.

[2] KEGEL, Kommentar, no. 480 preceding art. 7 EGBGB. The interzonal cases cited in support (at n. 1) are irrelevant since German substantive (as distinct from currency) law was uniform at the time.

[3] RG 14 Nov. 1929, RGZ 126, 196, 201.

[4] *See* KEGEL, Kommentar, no. 480 preceding art. 7 EGBGB. *Contra* (i.e., law governing foreign exchange regulations): SEETZEN, AWD 1969, 253–57, 255–56.

Fund seems to be doubtful.[5] Apart from these special situations, the German courts seem to be unconcerned with the logic of conflicts law; they themselves fix the money of account unless the parties have done so.

(a) *Contracts.*—Freedom of the parties to fix the money of account in any currency has always been recognized implicitly and on principle unless it is restricted or excluded by statute. In Germany, § 3 sentence 1 of the so-called Currency Act of 1948[6] prohibits the contracting of any debts in a foreign currency unless an authorization is obtained from the German Federal Bank. However, since 1961 the Law on Foreign Commerce has expressly exempted from this prohibition all transactions between residents of Germany and persons residing abroad.[7] Consequently, only contracts between residents of Germany must presently comply with the aforementioned restriction; as a rule, therefore, they must be concluded in German marks.[8] The relevance of foreign restrictions of this nature has already been mentioned (*supra* at n. 5).

In view of this present legal situation in Germany, most of the illustrations have to be drawn from pre-War cases. The monetary convulsions of the twenties and thirties, especially of the German mark, afforded the courts unusual opportunities to pass on contractual clauses by which creditors had attempted to secure themselves against devaluation.

An unequivocal promise to pay in foreign currency has always been honored by the German courts, absent express statutory prohibitions, irrespective of the creditor's nationality.[9] A currency option entitles the creditor to choose the money of account.[10] Complications may arise if the value of the money of account is determined by reference to other standards, for example, another currency,[11] the gold

[5] OLG Karlsruhe 15 Dec. 1965, WM 1966, 1312, has disregarded a Brazilian prohibition of this kind, based on information received from the Fund's Legal Department.

[6] Law of June 20, 1948, BGBl. III 7600–1–a.

[7] § 49 I Aussenwirtschaftsgesetz of April 28, 1961, BGBl. III 7400–1.

[8] However, a General Permit of the German Federal Bank has admitted certain exceptions. Thus contracts in foreign currency may be concluded, e.g., for the keeping of bank accounts; for bank loans up to a limited period of time; for the acquisition of accounts receivable and securities; for certain transit dealings; for guarantees and sureties for foreign residents or as security for obligations in foreign currency; and for certain categories of insurance contracts. For details, *see* General Permit 1009/61 of Aug. 24, 1961, BAnz. 1961 no. 167. A special permit may be applied for in other cases.

[9] RG 13 May 1935, RGZ 147, 377; 28 June 1934, RGZ 145, 51; 4 July 1929, JW 1929, 2709; 2 Feb. 1928, JW 1928, 1385; 27 June 1923, JW 1924, 173.

[10] RG 15 Jan. 1942, RGZ 168, 240, 247; 15 Mar. 1937; RGZ 154, 187; 5 Oct. 1936, RGZ 152, 213; 22 Dec. 1927, IPRspr. 1928 no. 66; 1 July 1926, JW 1926, 2675.

[11] Obligation in Czech crowns, to be fixed according to the rate of exchange for the dollar, RG 20 Apr. 1940, RGZ 163, 324, 328–333.

value,[12] the gold value of another currency,[13] and so on. In these cases the amount of money, expressed in the money of account, is determined by the fate of the external standard.

Sometimes the agreement of the parties is not clear. In the late twenties many contracts concluded between Germans provided for payment in "gold marks." This fictional unit was frequently defined as 1 GM = 10/42 of the dollar or 1/2790 kilogram of gold. After the totally unexpected depreciation of the dollar in consequence of the Joint Resolution of the United States Congress of June 5, 1933, debtors were invariably held bound to pay marks on the basis of the exchange rate for the gold dollar. The courts interpreted the clause as creating an obligation in gold dollars[14] or gold marks[15] or as intended only to secure against an expected devaluation of the mark.[16] After this event occurred in 1949, import contracts on a dollar basis remained unaffected by the indication in the import permit of the rate of conversion from dollars to marks (DM); the importer had to pay dollars at the new, higher rate.[17]

In the absence of any express choice by the parties, the courts determine the money of account according to the circumstances and the nature of the transaction. The creditor of a bank deposit made before World War II in Palestine in local pounds was permitted to recover after the War in English pounds since the parties had settled other debts in this currency.[18] And the *Reichsgericht* ordered a German broker who had sold his German customer's South African securities on the London stock exchange to pay the purchase price to his customer in English pounds.[19]

Generally speaking, the courts have ordered an agent or mandatory to deliver money received to his principal in the currency in which it was received.[20] There is even a subsidiary statutory rule of interpretation for commercial transactions: according to § 361 HGB the

---

[12] *See* the obligations contracted in "gold marks" after the German inflation of the twenties, *infra* next paragraph.

[13] Sales contract between German parties based on the gold value of the English pound, RG 6 Oct. 1933, JW 1933, 2583.

[14] RG 22 Oct. 1936, RGZ 152, 166, 172.

[15] RG 31 Jan. 1936, RGZ 150, 153, 156.

[16] RG 14 Dec. 1934, RGZ 146, 1, 5; 24 Sept. 1934, JW 1934, 3198; *see also* 5 July 1935, RGZ 148, 42; 23 Oct. 1934, IPRspr. 1934 no. 90. *See also* RG 28 May 1937, RGZ 155, 133 and 21 June 1933, RGZ 141, 212 (debts in pounds).

[17] LG Offenburg 19 May 1953, IPRspr. 1952/53 no. 273.

[18] LG Tübingen 16 Feb. 1966, IPRspr. 1966/67 no. 22. *See also* LAG Stuttgart 31 Mar. 1955, IPRspr. 1954/55 no. 19 (payment of wages in Italian lire since labor contract concluded and performed in Italy).

[19] RG 11 July 1923, RGZ 108, 191, 193. The securities had been deposited in London and were quoted only there.

[20] BGH 30 Sept. 1968, WM 1969, 26, 27; RG 29 Mar. 1927, RGZ 116, 330, 332, 336.

currency of the place of payment prevails unless otherwise provided. However, this rule plays no rôle in practice.

The rules concerning the money of account in contracts apply merely to primary contractual obligations to pay money, for example, the purchase price, the repayment of a loan, and the like. They do not apply to secondary obligations, such as the reimbursement of expenses or advances or the payment of damages, which have to be considered separately (*infra* (b)).

(b) *Expenses and damages.*—Expenses incurred within the framework of a contract are determined in the currency in which they have arisen. Thus outlays made in foreign currency by German forwarding or commission agents or banks in favor of either German or foreign customers are calculated in the foreign currency. The underlying theories differ, however; while some decisions view the claim for reimbursement as arising in the foreign currency (even though it may be paid in German marks, *see infra* (2)(b)),[21] another holds that it arose in German currency, the expense being merely an item of the account.[22] There is one important difference: under the first theory conversion is made at the rate of exchange on the day of payment, and under the second at the rate on the day the expense is incurred. The first theory was applied when the German mark was depreciating, and the latter when it was the foreign currency which had depreciated, the German currency having recovered. The guiding principle therefore seems to be the protection of the creditor, who may choose the date of conversion.

Damages for breach of contract are not reimbursed in the money of account. The German courts tend to award damages in German currency even if the creditor's loss has been incurred in foreign currency.[23] However, in two instances they are prepared to compensate on the basis of a foreign currency: if the creditor has in fact spent such currency (the payment constituting the creditor's loss or, presumably, being made in reparation of his loss),[24] or if he can prove that he would have used the value lost to purchase foreign currency and thereby would have fared better than by retaining German money.[25]

The reparation of tort damages follows similar lines. The courts

---

[21] RG 6 May 1933, IPRspr. 1933 no. 74; 22 Oct. 1924, RGZ 109, 85, 88–89; 28 Apr. 1924, JW 1924, 1593.

[22] RG 27 Jan. 1928, RGZ 120, 76, 81; *see also* BGH 3 Mar. 1965, LM no. 18 on § 116 BEG.

[23] RG 7 Dec. 1923, JW 1924, 672; 8 Apr. 1921, RGZ 102, 60, 62; 4 June 1919, RGZ 96, 121, 123; OLG Hamburg 30 Dec. 1952, IPRspr. 1952/53 no. 21 at p. 66.

[24] RG 27 Feb. 1924, JW 1925, 1477 (shipowner had to pay fine of 5,000 guilders because of an incorrect declaration of goods by shipper).

[25] *See infra* (3) (c) and (d).

award damages in German currency.[26] Expenses incurred by the injured person in foreign money are items of the account and are converted into marks at the rate of exchange on the day of payment.[27] Compensation for other damage is calculated on the basis of the prices obtaining at the place where the injured person will seek replacement or repairs.[28]

(c) *Support claims.*—Alimony and support are usually fixed in the currency of the creditor's residence.[29] This is only reasonable since the creditor's demand will be satisfied at his place of abode.

(d) *Charges on land and ships.*—In the entries of charges on land in the land register, the amounts secured have to be indicated in German currency.[30] This may cause difficulties to foreign creditors who desire to make loans to German debtors in foreign currency.[31] On the other hand, mortgages on German ships may be entered in the ship registry in a foreign currency.[32]

(e) *Corporate share capital and accounting.*—The capital of German stock corporations must be expressed in German currency. This is also true of the balance-sheets of merchants.[33]

(f) *Money judgments.*—By distinct contrast to Anglo-American law, the German courts may render decisions expressed in foreign currency.[34]

---

[26] BGH 30 Sept. 1968, *supra* n. 20; 10 July 1954, BGHZ 14, 212, 217; RG 12 May 1923, RG Warn. 1923/24 no. 60; LG Mannheim 6 June 1956, IPRspr. 1956/57 no. 173; 18 Sept. 1953, IPRspr. 1954/55 no. 162.

[27] RG and LG Mannheim 6 June 1956, *supra* n. 26; LG Bayreuth 5 July 1950, IPRspr. 1950/51 no. 23; *see also* BGH 6 Nov. 1951, BGHZ 3, 321, 327–28, and, in the same case, OGH Köln 17 Nov. 1949, OGHZ 2, 379, 387–88. If an adequate rate of exchange is lacking, the conversion has to be computed on the basis of the relative purchasing powers, BGH 10 July 1954, BGHZ 14, 212, 219–20.

[28] BGH 14 Jan. 1953, BGHZ 8, 288, 297; 14 Feb. 1952, BGHZ 5, 138, 142, 143.

[29] LG Düsseldorf 13 June and 24 Oct. 1952, IPRspr. 1952/53 nos. 203 and 207; LG Berlin 12 July 1952, *id.* no. 204, 3 Apr. 1950, IPRspr. 1950/51 no. 69; LG Hagen 11 Jan. 1951, *id.* no. 102. *Cf.* as to the amount of support claims, *supra* ch. 4 sub B II (2) (a) at n. 304.

[30] § 28 sent. 2 GBO (BGBl. III 315–11). Certain special statutes enacted in 1920 and 1923 granted dispensation from this rule, but they have lapsed.

[31] An Englishman had given £5,000 secured by a charge expressing the amount in gold marks; the debtor had promised repayment of pounds in kind. The Reichsgericht remanded the case for further findings as to whether the parties had intended an option clause or an obligation in pounds, the gold mark feature of the charge merely being forced on them by § 28 GBO, RG 5 Oct. 1936, RGZ 152, 213, 219.

[32] Art. III of the Law of May 8, 1963 (BGBl. I 293).

[33] § 6 Aktiengesetz 1965 (BGBl. I 1089, BGBl. III 4121–1), § 40 I HGB (BGBl. III 4100–1).

[34] *See* e.g., BGH 14 Jan. 1953, BGHZ 14, 288, 296; LG Mainz 16 May 1952, IPRspr. 1952/53 no. 66 (bank that had converted accounts of American creditor

(2) **Foreign Money as Money of Payment**

(a) *Nature of foreign money.*—After initial difficulties the *Reichsgericht* recognized in 1920 that foreign money is not merely a commodity but, although not legal tender in Germany, has most of the properties of "money."[35] This is the general opinion today. Whether foreign money is legal tender in the country of issue (and therefore entitled in Germany to protection against counterfeiting)[36] or whether it will be converted into another currency,[37] depends upon the law of the issuing state.

(b) *Payment in German money.*—A special statutory rule provides that the debtor may pay a debt, expressed in foreign currency and payable in Germany, in local currency; the conversion is at the rate of exchange of the time and place of payment; however, conversion may be excluded by the parties by express agreement for payment of the foreign currency in kind (§ 244 BGB).[38] Only the debtor and not the creditor may avail himself of this opportunity.[39] An express agreement to pay foreign money in kind will not be found where the contract simply provides for a purchase price in foreign currency and the seller's bill is so written.[40] But a clause providing "$5,000 only U.S. currency" is clear, and so is a "bailment" of a sum in foreign money.[41] According to the prevailing and better view, § 244 BGB obtains irrespective of the law governing the obligation; the provision is a "hidden" conflicts rule.[42]

---

expressed in reichmarks, pounds and dollars, condemned to pay amounts in these three currencies).

[35] *Expressly,* RG June 1920, JW 1921, 22.

[36] BGH 7 July 1964, BGHSt 19, 357, 358–359; 27 Jan. 1959, BGHSt 12, 344, 345 (English gold sovereign).

[37] BGH 28 Oct. 1959, LM no. 9 on § 56 BEG.

[38] *See also* art. 41 WG (BGBl. III 4133–1) and art. 36 ScheckG (BGBl. III 4132–1). These special provisions for bills of exchange and cheques in foreign currency differ in one respect from § 244 BGB: on late payment the creditor is entitled to choose for the conversion the rate of exchange on the date of maturity or that of payment. This affords him protection against a decrease of the exchange rate. *See* art. 41 I 2 WG and art. 36 I 2 ScheckG.

[39] OLG Nürnberg 25 Apr. 1967, IPRspr. 1966/67 no. 17; OLG Celle 4 Jan. 1963, IPRspr. 1962/63 no. 207; LG Frankfurt 3 May 1955, NJW 1956, 65 (creditor of German judgment condemning debtor to pay in Swiss francs may not levy execution on the latter's goods since this presupposes conversion into DM!). But under exceptional circumstances, especially in view of stringent exchange restrictions in the country of the money of account, the debtor of a contract governed by German law may be required to pay German currency, calculated on the basis of the foreign currency of account, BGH 30 Sept. 1968, WM 1969, 26, 27.

[40] RG 6 July 1923, JW 1924, 172.

[41] LG Berlin 7 Apr. 1959, IPRspr. 1958/59 no. 167; RG 22 Feb. 1937, RGZ 153, 384, 385.

[42] LG Stuttgart 14 Mar. 1957, IPRspr. 1956/57 no. 29; RAAPE 531; KEGEL, Kommentar, no. 488 preceding art. 7 EGBGB.

(c) *Set-off.*—Under German law, a set-off will be made only if the two obligations are of the same kind (§ 387 BGB). This provision is interpreted as excluding a set-off between two debts expressed in different currencies.[43] It may well be doubted whether this narrow view is in keeping with the interests of the parties and the opportunities offered by a well-functioning foreign exchange market, at least as between fully convertible currencies. Under a broader view, even a clause to pay foreign currency would not prevent a set-off provided it was the creditor who declared it (§ 388).[44] Prevailing opinion is less flexible. It offers some relief to a debtor who owes an obligation in foreign money payable in Germany and who has a counterclaim in German money; § 244 BGB allows the debtor of such a claim (not a claim to be paid in kind) to convert his obligation into German currency and thus to achieve equality in kind. In this case, the rate of exchange for the conversion is determined as of the day when the debtor makes his declaration of set-off.[45]

(3) Devaluation and Depreciation of Currencies

(a) *International scope of the German conversion of 1948.*—The laws of 1948 decreeing the conversion of the Reichsmark obligations into German marks (DM), generally on the basis 10 : 1,[46] do not specify their international scope, which has been much debated in legal writing.[47] The so-called private-law theory seems finally to have prevailed: the different devaluation rules apply to debts expressed originally in Reichsmarks, provided the obligation itself is subject to German law.[48] One American court has shared this view,[49] and in another case a claim for compensation for devaluation brought against the United States by an American depositor in a German bank was correctly denied.[50]

---

[43] RAAPE 532. This is the general opinion.

[44] BIRK, AWD 1969, 15–16.

[45] RG 16 May 1941, RGZ 167, 60, 63 (dollar debt), 20 Dec. 1922, RGZ 106, 99, 100.

[46] F. KLOPSTOCK, Monetary Reform in Western Germany, 57 J. Pol. Ec. 277–92 (1949).

[47] *See, especially,* STOLL, Zum Anwendungsbereich der westdeutschen Umstellungsgesetze, RabelsZ 21 (1956) 575–609, with references.

[48] BGH 24 Mar. 1960, WM 1960, 940. *See also* KG Berlin 16 Aug. 1956, NJW 1957, 347; BFH 26 Mar. 1954, IPRspr. 1954/55 no. 21.

[49] Reissner v. Rogers, 276 F.2d 506, 512–13 (D.C. Cir.), *cert. denied,* 364 U.S. 816 (1960). *See also* the debt claim proceedings of the Office of Alien Property, cited by DOMKE 39 n. 182.

[50] Eisner v. United States, 117 F. Supp. 197 (Ct. Cl. 1954). In 1928 the German Reichsgericht held that the general denial of "revalorization" of bank deposits does not violate rights of a foreign creditor under art. I (4) of the American-German Friendship Treaty of 1923 (Treaties B 55) because not involving an expropriation, RG 6 June 1928, RGZ 121, 203.

(b) *Protective contract clauses.*—Apart from expression of the money of account in foreign currencies (*supra* (1)(a)), creditors have invented many other protective clauses designed to secure payment of the full equivalent of the sum originally agreed upon. The most popular are gold, currency and index clauses. The validity of protective clauses is determined by the law governing the contract,[51] which law, in turn, will usually refer to the law governing the currency.[52]

(i) The original freedom under German law to agree on protective clauses was severely curtailed by § 3 sentence 2 of the Currency Law (*supra* n. 6). This provides that an authorization is necessary if the amount of a debt in German marks is to be determined by the rate of exchange of another currency or by the price or quantity of gold or of other goods or services. As distinct from contracting in a foreign currency, transactions concluded in DM between German residents and persons residing abroad are not exempted from the prohibition of protective clauses. On the other hand, the prohibition obtains only if the debtor resides in West Germany.[53] The statute has been implemented by the German Federal Bank which has issued regulations designating those clauses that will not be permitted.[54]

(ii) The German courts were confronted with a foreign prohibition of gold clauses when the United States Congress adopted the Joint Resolution on June 5, 1933. Two appellate courts did not hesitate to apply the prohibition to loans to German debtors governed by New York law.[55] The *Reichsgericht,* however, found it to be irreconcilable with German public policy in a case where a German creditor had acquired a bond issued by a German debtor before adoption of the Joint Resolution.[56] This decision, however, was quickly neutralized by a legislative provision calling for payment of all international obligations expressed in depreciated currencies according to their nominal value.[57] This result was confirmed, for obligations created before May 8, 1945 and expressed in United

---

[51] BGH 24 Mar. 1960, *supra* n. 48; RAAPE 540–43; *see also* HENN, AWD 1961, 61, 62; *contra* (*i.e.*, law of place of performance): KEGEL, IPR 404; SCHULZE, AWD 1962, 89–94, 93; SEETZEN, *supra* n. 4, at 257.

[52] KEGEL, Kommentar, no. 481 preceding art. 7 EGBGB.

[53] *See* the standard text of DÜRKES, Wertsicherungsklauseln (7th ed. 1966) 28 at B 8, 84 at C 67; SCHULZE, *supra* n. 51 at 92, 94. More differentiated is SEETZEN, *supra* n. 4 at 254, 255.

[54] BAnz. 1964 no. 160. Text and commentary, DÜRKES, *supra* n. 53, especially 283.

[55] OLG Köln 13 Sept. 1935, JW 1936, 203; OLG Düsseldorf 26 Sept. 1934, IPRspr. 1934 no. 93 b.

[56] RG 28 May 1936, JW 1936, 2058.

[57] Law of June 26, 1936 (RGBl. I 515) and Regulation of Dec. 5, 1936 (RGBl. I 1010).

States gold dollars, by the London agreement on German external debts of 1953.[58]

Today it seems that international respect for national rules concerning the validity of protective clauses follows from article VIII (2)(b) of the Bretton Woods Agreement (Treaties M 109), at least as among the member states of the International Monetary Fund. But even the rules of non-member states should be respected internationally, unless they discriminate against foreigners.

(c) *Damages for delayed payment.*—Late payment, of itself, entitles the creditor under German law neither to interest nor to additional damages. Both may be claimed only if the debtor is in delay (*Verzug*); this, as a rule, means after payment has fallen due and the creditor has sent a warning to the debtor.[59] It follows that a creditor who is entitled to a payment in German money is entitled to damages for currency depreciation only if his debtor is in delay and only from the date of such delay.

The crucial point is the proof of actual damages. The creditor sustains a loss if he would have avoided the consequences of the depreciation of German marks by converting the amount due to him into a stable foreign currency. In administering this proof, the courts have rightly distinguished between creditors residing abroad and those residing in Germany. The former are more easily presumed to have made the conversion[60]; for the latter, the burden is not so easy to discharge.[61]

(d) *Depreciation of foreign currencies.*—A debt expressed in a foreign currency is, just like one in German money, normally repaid according to its nominal value irrespective of the depreciation of its real value. Where German law governs the contract, the courts have considered applying the doctrine of "revalorization" to obligations in pounds and dollars. But they have refused to do so since the depreciation of these currencies in the thirties was incomparably lower than the complete disintegration of the German mark in the early twenties.[62] Instead the courts have in some cases, especially sales contracts, considered allowing the seller to bring an equitable claim aimed at restoring the implied balance between his delivery of goods and the buyer's payment of money.[63] The exact contours of this equitable remedy are not quite clear.

---

[58] Treaties M 194, art. 12 (a).

[59] For details, *see* 1 Cohn no. 226.

[60] RG 12 May 1923, RG Warn. 1923/24 no. 60; 16 Mar. 1920, JW 1920, 704; June 1920, JW 1921, 22; 25 Sept. 1919, RGZ 96, 262.

[61] RG 7 Dec 1923, JW 1924, 672; 22 Nov. 1923, RGZ 107, 212, 213; 8 Apr. 1921, RGZ 102, 60, 63.

[62] *Dollars*: RG 20 Apr. 1940, RGZ 163, 324, 333; 13 May 1935, RGZ 147, 377, 380; *pounds*: RG 28 June 1934, RGZ 145, 51.

[63] *See*, e.g., RG 28 May 1937, RGZ 155, 133, 137–38; 9 July 1935, RGZ 148,

Damages for delayed payment of obligations in foreign currency may include compensation for depreciation of the foreign currency. The rule described above (*supra* (c)) applies *mutatis mutandis*. Its application presupposes, of course, that German law governs the contract. Its application has been considered for debts in dollars and pounds.[64]

(4) **Exchange Regulations**

(a) *German exchange rules.*—The German courts have applied German exchange rules to a contract irrespective of the private law governing it. This is in keeping with the general principle of priority of the prohibitory rules of the *lex fori* (*supra* ch. 8 sub VI (1)). At the present time, however, Germany has abrogated almost all exchange regulations.

(b) *Foreign exchange regulations.*—One of the most debated topics at one time, namely, the application of foreign exchange rules enacted by other states, came to rest through article VIII (2)(b) of the Bretton Woods Agreement (Treaties M 109), already referred to (*supra* (3)(b)(ii)). This article makes unenforceable all contracts involving the currency of any member state of the International Monetary Fund that are contrary to that member's "consistent" exchange regulations. This provision guarantees the mutual respect for exchange restrictions between member states. It does not seem to have played any practical rôle between the United States and West Germany,[65] but the German courts have applied it not infrequently to contracts affecting the exchange rules of other nations.[66]

The attitude of the German courts vis-à-vis foreign exchange provisions of non-member states has been shaped by their rich experience with East German law. In 1959, the Federal Supreme Court disregarded East German exchange rules in a very broadly phrased opinion,[67] but this case does not reflect the present state of the law. A close analysis of the judicial practice shows that the courts take into account the rigid East German exchange restrictions if and only if either the debtor or the creditor is inextricably exposed to them.[68]

33, 37–42; 2 Apr. 1935, RGZ 147, 286, 289–92; 28 June 1934, RGZ 145, 51, 55–56; 21 June 1933, RGZ 141, 212, 216–20.

[64] RG 4 Jan. 1938, JW 1938, 946; 13 May 1935, RGZ 147, 377, 381; OLG Hamburg 5 Oct. 1932, IPRspr. 1933 no. 77.

[65] However, it was invoked in an administrative case decided by the Office of Alien Property of the U.S. Department of Justice, In the Matter of Brecher-Wolff, 22 I.L.R. 718 (1955).

[66] BGH 21 May 1964, WM 1964, 768; 19 Apr. 1962, WM 1962, 601; 20 Mar. 1956, WM 1956, 1265; OLG Frankfurt 27 Feb. 1969, WM 1969, 508; OLG Schleswig 1 Apr. 1954, IPRspr. 1954/55 no. 163; LG Hamburg 28 Dec. 1954, *id.* no. 164.

[67] BGH 17 Dec. 1959, BGHZ 31, 367.

[68] For details, *see* DROBNIG, Die Anwendung des Devisenrechts der Sowjetzone durch westdeutsche Gerichte, NJW 1960, 1088–1093.

The American courts, as might be expected, have had more frequent occasion to consider the application of German foreign exchange rules, both before and after Bretton Woods. In general, they have been liberal in recognizing these rules, whether enacted by the Nazi government[69] or by the Military Government,[70] and they will certainly recognize those enacted by the post-War German government. It is to be hoped that in doing so they will follow more closely than they have in the past the German concepts of the scope of prohibited transactions and of the retroactive effect of a subsequent license (*supra* ch. 1 at nn. 13 and 14).

If economic conditions in the United States and Germany continue to thrive in the future, it will be unlikely that restrictions on foreign exchange will hamper international monetary movements. If adverse circumstances should necessitate their introduction, both countries are bound to observe certain conventional rules.[71] These aim at the fairest possible treatment of the interests of nationals of the other country.

---

[69] *See* the administrative decisions of the Office of Alien Property, cited by DOMKE 45 nn. 209, 210, and *supra* n. 65. *Contra*: some court decisions where assets located in the United States were in dispute, e.g., Loeb v. Bank of Manhattan Co., 18 N.Y.S.2d 497 (Sup. Ct. 1939).

[70] Callwood v. Virgin Islands National Bank, 221 F.2d 770, 775 (3d Cir. 1955); Kent Jewelry Corp. v. Kiefer, 119 N.Y.S.2d 242, 248 (Sup. Ct. 1952); *In re* Muller's Estate, 199 Misc. 745, 749, 104 N.Y.S.2d 133, 135 (Sur. Ct. 1951).

[71] Art. XII of the Treaty of Friendship of 1954 (Treaties B 117) in connection with nos. 14–17 of the Protocol.

Chapter X.

COMPANIES AND OTHER ORGANIZATIONS*

Companies are the primary organizational form for conducting business, particularly on the international scene. We shall discuss first general problems of international company law and then some organizational aspects of establishment in Germany.

I. GENERAL CONFLICTS RULES

(1) Governing Law

(a) *Basic Rule.*—Companies and all other organizations (including foundations (*Stiftungen*), state enterprises,[1] public corporations, and so forth) are, according to long-standing German court practice, governed by the law of their principal office (*Sitz*, corporate domicile, literally "seat").[2] The principal office for conflicts purposes is the actual center of the administration.[3] Thus the place indicated in the company's formal documents or in the commercial register as the principal office of the company or as the center of its administration may be ignored as an arbitrary choice of law by the founders.

It is queer that Germany, while adopting the nationality principle for natural persons (*supra* ch. 3 sub A), follows the principle of

---

* For general surveys of German company law, *see* STEEFEL, German Commercial Law (3d ed. New York 1963) 78–127; SPETHMANN, West Germany, *in* Legal Aspects of Foreign Investment (Friedmann and Pugh, eds. 1959) 670–90.

[1] That state enterprises are treated the same as private organizations, even if their creation is a consequence of preceding expropriations, has been expressly recognized for a Czech state enterprise (BGH 9 July 1965, NJW 1965, 1664), and a state enterprise of (unrecognized) East Germany (*see* cases cited *supra* ch. 1 n. 85).

[2] *Corporations*: RG 9 Mar. 1904, JW 1904, 231 (Washington company doing business in Mexico, but administered in Hamburg, held without legal personality); 16 Dec. 1913, RGZ 83, 367 (Wisconsin corporation).

Partnerships: BGH 26 Sept. 1966, NJW 1967, 36, 38.

Foundations (*corporate trusts*): BayObLG 17 Mar. 1965, BayObLGZ 1965, 77, 80–81.

State enterprises: BGH 9 July 1965, NJW 1965, 1664.

See also infra n. 5.

[3] BGH 27 May 1957, WM 1957, 999, 1000; OLG Nürnberg 25 Apr. 1967, AG 1967, 362; OLG Frankfurt/M. 3 June 1964, AWD 1965, 175. In the two latter cases, corporations founded in Austria and Liechtenstein, respectively, were held void since administered in fact from a place in Germany. *Accord*: BGH 30 Jan. 1970, BGHZ 53, 181.

domicile in the field of organizations.[4] The United States, of course, is guilty of the reverse inconsistency in looking to the law of the domicile for human beings and to the law of incorporation for companies. In fact, however, the difference between the two approaches is not great and it is minimized by recourse to renvoi. Under German corporation law, as under that of most Continental countries, the domicile of a corporation subject to German law must as a rule be located in Germany.[5] And the use of renvoi to avoid a clash with the Anglo-American principle of incorporation is illustrated by a case where, since the law of Kentucky, the corporate domicile according to the German concept, referred to Delaware law as the law of the state of incorporation, the German court followed this reference over (art. 27 EGBGB).[6]

It is submitted that these general conflicts rules are inapplicable to American-German relations by virtue of article XXV (5) of the Treaty of Commerce of 1954 (Treaties B 117). Sentence 2 provides that "companies constituted under the applicable laws and regulations within the territories of either Party . . . shall have their juridical status recognized within the territories of the other Party." This rule is based on the principle of incorporation. If it speaks of recognition rather than governing law, this is only an outdated mode of referring to the applicable law (*infra* (c)). Admittedly, this interpretation of the conventional rule is novel.

(b) *Nationality.*—It is generally admitted today that organizations do not have a "nationality" or citizenship in the same sense as human beings.[7] The term is still used occasionally for conflicts purposes in order to designate, indirectly, the governing law. This is misleading. Frequently, however, it is necessary to qualify an organization as a "citizen" or a "foreigner" where a conflicts rule, international convention, or statutory provision uses these terms.

---

[4] However, the relation of organizations to the state of their seat has often been called their nationality, *see infra* (b). Numerous writers have urged adoption of the Anglo-American principle of incorporation, but so far in vain. *See, e.g.*, BEITZKE, Juristische Personen im Internationalprivatrecht und Fremdenrecht (1938) 92–99.

[5] *Germany*: BGH 21 Nov. 1955, BGHZ 19, 102, 105; RG 10 July 1934, JW 1934, 2969; 29 June 1923, RGZ 107, 94, 97. In exceptional circumstances, legal personality according to German law may be granted to organizations domiciled abroad, *see* §§ 22, 23 and 80 BGB; *cf.* OVG Münster 20 Sept. 1961, IPRspr. 1960/61 no. 20. *See also* 2 RABEL 38 n. 20 b.

[6] On this theory, RAAPE 199 justifies the Eskimo Pie case (RG 3 June 1927, RGZ 117, 215, 217). The court had determined the legal personality of the Eskimo Pie Co., a Delaware company with its business residence in Louisville, Ky., under Delaware law, since the charter had fixed Wilmington, Del., as the corporate domicile. *See also* KEGEL, Kommentar, no. 48 on art. 10 EGBGB.

[7] In German this is often expressed by modifying the word "Staats*an*gehörigkeit" into "Staats*zu*gehörigkeit" for organizations.

The process of qualification in each case depends upon the purposes of the rule in question. Usually, especially for a rule such as article 12 EGBGB regarding unlawful acts committed abroad by "a German," and for other provisions of private law, the same criterion is used as under the general conflicts rule; in other words, the organization is considered to be a national of the country in which its actual center of administration is located.[8] As we have seen (*supra* (a)), a special rule obtains under the Treaty of 1954 whereby incorporation alone is decisive. However, its juxtaposition to the immediately preceding definition of the term "companies" shows that this rule is limited to interpretation of the Treaty.[9]

(c) *Recognition.*—Court decisions of an older vintage frequently spoke of "recognition" of foreign companies, and this tradition was preserved in the American-German Treaty of Commerce.[10] This terminology was justified as long as special legislation made recognition of foreign organizations dependent upon governmental approval,[11] but such legislation no longer exists in Germany. Therefore modern German writers have rightly discarded the term "recognition" with respect to companies, at least as a separate notion. The German conflicts rule referring to the law of the place of an organization's principal office impliedly "recognizes" the organization, just as the *lex situs* rule "recognizes" real rights created under the law of the foreign situs of movables.[12] Similarly, contemporary decisions and conventional rules that still use the outdated language of recognition must be understood merely to refer to the ordinary conflicts rule regarding companies.

(2) Scope of the Governing Law

The law governing an organization determines most issues relating to its status and operation, although there are exceptions.

---

[8] *See,* for § 110 ZPO (security for costs by foreigners), OLG Düsseldorf 8 Jan. 1953, IPRspr. 1952/53 no. 279; LG Düsseldorf 26 Feb. 1958, IPRspr. 1958/59 no. 24.

[9] BGH 30 Nov. 1959, WM 1960, 193, 194; German Patent Office 15 Mar. 1954, IPRspr. 1954/55 no. 142.

[10] *See supra* (a), last paragraph.

[11] Art. 10 EGBGB denied legal personality to foreign "associations" (Vereine) with separate entity, unless recognized by the Bundesrat. The provision was scrapped in 1964 and replaced by rules designed to regulate the activities of foreign associations in Germany, *see infra* ch. 11 sub III.

In 1903/04, the legal status of American business corporations was temporarily clouded: One division of the OLG Hamburg (23 June 1903, NiemZ 14 (1904) 64) extended art. 10 EGBGB to a Tennessee business corporation and therefore denied its legal personality. However, other divisions of the same court vigorously opposed this view (OLG Hamburg 7 and 20 Nov. 1903, 23 Mar. 1904, NiemZ 14 (1904) 69, 163 and 476), so that the lonely dissenter ruefully recanted, OLG Hamburg 22 Nov. 1904, NiemZ 15 (1905) 320.

[12] For details, *see* Drobnig, ZHR 129 (1966) 93–120; *see also* Kegel, IPR 206–07; Raape 199–200.

(a) *Personality.*—Legal personality and access to courts are subject to the law of the place of the principal office.[13] However, limitations imposed upon the legal personality or capacity of corporations by the Anglo-American ultra vires doctrine are frowned upon in Germany.[14] German writers advocate disregard of such limitations, at least for transactions entered into in Germany, analogizing to article 7 III 1 EGBGB.[15] The courts also tend to invest foreign organizations with suability irrespective of their "personal law" if German plaintiffs would otherwise encounter great difficulties in enforcing their rights.[16] One writer invokes even here the aforementioned article 7 III 1 EGBGB and postulates that any organization doing business in Germany is suable in accordance with German law irrespective of the personal law of the organization.[17] The personal law, on the other hand, determines whether an organization is to be considered a merchant,[18] and it also governs the dissolution, liquidation, and termination of an organization,[19] except by way of expropriation.[20]

It might be expected that the existence of a foreign entity must be proved in Germany in the German form, that is, by an extract from a commercial register (*infra* II (3)(b)). In practice, however, it is well established that companies from countries lacking a commercial register may establish their existence in the form customary under the law of their principal office. By legislation adopted in 1970, German law has drawn closer to American law in permitting a German notary to issue a certificate attesting to the existence, the seat, and other relevant facts affecting a German company, provided

---

[13] Eskimo Pie case, *supra* n. 6; OLG Frankfurt/M. 21 Feb. 1933, IPRspr. 1933 no. 4 (dissolved New York corporation); OLG Hamburg 14 June 1904, OLG 9, 253 (New York partnership).

[14] *See* OLG Düsseldorf 21 Apr. 1964, AG 1965, 16.

[15] According to this provision, a foreigner contracting in Germany who has not full capacity according to his national law, is deemed fully capable if he would be so under German law (*see supra* ch. 4 sub C(1)). *See* KEGEL, Kommentar, no. 10 on art. 10 EGBGB, with further references.

[16] *See*, especially, BGH 28 Jan. 1960, NJW 1960, 1204 (Dutch foundation whose legal personality under Dutch law was doubtful). On the other hand, *see* OLG Hamburg, *supra* n. 13, which refused to permit a New York partnership to be sued and correctly required plaintiff to sue the partners individually.

[17] KEGEL, Kommentar, no. 15 on art. 10 EGBGB. This view lacks support in the cases; *see*, e.g., OLG Hamburg, *supra* n. 13.

[18] LG Hamburg 12 Nov. 1957, IPRspr. 1958/59 no. 22. However, OLG München 14 Nov. 1966, NJW 1967, 1326, 1328, determined the status of an American business corporation by reference to German law. If, exceptionally, a branch office of a foreign company has been entered in the German commercial register, German law governs, BRÜGGEMANN, *in* Handelsgesetzbuch, Grosskommentar, vol. I (3d ed. 1967) no. 41 of the Introduction. Being a "merchant" has important consequences in German commercial law.

[19] *See* OLG Frankfurt/M., *supra* n. 13.

[20] *See supra* ch. 6 at nn. 71–73.

the certificate is to be used abroad.[20a] In the case of an American company the certificate of incorporation[21] or an extract from a register or a confirmation of the company's creation and existence by an American attorney (based upon an examination of the relevant documents), is usually held sufficient.

(b) *Representation.*—The powers of the directors or officers to represent an organization are also, as a rule, subject to the law of the place of the principal office.[22] However, for transactions in Germany, the courts and writers tend to disregard any limitation upon these powers that is unknown to German law and has not been entered in the German commercial register.[23] When this rule applies, or when the rule respecting a power of attorney issued by an organization (*supra* ch. 8 sub IV (1)) applies, is not quite clear.[24] The following line of demarcation is proposed: The rules on powers of attorney govern where the action taken requires one to hold a special power of attorney in order to represent the organization in the matter at hand. By contrast, the rule on company powers prevails where the power to represent the organization derives exclusively from statutory company law. Special rules prevail in the exceptional situation where a branch office of a foreign company has been entered into the German commercial register. Limitations upon the power of representation which German law requires to be, but which have not in fact been, entered there cannot prevail against an innocent third person.[25] On the other hand, if such a limitation has been entered, third persons are bound if they knew or ought to have known of it (§ 15 II, III HGB). Where the power of representation of liquidators[26] or of a trustee in bankruptcy[27] are concerned, again it is the law of the place of the principal office which applies.

The modes of proof of the powers of corporate representatives differ profoundly. In Germany the most efficient and authentic

[20a] § 22a BNotO, as inserted by the Beurkundungsgesetz of August 28, 1969 (BGBl. I 1513).

[21] Eskimo Pie case, *supra* n. 6.

[22] BGH 23 Oct. 1963, BGHZ 40, 197, 199 (foreign state); 5 May 1960, BGHZ 32, 256, 258; KG Berlin 8 Mar. 1929, JFG 6, 195, 197.

[23] *See* OLG Hamm 6 June 1957, IPRspr. 1956/57 no. 27 (power of president of American corporation); KEGEL, Kommentar, no. 20 on art. 10 EGBGB, with references, based again on an analogy to art. 7 III 1 EGBGB. *Contra*: OLG Hamburg 21 Jan. 1932, IPRspr. 1932 no. 14.

[24] OLG Hamm, *supra* n. 23, probably exemplifies the confusion.

[25] § 15 I, III HGB; on the limits to the registration of foreign limitations, *see* KG Berlin, *supra* n. 22.

[26] OLG München 17 July 1928, IPRspr. 1929 no. 23 (English company).

[27] BGH 7 Dec. 1961, WM 1962, 263, 266; RG 5 Jan. 1937, RGZ 153, 200, 205–07. In this respect, § 237 KO, declaring a foreign bankruptcy ineffective in Germany (*see infra* ch. 14 sub IV (3)) does not obtain because the issue is one of company, not of bankruptcy, law.

means is an extract from the commercial register. Recently German notaries have been authorized to issue certificates as to the power of representation of corporate officers.[27a] In the case of American companies, German practice has by and large accepted the usual American procedure, namely, a certificate of the company's secretary confirming a meeting of the board of directors, its regularity, and its resolutions.[28]

(c) *Other issues.*—Issues of organization, capital and management are subject to the law at the place of the principal office.[29] This law governs the liability of the members of partnerships[30] as well as of corporations.[31] Changes in the structure of a company, such as merger, consolidation, scission, and so on, are also governed by this law, and it extends to the transfer of assets and liabilities as a whole provided the transfer is authorized by statute; in this case, assets or liabilities situated in Germany need not be transferred piecemeal.[32] The courts have, however, rightly permitted the German partners of partnerships formed abroad to choose German law for their internal relations.[33]

(3) **Transfer of Seat**

Since a transfer of the seat or principal office entails a change in the governing law, difficult problems are bound to arise from such a move. On the other hand, as a consequence of the two World Wars, many German companies domiciled in lost territory have sought to repatriate themselves. The following picture has emerged. Some of the older cases have held that the adoption of a resolution by a German company to transfer its seat abroad has the effect of dissolving the company.[34] Although regrettable, this solution seems

---

[27a] § 21 I 1 BNotO, as amended, *supra* n. 20a.

[28] A detailed description of the American rules in JACOB-STEINORTH, Die Vertretungsmacht bei den wichtigsten amerikanischen Handelsgesellschaften, DNotZ 1958, 361–377.

[29] RG 27 May 1910, RGZ 73, 366, 367; KG Berlin 8 Mar. 1929, JFG 6, 195, 197.

[30] BGH 13 July 1959, WM 1959, 1110; 17 Dec. 1953, LM no. 7 on § 105 HGB; RG 2 Jan. 1920, HansGZ 1920 HBl. 106 (Texas partnership). To the effect that the parties may choose another law, *see* the decisions of the BGH.

[31] BGH 10 June 1965, WM 1965, 787, 788; 11 July 1957, WM 1957, 1047, 1049; OLG München, *supra* n. 26; LAG Stuttgart 31 Mar. 1955, IPRspr. 1954/55 no. 19.

[32] *Cf.* OLG Frankfurt/M. 21 Feb. 1933, IPRspr. 1933 no. 4 (general assignment). The interesting advisory opinion on which the court relies is published in 25 Jahre Kaiser Wilhelm-Gesellschaft zur Förderung der Wissenschaften (1937) III 152–157.

[33] *See* BGH, *supra* n. 30; *see also* RG 27 Feb. 1931, HansRGZ 1931 B 295; OLG Hamburg, *supra* n. 23.

[34] The only international case is RG 5 June 1882, RGZ 7, 68. Interstate cases are BGH 6 July 1955, WM 1955, 1318; RG 22 Jan. 1916, RGZ 88, 53.

unavoidable in the interest of German shareholders and creditors as long as no procedure for an orderly emigration of companies is available.[35] On the other hand, the loss of two wars has produced liberal rules on the immigration of companies. After World War I, the courts recognized the continuity of companies that had transferred their seat from the lost territories to the territory which remained.[36] The same rule was applied after World War II when hundreds of companies transferred their seats from Eastern to Western Germany, notwithstanding Eastern prohibitions.[37] This principle was extended to companies domiciled in other East European countries, whether created under German or foreign law.[38]

II. ORGANIZATIONAL ASPECTS OF ESTABLISHMENT IN GERMANY[39]

(1) Economic Background

At the end of 1968, the nominal value of shareholdings (in the widest sense of the word) held by Americans in German enterprises amounted to almost two billion dollars, about 44% of all foreign-held shares. If loan capital, surplus and surplus reserves were included, the amount would be doubled. The market value of the shares was, of course, considerably higher. As related to the nominal value of the capital of all industrial and commercial enterprises in Germany, the amount in foreign hands was estimated to be well under 10%; in companies with publicly traded shares (*Aktiengesellschaften*), about 14.5%; in limited liability companies, more than 24.5%. Of the 5,375 enterprises with more than negligible foreign participation, some 4,440 were in the form of German business corporations, about 840 were in German partnerships or sole proprietorships, and 86 in branches or agencies of foreign enterprises. These few figures[40] may serve to indicate the magnitude in economic terms of the

---

[35] The countries of the European Economic Community are working on a draft convention for transfers of seat within the Community.

[36] E.g., RG 29 June 1923, RGZ 107, 94.

[37] E.g., BGH 14 Feb. 1958, NJW 1958, 671; OLG Düsseldorf 14 Dec. 1961, NJW 1962, 869. An American court recognized such a transfer in Carl Zeiss Stiftung v. V.E.B. Carl Zeiss, Jena, 293 F. Supp. 892, 915 (S.D.N.Y. 1968), 433 F.2d 686, 703 (2d Cir. 1970).

[38] *See*, e.g., BGH 11 July 1957, BGHZ 25, 134, 136, 148; *see also* KG Berlin 28 Apr. 1927, JW 1927, 1701.

[39] Still relevant although slightly outdated is OPPENHEIMER, Foreign Persons, Firms and Corporations Doing Business in Germany, 30 Colum. L. Rev. 986–1009 (1930); for an interesting general description, *see* H. HARTMANN, Amerikanische Firmen in Deutschland (1963).

[40] The figures are drawn from a report of the German Federal Bank in "Monatsberichte der Deutschen Bundesbank" 1969 no. 5 pp. 22–27; *see also id.* 1966 no. 11 pp. 15–24 and 1965 no. 5 pp. 51–60.

organizational issues arising in connection with foreign establishment in Germany.

(2) Freedom to Organize

The freedom to create organizations in Germany is guaranteed to American nationals and companies by the Commercial Treaty of 1954 (Treaties B 117). Americans engaged in any type of activity for gain are to be treated on a par with Germans (or with the nationals of the most favored nation) if they

—establish or maintain branches, offices or other business establishments in Germany;

—organize companies under German general company law or acquire majority interests in German companies; or

—control or manage enterprises in Germany which they have established or acquired.[41]

Certain limitations upon activities which are of particular public interest will be discussed later (ch. 11 sub II (2)(b)).

Outside the area of business activities Americans may, like Germans themselves, or other "most favored" foreigners, engage in scientific, educational, religious and philanthropic (but not political) pursuits, and for that purpose they may form associations under German law (art. VIII (2), *see infra* ch. 11 sub III). Since German law does not discriminate against foreigners in these matters, the conventional rules have little relevance.

(3) Form of Organization

Two initial questions confront one advising a businessman who desires to set up an enterprise in Germany: Is the business to be established as a subsidiary or a branch? If the former, what form of company is to be chosen?

(a) The choice between subsidiary and branch in most cases will depend primarily upon tax considerations, influenced by German as well as American revenue laws and the Tax Convention (*infra* ch. 16 sub (2)). For instance, an expected initial period of losses may make it desirable to start with a branch to permit deduction of these losses from profits at the home base. However a subsequent conversion of the branch into a German subsidiary may attract the attention of the German tax authorities if the branch has accumulated hidden reserves. Apart from taxes, peculiar conditions of certain types of business may come into play and sway the balance. Thus American banking and insurance companies usually operate by way of branches in Germany. Why? German subsidiaries in these two

---

[41] Art. VII (1) and (4). Most-favored-nation treatment is also assured to non-American enterprises controlled by Americans. Only special formalities, if non-harassing, may be prescribed, para. 3.

categories would be subject to the stringent regulatory requirements established for German corporations, while the guarantees required from the German branches of foreign firms are more lenient (*infra* ch. 11 sub II (2)). In addition, for the customer, especially an American doing business in Germany, it may be more attractive to deal with a legally integrated outpost of a large American bank than with a small local subsidiary.[42] A third consideration, operating in the other direction, is the requirement that branches of foreign corporations obtain government permits to do business in Germany. German corporations, even when founded by foreigners, are generally free from this requirement (*see infra* ch. 11 sub II (2)(b)). As a net result of these various considerations, at the end of 1968, there were 2,890 fully foreign-owned subsidiaries in Germany, including German partnerships and sole proprietorships, with a nominal capital of more than 3.1 billion dollars, as against only eighty-six branches with a capital of 217 million dollars.[43] It may well be assumed that American business conforms to this general pattern.

(b) If a subsidiary is to be created, the further question arises, what form should it take? Germany offers a wide variety of choices, at least two for each of the basic forms of organization.

There are three forms of partnership: general, limited and silent.[44] The limited partnership (*Kommanditgesellschaft*, KG) is quite popular because of its tax advantages, especially if the general partner is a corporation (in the form of a limited liability company) whose shares are held by the limited partners (GmbH & Co. KG).[45] Although not formally legal entities, general and limited partnerships enjoy many of the same rights. They can hold property and can sue and be sued under their trade name.

Of greater interest for the foreign investor are the two main forms of business corporation, the stock corporation (*Aktiengesellschaft*, AG) and the limited liability company (*Gesellschaft mit beschränkter Haftung*, GmbH).[46] The division corresponds roughly to the American division between a corporation floating securities

---

[42] *See also* Dahl, International Operations of U.S. Banks, 32 Law & Contemp. Prob. 100–30, 106 (1967).

[43] *See* report, *supra* n. 40, at 23 and 26.

[44] Offene Handelsgesellschaft, Kommanditgesellschaft, Stille Gesellschaft. *See* Steefel 78–88.

[45] Laundry, The GmbH & Co. Kommanditgesellschaft: German Partnership Vehicle for Joint Ventures, 23 Bus. Law. 213–29 (1967).

[46] There are a few other forms: the partnership limited by shares (Kommanditgesellschaft auf Aktien), rarely used (there are about 25); the mining company (bergrechtliche Gewerkschaft), existing in some states under state law; and cooperatives (Genossenschaften) and mutual insurance companies (Versicherungsvereine auf Gegenseitigkeit).

for public offering and a close corporation.[47] The stock corporation[48] is the more cumbersome and expensive form, subject to greater disclosure and as a rule chosen only if securities are to be offered to the public. The limited liability company[49] is the ordinary business corporation, usually with only a few members and a great degree of flexibility and informality. At the end of 1968, there were 2,328 stock corporations with a fixed capital of nearly 13 billion dollars as against 67,416 limited liability companies with a fixed capital of slightly more than 9 billion dollars. Compared with the end of 1966, the former had decreased by 92, the latter increased by 9,390.[50] Interestingly enough, the statistics on the form of foreign shareholdings in corporations reflect considerably less disproportion, namely 349:4,097 (as of the end of 1968) as compared with 381:3,506 (as of the end of 1965).[51] The reason for the difference is probably that a relatively larger number of big foreign corporations operate in Germany and prefer the form of the stock corporation (thus, *inter alia*, Ford, General Motors, Mobil Oil).

(c) A peculiar formal feature of German business law to be mentioned finally is the commercial register. In it are entered the names of all businessmen, trading individually or organized, incorporated or unincorporated. However, the greatest importance attaches to the registration of corporations; only with registration, published in the Federal Bulletin and in a local paper, does a corporation as such come into existence.[52] Into the register are entered the name of the company (*Firma*), its registered office (which is not necessarily the principal office for purposes of conflicts law (*supra* (1)(a)), its object, the amount of the fixed capital, and the

---

[47] STEEFEL 90–91 contrasts 18 basic features of the two German forms.

[48] *See* two English translations (with German text) of the Stock Corporation Act of 1965: JUENGER/SCHMIDT, German Stock Corporation Act (Commerce Clearing House 1967), and MUELLER/GALBRAITH, The German Stock Corporation Law (Frankfurt 1966), each with a brief introduction. *See*, further, STEEFEL/v. FALKENHAUSEN, The New German Stock Corporation Law, 52 Cornell L. Q. 518–50 (1967); VAGTS, Reforming the "Modern" Corporation: Perspectives from the German, 80 Harv. L. Rev. 23–89 (1966). STEEFEL 89–114 is superseded by the new Act of 1965. Partly outdated also is v. FALKENHAUSEN/STEEFEL, Shareholders' Rights in German Corporations (AG and GmbH), 10 Am. J. Comp. L. 407–31 (1961).

[49] For an English translation of the Law of 1892, *see* MUELLER, GmbH. German Law Concerning the Companies with Limited Liability (Frankfurt 1967), with brief introduction and sample articles. *See also* DE VRIES/JUENGER, Limited Liability Contract: The GmbH, 64 Colum. L. Rev. 866–86 (1964); STEEFEL, 114–24; v. FALKENHAUSEN/STEEFEL, *supra* n. 48.

[50] Statistisches Jahrbuch der Bundesrepublik Deutschland 1969, 181, 183; 1967, 201.

[51] *See* report *supra* n. 40, at 24.

[52] § 41 I 1 AktG, § 11 I GmbH-Ges. For specimens of publications in the Federal Bulletin, *see* STEEFEL 80, 104 and 117.

names of the officers representing the corporation (including any admissible limitations on the power of representation).[53] Since anybody may inspect the register or ask for extracts or for a certificate that there are no (or no further) entries relating to some particular, the legal existence of a corporation and the powers of its representatives are easy to ascertain.[54] The registration of companies and sole proprietorships follows similar, though simpler, lines.

(4) **Firm Name**

The strict German rules on the firm name (*Firma*) affect foreign business activities in two ways: Whoever uses a trade name violating the rights of another may be sued by the latter under the general rules on unfair competition (*infra* ch. 12 sub V). In addition to such repressive actions, the foreigner whose business is entered, in whatever form, in a German commercial register is subject to preliminary examination exercised on registration. We shall deal here with this latter aspect only.

A branch will usually carry the firm name of the main enterprise, although it need not do so.[55] The validity of the firm name is determined, on principle, by the law governing the company (*supra* I (1)(a)), but two concessions to the German rules are enforced: In the first place, the prohibition of trade names that are apt to deceive as to the nature or the size of the business or the circumstances of the entrepreneur has been declared by the courts to be of public policy.[56] And there is another rule designed to avoid confusion which will also apply to branches of foreign enterprises: each new firm name must distinguish itself clearly from names already existing and registered for the same locality (§ 30 I HGB);[57] however, branches of foreign enterprises will rarely create such confusion in view of the different language employed.

If a German subsidiary is created, its firm name is subject solely to German law. However, the foreign connection of the enterprise is relevant where the subsidiary chooses, as it often does, to adopt the name of its foreign parent company. That name must be copied

---

53 § 39 AktG, § 10 GmbH-Ges.

54 The effects of an entry or the omission of an entry are set out *supra* I (2) (b) at n. 25.

55 The German branch of "Deere & Co." has the firm name "John Deere Werke Zweigniederlassung der Deere & Co." Such additions are impliedly authorized by § 13b II HGB.

56 § 18 HGB; *see* BayObLG 2 May 1913, RJA 13, 37, 39–40; KG Berlin 16 June 1911, KGJ 42, 159. Thus the firm name "German X. Corporation Y. & Co." for a German partnership was declared deceptive as connoting a corporation, Mitteilungen der Industrie- und Handelskammer Berlin 1925, 706.

57 Balser/Pichura, Zweigniederlassungen ausländischer Kapitalgesellschaften in Deutschland (1958) 11; Keidel/Schmatz, Registerrecht (2d ed. 1960) 13; Brüggemann, no. 42 preceding § 1 HGB.

as closely as possible in its original language,[58] provided it is neither deceptive nor confusing (§§ 18 II, 30 HGB, *supra*). The designation of the foreign legal form of company (Ltd., Inc., Corp.) may be and usually is dropped.[59] On the other hand, an addition indicating restriction of the business to German territory is permissible and frequent.[60]

Since the commercial register is maintained by the local court (*Amtsgericht*), the whole procedure for entries is judicial. The court examines each application for registration; if a new firm name is to be entered, the local chamber of commerce is asked for its opinion on the firm, especially whether its name is deceptive or confusing under §§ 18 II, 30 HGB (*see supra*).

(5) **Registration in the Commercial Register**[61]

The rules on registration of a German subsidiary are closely similar to those on registration of a branch in Germany, since the office of the latter is technically considered to be the corporate domicile (*see* § 13b III HGB, § 44 V AktG).

The following documents are required for registration of a German stock corporation or the German branch of a foreign stock corporation:

—the application for registration, containing the firm name and the corporate domicile; the object of the corporation; its issued capital; the classes and nature of the shares; the composition of the board of managers; the form of notices and designation of a medium of publication;[62]

—a certified copy of the charter and by-laws (§ 44 I 2 AktG);

—proof of the legal existence of the foreign corporation as such;[63]

—a permit to do business, if necessary;[64] and

—the signatures of all the members of the "board of managers" (§ 35 HGB).

---

[58] *See* the examples quoted by OPPENHEIMER, *supra* n. 39, at 992 n. 34. But the addition of a German translation is permitted, e.g., "IBM Deutschland Internationale Büromaschinen Gesellschaft mbH."

[59] OLG Düsseldorf 11 July 1956, DNotZ 1956, 611. *Examples*: "Honeywell GmbH," "Schick Eversharp GmbH," "Digital Equipment GmbH," "Avon Cosmetics GmbH."

[60] *Examples*: "Deutsche Goodyear GmbH," "General Motors Deutschland GmbH," "Mobil Oil AG in Deutschland." *See* RG 17 Jan. 1944, DR 1944, 579, as against RG 12 Jan. 1937, JW 1937, 1876 (the reasons given in both decisions are heavily impregnated by the spirit of their time); KNÖCHLEIN, DB 1960, 746–49, 748.

[61] For details, *see* BALSER/PICHURA, *supra* n. 57.

[62] § 44 II 2 AktG in connection with §§ 23 III, 24 and 25 sent. 2 AktG.

[63] § 44 II 1 AktG; *see supra* nn. 21 and 22.

[64] § 44 II 1 AktG and LG Berlin 27 Aug. 1927, IPRspr. 1928 no. 151. This requirement primarily affects branches, *see infra* ch. 11 sub II (2) (a).

Registration of a German limited liability company or the German branch of a foreign company of this type similarly requires:

—the formal application for registration;

—the documents mentioned above (sub (2) to (5)); and

—a list of the members of the company.[65]

German law determines under what circumstances and in what form the first registration and subsequent entries have to be made.[66]

(6) **Bookkeeping**

A foreign enterprise doing business in Germany as a branch is subject to the German rules on bookkeeping, preservation of documents, and so forth (§§ 38–44b HGB), including the civil and criminal sanctions for violation of these duties.[67] It may be remarked that financial statements differ widely in the two countries. This makes it very difficult to understand the true import of a statement coming from the other side of the Atlantic. Branches and subsidiaries therefore usually establish, on the basis of one set of figures, two statements, one for local purposes and another for foreign consumption. The use of American technical experts, especially accountants, for this purpose is facilitated by a special provision of the Commercial Treaty (Treaties B 117) (art. VIII (1) sent. 2), which permits the employment of such persons, even if they do not qualify for the practice of their profession in Germany, to prepare for domestic use audits, examinations and reports relating to American business interests in Germany.

(7) **Special Rules for German Corporations with Foreign Contacts**

Whether and to which degree the rules of German company law may have to be modified on account of specific organizational contacts of a German corporation with foreign countries, is a broad and important, but unfortunately little-explored, field. Two typical questions may illustrate the problem: Can the constitutive documents for a German corporation be drafted outside Germany? Can a general assembly of all members be convened outside Germany? The answer to these questions hinges largely on the central rôle of the notary who is required for the drafting of most of the corporate documents. Since American law does not provide a true equivalent and German notaries are not permitted to practice outside Germany (*infra* ch. 14 sub V (1)(a)), it would seem that these questions must be answered in the negative.

Only where foreign contacts of German "connected" and "com-

---

[65] Balser/Pichura, *supra* n. 57, at 35–36.

[66] §§ 13b III HGB, 44 V AktG; KG Berlin 3 Oct. 1940, DR 1940, 2007.

[67] RG 2 Feb. 1914, Bad.Rspr. 16 (1914) 75.

bined" enterprises are concerned has the legislature created specific rules.[68]

---

[68] Brief accounts in the introduction to MUELLER/GALBRAITH, *supra* n. 48, at 18–20, and in WÜRDINGER, Aktien- und Konzernrecht (2d ed. 1966) 21–22. Analysis (and reprint) of some new contracts between German subsidiaries and American enterprises by MEILICKE, Korporative Versklavung deutscher Aktiengesellschaften, *in* Berliner Festschrift für Ernst E. Hirsch (1968) 118–26. *See also* HASKELL, The New West German Law of "Related Business Units," 24 Bus. Law. 421–33 (1969).

Chapter XI.

LAW OF ALIENS

One of the important and generally recognized attributes of sovereignty is the right of every state freely to grant or deny admission to aliens and to regulate their exercise of professional or business activities within its territory. However, there is a growing tendency to restrict the discretion of the states in these matters, both by national legislation and, more effectively, by bilateral treaties or multilateral instruments of public international law.

I. ENTRY AND SOJOURN; RIGHT OF ASYLUM; EXIT AND EXPULSION*

The central body of German rules on the admission and expulsion of aliens has been consolidated in the Law on Aliens of 1965 (*Ausländergesetz*, AuslG).[1] The aliens to whom the statute applies are defined as "everybody who is not a German"[2]; this includes stateless persons.[3] The text of the very first sentence implies, and the history and preparatory materials confirm, that entry and sojourn are not granted by some general rule, but only within the framework of the statute.[4] Although the statute expressly reserves the position of certain persons and also gives precedence to international agreements (§§ 49, 55 III AuslG), this reservation is of small import for Americans since the Friendship Treaty of 1954 (Treaties B 177) expressly subjects freedom of entry and residence "to the laws relating to the entry and sojourn of aliens" (art. II (1) sent. 1).[5]

* For texts and comments, *see* SCHIEDERMAIR, Handbuch des Ausländerrechts der Bundesrepublik Deutschland (1968) 82–376; KANEIN, Das Ausländergesetz und die wesentlichen fremdenrechtlichen Vorschriften (1966); KLOESEL/CHRIST, Deutsches Ausländerrecht (loose-leaf, 1965); MARXEN, Deutsches Ausländerrecht (1967); WEISSMANN, Ausländergesetz (1966).

[1] Of Apr. 25, 1965, BGBl. I 353, with several pieces of subsidiary legislation, all reprinted in SCHIEDERMAIR 82–376.

[2] § 1 II AuslG. For the definition of a "German," the provision refers expressly to art. 116 I GG, *see supra* ch. 3 sub A II (1) (c), following n. 16.

[3] Germans who have dual nationality are not aliens. However, § 27 AuslG requires them to report their foreign nationality.

[4] § 1 I AuslG: "may according to the provisions of this law . . . ." *See also* § 2 I 2: "the permit to reside may be granted . . . ." *See further* nos. 2 and 4 of the official motives, reprinted in SCHIEDERMAIR 87–89 and *id.* 27–28 and 35.

[5] Sentence 2 specifies this clause so as to reflect the treaty-trader/treaty-investor clauses of the Immigration Law, *see* WILSON 35–56. *See also* art. XXIV (6) of the Treaty.

(1) **Entry and Sojourn**

Quite apart from asylum, which receives separate treatment (*see infra* (2)), entry and sojourn of an alien as a rule require a "residence permit" (*Aufenthaltserlaubnis*, § 2 I 1 AuslG). However, this requirement is actually reversed in practice, since the statute itself and various special regulations enumerate many exemptions. Under general exemptions, no permit is necessary for the following persons:

—minors under sixteen years of age and aliens recognized by West Germany as aliens without a home country (*heimatloser Ausländer*) (§ 2 II AuslG);

—subject to reciprocity, the personnel and certain servants of a foreign consulate, and members of the families of the consul and personnel, as to whom the appropriate German authority must merely be notified (§ 49 II AuslG);

—certain groups of persons, especially the crew and passengers of ships and aircraft in transit (§ 1 I DV/AuslG);

—nationals of some ninety states, among others, United States citizens,[6] holding passports[7] or equivalent documents,[8] provided: (i) they do not stay for more than three months and do not intend to work; (ii) their employment in Germany by an employer located outside Germany is provisional and does not exceed two months; (iii) they engage, while still habitually residing abroad, in lectures or in artistic, scientific or sporting events for a period not exceeding two months; or (iv) they are sailors duly qualified by documents isued in Germany and their stay is in the exercise of or in connection with this calling (§ 1 II DV/AuslG). Certain of these exempt aliens, notably those under (iii) and (iv), must give notice of their stay to the appropriate German authority (§ 2 DV/AuslG).

If no exemption can be claimed, a residence permit is necessary. Whether it should be issued is discretionary with the German authorities. It may be issued if the presence of the alien does not adversely affect the public interest (§ 2 I 2 AuslG); administrative rules prescribe certain flexible criteria, mentioning as the usual grounds for refusal the fact that the alien would be liable to expulsion (*infra* (c)), or that he is affected by a certain contagious disease, or that he intends to study but either has not been admitted to a program or cannot prove sufficient financial means.[9] In addition,

---

[6] *See* Appendix to the Regulation in Execution of the Law of Aliens, DV/AuslG, BGBl. 1969 I 207.

[7] The obligation to produce a passport is prescribed in § 3 AuslG, but § 3 DV/AuslG exempts nine groups of persons from the obligation to hold a passport.

[8] § 4 DV/AuslG enumerates 17 documents that are recognized as equivalent to a passport, *inter alia*, "Cards/Certificates of Identity and Registration" issued to U.S. citizens for a stay in West Germany (§ 4 I no. 16).

[9] Nos. 4, 5 and 17 of the Administrative Rules for the Execution of the Law of Aliens (Allgemeine Verwaltungsvorschrift zur Ausführung des Ausländergesetzes, AuslG/Vwv), reprinted in SCHIEDERMAIR 307–67.

all "relevant" circumstances may be taken into account, such as the health of the applicant, the condition of the German labor market,[10] and political and economic factors in general.[11] In practice, a health certificate from a German medical authority (*Gesundheitsamt*) is demanded. In view of the shortage of labor, regard for the labor market is no obstacle, at least at present. The other considerations do not affect Americans, who almost always receive the permit.

The residence permit may be issued, initially or subsequently, for either a limited or an unlimited period of time, subject to conditions or charges, or with geographical restrictions (§ 7 AuslG). Only where an alien has resided lawfully for at least five years in West Germany and has been integrated into the economic and social life of the country may the permit not be so restricted (§ 8 AuslG). The law at present allows the application for a permit to be made immediately after entry.[12] Of the exceptional circumstances in which the permit must be obtained in the form of a passport visa before entry, the only one which might apply to an American (*i.e.*, sojourn with intent to work (§ 5 I no. 1 DV/AuslG)) is superseded by an executive agreement between the United States and West Germany of 1952/53.[13] Thus, in effect, Americans never need a visa; it suffices if they apply for the residence permit, where necessary, immediately after entering West Germany.

Any alien who has entered the country by virtue of a permit (and also certain others (*supra*)), has to report his residence (§ 21 I 1 AuslG).

(2) Right of Asylum

Deeply impressed by the Nazi persecutions and the flight of thousands of persecutees from Germany, the West German Constitution grants the right of asylum to political persecutees (art. 16 II 2 GG). To this group are added international, that is, non-German, "refugees" as defined by the Geneva Convention on Refugees of 1951[14] (now § 28 AuslG). An alien claiming the right of asylum

---

[10] In practice, therefore, the labor authorities are asked for their opinion. This is in addition to the separate "employment permit" to be issued by them (*infra* II (1)). The purpose of this double-check is to avoid even the entry of aliens intending to work.

[11] No. 6 AuslG/Vwv.

[12] §§ 5 I, 21 I 2, 21 III AuslG.

[13] Para. II of the Agreement (Treaties B 95). The agreement is somewhat one-sided since it does not reciprocate in the treatment of German non-immigrants who continue to require a visa. However, the latter is issued without charge (para. I) and today in practice often for life.

[14] BGBl. 1953 II 559, GVBl. Berlin-West 1954, 284, Verträge A 28, 189 UNTS 137, 150. The United States, by ratifying the 1967 Protocol to the Convention (Treaties M 308), has become practically a party to this Convention. On the definition of the status of refugees, *see* the exhaustive, comparative

has to submit an application; the procedure is laid down *in extenso* (§§ 29–45 AuslG). If an alien is recognized as being entitled to asylum, he is also entitled to the residence permit (§ 43 AuslG). His legal status is governed by the Geneva Convention on Refugees (§ 44 AuslG). Between 1953 and 1966, more than 20,500 aliens were granted asylum, among these about 14,000 refugees from Hungary.[15] In this connection the application of the American exchange student S. W. Kellogg is worth mentioning. He had participated in the Hungarian struggle of November 1956, wearing a United States Army uniform. The United States government requested his immediate return, charging him with armed service for a foreign power and abuse of the American uniform. Asylum in Germany was refused by two administrative boards, which held that the risk of a criminal prosecution does not amount to "persecution" if due process is guaranteed and political convictions are not penalized.[16]

(3) **Exit and Expulsion**

An alien is as a rule free to leave the country (§ 19 I AuslG). This right, however, is abridged in certain cases, and he may be prevented from leaving or, on the other hand, required and even forced to depart. His departure will be prohibited if his presence abroad would endanger the security of West Germany, or if he intends to flee from criminal justice or to breach a support obligation such as the duty to support an illegitimate child, or if he has violated provisions dealing with taxation, customs, or import or export controls (§ 19 II AuslG). Even if one of these conditions is fulfilled, issuance of the prohibition lies in the discretion of the authorities. An alien may be required to leave Germany if he has no residence permit or if it has expired or if he has been expelled (§ 12 I AuslG).

Apart from expiration under its own terms, a permit lapses if the alien no longer possesses a valid passport or equivalent document, if he loses or changes his nationality, or if he is expelled (§ 9 I AuslG). The law enumerates eleven grounds for expulsion, among which are: security reasons; conviction of an aggravated crime; violation of provisions dealing with taxation, customs, import or export controls, or residence; making of false statements about his personal or economic relations; and inability to support himself and his family (§ 10 AuslG). Aliens who have lived lawfully for at least five years in West Germany and have become integrated into the

---

treatise by GRAHL-MADSEN, The Status of Refugees in International Law, vol. 1 (1966).

[15] Detailed figures *in* KIMMINICH, Asylrecht (1968) 126–32, 128, and 26–27. Only one American citizen has applied (KIMMINICH 27)—apparently Mr. Kellogg (*see* text following).

[16] *See* ZaöRV 20 (1959/60) 103–04.

economic and social life of the country may be expelled only for reasons of security or aggravated instances of the other grounds mentioned (§ 11 I AuslG).

An alien who is required to leave the country may be deported if he does not depart voluntarily or if the public interest necessitates supervision of his departure. Deportation must be announced in writing and a time limit allowed (§ 13 AuslG). Normally an alien may not be deported to a country where he is liable to persecution for political reasons (§ 14 AuslG). In order to secure the deportation, the alien may be taken into custody (§ 16 AuslG).

II. WORK; PROFESSIONAL AND BUSINESS ACTIVITIES

(1) Work and Exercise of Professions

(a) Any non-German (*supra* ch. 3 sub A II (1)(c)) desiring to work requires an employment permit (*Arbeitserlaubnis*). An employer may not employ an alien without it (§ 43 I AVAVG). If the parties, although knowing of the requirement, intend not to apply for a permit, their labor contract is void, and this is also the result if the permit is refused. Where an application is made before commencement of the employment, the validity of the contract is in suspense.[16a] Details on the issuance of this permit are laid down in a special regulation,[17] but the following points are worthy of note: An employment permit can be granted and is valid only while the alien has the residence permit.[18] Those who are exempted include members of a partnership and officers of a corporation; workmen temporarily engaged in repair work; artists and scientists performing and lecturing for no longer than eight days in a single place; teachers, assistants and other personnel of schools, universities and institutes; and students and pupils engaged in temporary vacation work within the framework of international exchanges (§ 10 DVO no. 9/AVAVG).

The granting of the permit depends upon the German labor market and upon certain priorities of a political nature, favoring, for example, the Common Market countries and certain Mediterranean countries with which bilateral agreements on employment of foreign labor have been concluded (*see also infra*). The permit may be restricted to a defined occupation in a specific enterprise (§ 4), and although it is limited to one year it is renewable (§ 7 I). Permission is given without regard to the labor market and without occupational restrictions to one who has been working in West Germany lawfully and without interruption for at least five years, who has resided lawfully in the country for eight years, or who is married to a German residing habitually in West Germany (§ 5 I). In these cases

---

[16a] BAG 30 May 1969, NJW 1969, 2111.

[17] Ninth Implementing Regulation to the AVAVG, BGBl. 1959 I 689.

[18] §§ 3 and 9 III DVO no. 9/AVAVG and *supra* I (1).

the permit is issued for three years with the possibility of renewal. If an alien has resided lawfully in the country for at least ten years, it may be granted without limitation in time (§ 7 III).

Although article VII of the American-German Friendship Treaty of 1954 (Treaties B 117) requires national treatment of those engaging in gainful activity, the imposition of an employment permit is expressly admitted. However, it is to be granted liberally (no. 8 sentence 1 of the Protocol), and liberal treatment is in fact accorded by Germany to American applicants.

(b) For the exercise of certain occupations and professions by an individual alien, additional requirements have to be met. Such requirements are in derogation of the general principle laid down in § 1 I Industrial Code (*Gewerbeordnung*, GewO, BGBl. III 7100–1): "Anybody may exercise a trade to the extent that this statute does not establish or admit exceptions or restrictions."[19]

(i) A license is required for many occupational and professional activities irrespective of the nationality of the applicant. This is true of operators of hospitals; captains, mates, and pilots; operators of game machines and game halls; pawnbrokers; guardians of the person or property of others; auctioneers; artisans; operators of automobiles for the transportation of persons or goods; operators of hotels, restaurants, rooming-houses, and so on; and operators of retail businesses including mail-order businesses.[20] The extension of this general license requirement to Americans is in keeping with the "national treatment" demanded by article VII (1) sentence 1 of the Friendship Treaty of 1954 (Treaties B 117). The most-favored-nation treatment accorded by article VII (4) apparently adds nothing, in the absence of additional privileges accorded to nationals of third countries.

(ii) Special requirements have been set up for aliens intending to engage in an itinerant trade (as defined in § 55 I GewO). A regulation lays down the following rules:[21] A permit, called an "itinerant trade card" (*Reisegewerbekarte*) is required. This card may be refused not only if the alien has no residence permit (*supra* I (1)) and no employment permit, provided one is required (*supra* (a)), but it may also be refused if there is no economic necessity for the activity in the proposed area (§ 3 I AuslReisegewVO). The card

[19] American (state) restrictions are described in Konvitz, The Alien and the Asiatic in American Law (1946) 171–211. The bearing of treaty clauses is analyzed in a note by Hunt, International Law—Reservations to Commercial Treaties Dealing with Aliens' Rights to Engage in the Professions, 52 Mich. L. Rev. 1184–98 (1954); *see also* Wilson 86–91.

[20] *See* §§ 30, 31, 33a, 33d, 33i, 34, 34a and 34b GewO; for further details, *see* Schiedermair 531–32.

[21] Verordnung über die Ausübung des Reisegewerbes durch Ausländer, as revised August 3, 1965, BGBl. III 7105–1.

is limited to one year, or three years if the applicant has resided permanently in West Germany for at least five years. It is restricted to the territory over which the issuing authority has jurisdiction (§ 5 AuslReisegewVO). The last-mentioned limitations and restrictions and the requirement of necessity are dispensed with if the alien merely visits businessmen or soldiers of his own country and their families, or if he has resided permanently for at least ten years in West Germany (§ 5 a AuslReisegewVO).

These general rules are expressly made subject to international agreements (§ 55 d I GewO, § 1 I AuslReisegewVO). For commercial travelers, however, article XIII of the American-German Friendship Treaty of 1954 (Treaties B 117) requires "conformity with the applicable laws and regulations" and merely grants most-favored-nation treatment, which is apparently meaningless since privileges in favor of nationals of third countries do not seem to exist. The activities of peddlers and itinerant artisans are expressly excluded from the conventional régime (no. 13 of the Protocol).

(iii) Aliens are barred entirely from certain licensed occupations: specifically, they may not be bookmakers, chiropractors or notaries.[22] On principle, only Germans are permitted to serve as naval officers and pilots,[23] and public offices are of course reserved to Germans (art. 33 II GG). These exclusions and restrictions have been legitimated by the American-German Friendship Treaty (Treaties B 117) for state-licensed professions (Protocol no. 8 sent. 2).

(iv) Some professions admit aliens only exceptionally. Tax counselors and certified accountants are licensed only following an examination; non-Germans may be excluded from the examinations, but provisions contained in international agreements are reserved.[24] This exclusion also seems to be authorized by the provisions of the Protocol referred to above ((iii)). However, foreign accountants and other technical experts, even though not qualified to practice in Germany, may, "for internal purposes" only, make examinations, investigations, audits, and reports as to German enterprises, destined for an American client financially interested in these enterprises (art. VIII (1) sent. 2 of the Friendship Treaty of 1954, Treaties B 117). Foreign doctors of medicine, dentists and veterinary surgeons may be licensed on the basis of foreign examinations that are deemed equivalent to the German examinations, and similar rules obtain for pharmacists.[25] An alien may also be admitted as a patent attorney[26]

---

[22] For details, *see* SCHIEDERMAIR 539, 544. For notaries, *see* § 5 BNotO, BGBl. 1961 I 98.

[23] § 20 Schiffsbesetzungsordnung of June 29, 1931, RGBl. II 517, as revised, and § 10 II 2 of the Law on Maritime Pilots of Oct. 13, 1954, BGBl. I 1035.

[24] For details, *see* SCHIEDERMAIR 545–46.

[25] For details, *see* SCHIEDERMAIR 539–43. For pharmacists, *see* § 2 I Gesetz über das Apothekenwesen of August 20, 1960, BGBl. I 697, and § 4 Bundes-Apothekerordnung of June 5, 1968, BGBl. I 601.

[26] § 14 I no. 12 and II Patentanwaltsordnung of Sept. 7, 1966, BGBl. I 557.

upon compliance with the additional requirement of local residence. These restrictions are also justified vis-à-vis Americans by the above-mentioned provision of the Protocol.

For the admission of attorneys to the bar no exclusionary provisions exist.[27] However, since an applicant must have passed two German state examinations and since part of the training period as a clerk is spent in the civil service, for which German nationality is required,[28] almost every attorney will in fact be a German. Nevertheless, the subsequent acquisition of foreign nationality is possible and, indeed, many German lawyers who had to leave the country under Hitler and acquired foreign nationality after the War have been readmitted to the German bar, being exempted from the requirement of residence.[28a] Aliens may also be admitted as counselors-at-law (*Rechtsbeistand*); but they may represent a client in court only where representation by an attorney is not necessary, as in the local courts (*Amtsgerichte*). The operation of a branch office by a foreign lawyer or law firm requires a permit under the *Rechtsberatungsgesetz;* an additional permit is necessary for appearance as a *Rechtsbeistand* before the lower courts (*see supra*).[28b] Full status before the German courts can be attained by a foreign lawyer only by becoming an employee of a duly admitted German attorney,[29] or by forming a separate German firm of attorneys while at the same time remaining a partner of the foreign firm.

(2) **Business Activities**

In the business field proper, isolated restrictions as to certain activities are outweighed by the general requirement that foreign companies be admitted.

(a) *Admission of foreign companies.*—Paragraph 12 of the Industrial Code[30] requires a permit for any gainful activity of a

---

[27] Summary (in German) by BRANGSCH, Eleventh Conference of the International Bar Association, Lausanne 1966 (1966) 39–41. SCHIEDERMAIR 545 confuses the general qualification to become a judge, which is required even of an attorney, §§ 5–7 DRiG, BGBl. III 301–1, with that to be appointed as a judge, § 9 DRiG.

[28] *See* the provisions cited by SCHIEDERMAIR 528–529.

[28a] In the United States residence is generally required. Thus an attorney admitted to the New York bar, but practicing law in the American sector of West Berlin and without an office in New York, was denied compensation for his services to an American client, Estate of Fordan, 5 Misc.2d 372, 158 N.Y.S.2d 228 (Sur. Ct. 1956).

[28b] BGH 31 Mar. 1969, Rpfl. 1969, 239.

[29] Criticism *in* Note, Foreign Branches of Law Firms, 80 Harv. L. Rev. 1284–1302, 1291 (1967).

[30] Gewerbeordnung, GewO *supra* text at n. 19. The provision was revised in 1965 and now embodies essentially the practice under the preceding, quite

foreign legal entity in Germany, subject to the provisions of international agreements. It may be refused only if the activity would run counter to the public interest (§ 12 II GewO). Two instances of such incompatibility are specifically enumerated: The first is lack of reciprocity, which comes into play to the extent that article VII of the American-German Friendship Treaty of 1954 (Treaties B 117) does not guarantee freedom of establishment to American enterprises in Germany. The second is failure of the foreign entity to comply with the capital requirements prescribed by German law for comparable German legal entities. One purpose of this latter provision is to avoid the circumvention by German incorporators of the relatively strict German rules on the establishment of corporations, especially marketable-share companies whose center of business activity is in Germany. Another objective is protection of the German public against under-capitalized foreign entities doing business within the country. In practice, American close corporations are required to comply with the rules obtaining for the German GmbH (that is, subscribed capital of $5,465, 25% of which must be paid up in cash), and other corporations with those for the German AG (namely, paid-up capital of $6,830). The treatment of organizations which have no counterpart in German law, such as Massachusetts business trusts, is controversial.[31] As a further example of incompatibility with the German public interest mention has been made of unreliability of the representative or representatives of the foreign company in Germany.[32] By contrast, admission may not be refused on grounds such as a desire to protect domestic competition, or the fact that the company's representatives in Germany are aliens, or objections against the trade name of the foreign company.[33]

A gainful activity necessitating a permit to do business would undoubtedly include the establishment of a branch, sales office, agency, depot, service station, or representation in Germany; it would probably also include the employment of (dependent) commercial travelers and the admission, as either a general or a limited partner, in a partnership. The following do not constitute business activity within the country: the engagement of independent German com-

---

general, version (*see* Note *in* Gewerbe-Archiv 1955/56, 171). Excellent commentary by JEPSEN, Die Genehmigung des Gewerbebetriebes ausländischer juristischer Personen in der Bundesrepublik Deutschland, AWD 1966, 21–29.

[31] JEPSEN, *supra* n. 30, at 26 is of the opinion that in case of incompatibility with a German form of organization no minimum capital at all can be demanded. Correctly against this narrow and irrational interpretation is GLIECH, AWD 1967, 22–23.

[32] Unless reliability is examined in connection with the granting of a necessary additional permit or license, JEPSEN, *supra* n. 30, at 26. In practice, this aspect apparently does not play any rôle.

[33] JEPSEN, *supra* n. 30, at 26; in part, also, ARNOLD/HILL/KERN, note (d) on art. VII of the Friendship Treaty of 1954.

mercial agents, the temporary stay for an assembly or conference, or the mailing or transportation of goods to a customer in response to orders sent to a seller abroad.[34] A permit is granted by the highest authority competent in economic matters (usually the Ministry for Economics) of the German state where the foreign company desires to start its business activity (§ 12 III GewO). A number of documents should accompany the application.[35] The permit is granted for a specific branch of business and is valid for the whole of West Germany. It is usually expressly subject to revocation, if the legal requirements are found not to have been or no longer to be satisfied, and it may require supplementation by other permits or licenses (*see supra* (1)(b)). Refusal of the permit may be attacked in the administrative courts. On the other hand, commencement of business activity without permission may be prevented by force and may provoke penal sanctions against the persons responsible (§§ 15 II 1 and 147 I GewO).

It is not entirely certain whether these rules on admission are fully applicable to American legal entities in view of the Friendship Treaty of 1954 (Treaties B 117).[36] Article VII (3) merely allows "special formalities in connection with the establishment of alien-controlled enterprises," but goes on to say that "such formalities may not impair the substance of the rights set forth. . . ." Also, provisions of the Protocol reserving the imposition of employment permits (no. 8) and special requirements to insure the responsibility and solvency of foreign insurance companies (no. 10) indicate that such regulations are not generally permissible under the Treaty. One competent author has concluded therefore that the German authorities are "more or less" obliged to grant to American legal entities permission to do business.[37] On the other hand, an administrative court and the semi-official commentators of the Friendship Treaty have stated that § 12 GewO merely requires compliance with German law and therefore remains relevant for American

---

[34] JEPSEN, *supra* n. 30, at 23–25. As to the representation of an American company, *see* VG Köln 6 July 1967, Gew.Arch. 1968, 57.

[35] (1) Certified copy of the charter and by-laws;
(2) certificate of incorporation or copy of the entry in a (commercial) register;
(3) balance-sheets of the preceding years;
(4) power of attorney for the person representing the applicant in the proceeding; and
(5) names of the persons responsible for the enterprise in Germany; *see* JEPSEN, *supra* n. 30, at 26–27.

[36] The treaty rules would prevail over the (subsequent) statute by virtue of the express reservation in § 12 I 2 GewO, *supra* n. 30.

[37] JEPSEN, *supra* n. 30, at 29. This position in itself appears to be hardly logical, since precedence of the treaty rules would demand complete exemption from the requirement.

entities.[38] This interpretation is not borne out by the text of article VII (1) or by German law. The former guarantees freedom of business activity, whether or not the entrepreneur is organized as a juridical entity. It would be artificial to import into this text a requirement that a business organization comply with German rules. Moreover, German law, with few exceptions (*infra* (b)), contains no requirement that business be carried on in corporate form in general or in any specific type of company. I conclude therefore that American entities do not need the permit prescribed by § 12 GewO. However, administrative practice applies this provision without hesitation. As of June 30, 1969, 142 American corporations had been admitted.[38a]

(b) *Special business activities.*—Article VII (2) of the American-German Friendship Treaty of 1954 (Treaties B 117) authorizes each country to restrict or exclude the right of nationals of the other country to establish, acquire interests in, or carry on, enterprises in certain sensitive areas:

(i) Communications are mentioned in item no. 11 of the Protocol. Mail, telephone, telegraph, radio, and television are state monopolies in Germany. Therefore the installation of American radio stations in Germany requires special agreements (Treaties B 91 and 204);

(ii) Air transport by domestic or foreign carrier is subject to approval, but the latter may in addition be conditioned upon reciprocity. German-registered aircraft may be owned only by Germans or by German business entities (that is, entities in which Germans own the majority of the capital and control the management and administration).[39] In fact, some American airlines have been admitted for international transportation to and from Germany (in conformity with para. 2 sent. 3 of art. VII), and one has preserved its special status in intra-German traffic, namely, with West Berlin;[40]

(iii) Water transport as such is not closed to foreigners. However, coastal shipping between German ports is reserved primarily to Germans.[41] The ownership of ships flying the German flag is, as a rule, limited to Germans and German business entities (namely, entities in which Germans control the management and administration);[42]

---

[38] VG Köln 6 July 1967, Gew.Arch. 1968, 57; ARNOLD/HILL/KERN notes (d) and (f) on art. VII of the Treaty.

[38a] Communication of the Federal Ministry of Economics.

[39] §§ 23 a and 3 Luftverkehrgsesetz, BGBl. III 96–1. *See also* the corresponding definition of "German airline" in Chap. XII art. 4 para. 3 of the Settlement Convention (Treaties M 184).

[40] By virtue of Chap. XII art. 5 of the Settlement Convention (Treaties M 184).

[41] Law on Coastal Shipping of July 26, 1957, BGBl. I 738.

[42] § 1 Flaggenrechtsgesetz, BGBl. III 9514–1. A trust arrangement in favor

(iv) The acceptance and administration of trusts is a peculiarly Anglo-American line of business that has no direct equivalent in Germany. To some degree it is assumed by banks;

(v) Banking involving depository functions is generally subject to official approval,[43] which may be refused not only because of insufficient funds or unreliability or incompetence of the managers, which provision also affects domestic banks, but also because of the absence of any economic necessity (§ 53 II no. 5 KWG; *see infra*). A permit is necessary to open a branch in Germany,[44] and the whole banking business of each German branch is subject, with certain modifications, to the regulatory provisions of the Banking Law (*Gesetz über das Kreditwesen,* KWG, BGBl. III 7610–1). At least one person domiciled in Germany must be responsible for the internal management and representation of each branch, and upon him fall the responsibilities of a representative under the Banking Law. The branch has to keep separate books according to German rules, and these are subject to examination by German certified accountants (§ 53 II KWG). For litigation relating to the business of the branch, the statutory competence of the local courts (§ 21 ZPO) may not be excluded by agreement (§ 53 III KWG). Sixteen branches of six American banks have been admitted so far,[45] while the American Express Company has founded a German subsidiary;

(vi) The regulation of insurance, expressly mentioned in number 10 of the Protocol, is similar to though stricter than that of banking. Like German insurers, a foreign insurance company requires approval in order to do business (except the underwriting of transportation insurance) in Germany through representatives, agents or brokers, but not by mail.[46] Apart from the requirements which also obtain for German enterprises (reliability and competence of the managers, sufficient protection of the insured, and economic necessity), a foreign enterprise must be a legal entity under the law of its seat, must register a branch in Germany (*see supra* ch. 10 sub II (5)), and must appoint a "chief representative" domiciled in Germany.[47] The

---

of American citizens was held void by RG 10 June 1905, NiemZ 16 (1906) 258; *but cf.* OLG Kiel 19 Mar. 1934, IPRspr. 1934 no. 145.

[43] *See* Wilson 82–85.

[44] It replaces the general permit to do business required under § 12 GewO, *supra* n. 30, by all foreign legal entities, § 12 IV no. 1 GewO.

[45] Letter from the Federal Supervisory Office for Banking of Nov. 4, 1968. *See also* Dahl, International Operations of U.S. Banks, 32 Law & Contemp. Prob. 100–30 (1967); Bergmann, Ausländische Banken in der Bundesrepublik, Der Volkswirt 1966, 2394–2400.

[46] § 105 of the Statute on Inspection of Insurance, Versicherungsaufsichtsgesetz, VAG, BGBl. III 7631–1. *See* Aschauer, VersR 1967, 835–38, and *supra* n. 44.

[47] *See* the Circular explaining the required status of the branch and the chief representative, VerBAV 1962, 74 sub I and II; *see, further,* Rotkies, *id.* 1953, 202–04.

latter is deemed the exclusive representative for all aspects of its German business. But even if all these requirements are met, the admission or expulsion of the foreign insurer lies within the discretion of the Federal Minister of Economics (§§ 106, 108, 111 II VAG), who may take into account considerations of substantive reciprocity.[48] Following admission, a foreign insurer is subject to most of the rules of the Statute on Inspection of Insurance[49] and to the supervision of the regulatory authorities (§§ 110, 111 I VAG).[50] For litigation arising from its German insurance business, the statutory competence of the courts at the situs of the branch office may not be excluded by agreement (§ 109 VAG). Number 10 of the Protocol to the American-German Friendship Treaty of 1954 (Treaties B 117) expressly sanctions the application of special regulations to foreign insurance companies in order to insure "the degree of responsibility and solvency required of similar domestic companies." However, "these regulations may not in their effect result in discrimination in substance" against the foreign insurers. This would seem to restrict the discretion of the approving authority to grant or withdraw permission to do business. Seven American insurance companies have been admitted, one of which—in spite of such supervision—has become bankrupt;[51]

(vii) The distribution of foreign investment shares has been regulated in detail by a recent statute.[51a] Advertising and selling in Germany require not a permit, but notification to the proper authority; if the statutory conditions are not met (§§ 2–7), distribution may be prohibited. The foreign fund must appoint a German domiciliary to represent it both in and out of court. The court at the domicile or seat of the German representative has competence in litigation arising from the German business, and this competence cannot be excluded by agreement (§ 6);

(viii) There are no general rules excluding foreigners from the exploitation of land or other natural resources.[52] Only for the extraction of certain minerals, oil and phosphorus are there generally

---

48 *See* Annual Report 1966 of the Federal Supervisory Office for Insurance and Buildings Savings (1967) 33, where the procedure for admission is also explained in detail.

49 *Cf. supra* n. 46.

50 *See* the duties of accounting spelt out in the Circular, *supra* n. 47.

51 Letter from the Federal Supervisory Office for Insurance and Buildings Savings of Oct. 31, 1968.

51a Law concerning the distribution of foreign investment shares, July 28, 1969, BGBl. I 986. *English translation*: Brücher/Pulch, The German Law Concerning the Distribution of Foreign Investment Shares (1970). *See also* Note, West German Regulation of Foreign Mutual Fund Distributions, 3 N.Y.U. J. Int'l L. & Pol. 323–342 (1970).

52 *See* Wilson 82, 126–55, especially 150 and 153. There are, however, certain restrictions on the acquisition of land by foreign legal entities, *see supra* ch. 6 n. 47.

applicable restrictions, some for the whole territory but most only for certain parts of the country.[53] In the former Prussian territories (*see* ch. 6 n. 47), a Prussian Law of June 23, 1909 required government approval for the acquisition or exploitation of rights in minerals.[54]

(3) **East Germany**

An essential consequence of the Socialist character of the state has been the state monopoly of foreign trade. This monopoly as a rule implies state ownership of all organizations directly engaged in foreign trade and a high degree of planning, direction and supervision by the state. Foreign trade activities within East Germany by foreigners are heavily curtailed, and investment of foreign capital is practically impossible.[55]

III. ASSOCIATIONS

The Statute on Associations (*Vereinsgesetz*, BGBl. III 2180–1) distinguishes between a domestic association of foreigners (*Ausländerverein*) and an association with a seat abroad but active in Germany (*ausländischer Verein*). Both types are required to register their charters, the names and addresses of their board members and their foreign organizations (§§ 19, 21 DVO/*Vereinsgesetz*, BGBl. 1966 I 457), and on request they have to submit information about their activities and, if these are political, about their members and the financial means of the latter (§§ 20, 21 DVO/*Vereinsgesetz*). Both categories of association may be prohibited, apart from the reasons generally obtaining for German associations,[56] if their political activity violates or endangers internal or external security, public order or other important interests of the Federal government or of a state (§§ 14, 15 *Vereinsgesetz*). But a foreign association a majority of whose members and board are Germans may be prohibited only on the grounds applicable to German associations (§ 15 II).

---

[53] For details, *see* WILLECKE, Grundriss des Bergrechts (1958) 22–27.

[54] Preussische Gesetz-Sammlung 1909, 619, reprinted in REUSS/GROTEFEND/DAPPRICH, Das Allgemeine Berggesetz (11th ed. 1959) 256–57.

[55] For details, *see* DROBNIG/WAEHLER, Legal Aspects of Foreign Trade in East Germany, 2 J.W.T.L. 28–46, 33–41 (1968).

[56] "Prohibited are associations whose purposes or activities run counter to the penal laws or that are directed against the constitutional system or the idea of understanding of the peoples" (art. 9 II GG).

Chapter XII.

COPYRIGHT, INDUSTRIAL PROPERTY, AND UNFAIR COMPETITION

The three topics covered in this chapter are essentially "internationally" orientated. They have therefore enjoyed for decades exceptionally intensive and successful international legislation, both bilateral and multilateral. The multiple interactions between these international agreements and domestic law are noteworthy but also create complications.

I. COPYRIGHT AND RELATED RIGHTS*

(1) German Domestic Legislation

Copyright protection may be granted to all works of literature, research and art.[1] Apart from copyright proper, certain related or neighboring rights, such as those of performing artists, of radio and television enterprises and of sound recorders, receive special protection (§§ 70–87 UrhG).

The statute distinguishes between universal rights, rights of Germans and rights of aliens. There are certain rights of authors which are of a highly personal nature, namely, the decision whether and how his work should be communicated or published and he himself be designated, and also his protection against certain distortions and infringements (§§ 12–14 UrhG). This bundle of inalienable rights is granted to any author, regardless of nationality (§§ 121 VI, 122, 123 UrhG). If he is a German (*see supra* ch. 3 sub A II (1)(c)), he always enjoys protection under the statute, irrespective of whether and where the work has been published (§ 120 UrhG). By contrast, the copyright protection of foreigners, apart from the universal rights mentioned above, is limited. Protection under German law is granted only if a work is first published in Germany,

---

* *See* ULMER, The New German Copyright Act, "Copyright" no. 12 pp. 275–86 (1965); TOURNIER, The draft of german [*sic*] law on copyright and companies handling copyrights, Revue internationale du droit d'auteur no. 5 pp. 52–76 (1954), no. 6 pp. 46–98 (1955). For texts of American statutes (with translations) and brief introduction, *see* MÖHRING/SCHULZE/ULMER/ZWEIGERT, Quellen des Urheberrechts (looseleaf 1961——), USA.

[1] § 1 UrhG 1965 (Copyright Act, Urheberrechtsgesetz, BGBl. I 1273); 1 Copyright Laws and Treaties of the World (looseleaf 1956——), German Federal Republic Item 1. §§ 2–4 enumerate, but not exhaustively, the protected works.

or published in Germany not later than thirty days after its first publication abroad (§ 121 I UrhG). And this protection may be restricted even further if the author is a citizen of a state that is not a member of the Berne Copyright Convention, unless he resides either in Germany or another signatory state and unless that state accords adequate protection to the works of German nationals (§ 121 III UrhG). But these provisions, which would deny protection to an American author residing in the United States and publishing first in that country, are superseded by the rules of the Universal Copyright Convention (*infra* (2)(c)). In general language, § 121 IV 1 UrhG expressly reserves international agreements. Only the "*droit de suite*," still a rare exception, is exempted; a foreign author enjoys this right only if his home country grants reciprocity and if this fact has been formally confirmed by a notice published in the Federal Gazette (§ 121 V UrhG). No such notice has appeared so far.

These rules, in general, apply also to the holders of neighboring rights (§§ 125–128 UrhG).

(2) **International Agreements**

(a) Soon after the enactment of the American Copyright Act of 1891 (which, for the first time, made copyright protection accessible to foreigners), the United States concluded the Copyright Treaty of 1892 with Germany (Treaties B 41). It assured national treatment to American citizens in Germany for the protection of their literary and artistic works and photographs. The President of the United States reciprocated by issuing a Proclamation extending national treatment to German citizens.[2] The Treaty of 1892 was expressly yet unilaterally confirmed by Germany after the two World Wars (*supra* ch. 2 nn. 14 and 51), and the time limits for filing and other formalities were extended.[3] It has now become obsolete through the adherence of both countries to the Universal Copyright Convention (*infra* (c)).

(b) Although the United States is not a party to the Berne Copyright Convention,[4] this Convention may affect American citizens publishing for the first time in Germany or in another convention country, since article 6 (1) of the Convention grants to every person

---

[2] Proclamation of Apr. 15, 1892, 27 Stat. 1021. The proclamation was renewed after enactment of the new American Copyright Act of 1909 (*see* 36 Stat. 2685) and extended to musical works in 1910 (36 Stat. 2761).

[3] *See* the German statute of May 18, 1922 and the Presidential Proclamation of May 25, 1922, *supra* ch. 2 n. 14. *See*, further, Law No. 8 of the Allied High Commission of Oct. 20, 1949, Off. Gaz. HICOG 1949, 18, and the Treaty of Nov. 20, 1964/July 12, 1967 (Treaties B 198A), resulting in the Presidential Proclamation of July 12, 1967 (32 Fed. Reg. 10341).

[4] As revised in Brussels in 1948. The Stockholm revision of 1967 will not change significantly the situation for nationals of non-member states.

national treatment in the country of publication and conventional protection in the other member states. Germany has not made use of the reservations allowing restrictions upon these rights.

(c) Of more direct importance to American-German copyright relations is the Universal Copyright Convention of 1952 (Treaties M 189), which supersedes the Copyright Treaty of 1892 (art. XIX UCC). The Convention is not self-executing but obligates each member state to guarantee by appropriate means the enumerated rights to citizens of another member state (art. I). National treatment is granted to both published and unpublished works[5] of such citizens as well as to works of any author first published in a member state (art. II). The only formality required for published works is the symbol © accompanied by the author's name and the year of publication (art. III (1)). The duration of protection is governed, as a rule, by the law of the country in which protection is demanded (art. IV (1)). However, the limitations contained in paragraphs 4 through 6 of article IV have expressly been declared applicable in Germany (§ 140 UrhG).[6]

(3) **German Judicial Practice**

Certain points of international copyright protection that are covered neither by German domestic legislation nor by international conventions have been settled by the courts. They have held correctly that the existence and the contractual transfer of German copyrights are governed by German law; only the underlying contract is subject to the usual choice of law rules for contracts (*supra* ch. 8 sub II B).[7] Thus in a case where a German composer had twice assigned his German copyright to different German assignees and the second assignee had transferred the copyright to an American company, which registered the copyright formally in the United States, the court determined ownership of the American copyright according to American law; but once it was found that the American company had acquired the copyright, thus injuring the first assignee, the latter's action in tort for damages against the second assignee was decided according to German law, the tort having been committed in Germany between two German parties.[8]

---

[5] Additional Protocol no. 1 equates stateless persons and refugees usually residing in a member state to a citizen of that state.

[6] For further details, *see* the thorough comment by Bappert/Wagner, Internationales Urheberrecht (1956) 187–293, and especially the summary of the new American-German relations, at 275–92.

[7] OLG Hamburg 27 Mar. 1958, IPRspr. 1958/59 no. 152; OLG München 29 Jan. 1959, *id.* no. 153; *see also* OLG Koblenz 14 July 1967, GRUR/Ausl. 1968, 164.

[8] LG Berlin 19 Oct. 1959, IPRspr. 1958/59 no. 154.

II. PATENTS AND UTILITY MODELS*

(1) Patents

German patent law is in full evolution, as witnessed by the frequent modifications it has undergone since 1961. The latest revision, which dates from January 2, 1968, has already been modified.[9] The revision introduced two important changes: the so-called "deferred examination," which is also being discussed in the United States, and unrestricted protection for chemical and pharmaceutical inventions.[9a] The actual importance of the American-German patent "traffic" results from the fact that in 1968 some 12,000 applications for patents were filed by Americans in Germany and about 3,800 patents granted, while 6,450 applications by Germans were filed in the United States and 3,400 patents granted.[10] The annual royalties for licenses on patents, inventions and know-how paid from German sources to Americans increased between 1964 and 1967 from sixty-five million to more than ninety million dollars, amounting to between 40 and 50% of the total royalty payments to licensors abroad.[11]

(a) *National treatment.*—In contrast to the law on copyright and the other industrial property rights, the patent protection of foreigners is not substantially restricted in German domestic law. This complies, as far as citizens or residents of the member states are concerned, with articles 2 and 3 of the Paris Convention on Industrial Property of 1883 as revised, the latest revision dating from 1967 (Stockholm—Treaties M 315B). The only formal burden imposed upon persons or institutions domiciled abroad is imposed regardless of nationality: this is the requirement, in proceedings before the Patent Office or the Patent Tribunal, of representation by a German patent attorney or attorney at law (§ 16 PatG).

(b) *Priority.*—The Paris Convention, although it did not create

---

* Brief surveys in English on German patent law by BERKENFELD, Germany, *in* DURHAM, World Patent Litigation (looseleaf 1967—), and by CARLBERG, Guide to Patents, Trademarks and Designs (looseleaf, 2d ed. 1958—) 96–100; BUSSE, Procedure and Practice in the German Patent Office, 38 J.P.O.S. 683–704 (1956) (slightly outdated). *See also* the comparative analysis in *Ex parte* Gruschwitz, 138 USPQ 505 (Pat. Off. Bd. App. 1961). A recent detailed description of American patent law is given by AVERY, Das US-Patent (1967).

[9] Patent Law of May 5, 1936, as revised Jan. 2, 1968 (BGBl. 1968 I 2); v. UEXKÜLL, German Patent Law, Utility Model Law and Trade Mark Law (2d ed. 1968) 9–65; VOSSIUS/JUNG, Patent Act, Trade Mark Act, Gebrauchsmuster Act of the Federal Republic of Germany (2d ed. 1968) 9–62, with certain subsequent modifications.

[9a] KRIEGER, The New German Patent and Trademark Law, 1968 Ind. Prop. 155–62.

[10] 1969 Ind. Prop., annex to no. 12, pp. 5, 8.

[11] *Statistics*: Monatsberichte der Deutschen Bundesbank 1968 no. 7 p. 24, and 1966 no. 4 p. 32.

a single international patent but retained the system of independent national patents (art. 4*bis*), nevertheless established a certain interdependence by introducing the right to claim a priority based upon a foreign application. The period during which priority may be claimed is twelve months, dating from the foreign application (art. 4-C). Any facts occurring within this period, such as another patent application or use of the invention by another person, do not exclude patentability (art. 4-B; *see also* § 7 III PatG). An applicant must first indicate, within two months from the filing of his application, the date and place of his prior foreign application. On request by the Patent Office, he must furnish, again within two months, the file number and a copy of the prior application. If this information is not given on time, the claim for priority is forfeited (§ 27 PatG). However, it must be noted that this information does not dispense with the documents necessary for a German application. An application which does not describe the subject matter clearly, but merely refers to the file (or serial) number of an unpublished foreign application, has rightly been denied.[12]

(c) *Novelty.*—Of the several conditions of patentability (namely, novelty, standard of invention, advance in the art, and industrial applicability), the first has international aspects. An invention lacks the required novelty if it has been sufficiently disclosed to the public either by printed publications or by domestic use (§ 2 PatG). Since 1953 the Patent Office has included in this definition prior patent applications which are accessible to the public. Applications submitted abroad are equated with domestic applications, provided their public accessibility is similar to that at home. The courts have assumed such similarity for Swedish, Belgian, and French applications;[13] it is controversial for Austria.[14] For the United States this question cannot arise since applications are kept secret until the patent is granted.[15]

(d) *Non-user.*—In contrast to other countries there is no German obligation to use a patented invention. A compulsory license may be imposed only in the public interest (§ 15 I PatG) and not merely for non-user; but no such license has been imposed since World War II. Nor has a patent that is being worked exclusively or mainly outside Germany (§ 15 II PatG) been revoked within the past fifty years. Therefore the American-German Treaty on Industrial Property of 1909 (Treaties B 49, maintained in force after both World Wars,

---

[12] BGH 24 Mar. 1966, GRUR 1966, 488.

[13] BPatG 2 Nov. 1962, BPatGE 2, 164; BGH 25 Nov. 1965, BGHZ 44, 263 (U.S. priority claimed); BGH 21 May 1963, GRUR 1963, 518.

[14] *In the affirmative*: Patent Office 23 Nov. 1956, GRUR/Ausl. 1957, 179, and BPatG 10 Oct. 1963, BPatGE 4, 117; *in the negative*: VG München 20 Jan. 1960, Mitteilungen der Deutschen Patentanwälte 1961, 94.

[15] *See* AVERY 93.

supra ch. 2 nn. 13 and 49), providing that the use of an industrial property right in one country is equivalent to its use in the other,[16] and stipulating national treatment with respect to the sanctions for non-user, has become obsolete for Germany. On the other hand, the treaty rule on non-user does not protect American citizens against the imposition of a compulsory license on another ground, such as the public interest.[17]

(e) *Infringement of a patent.*—As in the United States, a German patent is protected against infringing acts perpetrated within the country. However, this principle of territoriality is broadly construed by the German courts. It has been held that a German patent is infringed in Germany if a German firm makes imitative drawings in Germany for production abroad and then instructs, supervises, and inspects the foreign production.[18] Similarly, if a German firm sells a patent-free machine in Germany while promising the foreign purchaser that it will make certain changes abroad in imitation of a competitor's German patent, this constitutes an infringement.[19] Finally, a German patent is infringed if a dealer imports patented goods which he has acquired abroad from the holder of a corresponding foreign patent. The holder of the German patent, even if identical with the holder of the foreign patent, may prevent interference with his German patent and ask for damages[20]; if the use of the foreign patent was unlawful, he may also ask damages for infringement of both the foreign and the German patents.[21]

Whether an action for the infringement of a foreign patent committed abroad may be brought before a German court is doubtful. The *Reichsgericht* always refused jurisdiction over such an action[22] unless based on a contract between two German parties residing in Germany and subject to German law.[23] Recently some German courts have held, correctly, that German jurisdiction exists, at least in damage actions, if they are competent according to the general rules of competence (*infra* ch. 14 sub I (2)).[24] Inevitably, this new

---

[16] The treaty rule came just in time to protect a German patent of the National Cash Register Company, already revoked by the Patent Office. *see* RG 20 Nov. 1909, RGZ 72, 242.

[17] RG 27 June 1928, RGZ 121, 328.

[18] RG 12 June 1929, RGZ 124, 368.

[19] BGH 29 Mar. 1960, NJW 1960, 1154.

[20] RG 4 Apr. 1914, RGZ 84, 370, 375–376; RG 2 May 1902, RGZ 51, 263, 266–67. Recently followed by BGH 29 Feb. 1968, BGHZ 49, 331, 334–35. To the same effect, *see* the American-German case, Boesch v. Gräff, 133 U.S. 697, 702–03 (1890).

[21] RG 4 Apr. 1914, *supra* n. 20, at 377–78.

[22] The leading case is RG 18 June 1890, JW 1890, 280; *see,* further, RG 6 June 1934, GRUR 1934, 657, 664.

[23] RG 1 July 1931, LZ 1931, 1316.

[24] OLG Düsseldorf 25 Mar. 1966, OLGZ 1967 no. 18; LG Düsseldorf 27 Oct. 1966, GRUR/Int. 1968, 101; AUERSWALD, Festschrift Werner vom Stein (1961)

approach opens up new areas of conflict of laws which the normal rules on torts do not fit. If the parties are both Germans, German law is applicable under the general tort regulation enacted in 1942 (*supra* ch. 7 sub (1)(b)(ii)). However, the existence and scope of the patent itself must be judged by its proper law, since its effect is limited to the territory of the issuing state.[25] For the same reason, the ordinary tort rule where only the defendant is a German must be modified: While the defendant's maximum obligation under article 12 EGBGB (*supra* ch. 7 sub (1)(b)(i)) is determined by assuming that he has violated an imaginary German patent corresponding to the existing foreign patent, nevertheless the existence and scope of the latter derive solely from the law of the state where issued (*see also infra* IV (1)(c)).

(f) *Contractual license.*—A contractual license for a patent is governed by the law of the patent,[26] which determines the existence, limitations, and scope of the license and, absent a choice of law by the parties, even of the additional contractual clauses.[27]

(2) Utility Models

The utility model (*Gebrauchsmuster*), a German legal invention shared by few other nations, is a "petty patent." It is registered without any examination as to novelty, obviousness or utility and can therefore be obtained quickly and cheaply. The registration may be canceled if an interested party proves that the requirements for registration have not been fulfilled. The popularity of the device in Germany is illustrated by over 52,000 applications and more than 22,000 registrations in 1968, among these about 3,600 being applications from, and some 450 registrations for, Americans.[28] The Law on Utility Models[29] is a brief enactment of little more than twenty provisions that is extensively supplemented, to the extent applicable, by the explicit rules of the Patent Law, particularly with regard to its international aspects. The need for representation of an applicant domiciled abroad by a domestic attorney is fixed by § 20 GebrMG

8–12. American courts have recently been confronted for the first time with the same problem, *see* Ortman v. Stanray Corp., 371 F.2d 154 (7th Cir. 1967), *noted in* 66 Mich. L. Rev. 358–72 (1967).

[25] KEGEL, Kommentar, nos. 27 and 41 on art. 12 EGBGB; AUERSWALD, *supra* n. 24, at 12. *Contra*: LG Düsseldorf 27 Oct. 1966, *supra* n. 24 which eliminates the regulation altogether.

[26] OLG Düsseldorf 4 Aug. 1961, GRUR/Ausl. 1962, 256.

[27] For details, *see* HAVER/MAILÄNDER, Lizenzvergabe durch deutsche Unternehmen in das Ausland (1967) 35–40; *see also* HENN, Problematik und Systematik des internationalen Patent-Lizenzvertrages (1967) 86–93.

[28] *See* the statistics, *supra* n. 10, at 12–13.

[29] Gebrauchsmustergesetz (GebrMG) of May 9, 1961, as revised on Jan. 2, 1968 (BGBl. 1968 I 24; v. UEXKÜLL, *supra* n. 9, at 67–76; VOSSIUS/JUNG, *supra* n. 9, at 63–93).

in terms similar to those of § 16 PatG (*supra* (1)(a)). Paragraph 2 I 2 GebrMG refers expressly to the priority rules for patents derived from foreign applications (*supra* (1)(b)). In addition, the Paris Convention permits a priority claim for a utility model to be based upon an earlier foreign patent application, and *vice versa* (art. 4 E (2)). This equation of German utility models with foreign patents is also followed in American patent law and practice.[30] In Germany a claim for priority may even be based on a foreign design (*infra* n. 40).

(3) **Plant Varieties and Seeds**

The protection of plant varieties has recently been introduced, and that of seeds reformed.[31] The first is a variety of patent protection. The rules on priority and on domestic representation of foreign domiciliaries (§§ 33 and 23 II *Sortenschutzgesetz*) are similar to those of the Patent Law (*supra* (1)(a) and (b)). However, the new Law withholds national treatment from foreigners, except those whose country of nationality or domicile either is a member of the International Convention for the Protection of Plant Varieties of 1961 or, according to a formal notice, grants corresponding protection to Germans or aliens domiciled in Germany (§ 23 I *Sortenschutzgesetz*). Foreigners are also excluded from the protection of seeds, in the absence of formal reciprocity (§ 64 I *Saatgutverkehrsgesetz*). A statement of reciprocity in favor of United States citizens has been published for seeds,[32] and for some plants;[32a] in addition, seeds "certified" by certain American boards are recognized in Germany.[33]

The protection of German plant varieties against infringement in general follows the rules established for patents.[34]

III. DESIGNS

As in the United States, the protection of designs is of a hybrid nature in Germany, having characteristics of both copyright and industrial property rights. The underlying statute,[35] although nearly

---

[30] American Infra-Red Radiant Co. v. Lambert Industries, Inc., 360 F.2d 977, 991–94 (8th Cir.), *cert. denied*, 385 U.S. 920 (1966); § 901.05 (b) para. 3 of the Manual of Patent Examining Procedure. For the reason for insertion of this provision, *see* notice of the Patent Office, Sept. 27, 1965, Off. Gaz. Pat. Off. 1965, 1335.

[31] Sortenschutzgesetz of May 20, 1968, and Saatgutverkehrsgesetz of the same date (BGBl. I 429 and 444).

[32] BAnz. 1968 no. 225 p. 2.

[32a] BGBl. 1970 I 1123.

[33] *See* no. 17 of annex 1 to the Regulation of June 19, 1968 (BGBl. I 703).

[34] BGH 29 Feb. 1968, *supra* n. 20, at 335–36.

[35] Geschmacksmustergesetz (GeschmMG) of 1876 (BGBl. III 442–1; *English translation*: 1 Design Laws and Treaties of the World (looseleaf 1960——), German Federal Republic item 1).

one hundred years old, is practically unchanged and therefore somewhat outdated. Nevertheless over 67,000 designs were registered in 1968, some 1,100 of these belonging to foreigners and only about 270 to Americans.[36] This disproportion between foreign and domestic registrations may seem to result from the xenophobic provisions of the statute. It grants full protection to Germans provided the protected products are made within Germany (§ 16 I GeschmMG), while, according to § 16 II, foreigners are to be protected only if they reside in Germany and if protection is sought for German-made products. But international agreements are reserved (§ 16 III), and, as far as American-German relations are concerned, the Paris Convention on Industrial Property (Treaties M 244) abolishes the requirements of national residence (art. 2 (2)) and German production (art. 5 B).[37] Thus in effect national treatment is achieved.

The required novelty is lost by distribution of the design, even abroad, before application for filing and deposit.[38] Novelty is also lacking if the design has been used in a foreign country by somebody whose design developments in the specific line of production are known to German producers.[38a] Since filing is to take place at the *Amtsgericht* located at the business residence (§ 9 II GeschmMG), a central filing-place had to be provided for persons not domiciled in Germany; this is now the Patent Office in Munich.[39] Priority for a foreign deposit within the preceding six months may be claimed under article 4 of the Paris Convention without regard to the nature of the foreign industrial right. Conversely, an American or any other design may be used as the basis for a priority claim for a German utility model.[40]

IV. TRADEMARKS

German law protects both the registered and unregistered trademark. The former (*Warenzeichen*) comes into being through registration, the latter, the so-called "presentation" of merchandise (*Ausstattung*), is a right acquired through qualified use. Both rights are regulated in the Trademark Law of 1936, as revised on January 2, 1968.[41]

---

[36] *See* statistics, *supra* n. 10, at 27–29.

[37] OLG Stuttgart 10 Jan. 1956, GRUR 1956, 237; FURLER, Das Geschmacksmustergesetz (3d ed. 1966), no. 7 on § 16 GeschmMG; *see also* v. GAMM, Geschmacksmustergesetz (1966), no. 4 on § 16 GeschmMG.

[38] *See* § 7 II GeschmMG; BGH 26 Oct. 1966, GRUR 1967, 533, 535.

[38a] BGH 8 May 1968, BGHZ 50, 340, 356.

[39] Art. 4 § 4 of the Law of July 18, 1953 (BGBl. I 615).

[40] BPatG 10 Nov. 1967, BPatGE 9, 211, and GRUR/Int. 1968, 206 (two cases).

[41] Warenzeichengesetz (Trademark Law) of 1936, as revised Jan. 2, 1968

(1) **Registered Trademarks**

The importance of trademarks may be gathered from the fact that in 1968 there were almost 22,000 applications for registration and over 11,000 registrations were made; these included more than 1,400 applications by and 850 registrations for Americans, amounting to 50% of those of foreign origin.[42]

The German Trademark Law does not deny national treatment to foreigners, except for collective marks and as to certain formalities. Of these exceptions, only two of the formal kind need be mentioned. Paragraph 35 II WZG prescribes that any holder of a trademark who is not domiciled in Germany must be represented by a German patent attorney in any proceeding, administrative or judicial, relating to the mark. The further requirement of § 35 III 1 WZG, that the holder of a foreign trademark applying for German registration must prove that he has received trademark protection in his home country, has become obsolete for Americans on two grounds: *First,* a dispensation from this requirement depends upon a formal notice of reciprocity, and such a notice was in fact published in 1952 with respect to trademark applications by Germans in the United States (BGBl. 1952 I 368); and, *second,* article 6 (2) of the Paris Convention, as revised in Lisbon in 1958, now generally eliminates the requirement of protection in the home country.

These national provisions are supplemented by the important rules of the Paris Convention on Industrial Property (Treaties M 244) which extend trademark protection considerably beyond the national régime. While § 35 III 3 WZG requires expressly that foreign trademarks comply with German standards, the Paris Convention extends registrability to marks registered in the home country, provided this is a convention state (art. 6*quinquies*, "*telle-quelle*" marks). Thus an American may register a sign as a trademark in Germany, although a German would not be permitted to do so because the sign does not qualify as a trademark under German law.[43] However, the permissible grounds of refusal, reserved by article 6*quinquies* letter B of the Paris Convention, will also apply in the case of an American "*telle-quelle*" application. The *Reichsgericht* has held that German public policy, under number 3 of this provision, requires cancellation of such a mark if the business to which the mark pertains is no longer carried on by its holder (*see* § 11 I no. 2 WZG).[44] Cancellation is also required under number 2 of the same treaty provision if a wordmark (like "Easy") merely refers to the nature of the goods,

---

(BGBl. I 29; v. UEXKÜLL, *supra* n. 9, at 77–94; VOSSIUS/JUNG, *supra* n. 9, at 94–103). *See* BEIER, 1968 Ind. Prop. 301–11.

[42] *See* statistics, *supra* n. 10, at 16–19.

[43] German Patent Office 1 and 22 Dec. 1932, IPRspr. 1933 no. 65a and b.

[44] RG 18 Jan. 1935, RGZ 146, 325, 330–32.

unless the mark has acquired distinctiveness in Germany.[45] The Convention grants national treatment for collective marks (art. 7*bis*).

Priority may be claimed on the basis of a trademark application made within the preceding six months in a convention state (art. 4). According to § 12 I 1 WZG, the German procedure in this respect is the same as that for patents (*see* § 27 PatG, and *supra* II (1)(b)).

Details on seizure at the border of goods infringing protected trademarks are laid down, in conformity with article 9 of the Paris Convention, in § 28 WZG.

Other international aspects of trademark law have been worked out by the courts, especially with respect to transfer and, above all, infringement.

The substantive requirements and effects of assignment of a trademark are governed by the law of the place of registration.[46] The legal protection afforded by a trademark is limited to the territory of the granting state. Therefore, generally speaking, a German trademark cannot be infringed by acts committed abroad,[47] and a foreign trademark cannot be infringed in Germany.[48] However, this principle is narrowed for typical export trade: thus, a foreign trademark is infringed in Germany if merchandise bearing the infringing mark is sent in transit to the foreign country through Germany[49] or is prepared in Germany for export to the granting state.[50] On the other hand, an American firm has been held to have infringed a German mark in Germany by failing to require its Swiss importer to prohibit re-export to Germany.[51] Strict territoriality is also mitigated by the rules on unfair competition, under which the German competitor of an American firm using an allegedly world-renowned mark "Modess" was forced to abandon a similar wordmark which he had registered in Germany intending to prevent future use of the American firm's mark in Germany.[52]

---

[45] German Patent Office 11 May 1931, IPRspr. 1931 no. 106, *see also* BPatG 29 Apr. 1965, BPatGE 7, 215, 218–20.

[46] BGH 21 Oct. 1964, GRUR/Ausl. 1965, 504, 506.

[47] BGH 11 Jan. 1955, GRUR 1955, 411, 413; RG 20 Sept. 1927, RGZ 118, 76, 80–82; 20 Apr. 1928, JW 1928, 1456.

[48] OLG Freiburg 18 Jan. 1951, GRUR 1952, 524.

[49] BGH 15 Jan. 1957, GRUR 1957, 352, 353–54; 15 Jan. 1957, GRUR 1957, 231, 235–36. But a German trademark is not infringed by mere transportation through Germany to a foreign destination, *see* GRUR 1957, 353 and especially 233–35.

[50] RG 5 Jan. 1932, JW 1933, 1844, 1846.

[51] OLG Düsseldorf 30 May 1958, GRUR 1959, 540.

[52] BGH 23 Mar. 1966, NJW 1967, 495. *See also* BGH 28 Jan. 1966, GRUR 1966, 427 (prior registration of defense mark by German forfeited as against subsequent registration of mark by American company that had acquired world renown for its mark).

Territorial limitation of a foreign trademark does not exclude German jurisdiction in actions for damages and restraint provided the German courts are competent under general rules.[53] If the defendant is a German, article 12 EGBGB limits recovery to the damages which would be recoverable in Germany if an imaginary German mark similar to the actual foreign mark were infringed in Germany.[54] These rules are well settled, in curious contrast to the uncertainties relating to the infringement of foreign patents (*supra* II (1)(e)).

The much-debated question of the importation of genuine goods has recently been clarified in judicial practice. Neither the foreign producer nor his German sole agent may, by virtue of a German trademark, prohibit the importation of merchandise which the producer has sold under a corresponding foreign trademark in another country.[55] The same result is reached where the German trademark of a foreign producer has been registered for his German subsidiary.[55a] The principle of territoriality of trademarks is no hindrance to this result since no protection of trademark rights is at issue. On the other hand, the territoriality rule does prevent the expropriation of a foreign mark from affecting the title to an identical German trademark belonging to the expropriated owner, even if the latter's registration is based on an international registration in Geneva.[56]

(2) "Presentation" of Merchandise

According to § 35 I WZG a foreigner domiciled outside Germany enjoys protection for his designations of the origin of merchandise[57] under the Trademark Law only if his home country extends the same protection to Germans and this has been officially announced. Such an announcement was published for the United States in 1894 (RGBl. 521). The same right is now also guaranteed by article 2 of the Paris Convention. The protection afforded by § 25 WZG to the "presentation" (*Ausstattung*) of merchandise is subsumed either under the term "trademark" in article 1 or under the definition of "unfair competition" in article 10*bis* (2) number 3 of the Paris Con-

---

[53] BGH 15 Jan. 1957, *supra* n. 49; *see also* BGH 13 July 1954, BGHZ 14, 286, 289–90.

[54] BGH 2 Oct. 1956, BGHZ 22, 1, 13–15; RG 8 July 1930, RGZ 129, 385, 388; OLG Hamburg 12 May 1933, IPRspr. 1933 no. 102.

[55] BGH 22 Jan. 1964, BGHZ 41, 84; OLG Hamburg 3 Oct. 1952, GRUR 1953, 177.

[55a] *See* the decisions in the pending litigation concerning the importation of "Revlon" products, OLG Düsseldorf 29 Mar. 1963, GRUR 1964, 207; 14 July 1964, GRUR/Ausl. 1965, 204.

[56] BGH 8 Mar. 1963, BGHZ 39, 220; 7 June 1955, BGHZ 18, 1.

[57] "Warenbezeichnungen," not "Warenzeichen" (trademarks). The translation by v. UEXKÜLL, *supra* n. 9, at 94, is incorrect.

vention.[58] While many details of the international protection of "presentation" are still unclear, it would seem that nationals of the convention states actually receive the full protection provided by § 25 WZG.[59]

V. TRADENAME

Because § 12 BGB, the basic rule, applies to Germans and foreigners alike,[60] German domestic legislation in effect does not discriminate against foreigners in the adoption of tradenames in Germany or the protection of foreign names there. Although protection under § 16 UWG, the subsidiary rule, is conditioned upon a formal notice of reciprocity for foreigners not domiciled in Germany (§ 28 UWG), Americans are unaffected since article 2 of the Paris Convention on Industrial Property (Treaties M 244) guarantees national treatment.[61] Moreover, article 8 of this Convention expressly prescribes protection of the tradename and relieves the owner from any requirement of deposit or registration.

Despite these seemingly clear statutory rules, the German courts have vacillated somewhat in their attitude, especially in the really crucial situation of a foreign newcomer to the German market. Under what conditions should his tradename be put on a par with an already recognized German tradename? In the *Eskimo Pie* case, the *Reichsgericht* in 1927 recognized the "American" priority of the Delaware Eskimo Pie Corporation as against a German firm on the ground that, although the American company had not yet sold any of its products in Germany, it had sufficiently proved its intention to come into the German market by registering a trademark together with its firm name.[62] Later, the court retreated from this position and insisted that a foreign tradename must have gained some recognition in Germany as a distinctive designation of the foreign firm.[63] More recently, the courts have become somewhat more lenient toward foreigners without, however, fully returning to the standard of the *Eskimo Pie* case. Protection and rank now commence with user by the foreign company in Germany, if the tradename is distinctive[64]; if the tradename is merely descriptive (for

---

[58] HEYDT *in* REIMER, Wettbewerbs- und Warenzeichenrecht (4th ed. 1966) I 764.

[59] *See*, e.g., LG Berlin 2 June 1956, GRUR 1957, 374, 375–76; RG 26 May 1933, RGZ 141, 110, 120–22.

[60] RG 3 June 1927, RGZ 117, 215, 218.

[61] RG 3 Mar. 1905, RGZ 60, 217; 3 June 1927, *supra* n. 60, at 222; *cf. also* BGH 16 Nov. 1954, GRUR 1955, 342.

[62] RG 3 June 1927, *supra* n. 60, at 220–21, 224.

[63] RG 30 Apr. 1931, RGZ 132, 374, 380; 28 Jan. 1943, RGZ 170, 302, 306–07; LG Berlin 2 June 1956, GRUR 1957, 374, 376.

[64] BGH 4 Nov. 1966, GRUR 1967, 199, 202; 7 June 1965, GRUR 1966, 267,

example, "Teenform"),[65] protection requires recognition as a distinctive designation.

There are two important German post-War decisions dealing with the tradenames of subsidiaries and branches which have become estranged from their parent companies. During World War I the German branch of Dun & Co., New York, together with the firm name, was sold by the German Enemy Property Custodian. The new owner, who used his own firm name, adding "formerly Dun & Co.," during the years between 1921 and 1949 collaborated with Dun & Co., later Dun & Bradstreet, New York, in the collection and exchange of information on an "exclusive" basis. In 1949, the American company had founded a German subsidiary in which it held the majority of shares; it authorized the use of the name "Dun" and concluded an agreement for the exclusive exchange of information; later, it terminated the earlier contract. The German party to this contract was held by the Federal Supreme Court to be precluded from further using the reference to "Dun & Co." on the ground that this tradename had gained world-wide reputation and that therefore customers would be misled in assuming a connection between the two firms.[66] A somewhat similar reverse situation was presented in the *Hellige* case. A New York subsidiary of a German company was founded in 1927 as Hellige, Inc. A German successor to the original German company was founded in 1949 as Fritz Hellige GmbH & Co. When, in 1960, the New York company in turn established a German subsidiary as Hellige, Inc., the German successor to the original German company sought to enjoin it from using the tradename "Hellige" in any combination whatsoever. The Federal Supreme Court refused to prohibit general use of the firm name "Hellige," but it ordered the defendant to seek a distinctive addition in order to respect the plaintiff's priority in the use of the tradename; the defendant's desire to make clear its connection with the American parent company could not dispense with this obligation.[67]

VI. UNFAIR COMPETITION*

(1) Protection of Foreigners

Whether or not a foreigner is protected against acts of unfair

---

269; LG Düsseldorf 1 Mar. 1962, GRUR/Ausl. 1962, 508, 509. The Federal Supreme Court has even questioned whether use of the foreign tradename is indispensable if it is already known in Germany, BGH 5 Feb. 1969, GRUR 1969, 357, 360.

[65] OLG München 28 Feb. 1963, GRUR/Ausl. 1964, 321.

[66] BGH 9 June 1953, BGHZ 10, 196, 201–02. The decision is based on § 3 UWG which prohibits *inter alia* deceitful information on business conditions.

[67] BGH 20 Sept. 1967, GRUR 1968, 212.

* WENGLER, Laws Concerning Unfair Competition and the Conflict of Laws,

competition through the special rules of the German Law of 1909[68] depends upon a formal notice of reciprocity (§ 28 UWG). However, article 2 of the Paris Convention on Industrial Property (Treaties M 244) guarantees national treatment to the citizens of the member states (*supra* n. 51), and the Convention expressly includes unfair competition (art. 10*bis*).

(2) **Governing Law**

The main problem in international cases of unfair competition is choice of law. Unfair competition is regarded in Germany as a special kind of tort, and international acts of unfair competition are therefore subject to the general conflicts rules on torts (*supra* ch. 7). However, experience has proved that an indiscriminate application of these rules is not fully appropriate to the special conditions of unfair competition. The courts are starting, under the influence of the legal writers,[69] to work out adjustments to fit the different situations.

If two foreign firms, even of the same nationality, compete on the German market, the German courts have jurisdiction as the courts of the place of injury (§ 32 ZPO) and German law is applied as the law of the "marketplace."[70] Competition on the German market is deemed to exist if goods manufactured abroad are exported to and sold in Germany.[71] The German courts are also competent[72] and German law is also applicable[73] if goods are shipped through Germany in order to compete unfairly on a foreign market.

If a German firm and a foreign firm are competing both in Germany and abroad and the foreign competition is a direct consequence of acts performed in Germany (for example, production in Germany, followed by export), then the courts will apply German law to all the acts of competition.[74]

---

4 Am. J. Comp. L. 167–88 (1955); HEFERMEHL *in* 1 PINNER, World Unfair Competition Law (1965) 86–88. On the substantive German law, *see* 1 *id.* at 13–14 and its eighty titles; BEIER, 1968 Ind. Prop. 341–49.

[68] Gesetz gegen den unlauteren Wettbewerb (UWG) of June 7, 1909, BGBl. III 43–1.

[69] WIRNER, Wettbewerbsrecht und internationales Privatrecht (1960); DEUTSCH, Wettbewerbstatbestände mit Auslandsbeziehung (1962); K. TROLLER, Das internationale Privatrecht des unlauteren Wettbewerbs (1962); WENGLER and HEFERMEHL, *supra* asterisked note; BEITZKE, Auslandswettbewerb unter Inländern, JuS 1966, 139–147, discussing BGH 20 Dec. 1963, BGHZ 40, 391.

[70] Expressly, in OLG Hamburg 22 Feb. 1962, IPRspr. 1962/63 no. 159, *aff'd* (implicitly), BGH 6 Nov. 1963, BGHZ 41, 55.

[71] *See* cases *supra* n. 70, and RG 13 Apr. 1932, IPRspr. 1932 no. 106.

[72] BGH 24 July 1957, GRUR 1958, 189, 196–97.

[73] BGH 15 Jan. 1957, GRUR 1957, 352, 353, and 231, 235–36.

[74] BGH 13 July 1956, BGHZ 21, 266, 270–71; *see also* 22 Jan. 1964, IPRspr. 1964/65 no. 182.

German law is also frequently applied if two German firms engage in competition both in Germany and abroad. This is no longer based upon the general principle which once prevailed and which subjected Germans domiciled in Germany to the German rules of unfair competition,[75] wherever they acted. Criticism by German legal writers led the Federal Supreme Court in 1963 to limit the application of German law between domiciled Germans in several respects: *First,* there must be a special connection between the two German competitors, as, for example, the fact that only Germans compete in the foreign market or the fact that the act in question was specifically directed against the German competitor.[76] *Second,* even if German law applies, the court may have to take the foreign circumstances into account, especially where more liberal customs prevail on the foreign market. *Finally,* there is the possibility that certain German rules may be restricted territorially to acts committed on the German market.[77] These restrictions appear to be sound because they seek to strike a balance between the conditions prevailing on a foreign market and the stricter rules to which Germans are subject at home.

Competition between a German firm and a foreign firm exclusively on foreign markets is subject to the laws of those markets. But the general limitation on the tort liability of a German defendant (*see* art. 12 EGBGB) will be observed.[78]

(3) German Substantive Law

There is only one of the judicial rules of the German substantive law on unfair competition which deserves attention here: The courts have repeatedly dealt with advertisements in which a competitor has been, truthfully, designated as an alien; after some hesitation, they have held this reference to constitute unfair competition.[79]

(4) Procedure

In Germany enforcement of the rules governing unfair competition is almost exclusively in private hands. Outside the area

---

[75] BGH 2 Oct. 1956, BGHZ 22, 1, 18; 11 Jan. 1955, GRUR 1955, 411, 413; 13 July 1954, BGHZ 14, 286, 291; RG 14 Feb. 1936, RGZ 150, 265, 270–71 (competition by two German firms in the United States).

[76] BGH 20 Dec. 1963, *supra* n. 69, at 397; 27 Mar. 1968, NJW 1968, 1572, 1574.

[77] BGH 20 Dec. 1963, *supra* n. 69, at 399–400; *see also* 24 July 1957, *supra* n. 72, at 197; 27 Mar. 1968, *supra* n. 76, at 1574–75.

[78] BGH 30 June 1961, BGHZ 35, 329, 334, 336 (American-German case); OLG Hamm 11 Nov. 1969, AWD 1970, 31.

[79] RG 25 Nov. and 20 Dec. 1939, RGZ 163, 164 and 176; 7 Jan. and 25 Feb. 1936, RGZ 150, 55 and 298. *Contra*: some earlier decisions, e.g., RG 10 Mar. 1933, JW 1933, 1578.

of antitrust law, no state organs exist for the purpose. Sanctions are private actions for damages or injunctions, although for certain aggravated acts penal prosecutions may be brought.

Venue for actions based on the Law of Unfair Competition exists at the defendant's business domicile in Germany or, if lacking, at his residence in Germany, if any. In addition, § 24 UWG (as amended by a Law of June 26, 1969, BGBl. I 633) gives venue to the court at the place of the tortious act, and this is the only one available against a defendant neither domiciled nor resident in Germany. Since the new article no longer provides that the jurisdiction of the German courts is exclusive, this particular obstacle to recognition of a foreign judgment based upon a claim for unfair competition committed in Germany has now disappeared.[80]

VII. EAST GERMANY

East Germany has its own statutes on copyrights, patents, and trademarks.[81]

(1) International Régime

(a) *Copyright.*—The Copyright Act of the German Democratic Republic (§ 96 UrhG) extends the protection of the statute to all East German authors, whether or not and wherever publication has taken place, and to aliens, if the first publication was in East Germany. For works and performances by aliens first published outside the country, protection is granted on the basis of reciprocity. Whether the United States will grant reciprocity, however, is unsettled.[82]

(b) *Industrial property rights.*—East Germany has revived the Paris Convention on Industrial Property and adhered to the revisions of Lisbon (1958) and Stockholm (1967) (*supra* ch. 2 at nn. 63 and 68). West Germany, on the other hand, has challenged the East German claim to membership (*supra* ch. 2 at nn. 72 and 73), and the same position will probably be taken by the United States. This has not prevented West Germany since early 1968 from treating East Germany internally as if it were a member of the Convention.[83]

---

[80] *Cf.*, for a case denying recognition under the earlier version, OLG Dresden 23 June 1932, IPRspr. 1932 no. 156. The result follows from § 328 I no. 1 ZPO, *see infra* ch. 14 sub II (8) (a) (i).

[81] Copyright Act of Sept. 13, 1965 (GBl. 1965 I 209; Law and Legislation in the German Democratic Republic 1966, 73–87); Patent Law of Sept. 6, 1950 (GBl. 1950, 989; 49 Pat. & T.M. Rev. 215–23, 264–71 (1951)), as modified by the Law of July 31, 1963 (GBl. 1963 I 121; 62 Pat & T.M. Rev. 119–23 (1964)); Trademark Act of Feb. 17, 1954 (GBl. 1954, 216; 55 Pat & T.M. Rev. 42–45, 65–74 (1956)), as revised Nov. 15, 1968 (GBl. 1968, 360). Utility models were abolished by the Law of July 31, 1963, §§ 10–12.

[82] *In favor*: GLÜCKSMANN, NJ 1965, 691; *against*: KAUL, NJ 1965, 760.

[83] Notice of the Patent Office, Jan. 5, 1968, Bl.f.PMZ 1968, 2. East German comment by SEIFFERT, Neuerer 1968 B 259–63.

In judicial practice, too, East Germany is treated in certain respects like a *de facto* foreign country. Thus the tradename of an East German firm, like a foreign tradename, does not gain priority until it is in fact used in West Germany.[84] On the other hand, the clearly earlier use of an invention in East Germany destroys its novelty in West Germany also.[85]

East Germany itself grants the conventional protection even to citizens of member states that refuse to do so vis-à-vis East Germany (*supra* ch. 2 at nn. 65–67).

(2) **Expropriation**

Expropriations of patents, trademarks or any other industrial property rights ordered in East Germany have been denied any effect whatever in West Germany. To bring about this result, the courts developed the doctrine that these rights have their situs in the whole German realm and therefore that they are not affected in West Germany by the expropriatory measures in the Eastern part of the country.[86]

The American government has also sought to protect the rights of expropriated owners of trademarks. Those that were not sold by the Alien Property Custodian or his successor, the Attorney General, and that were registered on the date of vesting in the name of a person in East Germany, were to be returned to the owner in West Germany. The exercise of rights in such marks by a resident of East Germany requires special permission.[87]

---

[84] BGH 19 Dec. 1960, BGHZ 34, 91, 96–98.

[85] BGH 12 July 1968, BGHZ 50, 213.

[86] BGH 30 June 1961, GRUR 1962, 91; 7 Mar. 1961, GRUR 1961, 420; 14 Feb. 1958, WM 1958, 353. There are many other cases to the same effect.

[87] 50 U.S.C. App. § 43 (d) (1964); 8 C.F.R. § 507.46 (a), (b).

Chapter XIII.

ANTITRUST LAW*

The international aspects of antitrust law in the United States and Germany differ considerably and have produced frequent conflicts, unresolved by the loose treaty rules existing in this area. The national law is paramount.

(1) Treaty Rules

In concluding the Economic Cooperation Agreement of 1949 (Treaties B 87) so essential for its economic recovery, West Germany undertook *inter alia* to prevent restraints of competition affecting international trade (art. II (3)). However, since this undertaking was limited to interferences with the joint program of European recovery, it would now seem to be obsolete.[1] In its place we must look to article XVIII (1) of the Friendship Treaty of 1954 (Treaties B 117), which affirms the agreement of the two countries that restrictive business practices may harm commerce between them. Each then undertakes to consult upon request of the other and to take appropriate measures within the framework of its existing legislation.[2] It has been held by American courts that the corresponding provision in the American-Japanese Treaty of Friendship does not preclude criminal antitrust investigations involving citizens of the other country, even where they are ordered to produce documents.[3] In practice, however, apparently no formal consultations have yet taken place; instead, there have been informal contacts between the Antitrust

---

* For an English translation of the Act Against Restraints of Competition of July 27, 1957 (as amended up to Sept. 15, 1965), explanatory notes, and case summaries, *see* O.E.C.D., Guide to Legislation on Restrictive Business Practices (looseleaf, 2d ed. 1962——) vol. 2 sub D; C. D. EDWARDS, Trade Regulations Overseas. The National Laws (1966) 153–221; SCHWARTZ, Antitrust Legislation and Policy in Germany, 105 U. Pa. L. Rev. 617–90 (1957); FIKENTSCHER, Statement on German antitrust law, June 10, 1966, Hearings on International Aspects of Antitrust Before the Subcomm. on Antitrust and Monopoly of the Sen. Comm. on the Judiciary, 89th Cong., 2d Sess., pt. 1, at 416–38.

[1] Nevertheless, BAUMBACH/HEFERMEHL, Wettbewerbs- und Warenzeichenrecht II (9th ed. 1967) 746 reprints the provision, apparently believing it still in force.

[2] On this clause, *see* the informative note by HAIGHT, The Restrictive Business Practices Clause in United States Treaties, 70 Yale L. J. 240–57 (1960).

[3] United States v. R. P. Oldham Co., 152 F. Supp. 818, 822–23 (N.D. Cal. 1957); *In re* Grand Jury Investigation of the Shipping Industry, 186 F. Supp. 298, 320 (D.D.C. 1960).

Division of the Department of Justice and the Federal Cartel Office in Berlin, in which individual cases have been discussed, the details of which have been kept confidential.

The Council of the OECD on October 5, 1967 adopted a resolution recommending that the member states exchange information and cooperate in antitrust proceedings affecting the interests of another member state.[4] The German government accepted the recommendation, stressing that all measures proposed would be undertaken voluntarily, within the framework of German legislation and on the basis of reciprocity; at the same time it published guidelines for the giving of information.[5]

(2) German Conflicts Rule

The German Act on Restraints of Trade of 1957 (GWB, BGBl. III 703–1) is strongly influenced by American antitrust law, a facsimile of which had been enacted by the three Western Military Governors in 1947 (*see* Mil. Gov. Gaz. Germany C 2). The conflicts provision of the new statute was also inspired by the American model, except for the latter's extraterritorial scope, which the Germans view as excessive. Paragraph 98 II GWB limits the territorial application of the statute to acts wherever occurring that produce an effect in West Germany.[6] This provision has not yet been construed judicially. There is a general feeling, however, that § 98 II GWB should be expanded beyond its literal text into a general conflicts rule to govern the application of foreign antitrust law also and even the recognition of foreign antitrust decrees; at least the private law sanctions of the American antitrust laws should be applied in Germany, provided the restrictive practices in question have affected only the American market and also provided there is no conflict with an express rule of German antitrust law.[7] Illustrations for these

---

[4] Recommendation of the Council of the O.E.C.D., Oct. 5, 1967 (Doc. C (67) 53, final version), BAnz. 1968 no. 171.

[5] Notice of Sept. 6, 1968, BAnz. 1968 no. 171.

[6] § 98 GWB provides: "This Act is applicable to all restrictive trade practices that have an effect in the area for which this Act is valid, even when they are caused outside the area for which this Act is valid." For American comment, *see* SCHAPIRO, The German Law Against Restraints of Competition—Comparative and International Aspects, 62 Colum. L. Rev. 1, 201, 236–48 (1962); on the practice of the German Federal Cartel Office under § 98 II GWB, *see* the illuminating articles by MARKERT, The Application of German Antitrust Law to International Restraints of Trade, 7 Va. J. Int'l L. no. 2 at 47–67 (1967); Die Anwendung des Gesetzes gegen Wettbewerbsbeschränkungen, *in* Zehn Jahre Bundeskartellamt (1968) 205–29.

See also the following general German monographs: I. SCHWARTZ, Deutsches internationales Kartellrecht (1962); E. REHBINDER, Extraterritoriale Wirkungen des deutschen Kartellrechts (1965).

[7] In a similar vein is MERTENS, Ausländisches Kartellrecht im deutschen Internationalen Privatrecht, RabelsZ 31 (1967) 385–411; SCHWARTZ, *supra* n. 6,

two exceptions are offered in the following discussion of the American rules.

(3) **Reactions to the American Conflicts Rules**

German firms have repeatedly come into conflict with the American federal antitrust laws.[8] Their application to restrictive agreements of German enterprises which affect only the American market is in keeping with the general conflicts principle recognized in Germany (*supra* (2)) and therefore does not raise any objection. The German reaction to the notorious extraterritorial application of the American antitrust legislation is quite different. Two illustrations may be given:

In connection with the investigation of the post-War international quinine and quinidine cartel in which a German and a New York firm had participated, a federal grand jury subpoenaed the First National City Bank in New York to produce certain documents of the German firm on deposit in the bank's Frankfurt branch. The courts overruled the bank's objections, based on the German rules of bank secrecy, the threat of civil action by the customer, and potential loss of business generally.[9] The courts held, correctly, that the production of the records would not entail criminal liability on the part of the bank and they noted that no German public interest in the matter had been indicated (this in spite of the concurrent German antitrust investigation which, however, was apparently not known to the American courts). The courts further discounted, again correctly, the chances of a German damage suit by the customer against the bank.

Another controversy of wider general concern has arisen in the field of international shipping. It opposes the United States to more than ten European maritime countries and also to Japan. The basis of the controversy is the approach to shipping regulation advocated by the United States, due in part to high government subsidies, and considered undesirable by other nations, where shipping is subsidized much less. The dispute came into the open when the Federal Maritime Board initiated a judicial antitrust investigation and ordered the production of numerous documents located partly

at 221–25; KEGEL, IPR 409, 415; REHBINDER, *supra* n. 6, at 285–92. The application of the sanctions contained in American antitrust acts would be excluded, e.g., for export cartels, expressly authorized by § 6 I GWB. *Cf.* STEINDORFF, NJW 1954, 374–76. *Contra*: WENGLER, RabelsZ 19 (1954) 424–25.

[8] *See* General Aniline & Film Corp. v. Bayer Co., 305 N.Y. 479, 113 N.E. 2d 844 (1953); United States v. Bayer Co., 135 F. Supp. 65 (S.D.N.Y. 1955).

[9] *In re* First National City Bank, 285 F. Supp. 845 (S.D.N.Y.), *aff'd sub nom.* United States v. First National City Bank, 396 F.2d 897 (2d Cir. 1968). *See* Note by EISNER, WM 1969, 198. On this cartel, *see*, generally, SENATE SUBCOMMITTEE ON ANTITRUST AND MONOPOLY, Prices of Quinine and Quinidine (1967); MARKERT, BB 1968, 218, indicating that the E.E.C. Commission in Brussels and the German Federal Cartel Office are also investigating this agreement.

in the United States and partly overseas. In 1960, a District Court affirmed the subpoenas, insofar as they related to documents located in the United States, over diplomatic protests and many legal objections, while production of those located abroad was deferred.[10] During the years that diplomatic negotiations have been going on,[11] some of the European governments have reacted against the threat that an American court might order production of documents of their shipping companies located in their home countries. In Germany, for one, a regulation was enacted requiring approval by the Federal Minister of Traffic for the transmittal of information on shipping to foreign authorities,[12] and similar laws were enacted in the United Kingdom and France. A prohibition by the competent minister would under the American conflicts rules clearly exempt the shipping line from compliance with the American court's order.

---

[10] *In re* Grand Jury Investigation of the Shipping Industry, *supra* n. 3, at 318.

[11] *See* JOHNSON, Foreign Policy and the Regulation of International Shipping, 51 Dep't State Bull. 314–17 (1964): GEREN, Diplomatic Adjustment by the Maritime Nations, 54 *id.* 78–85 (1966).

[12] Regulation of Dec. 14, 1966 (BGBl. 1966 II 1542).

Chapter XIV.

CIVIL PROCEDURE*

This chapter on enforcement of private rights will deal with jurisdiction (I), procedure proper (II), arbitration (III), bankruptcy (IV), formal documents (V), and, briefly, East Germany (VI). The great practical importance of these matters as well as the negligible attention paid to them in German writings justify a rather broad coverage here.

German procedural law distinguishes between contentious civil procedure, dealt with in the Code of Civil Procedure (ZPO, BGBl. III 310–4), and non-contentious civil procedure, regulated mainly in the Statute regarding Non-Contentious Civil Procedure (FGG, BGBl. III 315–1). There is no clear-cut or logical distinction between the two. The objects of non-contentious civil procedure have been defined as those civil matters not regulated by the law of contentious civil procedure for which government or court action is necessary in order to produce a legal effect.[1] It may be more descriptive to say that the functions of the courts which are particularly protective, distributive or administrative are usually performed in non-contentious proceedings; these include guardianship, adoption, distribution, bankruptcy, the keeping of the various judicial registers, and the like. Because of the diffuse subject-matter and the lack of uniform rules, the following survey will emphasize contentious procedure, and only the more remarkable special features of non-contentious procedure will be mentioned at the end of each section.

---

* The only important broad treatment is in RIEZLER, Internationales Zivilprozessrecht und prozessuales Fremdenrecht (1949). *See also* NAGEL, Die Grundzüge des Beweisrechts im europäischen Zivilprozess (1967) 403–83.

On judicial assistance, *see* BÜLOW/ARNOLD, Der internationale Rechtsverkehr in Zivil- und Handelssachen (looseleaf 1954—); OESTERHELT/SMIT, International Co-operation in Litigation: The Federal Republic of Germany, *in* International Co-operation in Litigation: Europe (ed. Smit 1965) 171–211; VOLLKOMMER, Disharmonien und Spannungen im internationalen Rechtshilfeverkehr zwischen den USA und Deutschland, ZZP 80 (1967) 248–63.

On German civil procedure, *see* commentaries by BAUMBACH/LAUTERBACH, STEIN/JONAS/SCHÖNKE and WIECZOREK.

[1] JANSEN, FGG (1959) no. 1 on § 1 FGG; KEIDEL, Freiwillige Gerichtsbarkeit (9th ed. 1967) no. 1 on § 1 FGG; SCHLEGELBERGER, Gesetz über die Angelegenheiten der Freiwilligen Gerichtsbarkeit (2 vols. 7th ed. 1967) I no. 6 on § 1 FGG. A different approach is taken by BAUR, Freiwillige Gerichtsbarkeit (1955) vol. 1 p. 30.

I. JURISDICTION

The term "jurisdiction" is ambiguous. It will be employed here for the international delimitation of the power of the courts to adjudicate, as distinct from the local venue of a specific court (*örtliche Zuständigkeit*). The international adjudicatory power of the courts of one state as distinct from those of another state (*internationale Zuständigkeit*) is also to be distinguished from those limitations imposed upon the adjudicatory powers of a state's courts either by international law (immunities) or by national law (other restraints on international jurisdiction). We shall deal with these latter restrictions first, before looking into international jurisdiction proper.

(1) **Immunities under International Law***

The German courts and writers distinguish clearly between the international jurisdiction of German courts in general and the restrictions imposed upon that jurisdiction by international law. If this latter kind of restriction comes into play, the "*Gerichtsbarkeit*" of German courts (as distinguished from their "*internationale Zuständigkeit*") is at issue.[2] The distinction is based not only on the different nature of the underlying principles, but also on certain differences in the legal consequences.

(a) *Diplomatic immunity.*—On diplomatic immunity, a special branch of the immunities of international law, a few rules are expressly laid down in § § 18–20 GVG (BGBl. III 300–2).[2a] These rules exempt from German *Gerichtsbarkeit* the members of the diplomatic missions duly accredited by the German government, including their families, employees and their non-German servants (§§ 18, 19). Also exempted are all those persons who enjoy this privilege by virtue of the generally recognized rules of customary international law or of a treaty; especially in the post-War period, a great number of such treaty rules have come into existence.[3] An

---

* Theses and reports of a special committee of the GERMAN SOCIETY FOR INTERNATIONAL LAW: Die Immunität ausländischer Staaten nach Völkerrecht und deutschem Zivilprozessrecht (Berichte der Deutschen Gesellschaft für Völkerrecht no. 8, 1968). The booklet by E. W. ALLEN, The Position of Foreign States before German Courts (New York 1928) is outdated. *See also* WALCHSHÖFER, Die deutsche internationale Zuständigkeit, ZZP 80 (1967) 165–229.

[2] BGH 24 July 1957, GRUR 1958, 189, 196; RG 16 May 1938, RGZ 157, 389, 392–93; thesis no. 43 of a committee of the GERMAN SOCIETY FOR INTERNATIONAL LAW, Berichte no. 8 (1968) 292; RIEZLER 201–02; WALCHSHÖFER 168–82.

[2a] Elaborate administrative regulations are laid down in a circular of the Federal Minister of the Interior, *see* GMBl. 1970, 218–242.

[3] *See* texts reprinted by WIECZOREK, V (1957) 182–229, VII (1963) 414–15;

exception is made for those provisions conferring exclusive jurisdiction upon a German court for actions concerning an immovable (§ 20 GVG); such an exclusive *forum rei sitae* is contained in § 24 ZPO and in similar provisions.[4] The Federal Constitutional Court has ruled with binding effect that there is no overriding general rule of international law (*see* art. 25 GG and *supra* ch. 2 sub B I (1)) under which immovables used by the diplomatic mission of a foreign state are in all circumstances immune from suit. More specifically, an action directed at changing the owner entry in the land register has been permitted.[5] Similarly, the Supreme Restitution Court in Berlin, an international tribunal similar to the one in West Germany proper (*see supra* ch. 1 sub II (1)(b) at n. 41), has held that even realty belonging to foreign diplomatic missions in Berlin, if no longer occupied, is subject to restitution proceedings.[6]

(b) *Consular immunity.*—Consuls of foreign states are subject to German *Gerichtsbarkeit* unless treaty rules provide otherwise (§ 21 GVG).[7] Such special rules are indeed contained in that part of the American-German Friendship Treaty of 1923 (Treaties B 55) dealing with consular relations and continued in force by article XXVIII of the 1954 Friendship Treaty (Treaties B 177). The 1923 Treaty contains a most-favored-nation clause (art. XVII (2) sent. 1). However, for American consular officers in Germany this means little, since consular treaties with other nations merely confer immunity for acts done in the consuls' official capacity within the range of their competence.[8] In addition, the 1923 Treaty expressly subjects consular officers to the jurisdiction of the receiving state's courts in civil matters. The only exception concerns the taking of testimony by such an officer; while he "should" give his testimony in court, the officer may demand that it be taken in his home or office, provided he is a citizen of the sending state and is not engaged in private gainful activity.[9]

(c) *Sovereign immunity.*—State immunity has not been regulated expressly, so that by virtue of article 25 GG the general principles of public international law apply (*supra* ch. 2 sub B I (1)). While before

---

see, further, art. 1 (2) of the Agreement on the "Fulbright Commission" in Germany (Treaties B 193).

[4] *See* LG Bonn 25 July 1958, NJW 1958, 1685.

[5] BVerfG 30 Oct. 1962, BVerfGE 15, 25.

[6] ORG Berlin 10 July 1959, ORGE Berlin 13, 36 (and 236), 53 (and 252); NJW/RzW 1959, 526 (three cases).

[7] A useful collection of texts on the status of foreign consuls is OHLENDORF/LOTTIG, Konsularrecht (1960).

[8] Art. 10 of the Consular Treaty with Turkey of 1929, reinstated in 1952. *See* text reprinted by WIECZOREK V 231.

[9] Art. XVIII (2) sent. 3 of the 1923 Treaty. Art. XXIV (3) affirms this rule in case a consular officer has accepted his appointment as administrator of the estate of a deceased compatriot.

World War II foreign states were granted unlimited immunity, the post-War period has seen the adoption of the restrictive theory. The Federal Constitutional Court has expressly denied the existence of a general rule of international law granting absolute immunity to foreign states.[10] The court distinguishes between acts *iure imperii* and *iure gestionis* according to the nature rather than the motive or purpose of the act in question, as seen by German law, although with certain restrictions derived from international law.[11] Therefore, a claim for payment of a bill for repair work on the heating system of an embassy building has been held not barred. The way was prepared by some of the lower courts.[12]

Even East Germany, although not recognized by West Germany, is usually accorded immunity under the same rules.[13] On the other hand, foreign or East German state enterprises are denied any immunity as such,[14] although exceptionally their acts may qualify for exemption *ratione materiae* (*see infra* (e)).

For American-German relations, article XVIII (2) of the Friendship Treaty of 1954 (Treaties B 117) contains a special rule based on the restrictive theory of state immunity.[15] No publicly owned or controlled enterprise of either state, whether a government agency or a separate corporation, is to enjoy immunity in the other state if it engages in business activities there. This submission to jurisdiction is very broad since it extends to taxation, suit and execution, and other liability. This treaty rule would seem to be in accord not only with general German law[16] but also with the policy of the Tate letter.[17] At present, however, in view of the small number of state

---

[10] BVerfG 30 Apr. 1963, BVerfGE 16, 27.

[11] BVerfG, *supra* n. 10, at 61–64.

[12] *No immunity*: LG Kiel 19 Mar. 1953, NJW 1953, 1718 (traffic accident of bus of Danish State Railways); *immunity*: OLG Hamburg 11 Nov. 1952, IPRspr. 1952/53 no. 286 (services of attorney for the Danish Ministry of Defense); OLG Schleswig 26 Mar. 1957, IPRspr. 1958/59 no. 175 A (services of carrier hired by British officers for hauling military objects).

[13] *Immunity granted for claims arising out of expropriations*: BGH 13 July 1961, IzRspr. 1960/61 no. 1 b; OLG Frankfurt 30 May 1963, IzRspr. 1962/63 no. 1 a; *immunity denied*: OLG Braunschweig 21 Sept. 1954 and 27 Oct. 1953, IzRspr. 1954/57 no. 1 and IzRspr. 1945/53 no. 25 (however, the court declared itself incompetent *ratione materiae*, *see infra* (e)).

[14] BGH 7 June 1955, BGHZ 18, 1, 9; 24 July 1957, GRUR 1958, 189, 193; OLG Frankfurt 16 Jan. 1964, IzRspr. 1962/63 no. 1 b; LAG München 16 May 1950, IzRspr. 1950/51 no. 21.

[15] On this rule, *see* the interesting observations of SETSER, The Immunity Waiver for State-Controlled Business Enterprises in United States Commercial Treaties, *in* Proceedings of the American Society of International Law, 55th Annual Meeting (1961) 89–105.

[16] *Expressly*: BVerfG, *supra* n. 10, at 53.

[17] Letter by the Acting Legal Adviser to the State Department, JACK B. TATE, to Attorney General Philip B. Perlman, May 19, 1952, 26 D.S. Bull. 984 (1952), JIR 7 (1957) 403.

enterprises engaged in extraterritorial business activities, the treaty rule does not play an important rôle.

Even if immunity does exist, it may be waived, especially by bringing an action in a German court.[18] But this waiver is restricted to the action as such (and the necessary incidental steps); it does not extend automatically to execution against the foreign state nor does it imply consent to a counterclaim by the defendant.[19] The procedural details are controversial.[20]

(d) *Immunity of state vessels.*—The immunity of state vessels is regulated for Germany in the Convention on Uniform Rules for the Immunities of Seagoing State Vessels of 1926.[21] The Convention creates uniform rules that apply not only between the contracting parties but against third states as well, unless a convention state excludes this result (art. 6 (1)). Germany, not having made such a reservation, gives effect to the conventional rules even in favor of non-signatories[22] like the United States. The Convention thus overrules certain older German cases in which the United States as owner of merchant vessels successfully invoked sovereign immunity before the German courts.[23]

(e) *Immunity "ratione materiae."*—This is a recent and not yet fully developed type of exemption under international law, akin in certain respects to the American "Act of State" doctrine. As the name indicates, this species of immunity is accorded to certain acts done abroad, even though personal immunity of the defendant foreign state or government agency may not exist.

The most important cases in this category are claims based on foreign public law (examples being a foreign civil servant's claim for payment of salary or a foreign state's claim for repayment of social security benefits)[24] or claims directed against foreign acts (such as a claim for compensation based on a foreign expropriation

---

[18] RG 23 June and 13 Oct. 1925, RGZ 111, 149 and 375, 380, and cases *infra* n. 19; *cf.* LG Bremen 15 June 1955, NJW 1955, 1450 (ordering customs inspection by Germans constitutes waiver by American occupation authorities).

[19] KG Berlin 13 Oct. 1932, IPRspr. 1933 no. 97; Prussian Tribunal for the Decision of Conflicts of Competence 10 Mar. 1928, JW 1930, 213.

[20] *See* RG 16 May 1938, RGZ 157, 389, 393–394; OLG Hamburg 11 Nov. 1952, *supra* n. 12, and OLG Braunschweig 27 Oct. 1953, *supra* n. 13. For details, *see* HABSCHEID, Die Immunität ausländischer Staaten nach deutschem Zivilprozessrecht; *see* theses and report, *supra* second asterisked note, at 159–281.

[21] 176 LNTS 199, supplemented by the protocol of 1934, 176 LNTS 214.

[22] RG 16 May 1938, *supra* n. 20, 394–395. Misleading, if not wrong, are RIEZLER 412 and WIECZOREK V 182 sub B II b.

[23] RG 10 Dec. 1921, RGZ 103, 274 ("Ice King"); *see also* decision under same date, RGZ 103, 280 ("West Chatala"). *See also,* on these cases and their aftermath, ALLEN 28–39.

[24] BGH 13 July 1961, IzRspr. 1960/61 no. 2; LG Offenburg 30 Dec. 1960, IPRspr. 1960/61 no. 172.

or a refusal of a foreign exchange license).[25] Contrary to American usage, the executive in Germany has no voice in establishing this immunity. Reasons based on foreign private law may also exclude the jurisdiction of the German courts, especially the complete irreconcilability of a foreign institution, such as polygamy, with German law. It is significant that many formerly incompatible institutions, as established in 1949 by Riezler (at 233–43), have vanished in the meantime thanks to the increasing pressure of practical needs and the growing liberality of German judges.

(f) *Procedure.*—In concluding, a few words on the procedural treatment of the immunities of international law are in order. These immunities have to be taken into account *ex officio* at any stage of the proceeding.[26] According to prevailing opinion a court, if convinced of a defendant's immunity, must refrain from any act whatsoever. If, however, there are any doubts as to immunity a hearing has to be held and for that purpose the plaintiff's statement of claim must be served on the defendant.[27] The court will usually decide the issue by an interlocutory judgment subject to appeal and second appeal.[28] Some writers claim that a decision adjudicating the litigation despite the defendant's immunity is a nullity. But at least for purposes of rectification, be it by ordinary appeal or by extraordinary action for annulment, an incorrect decision must be considered as existent.[29]

(g) *Non-contentious proceedings.*—In non-contentious civil procedure the principles already described (*supra* sub (a)-(f)) apply. Although §§ 18–21 GVG (*supra* sub (a) and (b)) were enacted for contentious civil proceedings only,[30] the courts, supported by common legal opinion,[31] decline unanimously to exercise any power over persons exempt from German jurisdiction acting *iure imperii.*[32] In an application to the court, a waiver of immunity from German

---

[25] OLG Braunschweig 21 Sept. 1954, *supra* n. 13; OLG Frankfurt 16 Jan. 1964, *supra* n. 14.

[26] BGH 10 Jan. 1956, BGHZ 19, 341, 345; 7 June 1955, BGHZ 18, 1, 5.

[27] Special precautions have been taken administratively in order to examine requests for service of writs and other documents on a foreign state; the court has to send the request for service with an extensive report to the state Ministry of Justice, § 35 ZRHO, *infra* n. 111; *see* BÜLOW/ARNOLD D 701.25, nn. 128 and 129.

[28] RG 16 May 1938, *supra* n. 20, at 394. For further details, *see* HABSCHEID, *supra* n. 20, at 182; *see also* theses nos. 52–55 at p. 294.

[29] *See,* for details, HABSCHEID, *supra* n. 20, at 239–41, 242–45, and also thesis no. 60 at p. 295.

[30] *Cf.* § 2 EGGVG.

[31] SCHLEGELBERGER I no. 1 on § 3 FGG; JANSEN no. 5 on § 3 FGG; KEIDEL, nos. 2 and 7 on § 3 FGG.

[32] OLG Hamburg 14 Oct. 1925, OLG 45, 94.

jurisdiction may often be found.[33] To the extent that exempt persons act *iure gestionis,* they are subject to German jurisdiction.[34]

(2) **International Jurisdiction of German Courts**

The international jurisdiction of a German court is not based, as in the traditional "American" law for personal actions, upon the service of the summons on the defendant within the territory covered by the court. Service is considered a secondary element. Primary importance attaches to the substantive connection of the parties or of the controversy with the territory through various points of contact, comparable to the criteria used by the modern American "long-arm" statutes.

German law has only a few rules expressly regulating the international jurisdiction of the German courts (*internationale Zuständigkeit*). Such rules exist for domestic relations and succession and have already been dealt with in connection with them.[35] For the wide field of proprietary relations, such as property, contract, tort, and so forth, with which we shall deal here, there are almost no express provisions in existence. In the absence of special rules, the ordinary provisions on local venue of the courts (*örtliche Zuständigkeit* or *Gerichtsstand*) are regarded as impliedly delimiting the international scope of the jurisdiction of German courts.[36] The Code of Civil Procedure contains a catalogue of statutory fora which is supplemented by special rules in a number of other statutes. In addition, provision is made for the parties' choice of a forum.

(a) *Statutory rules of local venue.*—The key provisions are §§ 12–19 ZPO, determining the local court which has general competence: this is the court of the defendant's domicile or, in the absence of such domicile in Germany or abroad, of his present residence in Germany or, as a last resort, of his last German domicilc. The domicile and residence of a person for the purpose of determining German jurisdiction are judged by the standards of German substantive law.[37]

---

[33] SCHLEGELBERGER I no. 3 on § 3 FGG.

[34] Restitution cases, *supra* n. 6. Restitution procedure was subject to the rules of the FGG.

[35] On divorce and annulment of marriage, *see supra* ch. 4 sub A V (1) and (4); on litigation and proceedings concerning support and maintenance of children, *see supra* ch. 4 sub B I (5) (d), II (3); on succession, *see supra* ch. 5 sub III (2).

[36] This is court practice of long standing, *see* BGH (Great Senate in Civil Matters) 14 June 1965, BGHZ 44, 46, 47; RG 14 Feb. 1936, RGZ 150, 265, 268; 14 Nov. 1929, RGZ 126, 196, 199–200; RIEZLER 219; *but see also* WALCHSHÖFER 183–190, 191–204.

[37] BayObLG 31 May 1966, BayObLGZ 1966, 203, 205–06; KG Berlin 16 Feb. 1961, FamRZ 1961, 383; RIEZLER 196. German law is also applied at present if German jurisdiction depends upon a domicile abroad, *see supra* ch. 3 sub B (2) (a) n. 67.

Contra: RG 12 Jan. 1939, RGZ 159, 167, 169 (generally disapproved).

For legal entities of all kinds it is the "seat," ordinarily the center of administration. The federal state or any federated state may be sued at the seat of the agency representing the state in the specific field of the litigation (§ 18 ZPO). In all these courts of general competence, all claims of whatever nature may be brought against a person unless the contrary is expressly provided.

The courts of special competence are only open to controversies of a more or less limited sort. Claims of a proprietary nature may, in addition to the generally competent court, also be brought before the court of a person's residence, if the latter is expected to be of some duration (§ 20 ZPO), or before the court of the place of his business establishment, if relating to the business (§ 21 ZPO). For certain actions concerning interests in immovables, the *forum rei* is the exclusive venue (§ 24 ZPO), and certain related claims may also be brought there (§ § 25, 26 ZPO). Claims concerning succession may be brought at the court of general competence of the decedent (§§ 27, 28 ZPO). According to § 29 ZPO, all claims arising from a contract may be brought at the place where the litigated obligation is to be performed. Claims arising from contracts concluded at a trade fair may be brought before the local court if the defendant or his representative (provided the latter is empowered to bind his principal by litigation) is present at the commencement of the suit (§ 30 ZPO). Actions arising from torts may be brought at the *locus delicti commissi* (§ 32 ZPO). For a counterclaim the court of the principal action is open provided the counterclaim is connected with the principal claim (§ 33 ZPO). This rule applies even where the parties have chosen a foreign forum for the bringing of the counterclaim.[38] A comparable forum is the one for an attorney's fees at the court of the principal action (§ 34 ZPO). The plaintiff may choose among the several competent courts (§ 35 ZPO).

Of particular importance to non-resident defendants lacking any of the foregoing contacts with Germany is the venue created by § 23 ZPO.[39] An action in personam (not merely an attachment suit limited to the value of the property attached) of a proprietary nature may be brought against a defendant without a German domicile in a district where he has assets. A claim for the payment of money is deemed located at the debtor's domicile and, if it is secured, also at the place of the security (§ 23 sent. 2 ZPO). Industrial property rights of persons lacking a German domicile or residence are deemed situated at the place where the compulsory domestic representative

---

[38] BGH 22 Nov. 1962, WM 1963, 23, 24; LG Stuttgart 12 Aug. 1952, IPRspr. 1952/53 no. 292 a.

[39] On this provision and its history, *see* NADELMANN, Jurisdictionally Improper Fora, *in* XXth Century Comparative and Conflicts Law (1961) 321–35, 329 ff.; v. MEHREN/TRAUTMAN, The Law of Multistate Problems (1965) 673–74.

has his business residence, or else at the seat of the Patent Office in Munich.[40] Any asset of the defendant, regardless of its value or connection with the suit, is deemed sufficient; it may even be a claim of the defendant against the plaintiff.[41] Such a claim may, for instance, have arisen from a prior unsuccessful action of the plaintiff against the defendant, entitling the latter to compensation for his expenses (§ 91 ZPO). To avoid abuse by the plaintiff, who might bring a suit for the sole purpose of creating an asset of the defendant that would entitle plaintiff to bring another suit under § 23 ZPO, the courts refuse to accept this venue if the first suit was commenced without any factual basis for assuming the presence of assets of the defendant.[42] If the parties agree that a foreign court shall have exclusive jurisdiction, venue under § 23 ZPO should be regarded as excluded, at least if the foreign judgment would be recognized in Germany.[43] Recognition abroad of decisions rendered on the basis of § 23 ZPO cannot be and is not expected. It is precisely because of the existence of restrictions on the enforcement of foreign judgments (*see infra* II (8)) in Germany that the special forum of § 23 ZPO is deemed necessary and justified.

Jurisdiction of the German courts cannot be based on mere service on a non-resident defendant passing through Germany or residing there only briefly. Therefore the demand for a restrictive doctrine like that of *forum non conveniens* has not been strong. Only a few writers have suggested that a German court should decline jurisdiction if its decision can be enforced neither at home, because the defendant has insufficient assets, nor abroad, because of non-recognition.[44]

(b) *Choice of forum.*—German law permits the parties to choose the competent court in derogation of the venues established by statute. This may be done expressly or impliedly, especially if the defendant pleads to the merits without objecting that the court lacks competence. An express agreement is ineffective if it does not relate to possible litigation arising from a specified legal relationship or if the claim is not of a proprietary nature or if a specific court

---

[40] Sentences 3 of § 16 PatG, § 20 GebrMG, § 23 II SortSchG, § 35 II WZG. This is also true for a trademark whose German registration is based on an international registration in Berne, *cf.* LG München 17 Dec. 1957, GRUR 1959, 156. *See also supra* ch. 12.

[41] RG 20 Oct. 1929, JW 1930, 263.

[42] *Compare* KG Berlin 6 May 1939, HRR 1939 no. 1047, *with* OLG Darmstadt 21 May 1924, JW 1929, 121.

[43] This point is controversial. For exclusion without regard to recognition, *see* BGH 13 Dec. 1967, NJW 1968, 356; OLG Hamburg 20 May 1958, IPRspr. 1958/59 no. 179. Two other cases support, at least implicitly, the thesis of the text: OLG München 2 Aug. 1956, IPRspr. 1956/57 no. 187 (no treaty of recognition, no exclusion); RG 9 June 1936, JW 1936, 3185 (treaty of recognition, exclusion).

[44] *See* WALCHSHÖFER 205–08, and the authors cited there in n. 181.

has exclusive competence (§§ 38–40 ZPO). These rules, although designed primarily for the *prorogatio fori* among German courts, have been extended to the international choice of forum as well, although hesitantly at times.

The substantive as distinguished from the procedural validity of a choice of forum is subject to the law governing the agreement to which the clause refers and into which it may be incorporated.[45] But at the same time, since it is also an act affecting procedure, the clause is severable from the underlying agreement, so that the chosen forum is competent to adjudicate the validity of that agreement, even if it finds it to be invalid.[46]

An international contractual choice of forum may take one of several forms having quite different legal connotations:

First, the parties may elect a German court although the German courts would not otherwise have international jurisdiction in the case. Such a choice is valid[47] if it complies with the rules of §§ 38–40 ZPO. It has not yet been decided whether the exclusive jurisdiction of a foreign court under the foreign law would invalidate the choice of a German court. The interests of international legal cooperation would seem to require this result. Some writers also doubt whether the choice of a German court is legitimate if neither the parties nor the subject-matter have any connection with Germany.[48] As in the case of choice of law (*supra* ch. 8 sub II (1) at n. 15), however, there would appear to be no reason to invalidate a choice of forum if the parties wish to select the courts of a country completely neutral to both of them;

Secondly, the prorogation of a foreign court does not create any problem if it is not in derogation of an existing statutory forum in Germany. Thus the choice of a foreign court as an additional forum is valid;

Thirdly, the validity of a choice of a foreign forum to have exclusive competence in derogation of an existing German statutory competence is less certain. Contrary to prevailing American judicial practice,[49] the German courts usually admit a clause ousting their

---

[45] BGH 29 Feb. 1968, BGHZ 49, 384, 386–87, contrary to the practice of the Reichsgericht, as to which *see* RG 16 Feb. 1939, RGZ 159, 254, 255.

[46] OLG Frankfurt 14 June 1960, IPRspr. 1960/61 no. 39a, *aff'd,* BGH 30 Jan. 1961, NJW 1961, 1061; KG Berlin 6 Dec. 1955, IPRspr. 1954/55 no. 186; LG Hamburg 28 Dec. 1954, *id.* no. 164.

[47] *See,* e.g., BGH 26 Nov. 1964, BGHZ 42, 385, 387–88; RG 21 Jan. 1926, JW 1926, 1337.

[48] WALCHSHÖFER 219–21; *see also* RIEZLER 308.

[49] *See,* e.g., *In re* Hamburg-American Line, 135 Misc. 715, 238 N.Y.Supp. 331 (Sup. Ct.), *aff'd,* 228 App. Div. 802, 239 N.Y.Supp. 914 (1930); Sudbury v. Ambi Verwaltung Kommanditgesellschaft auf Aktien, 213 App. Div. 98, 210 N.Y. Supp. 164 (1925) (both American-German cases). New York law has shown

jurisdiction, though within the limits of § 40 ZPO. Therefore the choice is valid if it relates to litigation arising from a specified legal relationship, if the claim is of a proprietary nature, and if no German court has exclusive jurisdiction.[50] Whether the choice of a foreign forum is exclusive, however, is unfortunately not always clear from the agreement, but the concurrent choice of the foreign law argues in favor of this construction.[51]

It might be logical to require in a prorogation case that the foreign court "accept" the choice by the parties or have jurisdiction on other grounds. But this argument seems rarely to have been made to the courts or adopted by them, probably because it involves the troublesome application of foreign jurisdictional rules.[52] Nor is the ultimate German recognition of the resulting foreign decision required, if the parties contemplate enforcement at the foreign forum;[53] if, on the other hand, enforcement is possible only in Germany, exclusion of German jurisdiction will be ineffective.[54]

(c) *Procedure.*—The procedural treatment of the court's international jurisdiction gives rise to certain questions. Thus it is not clear whether the court must take it into account *ex officio* or not. Again, it would seem that the court may decide the issue by interlocutory judgment.[55] Another once highly controversial question has now been settled: In actions of a proprietary nature, neither appeal nor second appeal may be based on the court's assumption of local venue (§§ 512 a, 549 II ZPO); between 1915 and 1964 some ten published decisions of the highest court in civil matters extended this rule to the assumption of international jurisdiction, against the indefatigable opposition of the legal writers; finally, the Great Senate in Civil Matters of the Federal Supreme Court reversed the standing court practice, admitting appeal and second appeal against a decision assuming international jurisdiction, especially in the interest of the foreign defendants who were usually involved.[56]

---

recently a marked trend towards recognition of jurisdictional clauses, but the exact contours are quite uncertain as yet; *see* REESE, 13 Am.J.Comp.L. 187–92 (1964).

[50] BGH 13 Dec. 1967, *supra* n. 43; 30 Jan. 1961, NJW 1961, 1061; RG: 9 June 1936, *supra* n. 43; 16 May 1926, JW 1926, 1336.

[51] BGH 8 Feb. 1968, WM 1968, 369, 370; OLG Frankfurt 14 June 1960, *supra* n. 46.

[52] *See,* however, OLG München 30 June 1965, OLGZ 1966 no. 18, ascertaining that the chosen court in Montreal has jurisdiction under its own law.

[53] BGH 13 Dec. 1967, *supra* n. 43; RG 16 May 1926, *supra* n. 50; *cf.* OLG München 30 June 1965, *supra* n. 52.

[54] KG Berlin 27 Nov. 1929, JW 1930, 652; 6 Feb. 1926, JW 1926, 1353; OLG München 2 Aug. 1956, IPRspr. 1956/57 no. 187.

[55] For details, *see* WALCHSHÖFER 223–25.

[56] BGH 14 June 1965, BGHZ 44, 46, JZ 1966, 237, with approving note by NEUHAUS, who retraces also the history of the issue.

(d) *Non-contentious proceedings.*—With respect to international jurisdiction of the German courts in non-contentious civil proceedings three principles are firmly established: *first,* there is no choice of forum[57] because §§ 38–40 ZPO do not apply[58]; *second,* international jurisdiction must be ruled upon by the courts *ex officio;*[59] and *third,* there is no general rule as to when the German courts may assume German international jurisdiction; each subject-matter has its own jurisdictional rule, which may be summarized by stating that, as in contentious civil procedure (*supra* sub (a)), the local venue provisions settle incidentally the question of German international jurisdiction.[60] It must be emphasized, however, that the frequent coincidence of the two is not automatic; two special features of non-contentious procedure are important in this connection.

One peculiarity is that often the substantive law and the rules of non-contentious procedure are too closely entwined to be separated.[61] Therefore the German courts may precipitately decline jurisdiction if they would have to apply not only a foreign substantive law, designated by the German conflicts rule, but also a foreign procedural law differing from German procedure.[62] It has even been urged that the German courts should take jurisdiction in non-contentious civil proceedings only if the German substantive law is applicable under the German conflicts rule.[63] In recent times the courts have become more liberal and at least minor differences between procedural laws do not bar German jurisdiction.[64] One example of this changed attitude was discussed in connection with problems of adoption (*supra* ch. 4 sub B III (3) at n. 357 and *supra* n. 62). Nevertheless, the substantive law does influence the decision as to jurisdiction, and here another peculiarity of non-contentious proceedings becomes important: many of the matters decided in

---

57 LG Schweinfurt 19 Feb. 1957, IPRspr. 1956/57 no. 138; Swoboda, Das internationale Recht der freiwilligen Gerichtsbarkeit (1934) 57.

58 BGH 29 Apr. 1952, NJW 1952, 1055; Keidel, no. 6 preceding § 3 FGG.

59 BayObLG 16 Jan. 1959, BayObLGZ 1959, 8, 10; KG Berlin 13 July 1959, NJW 1960, 248, 250.

60 E.g., BayObLG 19 Apr. 1962, BayObLGZ 1962, 151, 154; *cf. also* Heldrich, NJW 1967, 417–422.

61 Dölle, Über einige Kernprobleme des internationalen Rechts der freiwilligen Gerichtsbarkeit, RabelsZ 27 (1962) 201, 203–04.

62 E.g., KG Berlin 10 Mar. 1933, IPRspr. 1933 no. 53 a, where the court erroneously declined jurisdiction primarily because it would not apply New York law which, unlike German substantive law, requires that the judge take into account considerations of policy (ch. 4 sub B III (3) at n. 356). Another reason may have been the slight procedural difference between the law of New York and Germany where an adoption is not decreed by court order but contracted by the parties and only affirmed by the court (ch. 4 sub B III (1)).

63 *Cf.* critically, Neuhaus, Zur internationalen Zuständigkeit in der Freiwilligen Gerichtsbarkeit, NJW 1967, 1167–68.

64 Dölle, *supra* n. 61, at 225–33.

such proceedings, such as legitimation and adoption, deal with personal status. In order to prevent "limping" relations, the substantive law governing this status has to be taken into account. If the foreign law designated by the German conflicts rule would not recognize a German decision, the German courts will usually abstain from claiming jurisdiction.[65] On the other hand, if German substantive law applies, the courts will assume jurisdiction without further inquiry.[66] This bifurcation is (and not merely accidentally) comparable to the rules on divorce jurisdiction (*supra* ch. 4 sub A V (1)(b)). However, it will be disregarded in cases of urgency[67] as, for example, where a guardian must be appointed for a foreigner in Germany (*supra* ch. 4 sub C (1)(d)(ii)).

By virtue both of renvoi and of German venue provisions which generally confer competence upon the court at the place where personal relations are centered, the question of foreign recognition has seldom proved a stumbling block, and the German courts almost never refuse to take jurisdiction.[68] The situation may be summarized as follows: Absent special provisions, Germany generally has international jurisdiction in non-contentious civil proceedings if the German courts have local venue. Except in cases of urgency, jurisdiction depends further upon recognition of the resulting German decree by the foreign law which governs according to the German conflicts rule.

II. PROCEDURE PROPER*

The differences between American and German civil procedure are at least as deep as those between the substantive law of the two countries, if not deeper. The court and the judge play a much more active rôle in Germany. It is the court which serves the plaintiff's statement of claim on the defendant. The judge is not the arbiter of a duel fought in court by the parties, but he directs and conducts the proceeding. He may ask the parties to clarify their allegations and demands; he calls and examines witnesses and experts, the parties having only an indirect right of questioning and cross-examining; he drafts orders and decisions. Moreover, since there is no jury in civil cases, no separation of factual from legal issues in the pre-trial period is necessary nor is there a need for rules excluding certain evidence; instead, the judge is entrusted with an

---

65 *Cf.* OLG Celle 14 Apr. 1954, JZ 1954, 702, 703; BayObLG 22 Mar. 1957, BayObLGZ 1957, 118, 123, where the court emphasized that foreign countries do not claim exclusive international jurisdiction.

66 E.g., KG Berlin 7 June 1929, IPRspr. 1929 no. 88.

67 DÖLLE, *supra* n. 61, at 220–25; NEUHAUS, *supra* n. 63, at 1168.

68 *Cf.* the exception, KG Berlin 4 June 1959, IPRspr. 1958/59 no. 209.

* For material on German procedure, *see supra* ch. 2 sub II (2) (a) asterisked note.

almost unlimited power to weigh the evidence. As the net result of these and other differences, German court proceedings are usually quicker, cheaper and more informal than American proceedings, but they do not employ the same care and thoroughness in bringing out the facts.

These differences are even more pronounced in areas that, in Germany at least, are outside the jurisdiction of the ordinary courts. Non-contentious jurisdiction, usually exercised by special sections of the lowest courts or *Amtsgerichte,* comprises such matters as the legal protection of minors and other incompetents, adoption, the keeping of the various registers (commercial, matrimonial and land), succession, bankruptcy, and the like. All of these matters are deemed to be in the public interest, and the courts therefore act more or less as judicial administrators. This involves certain special rules of procedure, especially those authorizing intervention or at least proceeding *ex officio.*

(1) **Governing Law**

The basic rule in Germany, as everywhere else, subjects procedure, including jurisdiction, to the *lex fori.* Thus German law determines whether the German courts have international jurisdiction (*supra* I (2)) and which German court is competent;[69] the form of the action;[70] and the whole procedure of the court, including execution.[71]

The *lex fori* rule does not work unilaterally, although this is sometimes asserted. Thus the procedural effects of a proceeding in a foreign court, such as *lis pendens* and *res judicata,* are subject to the law of the foreign court (*see infra* (7) and (8)); and foreign rules on proof-taking may be followed where evidence is taken for foreign court proceedings (*see infra* (4)(b) and (c)).

A more difficult question is the delimitation of procedural matters from problems of substantive law. Although no fixed formula has been developed for this purpose, it may be said that in general the label "procedure" is affixed more reluctantly in Germany than in the United States. Particularly noteworthy in this respect are statutes of limitations, qualified as pertaining to substantive law rather than procedure by the German and the other civil law systems (*see supra* ch. 8 sub III (5)). The same is true of set-off (*see supra* ch. 8 sub III (6)). The qualification of the rules of evidence will be discussed later (*infra* (4)(a)). The concepts of domicile and residence, when used in connection with the jurisdiction or other

---

[69] OLG Bremen 4 Sept. 1963, FamRZ 1964, 219; OGH Köln 22 Sept. 1950, OGHZ 4, 251, 252 (competence of ordinary civil courts, or courts of non-contentious jurisdiction).

[70] LG Kiel 13 Dec. 1956, IPRspr. 1956/57 no. 130 (admissibility of declaratory judgment).

[71] For details, *see* RIEZLER 91–101.

procedure of the German courts, are understood in the light of German substantive law.[72] Whether suit may be brought in the firm name by a foreign merchant or partnership is answered in the affirmative, on the basis of German law.[73] The special rate of interest granted by statute as soon as a pecuniary claim is pending in court (§ 291 BGB) appears also, and correctly, to be subject to German law, without regard to the law otherwise governing the obligation in question,[74] but the details are unsettled.[75]

(2) **Access to the Courts**

Following general American treaty practice,[76] article VI (1) of the American-German Treaty of Friendship of 1954 (Treaties B 117) provides for national treatment with respect to access to courts and administrative tribunals and agencies. This right is accorded to companies as well as to nationals of either country,[77] and the second sentence makes it clear that companies not engaged in business in the territory of the other country shall enjoy access without complying with any of the requirements established for the doing of business (*cf. supra* ch. 11 sub II). In the United States, but not in Germany, this right of access must be understood as not extending to nonresident enemy plaintiffs in time of war.[78]

Apart from its general aspects, access to courts comprises procedural capacity, security for costs, and actions *in forma pauperis.* All of these special aspects are also covered by the Friendship Treaty, directly or indirectly.

(a) *Procedural capacity.* German law distinguishes between capacity to be a party (*Parteifähigkeit*) and capacity to conduct proceedings in one's own name or through an attorney (*Prozessfähigkeit*). The distinction is inspired by and is largely identical with the substantive law distinction between the general legal capacity belonging to all human beings and legal entities (*Rechtsfähigkeit*), and the

---

[72] *See supra* I (2) at n. 37; BGH 29 Nov. 1961, IPRspr. 1960/61 no. 190 (time for appeal depending on the domicile of appellant inside or outside Europe); RG 16 Oct. 1934, RGZ 146, 8, 14 (domicile for purposes of determining obligation to give security for costs).

[73] OLG Hamburg 24 Sept. 1901, OLG 3, 274 (merchant from Indiana); OLG Zweibrücken 18 May 1904, OLG 9, 252.

[74] LG Aschaffenburg 7 July 1953, IPRspr. 1952/53 no. 38, p. 141.

[75] Details are discussed by RIEZLER 101–18.

[76] *See* WILSON 209–43, especially 239–42.

[77] What makes a national or a company belong to either country is discussed *supra* ch. 3 sub A and ch. 10 sub I (1) (b).

[78] *See* DOMKE, Trading with the Enemy in World War II (1943) 220–29, 233–34; DOMKE 81–84. After World War II, Germans were denied access to American courts as late as 1957, *see* Farbenfabriken Bayer, A.G. v. Sterling Drug Inc., 148 F.Supp. 733 (D.N.J.1957), *rev'd,* 251 F.2d 300 (3d Cir.), *cert. denied,* 356 U.S. 957 (1958).

special capacity to contract, to testate, and the like (*Geschäftsfähigkeit*); this latter is denied to minors and certain others. Paragraph 50 I ZPO accordingly describes as "*parteifähig*" one who has legal personality, and § 52 I ZPO as "*prozessfähig*" only one who can bind himself by contract.

The reference in § 50 I ZPO to legal personality, a concept of private law, is usually understood as including the rules of German conflicts law on the status of human beings or legal entities.[79] However, in the case of organizations, it is given a broader interpretation. In purely local cases the different forms of partnership, although devoid of legal personality, are granted standing in court by a special provision (§ 124 I HGB). Accordingly foreign partnerships also, whether or not they are legal entities, are accorded the same standing in court as they have under their governing law.[80] Under the Friendship Treaty this result would seem to follow from article XXV (5) sentence 2 providing for "recognition" in each country of the "juridical status" of companies constituted in the other (*supra* ch. 10 sub I (1)). The courts tend to be liberal in other cases also, especially if the suability of a foreign organization is involved.[81]

There is a similar interaction between the rules on "*Prozessfähigkeit*" and those on capacity to contract.[82] Of particular interest is the special conflicts rule of § 55 ZPO, which declares that a foreigner lacking procedural capacity under his national law shall be "*prozessfähig*" if he is so according to the internal law of the forum.[83] This rule is the procedural equivalent of article 7 III 1 EGBGB which deals with foreigners lacking full capacity to contract (*supra* ch. 4 sub C (1)).

The court must take into account *ex officio* any party's lack of procedural capacity (§ 56 ZPO).

(b) *Security for costs*

(i) *In general.*—In Germany, as in the United States,[84] nonresident or alien plaintiffs may have to post security for costs (*cautio judicatum solvi*). However, there are certain differences. According to § 110 ZPO, in ordinary civil proceedings a national of a foreign

---

[79] BGH 17 Oct. 1968, BGHZ 51, 27, 28–29; RIEZLER 414. *See*, for human beings, *supra* ch. 4 sub C (1), and, for legal entities, *supra* ch. 10 sub I.

[80] RG 25 Nov. 1895, RGZ 36, 393, 394, 397; OLG Hamburg 14 June 1904, OLG 9, 253 (New York partnership); LG Berlin 13 Dec. 1929, IPRspr. 1930 no. 20.

[81] BGH 28 Jan. 1960, NJW 1960, 1204 (Dutch business "foundation").

[82] RIEZLER 420.

[83] An English partnership which was not permitted to sue on its contracts because of failure to register was nevertheless deemed "prozessfähig," LG Berlin 13 Dec. 1929, *supra* n. 80.

[84] *See* MCPHAIL, Security for Costs and its Treatment in United States Treaties, 37 Tul. L. Rev. 461–80 (1963), especially pp. 469–70 (German law) and 476 (Friendship Treaty of 1954).

state, or a stateless person not domiciled in Germany, may be required to give security; exceptions are made in certain kinds of actions[85] and for those plaintiffs whose national law would not require a German to post security in the same situation (§ 110 II no. 1 ZPO). Security may be demanded by the defendant, irrespective of his nationality,[86] for his costs. Security for court costs (*Gerichtskosten*), as distinguished from other costs which may be incurred by the losing party, was abolished for foreign plaintiffs and non-domiciled stateless persons in 1957.[86a] Only in proceedings before the Patent Court must any plaintiff domiciled abroad, irrespective of nationality and reciprocity,[87] give security (§ 37 VI PatG).

(ii) *Exemptions.*—The German courts have held consistently that a treaty guarantee to foreigners of free access to the courts, like that in article VI (1) of the American-German Friendship Treaty of 1954 (Treaties B 117), even though combined with the grant of national treatment, does not imply a derogation from the statutory obligation to give security.[88] Therefore item number 6 of the Protocol to the Friendship Treaty provides expressly for a limited exemption "in such instances as nationals or companies of the other Party would be exempt"; this applies, however, only if a citizen has his permanent residence or a company its main or branch establishment in Germany or if they have sufficient real property "in the territory" (according to the German text, "*im Bezirk*" or "in the district") to cover the costs of the court proceeding. The different wording in the texts, both of which are authentic, has given rise to some doubt in Germany, but the prevailing view correctly prefers the English text.[89] Broadly

---

[85] Actions in a "documentary proceeding" (based, e.g., on a bill of exchange), counterclaims, actions based on interests entered in a German land register, and actions where service is made publicly on the defendant, § 110 II nos. 2–5 ZPO; also where the plaintiff proceeds in forma pauperis, § 115 I no. 2 ZPO and *infra* (c). In addition, the courts have held that security may not be demanded in proceedings for which § 110 ZPO is not declared applicable; *see*, for example, OLG Stuttgart 26 Jan. 1962, IPRspr. 1962/63 no. 3 (non-contentious proceeding); BVerwG 28 Sept. 1965, RzW 1966, 239 (proceedings for restitution of property or reparation in form of damages instituted by former Germans who had left the country as persecutees and acquired a foreign nationality).

[86] RG 16 Oct. 1934, RGZ 146, 8, at 9 (defendant a compatriot of the foreign plaintiff).

[86a] § 85 I Gerichtskostengesetz (GKG) of 18 June 1878, RGBl. S. 141, replaced 26 June 1957, BGBl. I S. 861, 939.

[87] BGH 31 May 1960, GRUR 1960, 429.

[88] *See*, in particular, RG 16 Oct. 1934, *supra* n. 86, at 14–26; RG 18 Mar. 1922, RGZ 104, 189; OLG Karlsruhe 14 Jan. 1931, JW 1931, 751.

[89] OLG Nürnberg 18 June 1964, AWD 1964, 302; 24 Oct. 1963, IPRspr. 1962/63 no. 168; LG München I 18 Dec. 1963, WM 1964, 779; BÜLOW/ARNOLD B I no. 391.5 n. 16 and E no. 991.81 b n. 23a; MÜLLER, RabelsZ 30 (1966) 75 n. 52. *Contra*: SCHWENK 200. While the German text would make sense in the United States (SCHWENK), only the English text makes sense in Germany (BÜLOW/ARNOLD), and this is decisive.

speaking, the exemption is limited to American citizens domiciled in Germany[90] or American enterprises with branches there.

The statutory rules govern in all cases not covered by the Friendship Treaty, and only in these cases.[91] This means that an exemption from the general obligation to post security may result from § 110 II no. 1 ZPO if the American plaintiff can establish that his home state grants reciprocity, but an American domiciled in neither the United States nor Germany can never invoke reciprocity.[92] From a practical standpoint, however, this rule has little or no effect. Since in a few American states[93] security may be required from any plaintiff, thus precluding reciprocity, while in most of the American states security may be required from any non-resident plaintiff, thus limiting reciprocity to a situation already covered by the Treaty, § 110 II no. 1 ZPO provides no relief beyond that available under the Treaty. Accordingly, the German courts have denied reciprocity in several instances.[94]

(iii) *Procedure.*—Security for costs is a so-called "plea in bar," which means that defendant has to raise it. This must be done before he pleads to the merits unless he satisfies the court that he has been unable, without fault on his part, to raise it earlier (§ 274 ZPO). A subsequent plea is only admissible if the obligation to furnish security arises in the course of the proceeding, as where there is a change of nationality or a change in the nature of the proceeding and no part of the claim sufficient to cover the costs is undisputed (§ 111 ZPO). The amount of the security is fixed by the court following a free evaluation of the costs that defendant will probably incur in the proceeding. This amount may be increased or decreased subsequently (§ 112 ZPO). The amounts involved may be substantial since they are based not only on the court costs of the defendant but also on the fee of his attorney.[95] If the plaintiff fails to post security

---

[90] LG München I 18 Dec. 1963, *supra* n. 89.

[91] Some German courts do not appreciate the relationship between the special treaty rule and the general statutory provision, applying only the latter, instead of the former, or both cumulatively, *see* OLG Köln 30 Nov. 1956, IPRspr. 1956/57 no. 180; LG München I 18 Dec. 1963, *supra* n. 89.

[92] OLG Frankfurt 5 June 1957, IPRspr. 1956/57 no. 181.

[93] For the state legislation, *see* the slightly outdated compilation by BÜLOW/ARNOLD E 991.82–991.92.

[94] *District of Columbia*: OLG Köln 30 Nov. 1956, *supra* n. 91; *Illinois*: RG 13 Oct. 1934, IPRspr. 1934 no. 108; 29 Jan. 1930, RGZ 127, 194; *Indiana*: LG Düsseldorf 10 Dec. 1958, IPRspr. 1958/59 no. 174; *New York*: OLG Nürnberg 24 Oct. 1963, *supra* n. 89; RG 22 Mar. 1930, IPRspr. 1930 no. 119; *Pennsylvania*: BGH 20 Nov. 1961, WM 1962, 270; *Texas*: LG Düsseldorf 10 Dec. 1958, *supra.*

[95] In BGH 20 Nov. 1961, *supra* n. 94, the plaintiff Pennsylvania corporation sued for $28,570. The security successively demanded from it for five instances amounted to $3,800.

within the time limit fixed by the court, the action must, on motion of the defendant, be declared withdrawn (§ 113 ZPO).

(c) *Assistance to poor litigants*

(i) *German system.*—For decades German law has possessed an elaborate, comprehensive and satisfactory system of legal aid financed mainly through public funds.[96] Legal aid may be granted to either party at any stage of the proceeding by order of the court if (1) the applicant shows that he would be unable to bear the costs without jeopardizing support for himself and his family, and if (2) the intended action or defense offers sufficient prospect of success and does not appear to be unreasonable (§ 114 I ZPO). Incidentally, if there is a public interest in the action or the defense, even a domestic legal entity may be granted legal aid (see § 114 IV ZPO).[97] A foreign national will usually be granted legal aid only upon condition of reciprocity.[98] A stateless person may at the court's discretion be granted legal aid upon the same conditions as a German (§ 114 II ZPO).

(ii) *Treaty provisions.*—A treaty guarantee to foreigners of free access to courts, like article IV (1) of the American-German Treaty of Friendship of 1954 (Treaties B 117), does not secure national treatment with respect to obtaining legal aid.[99] Therefore item number 7 of the Protocol provides expressly for national treatment but, due to the federal structure of the United States, only to a limited extent. Germans are accorded national treatment in proceedings before the federal courts of the United States (no. 7 lett. (a)), and Americans are granted national treatment before the German courts[100] provided the case is of a type which in the United States would fall within the federal jurisdiction or could, upon application, be brought[101] before a federal court (no. 7 lett. (b)). This latter formula has been devised to maintain equilibrium between the

---

[96] Detailed description in STOHR, The German System of Legal Aid, 54 Calif.L.Rev. 801–08 (1966).

[97] According to § 14 FGG the same principles apply in non-contentious procedure.

[98] As in the case of security for costs, *supra* n. 85, exceptions have been made for restitution proceedings (OLG Celle 15 Feb. 1954, IPRspr. 1954/55 no. 44) and proceedings of political persecutees for reparation of damages, § 209 II BEG (BGBl. III 251–1).

[99] RG 17 Sept. 1935, RGZ 149, 83, 86, invoking two cases decided on exemption from the duty to post security, *see supra* n. 88. *See also* RIEZLER 442, who personally objects to this view.

[100] The phrase "before the courts of the Federal Republic of Germany" must not be read as referring to the (few, *see supra* ch. 2 sub III (2)) federal courts only, but to state courts as well, BÜLOW/ARNOLD E 991.72 n. 18; *see also* SCHWENK 200.

[101] *See* SCHWENK 201 and ARNOLD/HILL/KERN 3.

mutual concessions. It requires the German courts to ascertain the jurisdiction of the United States federal courts.[102]

(iii) *Reciprocity.*—In all cases not falling within the jurisdiction of their own federal courts, American citizens may obtain German legal aid according to German rules only if their home states grant reciprocity (§ 114 II sent. 1 ZPO). The legal aid systems of the American states differ widely, many states having no such system at all. Other states grant limited legal aid, some to a plaintiff,[103] some to a resident;[104] reciprocity would be limited to these situations. Finally, some states grant legal aid generally,[105] but in view of the great differences between the German and the American systems, those German courts that have looked carefully into the matter have denied the existence of reciprocity even there, and especially with respect to California and New York.[106]

(iv) *Procedure.*—An applicant for legal aid proves his economic need by exhibiting a certificate from a public authority (§ 118 II ZPO) which, however, does not bind the court. An American citizen residing in the United States has been required to produce a certificate of necessity legalized by a German diplomatic or consular representative, or at least an Internal Revenue notice of assessment.[107] His prospect of success is examined by the court at a preliminary hearing in which the adversary party is usually heard. The court may demand that the applicant establish his factual allegations and it may ask for the production of documents or for information from public authorities. Witnesses are heard only under special circumstances (§ 118 a I ZPO). A grant of legal aid by the court, which is valid only for the pending instance, exempts the applicant from the payment of court costs and costs for witnesses and from posting security for costs; it entitles him to the gratuitous services of a sheriff (for the service of documents and for execution)

---

[102] *Sedes materiae* is 28 U.S.C. §§ 1331–59. For a brief comment, see BÜLOW/ARNOLD E 991.5–991.9. *See also* Buechold v. Ortiz, 401 F.2d 371 (9th Cir. 1968), and Brandtscheit v. Britton, 239 F.Supp. 652 (N.D.Cal. 1965), closing the federal courts to the action of a German child against a California citizen to establish paternity and to obtain support.

[103] Missouri, Montana, New Jersey, New Mexico, New York, North Carolina, Oklahoma, and Texas, *see* BÜLOW/ARNOLD E 991.73 a–991.80 and WIECZOREK I 2 no. D on § 110 ZPO.

[104] Kansas, Kentucky, Louisiana, Michigan, Oregon, Tennessee, and Wisconsin, *see* BÜLOW/ARNOLD and WIECZOREK, *supra* n. 103.

[105] Arkansas, California, Colorado, Illinois, Indiana, Nebraska, Utah, Virginia, and West Virginia, *see* BÜLOW/ARNOLD and WIECZOREK, *supra* n. 103.

[106] *California*: LG Kassel 4 June 1954, IPRspr. 1954/55 no. 171; *contra*: OLG Frankfurt 25 Feb. 1954, *id.* no. 170; *New York*: LG Essen 5 Nov. 1954, NJW 1955, 592; LAG Frankfurt 24 Feb. 1954, NJW 1955, 1375.

[107] LAG Frankfurt 24 Feb. 1954, IPRspr. 1954/55 no. 167 (applicant's affidavit about his conditions held insufficient).

and of an attorney or court officer (§§ 115–116 a ZPO), who will be compensated by the state.

(3) **Service of Process and of other Documents**[108]

In the absence of treaty rules,[109] the international service of documents between the United States and Germany is governed by municipal law and by comity.

(a) *Service of German documents in the United States.*—Apart from special situations,[110] service upon a person residing outside Germany cannot be made by mailing in Germany but only through service effected abroad. Paragraph 199 ZPO indicates that assistance may be sought for this purpose either from the competent authorities of the foreign state or from the German representatives abroad. Administrative details of this aspect of international judicial assistance, among others, are laid down in elaborate rules on judicial assistance in contentious and non-contentious civil matters.[111]

These rules regulate in great detail the form and content of a request for service (§§ 16–26, 32–35 ZRHO). It must be drafted in the German language and translated by a sworn translator in Germany or in the United States if assistance by an American authority is desired; translation is also recommended if service is to be made through the German official representative and if the addressee is believed not to know German (§§ 25, 26 ZRHO). The request for service must indicate the nature of the document to be served, the name and address of the addressee, the court's file number and the names of the parties (§ 32 II ZRHO). In summonses to appear on a specified date, the time limit for appearance must be fixed by the court with due regard to the delays involved in international

---

[108] OESTERHELT/SMIT 173–81, 190–200; VOLLKOMMER 252–63.

[109] The Hague Convention on Civil Procedure of Mar. 1, 1954 (BCBl. 1958 II 576, 286 UNTS 265) is binding upon Germany but not the United States. On the other hand, the United States but not Germany has ratified the Hague Convention on the Service Abroad of Judicial and Extrajudicial Documents in Civil or Commercial Matters of Nov. 15, 1965 (20 UST 361, TIAS 6638), which in part supersedes the former.

[110] A nonresident who is not represented by counsel residing within the district of the court must appoint a representative authorized to accept service, § 174 II ZPO. Failing such an appointment, service may be made by the mailing of the documents to the addressee by the sheriff, § 175 I 2 ZPO.

Some special laws provide for service by registered mail against return receipt if the addressee's address is known; *see* the instructive case, BayObLG 17 Nov. 1967, BayObLGZ 1967, 443, 446–47, interpreting such a special provision.

Such service effected in New York has been held valid even if American law would oppose the service, which it does not, OLG Stuttgart 25 Feb. 1965, IPRspr. 1964/65 no. 207.

[111] Rechtshilfeordnung für Zivilsachen (ZRHO) of Oct. 19, 1956 (looseleaf), a uniform regulation enacted separately for the federal courts and the several states' court. It has been extended to labor matters also.

service.[112] In such summonses the procedural disadvantages of non-appearance may be pointed out, especially the risk of a default judgment, but no penalties may be threatened for non-compliance (§ 33 IV ZRHO) as this is thought to violate foreign sovereignty. Each outgoing request has to be submitted for examination to an office of inspection which ensures that all provisions and rules of German law and of any applicable treaties have been observed and that the form and content of the request are likely to be understood abroad (§§ 9, 27–29 ZRHO).

(i) Contrary to the sequence indicated by § 199 ZPO (*supra* text at n. 111), the primary agents for the transmittal of requests for service are German representatives abroad (§§ 11, 13 II, III, 15 sent. 1 ZRHO). These are empowered under German law (§ 19 *Konsulargesetz,* BGBl. III 27–1) to make service on any person residing within their jurisdictions. Although no treaty provision deals with this matter, American law seems to admit such service by a foreign consul,[113] and the German regulations therefore allow German consuls to make service on any person, irrespective of nationality, provided the addressee is willing to receive the document.[114] In practice service is usually made by the consulate through registered mail against return receipt, service being proved by a certificate of the German consul (§§ 202 II ZPO, 19 sent. 2 *Konsulargesetz*) issued on the basis of the addressee's receipt.

(ii) If service by a German representative is impossible or inadvisable,[115] assistance must be sought from the competent foreign authority (§ 15 sent. 1 ZRHO). In the case of the United States, where this happens rarely, the request is addressed to "the appropriate judicial authorities" and sent to the German Embassy in Washington for transmittal.[116] The State Department is now expressly authorized to receive such requests and transmit them to the "appropriate" court,[117] and the federal district courts are empowered to order service of any document issued in connection with a proceeding in

---

[112] §§ 262 II, 499 II, 339 II, 700 sent. 2 ZPO and § 33 II, III ZRHO.

[113] 28 U.S.C. § 1696 (b) (1964 ed.); and § 2.04 (b) Uniform Interstate and International Procedure Act, 1962, 9B U.L.A. 305. The latter has been adopted (as of 1968) by Arkansas, Massachusetts, Michigan, Nebraska, Oklahoma, and the Virgin Islands, Handbook of the National Commissioners on Uniform State Laws (1968) 293. *See also* McCusker, 37 D. S. Bull. 809 (1957); 2 Hackworth 118–19.

[114] Such "informal service," defined in § 5 no. 1 lett. a) ZRHO, is the only form of service allowed to German representatives, §§ 13 I no. 1, 32 IV ZRHO.

[115] Where recognition of the ensuing German decision is possible, service through the competent foreign authorities may be advisable if this insures recognition (§ 13 III ZRHO). For the United States, this consideration seems to be irrelevant.

[116] ZRHO, sub "Vereinigte Staaten von Amerika," A no. 3.

[117] 28 U.S.C. § 1781, as revised in 1964 (1964 ed.).

a foreign tribunal.[118] The form of service is governed by the law of the jurisdiction in which it is made.[119] Under the narrow and formalistic view which German law takes of the matter, any other form of service, although offered or admitted by American law even for foreign proceedings, is precluded.

(iii) If service abroad is impossible or if a person's address is unknown, service by publication may be authorized by the court (§§ 203–207 ZPO). Publication in the federal bulletin (*Bundesanzeiger*) is obligatory only for summonses; other documents are usually only affixed to a board in the court building (§ 204 II ZPO). However, it should be kept in mind that this method of "constructive notice" without more normally precludes recognition abroad of the ensuing judgment (*see infra* (8)(b)(i)).

(b) *Service of American documents in Germany.*—On the requesting side, too, American law is liberal in permitting a great variety of forms of service.[120]

(i) Although there is almost no basis in United States law for service of documents by American consuls,[121] German law would permit them to make service in Germany irrespective of the addressee's nationality as long as service is not "compulsory."[122] This probably means that service is admitted by personal delivery to a person willing to accept it,[123] provided it is not accompanied by any threat of compulsion.[124]

(ii) Foreign officials other than consuls are forbidden to act in Germany.[125] Therefore service by American marshals, sheriffs or special court appointees is out of the question.[126] Nor may service be made by registered mail, against receipt, if the document is dispatched by an American court official in the United States, since not only the United States postal services but also the German postal services would have to act as agent for the American court,

---

118 28 U.S.C. § 1696 (a); § 2.04 Uniform Act, *supra* n. 113.

119 *See* § 202 II ZPO, § 20 sent. 1 ZRHO.

120 Rule 4 (i) FRCP; §§ 2.01 and 2.02 of the Uniform Act, *supra* n. 113.

121 22 C.F.R. §§ 92.85–92.92 (1970). Section 92.86 permits service on a national or resident of the United States only by specific direction of the State Department and subject to the consent of the foreign country. American consulates in Germany rarely make such service.

122 BÜLOW/ARNOLD E 991.68 n. 11; NEHLERT, JR 1958, 124.

123 So-called "informal service," *see supra* n. 114. OESTERHELT/SMIT 195–96, invoking a private statement of Professor BÜLOW in n. 183; *also* VOLLKOMMER 254, invoking an inconclusive note by BÜLOW/ARNOLD.

124 OESTERHELT/SMIT 196, stating that the service of documents threatening punishment is permissible. *But see* RIEZLER 684.

125 This is an unwritten but firmly established general principle, RIEZLER 672; VOLLKOMMER 258.

126 VOLLKOMMER 258; *see also* OESTERHELT/SMIT 196–97, with untenable objections.

both by delivery of the document and by requesting signature of the receipt[127] (*see infra* (iv)).

(iii) Service by private persons, although officially disapproved,[128] must be held admissible and is in fact widely used. No violation of German sovereignty can possibly be claimed and compulsion is excluded.[129] However, a private attorney may not transmit a document connected with a foreign proceeding to a German process server for service according to the German rules since this might involve compulsion.[130] If an affidavit is required of the individual who made the service,[131] an American consul will administer the oath.

(iv) Assistance by German officials may be obtained only upon formal request in the form of a letter rogatory and will be granted only on a limited scale. Each incoming request is submitted to an office of inspection (§§ 57, 59 ZRHO), and a German translation must be enclosed or procured. Legalization of the signature of the requesting foreign official is not necessary (§§ 60, 61 ZRHO). If the request is unobjectionable, it is transmitted to the competent court, which is the local court (*Amtsgericht*) of the district where the recipient is living (§ 66 ZRHO). Since treaty rules are lacking, documents of American origin may only be served informally, in other words, through manual transmission to an addressee willing to accept.[132] The normal forms of service under German law, such as service by mail and substituted service, are excluded.[133] The document must be shown to the addressee so that he can decide whether or not to accept, and he must be informed of his freedom to refuse, even though the foreign proceeding may nevertheless continue and he may be exposed to other disadvantages (§ 69 III ZRHO). The registrar of the court either asks for a dated receipt or, if delivery has been made by an agent, issues a certificate of

---

[127] *See also* VOLLKOMMER 259–60, and a private statement by Professor BÜLOW quoted in OESTERHELT/SMIT 197 n. 90. *See* United States apology for violation of Swiss law, which is in this respect as in others very similar to German law (OESTERHELT/SMIT 362–64), committed by the dispatch of mail to a person in Switzerland, 56 A.J.I.L. 794 (1962).

[128] *See* the statement of Professor BÜLOW quoted in OESTERHELT/SMIT 192 n. 160. Service of foreign decisions that have been declared enforceable in Germany is, of course, admitted, § 81 IV ZRHO, and *infra* (8).

[129] VOLLKOMMER 260; *see also* OESTERHELT/SMIT 192.

[130] § 81 I, III ZRHO. § 12 of the Directives for Sheriffs (Geschäftsanweisung für Gerichtsvollzieher) expressly directs a sheriff not to execute such a request. The supervisory authority, however, usually consents to its execution. OESTERHELT/SMIT 193, basing its conclusion on American rather than German law, is incorrect; *but see id.* at 197–98 and n. 196.

[131] *See*, e.g. § 2.01 (b) of the Uniform Act, *supra* n. 113.

[132] §§ 70 II, 67 I no. 1, 68 II ZRHO. *See also supra* n. 114.

[133] VOLLKOMMER 261–62 makes a good argument for permitting such service on American citizens.

service on the basis of a receipt obtained by the agent (§ 75 ZRHO). If service is impossible, for example, because of the addressee's refusal to accept it, the registrar will issue a certificate explaining the reason (§ 79 I ZRHO).

The receipt, certificate and other documents are then returned to the office of inspection, which ascertains whether the request has been complied with fully and properly. The documents will thereafter be transmitted to the foreign requesting court (§ 64 ZRHO).

In choosing between the various forms of service, it is important to keep in mind the rule of § 328 I no. 2 ZPO which excludes recognition of a foreign judgment rendered against a German defendant if, *inter alia,* service has not been made upon him through German judicial assistance (*see infra* (8)). However, since there are other obstacles to recognition and since there is the faster and cheaper method of service through a private person, letters rogatory from an American court requesting service are almost never issued.

(4) **Evidence**

International rules of evidence are important, complex and largely unexplored.

(a) *Law applicable.*—Perhaps nowhere is the limit between substantive and adjective law more blurred than in the field of international evidence. No clear boundary exists between the *lex fori* and other laws that may be applicable, but the following line of demarcation may be asserted as accepted by prevailing practice and opinion in Germany. Although most questions pertaining to evidence are subject to the *lex fori,* some fall outside its scope. Thus the burden of proof is generally governed by the law applicable to the underlying legal relation,[134] but is subject to the *lex fori* if the consequences of a procedural act are in issue.[135] Presumptions,[136] too, are viewed as subject to the *lex causae* unless they relate solely to procedure.[137] The *lex fori* governs the technicalities of the administration of evidence, especially the admissible modes of proof, the production of documents, the taking of evidence and its evaluation,[138] including what constitutes sufficient evidence to make out a prima facie case.[139] The qualification of provisions comparable to the Anglo-American statutes of frauds is controversial. The Federal

---

134 BGH 14 Apr. 1969, WM 1969, 858; 8 Nov. 1951, BGHZ 3, 342, 346; RG 6 Feb. 1930, JW 1930, 1003; LG II Berlin 24 Jan. 1930, IPRspr. 1930 no. 6.

135 Riezler 465.

136 LG II Berlin 24 Jan. 1930, *supra* n. 134.

137 Riezler 489–90, emphasizing the fact that the qualification is made according to the *lex fori.*

138 BGH 30 July 1954, JZ 1955, 702.

139 Riezler 466.

Supreme Court has qualified the French rule as procedural and has therefore avoided applying it, but the German writers have adopted the opposite solution.[140]

(b) *Taking of evidence in Germany for use in the United States.*— In the absence of treaty rules, the taking of evidence for use abroad is governed in both countries by municipal law. We shall restrict ourselves here to one particularly important class of evidence, namely, testimony. Three methods are available to Americans to obtain testimony in Germany.

(i) American consuls are authorized to examine witnesses regardless of their nationality under both American[141] and German law,[142] if no compulsion is used.[143] Such a deposition will be made in the "American" form,[144] usually on written interrogatories and cross-interrogatories.[145] American consulates in Germany receive up to fifty such requests per annum.

(ii) Depositions are frequently taken before a German notary, except pursuant to a commission.[146] This official, as distinguished from the American "notary public," is a highly qualified and particularly respected member of the legal profession.[147] Although German notaries may not administer oaths for internal purposes, they have been expressly authorized to record depositions under oath if necessary under the foreign law or for the protection of interests abroad.[148]

---

[140] BGH 30 July 1954, *supra* n. 137. *Contra*: RIEZLER 471; GAMILLSCHEG, JZ 1955, 703–04; RAAPE 226; NEUHAUS 81. *But see also* NAGEL 426, 433.

[141] 22 C.F.R. § 92.49–92.64 (1970), permitting consular officers to take depositions on notice or to execute commissions to take depositions.

[142] Note of German government of Jan. 13, 1956, cited by OESTERHELT/SMIT 202; *see also* BÜLOW/ARNOLD E 991.68 n. 11 and NEHLERT, JR 1958, 126. The more restrictive provision of art. XXII of the American German Friendship Treaty of 1923 (Treaties B 55, maintained by art. XXVIII of the Friendship Treaty of 1954, Treaties B 117) that limited the taking of testimony to nationals of the consul's country (*see also* 2 HACKWORTH 102–03), is thus in effect abrogated.

[143] In United States v. Hofmann, 24 F. Supp. 847, 850, 851 (S.D.N.Y. 1938), the court required the witness in Germany to file with the American consul a consent to appear voluntarily and testify under oath.

[144] *See* the detailed rules *in* 22 C.F.R. § 92.56–92.64.

[145] *See*, e.g., Estate of Scharl, N.Y.L.J. Aug. 9, 1956, p. 3 col. 7 (Sur. Ct.); Demov & Morris v. Fontheim, N.Y.L.J. May 22, 1958, p. 8 col. 4 (City Ct.); McQuade v. Sztykgold, 1 A.D.2d 872, 149 N.Y.S.2d 378, 379 (1956); Ferro Metals Chemicals Corp. v. Monroe Smelting Corp., N.Y.L.J. May 11, 1956, p. 7 col. 7 (City Ct.), on problems of translation.

[146] In 1903, the Prussian Ministry of Justice in a lengthy opinion (JW 1906, 631–32) held inadmissible the taking of evidence by a Prussian notary on an American court's commission, but admitted action on the parties' request.

[147] Careful analysis in SCHLESINGER, The Notary and the Formal Contract in Civil Law, *in* STATE OF NEW YORK, Report of the Law Revision Commission for 1941 (Leg.Doc. no. 65 (M)) 59–70; *see also* SCHLESINGER, Comparative Law (3d ed. 1970) 15–20.

[148] § 22 I Bundesnotarordnung, BGBl. III 303–1.

Since the German form of examining witnesses differs greatly from the American, the preparation of written interrogatories is recommended unless American counsel is to be present.

(iii) Although depositions before a private person are not expressly prohibited,[149] such a person may not administer an oath under German law, and it would seem impossible to derive this authorization from American law.[150]

(iv) The last, most formal and slowest way is through letter rogatory issued by an American court to a German court. The general procedure is the same as described (*supra* (3(b)(iv)) for service through a German court. In the absence of a treaty, the German court may not employ compulsion (§ 83 I 2 ZRHO).[151] The deposition will be taken in accordance with German requirements as to form unless the request specifies another form which does not contravene mandatory rules of German law (§ 83 I 1 ZRHO). Paragraph 87 ZRHO stands for the general rule that privileges of witnesses are governed by German law.[152] Although German law is unfamiliar with either the examination and cross-examination of witnesses by the parties, the verbatim transcript, or other refinements of the Anglo-American method of taking depositions,[153] nothing prevents compliance with these formalities by a German court except its ignorance of these devices.[154] It is thus advisable to submit written interrogatories.[155] The administration of an oath is admissible except in the two cases indicated in § 393 ZPO.[156] In practice, letters rogatory from American courts are rarely received.

(c) *Taking of evidence in the United States for use in Germany.*— German procedure envisages three forms in which evidence may be taken abroad: preferably, through a German consul; otherwise, by assistance through the competent foreign authority, on request either of the court or of the party charged with adducing the proof.[157]

---

[149] However, Professor BÜLOW contends that they are illegal, *see* OESTERHELT/SMIT 201 n. 229.

[150] Of this opinion is, however, OESTERHELT/SMIT 202. The authors fail to recognize the official character of the taking of oaths in Germany.

[151] AG Schöneberg 3 Aug. 1955, file no. 18 AR 1192/55, *cited by* NEHLERT, JR 1958, 122–123.

[152] *See also* EISNER, WM 1969, 199–200.

[153] *See* the brief description *in* OESTERHELT/SMIT 203–04.

[154] NEHLERT, JR 1958, 125, tends to think that a cross-examination would run counter to basic principles of German procedure and therefore is inadmissible.

[155] OESTERHELT/SMIT 203.

[156] *See* § 86 ZRHO. Subsection 3 expressly admits forms of an oath that are unknown to German law. § 393 ZPO excludes the administration of an oath from a person under 17 years of age or otherwise without a sufficient perception of the significance of an oath and from a person that has been declared unable to swear by a final penal decision of a German court.

[157] §§ 363, 364 ZPO; *see also* §§ 11, 13 and 15 ZRHO (on these rules, *supra* (3) (a)).

(i) Assistance by a German consul is limited by German law to situations in which no compulsion by him is needed.[158] The general provisions on outgoing requests apply.[159] German consuls may hear any person in the United States, irrespective of nationality.[160] In important proceedings, especially in major criminal cases, the German court, with the permission of the United States authorities, sometimes attends the taking of the testimony by the consul, but purely as an observer. If the witness is unwilling to appear, the German consul is entitled under American law to ask an American court for help; the court could appoint the consul as a commissioner and might then compel testimony.[161] However, the German prohibition against compulsion (§ 13 I 1 ZRHO) may well extend to this case. True, it is foreign and not German compulsion that would be invoked; but since Germany has no desire to reciprocate in the corresponding situation, even the invocation of foreign assistance may be construed to be covered by the general prohibition against the use of compulsion.

At least one case is known where an American court appointed the judges of the German court to serve as commissioners, thus authorizing them personally to take testimony in the United States. They were permitted to follow the German rules of procedure, to the extent these were deemed consistent with the rights and privileges of witnesses under American law.[162]

(ii) If the witness abroad is unwilling to testify, assistance by the competent foreign authorities is required under German law. In the case of the United States, this does not necessarily mean, however, that a formal letter rogatory has to be issued by a German court.[163]

The German consul, as we have seen (*supra* (i)), may arrange for a commissioner to be appointed. Under German practice, this appointment is made by the German requesting court in blank, the name of the commissioner to be filled in by the German consul.[164] The commissioner may turn to an American court if compulsion is needed, and the court may order the witness to testify.[165] The

---

158 § 13 I 1 ZRHO; *see also* 28 U.S.C. § 1782 (b) (1964 ed.); § 3.02 (b) Uniform Act, *supra* n. 113.

159 §§ 6–10, 16–31 ZRHO, *see supra* (3) (a).

160 McCusker, 37 D. S. Bull. 809 (1957); Bülow/Arnold E 991.68. *See also supra* n. 142.

161 Oesterhelt/Smit 6, 182–83.

162 *In re* Letters rogatory from Landgericht (Provincial Court) at Munich (N.D.Ill. 1966, no. 66 C 1369).

163 Bülow/Arnold E 991.71 is outdated.

164 Bülow/Arnold E 991.69–991.70, with a form which urges the requesting court to specify the questions to be put to the witness.

165 28 U.S.C. § 1782 (a) (1964 ed.); § 3.02 (a) Uniform Act, *supra* n. 113.

commissioner may, and if properly instructed will, follow German procedure in taking testimony.[166] This applies especially to the administration of an oath (§ 37 I ZRHO). As far as privileges are concerned, both American and German rules are applicable.[167] If the German procedure is not set forth in the request, however, the testimony will be taken according to the rules of procedure of the requested court.[168] Even if the taking of the testimony does not comply with the rules of procedure of the requested court, it may be allowed if it is valid under German law (§ 369 ZPO).

As an alternative to the use of a commissioner, the German court may issue a letter rogatory to the "appropriate judicial authority." These requests are usually transmitted through the German Embassy and the State Department to a federal court. While it is also possible for a German consul to apply directly to one of the state courts, the willingness of the latter to execute such letters rogatory is not fully assured everywhere.

(iii) Paragraph 364 ZPO authorizes the German court to ask the party who has the burden of proof to transmit the court's request to the competent foreign authority and to attend to its execution. However, the provision is narrowly interpreted and very rarely used. The commentators hold that it applies only if the other channels for obtaining testimony cannot be used.[169] Moreover, § 36 ZRHO warns expressly that foreign authorities may offer resistance and recommends that this way be chosen only if experience has proven that it will succeed. There is no official information available, but two authors have applauded this procedure as "eminently useful and effective" for obtaining evidence in the United States.[170] It is doubtful, however, whether the procedure referred to by these authors coincides with that of § 364 ZPO, since the latter necessarily contemplates a court proceeding, initiated by private request. It is unlikely that a transcript of an examination taken by a private person without court intervention would comply with the requirement of § 364 II ZPO.[171]

(d) *Documentary evidence.*—Since documentary evidence is relevant not only in litigation, it will be discussed later (*infra* V).

(e) *Non-contentious civil procedure.*—In non-contentious civil procedure, even facts have to be ascertained *ex officio* by the courts

---

166 *See* 28 U.S.C. § 1782 (a) (1) sent. 4; § 3.02 (a) sent. 2 Uniform Act, *supra* n. 113.

167 28 U.S.C. § 1782 (a) (2); § 37 II–IV ZRHO and OESTERHELT/SMIT 184.

168 28 U.S.C. § 1782 (a) (1) sent. 5; § 3.02 (a) sent. 3 Uniform Act, *supra* n. 113.

169 WIECZOREK II 2, no. A I on § 364 ZPO; BAUMBACH/LAUTERBACH no. 1 on § 364 ZPO.

170 OESTERHELT/SMIT 181; *see also* COHN, ZZP 80 (1967) 234, for England.

171 As asserted by OESTERHELT/SMIT 184.

(§ 12 FGG). The ZRHO applies to the taking of evidence abroad and to judicial assistance in the taking of evidence in Germany for foreign tribunals (§ 1 I ZRHO).

(5) Application of Foreign Law*

Pleading and ascertainment of foreign law as well as review of its application stand at the crossroads between procedure and conflict of laws. Because of the different approaches of American and German law to both fields, there is small wonder that the procedural application of foreign law also diverges greatly and at every stage.

(a) *Conflicts rules of the lex fori.*—The conflicts rules of the *lex fori* determine, in theory at least, when foreign law is to be applied. In fact, however, the judge's attention must be drawn specifically not only to the content of the foreign law, but even to the conflict of laws rule which requires its application. This is not uncommon in the United States, where the application of foreign law is a relatively rare occurrence, and where in many cases the conflicts rules are disregarded and American law is applied instead of the properly applicable foreign law.[172]

In Germany it is clear in principle that German conflicts rules, as a part of German domestic law, must be applied *ex officio* by the court,[173] which is supposed to know its own law (*iura novit curia*). An incorrect application of German conflicts rules is a violation of German law and thus fully subject to review on both first and second appeal (*infra* (b)(iii)). However, since in civil proceedings matters other than personal status are usually controlled by the parties, who determine the issues by their allegations and proof, it is at least advisable for them expressly to invoke the German conflicts rule.[174] Otherwise, they risk the application of German internal law either through simple ignorance on the part of the court or, in contract and tort cases, as being the law tacitly chosen by them (*supra* ch. 7 sub (1)(c) and ch. 8 sub II (2)(a)).

The procedural treatment of the points of contact—such as nationality, domicile or place of making a contract—contained in the conflicts rules reflects the nature of the proceeding. In matters of

---

* DOMKE, Proof of Foreign Law in (Western) Germany, *in* American Bar Association, Section of International and Comparative Law, Proceedings 1960, pp. 162–65; SOMMERICH/BUSCH, Foreign Law (1959) 114–16; D. MÜLLER, Deutschland, *in* Die Anwendung ausländischen Rechts im internationalen Privatrecht (1968) 66–80; *see also* KEGEL, *in id.* 157–84.

[172] *In re* Meyer's Estate, 107 Cal. App. 2d 799, 238 P.2d 597 (1951) (succession of German citizen residing in Germany held governed by California law; *see, similarly, In re* Herter's Estate, *supra* ch. 5 n. 109; *see also* 1 EHRENZWEIG § 100.

[173] RAAPE 122; RIEZLER 492; KEGEL, *supra* asterisked note, at 159.

[174] MÜLLER 66; KEGEL, *supra* asterisked note, at 163.

personal status, the court follows an inquisitorial procedure, ascertaining for itself the relevant facts and circumstances. In all other matters, it is the party who would be benefited by the application of the German conflicts rule who must take control, alleging and proving those facts and circumstances.[175]

The German courts sometimes expressly leave open the question of the law on which they rely, preferring to stand upon two or more legal systems that conform on the point at issue. This method is quite legitimate for courts of all degrees and only one situation raises any difficulty: if a court of first appeal fails to state whether its decision is based on German or foreign law, a second appeal cannot as a rule be based on the violation of foreign law (*infra* (b)(iii)); hence the courts of second appeal have often said that appellate courts must declare unambiguously which law they are applying.[176] Today, however, a violation of this duty will not result in reversal and remand of the case (*see* cases cited in n. 176). Legal writers, thinking more pragmatically on this point, openly defend the right of an appellate court to reason alternatively on the basis of both German and foreign law,[177] provided it finds that the legal systems potentially applicable come to the same result.[178]

(b) *Application of foreign law.*—The application of foreign law involves pleading, ascertainment and review.

(i) The pleading of foreign law is intimately bound up with the procedural treatment of the *lex fori's* conflicts rules. Since these have to be applied *ex officio* in Germany (*supra* (a)), it follows that the foreign law indicated by the conflicts rules must also be applied irrespective of the attitude of the parties. Neither need plead foreign law, and even their agreement on the applicable law does not bind the court except in contract and tort cases.[179]

(ii) Ascertainment of foreign law is governed by § 293 ZPO.[180] This rule is interpreted extensively. It is understood as requiring

---

[175] KEGEL, *supra* asterisked note, at 160.

[176] BGH 29 Oct. 1962, NJW 1963, 252, 253; 14 May 1959 and 30 Oct. 1958, IPRspr. 1960/61 nos. 3 and 2; 11 May 1956, NJW 1956, 1155.

[177] M. WOLFF 85; KEGEL, Kommentar, nos. 85–87 preceding art. 7 EGBGB; STEINDORFF, JZ 1963, 202; HOFFMEYER, JZ 1957, 467–68.

[178] If no such finding has been made, the matter is usually remanded, *see* BGH 7 Nov. 1963, WM 1964, 83, 84; KG Berlin 28 Feb. 1958, IPRspr. 1962/63 no. 1.

[179] DOMKE, *supra* asterisked note, at 164; RIEZLER 492; MÜLLER 67. In contract and tort cases the parties may agree in court on the governing law, *see supra* ch. 7 sub (1) (c) and ch. 8 at n. 21, and also n. 24.

[180] "The law prevailing in another country, customary law and charters of public bodies require proof only insofar as they are unknown to the court. In ascertaining these legal rules, the court is not confined to the evidence adduced by the parties; the court may also use other sources of information and may make any orders necessary for such utilization." *See* also translation by DOMKE, *supra* asterisked note, at 163; SCHLESINGER, Comparative Law, *supra* n. 147, at 185.

the court to inform itself of the applicable foreign law, although it may ask the parties for assistance. If the court violates the duty to inform itself, the case has to be reversed and remanded.[181] The same obligation exists in non-contentious proceedings; although § 293 ZPO is not binding there, the general inquisitorial maxim laid down in § 12 FGG includes a duty on the part of the court to ascertain the applicable foreign law *ex officio*, without relying on the assistance of the parties.[182] A general presumption of identity between an applicable foreign law and the German *lex fori* is not recognized, and the use of similar formulas not based on substantiated statements respecting the content of the foreign law has resulted in reversal and remand.[183]

The ascertainment of foreign law does not constitute an issue of fact and is not therefore governed by the ordinary rules relating to proof of facts.[184] Consequently the judge is not bound by offers of proof submitted by the parties,[185] but is free to use whatever means of proof are available.[186] He is supposed to use his own knowledge and the sources directly accessible to him. If such immediate resources are lacking, only a few courses are open. One method is to seek information from the competent Ministry of Justice, but only Baden-Württemberg has made arrangements to collect relevant material. Another method is to turn to a German diplomatic representative abroad who in difficult questions will ask advice from local counsel. The most popular method, and the most surprising to the American reader, is to send the court file to one of the five major German research institutes on foreign law and to ask for an opinion.[187] These opinions are given quickly, are relatively inexpensive for the courts and enjoy a great authority with them.[188] Finally, the court may ask the parties, or one of them, to furnish the necessary information, and they, too, may use any of the

---

181 BGH 23 June 1964, NJW 1964, 2012; 24 Nov. 1960, NJW 1961, 410; 5 May 1956, IPRspr. 1958/59 no. 62 A.

182 KG Berlin 10 Feb. 1933, IPRspr. 1933 no. 47; 24 Mar. 1932, JW 1932, 2815; 12 Dec. 1929, IPRspr. 1930 no. 4.

183 RG 4 Nov. 1933, JW 1934, 835, 836; KG Berlin 28 Feb. 1958, IPRspr. 1962/63 no. 1.

184 KG Berlin 21 Apr. 1932, IPRspr. 1932 no. 44 (the restrictions on the admission of proofs in "documentary proceedings" do not affect the ascertainment of foreign law); 24 Sept. 1932, *id.* no. 2 (no formal taking of evidence if the parties, following the invitation of the court, submit information on foreign law).

185 BGH 29 Nov. 1961, JZ 1963, 167, 169.

186 BGH 28 Oct. 1965, NJW 1966, 296, 298.

187 The largest is the Max-Planck-Institute for Foreign Private Law and Private International Law (Prof. Zweigert) in Hamburg; four other major institutes are at the universities of Berlin (Prof. Wengler), Cologne (Prof. Kegel), Kiel (Prof. Menzel) and Munich (Prof. Ferid).

188 A recent collection of such opinions is IPG 1965/66 and 1967/68.

preceding methods or may submit opinions from foreign experts.[189] The courts themselves are not permitted to turn to foreign diplomatic representatives in Germany[190] or to foreign authorities or private persons abroad (§§ 40 I, 48 I ZHRO), but these prohibitions are not always strictly observed in practice.

Foreign law comprises not only statutory law, but also judicial and textbook law.[191] The conflicting views of courts and writers must be weighed according to the relative authority attached by the foreign law to the various sources.[192]

If all efforts to ascertain the applicable foreign law fail, the courts usually decide the point against the party relying on it.[193] It has been suggested by legal writers that they should search instead for the most closely related system of law, or apply the *lex fori.*[194]

(iii) Review of the application of foreign law does not as in many countries depend upon its qualification as "fact" or "law." In civil matters at least, a first appeal can always be based on a violation of the applicable foreign law.[195] The matter is different on the second appeal. In civil litigation, a second appeal may be based only on a rule of "federal law" or on certain other special laws (§ 549 I ZPO). A similar provision limits second appeals in administrative matters. These norms have been understood literally as excluding a second appeal based on a violation of foreign law.[196] This is so even if the content of the foreign law is identical with that of German law,[197] or if another interpretation of the foreign law is urged under the guise of an attack on the insufficiency of the proof.[198] On the

---

[189] The certificate of a New York notary public on American law has been correctly declared irrelevant as long as his legal training has not been proved, OLG Darmstadt 27 May 1910, Hess.Rspr. 11 (1910/11) 100.

[190] American consuls would seem to be prohibited from giving legal information, *see* 22 C.F.R. § 92.81 (1970).

[191] BGH 29 Oct. 1962, NJW 1963, 252–53; 4 Feb. 1960, WM 1960, 374, 375; OLG Hamburg 5 May 1934, IPRspr. 1934 no. 3. Thus one court relied on the case of Schneider v. Rusk, 377 U.S. 163 (1964), in order to demonstrate that § 352 (a) I.N.S. is unconstitutional, BayObLG 6 Nov. 1967, BayObLGZ 1967, 418, 422.

[192] RG 14 Nov. 1929, RGZ 126, 196, 201; OLG Bremen 21 Aug. 1959, IPRspr. 1958/59 no. 7 A p. 752.

[193] BGH 24 Nov. 1960, NJW 1961, 410–11; OLG Bremen 21 Aug. 1959, IPRspr. 1958/59 no. 7 A pp. 753–54.

[194] *Most closely related system of law*: KEGEL, Kommentar no. 115 preceding art. 7 EGBGB, with references in nn. 82 and 83; RAAPE 123. *Lex fori*: RIEZLER 497–98.

[195] RIEZLER 502.

[196] *See,* e.g., BGH 21 Feb. 1962, BGHZ 36, 348, 350, 353–54; 19 Mar. 1958, BGHZ 27, 47, 49; BVerwG 10 May 1961, NJW 1961, 2225.

[197] BGH 29 Oct. 1962, NJW 1963, 252; 4 Feb. 1960, WM 1960, 374, 375 (both cases on the Geneva uniform bills of exchange law); BGH 13 July 1959, WM 1959, 1110 (German Commercial Code in Austria).

[198] BGH 4 Feb. 1960, *supra* n. 197; 5 May 1960, WM 1960, 717; 8 Nov.

other hand, there is no unauthorized review of foreign law where the first appellate court has not even considered foreign law. In this case the court of second appeal may itself apply the foreign law or may remand the case for its ascertainment by the first appellate court.[199] A similar situation exists where, after the decision of the first appellate court, a new foreign statute is enacted.[200]

A true judge-made exception to the exclusionary provision is presented where the foreign rule is a conflicts rule and its correct application would result in a renvoi to German law.[201] But in the related situation where the international jurisdiction of the German courts derives from the foreign law, for instance, upon recognition of a German divorce by the national law of a foreign husband (*see supra* ch. 4 sub A V (1)(b)), review of the foreign law has been refused![202] Another judge-made exception exists for second appeals in non-litigious matters; since these are not governed by § 549 ZPO, the courts have finally held that a second appeal may be based upon a violation of foreign law.[203]

(6) **Temporary Relief***

German law offers two mutually exclusive forms of temporary relief where no litigation is pending: attachment to secure a monetary claim, and a restraining order to secure some other performance (§§ 916 ff., 935 ff. ZPO). The first is the more important.

Attachment is justified if there is a danger that otherwise execution of the judgment to be rendered will be impossible or will become substantially more difficult. The fact that the judgment would have to be enforced abroad is a sufficient justification (§ 917 ZPO). The commonest example is attachment of a foreign ship in a German port to secure a claim against the foreign owner. It is unsettled whether the existence of an immovable in Germany of ample value to cover the judgment prevents attachment, at least where there is no

---

1951, BGHZ 3, 342, 346, 347. The attack is admissible if the lower courts neglected facts which under their interpretation of the foreign law are relevant, BGH 22 Nov. 1962, WM 1963, 196, 197; 8 Nov. 1951, *supra*.

[199] BGH 29 Feb. 1968, BGHZ 49, 384, 387; 23 Oct. 1963, BGHZ 40, 197, 200–01; 14 May 1959, IPRspr. 1960/61 no. 3, and 15 Nov. 1956, *id.* no. 1.

[200] BGH 21 Feb. 1962, BGHZ 36, 348, 351–56.

[201] BGH 2 May 1966, BGHZ 45, 351, 354–55; 5 June 1957, BGHZ 24, 352, 354; RG: 5 July 1934, RGZ 145, 85, 86; 2 June 1932, RGZ 136, 361, 362.

[202] BGH 19 Mar. 1958, BGHZ 27, 47, 49–51; *contra*: RG 24 Feb. 1936, RGZ 150, 293, 295.

[203] BGH 12 July 1965, BGHZ 44, 121, 127; 4 Mar. 1960, FamRZ 1960, 229, 230; OLG Düsseldorf 14 Nov. 1961, IPRspr. 1960/61 no. 113; KG Berlin 24 June 1937, JFG 16, 23, 28–29.

* See BAUR, Present German Practices in the Application for Temporary Relief, 14 Am. J. Comp. L. 247–65 (1965).

indication of the debtor's intention to sell; the better view would exclude attachment in this case.[204]

The nationality and domicile of the parties to the proceeding are irrelevant. Even claims of a foreign creditor against a foreign debtor may be secured.[205] Only if both parties are domiciled in the same country, the debtor has sufficient property there, and the creditor has already obtained a judgment there, will attachment in Germany be deemed unjustified.[206] The attachment order fixes the sum of money which the debtor must deposit before the attachment will be quashed (§ 923 ZPO). The posting of this security creates an asset of the debtor in Germany and thus confers jurisdiction upon the German courts to entertain a suit against him (§ 23 ZPO, *see supra* I (2)(a)).[207]

The duty of the court to ascertain a relevant foreign law is somewhat relaxed in these as in other urgent proceedings. If its proof would require considerable effort, the German *lex fori* may be applied.[208] However, in commercial matters the courts often demand that the applicant establish credibly the content of the foreign law; if he fails, temporary relief will be refused.[208a]

(7) Foreign Lis Pendens

If an action with the same object and between the same parties is pending in another court, having been commenced there earlier, a new action must be dismissed *ex officio* (*see* § § 263 II no. 1, 274 II no. 4 ZPO). It is firmly settled that this rule also covers prior proceedings in a foreign court, provided only that the ultimate foreign judgment presumably would be recognized in Germany.[209] The treatment of a foreign *lis pendens* thus depends entirely on the rules concerning recognition and enforcement of foreign judgments (*infra* (8)).

---

[204] RG 30 Oct. 1907, RGZ 67, 22, 26; KG Berlin 26 Sept. 1927, IPRspr. 1928 no. 104; LG Dortmund 26 Nov. 1929, JW 1930, 1887. *Contra*: OLG Darmstadt 21 Feb. 1928, IPRspr. 1928 no. 105; LG München 5 July 1928, JW 1928, 2881.

[205] OLG München 18 Sept. 1959, IPRspr. 1958/59 no. 199; OLG Stuttgart 19 May 1952, NJW 1952, 831; KG Berlin 26 Sept. 1927, *supra* n. 204.

[206] KG Berlin 24 June 1910, OLG 21, 93 and 23, 227; *see also* LG Düsseldorf 19 Sept. 1958, IPRspr. 1958/59 no. 197.

[207] *See* OLG Hamm 18 Feb. 1928, JW 1928, 2034.

[208] OLG Düsseldorf 19 Aug. 1965, FamRZ 1965, 616; KG Berlin 25 May 1936, JW 1936, 3577. *Cf. also supra* ch. 4 sub A V (1) (c), concerning provisional orders during a divorce suit.

[208a] OLG Hamm 11 Nov. 1969, AWD 1970, 31; OLG Frankfurt 7 Nov. 1968, NJW 1969, 991.

[209] RG 18 Mar. 1930, IPRspr. 1930 no. 36; OLG Hamburg 26 Feb. 1929, HRR 1929 no. 1393 (both disregarding prior instituted American proceedings); RG 25 Aug. 1938, RGZ 158, 145, 147. *See also* Oakland Truck Sales, Inc. v. United States, 149 F. Supp. 902 (Ct.Cl.1957) where American suit was stayed until determination of German suit between, in effect, the same parties.

Non-contentious civil proceedings have adopted the same principles to prevent conflicting decisions on the same issue. In cases of urgency, however, as in certain custody cases (*supra* ch. 4 sub B I (5)(b)(i)), an earlier foreign application should not bar a German court from acting, particularly as the German court could alter the foreign decree even though recognized in Germany (*supra* ch. 4 sub B I (5)(b)(iv)).

(8) **Recognition and Enforcement of Foreign Judgments***

One of the most crucial aspects of international procedure is the recognition and enforcement of foreign judgments. This problem will be treated here in its general aspects, with particular emphasis on money judgments. The special problems of recognition of divorce and alimony decrees were dealt with earlier (ch. 4 sub A V (3), B I (5)(d) and II (3)(c)).

(a) *General rules.*—The grounds for refusal of either recognition or enforcement of a foreign judgment are laid down in §§ 328 and 723 ZPO. With one exception, they are mandatory; no agreement of the parties can change them.[210] There are four generally applicable grounds, and two special grounds protecting German parties.

The general grounds are as follows:

First, where the state of rendition lacked international jurisdiction according to German law (§ 328 I no. 1 ZPO). Generally speaking, the German rules (*supra* I (2)) allow a court to take jurisdiction if there is a reasonable connection with the persons or the subject-matter of the litigation, which means more than mere service of process on a transient. Since the German rules are on the whole, with this one exception, more liberal than American rules, the jurisdictional requirement will not usually be an obstacle to the recognition of American judgments in Germany (*see also infra* (b)(i)). A difficulty may arise, on the other hand, because of the liberality with which the German courts uphold contractual clauses conferring

* Heidenberger, Similarities and Differences in the Enforcement of Foreign Decrees and Judgments in the Federal Republic of Germany and the United States, 33 Journal of the Bar Association of the District of Columbia 433–45 (1966); Mowitz, The Execution of Foreign Judgments in Germany, 81 U. Pa. L. Rev. 795–805 (1933); Deutsch, Die Anerkennung ausländischer Urteile in den Staaten der USA, ZZP 71 (1958) 321–39; Harder, Die Anerkennung und Vollstreckung deutscher Urteile . . . im Staate New York (diss. Frankfurt 1967); *id,* Vollstreckung deutscher Urteile in USA, insbesondere in New York, AWD 1963, 36–39; Aus der Schule der Diplomatie (1965) 508–18; Heidenberger, Vollstrekkung deutscher Urteile in den Vereinigten Staaten, N.J.W 1958, 1117–19; Krohn, Anerkennung und Durchsetzung deutscher Urteile sowie von Schiedsvereinbarungen und Schiedssprüchen in den USA, Monatsschrift der Vereinigung Deutscher Auslandsbeamten 26 (1963) 101–18; Peterson, Die Anerkennung ausländischer Urteile im amerikanischen Recht (Arbeiten zur Rechtsvergleichung no. 18, 1964).

[210] RG 22 Nov. 1895, RGZ 36, 381, 384–86.

exclusive jurisdiction upon a foreign court. If an American court, as it is apt to do (*supra* I (2) at n. 49), disregards a clause ousting its jurisdiction and proceeds to decide the case, the resulting American decision will be denied recognition and enforcement in Germany[210a];

Second, where recognition of the foreign judgment would run counter to German public policy (§ 328 I no. 4 ZPO). Applications of this exclusionary provision are rare. A serious violation of due process or a fraud on the foreign court would qualify[211]; so would a foreign decision disregarding the German rules on foreign exchange and posing a threat to the German foreign exchange market,[212] or a decision violating other basic statutory regulations.[213] Recognition of a contradictory foreign judgment is also excluded if there has been an earlier German decision involving the same subject-matter and the same parties.[214] Not only do these applications of German public policy demonstrate great restraint, but most of them correspond to specific grounds found in American law for non-recognition of foreign judgments (*see infra* (b)(i));

Third, where reciprocity is lacking (§ 328 I no. 5 ZPO). This requirement is dispensed with for non-pecuniary cases under certain circumstances (§ 328 II ZPO). The requirement of reciprocity is actually the largest single obstacle to the recognition of foreign judgments, although recent decisions of the Federal Supreme Court have been considerably more liberal in interpreting it (*infra* sub (b));

Fourth, where the foreign judgment, according to the law of the foreign court, is no longer subject to appeal. This is expressly spelt out as a prerequisite for the German judgment of execution (§ 723 II 1 ZPO, *see infra*), but it obtains as well for mere recognition.[214a]

In addition to these four general grounds the law has established two special grounds for the protection of German parties:

First, where the losing German defendant in the foreign proceeding failed to receive proper notice. Proper notice requires personal service of legal process in the foreign state or elsewhere through German judicial assistance (*see supra* II (3)(a)), unless the German defendant appeared (generally or even specially[215]) in the foreign proceeding (§ 328 I no. 2 ZPO). Thus an Ohio divorce decree was

---

[210a] BGH 26 Mar. 1969, BGHZ 52, 30 (American buyer had brought counterclaim against German seller's suit in New York, although buyer was obliged under seller's conditions to bring all claims in German court; New York judgment not enforced in Germany).

[211] WIECZOREK II 1, no. E IV b 2 on § 328 ZPO.

[212] BGH 11 Oct. 1956, BGHZ 22, 24, 29–31; KG Berlin 6 Dec. 1955, IPRspr. 1954/55 no. 186.

[213] *German antitrust law*: KG 6 Dec. 1955, *supra* n. 212.

[214] RG 12 May 1915, JW 1915, 1264; *see also* BGH 15 Nov. 1967, BGHZ 49, 50, 55.

[214a] RIEZLER 531.

[215] RG 21 Apr. 1891, JW 1891, 272.

refused recognition where a certified copy of the plaintiff American husband's summons was mailed by the court to the local German consulate which in turn passed it on informally to the defendant German wife residing in Germany.[216] Since this protective clause was established exclusively for the defendant's protection,[217] he must invoke it expressly;

Second, where the foreign judgment violated a German conflicts rule relating to the personal status of a German (§ 328 I no. 3 ZPO). Although this provision is aimed at the recognition of foreign judgments and decrees relating to personal status (*cf. supra* ch. 4 sub A V (3)(b)(iii), B III (4), C (1)(d)(iv) and (5)(c), and *infra* (d) at n. 254), it may occasionally, on incidental points, become relevant in other cases as well.

The effect of recognition is determined by the legal consequences which the law of the foreign forum attaches to its judgment.[218] Thus the collateral estoppel attached to a judgment by most American jurisdictions will probably operate in Germany also.[219] The simple recognition of the res judicata effect of a foreign judgment does not require any German proceeding, but possible doubts may be settled by a (positive or negative) declaratory action, which follows the general rules governing this form of action.[220] Enforcement, on the other hand, necessitates a so-called judgment of execution (*Vollstreckungsurteil,* § 722 I ZPO), pronouncing the enforceability of the foreign judgment; this may be restricted to portions of the foreign judgment, especially the enforceable aspects of an otherwise unenforceable judgment, such as the provisions for alimony or costs in a divorce decree.[221] The German court must ascertain that there are no objections to recognition; but it may not examine the "legality" —meaning the merits—of the foreign decision (§ 723 I and II 2). The defendant may raise defenses against the original claim arising

---

[216] RG 15 June 1936, JW 1936, 2456. The court rightly held that this procedure (prescribed by Ohio law) was not service through German judicial assistance; the latter would have required in this case a request to a German court.

[217] WIECZOREK II 1, no. E II a on § 328 ZPO; BAUMBACH/LAUTERBACH no. 3 C on § 328 ZPO.

[218] RG 17 May 1929, IPRspr. 1929 no. 151; OLG Saarbrücken 9 Dec. 1957, NJW 1958, 1046.

[219] In investigating the prospective recognition in the United States of German divorce decrees to be rendered against American citizens (as a condition for the assumption of German jurisdiction, § 606 b no. 1 ZPO), the German courts have already evaluated the actions of the parties according to the American rules of estoppel, *see supra* ch. 4 sub A V (1) (b) at n. 139.

[220] RG 5 Jan. 1925, RGZ 109, 383, 385–86, and 31 Oct. 1941, RGZ 167, 373, 380–81. On the technicalities of such a declaratory action, nothing need be said here.

[221] RG 5 Jan. 1925, RGZ 109, 383, 386–87.

too late to be raised in the foreign proceeding.[222] If they arise after the German judgment of execution has been rendered, a separate action must be brought, according to the general rule of § 767 ZPO, against the carrying out of the judgment of execution.[223] Here again, a negative declaratory action may be brought by the judgment debtor, while the creditor usually will not be permitted under the German rules of procedure to bring an action for a positive declaration instead of the statutory action for execution (*see supra* at n. 220). Venue for the action of execution lies initially at the debtor's domicile or residence in Germany; failing these, venue lies at any place in Germany where the debtor has assets (§ 722 II ZPO; *see* § 23 ZPO, *supra* I (2)). Since the only purpose of this proceeding is enforcement of the foreign judgment, a decision dismissing this action is not res judicata against a new action in Germany based not on the foreign judgment but on the underlying claim.[224]

(b) *Reciprocity.*—The most recent cases construing § 328 I no. 5 ZPO assume the existence of reciprocity where the recognition and enforcement of German judgments abroad do not meet with difficulties essentially greater than the obstacles imposed by Germany in the converse situation. Partial reciprocity suffices, meaning reciprocity for the particular class of judgment at issue. It is not necessary that the foreign rules be identical with the German rules but merely, if looked at as a whole, that they be essentially equivalent; a negative factor in one respect may be compensated for by a positive factor in another.[225]

Comparison with American rules is complicated both by the diversity from state to state and the lack of statutory enactments. Each jurisdiction must of course be regarded separately.[226] Somewhat outdated statutory rules of general application exist in California, Montana, New Jersey, and Oregon; these are supplemented by rules on incidental matters, such as the period of limitation for suits on

---

[222] RG 25 June 1926, RGZ 114, 171, 173.

[223] Venue is with the German court that rendered that judgment, RG 21 Jan. 1941, RGZ 165, 374, 379–83.

[224] LG München I 14 June 1962, IPRspr. 1962/63 no. 128.

[225] BGH 30 Sept. 1964, BGHZ 42, 194, 196–97; *see also* BGH 15 Nov. 1967, BGHZ 49, 50, 53; 8 May 1968, BGHZ 50, 100 and 103; 9 July 1969, WM 1969, 1090.

[226] *Expressly*: KG Berlin 2 Feb. 1962, IPRspr. 1962/63 no. 185; 14 Oct. 1932, JW 1932, 3822 (Nevada divorce of German couple domiciled in New York not recognized); OLG Colmar 13 Nov. 1908, Rhein.Z 1 (1909) 339–40, all representing the standing practice. *Contra*: only MENDELSSOHN-BARTHOLDY, Rhein.Z. 12 (1923) 202–03. When certain courts stated that reciprocity with the "United States" was lacking (RG 18 Mar. 1930, IPRspr. 1930 no. 36; OLG Hamburg 26 Feb. 1929, HRR 1929 no. 1393), this was probably meant as a shorthand expression for all the states of the Union. *But see also infra* n. 260.

foreign judgments or their authentication.[227] A modern and complete set of rules is available only in those seven states that have adopted the Uniform Foreign Money-Judgments Recognition Act of 1962, namely, California, Illinois, Maryland, Massachusetts, Michigan, New York[227a] and Oklahoma. In the other states, case law must be relied upon.[228] The following examination will be based primarily on the provisions of the Uniform Act, with side glances at the law of other American jurisdictions. While there are not yet any cases construing the Act, the Act is itself based largely on prior case law.

(i) *Uniform Act.*—The Act, which is inapplicable to claims for support, taxes, or fines (§ 1 (2)), enumerates ten grounds on which recognition must be or may be denied. The compulsory grounds are:

—Non-finality or non-enforceability of the foreign judgment according to the law of the court of decision (§ 2). Finality means that the judgment must not be subject to amendment by the rendering court; the possibility or pendency of an appeal is irrelevant, as § 2 itself says. However, according to § 6, the proceedings may be stayed if an appeal is pending or the defendant satisfies the court that he is entitled and intends to appeal from the foreign judgment. German law goes even further, requiring not only finality but also expiration of the right to appeal.[229] Enforceability is not expressly demanded by German law, but it is a necessary attribute of judgments to pay money and is implied in the requirement of non-appealability;

—Partiality of the tribunal or lack of due process (§ 4 (a)(1)). These two general grounds for non-recognition are clearly covered in Germany by the public policy clause of § 328 I no. 4 ZPO;[230]

—Lack of personal jurisdiction over the defendant (§ 4 (a)(2)). The Uniform Act itself enumerates various bases of personal jurisdiction any of which suffices for purposes of recognition; these bases not only reflect the current trend toward broadening personal jurisdiction, but they are also expressly stated not to be exclusive (§ 5 (b)). In the framework of our inquiry, however, we merely have to satisfy ourselves that these grounds are no narrower than the rules creating German jurisdiction (*supra* I (2)), and this is certainly true of personal service (§ 5 (a)(1)); of submission (§ 5 (a)(3)); of domicile, or place of incorporation or principal place of business of a legal entity (§ 5 (a)(4)); of business office coupled with a claim arising

---

[227] Rules with respect to the first question are to be found in Florida, Georgia, Kentucky, Louisiana, Nebraska, Virginia and West Virginia, and with respect to the second question in Iowa, Louisiana, Vermont, *etc.*

[227a] Adopted 19 May 1970, effective 1 Sept. 1970, by L. 1970 ch. 981, which added art. 53 to the Civil Practice Law and Rules.

[228] *See* the helpful tabulation *in* PETERSON 107–48 and 20 n. 47.

[229] BGH 30 Sept. 1964, BGHZ 42, 194, 199, 200 (finality of South African judgment).

[230] BGH 30 Sept. 1964, *supra* note 229, at 202.

out of business done through that office (§ 5 (a)(5)); and of a claim arising from the operation of a motor vehicle or airplane in the foreign state (§ 5 (a)(6)).[231] Section 5 (a)(2) mentions voluntary appearance in the proceedings by the defendant, unless limited to protecting property seized or threatened with seizure or to contesting the court's jurisdiction The former alternative has an exact equivalent in § 39 ZPO, but the latter is narrower than § 23 ZPO which creates jurisdiction on the mere basis of the location of assets of the defendant in Germany (*supra* I (2)(a)); however, since recognition abroad of German decisions rendered in this "improper" forum is not expected (*supra* I (2)(a), text following n. 43), the divergence between German and American jurisdictional rules on this particular point is innocuous.[232] It follows from the foregoing that the expressly admitted bases of foreign jurisdiction, with one unimportant exception, are no narrower than the corresponding German fora. The provision of the Uniform Act that the American courts may also recognize other bases of jurisdiction (§ 5 (b)), need not concern us as long as there is not sufficient case law to indicate the existence of such additional bases in German law. Of potentially greater importance for money judgments might be the additional fora of place of performance of a contract (§ 29 ZPO) and place of commission of a tort (§ 32 ZPO), but the Federal Supreme Court has specifically held that these two jurisdictional bases are considered undesirable and therefore do not prevent reciprocity even though German judgments rendered at these fora will not be recognized abroad;[233]

—Lack of jurisdiction over the subject matter (§ 4 (a)(3)). This is not defined in detail, but the rules on jurisdiction in rem and quasi in rem affecting interests in things are included. (Rules relating to status are irrelevant here.) Thus Mr. Justice Story while sitting as a circuit judge in 1838 recognized a decision of the marine court of Hamburg arising from a collision on the Elbe river between an American boat and a German boat; conclusive effect was given to the determination of the German court as to the cause and amount of the loss, and the contribution based on the

---

[231] § 5 (a) (1), (3)–(6) Uniform Act. The first case has no German equivalent; for (3), *see* §§ 38, 40 ZPO and *supra* sub I (2) (b); for (4), *see* §§ 13, 16 and 19 ZPO and *supra* I (2) (a); for (5), *see* § 21 ZPO and *supra* I (2) (a); for (6), *see* §§ 32 ZPO, 20 StVG, 56 I LuftVG, BGBl. III 96–1.

[232] BGH, *supra* n. 229, at 200.

Even if reciprocity exists in general, an American judgment rendered on the basis of defendant's assets in an American jurisdiction will not be recognized in Germany, because a corresponding German decision also would not be recognized, BGH 9 July 1969, WM 1969, 1090, 1091–92.

[233] BGH, *supra* n. 229. However, § 32 ZPO is not entirely inconsistent with the Uniform Act, *see* § 5 (a) (6) and *supra* n. 231.

rules of general average to be made by the two ships.[234] For the most important class of "real" actions, § 24 ZPO also provides that actions relating to "real" rights in immovables have to be brought exclusively at the *forum rei sitae*. That Germany does not provide a corresponding forum for movables is irrelevant from the standpoint of reciprocity.

As for optional grounds for denial of recognition, the Uniform Act lists the following:

—Lack of notice to the defendant in sufficient time for his defense (§ 4 (b)(1)). The requirement of notice is essentially that of § 328 I no. 2 ZPO, although the latter protects only Germans (*see supra* (a)). But § 328 I no. 4 supplies the additional protection of due process, without the limitation to Germans (*see supra* n. 211). Thus service by "publication" will not suffice. This form of service, however, is of the most subsidiary class and therefore used only rarely. Moreover, recognition of judgments based on this kind of service is not expected in Germany (*supra* (3)(a)(iii)). The Uniform Act introduces one additional element lacking in German law, namely, sufficiency of time for defense. This, however, is merely an additional refinement that does not go to the heart of the notice requirement;

—Fraud in the procurement of the foreign judgment (§ 4 (b)(2)). Under German law this obstacle is clearly taken care of by the general public policy clause in § 328 I no. 4 ZPO;[235]

—Contravention of public policy by the claim adjudicated (§ 4 (b)(3)). Public policy in this context is limited to objections to the subject matter of the foreign adjudication, while procedural flaws have been singled out in a number of separate clauses. Existing case law permits the conclusion that the American courts rarely invoke substantive public policy;[236]

—Incompatibility between the foreign judgment and another final and conclusive decision of the American forum (§ 4 (b)(4)). In this situation Germany invokes its public policy (*supra* (a) at n. 214);

—Disregard of an agreement of the parties designating another forum, in the widest sense of the word, for the settlement of their dispute (§ 4 (b)(5)). This case would be covered under German law by the plea of lack of jurisdiction (§ 328 I no. 1 ZPO, in connection with §§ 38 and 40 ZPO);

---

[234] Peters v. Warren Insurance Co., 19 F. Cas. 373 (No. 11,035) (C.C.D. Mass. 1838). Another point certified by the Circuit Court was settled by the Supreme Court, speaking again through Mr. Justice Story, in Peters v. Warren Insurance Co., 39 U.S. (14 Pet.) 99 (1840).

[235] BGH, *supra* n. 229, at 204–05; *see also supra* n. 211.

[236] *See* PETERSON 18, 97–100; *see also* BGH, *supra* n. 229, at 203–04.

—In the case of jurisdiction based only on personal service, the serious inconvenience of the foreign forum (§ 4 (b)(6)). Since German law does not base jurisdiction on service alone (*supra* I (2)(a)), the plea of *forum non conveniens* cannot apply to German judgments.

One final procedural difference must be mentioned: American law generally does not use the form of the German "action for execution" (*supra* (a)), but requires a separate new action on the judgment. However, this procedural, formal difference does not make execution more difficult and therefore is irrelevant for purposes of reciprocity.[237]

The foregoing comparison shows the almost complete equivalence of the Uniform Act and the German rules on recognition. I conclude therefore that for money judgments reciprocity exists with those American jurisdictions that have adopted the Act.[238] Earlier German decisions denying reciprocity, sometimes on untenable grounds, have lost their persuasive value.[239]

(ii) *Other jurisdictions.*—It is incomparably more difficult to determine whether reciprocity exists with other American jurisdictions. This is due to the scarcity of the relevant case law, most of which relates to matrimonial actions and which does not reveal whether the conditions for recognition are more stringent than the four requirements of § 328 ZPO. Uncertainty stems particularly from the rapid evolution of the "American" rules on personal jurisdiction, whose impact on the rules on recognition is as yet unknown.

The statutes of Montana and Oregon contain express language excluding reciprocity in cases of personal jurisdiction, by providing (following the Field Code) that the presumed right established by a foreign judgment may be overcome *inter alia* by evidence of a "clear mistake of law or fact."[240] The reexamination of the merits

---

237 BGH, *supra* n. 229, at 205.

238 On California, *see also infra* (ii). Massachusetts adds one important feature to the Uniform Act: in the provision corresponding to § 4 (b) of the Uniform Act an additional clause (7) requires reciprocity with the foreign state (ch. 235 § 23 A (3) (7) Annotated Laws of Massachusetts). Such an additional reciprocity requirement does not prevent assumption of reciprocity by Germany if the conditions are otherwise fulfilled, *see, impliedly,* BGH 15 Nov. 1967, BGHZ 49, 50, 51.

239 Reciprocity with California had been denied by RG 26 Mar. 1909, RGZ 70, 434, *see infra* n. 241. Reciprocity with Illinois had been denied by OLG Hamburg 27 May 1914, OLG 29, 181, but affirmed by KG Berlin 3 May 1935, JW 1935, 2570. The same is true of the general denial of reciprocity for all the United States by STEIN/JONAS/SCHÖNKE no. VIII E 53. WIECZOREK II/1, no. E Vb on § 328 ZPO, erroneously deduces reciprocity vis-à-vis the federal courts (?) from art. VI of the American-German Friendship Treaty of 1954 (Treaties B 117).

240 Repl. vol. 7, Revised Codes of Montana, 1947, § 93–1001–27 sub 2; Oregon Revised Statutes § 43.190 sub (2) (1967 repl. pt.).

thus implied is incompatible with § 328 ZPO and therefore excludes reciprocity in cases of personal jurisdiction.[241]

California formerly had the same rule as Montana and Oregon but amended it after the earthquake in 1907, apparently in order to establish reciprocity with Germany for suits against German insurance companies.[242] However, this amendment was not honored in Germany.[243] In connection with the enactment of the Uniform Foreign Money-Judgments Recognition Act, the provision was again amended in 1967 to make clear that it now applies only in cases not covered by the Uniform Act. Sections 1915 through 1917 of the Code of Civil Procedure lay down the following requisites for recognition: finality of the foreign judgment; jurisdiction of the foreign court, according to its own law and California law; and absence of collusion between the parties or fraud by the party invoking the judgment. The dual requirement with respect to jurisdiction, as revised in 1907, was interpreted in Germany as authorizing the California court to examine not only the international jurisdiction and local venue of the foreign court, but also its functional competence, and this was regarded as a reexamination of the merits, excluding reciprocity.[244] However, the California cases do not bear out this interpretation. The courts appear never to have checked a foreign court's jurisdiction according to its own rules, not to mention its functional competence. Moreover, the German Federal Supreme Court has held recently that a requirement of this kind usually amounts to a mere formality constituting no obstacle to reciprocity.[245] As for personal jurisdiction of the California courts in cases not covered by the Uniform Act, the grounds[246] are very similar to the catalogue of § 5 of the Uniform Act. The Federal Supreme Court has expressly affirmed reciprocity with South Africa, whose jurisdictional rules are based on the common law,[247] and this permits the conclusion that reciprocity exists with California also.[247a]

New Jersey's statutory rule on the recognition of foreign judgments applies in terms both to sister-state and foreign judgments.[248] It

---

241 PETERSON 104. *See also* RG 26 Mar. 1909, RGZ 70, 434, 435 on the original version of § 1915 California Code of Civil Procedure that had been identical with the provisions of Montana and Oregon.

242 § 1915 California Code of Civil Procedure, as amended 1907 (West 1955).

243 RG 26 Mar. 1909, RGZ 70, 434 denied reciprocity. *See* the bitter comment of the State Department *in* 2 HACKWORTH 88. Dealing with and criticizing this case and its background, *see* WITTMAACK, NiemeyersZ. 22 (1912) 1–121; *see also* FELLER, JW 1931, 112–14.

244 RG, *supra* n. 243, at 435–36.

245 BGH 15 Nov. 1967, BGHZ 49, 50, 51–55, especially 54.

246 *See, generally,* 1 WITKIN, California Procedure (1954) §§ 53–92.

247 BGH 30 Sept. 1964, BGHZ 42, 194, 198, 199–200.

247a *Accord*: SCHUMANN/LEIPOLD *in* STEIN/JONAS/SCHÖNKE/POHLE (19th ed. 1969), no. VIII D on § 328 ZPO.

248 New Jersey Statutes Annotated (1952) 2A:82–4.

expressly empowers the person affected by such a judgment to impeach it by showing that despite recitations to the contrary the defendant was not within the jurisdiction of the other court, was not summoned and did not appear. Of the various objections advanced against foreign judgments,[249] four—fraud, inadequate notice, absence of due process, and violation of public policy—are identical with provisions of the Uniform Act and therefore need not be discussed here. Lack of personal jurisdiction is also a replica of the Uniform Act, although the bases of jurisdiction are conceived differently. In addition, the New Jersey courts have refused recognition on the grounds that a prior action was pending in New Jersey, and that the six-year statute for ordinary contract obligations had run.[250] While the first of these grounds is not a serious deviation, the second constitutes a considerable restriction, and it follows that reciprocity with New Jersey exists merely for a period of six years after adjudication.

Indiana lacks any legislative provision on the subject, and it may be presumed that it follows the common law requirements. This presumption is confirmed by an unreported decision in an action brought in a federal district court sitting in Indiana for damages for injuries suffered in an accident in Hanau, Germany, in 1960.[251] Defendant pleaded in bar a German negative declaratory judgment rendered in 1962 and affirmed in 1963 between the same parties at the defendant's instance. Both parties were American citizens who were stationed in Germany at the time of the accident and of the German suit. The American court found that the German judgment was final, that the German court had jurisdiction over the parties and the subject matter, and that the defendant had had a full and fair trial. The judgment was recognized.

Like Indiana, Pennsylvania lacks any statutory provision and the case law is scarce, but apparently the general common law requirements are followed.[252] Proof of this assumption is an old decision of a county court awarding judgment to plaintiff in an action on a German money judgment. The court said: ". . . [O]ur courts never go into the merits, when the record of the foreign judgment shows on its face that the court rendering it had jurisdiction of the parties."[253] Apparently both parties resided in Germany when the German decision was rendered.

New York until 1970 had no statute on the subject, but it had a

---

249 Ernster, Recognition and Enforcement of Foreign Money Judgments, 22 Rutgers L. Rev. 327, 336–40 (1968).

250 Ernster, *supra* n. 249, at 339–40.

251 Powell v. Hand (N.D. Ind., Ft. Wayne Div., 1965, Civil no. 1527).

252 *See In re* Estate of Christoff, 411 Pa. 419, 192 A.2d 737 (1963), *cert. denied*, 375 U.S. 965 (1964).

253 Weiseberger v. Nevil, 11 Pa. County Ct. 40, 41 (1892).

body of case law in which the courts had evolved the following prerequisites for recognition: finality of the foreign judgment; jurisdiction of the foreign court; absence of fraud; due process; and compliance with public policy.[254] These conditions were largely identical with those of the Uniform Act. Only the jurisdictional requirement needs to be examined here. Where jurisdiction of the New York courts was concerned, §§ 301 and 302 of the Civil Practice Law and Rules, effective in 1963, applied. The first provision merely retained in force the earlier uncodified law which required domicile of the defendant within the jurisdiction of the court, personal service upon him, or his general appearance.[255] To these traditional bases § 302 added three important new ones: transaction of any business within the state; commission of a tort within the state, or without the state in certain circumstances; and ownership, use or possession of any real property within the state (§ 302). These new bases of jurisdiction were wider than the corresponding grounds in the Uniform Act; this means that New York law had come even closer to German law than has the Act. The conclusion that reciprocity exists in New York,[255a] and existed even before 1963, is borne out by New York cases recognizing or enforcing German judgments and decisions. In one, an award of a German institutional arbitration board was treated as emanating from a court of record and was recognized as final and enforceable, both parties residing at the time in Germany and having submitted to the board.[256] In another, an award of a German administrative authority demanding repayment of fraudulently obtained indemnification was recognized on the ground that the American-domiciled defendant, by applying for the indemnification, had submitted to German jurisdiction for all subsequent stages of the proceeding; due process was not violated since, although not heard on the issue of revocation, he had had ample time to contest it in court; nor was public policy offended since this was not a vindication of a public right but merely the restoration of an outlay wrongfully obtained.[257] German money judgments have also been enforced in two other reported cases.[258] The only

---

[254] *See*, e.g., Cowans v. Ticonderoga Pulp & Paper Co., 219 App. Div. 120, 121, 122, 219 N.Y. Supp. 284, 286, *aff'd*, 246 N.Y. 603, 159 N.E. 669 (1927). *See, further*, publications by HARDER.

[255] *See* WEINSTEIN/KORN/MILLER, New York Civil Practice (1966—) vol. 1, paras. 301.11–301.16.

[255a] *Accord*: SCHUMANN/LEIPOLD, *supra* n. 247a

[256] Coudenhove-Kalergi v. Dieterle, 36 N.Y.S.2d 313, 316–17 (Sup. Ct. 1942). The award was also recognized as an arbitral award, at 317–18.

[257] Regierungspraesident Land Nordrhein-Westfalen v. Rosenthal, 30 Misc.2d 768, 219 N.Y.S.2d 431 (Sup. Ct. 1961), *aff'd*, 17 A.D.2d 145, 232 N.Y.S.2d 963 (1962).

[258] Berliner Industriebank A.G. v. Remington Records, Inc., N.Y.L.J. Oct. 8, 1959, p. 13 col. 7 (Sup. Ct.); Stein v. Friedman, N.Y.L.J. Feb. 21, 1945, p. 691 col. 8 (City Ct.).

known case refusing enforcement of such a judgment fits into the picture: A German resident brought suit in Germany against his compatriot who had emigrated to New York on a debt created before the emigration; the defendant was served by publication and did not appear in the German proceeding; refusal of recognition was the unavoidable consequence,[259] citizenship alone being held insufficient to create jurisdiction.

Despite the foregoing, German court practice has so far usually denied reciprocity with New York, mostly on grounds that were not, or at least are no longer, tenable.[260] One court understood New York law as refusing recognition of a judgment by default where the defendant, although served personally, fails to appear generally or at least to plead in a personal writing to the merits of the case. The German court drew the conclusion that reciprocity for all money judgments had to be denied.[261] The first reason it gave, however, is wrong,[262] and the second has been superseded.[263] The only published German case that has considered the problem since initiation of the new liberal doctrine of the Federal Supreme Court has affirmed the existence of reciprocity in New York.[264]

(c) *Effects of unrecognized judgments.*—Even if a foreign judgment is denied recognition because it does not comply with the requirements of § 328 ZPO, this does not mean that it is without any legal effect in Germany. A new adjudication is required. It is not hampered by any such doctrine as merger; and even an agreement between the parties conferring exclusive competence upon the foreign court does not prevent the bringing of the new action in Germany at the defendant's private or business domicile or at

---

259 Grubel v. Nassauer, 210 N.Y. 149, 103 N.E. 1113 (1913).

260 LG Detmold 2 Aug. 1930, IPRspr. 1930 no. 152, relying on German cases, most of which denied reciprocity vis-à-vis other American states. KG Berlin 2 Feb. 1962, IPRspr. 1962/63 no. 185; 22 Oct. 1963, *id.* no. 196, both relying inter alia on the possibility of attacking foreign judgments on the ground of fraud. This objection had been superseded by the subsequent decisions of the Federal Supreme Court, *supra* n. 229.

Reciprocity had been found in the old decision, Oberappellationsgericht Jena, Blätter für Rechtspflege in Thüringen und Anhalt 19 (1872) 72.

261 KG Berlin, *supra* n. 260, invoking Bülow/Arnold E 991.97 for the latter argument.

262 Peterson 91 n. 340, noting expressly that American courts have recognized foreign default judgments, provided the foreign court had personal jurisdiction. One positive example from among the New York cases on American-German relations is Regierungspraesident Land Nordrhein-Westfalen v. Rosenthal, *supra* n. 257; a negative example is Grubel v. Nassauer, *supra* n. 259.

263 According to the extended divisibility doctrine of the Federal Supreme Court, *see supra* n. 225.

264 LG Hamburg 29 Aug. 1968, 13 O 156/66, unreported. *See also* Wieczorek II/1, no. E V b on § 328 ZPO, asserting reciprocity with New York, but on the inconclusive ground that enforcement is possible there by an action on the judgment.

any other statutory venue (*see supra* I (2)), if the parties did not contemplate enforcement in the foreign forum or if enforcement is possible only in Germany (*supra* I (2)(b) at nn. 35 and 36). In this new action in Germany the plaintiff may use the foreign judgment as proof of the facts determined abroad,[265] and also of the law applied if the foreign court applied its own law and this law is also applicable according to the German conflicts rule.[266] The faith accorded the foreign judgment depends on the conduct of the foreign proceeding, especially on the care invested in the finding of facts and on the persuasiveness of the legal rules applied.[267]

An unrecognized foreign judgment cannot interrupt the running of the statute of limitations if German law governs (*supra* ch. 8 sub III (3)).[268] But if foreign law governs, and that law attributes an interruptive effect to the bringing of an action or the rendering of a judgment, then the foreign action or judgment, even if not recognized in Germany, will still serve to interrupt the running of the German statute of limitations.[269]

It has also been held that the costs of a foreign judicial proceeding resulting in an unrecognized judgment may be made the object of a new suit in Germany. The courts base the claim for compensation for these costs either on the procedural law of the foreign forum which granted the compensation or on the underlying legal relationship of the parties.[270]

(d) *Non-contentious proceedings.*—No statutory provision states under what circumstances foreign decrees in non-contentious civil proceedings have to be recognized in Germany. For special cases, such as legitimacy and illegitimacy, adoption, guardianship, declaration of death, and succession, the problem of recognition has already been dealt with. There are, however, some principles which apply generally:

(i) Characterization of the foreign proceeding as contentious or non-contentious is decided under German concepts;

(ii) The rules of § 328 ZPO (*supra* sub (a)) do not apply to

---

[265] RG 8 July 1930, RGZ 129, 385, 387; OLG Celle 4 Jan. 1963, IPRspr. 1962/63 no. 207; OLG Hamburg 12 May 1933, IPRspr. 1933 no. 102.

[266] RG and OLG Celle, *supra* n. 265; LG Detmold, *supra* n. 260 (New York decree for (separation and) payment of support regarded as "source of law").

[267] *See* remark in RG 8 July 1930, *supra* n. 265, about the elaborate and careful finding of facts in the unrecognized Norwegian judgment, and OLG Celle, *supra* n. 265, emphasizing the elaborate reasoning of the unrecognized Lebanese judgment.

[268] RG 8 July 1930, *supra* n. 265, at 388–90, especially 389; RG 18 Sept. 1925, JW 1926, 374.

[269] BGH 30 June 1964, WM 1964, 879; OLG Celle, *supra* n. 265; OLG Breslau 19 Dec. 1938, JW 1939, 344.

[270] OLG Bremen 29 Nov. 1957, IPRspr. 1958/59 no. 187; OLG Hamburg 12 May 1933, *supra* n. 265; LG München I 2 Nov. 1956, NJW 1957, 878; *see also* BGH 30 June 1964, *supra* n. 269.

recognition of a decree in a non-contentious foreign civil proceeding;[271]

(iii) The foreign decree must be valid and final according to the foreign *lex fori;* if the *lex fori,* under German conflicts rules, differs from the *lex causae,* then the decree must comply with the *lex causae*;[272]

(iv) The foreign state must have had international jurisdiction according to German principles. This means, in short, that Germany must not have had exclusive international jurisdiction and that the foreign state must have had reasonably close contacts with the matter in issue;[273]

(v) The foreign decisional authority must have reached a result no less favorable to a German party than the result which would have followed application of the German conflicts provisions mentioned in § 328 I no. 3 ZPO;[274]

(vi) The foreign decree will not be recognized if it contravenes German public policy;[275]

(vii) Reciprocity is not required for recognition of a decree in a foreign non-contentious proceeding;[276]

(viii) If the foreign decree cannot be recognized in Germany, it must be determined in each individual case whether it may be validated by subsequent court action in Germany.[277]

(9) **Costs**

According to German law, the losing party has to bear all costs of a judicial proceeding. In particular, it must reimburse the "necessary" costs incurred by the winner of the lawsuit (§ 91 ZPO). These rules obtain in favor of foreigners residing abroad; it is immaterial if the foreigner would have a similar claim under his own law or rather, as in the United States, if reimbursement of the winner's costs is generally refused.[278]

Except in simple cases, the courts have usually held that a foreigner residing abroad was entitled to use the services of local counsel or trusted German counsel to cooperate with the German attorney

---

[271] BayObLG 18 Dec. 1968, BayObLGZ 1968, 331, 335; DÖLLE, *supra* n. 61, at 235; KEIDEL no. 55 on § 33 FGG.

[272] BayObLG 18 Dec. 1968, *supra* n. 271, at 335; DÖLLE, *supra* n. 61, at 236–38.

[273] E.g., BGH 7 Dec. 1955, BGHZ 19, 240, 243–44; KEIDEL no. 56 on § 33 FGG.

[274] *Cf.*, e.g., *supra* ch. 4 sub B III (4).

[275] E.g., OLG Köln 13 July 1962, FamRZ 1964, 466, 469; KEIDEL no. 55 on § 33 FGG.

[276] DÖLLE, *supra* n. 61 at 238; KEIDEL no. 55 on § 33 FGG. The courts do not even mention the question of reciprocity.

[277] As to foreign adoption decrees, *cf. supra* ch. 4 sub B III (4).

[278] OLG Schleswig 8 May 1959, IPRspr. 1960/61 no. 209.

representing the party before the court.[279] This is so as long as questions of fact or of foreign law are at issue.[280] In the case of Americans, it has also been pointed out that a trip by the client to confer with his attorney, to which any party in a complicated case is entitled, would usually be more expensive than the fee of an American lawyer.[281] If testimony is taken in the United States, attendance by American counsel is always held justified.[282] The amount of the fee of the foreign attorney is determined by the statutory or customary rules obtaining at the place where his office is located.[283] Since there is no fixed schedule and the American standard is considerably higher, the German courts usually require some assurance of the adequacy of the fee demanded.[284]

If the foreign party or counsel corresponds in his native language with the German attorney and neither understands the other's language, the costs of translating this correspondence are necessary and therefore must be borne by the losing party.[285]

Similar principles apply under § 13 c FGG with respect to costs incurred in non-contentious civil proceedings.

III. ARBITRATION*

The voluminous trade relations between the United States and Germany highlight questions of arbitration, since commercial parties

---

[279] OLG Frankfurt 15 Feb. 1963, NJW 1963, 961; KG Berlin 21 Dec. 1960, IPRspr. 1960/61 no. 215; OLG Schleswig, *supra* n. 278; LG Lübeck 28 Feb. 1962, IPRspr. 1962/63 no. 204. The last three decisions mentioned are American cases.

[280] But KG Berlin, *supra* n. 279, refused reimbursement of American counsel fees for an appellate proceeding since German counsel was by now sufficiently informed and could have corresponded directly with the American client.

[281] OLG Schleswig and LG Lübeck, *supra* n. 279.

[282] KG Berlin, *supra* n. 279; OLG Düsseldorf 25 Mar. 1959, IPRspr. 1958/59 no. 195.

[283] *See* cases cited *supra* n. 279, except the first.

[284] The courts accept an affidavit of the American attorney or an opinion of a German consul or a German expert on foreign law, *see* KG Berlin and LG Lübeck, *supra* n. 279; OLG Düsseldorf, *supra* n. 282.

[285] OLG Celle 12 Feb. 1960, NJW 1960, 1306; LG München I 13 Oct. 1960, IPRspr. 1960/61 no. 212.

* SCHWAB, The Legal Foundations and Limitations of Arbitration Procedures in the U.S. and Germany, *in* SANDERS, ed., International Arbitration. Liber Amicorum for Martin Domke (1967) 301–12; SCHOTTELIUS, Germany, *in* UNION INTERNATIONALE DES AVOCATS, Arbitrage International Commercial/International Commercial Arbitration (1956) vol. I, 35–59; GLOSSNER, German Federal Republic, *in id.* (1965) vol. III, 235–37; DOMKE, On the Enforcement Abroad of American Arbitration Awards, 17 Law & Contemp. Prob. 544, 557–65 (1952); KAHN, Arbitration in England and Germany, 12 J. Comp. Leg. & Int'l L. (3d ser.) 58–78, 228–47 (1930); BAUMBACH/SCHWAB, Schiedsgerichtsbarkeit (2d ed. 1960); KROHN, *supra* II (8) asterisked note; ARENDT, Die Vollstreckung privater deutscher Schiedssprüche in Handelssachen in den Vereinigten Staaten von Nordamerika

prefer this method for the settlement of their disputes. The United States, in contrast to Germany, is not yet a party to any of the important general conventions regulating private and commercial international arbitration.[285a] But agreed general rules exist in at least some bilateral treaties, and a specific class of arbitrations is covered by one multilateral convention. For the rest, recourse must be had to national sources.

(1) **Arbitral Clause**

(a) *Governing law.*—According to German concepts, the law applicable to the making, validity and interpretation of an arbitral clause is determined by the conflicts rules relating to contracts.[286] The parties are therefore free to choose the applicable law. Where no choice has been made, either expressly or tacitly, the center of gravity will be sought and, in the last analysis, the place of performance (*see supra* ch. 8 sub II (4)). As a rule the parties will subject the arbitral clause to the law governing their underlying legal relations, but this coincidence is not necessary[287] even if the arbitral clause is inserted in the body of the main contract.[288] Divisibility of the governing law for various issues accords with the general rules relating to contracts (*supra* ch. 8 sub II (1)). This doctrine would even permit the parties to subject the various aspects of the arbitral clause itself, such as making and validity, to different laws but, again, they will ordinarily want to choose only one law for their arbitral clause.[289] In any event, the legal system which is found to apply to the arbitral clause will govern, to the exclusion of any other law, even the law of one or both of the parties, the conclusion,[290] the validity[291] and the interpretation of the arbitral clause.[292]

---

und umgekehrt. (thesis Munich 1959); WALKER, Commercial Arbitration in United States Treaties, 11 Arb. J. 68–84 (1956); DOMKE, The Law and Practice of Commercial Arbitration (1968).

285a Although, effective 29 Dec. 1970, the United States ratified the U.N. Convention on the Recognition and Enforcement of Foreign Arbitral Awards (Treaties M 243 A), it has not been possible to take into account here the numerous changes occasioned by this event.

286 BGH 28 Nov. 1963, BGHZ 40, 320, 322; 28 June 1965, WM 1965, 1014; 20 May 1968, WM 1968, 803; 19 Dec. 1968, WM 1969, 216, 217; OLG Stuttgart 19 July 1962, IPRspr. 1962/63 no. 210; LG Bremen 24 Apr. 1952, IPRspr. 1954/55 no. 178.

287 BGH 28 Nov. 1963, *supra* n. 286, at 323; 19 Dec. 1968, *supra* n. 286.

288 BGH 28 Nov. 1963, *supra n.* 287.

289 BGH 19 Dec. 1968, *supra* n. 286.

290 OLG Stuttgart, *supra* n. 286.

291 BGH 19 Dec. 1968, *supra* n. 286; OLG Düsseldorf 12 Jan. 1961, IPRspr. 1960/61 no. 219.

292 OLG Hamburg 6 July 1961, IPRspr. 1960/61 no. 54 (American law decides whether reference in bill of lading to charter party includes arbitral clause contained therein).

Under common law and the older statutory law still in force in the majority of states of the United States, arbitral clauses relating to future controversies are freely revocable.[293] Moreover the American courts frequently determine the validity of such clauses by the *lex fori*. Thus any recognition of the binding character of an arbitral clause depends either upon the local arbitration law or the Federal Arbitration Act, where applicable.[294] Although the German courts are quite renvoi-prone, they should not, in passing upon a clause governed by "American" law, infer a tacit renvoi to the German *lex fori*.[295] It is at least doubtful whether the arbitrators themselves or the foreign court, especially an American court, would follow such a renvoi, and the result might be a most undesirable split of opinion on the validity of the clause.

The American-German Friendship Treaty of 1954 (Treaties B 117) touches upon the problem but gives very little relief. It provides that an arbitral clause shall not be unenforceable "merely on the grounds that the place designated for the arbitration proceedings is outside" the territories of one of the contracting parties or that the arbitrators are not nationals of that country (art. VI (2) sent. 1). This clause merely avoids discrimination on two narrow points,[296] but does not validate clauses that are invalid under the applicable law on other grounds.[297]

The validity of a contractual clause providing for conciliation or arbitration of an investment dispute between a contracting state and a national of another contracting state, and submitting the dispute to the "International Centre for Settlement of Investment Disputes," is established by article 25 (1) of the multilateral Convention of March 18, 1965 (Treaties M 292 A) to which both Germany and the United States are parties. In particular, such a clause is not revocable unilaterally.

(b) *Effects.*—If despite the existence of a valid arbitral clause,

---

[293] *See* DOMKE, The Law and Practice of Commercial Arbitration (1968) 16–21. In New York, arbitration clauses are enforced, *see* Giuffre v. The Magdalene Vinnen, 152 F. Supp. 123 (E.D.N.Y. 1957) (where the federal court issued a stay by virtue of a clause providing for arbitration in Bremen, agreed upon between the German shipowner and the charterer impleaded by the shipowner). *See also* Lowry & Co. v. S.S. Nadir, 223 F. Supp. 871 (S.D.N.Y. 1963) (arbitration in Hamburg).

[294] KROHN 111–13; WALKER 71, 74–78.

[295] Following the pattern established for other situations, *see supra* ch. 4 *passim*.

[296] In an American-German case arising prior to and therefore decided outside the framework of the Treaty, the court impliedly came to the same result as the treaty provision, Standard Magnesium Corp. v. Otto Fuchs, K.G. Metallwerke, 251 F.2d 455 (10th Cir. 1957).

[297] WALKER 75, 78; BAUMBACH/SCHWAB 275; BÜLOW/ARNOLD E 991.102; KROHN 110–12; SCHWENK 201.

suit is brought before the German ordinary courts, the arbitral clause must be invoked by the defendant before he pleads orally to the merits of the case (§ 274 ZPO). If thus properly invoked, the clause ousts the jurisdiction of the ordinary courts, irrespective of whether the tribunal is to sit in Germany or abroad.[298] The validity of the arbitral clause is also a prerequisite for the recognition and enforcement of a foreign arbitral award, both under the German-American treaty (art. VI (2) sent. 2)[299] and under German[300] and American[301] national law.

(2) Law of the Arbitration

There are two different sets of rules applicable to an arbitration proceeding, those relating to procedure and those relating to substance.

(a) *Procedure.*—According to German concepts, the parties are free to choose the procedural law to apply to their arbitration.[302] Since parties rarely make an express choice at the time of contracting, recourse must be had to the various methods of ascertaining intent (*see supra* ch. 8 sub II). The choice may be exercised either prior to or during the course of the arbitration. It is good practice for arbitrators in Germany to ask the parties right at the commencement of the proceeding what laws, procedural and substantive, they are to apply. A tacit choice of German law has been deduced from the designation of a German court to determine incidental matters, "according to § 1045 ZPO."[303] If the parties have not made a choice, express or implied, the courts attach particular importance to the place of the proceeding and, subsidiarily, to the residence of the arbitrators.[304] The first criterion will be decisive, especially if an institutional arbitration has been agreed upon.[305]

---

[298] OLG Hamburg 3 Sept. 1954, IPRspr. 1954/55 no. 179; WIECZOREK II 1, no. D III on § 274 ZPO; BAUMBACH/SCHWAB 78.

[299] LG Berlin 4 Dec. 1964, KTS 1966, 182, 183; BAUMBACH/SCHWAB 276, 277; KROHN 113–15, ARENDT 32–34. In the United States, *see* WALKER 79. Those who think that objections may be raised only on public-policy grounds are incorrect: BÜLOW/ARNOLD E 991.102–03, E 991.107 and n. 59; ARNOLD/HILL/KERN 4; HARDER, Thesis 158.

[300] BAUMBACH/SCHWAB 238; *see*, e.g., OLG Nürnberg 26 Nov. 1965, KTS 1966, 111, 112–14.

[301] *See* DOMKE, *supra* n. 293, at 306; DOMKE, RiW 1 (1954/55) 1.

[302] *See* BGH 22 Nov. 1962, WM 1963, 196, 197 (impliedly); RAAPE 557. BAUMBACH/SCHWAB 125 would let the law of the place of arbitration decide whether the parties may choose the applicable law.

[303] OLG Hamburg 8 Dec. 1960, IPRspr. 1960/61 no. 218.

[304] BGH 3 Oct. 1956, BGHZ 21, 365, 369; OLG Hamburg, *supra* n. 303; RAAPE 558. The parties may agree on alternate places for the proceeding depending on the domicile of the defendant or, according to an obiter dictum (BGH 27 Feb. 1969, WM 1969, 573, 575), even that of the plaintiff.

[305] RAAPE 557; SCHOTTELIUS, Das kaufmännische Schiedsgericht (1953) 50,

The applicable procedural law not only determines the procedure of the arbitration itself, but has a bearing upon the enforcement of the arbitral award. Both the "nationality" and the validity of the award depend upon the procedural law governing the arbitration (*infra* (3)).

(b) *Substance.*—The question, what law must be applied by the arbitrators to resolve the parties' dispute, presupposes an answer to the preliminary question, what conflicts rules should the arbitrators look to in selecting the governing law or laws? This preliminary question is an intricate and virtually insoluble theoretical question which has played almost no rôle in practice. Since the vast majority of arbitrations relate to contracts and since almost all legal systems today recognize party autonomy, the arbitrators will simply follow an express, tacit or implied choice of the applicable substantive law, or even of the applicable conflicts rules,[306] and the intention of the parties is usually ascertained at the commencement of the proceeding.

In the absence of any choice by the parties, their stipulation of arbitration is generally considered a tacit agreement to be bound by the substantive law obtaining at the place of the arbitration (*supra* ch. 8 sub II (2)(b)). In one instance, however, a Hamburg ad hoc arbitration board resorted to German conflicts law and even followed a reference over from Texas law to New York law to decide a claim for demurrage for delay in loading a ship in Texas.[307] And, for certain investment disputes, the Convention of March 18, 1965 Treaties M 292 A) directs recourse to the conflicts rules of the state where the investment has taken place (art. 42 (1)).

(3) Enforcement of Foreign Awards in Germany

Whether an arbitral award is German or foreign, in which latter case it must be enforced according to special rules, depends upon the procedural law under which the arbitration has taken place.[308] Although the general conditions for enforcement of foreign awards in Germany are laid down in § 1044 ZPO, where the parties are Americans and Germans their awards are subject primarily to the special rules embodied in article VI (2) of the American-German Friendship Treaty (Treaties B 117). Where certain investment

---

51. If the parties have chosen conciliation or arbitration by the International Centre for the Settlement of Investment Disputes, the conventional rules of procedure apply, *see* arts. 28–63 of the Convention of Mar. 18, 1965 (Treaties M 292 A).

[306] RAAPE 563–64. *See also* art. 42 (1) of the Convention, *supra* n. 305.

[307] Private arbitration, IPRspr. 1931 no. 41; *see also* RG 19 Nov. 1929, JW 1930, 1862.

[308] BGH 3 Oct. 1956, BGHZ 21, 365, 367–68; LG Berlin 4 Dec. 1964, KTS 1966, 182; RAAPE 559.

disputes are concerned, the German rules enacted in execution of the Convention of March 18, 1965[309] are controlling.

(a) *§ 1044 ZPO and the American-German Treaty of 1954.*—Unfortunately, it is not clear exactly how far the special treaty rules supersede the general provision of § 1044 ZPO. This statute establishes five conditions:

(i) The arbitral award must have become conclusive according to the law governing it (§ 1044 I sent. 1). In the light of § 1044 II no. 1, which deals with a related point (*infra* (ii)), the governing law is the procedural law applied by the arbitrators (*see supra* (2)(a)). However, this general conflicts rule is modified by sentence 2 of article VI (2) of the Treaty, testing the finality and enforceability of an award by the "laws of the place where rendered." In substance, this deviation from the rule of § 1044 I sentence 1 ZPO will not mean very much (*supra* (2)(a)). Of greater significance is the fact that the treaty rule demands not only finality but also enforceability. Whether enforceability has to be declared by a court decree rendered in the "home country" of the award or whether it suffices that the conditions for the rendering of such a decree are present, is disputed, but prevailing opinion in Germany correctly takes the latter view.[310] Proof of enforceability and finality is facilitated by a court decree declaring the award enforceable (in Germany)[311] or confirming it (in the United States[312]). If a foreign award, after having been declared enforceable in Germany, is later set aside abroad, the German declaration of enforceability may also be set aside (§ 1044 IV ZPO);

(ii) The arbitral award must be valid (*rechtswirksam*) according to the procedural law governing the arbitration (§ 1044 II no. 1 ZPO). This condition is not explicitly contained in article VI (2) of the Friendship Treaty, but is implied in the requirement of enforceability (*supra* (i)). The latter encompasses all the objections against validity that are admitted by the "home country" of an

---

[309] Treaties M 292 A. The rules are contained in the Law of Feb. 25, 1969, ratifying the Convention, BGBl. 1969 II 369.

[310] LG Berlin, *supra* n. 308; KROHN 117; ARENDT 44–45; *see also infra* n. 311. For the United States, *see* von Engelbrechten v. Galvanoni & Nevy Bros., Inc., 59 Misc.2d 721, 300 N.Y.S.2d 239 (Civil Ct. 1969); WALKER 81.

For the narrower view, *see* BAUMBACH/SCHWAB 276–77, on the ground that otherwise the words "final" and "enforceable" would be practically identical and hence redundant. However, this strictly logical interpretation is hardly appropriate for a treaty based on an Anglo-American draft nor is it even correct, *see infra* (2). *See also* BÜLOW, RiW 2 (1956) 37; LG Duisburg 9 Dec. 1966, IPRspr. 1966/67 no. 282 (New York award, rendered between a United States firm and a Spanish company and thus not subject to the Treaty; obiter dictum).

[311] KROHN and ARENDT, *supra* n. 310; BÜLOW/ARNOLD E 991.106; DOMKE, RiW 1 (1954/55) 2.

[312] LG Berlin, *supra* n. 308.

award,[313] a consequence usually overlooked in Germany.[314] In particular, article VI (2) sentence 2 itself permits examination of the validity of the arbitral clause (*see supra* n. 299);

(iii) The arbitral award must not contravene public policy (§ 1044 II no. 2 ZPO, art. VI (2) sent. 2 of the Friendship Treaty). This term will be understood in each country in the local sense. It has been held that the fact that an American award has been given without opinion does not violate German public policy since § 1041 II ZPO expressly authorizes the parties to waive an opinion.[315] Nor does it contravene German public policy that a German importer, who has undertaken to obtain a German import license but has been unsuccessful, is ordered by a foreign award to pay damages.[316] On the other hand, dealings in futures, even on a foreign exchange, contravene German public policy if motivated solely by speculation and not constituting genuine hedge transactions;[317]

(iv) The party against whom the arbitral award was rendered must have been properly represented, unless he approved, expressly or impliedly, the conduct of the case;

(v) The losing party must have been granted due process (§ 1044 II nos. 3 and 4).

These two latter objections do not appear in article VI (2) of the Treaty and they are therefore excluded as such. If, however, they amount to a violation of public policy, they may prevent enforcement under that rubric.[318]

Since the Treaty is silent on the procedure for declaring foreign awards enforceable, German law governs in this respect. According to § 1044 I ZPO, the applicable rules are those on the judicial declaration of enforcement of German awards, with a few modifications; the details are given in §§ 1042 a through 1043 ZPO. If recognition of the foreign award is precluded, the court will state that the award cannot be recognized in Germany, but it will not set it aside (§ 1044 III ZPO). As in the case of a foreign judgment, it is also possible for the award debtor to attempt to prevent

---

[313] ARENDT 32, 32 b, 53, 59, 69; *see also* SCHWENK 201. However, an American order confirming the award will cut off such objections; in this respect, such an order is itself recognized by art. VI (2) sent. 2 of the Treaty. *Contra*: ARENDT 71, invoking interpretations of the German general law of procedure, but not the Treaty.

[314] BÜLOW/ARNOLD E 991.107; BRÜCHER, AWD 1967, 338; *see also* the obiter dictum in BGH 16 Feb. 1961, BGHZ 34, 274, 277.

[315] LG Berlin 4 Dec. 1964, *supra* n. 308. The court does not even mention this provision. *See also* OLG Schleswig 30 Oct. 1959, IPRspr. 1958/59 no. 189, *aff'd on other grounds*, BGH 16 Feb. 1961, BGHZ 34, 274.

[316] BGH 27 Feb. 1964, WM 1964, 549; OLG Köln 30 July 1952, NJW 1952, 1420.

[317] OLG Hamburg 24 June 1932, IPRspr. 1932 no. 153.

[318] BÜLOW/ARNOLD E 991.107; ARENDT 71–73.

enforcement of the foreign award by asking for a negative declaratory judgment.[319] When declared enforceable in Germany, the foreign award has the status of a local award (art. VI (2) sent. 3 of the Treaty), and it is entitled to the same measures of enforcement. It is also exposed to the same objections that may be raised against a conclusive and enforceable German award, the most important being a set-off based on facts occurring after the award has been rendered.[320] Only objections that have arisen between the rendering of the award and the declaration of enforceability may be asserted in the enforcement proceeding,[321] and this rule has been extended to the enforcement of foreign awards, both under the general rules[322] and under the American-German Treaty.[323] If objections arise after an award has been declared enforceable, the debtor will have to bring an action under § 767 ZPO to set the judgment aside (*see supra* text at n. 223), just as he would if the claim had been adjudicated by a court.

(b) *Investment Convention.*—Since the Convention of March 18, 1965 (Treaties M 292 A) directly obligates the contracting states to enforce an arbitral award rendered according to its provisions (art. 54 (1)), a special procedure for enforcement was designed by the German law ratifying the Convention (*see supra* n. 309). It refers to the procedure for enforcement of a German arbitral award, while excluding any examination of the award on the merits (*see* arts. 2 and 3).

(4) Enforcement of Foreign Awards in the United States

The last sentence of article VI (2) of the American-German Friendship Treaty (Treaties B 117) provides that foreign arbitral awards that have been declared enforceable in the United States shall be entitled in any state court "only to the same measure of recognition as awards rendered in other States." This provision has not yet been construed judicially. It seems to reduce foreign awards to the status of sister-state awards even if the effects of the foreign award would reach further under its own law.[324] Of course, the American courts may go beyond this treaty rule and bestow greater effects on a foreign award.[325] Where they are not disposed to do so, the foreign

---

[319] OLG Nürnberg 26 Nov. 1965, KTS 1966, 111.

[320] Objections based on earlier facts are cut off, provided the arbitrators were competent and willing to decide upon these objections. If they were not and therefore refused to deal with them, the award does not cut off earlier objections, BGH 22 Nov. 1962, BGHZ 38, 259, 264–66; 7 Jan. 1965, WM 1965, 293.

[321] Baumbach/Schwab 202.

[322] BGH 22 Nov. 1962, *supra* n. 320, at 263.

[323] BGH 16 Feb. 1961, BGHZ 34, 274, 277–78.

[324] Bülow/Arnold E 991.107; Eisner, NJW 1968, 1560.

[325] Walker 80.

award cannot benefit from the statutory special proceedings for enforcement of arbitral awards, since these are designed only for awards rendered within the particular state.[326] Therefore, an action must usually be brought on the foreign award and plaintiff may, under favorable circumstances, obtain summary judgment.[327] For recognition, as distinct from enforcement of a foreign award, no special proceeding is necessary.[328]

(5) **East Germany***

Disputes arising from foreign trade contracts, and only these disputes, are settled almost invariably by arbitration. As in the other socialist countries, institutional arbitration is provided by the Arbitral Tribunal attached to the Chamber for Foreign Commerce in East Berlin. Legal bases for the functioning of the tribunal are §§ 1025 through 1048 ZPO and the Arbitration Rules of 1957.[328a] Jurisdiction must be conferred on the tribunal by a clause in a commercial contract, and at least one of the parties must be domiciled outside East Germany (Rules § 1). The tribunal also acquires jurisdiction if the defendant argues on the merits in the obligatory preliminary conciliation proceeding, without objecting to the jurisdiction of the tribunal (Rules, § 2). Each party selects an arbitrator from the established list of arbitrators, the umpire also being chosen by the two arbitrators from the list. Recognition and enforcement of foreign arbitral awards in East Germany is governed by § 1044 ZPO (*see supra* (3)(a)), unless a convention is in force.[328b]

For maritime matters, a special arbitration tribunal was created in 1959 by the Chambers of Foreign Commerce of Czechoslovakia, East

---

[326] EISNER, Die Durchsetzung von Schiedssprüchen des deutsch-US-amerikanischen Handelsverkehrs, KTS 1966, 129–37, 132.

[327] *See*, e.g., Coudenhove-Kalergi v. Dieterle, *supra* n. 256 (action on a German award).

[328] *See* the two cases of Birge-Forbes Co. v. Heye, 212 Fed. 112 (5th Cir.), *cert. denied*, 234 U.S. 759 (1914) and 248 Fed. 636 (5th Cir. 1918), *aff'd*, 251 U.S. 317 (1920), where a German agent of a Texas cotton exporter claimed reimbursement for payment of German arbitral awards rendered against the exporter in favor of his German customers. The awards were regarded as conclusive in both actions.

* LEMKE, German Democratic Republic, *in* UNION INTERNATIONALE DES AVOCATS, *op. cit. supra* n. 285, vol. 2 (1960) 155–67.

[328a] Arbitration Rules of July 3, 1957 (*reprinted in* "Aussenhandel" 1957 nos. 16/17 (appendix) *and in* FELLHAUER, Der Aussenhandelskaufmann und die Schiedsgerichte (1959) 127 ff.; *translation in* Law and Legislation in the German Democratic Republic 1966 no. 1 pp. 88–93).

[328b] East Germany has declared again in force the two Geneva Conventions of 1923 and 1927, *see* Regulation of Apr. 16, 1959 (GBl. DDR I 505) nos. 11 and 16. According to the general rule, these Conventions will probably be observed in East Germany vis-à-vis convention countries; but whether the latter will reciprocate is doubtful, *see supra* ch. 2 sub A II (2).

Germany and Poland. The tribunal sits in Gdynia, Poland, and may acquire jurisdiction in all private law disputes arising in maritime and inland navigation matters.[328c]

IV. BANKRUPTCY

German international bankruptcy law is characterized by a dearth of legislative rules. Abstract, general principles flourish, and doctrinal discussion usually centers around the dichotomy between the principle of territoriality ascribed to foreign bankruptcies, and the principle of universality seen in local bankruptcies. We propose to engage here in the more fruitful investigation of concrete situations.

(1) General Conflicts Rule

The German Federal Supreme Court has solved in the following manner the conflict between the all-inclusive claims of the state where bankruptcy is adjudicated, and the hostile attitude of other countries against a foreign bankruptcy: Whether a bankruptcy decree is intended to have effects beyond the forum must be determined by its own laws. If extraterritorial effects are in fact claimed, as is the rule, then it must be left to each foreign state where property of the bankrupt is situated to decide whether it accepts these extraterritorial effects or, as is more frequent, excludes them.[329] Since experience shows that neither principle, universality or territoriality, is pursued to its logical end, it is always necessary to investigate the particular situation.

(2) Local Bankruptcies

The international effects of a bankruptcy adjudicated in Germany are not generally fixed. According to § 238 I, II KO, there are two instances in which a bankruptcy may be adjudicated in Germany, without claiming extraterritorial effects: *first,* if the bankrupt has a business establishment but not his principal establishment in Germany; *second,* if he has neither his principal place of business nor a branch in Germany but merely has a farm there which he exploits as owner or lessee. Thus, in contrast to American law, the mere presence of assets of the debtor is insufficient for an adjudication of bankruptcy. The two cases mentioned in § 238 I, II KO are usually considered as exceptions to the unwritten general rule, similar to the rule in the United States, according to which a local bankruptcy adjudicated at the debtor's private or business domicile claims effectiveness throughout the world.[330] Of course, the recognition of

---

[328c] Arbitration Rules of June 17, 1959 (*reprinted in* "Aussenhandel" 1959 no. 1 (appendix p. 6) *and in* FELLHAUER, *supra* n. 328a, at 170 ff.), §§ 1 and 2.

[329] BGH 4 Feb. 1960, WM 1960, 347.

[330] RG 5 June 1931, IPRspr. 1931 no. 161.

this claim abroad depends upon the law of each country in which foreign assets are located.[331]

As will be explained (*infra* (3)), an adjudication of bankruptcy abroad, whether earlier or later, has only a limited effect in Germany. One incidental effect is that the debtor's inability to pay (the main prerequisite for an adjudication of bankruptcy, according to § 102 KO) need not be proved anew if a petition in bankruptcy is filed later in Germany (§ 238 III KO).

Foreign creditors are on a par with local creditors in a German proceeding (§ 5 I KO). Although § 5 II KO makes it possible for the government to deny national treatment to foreign creditors for retaliatory purposes, this power has never been exercised and is unlikely to be exercised in the future. Priority and preference rights of local or foreign creditors, even if based on contracts governed by foreign law, are qualified and satisfied according to German bankruptcy rules.[332] The preferences established by § 61 nos. 2 and 3 KO in favor of public treasuries have been held to be limited to claims of German public institutions, thus excluding foreign customs and social security claims.[333]

(3) **Foreign Bankruptcies**[334]

Under § 237 I KO, execution may be levied on the German assets of a debtor adjudicated a bankrupt abroad. The government may order an exception to this rule (§ 237 II KO), probably on the basis of reciprocity, but it has never yet done so. The rule of § 237 KO inures primarily to the benefit of the local creditors of the bankrupt, although foreign creditors are by no means excluded.[335] Apart from execution against individual assets, wholesale liquidation of the German assets through a German bankruptcy proceeding is also admissible (§ 238 III KO, *supra* (2)).

Whether § 237 KO expresses a general principle refusing to give any local effect to foreign bankruptcies or, on the contrary, whether it is merely an exception to the general principle of universality, has been much debated. Even the courts have differed, and a close analysis of their decisions shows that no uniform answer can be given. They have developed pragmatic rules in response to certain recurring situations.

---

[331] In American Ship Building Co. v. Willy H. Schlieker, K.G., 219 F. Supp. 905, 907 (S.D.N.Y. 1963), the court disregarded the German bankruptcy of the respondent German company, on the ground inter alia that the litigated funds were held in the United States.

[332] RG 5 June 1931, *supra* n. 330. *See also* §§ 50 and 56 KO.

[333] OLG Düsseldorf 8 Mar. 1933, IPRspr. 1933 no. 110; OLG Karlsruhe 14 Feb. 1929, JW 1929, 2362.

[334] Recent critical survey by MÜLLER-FREIENFELS, Auslandskonkurs und Inlandsfolgen, *in* Festschrift für Hans Dölle (1963) II 359–98.

[335] RG 5 Jan. 1937, RGZ 153, 200, 207.

One extension of § 237 KO is well settled. Not only may execution be made on local assets even though a debtor has been adjudicated a bankrupt abroad, but an action may also be brought against one who has been declared a bankrupt abroad.[336] Less certain are the rights of the foreign trustee in bankruptcy, where no local execution or bankruptcy is at issue and his powers under the foreign law (*supra* (1)) are extraterritorial. The courts distinguish, on hardly tenable grounds, between unincorporated and incorporated bankrupts. Where the bankrupt is unincorporated the foreign trustee is denied any powers in Germany, the bankrupt alone being permitted to assert his rights and being held responsible for his obligations.[337] In particular, the foreign trustee cannot claim for the bankrupt's estate abroad the assets located in Germany.[338] On the other hand, the trustee is held entitled to assert extraterritorially such claims of the bankrupt's estate as have been acquired since the foreign adjudication of bankruptcy.[339] These unsatisfactory rules are not followed for an incorporated bankrupt if under the law governing it (*supra* ch. 10 sub 10 I (1)) its ordinary representatives are replaced by a liquidator or a trustee in bankruptcy.[340] In fact, here it would be wholly artificial to declare the original representatives of the bankrupt preserved for proceedings in Germany.

V. FORMAL DOCUMENTS*

The rules on the formalities of documents, although most important for evidentiary purposes in judicial proceedings, are also relevant outside the courts.

(1) German Documents

Documents established according to German formal rules by or with the aid of German officials are deemed to be "German." A simple writing does not require intervention of any official (§ 126 BGB), but statutory rules sometimes require a formal document by insisting either that the author's signature be publicly certified (§ 129 BGB) or even that the document be publicly drawn (see § 128

---

336 BGH 30 May 1962, WM 1962, 782; RG 5 Jan. 1937, RGZ 153, 200, 205.

337 *See* cases *supra* n. 336.

338 BGH 4 Feb. 1960, *supra* n. 329; 30 May 1962, *supra* n. 336; 7 Dec. 1961, WM 1962, 263, 266, expressly overruling the contrary holding of OLG München 29 Sept. 1955, IPRspr. 1954/55 no. 210. Also to the contrary are RAAPE 678 and MÜLLER-FREIENFELS, *supra* n. 334, at 375–81.

339 RG 11 June 1926, RGZ 114, 82, 84–85.

340 BGH 7 Dec. 1961, *supra* n. 338; RG 5 Jan. 1937, *supra* n. 336, at 205–07; *cf.* RG 11 July 1934, JW 1934, 2845.

* BÜLOW, Die Legalisation öffentlicher Urkunden, DNotZ 1955, 9–49; BÄRMANN, Die Freizügigkeit der notariellen Urkunde, AcP 159 (1960/61) 1–40; HÖFER/HUHN, Allgemeines Urkundenrecht (1968); BLUMENWITZ, Zum Kollisionsrecht der notariellen Urkunde, DNotZ 1968, 712–50.

BGB). Signatures may be certified by any competent official, the most important being a notary, a court, or, outside Germany, a German consul.[341] Although this was true prior to 1970 for the public drawing of a document also,[342] a recent statute has established almost exclusive jurisdiction in notaries and consuls.[343] Sworn documents (affidavits) and acknowledgments of documents are not known in Germany, where oath-taking is infrequent.[343a]

(a) *Jurisdiction to draw documents.*—A German notary is not permitted to act outside the area for which he has been accredited, except in urgent cases or with the permission of his supervisory authority. Nevertheless, an "extraterritorial" act which he performs in Germany without complying with either condition is valid even if executed outside the territory of the German state in which he was admitted,[344] but if he acts outside Germany without authorization by the foreign country his act is invalid under German law as a transgression of the public powers bestowed by German law and as an invasion of foreign sovereignty.[345] Whether his conduct in certifying a signature may be split up into a non-official act of witnessing performed abroad and a subsequent official certification effected in his German office,[346] is disputed; while the validity of the certification is probable, it is also certain that the German notary would be liable to disciplinary action.

A German court would never be tempted to execute a notarial act outside of Germany but, if it ever did, its act would be void.

A German consul may perform his notarial functions in the United States, if the author of a unilateral legal act is a German; if at least one of the contracting parties is a German; if the document relates to the transfer or encumbrance of property of any kind within Germany; or, finally, if an agreement, even between Americans, relates to property located or business to be transacted within Germany.[347]

---

[341] §§ 20 I 1 BNotO; 17 KonsG (BGBl. III 303–1 and 27–1).

[342] §§ 20 I, 26–31, 33–37 BNotO; §§ 167–182 FGG; §§ 16, 16a, 37a KonsG.

[343] Law on Authentications (Beurkundungsgesetz) of Aug. 28, 1969 (BGBl. I 1513).

[343a] *See* KAPLAN/VON MEHREN/SCHAEFER, Phases of German Civil Procedure I, 71 Harv. L. Rev. 1193, 1244 (1958).

[344] §§ 11 II, III BNotO; 2 Beurkundungsgesetz.

[345] BÄRMANN 5; SEYBOLD/HORNIG, Bundesnotarordnung (4th ed. 1962) no. 5 on § 11; HÖFER/HUHN 75; BLUMENWITZ 715, 716; KG Berlin 17 Sept. 1937, JFG Erg. 17, 123, 125; RG 13 May 1927, JW 1927, 2126 (obiter dictum).

[346] *In the affirmative*: KG Berlin, *supra* n. 345, at 126; RG 13 May 1927, *supra* n. 345, at 2127; SEYBOLD/HORNIG, *supra* n. 345; SCHOETENSACK, DNotZ 1952, 271. *Undecided*: BÄRMANN 6, 14 n. 46. *Contra*: Letter of the President of the Bundesnotarkammer of Mar. 16, 1964, and letter of the Federal Minister of Justice of May 4, 1964, DNotZ 1964, 388 and 391; BLUMENWITZ 719–21.

[347] Art. XXII (1) sent. 2 of the American-German Friendship Treaty of 1923, *see supra* n. 142.

(b) *Formalities.*—A German official, and this includes a notary, must follow the strict and highly formalized rules laid down by German law for the official drawing up of documents. However, it is certainly permissible for him to go beyond the German formalities if this is desired in order to comply with requirements which are viewed as substantive under foreign law[348] or, perhaps even more importantly, in order to dispense with the onerous proof of the German formal rules in the foreign country.

Until 1970, German officials, including notaries, were permitted to draw instruments only in the German language (§§ 175 FGG, 16 II lett. a KonsG) except, but only under certain circumstances, last wills (§§ 2245 BGB, 16 a I 2 KonsG). A recent statute empowers notaries and consuls to draw documents in foreign languages.[349] In any event, the addition of a translation into a foreign language is permissible, as long as it is made clear that this is merely a translation from the German original.[350]

The original of any document drawn by a German notary is retained by him; only certified copies are delivered to the parties, although the original may be turned over if the document is to be used abroad and if all the parties agree;[351] this exception has been admitted in the interests of effective international legal cooperation. As for the United States, a state court has held that the mailing of a certified copy of a German notarial document complied with an American trust indenture requiring an "instrument in writing signed and acknowledged by the donor and delivered to the trustee," although the donor might have obtained the original document.[352]

(c) *Authentication of German documents for use abroad.*—Under American federal and state law, foreign official documents that are to be used before American authorities always require authentication by an American consul.[353] These rules are still operative since the

---

348 HÖFER/HAHN 83. The authors mention the presence of two witnesses and certain affirmatory phrases. These would seem to fall into the second category mentioned in the text.

349 §§ 5 II Beurkundungsgesetz; 16 II lett. a KonsG, as amended by the former (*see supra* n. 343). But a notary will not be obliged to do this (§ 15 II BNotO) and is merely expected to do it if he has a sufficient command of the foreign language.

350 Letter of the Federal Minister of Justice of Apr. 23, 1963, DNotZ 1963, 323–28. *See also* DUMOULIN, DNotZ 1964, 405–18, pleading for greater leeway.

351 § 45 I Beurkundungsgesetz, *supra* n. 343.

352 Hackley Union Nat. Bank v. Farmer, 252 Mich. 674, 234 N.W. 135 (1931).

353 *See, e.g.,* 28 U.S.C. § 1741 (1964 ed.) and Rule 44 FRCP; § 1454 California Evidence Code. *See also* BÜLOW 37. A German divorce decree, recognized by the Appellate Division of the New York Supreme Court (260 App. Div. 30, 20 N.Y.S.2d 206), was disregarded by the Court of Appeals because of the lack of authentication, Martens v. Martens, 284 N.Y. 363, 31 N.E.2d 489 (1940).

United States is not, like Germany, a party to the 1960 Hague Convention Abolishing the Requirement of Legalization for Foreign Public Documents.[354] Documents drawn by a German consul in the United States (*supra* (1)(a) and *infra* n. 362), on the other hand, are apparently excepted under article XXII (2) of the American-German Treaty of Friendship of 1923 (*supra* n. 101). In practice, authentication is almost always made directly, since the signatures and seals of most German officials, including notaries, whose documents are frequently used in the United States have been deposited with the American consul.[355] In this case, no German certification of the genuineness of the signature and of the official's position is necessary. If, on the other hand, the signature and seal have not been deposited with the consul or if American state law requires authentication to show that the foreign official is empowered to perform a particular act, one or more intermediary certifications by the German authorities are indispensable.[356]

Since the American authorities and courts, by force of statute[357] or by self-imposed limitation,[358] often refuse to recognize the signatures of officials of unrecognized foreign governments, utilization of East German official documents in the United States often poses difficult problems. In the absence of diplomatic relations between the two governments, no American representative is competent to authenticate East German official signatures, and documents emanating from East Germany are usually valueless in the United States.[359] There are two solutions: one is the practice of the West German authorities, who certify the signatures of East German administrative,

---

[354] BGBl. 1964 II 876, 1966 II 106; 527 UNTS 189.

[355] 22 C.F.R. § 92.37 (a). *See* Notice *in* StAZ 1967, 123 to the effect that the American Consulate General in Frankfurt authenticates directly the signatures of those German Civil Registrars that have been deposited with it. Similar arrangements have been made with many other groups of German officials.

[356] On the procedure, *see* 22 C.F.R. § 92.36–92.43.

Sometimes a chain of certifications on the German side is necessary until the signature of a German official appears which has been deposited with the American consulate. For judicial and notarial documents this is usually that of the President of the Landgericht, *see* the Regulation of the Ministry of Justice of Baden-Württemberg of May 22, 1968, Die Justiz 1968, 168 sub III A "USA"; Bülow 14. On the contents of the German certification, *see* the Regulation sub III (2); Bülow 39 n. 105.

[357] *See*, e.g., § 1454 California Evidence Code, which deals only with signatures effected in a "nation recognized by the executive power of the United States" and hence by implication excludes others.

[358] *See In re* Braunstein's Estate, 114 N.Y.S.2d 280 (Sur. Ct. 1952); *In re* Adler's Estate, 197 Misc. 104, 93 N.Y.S.2d 416 (Sur. Ct. 1949), *app. dismissed*, 279 App. Div. 745, 109 N.Y.S.2d 175 (1951); *contra*: *In re* Estate of Luberg, 19 A.D.2d 370, 372, 243 N.Y.S.2d 747, 750 (1963).

[359] Liebelt Estate, 13 Fid. Rptr. 63 (Orphan's Ct., Lackawanna County, Pa. 1962); Matter of Nezold, N.Y.L.J. Aug. 5, 1955, p. 4 col. 7 (Sur. Ct.).

as distinct from governmental, authorities; the other concerns notarial acts prepared by the one notary who was admitted before the division of Berlin and is still practising in both parts of the city;[360] her signature can consequently be certified by the West Berlin authorities and, in turn, by the American consul in West Berlin.

(2) **Foreign Public Documents in Germany**

German law invests "public documents" with special probative value, which is also granted to documents of foreign origin.

(a) *Classification.*—A foreign document is "public" if the three elements that make it so under German internal law (§ 415 I ZPO) are fulfilled according to the *lex loci actus.* It is this law of the place of making which determines whether a public authority or a person vested with "public faith" has drawn up the document, whether he has acted within his competence, and whether he has observed the locally prescribed formalities.[361] How is the existence of these three constitutive elements proved? This raises the problem of authentication.

(b) *Authentication.*—By virtue of a treaty provision, only documents drawn by American consuls in Germany are fully equated to German public documents.[362] Although German law does not as a rule require authentication of foreign public documents to be used in Germany,[363] the civil courts in ordinary proceedings must exercise their discretion in deciding whether a document drawn by a foreign authority or person of public faith may be regarded without further proof as genuine, in other words, as signed by the official (§ 438 I ZPO). If proof of genuineness is considered necessary, legalization by a German consul supplies it (§ 438 II ZPO).

The first provision—conferring discretion upon the court—is generally applicable, although as such nowhere codified.[364] The second provision—consular legalization—is also of general application, being based on a special statutory provision that closely resembles the wording of § 438 II ZPO.[365] It is impossible to ascertain how the

---

[360] Mrs. Ingeburg Gentz, 102 Berlin, Köpenicker Str. 91 (GDR).

[361] RG 26 June 1883, RGSt. 8, 372, 374–75; *see also* RG 5 Oct. 1926, JW 1927, 1096, 1097.

[362] Art. XXII (2) American-German Treaty of Friendship of 1923, *see supra* n. 142. *See* Bülow 42 n. 122 and also *supra* (2).

[363] The exception in § 5 a I PStG (requiring, for a foreign certificate of ability to marry, a confirmation by the German consul as to the foreign official's authority to issue such a certificate) is without importance for American-German relations, *see supra* ch. 4 sub A II (1) (b).

[364] Bülow 40–42; Baumbach/Lauterbach no. 2 C on § 438 ZPO. The rule is in conformity with the judge's general power freely to evaluate the evidence, § 286 II ZPO.

[365] § 2 of the Act of May 1, 1878 (RGBl. 89). *See also* § 109 DA.

first provision is applied in practice; it appears, however, that today authentication or other proof of the genuineness of the signature of a foreign official is seldom demanded in litigation but is normally required in non-litigious matters, especially in connection with transfers of real estate. Some commentators suggest that it is unnecessary if the parties do not contest the genuineness of the signatures.[366] Practice in the particularly formalistic proceeding before the land registry takes a stricter line: in each case the judge must investigate whether the genuineness of a foreign public document may be deduced from some other circumstance.[367] If an American notary public's signature has been certified by the clerk of an American court, formal authentication by a German consul may be dispensed with.[368]

Authentication of the signature, however, does not establish the other two elements of a foreign "public document," namely, authority of the issuing official and compliance with the proper formalities (*supra* (a)). It would appear that proof of these additional elements can be adduced in the same way as proof of the genuineness of the signature. However, in practice the courts usually do not require special proof of these additional circumstances since their existence is either deduced from the proper signing and authentication of the document,[369] or is investigated by the court *ex officio*.[370] If properly requested, the authentication by the German consul may be extended so as to cover also the authority of the issuing official and the observation of the necessary formalities ("extended authentication").

(c) *Status of foreign public documents.*—Foreign documents which comply with the requirements of § 415 I ZPO (*supra* (a)) enjoy to the full the probative value accorded to German public documents. Indeed, in defining a public document, § 415 ZPO does not distinguish between documents of German and those of foreign origin, and the latter are therefore held to be included.[371] Such public documents prove fully, but not irrebuttably, a declaration made before the issuer of the document, and also facts witnessed by the

---

366 NAGEL 427; WIECZOREK II 2, no. A I a on § 438 ZPO; *contra*: BAUMBACH/LAUTERBACH no. 1 on § 438 ZPO.

367 KG Berlin 2 Oct. 1930, DNotZ 1931, 29.

368 LG Berlin 19 Sept. 1966, DRpfl. 1967, 422. In another case, authentication of a power of attorney was not demanded since another document in the court file with the same signature had been authenticated, OLG Schleswig 19 Dec. 1961, IPRspr. 1960/61 no. 22.

369 KG Berlin 22 June 1939, JFG 20 no. 46 (p. 178); BAUMBACH/LAUTERBACH no. 2 A on § 438 ZPO.

370 KG Berlin 21 Dec. 1903, KGJ 27 A 250.

371 RG 10 Sept. 1934, RGSt. 68, 300, 302; 5 Oct. 1926, JW 1927, 1096, 1097; WIECZOREK no. C I b on § 415 ZPO.

official himself.[372] Official decisions or decrees, on the other hand, are deemed fully and irrebuttably proved.

The equation of foreign and domestic public documents also implies that the former enjoy the same criminal law protection against falsification as the latter.[373]

(3) Equivalence of American and German Notaries

Although foreign and German public documents may have the same probative value, this does not necessarily imply that, where German law governs, the German rules requiring notarial documents are satisfied by documents drawn by American notaries public. The significant differences between the notarial institutions in the two countries (*supra* n. 103) have given rise to difficult problems in German practice. Unless jurisdiction is expressly or impliedly conferred upon German notaries,[374] it is merely a matter of interpretation whether American notaries may be substituted. A distinction is properly made between a simple notarial act that can be performed by a person without legal training, such as certification of a signature, and one where the notary under German law performs an advisory function, such as the drawing up of a document. In practice, indeed, the certification of a signature by an American notary public is recognized as complying with § 129 BGB (*supra* (1)) and similar rules,[375] while wherever a notarial document is required (*see* § 128 BGB, *supra* (1)), a document drawn up by an American notary public is usually not considered fully equivalent,[376] since it is doubtful whether he is authorized under his own law to prepare instruments.

---

[372] For details, *see* §§ 415, 417, 418 ZPO. Special rules on the probative value of the civil register and documents from it are found in §§ 60 and 66 PStG.

[373] RG 10 Sept. 1934 and 26 June 1883, *supra* nn. 371 and 361 respectively.

[374] § 794 I no. 5 ZPO limits execution on the basis of a notarial or judicial "confession of judgment" to documents drawn up by a German notary or court. Prevailing opinion also interprets § 925 BCB (concerning the agreement of the parties to transfer title to an immovable) as requiring the presence of a German notary, *see supra* ch. 6 n. 42.

[375] KG Berlin 21 Dec. 1903, *supra* n. 370; *see also* OLG Schleswig 19 Dec. 1961, *supra* n. 368 (British Columbia). *Cf.* Blumenwitz 738; Reithmann, DNotZ 1956, 475; Wolff 128; Kegel, IPR 222.

[376] *See* BGH 10 June 1968, WM 1968, 1170, 1171; AG Eggenfelden 22 Sept. 1959, DAVorm. 32 (1959/1960) 229, 230 (obiter dictum); Opinion of the Max-Planck-Institute Hamburg, IPG 1965/66 no. 73; Mann, NJW 1955, 1177, 1178; Blumenwitz 738.

Contra for the important request to obtain a "certificate of inheritance" (*supra* ch. 5 sub III (3)): LG Berlin 19 Sept. 1966, DRpfl. 1967, 422 (impliedly); LG Mainz 12 June 1958, IPRspr. 1958/59 no. 205; Kegel, Kommentar no. 25 on art. 11 EGBGB. *Contra*: Firsching, Handbuch der amtsgerichtlichen Praxis, vol. VI, Nachlassrecht (2d ed. 1960) 30. *See also* LG Berlin 15 Aug. 1957, IPRspr. 1956/57 no. 140 (obiter dictum).

Conversely, a German notary is equated in the United States to an "officer having an official seal and authorized to administer oaths" (35 U.S.C. § 115). He has been held entitled, therefore, to take an inventor's oath for an American patent application.[377]

VI. EAST GERMANY

The majority of the legislative provisions cited in the preceding sections still obtain in East Germany and presumably the rules explained above apply also, although post-War authority is usually lacking. (On certain specific aspects of arbitration and on documents, *see supra* III (5) and V (1)(c) *in fine*, respectively.)

---

[377] Such oaths are recognized by the United States Patent Office, *see* communication of the German Federal Minister of Justice of Mar. 15, 1963, DNotZ 1963, 259; draft form of oath *in* HUHN/HÖFER 188–90.

Chapter XV.

SOCIAL SECURITY*

Compulsory social insurance was introduced into Germany by Bismarck in the last decades of the nineteenth century. The elaborate system of social security in force today includes workmen's compensation for injuries and benefits for illness, disability, old age, death, and unemployment, and covers most categories of workers and employees and certain groups of independent professionals. The multiplicity of institutions and forms of social security is matched only by the number and variety of their legal sources.

Article IV of the American-German Friendship Treaty of 1954 (Treaties B 117) prescribes national treatment in matters of workmen's compensation and social security. This provision means very little because of the disparity of conflicts rules on the subject.

(1) General Conflicts Rules

It is necessary to a proper understanding of the scattered existing conflicts rules to distinguish between the duty of contribution and the claim for benefits.

(a) *Duty of contribution.*—For some branches of social security, the international scope of the duty of contribution has been spelt out for certain cases. Two provisions extend this duty to Germans employed abroad as official representatives and also to Germans employed privately abroad for a limited period of time.[1] Offsetting this latter provision is one which exempts employees of foreign enterprises which engage in only temporary activities in Germany.[2] As for German sailors on foreign ships they may, on application by the shipowner, be insured if the state of the ship's flag does not object.[3] The general principle underlying these few scattered provisions has been designated by the courts and writers as "territoriality." Since German social security as a compulsory form of

---

* B. v. MAYDELL, Sach- und Kollisionsnormen im internationalen Sozialversicherungsrecht (Berlin 1967); JANTZ, Die Hauptgrundsätze der zwischenstaatlichen Sozialversicherung, *in* Die Sozialversicherung der Gegenwart 3 (1963) 21–32; WICKENHAGEN, Zwischenstaatliches Sozialversicherungsrecht (1957); *see also* the material in SCHWINGER, Vom nationalen zum internationalen und übernationalen Recht der Sozialversicherung (thesis Mainz 1964).

[1] §§ 1227 I nos. 2 and 7 RVO and 2 I nos. 2 and 10 AnVG (BGBl. III 820–1 and 821–1) (old age, disability, and death).

[2] § 168 V no. 4 RVO (illness).

[3] § 1227 II RVO, *see supra* n. 1.

insurance implies a duty of contribution, it is generally thought to be restricted to persons employed in Germany.[4] Nationality is irrelevant. Nevertheless, a limited exception to the principle of territoriality follows from the so-called doctrine of "radiation," according to which the interest of a German employee in his German social security is maintained if the German enterprise which employs him sends him abroad for a limited period of time,[5] which may be one year or perhaps even several years.[6] Locally resident workers employed abroad for limited purposes are no longer covered by German social security,[7] nor are persons formerly residing in Germany who are sent abroad to work for many years, even if the work is performed for a foreign branch of a German firm.[8] Conversely, a foreign enterprise's temporary activity in Germany is not subject to German social security provisions.[9]

The element of compulsion inherent in the duty to contribute to social security explains and justifies the foregoing rules. Any extension of international comity to this field usually depends upon express treaty provision.

(b) *Claim for benefits.*—The courts and writers, supported by a number of legislative provisions, have extended the principle of territoriality to the benefit side of social security. Obviously a person who has never worked in Germany, even though he has worked for a German employer, is not covered.[10] But the principle is also applied if the applicant, although he formerly lived and worked in Germany, now voluntarily resides outside Germany; he is excluded from receiving benefits unless a specific legislative rule provides otherwise.[11] This result finds some support in the structure of the legislative provisions themselves,[12] and it is also based on considerations

---

[4] This rule is self-evident today so that it has been confirmed in the post-War period only in obiter dicta, *see* BSG 23 Aug. 1967, BSGE 27, 129, 132; 26 June 1958, BSGE 7, 257, 263.

[5] *See supra* n. 1; BSG 4 July 1962, BSGE 17, 173, 177; BSG 30 Oct. 1963, BSGE 20, 69; WICKENHAGEN 25–31.

[6] BSG 4 July 1962, *supra* n. 5, at 181, 179. The Federal Minister for Labor would include periods of at least two years, *see* letter of Dec. 16, 1959, BArbBl. 1960, 7.

[7] BSG 26 June 1958, *supra* n. 4, at 265.

[8] BSG 8 Oct. 1964, BSGE 22, 31, 32.

[9] *See supra* n. 2.

[10] BSG 26 June 1958, *supra* n. 4; 8 Oct. 1964, *supra* n. 8; *see also* 30 Oct. 1963, *supra* n. 5, at 70–71 (benefits by virtue of the theory of "radiation," *supra* (a)).

[11] BSG 3 Feb. 1966, BSGE 24, 227–28. *Cf.* 42 U.S.C. § 402 (t), based on the same principle.

[12] *See* §§ 625 I no. 1, 1315 I no. 1 RVO, 94 I no. 1 AnVG (excluding foreigners residing abroad), and §§ 626, 1316 RVO, 95 AnVG (exception to the foregoing rule if the existence of reciprocity has been formally stated). *And see* §§ 1317 RVO and 96 AnVG (excluding Germans residing abroad) and §§ 1318–1323a RVO and 97–102 a AnVG (various exceptions to the foregoing rule).

of public finance (why should German public funds be spent on persons residing abroad?) and even on public international law (the receipt of benefits from social security is a reflection of its compulsory nature).[13] These notions appear to be rather outmoded today, and therefore the principle of territoriality as an unwritten principle restricting social security benefits has quite rightly come under attack.[14]

The few legislative rules excluding protection frequently distinguish between the residence abroad of Germans and of aliens.[15] One provision, however, dealing with unemployment benefits, differentiates between Germans and foreigners irrespective of residence, excluding the latter unless the existence of reciprocity has been formally stated or international agreements provide otherwise.[16] Still other provisions, for illness or accidents, deny benefits only when the beneficiary gives up his German residence, regardless of his nationality.[17]

(2) **American-German Relations**

The grant of national treatment[18] by article IV of the American-German Friendship Treaty of 1954 (Treaties B 117) affects only those rules that differentiate between Germans and aliens. Thus the principle of territoriality which governs the duty of contribution (*supra* (1)(a)) and the payment of benefits to beneficiaries residing outside of Germany,[19] are not touched at all. An American citizen who moves away from Germany cannot demand more than a German citizen residing abroad would be entitled to.[20]

---

[13] Thus BSG 23 Aug. 1967, *supra* n. 4, found no compulsion if a foreigner now residing abroad specifically applied for some benefit.

[14] *See, especially,* v. MAYDELL 68–72; PODLECH, NJW 1963, 1142–44; *see also* FENGE, Zeitschrift für Sozialreform 12 (1966) 257–68.

[15] *See* the provisions cited *supra* n. 12.

[16] § 144 AVAVG (as revised Apr. 3, 1957, BGBl. I 321) for unemployment benefits.

[17] If an ill person voluntarily departs abroad without the consent of the director of the board, certain sick benefits are suspended, § 216 I no. 2 RVO. If the insured moves abroad after falling ill or being accidentally injured, the board may capitalize the benefits (§§ 217 I, 616 RVO).

[18] It should be noted that no. 4 of the protocol restricts the grant of national treatment as to the matters covered by art. IV (2) (i.e., social security as opposed to workmen's compensation) to laws or regulations of national origin or inspiration. This restriction is inapplicable to Germany, and it limits the rights of Germans in the United States to federal statutes or state statutes that are based in whole or in part on federal requirements.

[19] ARNOLD/HILL/KERN 2 on art. IV.

[20] BSG 27 May 1964, Sozialrecht no. 2 on § 1318 RVO; 3 Feb. 1966, *supra* n. 11, at 230; LSG Nordrhein-Westfalen 17 Sept. 1963, Breithaupt'sche Sammlung von Entscheidungen der Sozialversicherung, Versorgung und Arbeitslosenversicherung 53 (1964), 784; no. VI, Circular of the Federal Minister for Labor, July 12, 1956, BArbBl. 1956, 488.

On the other hand, to the extent that certain provisions discriminate against foreign citizens residing abroad in favor of Germans in the same situation, they are no longer applicable to Americans. These individuals now have to be treated on the same footing as Germans residing abroad.[21] Accordingly, the rule excluding foreigners generally, whatever their residence, from unemployment benefits no longer applies to Americans.[22] The same is true of reimbursement of rent to a person residing abroad; an American citizen residing in the United States may demand payment on the same footing as a German residing outside Germany.[23]

---

[21] The Circular, *supra* n. 20, enumerates seven statutory provisions that have since been thoroughly revised. *See,* for the more important discriminatory provisions, *supra* n. 12.

[22] § 144 AVAVG, although not mentioned in the Circular, *supra* n. 20, surely no longer bars Americans from benefits, *see* HENTRICH, BArbBl. 1956, 515.

[23] BGH 11 July 1962, RzW 1963, 320, 322 (overruling prior decisions to the contrary).

Chapter XVI.

TAXATION*

To deal adequately here with the problems of taxation that have arisen between the two countries is well-nigh impossible. Another book would be required. But there is little genuine necessity since many aspects of American-German taxation have already been well covered in recent works. It will suffice, therefore, to refer here briefly to the most important legal, and especially the conventional, sources, and to the more comprehensive literature.

(1) General Rules

A few general rules and principles of taxation are contained in the American-German Friendship Treaties of 1923 and 1954. Article XI of the 1954 Treaty (Treaties B 117) guarantees national treatment with respect to the payment of taxes, fees or charges (para. 1). This provision, however does not apply to citizens or companies of one of the two countries who neither reside nor engage in trade or other gainful pursuit in the other; but the two countries have undertaken to apply to these categories of taxpayers "in general the principle" of national treatment (para. 2); and all are to enjoy most-favored-nation treatment (para. 3). The grant of special tax advantages on the basis of reciprocity or double taxation agreements is reserved, and so is the allowance of personal exemptions from income and inheritance taxes to nonresidents (para. 5). Turning to the international scope of the domestic tax laws, article XI (4) demands for the taxation of companies and nonresident nationals of the other country that no charges be imposed on income, capital or other sources that are not reasonably allocable to the taxing country; in the same way, at least those deductions and exemptions that are reasonably allocable to the taxing country are to be granted.

Immunity from taxation by the host country has been agreed upon

---

* H. J. GUMPEL, Taxation in the Federal Republic of Germany (2d ed. Chicago 1969); O. L. WALTER, Essentials of Direct Taxation in the Federal Republic of Germany (New York 1966); CCH Common Market Reporter (looseleaf) paras. 6641–52; CCH Common Market Reports; SCHMIDT/DÖSER/BELLSTEDT, German Added Value [Turnover] Tax Law (1967).

On East Germany, *see* HUISKAMP, Taxation in the Eastern Zone of Germany, 2 Law in Eastern Europe (1958) 102–31; SPILLER, Zum internationalen Steuerrecht im Rechtssystem der DDR, 22 Bulletin for International Fiscal Documentation 511–23 (1968).

for consular officers and for lands and buildings used exclusively for governmental purposes of the other country.[1] However, no immunity may be claimed by state enterprises or public corporations that engage in business activities in the host country (art. XVIII (2) Treaty of 1954).

(2) **Income and Property Taxes**

A Convention for the Avoidance of Double Taxation with Respect to Taxes on Income was concluded in 1954 (Treaties B 112). It was preceded by an arrangement concluded as early as 1923–1925 but limited to providing relief from double income taxation on shipping profits (Treaties B 53); after World War II, the domestic regulations that had been issued in execution of the arrangement were declared again applicable in Germany in 1952 (*supra* ch. 2 n. 47). After eleven years of operation, the Convention of 1954 was revised in 1965 (Treaties B 200). Its title was significantly extended by referring to "taxes on income and to certain other taxes"; it now covers on the German side taxes on income, corporations, trade (*Gewerbe*), and capital (*Vermögen*), whereas it is limited on the American side to the federal income tax, including surtaxes (art. I (1)). Future taxes of a substantially similar character are also to be included (para. (2)). The exclusion of state income and property taxes on the American side is due to the constitutional limitations of the treaty-making power in the United States. The literature on the Convention is abundant.[2]

(3) **Other Taxes**

In the absence of treaty rules for other taxes, only domestic rules[3] apply within the framework of the general principles mentioned

---

[1] Details in art. XIX (1) and (2) of the Treaty of 1923 (Treaties B 55).

[2] The most useful are the two following bilingual works: DEBATIN/WALTER, Handbuch zum deutsch-amerikanischen Doppelbesteuerungsabkommen/Handbook on the United States-German Tax Convention (Tax Treaty Guides vols. I and IA, International Bureau of Fiscal Documentation, Amsterdam, looseleaf 1967—); H.-TH. SCHUBERT, Deutsch-amerikanisches Doppelbesteuerungsabkommen/American-German Convention for the Avoidance of Double Taxation (Düsseldorf 1967).

[3] On German international taxation, *see* BÜHLER, Prinzipien des Internationalen Steuerrechts (Amsterdam 1964); R. C. A. SCHMITZ, Kommentar zum Internationalen Steuerrecht der Bundesrepublik Deutschland (2 vols. 1957); RÄDLER/RAUPACH, Deutsche Steuern bei Auslandsbeziehungen (1966); TEICHNER, Internationales Steuerrecht (1967); MERSMANN, Die Ertragsbesteuerung inländischer Betriebsstätten und Tochtergesellschaften ausländischer Kapitalgesellschaften (1966); JOHN E. BLYTH, Massnahmen zur Beseitigung der Doppelbesteuerung amerikanischer Unternehmen in der Bundesrepublik Deutschland (1964); WEBER-FAS, Corporate Residence Rules for International Tax Jurisdiction: A Study of American and German Law, 5 Harv. J. Leg. 175–251 (1968).

earlier (*supra* (1)). However, these general national rules on exemptions or deductions cannot do justice to the specific traits of any particular foreign country and therefore do not bring about the desirable mutual harmonization of the international aspects of taxation. This purpose can only be achieved by agreements. A treaty on inheritance taxes would be particularly desirable;[4] negotiations are under way.

---

[4] *See* CALLMANN, Die Auswirkungen der Doppelbesteuerung auf dem Gebiete der Erbschaftssteuer in den Vereinigten Staaten, AWD 1963, 43–45.

Chapter XVII.

CRIMINAL LAW AND PROCEDURE*

The distinction between penal and private law, between criminal and civil procedure, looms large in Germany, even though both are administered by one set of courts. Not only contacts with the more unified American system, but also exposure to the modern trend of the international administration of criminal justice, may be expected to promote closer links between the two branches. Hence we shall survey briefly the American-German legal relations in the penal field, looking first at applicable law and jurisdiction (I), next at recognition of foreign judgments (II), and finally at extradition and other judicial assistance (III).

I. APPLICABLE LAW, JURISDICTION AND PROCEDURE

(1) Applicable Law

In the present state of affairs, the German courts refuse to enforce foreign penal law. One may not be accused, convicted or sentenced by virtue of foreign law, but this rule does not preclude foreign penal law from being taken into account in applying German law or in determining whether German criminal law is applicable at all. The existing conflicts rules are unilateral; they merely determine when and whether German criminal law is to be applied by the German courts. The conflicts rules may be subsumed under three (or more) principles[1]:

(a) An offense committed in Germany is governed by German

---

* The German Penal Code of 1871 (American Series of Foreign Penal Codes No. 4, 1961); The German Draft Penal Code. E 1962 (*id.* No. 11, 1966); The German Code of Criminal Procedure (*id.* No. 10, 1965); NEUMANN, *in* 2 Manual of German Law (1952) 72–157; F. HONIG, Criminal Justice in Germany To-day, 5 Y.B. World Aff. 131–52 (1951); H. J. WOLFF, Criminal Justice in Germany, 42 Mich. L. Rev. 1067–88, 43 *id.* 155–78 (1944); G. O. W. MUELLER, German Draft Criminal Code 1960—An Evaluation in Terms of American Criminal Law, 1961 U. Ill. L. F. 25–77; OVERLAND/NEWHOUSE, Juvenile Criminal Law in the Federal Republic of Germany and in England, 4 Calif. West. L. Rev. 35–64 (1968); H. H. MEYER, German Criminal Procedure: The Position of the Defendant in Court, 41 A.B.A.J. 592–94, 666–68 (1955); JESCHECK, Principles of German Criminal Procedure in Comparison with American Law, 56 Va. L. Rev. 239–253 (1970).

[1] *See* DICKINSON, Introductory Comment to Jurisdiction With Respect to Crime, Harvard Research in International Law, 29 Am. J. Int'l L. Supp. 443, 445 (1935).

penal law irrespective of the nationality of the offender (§§ 3 I, 4 I StGB). This is an illustration of the so-called territorial principle;

(b) An offense committed by a German abroad is also subject to German law, unless it is not punishable according to the law of the place of commission because of special conditions obtaining there (§ 3 II StGB). This is an example of the nationality principle;

(c) Even an offense committed by a foreigner abroad is under certain conditions subject to German law: (i) if it affects special German interests (the protective principle), or (ii) if it affects certain universally recognized interests (the universality principle).

The protective principle ((c)(i)) calls for the application of German law provided the offense is punishable at the place of commission and provided, in addition, the offender has subsequently become a German, or the offense violates German interests, or the offender has been apprehended in Germany and cannot be extradited (§ 4 II StGB). Nevertheless, German law applies without regard to the law of the place of commission if the offender violated particularly vital German interests, for example, engaged in high treason; or committed certain "international" crimes, such as traffic in women or counterfeiting of money (§ 4 III StGB) (which may be viewed as falling within the universality principle). The broad sphere of application claimed by German criminal law for offenses committed abroad is mitigated somewhat by provisions expressly empowering the public prosecutor to refuse to bring charges against offenders, German or foreign, who have acted abroad (§ 153 b no. 1, 2 StPO), or foreign offenders who are being extradited for the same offense (§ 154 b I StPO).

The general provisions of the new Penal Code, which was adopted in 1969 (BGBl. I 717) but will not become effective until late 1973, will retain essentially the old conflicts rules. Thus the territorial and the universality principles ((a) and (c)(ii)) will be preserved, the latter with slight amendments.[1a] The nationality principle (b) has been somewhat restricted, the new law requiring that the offender be a German at the time of commission of the offense or before prosecution, and that the offense be punishable under the law of the place of commission.[2] The protective principle (c)(i) also has been further restricted: the offense must be punishable under the local law and must also have been committed against a German (sometimes called the passive nationality principle) or by a foreigner who has been apprehended in Germany and cannot be extradited.[3]

[1a] §§ 3, 5, 6 Penal Code 1969.
[2] § 7 II no. 1 Penal Code 1969.
[3] § 7 I, II no. 2 Penal Code 1969.

(2) **Jurisdiction**

As in civil procedure (*supra* ch. 14 sub I (2)), the rules on venue of the courts incidentally define the international jurisdiction of the German courts in criminal matters. The three places where venue (and therefore jurisdiction) may be laid are enumerated in §§ 7–9 StPO: the place of commission of the offense is primary; then comes the domicile, residence or last domicile of the offender in Germany; and, finally, the place of apprehension is looked to. These rules attempt to make sure that a German court will be available in all cases where German criminal law applies (*supra* (1)). To fill any remaining gap, § 13 a StPO empowers the Federal Supreme Court to name a competent court, if otherwise lacking.

These rules go considerably beyond the territorial basis on which the American courts exercise criminal jurisdiction. Therefore the State Department could not in 1910 promise that the American courts would try an offense committed by an American citizen in Germany.[4]

(3) **Procedure**

The American-German Friendship Treaty of 1954 (Treaties B 117) establishes in article III (2) certain minimal procedural safeguards for a national of either country taken into custody in the other. On his demand, the nearest consular representative of his country shall be notified and shall have the right to visit and communicate with him. The arrested person shall be treated humanely; shall receive formal and prompt information of the accusations against him; shall be brought to trial as promptly as is consistent with the proper preparation of his defense; and shall enjoy all means reasonably necessary to his defense, including the services of competent counsel of his choice.

II. RECOGNITION OF FOREIGN JUDGMENTS*

Foreign penal judgments are not executed in Germany, but this rule does not preclude their being taken into account in Germany.

---

[4] *See* 2 Hackworth 180; 1910 Foreign Relations 517–18. The German government had sought an assurance of reciprocity in order to undertake, on request of the United States, the prosecution in Germany of a German citizen for a theft committed in New York. Under the present versions of § 9 StPO and § 3 I StGB, the prosecution in Germany and the application of German law would not depend upon a request from a foreign government.

* On the international effects of penal sentences, *see* the national reports for Germany by Maurach and H. Mayer, Revue internationale de droit pénal 34 (1963) 15–32 and 33–49, and for the United States by Pye, *id.* 55–79. An English version of the latter's report, The Effect of Foreign Criminal Judgments, can be found in Mueller/Wise, eds., International Criminal Law (New York 1965) 479–506.

Thus § 7 StGB expressly provides that a punishment carried out abroad must be deducted from a German punishment subsequently imposed for the same offense. Therefore, if in the opinion of the public prosecutor a later sentence in Germany would not substantially exceed the sentence already served abroad, he may refrain from bringing the charge at all (§ 153 b no. 3 StPO). It should be noted that the German courts feel free to deduct, where appropriate under general rules, the period of detention an accused has undergone abroad while awaiting extradition to Germany.[5]

The American courts appear to lean in the same direction. In one case an order by the German police, who had placed an American ex-convict on board an American vessel, that the man be confined to his room while the vessel was in Hamburg, was recognized as justifying the captain's action, so that the shipowner was not liable for false imprisonment.[6] In another case, the pardon obtained by a German convict after serving part of his sentence in Germany was recognized as purging the prior criminal conviction and thus preventing deportation from the United States, but the order discharging him was reversed on a point of construction of the United States statute involved.[7]

III. EXTRADITION AND OTHER LEGAL ASSISTANCE*

(1) **Extradition**

Although only a species of international judicial assistance in criminal matters, extradition has so many peculiar features that it deserves special treatment.

Since the numerous treaties concluded in the nineteenth century with the German states on the "mutual delivery of criminals, fugitives from justice" (Treaties B 16–23, 25, 26) were not revived after World War I (*supra* ch. 2 sub A I), a new extradition treaty between the United States and Germany was negotiated in 1930 (Treaties B 63). It was reinstated after the termination of the occupation régime as of January 1, 1956 (*supra* ch. 2 n. 49), but recourse to it has been rare; in the slightly more than twenty years of its actual operation

---

[5] RG 6 Oct. 1905, RGSt 38, 182; SCHÖNKE/SCHRÖDER, Strafgesetzbuch (14th ed. 1969) no. 2 on § 60 StGB.

[6] Dick v. United States Lines Co., 38 F.Supp. 685 (S.D.N.Y. 1941).

[7] Hempel v. Weedin, 23 F.2d 949 (W.D.Wash.), *rev'd sub nom.* Weedin v. Hempel, 28 F.2d 603 (9th Cir. 1928).

* G. O. W. MUELLER, International Judicial Assistance in Criminal Matters, *in* International Criminal Law (New York 1965) 410–41; GRÜTZNER, Der Rechtshilfeverkehr in Strafsachen mit den Vereinigten Staaten von Amerika, Goltdammers Archiv für Strafrecht 1953, 14–23; GRÜTZNER, Internationaler Rechtshilfeverkehr mit dem Ausland in Strafsachen (looseleaf 1954—) II V 3; METTGENBERG, Ein neuer Auslieferungsvertrag mit den Vereinigten Staaten von Amerika, JW 1931, 706–07.

(between 1931 and 1940 and between 1956 and 1968) only five American and five German requests for extradition have been submitted and granted.[8]

Extradition under the treaty is expressly made conditional upon reciprocity (art. I (1)). In addition, the treaty establishes two general conditions for extradition:

First, the crime or offense covered by the charge or conviction must have been committed within the "territorial jurisdiction" of the requesting state; this term includes territory and territorial waters, merchant vessels on and aircraft over the high seas, and men of war wherever situated (art. I (2));[9]

Second, extradition is restricted to the twenty-eight extraditable crimes and offenses specifically enumerated in article III, provided these are punishable by the laws of both countries applicable to the case. Surrender shall take place only if there is sufficient evidence of criminality to justify commitment of the fugitive for trial under the law of the requested state if the crime or offense had been there committed (art. I (1)).[10] As is usual in such treaties, offenses of a political character are excepted (art. IV). Exceptions from prosecution or punishment under the law of the requested state based on lapse of time, prior trial, or any other cause, shall also dispense with surrender under the treaty (art. VI), and extradition may be deferred if the fugitive is under prosecution in the requested country (arts. VI, VII). The traditional principle that extradition is limited to the specific offense for which it has been requested and the resulting exemption of the extradited person are embodied in article V.

Citizens of the requested state are exempt from extradition[11] and, according to German constitutional law, so are persons entitled to political asylum.[12] A special problem is created by the constitutional abolition in Germany of the death penalty (art. 102 GG), still maintained in some of the American states; the Federal Constitutional Court, however, has held that extradition for a crime that

---

[8] *See* the German statistics published in DJ 1936, 1149 and subsequent volumes, and after the War in the Federal Gazette.

[9] This provision is obviously based on the American conception of territorial jurisdiction in criminal matters, *supra* (1).

[10] This requirement is also imported from American law and is therefore not familiar to German courts. Thus it has been overlooked in the Hinrichs case (KG Berlin 22 June 1932, JW 1933, 984), criticized on this account by METTGENBERG/DOERNER 155.

[11] Art. II of the Treaty. In Germany, this rule is now underpinned by a constitutional provision, art. 16 II 1 GG.

[12] This follows from art. 16 II 2 GG; *see supra* ch. 11 sub I (2). This exemption is fortunately of no practical importance in American-German legal relations.

is punishable by a death sentence in the requesting state is not precluded by article 102 GG.[13]

A request for extradition must be supported by a copy either of the sentence or, if the fugitive has merely been charged, of the warrant of arrest together with supporting evidence. All the documents must be duly authenticated (art. X (3)). The German authorities have been informed that the American authorities only recognize testimony given under oath.[14]

Arrest, detention, hearing and eventual surrender of the fugitive are all governed by the law of the requested state (art. X (2)). In Germany, the relevant rules are contained in the Extradition Law (DAG) of 1929 (as amended 1933 (BGBl. III 314–1) §§ 7–32), supplemented by the relevant provisions of the administrative regulations for the international aspects of criminal matters (nos. 26–58 RiVASt) (*see* n. 14). A provisional arrest may be made for one month and may be prolonged on request for another month. If no formal request for extradition has been received on expiration of these periods, the prisoner has to be released (art. X (4)).[15]

The treaty does not provide for transit of a fugitive apprehended in a third country through the territory of the requested state to that of the requesting state. This procedure is well known in Germany. Although there is no formalized procedure for transit in the United States, this country does not normally object to transit of a fugitive in the company of a German agent, but he may not be forcibly detained on American soil.[16] In special cases the German authorities may take the precaution of submitting a request for extradition so as to facilitate re-apprehension in case of escape.[17] In view of the principle of reciprocity governing the German Extradition Law (§ 4 no. 1), the formal transit through German territory of a person wanted in the United States is not possible.[18]

---

[13] BVerfG 30 June 1964, BVerfGE 18, 112. GECK, JuS 1965, 221–32, expresses approval.

[14] Richtlinien für den Verkehr mit dem Ausland in strafrechtlichen Angelegenheiten, Jan. 15, 1959 (RiVASt) appendix II sub Vereinigte Staaten von Amerika, lett. d; GRÜTZNER, Rechtshilfeverkehr II V 3, introductory note no. 3.

[15] The effect of this provision on the national legal systems is not quite clear. A United States federal district court held that 18 U.S.C. § 654 (now § 3188 (1964 ed.)) operated on the American-German Treaty and that therefore release had to be ordered after two months. *In re* Normano, 7 F. Supp. 329 (D. Mass. 1934). In Germany, no. 40 RiVASt declares the four months' delay of § 18 III DAG applicable even if a treaty provides for a shorter term.

On the requirements for a request for extension of time under art. X, *see* the State Department Note of Oct. 21, 1931, 4 HACKWORTH 114.

[16] *See* the undated State Department Note (1967) *in* GRÜTZNER II V 3, introductory note no. 5.

[17] GRÜTZNER, *supra* n. 16.

[18] The conditions of a formal transit are the same as those for extradition (§ 33 I DAG refers expressly to §§ 1–6 DAG) and thus include reciprocity. *See also* 4 HACKWORTH 219.

Non-admission of an immigrant or his subsequent expulsion often produce the same results as extradition. Since the American immigration authorities are extremely sensitive to an immigrant's criminal record, the German authorities may suggest that appropriate steps be taken in the United States.[19] In Germany, by contrast, extradition takes precedence over expulsion or any other measures which contain fewer guarantees for the fugitive.[20]

(2) **Other Legal Assistance**

Under German law other legal assistance in criminal matters, such as the supplying of information or the transmittal of objects, may be rendered to a foreign state only on condition of reciprocity (§§ 34 II, 41 I DAG). The requisite reciprocity was secured by an exchange of notes in 1960/1 (Treaties B 176). This agreement establishes reciprocal although not identical obligations in accordance with the specific needs and facilities of each party.

(a) *Information from the penal registers.*—Such information is in practice requested quite frequently. The conditions and the procedure for obtaining it have therefore received special attention in the Agreement. Information for purposes of a criminal proceeding is fully covered by the Agreement. Germany has undertaken to give information "in accordance with the German domestic provisions" (no. 1 of the German note). This phrase is ambiguous since German law restricts information from the penal register under certain conditions and vis-à-vis "ordinary" authorities, while the courts, public prosecutors and a few other "privileged" authorities may obtain full information.[21] On the other hand, it is also provided that foreign authorities, if they are entitled to receive any information, must be informed fully.[22] Germany interprets this requirement narrowly as meaning that an American authority shall receive information to the same extent as a comparable German authority.[23] Requests for information by the Federal Bureau of Investigation are to be forwarded by the Legal Attaché of the American Embassy directly either to the *Bundeskriminalamt* or to the Penal Register Authorities, usually according to a person's birthplace. Requests by other American authorities are, as a rule, to be transmitted through diplomatic channels (no. 3 of the German note). German requests

---

[19] GRÜTZNER, *supra* n. 14, at no. 7.

[20] RiVASt nos. 26 and 32 (1) sent. 2.

[21] Details in the Straftilgungsgesetz of Apr. 9, 1920 (RGBl. 507).

[22] § 37 Strafregisterverordnung of Feb. 17, 1934 (RGBl. I 140).

[23] No. 2 of Circular of the Federal Minister of Justice, June 27, 1961 (GRÜTZNER, *supra* n. 14, at II V 3 p. 17 b n. 2), interpreting the same phrase of the Agreement although in a slightly different context. The interpretation is probably influenced by the more explicit corresponding rule of the American Note, *see infra* n. 24. The "privileged" authorities that are entitled to full information are enumerated in § 4 of the Law of Apr. 9, 1920, *supra* n. 21.

by the *Bundeskriminalamt,* the courts or the public prosecutors are to be directed to the Legal Attaché of the American Embassy on behalf of the FBI. Requests from other German authorities are, again, as a rule, to be transmitted through diplomatic channels (no. 3 of the American note).

The Agreement also authorizes the obtaining of information from the penal register for non-criminal purposes. Such information is promised by both countries, more or less explicitly, to the extent that it would be given to the corresponding domestic authority.[24] In Germany this means that only privileged authorities will obtain full information (last paragraph).[25] A complicated special procedure has been devised for information required by American agencies in Germany for purposes of immigration and marriage; in these cases the individual concerned and the American agency both have to apply, and only limited information is given.[26]

(b) *Service.*—The service of documents, summonses, decisions, and so forth, follows essentially the rules observed in civil proceedings (*supra* ch. 14 sub II (3)).[27]

(c) *Taking of evidence.*—The taking of testimony is also governed by essentially the same rules as those obtaining in civil proceedings (*supra* ch. 14 sub II (4)(b) and (c)).[28] These rules apply also to the hearing of the accused.[29] For criminal matters, the attendance or active participation of German judges or officers at hearings abroad as well as of foreign judges and officers in Germany, is expressly authorized, subject, in each instance, to consent by the government of the requested state.[30]

---

[24] No. 2 of the American and no. 2 para. 2 of the German Note, *see supra* n. 23.

[25] *Expressly*: no. 2 of the Circular mentioned in n. 23.

[26] No. 2 para. 1 of the German Note, no. 1 of the Circular of June 27, 1961, *supra* n. 23, and no. 1 of the Circular of the Federal Minister of Justice of July 8, 1963, GRÜTZNER, *supra* n. 14, at I B 3.

[27] GRÜTZNER, *supra* n. 14, at nos. 17 and 26; MUELLER 416–19.

[28] GRÜTZNER, *supra* n. 14, at nos. 10, 16–18, 24, 26; MUELLER 420–27.

[29] Details in GRÜTZNER, *supra* n. 14, at nos. 19, 24, 26.

[30] RiVASt nos. 171 III and 191 I for activities of German judges abroad, no. 186 I for the acting of foreign judges in Germany.

APPENDICES

APPENDIX I

Conflict of Laws Rules in the Introductory Law to the Civil Code (EGBGB)*

August 18, 1896

Art. 7. The capacity (*Geschäftsfähigkeit*) of a person is governed by the law (*Gesetzen*) of the state of which he is a national.

If a foreigner who is of full age, or who has the legal status of a person of full age, acquires German nationality, he retains the legal status of a person of full age, even though he is not of full age according to German law.

If a foreigner enters into a legal transaction in this country as to which he lacks capacity or his capacity is limited, he is regarded as capable of entering into this legal transaction insofar as he would be capable under German law. This provision does not apply to legal transactions relating to family law or the law of succession, or to legal transactions which dispose of real estate situated abroad.

Art. 8. A foreigner may in this country be adjudged incompetent according to German law, if he has his domicile (*Wohnsitz*) or, having no domicile, his residence (*Aufenthalt*) in this country.

Art 9. [Abrogated; replaced by §12 Verschollenheitsgesetz of July 4, 1939, as revised, BGBl. III 401–6.]

Art. 10. [Abrogated by §30 I no. 4 Vereinsgesetz of August 5, 1964, BGBl. I 593.]

Art. 11. The form of a legal transaction (*Rechtsgeschäft*) is governed by the law which governs the substance of the legal transaction. However, compliance with the law of the place where the legal transaction is entered into is sufficient.

The provision of para. 1 sentence 2 does not apply to a legal transaction whereby a right to a thing is created or such a right is disposed of.

Art. 12. By reason of an unlawful act committed in a foreign country, no greater claims can be enforced against a German than those created by German law.

Art. 13. The conclusion of a marriage, even if only one of the parties is a German, is governed as to each of them by the law of the country of which he (or she) is a national. The same applies to foreigners who conclude a marriage in this country.

The conclusion of a marriage by the wife of a foreigner declared dead according to art 9 para. 3[1] is governed by German law.

The form of a marriage celebrated in this country is governed exclusively by German law.

Art. 14. The personal legal relations of German spouses *inter se* are governed by German law even if the spouses have their domicile in a foreign country.

---

*RGBl. 604, BGBl. III 400–1. Translation by the author.

[1] Article 9 para. 3 was abrogated and has been replaced by § 12 para. 3 Verschollenheitsgesetz.

German law applies even though the husband has lost his German nationality, provided the wife has retained hers.

Art. 15. The matrimonial property régime is governed by German law if the husband was a German at the time of the marriage.

If the husband acquires German nationality after marriage, or if the foreign spouses have their domicile in this country, the laws of the country of which the husband was a subject at the time of the marriage govern the matrimonial property régime; spouses may, however, enter into a marriage contract, even though this would not be permitted under the laws of that country.

Art. 16. If foreign spouses, or spouses who acquire German nationality after marriage, have their domicile in this country, the provisions of §1435[2] of the Civil Code apply mutatis mutandis; the foreign statutory property régime is deemed equivalent to a contractual property régime.

The provisions of § § 1247, 1362, and 1405[3] of the Civil Code apply, insofar as they are more favorable to third parties than the foreign law.

Art. 17. Divorce (*Scheidung*) is governed by the law of the country of which the husband is a national at the time when suit is brought.

A fact (*Tatsache*) which occurred while the husband was a national of another country can be asserted as a ground for divorce only if that fact is also a ground for divorce or for separation (*Trennung*) under the law of that country.

The divorce suit of the wife is governed by German law, even though at the time when the decision is rendered only the wife has German nationality; if in this case the marriage is dissolved, the wife may, on application of the husband, be declared to be at fault if the application would be justified under German law.

A divorce according to a foreign law may not be pronounced in this country, unless the divorce would be admissible under the foreign law as well as under German law.

Art. 18. The legitimacy of a child is governed by German law if the husband of the mother at the time of the birth of the child is a German or, where he died before the birth of the child, if he was a German at the time of his death.

The annulment of legitimacy is governed by German law even though only the mother has German nationality or, where she is dead, if she had German nationality at the time of her death, and provided further that the child is still a minor at the time of the annulment or, where the child is dead, if he would be a minor. If the child is subject to parental authority or to the guardianship of his mother, a curator has to be appointed insofar as this is necessary for the protection of his rights.

Art. 19. The legal relations between the parents and a legitimate child are governed by German law if the father, or, in case of the father's death, the mother, possesses German nationality. The same rule applies if the German nationality of the father or the mother is lost but the child is still a German national.

Art. 20. The legal relation between an illegitimate child and his mother is determined by German law if the mother is a German. The same rule applies if the mother has lost her German nationality while the child has retained his German nationality.

---

[2] §1435 BGB was abrogated by the Gleichberechtigungsgesetz of June 18, 1957, BGBl. I 609. It has been replaced by §1412 BGB.

[3] §1405 BGB was abrogated by the Gleichberechtigungsgesetz of June 18, 1957, BGBl. I 609. It has been replaced by §§1431 and 1456.

Art. 21. The father's duty to furnish maintenance to an illegitimate child and his duty to reimburse the mother for the costs of pregnancy, confinement and support are determined by the law of the country of which the mother is a subject at the time of the birth of the child; however, claims beyond those of German law cannot be asserted.

Art. 22. Legitimation of an illegitimate child as well as adoption of a child are governed by German law if the father at the time of the legitimation, or the adopter at the time of the adoption, possesses German nationality.

If the father or the adopter is a national of a foreign country, while the child possesses German nationality, the legitimation or adoption is ineffective if the assent required by German law, either of the child or of a third person with whom the child has a family relationship, is lacking.

Art. 23. A guardianship or curatorship may be established in this country even over a foreigner if the country of which he is a national does not assume his protection, provided the foreigner requires protection under the law of his country, or if he has been adjudged incompetent in this country.

The German guardianship court may take provisional measures as long as a guardianship or curatorship has not been established.

Art. 24. Succession to the estate of a German, even if he had his domicile abroad, is governed by German law.

If a German had his domicile abroad at the time of his death, his heirs may invoke the law at the domicile of the deceased with respect to their liability for the debts of the estate.

If a foreigner who has executed or revoked a disposition *mortis causa* acquires German nationality, the validity of the execution or revocation is determined by the law of the country of which he was a national at the time of the execution or revocation; he also retains the capacity to execute a disposition *mortis causa* even though he has not yet attained the age required by German law. The provision of article 11 para. 1 sentence 2 remains unaffected.

Art. 25. Succession to the estate of a foreigner who at the time of his death had his domicile in this country is governed by the laws of the country of which he was a national at the time of his death. Nevertheless, a German may assert claims arising from his right of succession on the basis only of German law unless, according to the law of the country of which the deceased was a national, succession to the estate of a German who had his domicile in that country is governed exclusively by German law.

Art. 26. If assets from an estate which has accrued abroad are transferred through German authorities to this country for the heirs or legatees entitled under the law of the foreign country, another person cannot object to the transfer on the ground that he has a claim to the assets as heir or legatee.

Art. 27. If German law is declared to be applicable by the law of a foreign country whose law governs according to article 7 para. 1, article 13 para. 1, article 15 para. 2, article 17 para. 1 and article 25, then German law applies.

Art. 28. The provisions of articles 15, 19, 24 para. 1, 25 and 27 do not apply to objects which are outside the territory of the country whose law is applicable according to these provisions, provided those objects, according to the law of the country within which they are located, are subject to special provisions.

Art. 29. Where the national law has been declared applicable, the legal relations of a stateless person are governed by the law of the state in which he has, or had at the relevant time, his usual residence (*gewöhnlichen Aufenthalt*) or, if such is lacking, his residence.

Art. 30. The application of a foreign law is excluded if this application would offend against good morals (*guten Sitten*) or would be contrary to the purpose (*Zweck*) of a German law.

Art. 31. The Chancellor may, with the consent of the Federal Council, order that a right of reprisal shall be exercised against a foreign country, its nationals and their legal successors.

APPENDIX II

Treaty of Friendship, Commerce and Navigation between the Federal Republic of Germany and the United States of America*

October 29, 1954

The Federal Republic of Germany and the United States of America desirous of strengthening the bonds of friendship existing between them and of encouraging closer economic and cultural relations between their peoples, and being cognizant of the contributions which may be made toward these ends by arrangements promoting mutually advantageous commercial intercourse, encouraging mutually beneficial investments, and establishing mutual rights and privileges, have resolved to conclude a Treaty of Friendship, Commerce and Navigation, based in general upon the principles of national and of unconditional most-favored-nation treatment reciprocally accorded, and for that purpose have appointed as their Plenipotentiaries:

The President of the Federal Republic of Germany:

Dr. Konrad Adenauer, Federal Chancellor and Federal Minister of Foreign Affairs, and

The President of the United States of America:

Mr. John Foster Dulles, Secretary of State of the United States of America,

who, having communicated to each other their full powers found to be in due form, have agreed as follows.

Article I

1. Each Party shall at all times accord fair and equitable treatment to the nationals and companies of the other Party, and to their property, enterprises and other interests.
2. Between the territories of the two Parties there shall be, in accordance with the provisions of the present Treaty, freedom of commerce and navigation.

Article II

1. Nationals of either Party shall, subject to the laws relating to the entry and sojourn of aliens, be permitted to enter the territories of the other Party, to travel therein freely, and to reside at places of their choice. Nationals of either Party shall in particular be permitted to enter the territories of the other Party and to remain therein:

*Text taken from 1956 BGBl. II 488. A few corrections for typographical errors have been made by referring to the text published in 7 UST 1839.

(a) for the purpose of carrying on trade between the territories of the two Parties and engaging in related commercial activities;

(b) for the purpose of developing and directing the operations of an enterprise in which they have invested, or in which they are actively in the process of investing, a substantial amount of capital.

2. Each Party undertakes to make available the best facilities practicable for travel by tourists and other visitors with respect to their entry, sojourn and departure, and for the distribution of information for tourists.

3. Nationals of either Party, within the territories of the other Party, shall enjoy freedom of conscience; and they shall be at liberty to hold religious services, both private and public, at suitable places of their choice.

4. Nationals of either Party shall be permitted, within the territories of the other Party, to gather information material for dissemination to the public, and shall enjoy freedom of transmission of such material to be used abroad for publication by the press, radio, television, motion pictures, and other means; and they shall be permitted to communicate freely with other persons inside and outside such territories by mail, telegraph and other means open to general public use.

5. The provisions of the present Article shall be subject to the right of either Party to apply measures that are necessary to maintain public order and protect the public health, morals and safety.

Article III

1. Nationals of either Party within the territories of the other Party shall be free from molestations of every kind, and shall receive the most constant protection and security. They shall be accorded in like circumstances treatment no less favorable than that accorded nationals of such other Party for the protection and security of their persons and their rights. The treatment accorded in this respect shall in no case be less favorable than that accorded nationals of any third country or that required by international law.

2. If, within the territories of either Party, a national of the other Party is taken into custody, the nearest consular representative of his country shall on the demand of such national be immediately notified and shall have the right to visit and communicate with such national. Such national shall:

(a) receive reasonable and humane treatment;

(b) be formally and immediately informed of the accusations against him;

(c) be brought to trial as promptly as is consistent with the proper preparation of his defense; and

(d) enjoy all means reasonably necessary to his defense, including the services of competent counsel of his choice.

Article IV

1. Nationals of either Party shall be accorded national treatment in the application of laws and regulations within the territories of the other Party that establish a pecuniary compensation or other benefit or service, on account of disease, injury or death arising out of and in the course of employment or due to the nature of employment.

2. Nationals of either Party shall furthermore be accorded national treatment with regard to the application of social security laws and regulations within the territories of the other Party under which benefits are provided without examination of financial need in the following cases:

(a) sickness, including temporary disability for work, and maternity;
(b) old age, invalidity, or occupational disability;
(c) death of the father, spouse, or any other person liable for maintenance;
(d) unemployment.

Article V

1. Property of nationals and companies of either Party shall receive the most constant protection and security within the territories of the other Party.

2. The dwellings, offices, warehouses, factories and other premises of nationals and companies of either Party located within the territories of the other Party shall not be subject to molestation or to entry without just cause. Official searches and examinations of such premises and their contents, when necessary, shall be made only according to law and with careful regard for the convenience of the occupants and the conduct of business.

3. Neither Party shall take unreasonable or discriminatory measures that would impair the legally acquired rights or interests within its territories of nationals and companies of the other Party in the enterprises which they have established, in their capital, or in the skills, arts or technology which they have supplied.

4. Property of nationals and companies of either Party shall not be taken within the territories of the other Party, except for the public benefit and in accordance with due process of law, nor shall it be taken without just compensation. Such compensation shall represent the equivalent of the property taken and shall be made in an effectively realizable form and without unnecessary delay. Adequate provision shall have been made at latest by the time of the taking for the determination and the giving of the compensation.

5. Nationals and companies of either Party shall in no case be accorded, within the territories of the other Party, less than national treatment and most-favored-nation treatment with respect to the matters set forth in paragraphs 2 and 4 of the present Article. Moreover, enterprises in which nationals or companies of either Party have a substantial interest shall be accorded, within the territories of the other Party, not less than national treatment and most-favored-nation treatment in all matters relating to the taking of privately owned enterprises into public ownership and to the placing of such enterprises under public control.

Article VI

1. Nationals and companies of either Party shall be accorded national treatment with respect to access to the courts of justice and to administrative tribunals and agencies within the territories of the other Party, in all degrees of jurisdiction, both in pursuit and in defense of their rights. It is understood that companies of either Party not engaged in activities within the territories of the other Party shall enjoy such access therein without any requirement of registration or domestication.

2. Contracts entered into between nationals or companies of either Party and nationals or companies of the other Party, that provide for the settlement by arbitration of controversies, shall not be deemed unenforceable within the territories of such other Party merely on the grounds that the place designated for the arbitration proceedings is outside such territories or that the nationality of one or more of the arbitrators is not that of such other Party. Awards duly rendered pursuant to any such contracts, which are final and enforceable under

the laws of the place where rendered, shall be deemed conclusive in enforcement proceedings brought before the courts of competent jurisdiction of either Party, and shall be entitled to be declared enforceable by such courts, except where found contrary to public policy. When so declared, such awards shall be entitled to privileges and measures of enforcement appertaining to awards rendered locally. It is understood, however, that awards rendered outside the United States of America shall be entitled in any court in any State thereof only to the same measure of recognition as awards rendered in other States thereof.

Article VII

1. Nationals and companies of either Party shall be accorded, within the territories of the other Party, national treatment with respect to engaging in all types of commercial, industrial, financial and other activity for gain, whether in a dependent or an independent capacity, and whether directly or by agent or through the medium of any form of lawful juridical entity. Accordingly, such nationals and companies shall be permitted within such territories:

(a) to establish and maintain branches, agencies, offices, factories and other establishments appropriate to the conduct of their business;

(b) to organize companies under the general company laws of such other Party, and to acquire majority interests in companies of such other Party; and

(c) to control and manage enterprises which they have established or acquired.

Moreover, enterprises which they control, whether in the form of individual proprietorships, companies or otherwise, shall in all that relates to the conduct of the activities thereof, be accorded treatment no less favorable than that accorded like enterprises controlled by nationals or companies of such other Party.

2. Each Party reserves the right to limit the extent to which aliens may establish, acquire interests in, or carry on enterprises engaged within its territories in communications, air or water transport, taking and administering trusts, banking involving depository functions, or the exploitation of land or other natural resources. However, new limitations imposed by either Party upon the extent to which aliens are accorded national treatment, with respect to carrying on such activities within its territories, shall not be applied as against enterprises which are engaged in such activities therein at the time such new limitations are adopted and which are owned or controlled by nationals or companies of the other Party. Moreover, neither Party shall deny to transportation, communications and banking companies of the other Party the right to maintain branches and agencies, in conformity with the applicable laws and regulations, to perform functions necessary for essentially international operations in which they engage.

3. The provisions of paragraph 1 of the present Article shall not prevent either Party from prescribing special formalities in connection with the establishment of alien-controlled enterprises within its territories; but such formalities may not impair the substance of the rights set forth in said paragraph.

4 Nationals and companies of either Party, as well as enterprises controlled by such nationals or companies, shall in any event be accorded most-favored-nation treatment with reference to matters treated in the present Article.

Article VIII

1. Nationals and companies of either Party shall be permitted to engage, within the territories of the other Party, accountants and other technical experts,

executive personnel, attorneys, agents and other specialists of their choice. Moreover, such nationals and companies shall be permitted to engage accountants and other technical experts regardless of the extent to which they may have qualified for the practice of these professions within the territories of such other Party, for the particular purpose of making for internal purposes examinations, audits and technical investigations for, and rendering reports to, such nationals and companies in connection with the planning and operation of their enterprises, and enterprises in which they have a financial interest, within such territories.

2. Nationals and companies of either Party shall be accorded, within the territories of the other Party, national treatment and most-favored-nation treatment with respect to engaging in scientific, educational, religious and philanthropic activities, and shall be accorded the right to form associations for that purpose under the laws of the country. Nothing in the present Treaty shall be deemed to grant or imply any right to engage in political activities.

Article IX

1. Nationals and companies of either Party shall be accorded within the territories of the other Party:

(a) national treatment with respect to leasing land, buildings and other real property appropriate to the conduct of activities in which they are permitted to engage pursuant to Articles VII and VIII and for residential purposes; and with respect to occupying and using such property; and

(b) other rights in real property permitted by the applicable laws of such other Party.

2. Nationals and companies of either Party shall be accorded, within the territories of the other Party, national treatment and most-favored-nation treatment with respect to acquiring, by purchase, lease, or otherwise, and with respect to owning and possessing, personal property of all kinds, both tangible and intangible. However, either Party may impose restrictions on alien ownership of materials dangerous from the standpoint of public safety and alien ownership of interests in enterprises carrying on the activities listed in the first sentence of paragraph 2 of Article VII, but only to the extent that this can be done without impairing the rights and privileges secured by Article VII or by other provisions of the present Treaty.

3. Nationals and companies of either Party shall be accorded national treatment, within the territories of the other Party, with respect to acquiring property of all kinds by testate or intestate succession or under judicial sale to satisfy valid claims. Should they because of their alienage be ineligible to continue to own any such property, they shall be allowed a period of at least five years in which to dispose of it.

4. Nationals and companies of either party shall be accorded, within the territories of the other Party, national treatment and most-favored-nation treatment with respect to disposing of property of all kinds.

Article X

1. Nationals and companies of either Party shall be accorded, within the territories of the other Party, national treatment with respect to obtaining and maintaining patents of invention, and with respect to rights in trade-marks, trade names, trade-labels, and industrial property of every kind.

2. The Parties undertake to cooperate in furthering the interchange and use

of scientific and technical knowledge, particularly in the interests of increasing productivity and improving standards of living within their respective territories.

Article XI

1. Nationals of either Party residing within the territories of the other Party, and nationals and companies of either Party engaged in trade or other gainful pursuit or in scientific, educational, religious or philanthropic activities within the territories of the other Party, shall not be subject to the payment of taxes, fees or charges imposed upon or applied to income, capital, transactions, activities or any other object, or to requirements with respect to the levy and collection thereof, within the territories of such other Party, more burdensome than those borne in like situations by nationals and companies of such other Party.

2. With respect to nationals of either Party who are neither resident nor engaged in trade or other gainful pursuit within the territories of the other Party, and with respect to companies of either Party which are not engaged in trade or other gainful pursuit within the territories of the other Party, it shall be the aim of such other Party to apply in general the principle set forth in paragraph 1 of the present Article.

3. Nationals and companies of either Party shall in no case be subject, within the territories of the other Party, to the payment of taxes, fees or charges imposed upon or applied to income, capital, transactions, activities or any other object, or to requirements with respect to the levy and collection thereof, more burdensome than those borne in like situations by nationals, residents and companies of any third country.

4. In the case of companies and of nonresident nationals of either Party engaged in trade or other gainful pursuit, within the territories of the other Party, such other Party shall not impose or apply any tax, fee or charge upon any income, capital or other basis in excess of that reasonably allocable or apportionable to its territories nor grant deductions and exemptions less than those reasonably allocable or apportionable to its territories. A comparable rule shall apply also in the case of companies organized and operated exclusively for scientific, educational, religious or philanthropic purposes.

5. Each Party reserves the right to:

(a) extend specific tax advantages on the basis of reciprocity;

(b) accord special tax advantages by virtue of agreements for the avoidance of double taxation or the mutual protection of revenue; and

(c) apply special provisions in allowing, to nonresidents, exemptions of a personal nature in connection with income and inheritance taxes.

Article XII

1. Nationals and companies of either Party shall be accorded national treatment and most-favored-nation treatment by the other Party with respect to the assumption of undertakings for, and the making of, payments, remittances, and transfers of moneys and financial instruments.

2. It is agreed that no provision of the present Treaty shall be applied in such a manner as to alter arrangements applicable to either Party by virtue of its membership in the International Monetary Fund.

3. Neither Party may, with respect to the other Party, in any manner impose exchange restrictions which are unnecessarily detrimental to or arbitrarily discriminate against claims, investments, transportation, trade or other interests of nationals and companies of such other Party or their competitive position. Should

either Party impose exchange restrictions with respect to the other Party, it will remove them as rapidly as it is able to do so considering its economic condition.

4. The two Parties, recognizing that the international movement of investment capital and the returns thereon would be conducive to the full realization of the objectives of the present Treaty, are agreed that such movments shall not be unnecessarily hampered. In accordance with this mutually agreed principle, each Party undertakes to afford to nationals and companies of the other Party reasonable facilities for the withdrawal of funds earned by them as a result of making or maintaining capital investments as well as for the transfer of capital investments. The same principle applies with respect to the compensation referred to in Article V, paragraph 4.

5. The term "exchange restrictions" as used in the present Article includes all restrictions, regulations, charges, taxes, fees, and other requirements imposed by either Party, which burden or interfere with the assumption of undertakings for, or the making of, payments, remittances, or transfers of moneys and financial instruments.

6. All questions arising under the present Treaty concerning foreign exchange restrictions will be governed by the provisions of the present Article.

Article XIII

Nationals and companies of either Party engaged in business within the territories thereof may operate as commercial travelers either directly or by means of agents or employees within the territories of the other Party, in conformity with the applicable laws and regulations. Such commercial travelers shall, upon their entry into and departure from the territories of such other Party and during their sojourn therein be accorded most-favored-nation treatment in respect of the customs and other matters, including, subject to the exceptions in Article XI, paragraph 5, taxes and charges applicable to them, their samples, their advertising material and the taking of orders, and regulations governing the exercise of their functions.

Article XIV

1. Each Party shall accord most-favored-nation treatment to products of the other Party, from whatever place and by whatever type of carrier arriving, and to products destined for exportation to the territories of such other Party, by whatever route and by whatever type of carrier, with respect to customs duties and charges of any kind imposed on or in connection with importation or exportation or imposed on the international transfer of payments for imports or exports, and with respect to the method of levying such duties and charges, and with respect to all rules and formalities in connection with importation and exportation.

2. Neither Party shall impose restrictions or prohibitions on the importation of any product of the other Party, or on the exportation of any product to the territories of the other Party, unless the importation of the like product of, or the exportation of the like product to, all third countries is similarly restricted or prohibited.

3. Either Party may impose prohibitions or restrictions on sanitary or other customary grounds of a non-commercial nature, or in the interest of preventing deceptive or unfair practices, provided such prohibitions or restrictions do not arbitrarily discriminate against the commerce of the other Party.

4. Nationals and companies of either Party shall be accorded national treatment and most-favored-nation treatment by the other Party with respect to all matters relating to importation and exportation.

5. If at any time a question should arise concerning the application of paragraph 2 of the present Article, the two Parties shall consult with a view to determining the application thereof. If such consultation, or consultation pursuant to Article XXIV, paragraph 5, does not lead to a mutually satisfactory conclusion, either Party may give written notice of termination of the present Article; and notwithstanding the provisions of Article XXIX, the present Article shall terminate three months following receipt of such notice by the other Party.

6. The provisions of the present Article shall not apply to advantages accorded by either Party by virtue of a customs union or free-trade area of which it may become a member, so long as it informs the other Party of its plans and affords such other Party adequate opportunity for consultation.

Article XV

1. Each Party shall promptly publish laws, regulations, and administrative rulings of general application pertaining to rates of duty, taxes or other charges, to the classification of articles for customs purposes, and to requirements or restrictions on imports and exports or the transfers of payments therefor, or affecting their sale, distribution or use; and shall administer such laws, regulations and rulings in a uniform, impartial and reasonable manner. As a general practice, new or more burdensome administrative requirements affecting imports shall not be enforced until after public notice thereof.

2. Each Party shall maintain an appeals procedure under which nationals and companies of the other Party, and importers of products of such other Party, shall be able to obtain prompt and impartial review, and correction when warranted, of administrative action relating to customs matters, including the imposition of fines and penalties, confiscations, and rulings on questions of customs classification and valuation by the administrative authorities. Penalties imposed for infractions of the customs and shipping laws and regulations concerning documentation shall be merely nominal in cases resulting from clerical errors or when good faith can be demonstrated.

3. With reference to marking requirements applicable to imported products, each Party shall as a general practice:

(a) allow required marks of origin to be affixed after importation;

(b) not permit markings that result in misrepresenting the true origin of the products; and

(c) not apply requirements that entail an expense which is economically prohibitive or that result in seriously damaging the product.

Article XVI

1. Products of either Party shall be accorded, within the territories of the other Party, national treatment and most-favored-nation treatment in all matters affecting internal taxation, sale, distribution, storage and use.

2. Articles produced by nationals and companies of either Party within the territories of the other Party or by companies of the latter Party controlled by such nationals and companies, shall be accorded therein treatment no less favorable than that accorded to like articles of national origin by whatever person or company produced, in all matters affecting exportation, taxation, sale, distribution, storage and use.

Article XVII

1. Each Party undertakes:

(a) that enterprises owned or controlled by its Government, and that monopolies or agencies granted exclusive or special privileges within its territories, shall make their purchases and sales involving either imports or exports affecting the commerce of the other Party solely in accordance with commercial considerations, including price, quality, availability, marketability, transportation and other conditions of purchase or sale; and

(b) that the nationals, companies and commerce of such other Party shall be afforded adequate opportunity, in accordance with customary business practice, to compete for participation in such purchases and sales.

2. Each Party shall accord to the nationals, companies and commerce of the other Party fair and equitable treatment, as compared with that accorded to the nationals, companies and commerce of any third country, with respect to:

(a) the governmental purchase of supplies;

(b) the awarding of concessions and other government contracts; and

(c) the sale of any service sold by the Government or by any monopoly or agency granted exclusive or special privileges.

3. Neither Party shall impose any measure of a discriminatory nature that hinders or prevents the importer or exporter of products of either country from obtaining marine insurance on such products in companies of either Party.

Article XVIII

1. The two Parties agree that business practices which restrain competition, limit access to markets or foster monopolistic control, and which are engaged in or made effective by one or more private or public commercial enterprises or by combination, agreement or other arrangement among such enterprises, may have harmful effects upon commerce between their respective territories. Accordingly, each Government agrees upon the request of the other Government to consult with respect to any such practices and to take such measures, not precluded by its legislation, as it deems appropriate with a view to eliminating such harmful effect.

2. No enterprise of either Party, including corporations, associations, and government agencies and instrumentalities, which is publicly owned or controlled shall, if it engages in commercial, industrial, shipping or other business activities within the territories of the other Party, claim or enjoy, either for itself or for its property, immunity therein from taxation, suit, execution of judgment or other liability to which privately owned and controlled enterprises are subject therein.

Article XIX

1. Vessels under the flag of either Party, and carrying the papers required by its law in proof of nationality, shall be deemed to be vessels of that Party.

2. So long as both Parties follow systems of tonnage measurement which are substantially similar, tonnage certificates issued by either Party shall be accepted by the other Party, and vessels shall not be subject to new measurements in the ports of such other Party.

3. The term "vessels", as used in the present Treaty, means all types of vessels, whether privately owned or operated, or publicly owned or operated; but this term does not include vessels of war.

Article XX

1. Vessels of either Party shall have liberty, on equal terms with vessels of the other Party and on equal terms with vessels of any third country, to come with their cargoes to all ports, places and waters of such other Party open to foreign commerce and navigation. Such vessels and cargoes shall in the ports, places and waters of such other Party be accorded in all respects national treatment and most-favored-nation treatment.

2. Vessels of either Party shall be accorded national treatment and most-favored-nation treatment with respect to the right to carry all cargo that may be carried by vessel to or from the territories of the other Party.

3. Goods carried by vessels under the flag of either Party to or from the territories of the other Party shall enjoy the same favors as when transported in vessels sailing under the flag of such other Party. This applies especially with regard to customs duties and all other fees and charges, to bounties, drawbacks and other privileges of this nature, as well as to the administration of the customs and to transport to and from port by rail and other means of transportation.

4. The coasting trade and inland navigation are excepted from the provisions of the present Article. However, the vessels of each Party shall be accorded by the other Party most-favored-nation treatment with respect to the coasting trade and inland navigation. Moreover, it is understood that vessels of either Party shall be permitted to discharge portions of cargoes at any ports, places or waters of the other Party open to foreign commerce and navigation, and to proceed with the remaining portions of such cargoes to any other such ports, places or waters, and they shall be permitted to load in like manner in the same voyage outward, at the various ports, places and waters open to foreign commerce and navigation; but a right to engage in the coasting trade or inland navigation may not thereby be claimed.

5. The provisions of the present Article shall not apply to fishing vessels.

Article XXI

If a vessel of either Party runs aground or is wrecked on the coasts of the other Party, or if it is in distress and must put into a port of the other Party, the latter Party shall extend to the vessel as well as to the crew, the passengers, the personal property of crew and passengers, and to the cargo of the vessel, the same protection and assistance as would have been extended to a vessel under its own flag in like circumstances; and shall permit the vessel after repairs to proceed with its voyage upon conformity with the laws applicable alike to vessels under its own flag. Articles salvaged from the vessel shall be exempt from all customs duties unless they pass into internal consumption; but articles not entered for consumption may be subject to measures for the protection of the revenue pending their exit from the country.

Article XXII

1. In all ports of either Party the masters of all vessels under the flag of the other Party, whose crews have ceased to be fully constituted on account of illness or for any other cause, shall be permitted to engage such seamen as may be necessary for the continuation of the voyage.

2. Nationals of either Party who are seamen may be sent to ports of the other Party to join national vessels, in care of consular officers, either individually or in groups on the basis of seamen's papers issued in lieu of passports. Likewise, nationals of either Party shall be permitted to travel through the territory of the other Party on their way to join vessels or to be repatriated on the basis of seamen's papers issued in lieu of passports.

Article XXIII

1. There shall be freedom of transit through the territories of each Party by the routes most convenient for international transit:

(a) for nationals of the other Party, together with their baggage;

(b) for other persons, together with their baggage, en route to or from the territories of such other Party; and

(c) for products of any origin en route to or from the territories of such other Party, with or without trans-shipment, warehousing, breaking bulk or change in the mode of transport.

2. The persons and things referred to in paragraph 1 of the present Article shall be exempt from customs duties, from duties imposed by reason of transit, and from unreasonable charges and requirements; and shall be free from unnecessary delays and restrictions.

3. The provisions of the present Article shall be subject to the right of either Party to apply measures referred to in Article II, paragraph 5, and nondiscriminatory regulations necessary to prevent abuse of the transit privilege.

Article XXIV

1. The present Treaty shall not preclude the application by either Party of measures:

(a) regulating the importation or exportation of gold, silver, platinum and the alloys thereof;

(b) relating to fissionable materials, to radioactive by-products of the utilization or processing thereof, or to materials that are the source of fissionable materials;

(c) regulating the production of or traffic in arms, ammunition and implements of war, or traffic in other materials carried on directly or indirectly for the purpose of supplying a military establishment;

(d) necessary to fulfil its obligations for the maintenance or restoration of international peace and security, or necessary to protect its essential security interests;

(e) denying to any company in the ownership or direction of which nationals of any third country or countries have directly or indirectly the controlling interest the advantages of the present Treaty, except with respect to recognition of juridical status and with respect to access to courts; and

(f) reserving rights and privileges with respect to its national fisheries and marine hunting, and the landing in its ports of fish or fish products or the catch of products of marine hunting taken on board the transporting vessel at sea.

2. The most-favored-nation provisions of the present Treaty relating to the treatment of goods shall not apply to advantages accorded by the United States of America or its Territories and possessions to one another, to the Republic of Cuba, to the Republic of the Philippines, to the Trust Territory of the Pacific Islands or to the Panama Canal Zone.

3. The most-favored-nation treatment provisions of the present Treaty shall not apply to advantages accorded by either Party to adjacent countries in order to facilitate frontier traffic.

4. The provisions of the present treaty relating to the treatment of goods shall not preclude action by either Party which is required or permitted by the General

Agreement on Tariffs and Trade during such time as such Party is a contracting party to the General Agreement. Similarly, the most-favored-nation provisions of the present Treaty shall not apply to special advantages accorded by virtue of the aforesaid Agreement.

5. If at any time the arrangements provided in the first sentence of paragraph 4 of the present Article should cease to be applicable, the provisions of Article XIV, paragraph 2, shall not apply for a period of twelve months to restrictions in effect at that time. During this period the two Parties will, upon the request of either of them, consult with a view to determining whether in the light of circumstances then prevailing, any further adjustment may be necessary.

6. The present Treaty does not affect provisions of statute under which aliens may be permitted entry into the territories of a Party subject to express conditions regarding their engaging in gainful occupations therein.

Article XXV

1. The term "national treatment" means treatment accorded within the territories of a Party upon terms no less favorable than the treatment accorded therein, in like situations, to nationals, companies, products, vessels or other objects, as the case may be, of such Party.

2. National treatment is accorded by the Federal Republic of Germany in the provisions of the present Treaty in consideration of the national treatment accorded by the United States of America to the nationals, companies, products, vessels or other objects, of the Federal Republic of Germany, with respect to the same subject matter.

3. National treatment accorded under the provisions of the present Treaty to companies of the Federal Republic of Germany shall, in any State, Territory, or possession of the United States of America, be the treatment accorded therein to companies created or organized in other States, Territories, and possessions of the United States of America.

4. The term "most-favored-nation treatment" means treatment accorded within the territories of a Party upon terms no less favorable than the treatment accorded therein, in like situations, to nationals, companies, products, vessels or other objects, as the case may be, of any third country.

5. As used in the present Treaty, the term "companies" means corporations, partnerships, companies and other associations, whether or not with limited liability and whether or not for pecuniary profit. Companies constituted under the applicable laws and regulations within the territories of either Party shall be deemed companies thereof and shall have their juridical status recognized within the territories of the other Party.

6. Without prejudice to other methods of establishing nationality, a person in possession of a valid passport issued by the competent authorities of either Party or a valid identity document named in the Protocol, shall be considered a national of that Party.

Article XXVI

1. The territories to which the present Treaty extends shall comprise all areas of land and water under the sovereignty or authority of each Party, other than the Panama Canal Zone and the Trust Territory of the Pacific Islands.

2. The present Treaty shall also apply from the date specified in Article XXIX, paragraph 2, to Land Berlin which for the purposes of the present Treaty comprises those areas over which the Berlin Senate exercises jurisdiction.

3. It is a condition to the application of the present Treaty to Land Berlin,

in accordance with the preceding paragraph, that the Government of the Federal Republic of Germany shall previously have furnished to the Government of the United States of America a notification that all legal procedures in Berlin necessary for the application of the present Treaty therein have been complied with.

Article XXVII

1. Each Party shall accord sympathetic consideration to, and shall afford adequate opportunity for consultation regarding, such representations as the other Party may make with respect to any matter affecting the operation of the present Treaty.

2. Any dispute between the Parties as to the interpretation or the application of the present Treaty which the Parties do not satisfactorily adjust by diplomacy or some other agreed means shall be submitted to arbitration or, upon agreement of the Parties, to the International Court of Justice.

Article XXVIII

The present Treaty shall replace and terminate provisions in force in Articles I through V, VII through XVI, and XXIX through XXXII, of the treaty of friendship, commerce and consular rights between Germany and the United States of America, signed at Washington December 8, 1923, as amended by an exchange of notes dated March 19 and May 21, 1925 and the agreement signed at Washington June 3, 1935, and as applied by the agreement of June 3, 1953, Article VI having terminated on June 2, 1954. Articles XVII through XXVIII of the said treaty, as amended by Article II of the agreement of June 3, 1953, shall continue in force between the Federal Republic of Germany and the United States of America, with territorial application to the same extent as that provided in Article XXVI of the present Treaty, until replaced by a consular convention beween the two Parties or until six months after either Party shall have given to the other Party a written notice of termination of the said Articles.

Article XXIX

1. The present Treaty shall be ratified, and the ratifications thereof shall be exchanged at Bonn as soon as possible.

2. The present Treaty shall enter into force one month after the day of exchange of ratifications. It shall remain in force for ten years and shall continue in force thereafter until terminated as provided herein.

3. Either Party may, by giving one year's written notice to the other Party, terminate the present Treaty at the end of the initial ten-year period or at any time thereafter.

In Witness Whereof the respective Plenipotentiaries have signed the present Treaty and have affixed hereunto their seals.

Done in duplicate, in the German and English languages, both equally authentic, at Washington this twenty-ninth day of October, one thousand nine hundred fifty-four.

For the Federal Republic of Germany:
/S/ Adenauer

[Seal]

For the United States of America:
/S/ John Foster Dulles

[Seal]

Protocol

At the time of the signing of the Treaty of Friendship, Commerce and Navigation between the Federal Republic of Germany and the United States of America, the undersigned Plenipotentiaries, duly authorized, have further agreed on the following provisions, which shall be considered integral parts of the aforesaid Treaty:

1. The spouse and unmarried minor children of a person permitted entry under the provisions of the second sentence of Article II, paragraph 1, shall also be permitted entry if accompanying him or following to join him.
2. The provisions of Article II, paragraph 1 (b), shall be construed as extending to nationals of either Party seeking to enter the territories of the other Party solely for the purpose of developing and directing the operations of an enterprise in the territories of such other Party in which their employer has invested or is actively in the process of investing a substantial amount of capital: provided that such employer is a national or company of the same nationality as the applicant and that the applicant is employed by such national or company in a responsible capacity.
3. The term "public health" in Article II, paragraph 5, and the term "sanitary grounds" in Article XIV, paragraph 3, comprise the protection of human, animal, and plant life and health.
4. The provisions of Article IV, paragraph 2, refer only to laws and regulations which either are national laws or regulations or are based in whole or in part on requirements of national laws or regulations.
5. The provisions of Article V, paragraph 4, shall apply to the property taken in the territories of either Party in which nationals and companies of the other Party have a direct or indirect interest.
6. With reference to Article VI, paragraph 1, nationals and companies of either Party appearing as plaintiff or intervening party before the courts of the other Party shall be exempt from obligation to post security for costs in such instances as nationals or companies of the other Party would be exempt; exemption, however, is only granted if:

   (a) the nationals have their permanent residence or the companies their establishment (main or branch), or

   (b) the nationals or the companies have sufficient real property to cover costs,

   in the territory of that Party before the courts of which the suit is pending.
7. With reference to Article VI, paragraph 1, nationals of either Party shall be accorded national treatment within the territories of the other Party:

   (a) With respect to suits in *forma pauperis,* in proceedings in the Federal courts of the United States of America;

   (b) With respect to the pauper's right (*Armenrecht*) in proceedings before the courts of the Federal Republic of Germany, in types of cases which in the United States of America would fall within the Federal jurisdiction or could be brought before Federal courts.
8. With reference to Article VII, paragraph 1, a Party may apply regulations under which alien employees within its territories are required to have employment permits; but, in keeping with the objectives of that paragraph, such regulations shall be administered in a liberal fashion as to nationals of the other Party. Furthermore, it is understood that legal provisions which reserve to nationals of the country the practice of state licensed professions or require state examinations and licenses and local residence are not precluded by the terms of that paragraph.

9. The provisions of Article VII do not obligate either Party to permit nationals and companies of the other Party to carry on businesses in its territories without fulfilling the requirements which are generally applicable by law.

10. The provisions of Article VII, paragraph 1, do not affect the right of either Party, in accordance with the agreements and objectives of the present Treaty, to apply special regulations to foreign insurance companies in order to ensure that such companies maintain the degree of responsibility and solvency required of similar domestic companies, but these regulations may not in their effect result in discrimination in substance against such foreign companies.

11. The term "communications" in Article VII, paragraph 2, includes radio and television, among other means of communication.

12. With reference to Article VII, paragraph 4, either Party may require that the granting of rights to engage in mining on the public domain shall be dependent on reciprocity.

13. The provisions of Articles VII, paragraph 1, and XIII shall not extend to the activity of peddlers and itinerant artisans in the exercise of their occupations as such.

14. Article XII, paragraph 1, is not concerned with rules regarding currencies as such and therefore does not preclude differential treatment of different currencies. It is only concerned with the rights of nationals and companies under whatever foreign exchange regulations may be in effect and is only designed to preclude discriminations against nationals and companies on a nationality basis in the application of the foreign exchange regulations.

15. The term "reasonable" in Article XII, paragraph 4, allows each Party to apply such measures as are required to fulfil its legal obligations, to secure goods and services essential to the health and welfare of its people, and to give consideration to special needs for other exchange transactions.

16. Either Party may, for the protection of its currency and in the interest of servicing investments and providing for their repatriation, make the importation of capital dependent on a license.

17. If more than one rate of exchange exists, the rate applicable to withdrawals under Article XII, paragraph 4, shall be a rate which is specifically approved by the International Monetary Fund for such transactions or, in the absence of a rate so approved, an effective rate which, inclusive of any taxes or charges on exchange transfers, is just and reasonable.

18. In matters affecting internal taxation the national treatment provision of Article XVI, paragraph 1, shall not apply within the territories of either Party to special treatment of products made in whole or in part of materials grown or produced within the territories of such Party. However, this provision shall apply only where such special treatment exists on the date of entry into force of the present Treaty. Any enactment or amendment made subsequent to that date shall not alter such special treatment in a manner detrimental to the interests of the other Party.

19. The provisions of Article XVII, paragraph 2 (b) and (c), and of Article XX, paragraph 2, shall not apply to postal services of either Party.

20. With reference to Article XX, the term "cargoes" in the meaning of the present Treaty includes both goods and passengers.

21. The provisions of Article XXIV, paragraph 2, shall apply in the case of Puerto Rico regardless of any change that may take place in its political status.

22. Identity documents within the meaning of Article XXV, paragraph 6, shall include, *inter alia,*
    (a) for the Federal Republic of Germany:
    The certificate of residence (*Heimatschein*) and the seaman's book (*Seefahrtsbuch*) issued by the authorities of the Federal Republic of Germany, if the bearer is designated therein as a German national;
    (b) for the United States of America:
    A card or certificate of identity and registration, or a United States merchant mariner's document, if the bearer is designated therein as a national of the United States.
23. Territories under the authority of a Party solely as a military base or by reason of temporary military occupation shall not be considered territories of that Party within the meaning of Article XXVI, paragraph 1.
24. It is agreed that after the Federal Republic of Germany becomes a member of the United Nations or a party to the Statute of the International Court of Justice, disputes to which Article XXVII, paragraph 2, refers, and which are not resolved by diplomacy or some other agreed means, shall be submitted to the International Court of Justice.

IN WITNESS WHEREOF the respective Plenipotentiaries have signed this Protocol and have affixed hereunto their seals.

DONE in duplicate, in the German and English languages, both equally authentic, at Washington this twenty-ninth day of October, one thousand nine hundred fifty-four.

For the Federal Republic of Germany:
signed: Adenauer

For the United States of America:
signed: John Foster Dulles

[EXCHANGE OF NOTES]

Department of State, Washington — October 29, 1954

His Excellency,
Dr. Konrad Adenauer,
Chancellor of the
Federal Republic of Germany.

Excellency:

I have the honor to refer to the treaty of friendship, commerce and navigation between the United States of America and the Federal Republic of Germany, signed today, and to set forth the further agreement as follows:

The present special position of the United States of America and its personnel in Germany shall not be affected by the aforesaid treaty.

The aforesaid treaty shall not modify or derogate from the provisions of the conventions signed at Bonn on May 26, 1952 or such agreement or agreements as may modify or replace them.

Accept, Excellency, the renewed assurances of my highest consideration.

signed: JOHN FOSTER DULLES
Secretary of State of the
United States of America

[The Note from Chancellor Adenauer to Secretary Dulles, also dated October 29, 1954, is not reproduced here as the body of the Note is merely the German version of the Note reproduced *supra*.]

Department of State, Washington October 29, 1954

His Excellency,
Dr. Konrad Adenauer,
Chancellor of the
Federal Republic of Germany.

Excellency:

During the discussion of Article XV, paragraph 1, of the treaty of friendship, commerce and navigation between the United States of America and the Federal Republic of Germany, signed today, the representatives of the two Governments exchanged views as to possible means available for affording protection to traders against sudden imposition of administrative measures adversely affecting their ability to plan and conduct their international business with reasonable assurance.

The representatives of the United States of America pointed out that under United States procedure new administrative measures affecting imports become effective, as a general practice, only upon the expiration of a transitory period of not less than 30 days after publication thereof. Types of administrative measures falling under this procedure include, for example, the imposition or reduction of quotas, the increase of duties as a consequence of "escape clause" action or of a change in a uniform and established classification, and the withdrawal of trade agreement concessions. They also explained that under Section 16.10a of the Customs Regulations a procedure exists whereby importers and foreign exporters may apply to the Commissioner of Customs for decisions of a binding character regarding the customs classification of particular articles intended for importation.

The German representatives stated that under German law and procedure importers and foreign exporters may, in advance of shipment, obtain binding customs information about tariff rates and expressly specified commodities valid as against any modification or cancellation, subject to the regulations of the *Allgemeine Zollordnung*, paragraph 86, subparagraph 3, for a period of three months. Moreover, paragraph 131 of the *Reichsabgabenordnung* affords the possibility for importers to apply for suspension or reduction of the customs duties payable by them, if a customs tariff modification affects them unfairly in individual cases. They further stated that upon promulgating new import restrictions or intensifying existing import restrictions the competent German government agencies will take into account in their administrative practices, as far as possible, the recommendations accepted by the Contracting Parties to the General Agreement on Tariffs and Trade, that is, the Standard Practices for Import and Export Restrictions and Exchange Controls.

The two Governments are agreed that neither has the intention of changing existing administrative procedures so as to provide less favorable facilities and treatment; and that, moreover, further progress should be sought on a broad international basis in the development of measures designed to increase the certainty with which traders can plan their international business as against administrative actions affecting the international movement of products.

Accept, Excellency, the renewed assurances of my highest consideration.

signed: JOHN FOSTER DULLES
Secretary of State of the
United States of America

APPENDIX III

Compilation of Treaties

[*Introductory Note*: This compilation of treaties lists separately the bilateral treaties concluded between the United States and Germany (abbreviated "Treaty B —" and divided into four groups) and those multilateral conventions to which the two countries are or have been parties (abbreviated "Treaty M —"). Where a treaty or convention is expressly declared applicable for West Berlin, the source of the relevant Berlin law is indicated (see ch. 1 sub II (2) (d)). The multilateral treaties which have been declared applicable by East Germany or of which it has purported to become a member are enumerated in ch. 2 nn. 63 and 68; see also n. 72. Finally, it may be pointed out that an instrument becomes effective on the day agreed upon for this purpose; this day may either coincide with, be prior to, or be subsequent to, the day of the coming into force of the treaty.]

BILATERAL TREATIES (B)

(1) With German States (1785–1870)*

1. Treaty of amity and commerce with Prussia, of Sept. 10, 1785 (effective Oct. 1786):

   8 Stat. 84, 18 Stat. part 2 p. 641, TS no. 292, 2 Malloy 1477, 2 Martens 566;

   Expired Oct. 1796.

2. Treaty of amity and commerce with Prussia, of July 11, 1799 (effective June 22, 1800):

   8 Stat. 162, 18 Stat. part 2 p. 648, TS no. 293, 2 Malloy 1486, Martens, 2 Supp. 226, 9 Martens NRG (3e sér.) 321;

   Expired June 22, 1810.

3. Convention of friendship, commerce, and navigation with the Hanseatic Republics (Bremen, Hamburg, and Lübeck), of Dec. 20, 1827 (effective June 2, 1828):

   8 Stat. 366, 18 Stat. part 2 p. 400, TS no. 157, 1 Malloy 901, Martens, 11 Supp. part 1 p. 362, Hamb.VO 10 (1827/28) 108;

   See additional article, no. 5.

4. Treaty of commerce and navigation with Prussia, of May 1, 1828 (effective Mar. 14, 1829):

   8 Stat. 378, 18 Stat. part 2 p. 669, TS no. 294, 2 Malloy 1496, Martens, 11 Supp. part 1 p. 615, Preuss.GS 1829, 25.

5. Additional article to convention of 1827 with the Hanseatic Republics (no. 3), of June 4, 1828 (effective Jan. 14, 1829):

---

*Postal conventions are excluded.

8 Stat. 386, 18 Stat. part 2 p. 403, TS no. 158, 1 Malloy 905, Martens, 11 Supp. part 1 p. 373, Hamb.VO 10 (1827/28) 206;

Superseded by no. 37.

6. Treaty of commerce and navigation with Hanover, of May 20, 1840 (effective Nov. 14, 1840):

   8 Stat. 552, 18 Stat. part 2 p. 387, TS no. 153, 1 Malloy 885, 1 Martens NRG 84, Hann. GS 1840 part 1 p. 505;

   Superseded by no. 12.

7. Convention abolishing droit d'aubaine and taxes on emigration with Hesse, of Mar. 26, 1844 (effective Oct. 16, 1844):

   9 Stat. 818, 18 Stat. part 2 p. 422, TS no. 170, 1 Malloy 947, 7 Martens NRG 570, Hess.RegBl. 1844 no. 34.

8. Convention abolishing droit d'aubaine and taxes on emigration with Württemberg, of Apr. 10, 1844 (effective Oct. 3, 1844):

   8 Stat. 588, 18 Stat. part 2 p. 809, TS no. 373, 2 Malloy 1893, 6 Martens NRG 373, Württ.RegBl. 1844, 52.

9. Convention abolishing droit d'aubaine and taxes on emigration with Bavaria, of Jan. 21, 1845 (effective Nov. 4, 1845):

   9 Stat. 826, 18 Stat. part 2 p. 41, TS no. 16, 1 Malloy 56, Bayer.RegBl. 1845, 851.

10. Convention abolishing droit d'aubaine and emigration taxes with Saxony, of May 14, 1845 (effective Aug. 12, 1846):

    9 Stat. 830, 18 Stat. part 2 p. 690, TS no. 317, 2 Malloy 1610, Sächs.GVOBl. 1846, 225.

11. Convention abolishing droit d'aubaine and emigration taxes with Nassau, of May 27, 1846 (effective Oct. 13, 1846):

    9 Stat. 849, 18 Stat. part 2 p. 531, TS no. 248, 2 Malloy 1231, VOBl. des Herzogthums Nassau 38 (1846) 212.

12. Treaty of commerce and navigation with Hanover, of June 10, 1846 (effective Mar. 15, 1847):

    9 Stat. 857, 18 Stat. part 2 p. 391, TS no. 154, 1 Malloy 890, 9 Martens NRG 191, Hann.GS 1847 part 1 p. 65;

    Supersedes no. 6; for accession, see no. 13; modified by no. 27.

13. Declaration of accession by Oldenburg to the treaty of commerce and navigation with Hanover (no. 12), of Mar. 10, 1847 (effective Mar. 10, 1847):

    9 Stat. 868, 18 Stat. part 2 p. 578, TS no. 263, 2 Malloy 1308, Oldenb.GBl. 2 (1845/48) 371.

14. Treaty of commerce and navigation with Mecklenburg-Schwerin, of Dec. 9, 1847 (effective June 29, 1848):

    9 Stat. 910, 18 Stat. part 2 p. 467, TS no. 199, 1 Malloy 1074, 10 Martens NRG 643, Meck.-Schwer.GS 5 (1800–1856) Supp. p. 937.

15. Consular Convention with the Hanseatic Republics (Bremen, Hamburg, and Lübeck), of Apr. 30, 1852 (effective Feb. 25, 1853):

    10 Stat. 961, 18 Stat. part 2 p. 404, TS no. 159, 1 Malloy 906, 17 Martens NRG part 1 p. 161, Hamb.VO 23 (1853) 20;

    Superseded by no. 37.

16. Convention for the mutual delivery of criminals, fugitives from justice, in certain cases with Prussia and other States of the Germanic Confederation (Saxony, Hesse, Saxe-Weimar-Eisenach, Saxe-Meiningen, Saxe-Altenburg, Saxe-Coburg-Gotha, Brunswick, Anhalt-Dessau, Anhalt-Bernburg, Nassau, Schwarzburg-Rudolstadt, Schwarzburg-Sondershausen, Waldeck, Reuss ä.L., Reuss j.L., Lippe, Hesse-Homburg, Francfort), of June 16, 1852, with additional article of Nov. 16, 1852 (effective May 30, 1853):

    10 Stat. 964, 18 Stat. part 2 p. 660, TS no. 296, 2 Malloy 1501, 19 Martens NRG 49, Preuss.GS 1853, 645, BGBl. 1868, 231;

    For accessions, see nos. 17, 19–23; for extension, see no. 29.

17. Declaration of accession of Bremen to the extradition convention with Prussia and other States of the Germanic Confederation (no. 16), of Sept. 6, 1853 (effective Oct. 14, 1853):

    10 Stat. 790, 18 Stat. part 2 p. 92, TS no. 37, 1 Malloy 155, 19 Martens NRG 49, Brem. GBl. 1853, 113.

18. Extradition convention with Bavaria of Sept. 12, 1853 (effective Nov. 1, 1854):

    10 Stat. 1022, 18 Stat. part 2 p. 42, TS no. 17, 1 Malloy 58, Bayer.-Reg.Bl. 1854, 1089.

19. Declaration of accession by Württemberg to the extradition convention with Prussia and other States of the Germanic Confederation (no. 16), of Oct. 13, 1853 (effective Mar. 2, 1854):

    10 Stat. 791, 18 Stat. part 2 p. 810, TS no. 374, 2 Malloy 1895, Württ.Reg.Bl. 1854, 31.

20. Declaration of accession by Mecklenburg-Schwerin to the extradition convention with Prussia and other States of the Germanic Confederation (no. 16), of Nov. 26, 1853 (effective Jan. 5, 1854):

    10 Stat. 971, 18 Stat. part 2 p. 472, TS no. 200, 1 Malloy 1080, Meck.-Schwer.Reg.Bl. 1854, 71, Meck.-Schwer.GS 5 (1800–1856 Supp. p. 497.

21. Declaration of accession by Mecklenburg Strelitz to the extradition convention with Prussia and other States of the Germanic Confederation (no. 16), of Dec. 2, 1853 (effective June 16, 1854):

    10 Stat. 970, 18 Stat. part 2 p. 473, TS no. 201, 1 Malloy 1081, GS Mecklenburg-Strelitzische Lande II 2 (1860) 500.

22. Declaration of accession by Oldenburg to the extradition convention with Prussia and other States of the Germanic Confederation (no. 16), of Dec. 30, 1853 (effective May 12, 1854):

    10 Stat. 971, 18 Stat. part 2 p. 579, TS no. 264, 2 Malloy 1309, Oldenb.GBl. 1854/55, 193.

23. Declaration of accession by Schaumberg-Lippe to the extradition convention with Prussia and other States of the Germanic Confederation (no. 16), of June 7, 1854 (effective July 26, 1854):

    10 Stat. 972, 18 Stat. part 2 p. 692, TS no. 318, 2 Malloy 1612, Schaumburg-Lippische Landesverordnungen 8 (1848–1855) 645.

24. Convention respecting the disposition of property with Brunswick and Lüneburg, of Aug. 21, 1854 (effective July 28, 1855):

    11 Stat. 601, 18 Stat. part 2 p. 93, TS no. 38, 1 Malloy 156.

25. Extradition treaty with Hanover, of Jan. 18, 1855 (effective Apr. 17, 1855):
    10 Stat. 1138, 18 Stat. part 2 p. 396, TS no. 155, 1 Malloy 896, Hann.GS 1855 part 1 p. 155.

26. Extradition convention with Baden, of Jan. 30, 1857 (effective Apr. 21, 1857):
    11 Stat. 713, 18 Stat. part 2 p. 37, TS no. 14, 1 Malloy 51, Bad.RegBl. 1857, 154.

27. Convention abolishing Stade or Brunshausen dues with Hanover, of Nov. 6, 1861 (effective Apr. 29, 1862):
    12 Stat. 1187, 18 Stat. part 2 p. 398, TS no. 156, 1 Malloy 898, Hann.GS 1863 part 1 p. 203.

28. Convention for the amelioration of the postal service with the Post Department of the North German Union, of Oct. 21, 1867 (effective Jan. 1, 1868):
    15 Stat. 577, 16 Stat. 979, BGBl. 1868, 26;
    Amended by nos. 34 and 35; supplemented by no. 37 A; superseded by Treaty M 3.

29. Naturalization convention with North German Union, of Feb. 22, 1868 (effective May 9, 1868):
    15 Stat. 615, 18 Stat. part 2 p. 575, TS no. 261, 2 Malloy 1298, 19 Martens NRG 78, BGBl. 1868, 228;
    Art. III extends no. 16 to all states of the North German Union.

30. Naturalization treaty with Bavaria, of May 26, 1868 (effective Sept. 18, 1868):
    15 Stat. 661, 18 Stat. part 2 p. 44, TS no. 18, 1 Malloy 60, Bayer.RegBl. 1868, 2153.

31. Naturalization convention with Baden, of July 19, 1868 (effective Dec. 7, 1869):
    16 Stat. 731, 18 Stat. part 2 p. 38, TS no. 15, 1 Malloy 53, Bad.GVOBl. 1869, 579.

32. Convention as to naturalization and extradition with Württemberg, of July 27, 1868 (effective Aug. 17, 1869):
    16 Stat. 735, 18 Stat. part 2 p. 811, TS no. 375, 2 Malloy 1895, Württ.RegBl. 1872, 172.

33. Naturalization convention with Hesse, of Aug. 1, 1868 (effective July 23, 1869):
    16 Stat. 743, 18 Stat. part 2 p. 423, TS no. 171, 1 Malloy 949, Hess.-RegBl. 1869, 599.

34. Additional convention to the convention of Oct. 21, 1867 with the Post Department of the North German Union (no. 28), of Apr. 7/23, 1870 (effective July 1, 1870):
    16 Stat. 1003, BGBl. 1870, 594;
    Amended by no. 35. Superseded by Treaty M 3.

(2) With Germany (1871–1945)

35. Additional article to the convention of Oct. 21, 1867 with the Post Department of the North German Union (no. 28), of Mar. 31/May 14, 1871 (effective Oct, 1, 1871):
    17 Stat. 859, BGBl. 1871, 245;
    Superseded by Treaty M 3.

36. Convention concerning the exchange of post office money orders with the Post Office Department of Germany, of July 22, 1871 (effective Oct. 1, 1872):

    See ABl.DRPVerw. 1872, 711;

    Superseded by no. 38.

37. Consular convention, of Dec. 11, 1871 (effective Apr. 29, 1872):

    17 Stat. 921, 18 Stat. part 2 p. 255, TS no. 99, 1 Malloy 550, 19 Martens NRG 34, RGBl. 1872, 95.

37A. Additional articles of agreement (relating to exchange of postal-cards) with the Post Office Department of Germany, of Oct. 31/Nov. 18, 1873 (effective Dec. 1, 1873):

    18 Stat. part 3 p. 802, see ABl.DRPVerw. 1873, 486;

    Supplements no. 28; superseded by Treaty M 3.

38. Convention concerning the exchange of post office money orders with the Post Office Department of Germany, of Oct. 9, 1897 (effective Apr. 1, 1880):

    21 Stat. 680, CBl. 1880, 110;

    Supersedes no. 36; supplemented by no. 39.

39. Additional agreement to the convention concerning the exchange of post office money orders (no. 38), of June 14/29, 1889:

    See ABl.RPA 1889, 216.

40. Agreement concerning mail by sea on the lines between Bremen and Hamburg on the one hand and New York on the other hand with the Post Office Department of Germany, of Dec. 24, 1890:

    Abrogated by no. 47.

41. Copyright agreement, of Jan. 15, 1892 (effective May 6, 1892):

    27 Stat. 1022, TS no. 100, 1 Malloy 557, 17 Martens NRG (2e sér.) 934, RGBl. 1892, 473, 475;

    See text, p. 29 and n. 14, p. 35 and n. 53.

42. Agreement concerning the exchange of parcel post with the Post Office Department of Germany, of Aug. 26, 1899 (effective Oct. 1, 1899):

    31 Stat. 1830, see notice in ABl.RPA 1899, 301;

    Superseded by no. 60.

43. Reciprocal commercial arrangement, of July 10, 1900 (effective July 13, 1900):

    31 Stat. 1935, TS no. 101, 1 Malloy 558, DRAnz. 1900 no. 184 of Aug. 4, Dt.Hand.Arch. 1900 I 488;

    Expired Feb. 28, 1906 (DRAnz. 1906 no. 53).

44. Agreement for the reciprocal protection of trade-marks in Morocco, of Sept. 28/Oct. 8, 1901 (effective Oct. 8, 1901):

    TS no. 473, 1 Malloy 559.

45. Agreement for the protection of trade-marks in China, of Dec. 6, 1905/Jan. 22, 1906 (effective Jan. 22, 1906):

    TS no. 481, 1 Malloy 560.

46. Commercial Agreement, of Apr. 22/May 2, 1907 (effective July 1, 1907):
    TS no. 460, 1 Malloy 563, 35 Martens NRG (2e sér.) 630, RGBl. 1907, 305;
    Expired Feb. 6, 1910.

47. Agreement concerning mail by sea with the Post Office Department of Germany, of Aug. 2, 1907:
    Supplemented by no. 48.

48. Postal convention concerning the reduction of fees for letters by sea mail with the Post Office Department of Germany, of Jan. 9/26, 1909 (effective Jan. 1, 1909):
    36 Stat. 21 97, see ABl.RPA 1908, 337;
    Supplements no. 47.

49. Patent convention, of Feb. 23, 1909 (effective Aug. 1, 1909):
    36 Stat. 2178, TS no. 531, 1 Malloy 578, 5 Martens NRG (3e sér.) 461, RGBl. 1909, 895;
    See text p. 28 and n. 13, p. 35 and n. 49.

50. Treaty restoring friendly relations, of Aug. 25, 1921 (effective Nov. 11, 1921):
    42 Stat. 1939, TS no. 658, Redmond 2596, 12 LNTS 191, 11 Martens NRG (3e sér.) 917, RGBl. 1921, 1318, 1369;
    See also no. 51.

51. Agreement for a Mixed Commission to determine the amount to be paid by Germany in satisfaction of Germany's financial obligations under the Treaty concluded between the two Governments on Aug. 25, 1921 (no. 40), of Aug. 10, 1922 (effective Aug. 10, 1922):
    42 Stat. 2200, TS no. 665, Redmond 2601, 26 LNTS 358, 11 Martens NRG (3e sér.) 924, RGBl. 1923 II 113;
    Extended by no. 61; see also no. 97.

52. Agreement about the importation of opium and similar narcotics, of Aug. 7/Oct. 10, 1923 (effective Oct. 10, 1923):
    Notice in 1 St.Archiv N.F. 45 no. 188.

53. Arrangement regarding relief from double income tax on shipping profits, of Sept. 5, 1923/Oct. 8, 1923/Jan. 19, 1924, May 5, 1924/Sept. 3, 1924/Nov. 29, 1924/Dec. 11, 1924/March 20, 1925 (effective Jan. 1, 1921):
    47 Stat. 2627, EAS no. 17, 119 LNTS 185, 28 Martens NRG (3e sér.) 499.

54. Convention for the exchange of money orders, of Sept. 10/Oct. 6, 1923.

55. Treaty of friendship, commerce and consular rights with Germany, of Dec. 8, 1923, amended through agreement of Mar. 19/May 21, 1925 (effective Oct. 14, 1925):
    44 Stat. 2132, TS no. 725, Trenwith 4191, 52 LNTS 133, 17 Martens NRG (3e sér.) 353, RGBl. 1925 II 795, 967;
    Amended by nos. 71, 103 and 104 and in part replaced by no. 117.

56. Convention for the prevention of smuggling of intoxicating liquors, of May 19, 1924 (effective Aug. 11, 1924):
    43 Stat. 1815, TS no. 694, Trenwith 4208, 41 LNTS 271, 17 Martens NRG (3e sér.) 492, RGBl. 1926 II 233.

57. Agreement regarding the direct exchange of information between the services in charge of the traffic in narcotic drugs, of Dec. 24, 1927/Feb. 14, 1928 (effective Feb. 14, 1928):

    79 LNTS 235, notice in RMBl. 1928, 364;

    Superseded by no. 118.

58. Treaty of arbitration, of May 5, 1928 (effective Feb. 25, 1929):

    45 Stat. 2744, TS no. 774, Trenwith 4210, 90 LNTS 177, 20 Martens NRG (3e sér.) 427, RGBl. 1929 II 3, 133.

59. Treaty of conciliation, of May 5, 1928 (effective Feb. 25, 1929):

    45 Stat. 2748, TS no. 775, Trenwith 4212, 90 LNTS 171, 20 Martens NRG (3e sér.) 423, RGBl. 1929 II 3, 133.

60. Agreement concerning the exchange of parcel-post with the Post Office Department of Germany, of June 25/Aug. 4, 1928 (effective July 1, 1928):

    45 Stat. 2701, notice in Dt. Hand.Archiv 1928, 3685;
    Supersedes no. 42; superseded by no. 72.

61. Agreement for the extension of the jurisdiction for the bringing of claims before the Mixed Claims Commission established by the agreement of Aug. 10, 1922 (no. 51), of Dec. 31, 1928 (effective same day):

    45 Stat. 2698, TS no. 766, Trenwith 4213, 20 Martens NRG (3e sér.) 460.

62. Agreement regarding the war debt of Germany to the U.S., of June 23, 1930 (effective same day):

    106 LNTS 121, 25 Martens NRG (3e sér.) 338, RGBl. 1930 II 385, 960.

63. Extradition treaty, of July 12, 1930 (effective Apr. 26, 1931):

    47 Stat. 1862, TS no. 836, Trenwith 4216, 119 LNTS 247, 24 Martens NRG (3e sér.) 487, RGBl. 1931 II 402;

    Extended by no. 73. On re-application with West Germany after Jan. 1, 1956, see text p. 35 and n. 51.

64. Agreement concerning customs inspection of passengers and their baggage on board American and German ships on the high seas, of Aug. 27/Sept. 5, 1931 (effective Aug. 31, 1933):

    34 Martens NRG (3e sér.) 533, RGBl. 1933 II 644.

65. Arrangement for the reciprocal recognition of load-line certificates, of Sept. 11/Dec. 16, 1931 (effective Dec. 16, 1931):

    47 Stat. 2695, EAS no. 31, 129 LNTS 129, 34 Martens NRG (3e sér.) 901, RMBl. 1931, 23, DRAnz. 1932 no. 22;

    Superseded by Treaty M 80.

66. Agreement for collect-on-delivery parcel post service, of Dec. 22, 1931/Jan. 5, 1932 (effective Jan. 1, 1932):

    47 Stat. 1966, see ABl.RPM 1931, 578;

    Superseded by no. 72.

67. Moratorium Agreement, of May 26, 1932 (effective July 1, 1931).

68. Agreement for the reciprocal reduction of passport visa-fees, of May 27/31, 1932 (effective June 10, 1932).

69. Arrangement regarding air navigation, of May 27, 30 and 31, 1932 (effective June 1, 1932):

    47 Stat. 2721, EAS no. 38, 133 LNTS 409, 26 Martens NRG (3e sér.) 364, DRAnz. 1932 no. 136.

70. Arrangement concerning the reciprocal recognition of certificates of airworthiness for aircraft imported from one country into the other as merchandise, of May 27, 30 and 31, 1932 (effective June 1, 1932):

    47 Stat. 2732, EAS no. 39, 133 LNTS 427, 26 Martens NRG (3e sér.) 375, DRAnz. 1932 no. 136.

71. Agreement concerning an amendment of the treaty of friendship, commerce and consular rights (no. 55), of June 3, 1935 (effective Oct. 14, 1935):

    49 Stat. 3258, TS no. 897, Trenwith 4221, 163 LNTS 415, 31 Martens NRG (3e sér.) 773, RGBl. 1935 II 743;

    Amended by nos. 103 and 104 and in part replaced by no. 117.

72. Agreement concerning the exchange of parcel-post, of Feb. 6/Mar. 16. 1939 (effective Jan. 2, 1939):

    53 Stat. 2183, 198 LNTS 237.

73. Agreement concerning extension of the extradition treaty (no. 63) to Austria, of July 22/Nov. 2, 1939 (effective Nov. 2, 1939):

    Foreign Relations, 1939, vol. II, pp. 566–567; notice in RGBl. 1940 II 39.

74. German-American standstill agreement of 1939, of Dec. 9, 1939 (effective Nov. 1, 1939):

    DRAnz. 1940 no. 72 p. 3;

    Replaced M 103; expired May 31, 1940; extended by no. 75.

75. German-American standstill agreement of 1940, of May 25, 1940 (effective June 1, 1940):

    DRAnz. 1940 no. 167 annex 2 p. 3;

    Expired Nov. 30, 1940.

76. Agreement respecting reciprocal application of the model agreement concerning repatriation and hospitalization of prisoners of war annexed to the convention of July 27, 1929 (Treaty M 77), of Mar. 4/30, 1942 (effective Mar. 30, 1942):

    56 Stat. 1507, EAS no. 255, 105 UNTS 219.

(3) With Occupation Powers*

77. Postal agreement concerning airmail service (incoming only) of Sept. 15, 1946 (effective same day):

    Expired.

78. Agreement between the International Refugee Organization and the United States Occupation Authorities, of July 28, 1947 (effective Jan. 1, 1948):

    Germany 1947–1949, p. 131.

79. Economic cooperation agreement with the French Military Government, of July 9, 1948 (effective same day):

    62 Stat. 2251, TIAS no. 1784, 24 UNTS 103;

    Assumed by Federal Republic, BGBl. 1955 II 511, 515.

---

*The Allied Control Authority, unless otherwise indicated.

80. Agreement respecting the application of most-favored-nation treatment to areas under occupation or control with the French Military Government, of July 9, 1948 (effective same day):

    62 Stat. 2891, TIAS no. 1824;

    Supplemented by no. 82.

81. Economic cooperation agreement with the United States/United Kingdom Military Governments, with exchange of notes, of July 14, 1948 (effective same day):

    62 Stat. 2279, TIAS no. 1785, Europa-Archiv 1948, 1561, Öffentlicher Anzeiger für das Vereinigte Wirtschaftsgebiet 1949 no. 26;

    Supplemented by nos. 83 and 87;

    Assumed by Federal Republic, BGBl. 1955 II 515.

82. Agreement respecting the application of most-favored-nation treatment to areas under occupation or control with the United States/United Kingdom Military Governments, of July 14, 1948 (effective same day):

    62 Stat. 2895, TIAS no. 1825;

    Supplemented by no. 80.

83. Economic cooperation agreement with United States/United Kingdom Military Governments and Trieste, of Oct. 15, 1948 (effective same day):

    62 Stat. 3026, TIAS no. 1845;

    Supplements no. 81; supplemented by no. 87;

    Assumed by Federal Republic, BGBl. 1955 II 515.

84. Agreement respecting duty-free entry and payment of transportation charges on relief supplies and packages for the United States/United Kingdom occupied areas in Germany, of Dec. 7/16, 1948 (effective Dec. 16, 1948):

    62 Stat. 3860, TIAS no. 1951;

    Supplemented by nos. 85 and 87.

85. Agreement respecting duty-free entry of and payment of transportation charges on relief supplies and packages for the French Zone of Occupied Germany, of Dec. 16, 1948/Feb. 7, 1949 (effective Feb. 7, 1949):

    63 Stat. 2802, TIAS no. 2049;

    Supplements no. 84.

86. Postal agreement concerning international money order service (incoming only) for remittance of a personal, family or charitable nature, of Jan. 31, 1949 (effective same day):

    Assumed by Federal Republic, BGBl. 1955 II 515.

(4) With Federal Republic of Germany*

87. Economic cooperation agreement, of Dec. 15, 1949 (effective Dec. 29, 1949):

    64 Stat. (3) B86, TIAS no. 2024, 92 UNTS 269, BGBl. 1950, 9, 79, GVOBl. Berlin 1953, 199;

    Supplements nos. 81 and 83. Amended by nos. 88 and 94;

    Supplemented by Treaty M 163 and 164.

---

*For treaties valid in West Berlin, the source of the West Berlin cover-law is indicated. See *supra* ch. 1 at n. 68.

88. Agreement amending the economic cooperation agreement (no. 87), of Feb. 27/Mar. 28, 1951 (effective Mar. 28, 1951):

    2 UST 1295, TIAS no. 2278, 141 UNTS 390;

    Amended by no. 194.

89. Agreement relating to duty-free entry into the Federal Republic of Germany of relief shipments and the defrayment of transportation costs of such shipments, with memorandum attached, of Apr. 10/May 25/June 7, 1951 (effective Dec. 29, 1949):

    5 UST 2820, TIAS no. 3135, 238 UNTS 161;

    Supplements nos. 84 and 85. Amended by no. 92.

90. Agreement relating to the assurance required under the Mutual Security Act of 1951, of Dec. 19/28, 1951 (effective Dec. 28, 1951):

    3 UST 4564, TIAS no. 2607, 181 UNTS 45.

91. Agreement regarding operation of certain radio installations from within the Federal Republic of Germany, of June 11, 1952 (effective May 5, 1955):

    7 UST 789, TIAS no. 3559, 273 UNTS 105, BGBl. 1953 II 516, 1955 II 764.

92. Agreement amending the Agreement relating to duty-free entry into the Federal Republic of Germany of relief shipments and the defrayment of transportation costs of such shipments (no. 89), of July 8/Sept. 6, 1952 (effective Sept. 6, 1952):

    5 UST 2835, TIAS no. 3137, 238 UNTS 167.

93. Agreement for financing certain educational exchange programs, of July 18, 1952 (effective same day):

    3 UST 4095, TIAS no. 2553, 165 UNTS 167;
    Amended by no. 152 and replaced by no. 193.

94. Agreement amending the economic cooperation agreement (no. 87), of Nov. 14/Dec. 30, 1952 (effective Dec. 30, 1952):

    3 UST 5323, TIAS no. 2736, 212 UNTS 329.

95. Arrangement relating to the waiver of visa fees by the United States and visa requirements by the Federal Republic of Germany, of Dec. 12/30, 1952/Jan. 9, 1953 (effective Feb. 1, 1953):

    4 UST 126, TIAS no. 2771, 212 UNTS 3, GemMBl. 1953, 575, notice in BAnz. 1953 no. 7 p. 5.

96. Agreement regarding the settlement of the claim of the United States for postwar economic assistance (other than surplus property) to Germany, of Feb. 27, 1953 (effective Sept. 16, 1953):

    4 UST 893, TIAS no. 2795, 224 UNTS 13, BGBl. 1953 II 492, 590;

    Supplements Treaty M 194; supplemented by nos. 97–99, 156, 178 and 208.

97. Agreement relating to the indebtedness of Germany for awards made by the Mixed Claims Commission, United States and Germany, of Feb. 27, 1953 (effective Sept. 16, 1953):

    4 UST 908, TIAS no. 2796, 244 UNTS 31, BGBl. 1953 II 487, 590;

    Supplements nos. 51 and 96.

98. Agreement regarding the validation of dollar bonds of German issue, of Feb. 27, 1953 (effective same day):

    4 UST 797, 5 UST 1, TIAS no. 2793, 223 UNTS 167, BAnz. 1953 no. 50;

    Supplements no. 96; supplemented by no. 109; amended by nos. 101 and 175.

99. Agreement regarding the settlement of the obligations of the Federal Republic of Germany to the United States for surplus property furnished Germany, of Feb. 27, 1953 (effective Sept. 16, 1953):

    4 UST 923, TIAS no. 2797, 205 UNTS 103, BGBl. 1953 II 497, 590;

    Amended by nos. 110 and 120.

100. Agreement concerning the settlement of claims against the United States forces and authorities which arose during the period of Aug. 1, 1945 to June 30, 1947, of Mar. 24/30, 1953 (effective Mar. 30, 1953):

    5 UST 2149, TIAS no. 3076, 235 UNTS 285.

101. Agreement regarding certain matters arising from the validation of German dollar bonds, of Apr. 1, 1953 (effective Sept. 16, 1953):

    4 UST 885, 5 UST 1, TIAS no. 2794, 224 UNTS 3, BGBl. 1953 II 301, 591, GVOBl.Berlin 1953, 1164;

    Amends no. 98; supplemented by nos. 109 and 175.

102. Agreement concerning cultural relations, of Apr. 9, 1953 (effective same day):

    4 UST 939, TIAS no. 2798, 204 UNTS 79, Bulletin 1953, 590.

103. Agreement terminating Art. VI of the treaty of friendship, commerce and consular rights of Dec. 8, 1923 (no. 55), of June 2, 1953 (effective June 2, 1954):

    5 UST 827, TIAS no. 2972.

104. Agreement concerning the treaty of friendship, commerce and consular rights of Dec. 8, 1923, as amended (no. 55), of June 3, 1953 (effective Oct. 22, 1954):

    5 UST 1939, TIAS no. 3062, 31 D.S.Bull. 713 (1954), 253 UNTS 89, BGBl. 1954 II 722, 1051, GVOBl.Berlin 1954, 619;

    Partly superseded by no. 117.

105. Agreement concerning certificates of origin for hogs' bristles, of Aug. 18/26, 1953 (effective Aug. 26, 1953):

    BAnz. 1953 no. 181, 1954 no. 76, notice in 19 Fed.Reg. 5655.

106. Agreement relating to the return to the Federal Republic of Germany of Tripartite Naval Commission vessels, of Aug. 20, 1953 (effective same day):

    4 UST 2815, TIAS no. 2891, 224 UNTS 49, BAnz. 1953 no. 161 p. 2.

107. Agreement relating to the purchase by the Federal Republic of Germany from the United States of certain equipment for police use, of Nov. 23, 1953 (effective same day):

    5 UST 170, TIAS no. 2911, 224 UNTS 107.

108. Agreement concerning assistance to be rendered by a German Red Cross hospital in Korea, of Feb. 12, 1954 (effective same day):

    5 UST 322, TIAS no. 2924, 223 UNTS 153.

109. Confirmation of effectiveness in Berlin of agreement relating to the validation of certain German dollar bonds, of Feb. 25/Apr. 9, 1954:

 5 UST 1, 223 UNTS 245.

110. Agreement relating to the deduction of $2,350,000 from the indebtedness of the Federal Republic to the United States for certain claims pursuant to arts. I and VII of the surplus property payment agreement of Feb. 27, 1953 (no. 99), of May 17/Aug. 17, 1954 (effective Aug. 18, 1954):

 5 UST 1476, TIAS no. 3021, 233 UNTS 31, 31 D.S.Bull. 319 (1954);
 Supplemented by no. 120.

111. Agreement relating to the exemption of U.S. airline companies from certain German taxes, of July 22, 1954 (effective July 22, 1954):

 TIAS no. 3003.

112. Convention for the avoidance of double taxation with respect to taxes on income, of July 22, 1954 (effective Jan. 1, 1955):

 5 UST 2768, TIAS no. 3133, 239 UNTS 3, BGBl. 1954 II 1118, 1955 II 6, GVOBl.Berlin 1955, 221;
 Amended by no. 200.

113. Agreement relating to the use of practice bombing range near Cuxhaven (Germany) by U.S. Air Force units temporarily stationed in the United Kingdom, of Aug. 6/28, 1954 (effective Aug. 28, 1954):

 5 UST 1957, TIAS no. 3063;
 Amended by nos. 114, 129 and 149.

114. Agreement amending the agreement relating to the use of practice bombing range near Cuxhaven (no. 113), of Sept. 21/24/Oct. 15/18, 1954 (effective Oct. 18, 1954):

 5 UST 1957, TIAS no. 3063;
 Amended by no. 129.

115. Agreement concerning tax relief to be accorded by the Federal Republic of Germany to United States expenditures in interest of the common defense, with annex and exchange of letters, of Oct. 15, 1954 (effective Nov. 8, 1955):

 6 UST 3081, TIAS no. 3360, 239 UNTS 135, BGBl. 1955 II 823, 943, GVOBl.Berlin 1956, 1067.

116. Agreement relating to the exchange of official publications, of Oct. 27, 1954 (effective same day):

 5 UST 2563, TIAS no. 3121, 234 UNTS 131, 31 D.S.Bull. 791 (1954), BAnz. 1955 no. 68 p. 1.

117. Treaty of friendship, commerce and navigation, with protocol and exchange of notes, of Oct. 29, 1954 (effective July 14, 1956):

 7 UST 1839, TIAS no. 3593, 273 UNTS 2, BGBl. 1956 II 488, 763, GVOBl.Berlin 1956, 1067;
 Supersedes in part nos. 55 and 104.

118. Arrangement concerning the exchange of information relating to the illicit traffic in narcotics, of Jan. 17/Aug. 24, 1955/March 7, 1956 (effective Mar. 7, 1956):

 7 UST 371, TIAS no. 3514, 271 UNTS 361, BGBl. 1957 II 709, GVOBl.Berlin 1957, 1625;
 Supersedes no. 57.

119. Agreement for the sale of feed grain and the purchase of building materials for United States defense purposes, of Feb. 18, 1955 (effective same day):

 6 UST 655, TIAS no. 3199, 247 UNTS 257.

120. Agreement for the final disposition of certain claims to be paid from the amount deducted from the indebtedness of the Federal Republic pursuant to art. I of the surplus property payments agreement of Feb. 27, 1953 (no. 99), of Mar. 11/Apr. 14, 1955 (effective Apr. 19, 1955):

 6 UST 1065, TIAS no. 3245, 263 UNTS 351.

121. Agreement relating to offshore procurement, of Apr. 4, 1955 (effective Feb. 7, 1957):

 8 UST 157, TIAS no. 3755, 279 UNTS 73, BGBl. 1956 II 2080, 1957 II 43, GVOBl.Berlin 1958, 301;

 Supplemented by no. 122.

122. Agreement on the model contract containing standard contract clauses referred to in art. 16 of the agreement of Apr. 4, 1955 relating to offshore procurement (no. 121), of Apr. 4, 1955 (effective Feb. 7, 1957):

 8 UST 497, TIAS no. 3804, 289 UNTS 326, BAnz. 1957 no. 136.

123. Agreement relating to the operation of the International Tracing Service, of June 6, 1955 (effective same day):

 6 UST 6169, TIAS no. 3471, 315 UNTS 155, BAnz. 1955 no. 241;

 Supplemented by treaties M 215 and 216; extended and amended by no. 172.

124. Mutual defense assistance agreement, of June 30, 1955 (effective Dec. 27, 1955):

 6 UST 5999, TIAS no. 3443, 240 UNTS 47, BGBl. 1955 II 1050, 1956 II 377;

 Supplemented by nos. 125, 138–141, 146, 157 and 187.

125. Agreement for the return of equipment pursuant to the mutual defense assistance agreement, of June 30, 1955 (effective Dec. 27, 1955):

 6 UST 6005, TIAS no. 3444, 240 UNTS 69, BAnz. 1956 no. 199 p. 1;

 Amended by no. 177.

126. Air transport agreement and exchange of notes, of July 7, 1955 (effective Apr. 16, 1956):

 7 UST 527, TIAS no. 3536, 275 UNTS 3, BGBl. 1956 II 404, 598;

 Amended by no. 213.

127. Agreement relating to the lease of air navigation equipment, of Aug. 2, 1955 (effective Aug. 2, 1955):

 6 UST 6111, TIAS no. 3464, 268 UNTS 121;

 Extended by no. 151; amended by nos. 169, 182, 196, 199, 209 and 218.

128. Agreement relating to external debts of the city of Berlin and of public utility enterprises owned or controlled by Berlin, of Aug. 13/29, 1955/ Feb. 29/Mar. 2, 1956 (effective Mar. 12, 1956):

 7 UST 635, TIAS no. 3545, 273 UNTS 209, Verträge A 92 (vol. 10 p. 4, 8, 13), notice in BGBl. 1956 II 658;

 Supplements Treaty M 194.

129. Agreement amending the agreement relating to the use of practice bombing range near Cuxhaven (no. 113), of Nov. 7/14/29, 1955 (effective Nov. 29, 1955):

6 UST 6073, TIAS no. 3443, 240 UNTS 79;

Supplemented by no. 147.

130. Surplus agricultural commodities agreement for the sale of poultry, of Dec. 23, 1955 (effective same day):

6 UST 6008, TIAS no. 3445;

Supplemented by no. 179.

131. Agreement to facilitate interchange of patent rights and technical information for defense purposes, and exchange of notes, of Jan. 4, 1956 (effective same day):

7 UST 45, TIAS no. 3478, 268 UNTS 143, BAnz. 1956 no. 73;

Supplemented by nos. 155 and 197.

132. Agreement for cooperation concerning civil uses of atomic energy, of Feb. 13, 1956 (effective Apr. 23, 1956):

7 UST 609, TIAS no. 3543, 279 UNTS 338, Bulletin 1956, 317;

Amended by no. 137; supplemented by no. 147; superseded by no. 148.

133. Agreement relating to the return of captured files and archives of the former German Foreign Office at present in the territory of the United Kingdom, of Mar. 14/Apr. 18, 1956 (effective Apr. 18, 1956):

7 UST 2119, TIAS no. 3615, 271 UNTS 319.

134. Agreement regarding the importation of foreign films into and the screen time quota for exhibition in the Federal Republic of Germany, of Apr. 26, 1956 (effective Aug. 17, 1957):

8 UST 735, TIAS no. 3829, 283 UNTS 267, BGBl. 1957 II 282, 1284, GVOBl.Berlin 1957, 1335.

135. Agreement concerning the payment of a financial contribution, of June 6, 1956 (effective same day):

Bulletin 1956, 1216.

136. Agreement relating to the waiver of immunity from legal process of members of the Arbitration Tribunal and the Arbitral Commission on property, rights and interests in Germany under the administrative agreement of July 13, 1956 (Treaty M 231), of July 24/27, 1956 (effective July 27, 1956):

7 UST 2773, TIAS no. 3657, 278 UNTS 3.

137. Agreement amending the agreement for cooperation concerning civil uses of atomic energy (no. 132), of June 29, 1956 (effective Feb. 18, 1957):

TIAS no. 3765, 279 UNTS 342;

Superseded by no. 148.

138. Agreement for reimbursable military procurement under section 106 of the Mutual Security Act of 1954, as amended, of Oct. 8, 1956 (effective same day):

7 UST 2787, TIAS no. 3660, 278 UNTS 9, notice BAnz. 1956 no. 201 p. 3.

139. Agreement relating to the sale to the Federal Republic of certain military equipment, materials, and services pursuant to sec. 106 of the Mutual Security Act of 1954, as amended, of Oct. 8, 1956 (effective same day):

7 UST 2787, TIAS no. 3660, 278 UNTS 9;

Amended by nos. 174 and 185.

140. Agreement relating to the training of German army personnel pursuant to the mutual defense assistance agreement (no. 124), of Dec. 12, 1956 (effective same day):

8 UST 149, TIAS no. 3753, 280 UNTS 63.

141. Agreement relating to the training of German navy personnel pursuant to the mutual defense assistance agreement (no. 124), of Dec. 12, 1956 (effective same day):

8 UST 153, TIAS no. 3754, 280 UNTS 71.

142. Agreement relating to the disbandment of the German element of the Civilian Service Organization maintained by American Forces in Germany under the Forces Convention (Treaty M 208), of Apr. 11, 1957 (effective same day):

8 UST 645, TIAS no. 3815, 283 UNTS 233;

Supplemented by no. 143.

143. Agreement supplementing the agreement relating to the disbandment of the German element of Civilian Service Organization maintained by American Forces in Germany under the Forces Convention (no. 142), of Apr. 11, 1957 (effective same day):

8 UST 645, TIAS no. 3815, 283 UNTS 237.

144. Agreement relating to the loan of certain naval vessels or small craft to the Federal Republic of Germany, of Apr. 30/May 1, 1957 (effective May 1, 1957):

8 UST 894, TIAS no. 3852, 284 UNTS 85;

Amended by no. 153, extended by nos. 191/2, 201, 212 and 217.

145. Agreement providing for a voluntary contribution to costs resulting from maintenance of United States troops in Germany, of June 7, 1957 (effective May 16, 1959):

37 D.S.Bull 129 (1957), BGBl. 1959 II 409, 818.

146. Supplemental agreement to the agreement on mutual assistance (no. 124), of June 7, 1957 (effective May 16, 1959):

BGBl. 1959 II 409, 412, 818.

147. Agreement for cooperation, on behalf of Berlin, concerning civil uses of atomic energy, of June 28, 1957 (effective Aug. 1, 1957):

8 UST 1225, TIAS no. 3874, 288 UNTS 339, BAnz. 1957 no. 182, GVOBl.Berlin 1958, 232;

Supplements nos. 132 and 137; amended by no. 188/9.

148. Agreement for cooperation concerning civil uses of atomic energy, of July 3, 1957 (effective Aug. 7, 1957):

8 UST 1265, TIAS no. 3877, 288 UNTS 305, BAnz. 1957 no. 181;

Supersedes no. 132; see also no. 157; amended by nos. 158 and 190.

149. Agreement supplementing the arrangement relating to the use of the practice bombing range Cuxhaven (Sandbank) (no. 113), of Aug. 5, 1957 (effective same day):

TIAS no. 3890.

150. Agreement relating to the transfer to the Federal Republic of the air bases at Landsberg, Kaufbeuren and Fuerstenfeldbruck and the air depot at Erding, of Dec. 10, 1957 (effective same day):

8 UST 2475, TIAS no. 3968, 307 UNTS 59.

151. Agreement extending agreement for the lease of air navigation equipment (no. 127), of Feb. 24/May 24, 1958 (effective May 24, 1958):

9 UST 958, TIAS no. 4062, 317 UNTS 340.

152. Agreement amending the agreement for financing certain educational exchange programs (no. 93), of May 14, 1958 (effective same day):

Notice in BAnz. 1958 no. 93 p. 4;

Replaced by no 193.

153. Agreement amending the agreement relating to the loan of certain naval vessels or small craft to the Federal Republic of Germany (no. 144), of Oct. 1/15, 1958 (effective Oct. 15, 1958):

9 UST 1334, TIAS no. 4125, 336 UNTS 402;

Extended by no. 201.

154. Agreement relating to certificates of airworthiness for imported aircraft, of Dec. 11, 1958 (effective same day):

9 UST 1478, TIAS no. 4145, 337 UNTS 31, BAnz. 1959 nos. 33, 51;

Supplemented by no. 180.

155. Agreement approving the procedures for reciprocal filing of classified patent applications in the United States and the Federal Republic of Germany, of Mar. 9/May 23, 1959 (effective May 26, 1959):

10 UST 2001, TIAS no. 4369, 361 UNTS 337, BAnz. 1956 no. 73;

Amended by no. 197.

156. Agreement relating to advance payment by Germany on its indebtedness to the United States for post-war economic assistance (other than surplus property) (no. 96), of Mar. 20, 1959 (effective same day):

10 UST 401, TIAS no. 4200, 341 UNTS 15, BAnz. 1960 no. 10.

157. Agreement for cooperation on uses of atomic energy for mutual defense purposes with the Federal Republic of Germany, of May 5, 1959 (effective July 27, 1959):

10 UST 1322, TIAS no. 4276, 355 UNTS 307;

Supplements no. 124; see also no. 148.

158. Agreement amending the agreement for cooperation concerning civil uses of atomic energy (no. 148), of July 22, 1959 (effective Sept. 22, 1959):

10 UST 1659, TIAS no. 4314, 358 UNTS 344, BAnz. 1959 no. 246 p. 3;

Amended by no. 190.

159. Agreement on the settlement of disputes arising out of direct procurement of goods and services from the German Federal Railways and the German Federal Post, of Aug. 3, 1959 (effective July 1, 1963):

    14 UST 689, TIAS no. 5352, p. 3, 490 UNTS 34, BGBl. 1961 II 1382, 1963 II 745;

    Supplements Treaty M 250.

160. Agreement on the status of persons on leave, of Aug. 3, 1959 (effective July 1, 1963):

    14 UST 689, TIAS no. 5352, p. 6, 490 UNTS 36, BGBl. 1961 II 1384, 1963 II 745;

    Supplements Treaty M 250.

161. Agreement implementing the customs and taxation provisions and the customs and consumer tax provisions of the supplementary agreement of Aug. 3, 1959 (Treaty M 250), with annexes, of Aug. 3, 1959 (effective July 1, 1963):

    14 UST 689, TIAS no. 5352, p. 8, 490 UNTS 40.

162. Administrative agreement on aerial photography, implementing article 42 of the supplementary agreement of Aug. 3, 1959 (Treaty M 250), with annex, of Aug. 3, 1959 (effective July 1, 1963):

    14 UST 689, TIAS no. 5352, p. 24, 490 UNTS 70.

163. Administrative agreement pursuant to paragraph 3 of article 74 of the supplementary agreement of Aug. 3, 1959 (Treaty M 250), with annex (Prevention of customs and tax abuses), of Aug. 3, 1959 (effective July 1, 1963):

    14 UST 689, TIAS no. 5352, p. 29, 490 UNTS 82.

164. Agreement relating to accommodation serving public transport and communications pursuant to article 48 of the supplementary agreement of Aug. 3, 1959 (Treaty M 250), with annexes, of Aug. 3, 1959 (effective July 1, 1963):

    14 UST 689, TIAS no. 5352 p. 34, 490 UNTS 94.

165. Agreement relating to rent-free accommodations (Property owned by Government Corporations) to be made available to the United States Forces, with annex, of Aug. 3, 1959 (effective July 1, 1963):

    14 UST 689, TIAS no. 5352, p. 40, 490 UNTS 108;

    Supplements Treaty M 250.

166. Understanding relating to maintenance claims for illegitimate children of members of foreign forces stationed in the Federal Republic of Germany, with annexes, of Aug. 3, 1959 (effective July 1, 1963):

    14 UST 689, TIAS 5352, p. 41, 490 UNTS 114, BAnz. 1966 no. 60;

    Supplements Treaty M 250.

167. Agreement relating to administrative agreements on construction works within the meaning of paragraphs 2 and 3 and sub-paragraph (i) of paragraph 6 of article 49 of the supplementary agreement of Aug. 3, 1959 (Treaty M 250), of Aug. 3, 1959 (effective July 1, 1963):

    14 UST 689, TIAS no. 5352, p. 50, 490 UNTS 132.

168. Agreement for the operation at the Birkenfeld High Altitude Traffic Control Facility of air traffic control services in the airspace above 20,000 feet, of Oct. 1, 1959 (effective same day):

    10 UST 1766, TIAS no. 4330, 358 UNTS 129, BAnz. 1960 no. 65;

    Expired Apr. 28, 1968 (BAnz. 1969 no. 53).

169. Agreement amending the agreement relating to the lease of air navigation equipment (no. 127), of Nov. 3, 1959/Jan. 8, 1960 (effective Jan. 8, 1960):

11 UST 1476, TIAS no. 4490, 376 UNTS 435;

Amended by nos. 182, 196 and 199.

170. Agreement relating to the return of the Emden-Cherbourg-Horta Submarine telegraph cable to German Ownership, of Nov. 4, 1959/Mar. 16, 1960 (effective Mar. 16, 1960):

11 UST 254, TIAS no. 4441, 371 UNTS 101.

171. Agreed procedures with regard to certification of cut jade stones, of Mar. 8, 1960 (effective Mar. 10, 1960):

BAnz. 1960 no. 66, notice in 25 Fed.Reg. 2088.

172. Agreement extending and amending the agreement relating to the operation of the International Tracing Service (no. 123), of Apr. 28/May 5, 1960 (effective May 5, 1960):

12 UST 444, TIAS no. 4736, BAnz. 1961 no. 244;

Supplemented by Treaties M 261 and 264 A.

173. Agreement relating to a weapons production program, of May 27, 1960 (effective same day):

11 UST 1606, TIAS no. 4504, 377 UNTS 45, BAnz. 1960 no. 223.

174. Agreement amending the agreement relating to the sale to the Federal Republic of certain military equipment, materials, and services (no. 139), of June 15/Oct. 24, 1960 (effective Oct. 24, 1960):

11 UST 2242, TIAS no. 4599, 393 UNTS 332;

Amended by no. 185.

175. Second agreement regarding certain matters arising from the validation of German dollar bonds, of Aug. 16, 1960 (effective June 30, 1961):

12 UST 943, TIAS no. 4798, 418 UNTS 235, BGBl. 1961 II 461, 1084, GVOBl.Berlin 1961, 1537 (with reservations);

Supplements nos. 98 and 101.

176. Agreement relating to reciprocal legal assistance in penal matters and information from penal register, of Nov. 7/Dec. 28, 1960/Jan. 3, 1961 (effective Jan. 3, 1961):

12 UST 1156, TIAS no. 4826, 416 UNTS 93, BGBl. 1961 II 471, GVOBl.Berlin 1961, 1628.

177. Agreement amending the agreement for the return of equipment pursuant to the mutual defense assistance agreement (no. 125), of Mar. 9, 1961 (effective same day):

12 UST 243, TIAS no. 4703, 405 UNTS 323, BAnz. 1961 no. 99.

178. Agreement relating to partial settlement of German post-war debt to the United States resulting from post-war economic assistance (other than surplus property), of Apr. 25, 1961 (effective same day):

12 UST 477, TIAS no. 4737, 410 UNTS 340, BAnz. 1961 no. 81 p. 3;

Supplements no. 96.

179. Agreement relating to the close-out of the collection account of the agricultural commodities agreement of Dec. 23, 1955 (no. 130), of May 19/Aug. 24, 1961 (effective Aug. 24, 1961):

12 UST 1276, TIAS no. 4848, 421 UNTS 304.

180. Application to Land Berlin of agreement of Dec. 11, 1958 relating to certificates of airworthiness for imported aircraft (no. 154), of May 24, 1961/Jan. 23, 1962 (effective Jan. 23, 1962):

13 UST 196, TIAS no. 4960, 435 UNTS 365.

181. Agreed procedures concerning the rectification of origin of menthol, of June 16/20, 1961 (effective June 20, 1961):

Notice in 26 Fed.Reg. 5473;

Amended by no. 184.

182. Agreement amending the agreement relating to the lease of air navigation equipment (no. 127), of Aug. 14/Sept. 11, 1961 (effective Sept. 11, 1961):

12 UST 1350, TIAS no. 4854, 421 UNTS 309;

Amended by nos. 196 and 199.

183. Agreement on cooperation in intercontinental testing in connection with experimental communications satellites, of Sept. 5/29, 1961 (effective Sept. 29, 1961):

12 UST 1682, TIAS no. 4885, 424 UNTS 113.

184. Agreement amending the agreed procedures concerning the certificates of origin of menthol (no. 181), of Oct. 4/31, 1961 (effective Oct. 31, 1961):

Notice in 26 Fed.Reg. 10, 943.

185. Agreement amending the agreement relating to the sale to the Federal Republic of certain military equipment, materials, and services (no. 139), of Nov. 24, 1961 (effective same day):

12 UST 3045, TIAS no. 4903, 434 UNTS 328.

186. Agreement providing compensatory concessions under the general agreement on tariffs and trade for certain tariff actions taken by the United States, of Jan. 29, 1962 (effective same day):

13 UST 939, TIAS no. 5032.

187. Agreement relating to the disposition of equipment and materials furnished to the Federal Republic on a grant basis under the mutual defense assistance agreement (no. 124), of May 25, 1962 (effective same day):

13 UST 1341, TIAS no. 5092, 458 UNTS 259.

188/9. Agreement amending the agreement for cooperation on behalf of Berlin concerning civil uses of atomic energy (no. 147), of June 29, 1962 (effective July 30, 1962):

13 UST 1486, TIAS no. 5109, 453 UNTS 380, BAnz. 1962 no. 211 p. 2, GVOBl.Berlin 1962, 663.

190. Agreement amending the agreement for cooperation concerning civil uses of atomic energy (no. 148), of July 5, 1962 (effective Aug. 7, 1962):

13 UST 1770, TIAS no. 5120, 458 UNTS 322, BAnz. 1962 no. 211.

191/2. Agreement extending the period of the loan of the "USS Anthony" in accordance with the agreement of Apr. 30/May 1, 1957 (no. 144), of Sept. 19/25, 1962 (effective Sept. 25, 1962):

13 UST 2178, TIAS no. 5181, 460 UNTS 315.

193. Agreement for conducting certain educational exchange programs, of Nov. 20, 1962 (effective Jan. 24, 1964):

15 UST 78, TIAS no. 5518, 505 UNTS 263, BGBl. 1964 II 27, 215, GVOBl.Berlin 1964, 708;

Replaces no. 93; supplemented by no. 219.

194. Agreement regarding the use of German territorial waters and ports by the N.S. Savannah, of Nov. 29, 1962 (effective same day):

13 UST 2567, TIAS no. 5223, 460 UNTS 169.

195. Agreement concerning the settlement of claims which have arisen through the non-duty use of private motor vehicles of members of the United States Forces insured by the Brandaris insurance company, of Feb. 28/Mar. 14, 1963 (effective Mar. 14, 1963):

14 UST 342, TIAS no. 5318, 474 UNTS 71, notice in BAnz. 1963 no. 61 p. 4.

196. Agreement amending the agreement relating to the lease of air navigation equipment (no. 127), of July 1/24, 1963 (effective July 14, 1963):

14 UST 1069, TIAS no. 5406, 487 UNTS 350;

Amended by no. 199.

197. Agreement amending the agreement approving the procedures for reciprocal filing of classified patent applications in the United States and the Federal Republic of Germany (no. 155), of Jan. 14/May 28, 1964 (effective May 28, 1964):

15 UST 765, TIAS no. 5601, 529 UNTS 350, BAnz. 1965 no. 144.

198. Administrative agreement concerning the status of Indiana University, Ohio State University and Boston University, of Mar. 6/17, 1964 (effective Mar. 23, 1964):

BAnz. 1964 no. 113;

Supplements Treaty M 250.

198 A. Agreement relating to the extension of time for fulfilling the conditions and formalities of the copyright laws of the United States, of Nov. 20, 1964/July 12, 1967 (effective July 12, 1967):

18 UST 2366, TIAS no. 6341.

199. Agreement amending the agreement relating to the lease of air navigation equipment (no. 127), of July 30/Aug. 25, 1965 (effective Aug. 25, 1965):

16 UST 1760, TIAS no. 5905, 573 UNTS 317.

200. Protocol modifying the convention of July 22, 1954, for the avoidance of double taxation with respect to taxes on income (no. 112), of Sept. 17, 1965 (effective Dec. 27, 1965):

16 UST 1875, TIAS no. 5920, 578 UNTS 224, BGBl. 1965 II 1609, 1966 II 92, 745, GVOBl.Berlin 1966, 560.

201. Agreement extending and amending the agreement relating to loan of certain naval vessels or small craft (no. 144), of Oct. 7, 1965 (effective same day):

16 UST 1626, TIAS no. 5883, 573 UNTS 324.

201 A. Administrative agreement concerning the procedure for the settlement of damage claims pursuant to art. VIII of the NATO status of forces agreement of June 19, 1951 (M 173) in conjunction with art. 41 of the supplementary agreement of Aug. 3, 1959 (M 250), of Oct. 8/26, 1965 (effective July 1, 1963):

BAnz. 1970 no. 85, appendix (no. 12) p. 4.

202. Agreement to support personnel from the Federal Republic of Germany stationed in the United States during emergencies, of Oct. 21/Dec. 18, 1965 (effective Dec. 18, 1965):

16 UST 1912, TIAS no. 5922.

203. Agreed procedures with regard to certification of human hair products, of Mar. 21/Apr. 12, 1966 (effective Mar. 25, 1966):

BAnz. 1966 no. 144, GVOBl.Berlin 1967, 441, notice in 31 Fed.Reg. 4973;

Amended by no. 205.

204. Agreement relating to the reciprocal granting of authorization to permit licensed amateur radio operators of either country to operate their station in the other country, of June 23/30, 1966 (effective June 30, 1966):

17 UST 1120, TIAS no. 6068.

205. Agreement amending the agreed procedures with regard to the certification of human hair products (no. 203), of Dec. 8, 1966 (effective same day):

See BAnz. 1967 no. 13, GVOBl.Berlin 1967, 441.

206. Agreement relating to the transfer of three paintings to the Federal Republic of Germany for the Weimar Museum, of Dec. 9/16, 1966 (effective Dec. 16, 1966):

17 UST 2279, TIAS no. 6169.

207. Agreed procedures for the certification of tussah silk piece goods, of Dec. 14, 1966/Apr. 11, 1967 (effective Mar. 16, 1967):

BAnz. 1967 no. 150 p. 2, GVOBl.Berlin 1967, 1502, notice in 32 Fed.Reg. 4141.

207 A. Administrative agreement concerning the legal status of the universities of Southern California, of Oklahoma, of Utah and of the Capitol Institute of Technology, of Dec. 23, 1966 (effective same day):

BAnz. 1968 no. 21.

208. Agreement relating to the prepayment of the remaining German debt to the United States resulting from post-war economic assistance (excluding surplus property), of Dec. 29, 1966 (effective same day):

18 UST 101, TIAS no. 6204;

Amends no. 96.

208 A. Administrative agreement pursuant to art. 44 of the Supplementary Agreement to the NATO status of forces agreement of Aug. 3, 1959 (M 250) concerning the cooperation .... in the settlement of disputes, of Jan. 30/Apr. 17, 1967 (effective July 1, 1963):

BAnz. 1970 no. 85, appendix (no. 12) p. 56.

209. Agreement extending agreement relating to the lease of air navigation equipment (no. 127), as extended, of Sept. 26/Oct. 24, 1967 (effective Oct. 24, 1967):

18 UST 2845, TIAS no. 6373.

210. Executive agreement on the legal status of credit unions of the American forces in the Federal Republic of Germany, of Oct. 24, 1967 (effective Nov. 15, 1967):

BAnz. 1967 no. 213;

Supplements Treaty M 250.

211. Agreement relating to the transfer of title of the United States destroyer, U.S.S. Charles Ausburne, to the Federal Republic, of Feb. 27, 1968 (effective same date):

19 UST 5015, TIAS no. 6502.

212. Agreement extending and amending the agreement relating to loan of certain naval vessels or small craft (no. 144), of Feb. 27/Mar. 5, 1968 (effective Mar. 5, 1968):

19 UST 5066, TIAS no. 6505.

213. Agreement amending the agreement of July 7, 1955, relating to air transport no. 126), of Apr. 5, 1968 (effective same day):

19 UST 4402, TIAS no. 6434.

214. Memorandum of understanding concerning aeronomy satellite, of June 10, 1969 (effective same date):

BGBl. 1970 II 166, GVOBl.Berlin 1970, 692.

215. Memorandum of understanding concerning "Project Helios," of June 10, 1969 (effective same date):

BGBl. 1970 II 171, GVOBl.Berlin 1970, 692.

216. Administrative Agreement concerning the legal status of the American "United Service Organization" in the Federal Republic of Germany, of June 18/24, 1969 (effective June 27, 1969):

BAnz. 1969 no. 156.

217. Agreement relating to the extension of the loan of certain vessels pursuant to the agreement of Apr. 30/May 1, 1957, as amended (no. 144), of July 7/ Sept. 19, 1969 (entered into force Sept. 19, 1969).

20 UST 4103, TIAS 6805.

218. Agreement extending the agreement relating to the lease of air navigation equipment (no. 127), as extended, of Nov. 12, 1969/Jan. 30, 1970 (effective Jan. 30, 1970):

21 UST 1326, TIAS 6888.

219. Agreement supplementing the agreement for conducting certain educational exchange programs (no. 193), of Mar. 11/June 5, 1970 (effective June 5, 1970):

20 UST 731, TIAS no. 6684.

MULTILATERAL CONVENTIONS (M)

to which the U.S. and Germany were or are parties

1. Convention on the amelioration of the condition of the wounded in time of war, of Aug. 22, 1864 (effective U.S.–Germany, June 12, 1906):

22 Stat. 940, TS no. 377, 2 Malloy 1903, 18 Martens NRG 607, notice in RGBl. 1907, 303;

Superseded by no. 36.

2. Convention concerning the Cape Spartel lighthouse, of May 31, 1865 (effective U.S.–Germany Mar. 4, 1878):

    14 Stat. 679, 18 Stat. part 2 p. 525, TS no. 245, 1 Malloy 1217, 20 Martens NRG (1ère sér.) 350;

    Abrogated by Protocol of Mar. 31, 1958 (9 UST 527, TIAS no. 4029, 320 UNTS 103).

3. Universal Postal Union, of Oct. 9, 1874 (effective U.S.–Germany July 1, 1875):

    19 Stat. 577, 1 Martens NRG (2e sér.) 651, RGBl. 1875, 223;

    Amended by nos. 5, 11, 18, 19 and 35;

    Superseded by no. 62.

4. Convention on the International Bureau of Weights and Measures, of May 20, 1875 (effective U.S.–Germany Aug. 2, 1878):

    20 Stat. 709, TS no. 378, 2 Malloy 1924, 1 Martens (2e sér.) 663, RGBl. 1876, 191, BGBl. 1970 II 1076;

    Declared applicable by art. 282 no. 20 Treaty of Versailles (see text p. 28);

    Amended by no. 64.

5. Universal Postal Union, of June 1, 1879 (effective U.S.–Germany April 1, 1879):

    20 Stat. 734, 3 Martens NRG (2e sér.) 699, RGBl. 1878, 83, 118;

    Amends no. 3; amended by nos. 11, 18, 19 and 35; superseded by no. 62.

6. Convention relating to the municipal administration of the city and district of Apia, of Sept. 2, 1879 (effective U.S.–Germany Aug. 27, 1880):

    6 Martens NRG (2e sér.) 409, 10 *id.* 605, St.Archiv 38 (1881) no. 7294;

    Extended by no. 9; abrogated by no. 14.

7. Convention as to diplomatic protection in Morocco, of July 3, 1880 (effective U.S.–Germany July 3, 1880):

    22 Stat. 817, TS no. 246, 1 Malloy 1220, 6 Martens NRG (2e sér.) 550, 624, RGBl. 1881, 103.

8. Convention for international protection of industrial property, of Mar. 20, 1883 (effective U.S.–Germany May 1, 1903):

    25 Stat. 1372, T.S. no. 379, 2 Malloy 1935, 10 Martens NRG (2e sér.) 133, RGBl. 1903, 147, 148;

    Supplemented and amended by nos. 17, 27 and 53. Declared applicable by art. 286 Treaty of Versailles (see text p. 28).

9. Additional convention to the convention of Apia (no. 6), of Sept. 29, 1883 (effective U.S.–Germany same day):

    10 Martens NRG (2e sér.) 608.

10. Convention for the protection of submarine cables, of Mar. 14, 1884 (effective U.S.–Germany May 1, 1888):

    24 Stat. 989, TS no. 380, 2 Malloy 1949, 11 Martens NRG (2e sér.) 281, RGBl. 1888, 151, Verträge A 324;

    Declared applicable by art. 282 no. 1 Treaty of Versailles (see text, p. 28), and as of May 1, 1952 by Federal Republic of Germany (BGBl. 1955 II 5); supplemented by nos. 12 and 13.

11. Universal Postal Union, of Mar. 21, 1885 (effective U.S.–Germany Apr. 1. 1886):

    25 Stat. 1339, 11 Martens NRG (2e sér.) 1, RGBl. 1886, 82, 122;

    Amends nos. 3 and 5; amended by nos. 18, 19 and 35.

12. Declaration respecting the interpretation of articles II and IV of the convention of Mar. 14, 1884, for the protection of submarine cables (no. 10), of Dec. 1, 1886 (effective U.S.–Germany May 1, 1888):

    25 Stat. 1424, TS no. 380–2, 2 Malloy 1956, 15 Martens NRG (2e sér.) 69, RGBl. 1888, 167, Verträge A 324.

    See further no. 13.

13. Final protocol of agreement fixing May 1, 1888, as the date of effect of the Convention concluded at Paris Mar. 1884, for the protection of submarine cables (no. 10), of July 7, 1887 (effective U.S.–Germany May 1, 1888):

    25 Stat. 1425, TS no. 380–3, 2 Malloy 1958, RGBl. 1926 II 135, Verträge A 324.

14. General Act of the Berlin Samoa Conference, of June 14, 1889 (effective U.S.–Germany same day):

    26 Stat. 1497, TS no. 313, 2 Malloy 1576, 15 Martens NRG (2e sér.) 571, DRAnz. 1890 no. 21 annex 3, St.Archiv 1891–92 no. 10, 085;

    Abrogated by no. 26.

15. General Act for the repression of African slave trade, of July 2, 1890 (effective U.S.–Germany Feb. 2, 1892):

    27 Stat. 886, TS no. 383, 2 Malloy 1964, 16 Martens NRG (2e sér.) 3, 17, *id.* 345, RGBl. 1892, 605, 660;

    Amended by nos. 20, 59, 60 and 70.

16. Convention concerning the formation of an international union for the publication of customs tariffs, of July 5, 1890 (effective U.S.–Germany July 10, 1904):

    26 Stat. 1518, TS no. 384, 2 Malloy 1996, 16 Martens NRG (2e sér.) 532, 18 *id.* 558, St.Archiv 1896 no. 11 086, BAnz. 1958 no. 51;

    Declared applicable by art. 282 no. 5 Treaty of Versailles (see text p. 28 and by the Federal Republic of Germany (BGBl. 1953 II 117);

    Amended by no. 165.

17. Supplementary industrial property convention, of Apr. 15, 1891 (effective U.S.–Germany May 1, 1903):

    27 Stat. 958, TS no. 385, 2 Malloy 1943, 22 Martens (2e sér.) 216, RGBl. 1903, 147, 164;

    Supplements no. 8; supplemented by nos. 27 and 53.

18. Universal Postal Union, of July 4, 1891 (effective U.S.–Germany July 1, 1892):

    28 Stat. 1078, 17 Martens NRG (2e sér.) 628, RGBl. 1892, 503, 595;

    Amends nos. 2, 4 and 8. Declared applicable by art. 283 Treaty of Versailles (see text p. 28);

    Amended by nos. 19 and 35; superseded by no. 62.

19. Universal Postal Union, of June 15, 1897 (effective U.S.–Germany Jan. 1, 1899):

    30 Stat. 1629, 28 Martens NRG (2e sér.) 488, RGBl. 1898, 1079, 1184;

    Amends nos. 2, 4, 8 and 14; declared applicable by art. 283 Treaty of Versailles (see text p. 28), amended by no. 35; superseded by no. 62.

20. Convention for the regulation of the importation of spirituous liquors into certain regions of Africa, of June 8, 1899 (effective U.S.–Germany Feb. 1, 1901):

    31 Stat. 1915, TS no. 389, 2 Malloy 1993, 29 Martens NRG (2e sér.) 401, RGBl. 1900, 823, 829;

    Amended by no. 37; superseded by no. 60.

21. Convention for the pacific settlement of international disputes, of July 29, 1899 (effective U.S.–Germany Sept. 4, 1900):

    32 Stat. 1779, TS no. 392, 2 Malloy 2016, 26 Martens NRG (2e sér.) 920, RGBl. 1901, 393, 482, 483, Verträge A 329;

    Superseded by no. 40.

22. Declaration as to launching of projectiles and explosives, of July 29, 1899 (effective U.S.–Germany Sept. 4, 1900):

    32 Stat. 1839, TS no. 393, 2 Malloy 2032, 26 Martens NRG (2e sér.) 994, RGBl. 1901, 470, 482;

    Expired after 5 years.

23. Convention for the adaptation to maritime warfare of the principles of the Geneva Convention of Aug. 22, 1864 (no. 1), of July 29, 1899 (effective U.S.–Germany Sept. 4, 1900):

    32 Stat. 1827, TS no. 396, 2 Malloy 2035, 26 Martens NRG (2e sér.) 979, RGBl. 1901, 455, 482, Verträge A 331;

    Superseded by no. 47.

24. Convention with respect to the laws and customs of war on land, of July 29, 1899 (effective U.S.–Germany Apr. 9, 1902):

    32 Stat. 1803, TS no. 403, 2 Malloy 2042, 26 Martens NRG (2e sér.) 949, RGBl. 1901, 423, 1902, 168, Verträge A 330;

    Superseded by no. 43.

25. Convention relating to settlement of Samoan claims between U.S., Germany and Great Britain, of Nov. 7, 1899 (effective U.S.–Germany Mar. 7, 1900):

    31 Stat. 1875, TS no. 315, 2 Malloy 1589, 32 Martens NRG (2e sér.) 408, St.Archiv 1901 no. 12070.

26. Convention to adjust the question between the U.S., Germany and Great Britain in respect to the Samoan Islands, of Dec. 2, 1899 (effective U.S.–Germany Feb. 16, 1900):

    31 Stat. 1878, TS no. 314, 2 Malloy 1595, 30 Martens NRG (2e sér.) 683, DRAnz. 1899 no. 298;

    Art. III abrogated by art. 288 Treaty of Versailles (see text p. 28).

27. Additional Act for the protection of industrial property, of Dec. 14, 1900 (effective U.S.–Germany May 1, 1903):

    32 Stat. 1936, TS no. 411, 2 Malloy 1945, 30 Martens NRG (2e sér.) 465, RGBl. 1903, 147, 167;

    Supplements nos. 8 and 17; amended by no. 53.

28. Final protocol entered into at the conclusion of the so-called "Boxer" Troubles in 1900, of Sept. 7, 1901 (effective U.S.–Germany same date):
    TS no. 397, 2 Malloy 2006, 32 Martens NRG (2e sér.) 94, DRAnz. 1901 no. 246 annex 1;
    Amended by no. 33.

29. International Sanitary Convention, of Dec. 3, 1903 (effective U.S.–Germany April 6, 1907):
    35 Stat. 1770, TS no. 466, 2 Malloy 2066, 1 Martens NRG (3e sér.) 78, RGBl. 1907, 425, 543;
    Amended by no. 54; declared applicable by art. 282 no. 19 Treaty of Versailles (see text p. 28); superseded by no. 69.

30. Agreement for the repression of the trade in white women, of May 18, 1904 (effective U.S.–Germany July 18, 1908):
    35 Stat. 1979, TS no. 496, 2 Malloy 2131, 1 LNTS 83, 32 Martens NRG (2e sér.) 160, RGBl. 1905, 695, 715, 1907, 721, 1908, 481, Verträge A 337;
    Declared applicable by art. 282 no. 17 Treaty of Versailles (see text p. 28).

31. Convention for the exemption of hospital ships in time of war from the payment of all dues and taxes imposed for the benefit of the state, of Dec. 21, 1904 (effective U.S.–Germany Mar. 26, 1907):
    35 Stat. 1854, TS no. 459, 2 Malloy 2135, 2 Martens NRG (3e sér.) 213, RGBl. 1907, 722, 730, Verträge A 338;
    Declared applicable by art. 282 no. 13 Treaty of Versailles (see text p. 28).

32. Convention for the creation of an International Institute of Agriculture, of June 7, 1905 (effective U.S.–Germany Feb. 25, 1908):
    35 Stat. 1918, TS no. 489, 2 Malloy 2140, 3 Martens NRG (3e sér.) 139, ZBl. 1908, 132;
    Declared applicable by art. 282 no. 23 Treaty of Versailles (see text p. 28); amended by no. 68.

33. New Agreement with China and certain powers for the Whang-Pu Conservancy, of Sept. 27, 1905 (effective U.S.–Germany same day):
    TS no. 448, 2 Malloy 2013, 6 Martens NRG (2e sér.) 685;
    Amends in part no. 28.

34. General Act of the international conference at Algeciras and an additional protocol of Apr. 7, 1906 (effective U.S.–Germany Dec. 31, 1906):
    34 Stat. 2905, TS no. 456, 2 Malloy 2157, 34 Martens NRG (2e sér.) 238, RGBl. 1906, 891; 1907, 19, 20.

35. Universal Postal Union, of May 26, 1906 (effective U.S.–Germany Oct. 1, 1907):
    35 Stat. 1639, 1 Martens NRG (3e sér.) 355, RGBl. 1907, 593, 719;
    Amends nos. 3, 5, 11, 18 and 19; declared applicable by art. 283 Treaty of Versailles (see text p. 28); superseded by no. 62.

36. International Red Cross Convention, of July 6, 1906 (effective U.S.–Germany Nov. 27, 1907):
    35 Stat. 1885, TS no. 464, 2 Malloy 2183, 2 Martens NRG (3e sér.) 620, RGBl. 1907, 279, 303;
    Supersedes no. 1; superseded by no. 76.

37. Convention revising the duties imposed by the Brussels Convention of June 8, 1899 on spirituous liquors imported into certain regions of Africa (no. 20), of Nov. 3, 1906 (effective U.S.–Germany Dec. 3, 1907):

    35 Stat. 1912, TS no. 467, 2 Malloy 2205, 1 Martens NRG (3e sér.) 722, RGBl. 1908, 5;

    Superseded by no. 60.

38. International wireless telegraph convention, of Nov. 3, 1906 (effective U.S.–Germany May 17, 1912):

    37 Stat. 1565, TS no. 568, Redmond 2889, 3 Martens NRG (3e sér.) 147, RGBl. 1908, 411, 462, 1912, 447;

    Superseded by no. 56.

39. Agreement respecting the unification of the pharmacopoeial formulas for potent drugs, of Nov. 29, 1906 (effective U.S.–Germany Dec. 29, 1906):

    TS no. 510, 2 Malloy 2209, 1 Martens NRG (3e sér.) 592, St.Archiv 1909 no. 14.027, Dt.Hand.Arch. 1933, 323;

    Declared applicable by art. 282 no. 21 of the Treaty of Versailles (see text p. 28); abrogated by no. 180.

40. Convention for the pacific settlement of international disputes, of Oct. 18, 1907 (effective U.S.–Germany Jan. 26, 1910):

    36 Stat. 2199, TS no. 536, 2 Malloy 2220, 54 LNTS 435, 3 Martens NRG (3e sér.) 360, RGBl. 1910, 5, 375, 378;

    Supersedes no. 21.

41. Convention respecting the limitation of the employment of force for the recovery of contract debts, of Oct. 18, 1907 (effective U.S.–Germany Jan. 26, 1910):

    36 Stat. 2199, TS no. 536, 2 Malloy 2220, 54 LNTS 435, 3 Martens 414, RGBl. 1910, 59, 375, 379;

    Applicable again as of May 1, 1952 for the Federal Republic of Germany (BGBl. 1953 II 125).

42. Convention relative to the opening of hostilities, of Oct. 18, 1907 (effective U.S.–Germany Jan. 26, 1910):

    36 Stat. 2259, TS no. 538, 2 Malloy 2259, 3 Martens NRG (3e sér.) 437, RGBl. 1910, 82, 375.

43. Convention respecting the laws and customs of war on land, of Oct. 18, 1907 (effective U.S.–Germany Jan. 26, 1910):

    36 Stat. 2277, TS no. 539, 2 Malloy 2269, 3 Martens NRG (3e sér.) 461, RGBl. 1910, 107, 375;

    Supersedes no. 24.

44. Convention respecting the rights and duties of neutral powers and persons in war on land, of Oct. 18, 1907 (effective U.S.–Germany Jan. 26, 1910):

    36 Stat. 2310, TS no. 540, 2 Malloy 2290, 3 Martens NRG (3e sér.) 504, RGBl. 1910, 151, 375,

45. Convention relative to the laying of automatic submarine contact mines, of Oct. 18, 1907 (effective U.S.–Germany Jan. 26, 1910):

    36 Stat. 2332, TS no. 541, 2 Malloy 2304, 3 Martens NRG (3e sér) 580, RGBl. 1910, 231, 375.

46. Convention respecting bombardment by naval forces in times of war, of Oct. 18, 1907 (effective U.S.–Germany Jan. 26, 1910):

    36 Stat. 2351, TS no. 542, 2 Malloy 2314, 3 Martens NRG (3e sér.) 604, RGBl. 1910, 256, 375.

47. Convention for the adaptation to naval war of the principles of the Geneva Convention, of Oct. 18, 1907 (effective U.S.–Germany Jan. 26, 1910):

    36 Stat. 2371, TS no. 543, 2 Malloy 2326, 3 Martens NRG (3e sér) 630, RGBl. 1910, 283, 375;

    Supersedes no. 23.

48. Convention relative to right of capture in naval war, of Oct. 18, 1907 (effective U.S.–Germany Jan. 26, 1910):

    36 Stat. 2396, TS no. 544, 2 Malloy 2341, 3 Martens NRG (3e sér.) 663, RGBl. 1910, 316, 375.

49. Convention concerning the rights and duties of neutral powers in naval war, of Oct. 18, 1907 (effective U.S.–Germany Feb. 1, 1910):

    36 Stat. 2415, TS no. 545, 2 Malloy 2352, 3 Martens NRG (3e sér.) 713, RGBl. 1910, 343, 382.

50. Arrangement for the establishment of the international office of public health, of Dec. 9, 1907 (effective U.S.–Germany Aug. 11, 1928):

    35 Stat. 2061, TS no. 511, 2 Malloy 2214, 2 Martens NRG (3e sér.) 913, RMBl. 1930, 2, St. Archiv 1913 no. 14.285.

51. Arrangement relative to the repression of the circulation of obscene publications, of May 4, 1910 (effective U.S.–Germany Sept. 15, 1911):

    37 Stat. 1511, TS no. 559, Redmond 2918, 7 Martens NRG (3e sér.) 266, RGBl. 1911, 209, 215;

    Declared applicable by art. 282 no. 18 Treaty of Versailles (see text p. 28).

52. Convention for the unification of certain rules of law with respect to assistance and salvage at sea, of Sept. 23, 1910 (effective U.S.–Germany Mar. 1, 1913):

    37 Stat. 1658, TS no. 576, Redmond 2943, 7 Martens NRG (3e sér.) 728, RGBl. 1913, 66, 89;

    Declared applicable by art. 282 no. 12 Treaty of Versailles (see text p. 28) and as of Nov. 1, 1953 by Federal Republic of Germany (BGBl. 1954 II 467).

53. Convention for the protection of industrial property, of June 2, 1911 effective U.S.–Germany May 1, 1913):

    38 Stat. 1645, TS no. 579, Redmond 2953, 8 Martens NRG (3e sér.) 760, RGBl. 1913, 209, 236;

    Amends nos. 8, 17 and 27; declared applicable by art. 286 Treaty of Versailles (see text p. 28); replaced by no. 67.

54. International Sanitary Convention, of Jan. 17, 1912 (effective U.S.–Germany Dec. 30, 1920):

    42 Stat. 1823, TS no. 649, Redmond 2972, 4 LNTS 282, 13 Martens NRG (3e sér.) 3, RGBl. 1922 II 5;

    Amends no. 29; superseded by no. 69.

55. Convention and final Protocol for the suppression of the abuse of opium and other drugs, of Jan. 23, 1912 (effective U.S.–Germany Jan. 10, 1920):
    38 Stat. 1912, TS no. 612, Redmond 3025, 8 LNTS 188, 11 Martens NRG (3e sér.) 247, RGBl. 1921, 6, BGBl. 1970 II 973;
    Supplemented by no. 81; amended by no. 115.

56. International wireless telegraph convention, of July 5, 1912 (effective U.S.–Germany July 1, 1913):
    38 Stat. 1672, TS no. 581, Redmond 3048, 1 LNTS 136, 11 Martens NRG (3e sér.) 270, RGBl. 1913, 373, 432;
    Supersedes no. 38; declared applicable by art. 284 Treaty of Versailles (see text p. 28); superseded by nos. 71 and 78.

57. Protocol relating to the abolition of the system of foreign settlements in Chosen, of Apr. 21, 1913 (effective U.S.–Germany same day):
    Redmond 3086, 18 Martens NRG (3e sér.) 405.

58. Constitution of the International Labor Organization, of June 28, 1919 (effective U.S.–Germany June 12, 1951):
    49 Stat. 2712, TS no. 874, Trenwith 5531, Redmond 3503, 11 Martens NRG (3e sér.) 321 (638), RGBl. 1919, 1269, 1925 II 161;
    Amended by nos. 114, 198 and 279.

59. Revision of the General Act of Berlin of Feb. 26, 1885, and the General Act of Brussels of July 2, 1890 (no. 15), of Sept. 10, 1919 (effective U.S.–Germany Oct. 29, 1934):
    49 Stat. 3027, TS no. 877, Trenwith 4849, 8 LNTS 25, 14 Martens NRG (3e sér.) 12, Dt.Hand.Arch. 1923, 359.

60. Convention relating to the liquor traffic in Africa, of Sept. 10, 1919 (effective U.S.–Germany Mar. 22, 1929):
    46 Stat. 2199, TS no. 779, Trenwith 4850, 8 LNTS 11, 14 Martens NRG (3e sér.) 19, Dt.Hand.Arch. 1923, 357;
    Supersedes nos. 20 and 37.

61. Treaty relating to Spitsbergen, of Feb. 9, 1920 (effective U.S.–Germany Sept. 7, 1925):
    43 Stat. 1892, TS no. 686, Trenwith 4861, 2 LNTS 7, 13 Martens NRG (3e sér.) 473, RGBl. 1925 II 763, 951, 1928 II 174;
    Declared applicable by the Federal Republic of Germany (BGBl. 1953 II 117).

62. Universal Postal Union, of Nov. 30, 1920 (effective U.S.–Germany Jan. 1, 1922):
    42 Stat. 1971, 15 Martens NRG (3e sér.) 722, RGBl. 1921, 1376;
    Supersedes nos. 3, 5, 11, 18, 19 and 35; superseded by no. 66.

63. Statutes of the International Hydrographic Institute, of June 21, 1921 (effective same day):
    1 Hudson 663.

64. Convention amending the convention to insure the unification and improvement of the metric system signed at Paris, May 20, 1875, and the regulation annexed thereto (no. 4), of Oct. 6, 1921 (effective U.S.–Germany Jan. 30, 1928):
    43 Stat. 1686, TS no. 673, Redmond 3088, Trenwith 4868, 17 LNTS 45, 13 Martens NRG (3e sér.) 286, RGBl. 1927 II 409, 1928 II 165, 617, BGBl. 1970, II 1076, Verträge A 320.

65. International Convention for the unification of certain rules relating to bills of lading, of Aug. 25, 1924 (effective U.S.–Germany Jan. 1, 1940):

51 Stat. 233, TS no. 931, Trenwith 4935, 120 LNTS 155, 31 Martens NRG (3e sér.) 56, RGBl. 1939 II 1049, Verträge A 385;

Applicable to Federal Republic of Germany as of Nov. 1, 1953 (BGBl. 1954 II 466).

66. Universal Postal Union, of Aug. 28, 1924 (effective U.S.–Germany Oct. 1, 1925):

44 Stat. 2221, TS no. 708 A, 40 LNTS 19, 19 Martens NRG (3e sér.) 345, RGBl. 1925 II 517, 947, 1927 II 326;

Supersedes no. 62; superseded by no. 75.

67. Convention for the protection of industrial property, of Nov. 6, 1925 (effective U.S.–Germany Mar. 6, 1931):

47 Stat. 1789, TS no. 834, Trenwith 4945, 74 LNTS 289, 25 Martens NRG (3e sér.) 820, RGBl. 1928 II 176, 1931 II 37, Verträge A 393;

Replaces no. 53; replaced by no. 91.

68. Protocol relative to the international convention of June 7, 1905 (no. 32), of Apr. 21, 1926 (effective U.S.–Germany Aug. 25, 1934):

49 Stat. 3350, TS no. 903, Trenwith 4959, 26 Martens NRG (3e sér.) 622; see also 88 LNTS 410.

69. International sanitary convention of June 21, 1926 (effective U.S.–Germany Aug. 6, 1930):

45 Stat. 2492, TS no. 762, Trenwith 4962, 78 LNTS 230, 26 Martens NRG (3e sér.) 162, RGBl. 1930 II 590, 1268, Verträge A 400;

Supersedes no. 54; supplemented by no. 86.

70. Convention to suppress the slave trade and slavery, of Sept. 25, 1926 (effective U.S.–Germany Mar. 21, 1929):

46 Stat. 2183, TS no. 778, Trenwith 5022, 60 LNTS 253, 19 Martens NRG (3e sér.) 303, RGBl. 1929 II 64, 178, 1931 II 233;

Amends nos. 15 and 59; supplemented by no. 231 A.

71. International radiotelegraph convention and general regulations, of Nov. 25, 1927 (effective U.S.–Germany Aug. 22, 1929):

45 Stat. 2760, TS no. 767, Trenwith 5031, 84 LNTS 97, 26 Martens NRG (3e sér.) 234, RGBl. 1929 II 266, 693;

Supersedes no. 56; superseded by no. 84.

72. Convention on the abolition of import and export prohibitions and restrictions, of Nov. 8, 1927/July 11, 1928 (effective U.S.–Germany Jan. 1, 1930):

46 Stat. 2461, 2499, TS no. 811, Trenwith 5104, 97 LNTS 391, RGBl. 1929 II 649, 1929 II 679, 1930 II 20;

Ineffective from July 1, 1930 (RGBl. 1930 II 959).

73. Treaty providing for the renunciation of war as an instrument of national policy, of Aug. 27, 1928 (effective U.S.–Germany July 24, 1929):

46 Stat. 2343, TS no. 796, Trenwith 5130, 94 LNTS 57, 21 Martens NRG (3e sér.) 3, RGBl. 1929 II 97, 631, Verträge A 412.

73A. Convention regarding international exhibitions, of Nov. 22, 1928 (effective U.S.–Germany June 24, 1968):

19 UST 5927, TIAS no. 6548, 111 LNTS 343, RGBl. 1930 II 727, 1931 II 11, BGBl. 1969 II 1466;

Amended by no. 138 A and 307.

74. International convention for the safety of life at sea with regulations, of May 31, 1929 with amendment of Dec. 31, 1930 (effective U.S.–Germany Nov. 7, 1936):

50 Stat. 1121, 51 Stat. 13, TS no. 910, 921, Trenwith 5134, 5350, 136 LNTS 81, 32 Martens NRG (3e sér.) 739, RGBl. 1931 II 235, 1938 II 902;

Superseded by nos. 139 and 140.

75. Universal Postal Union, of June 28, 1929 (effective U.S.–Germany Oct. 21, 1930):

46 Stat. 2523, 102 LNTS 245, RGBl. 1930 II 785, 1273;

Supersedes no. 66; superseded by no. 89.

76. Convention for the amelioration of the condition of the wounded and the sick of armies in the field, of July 27, 1929 (effective U.S.–Germany Aug. 21, 1934):

47 Stat. 2074, TS no. 847, Trenwith 5209, 118 LNTS 303, 30 Martens NRG (3e sér.) 827, RGBl. 1934 II 207, 208, Verträge A 415;

Supersedes no. 36; superseded by nos. 152 and 153.

77. Convention relating to the treatment of prisoners of war, of July 27, 1929 (effective U.S.–Germany Aug. 21, 1934):

47 Stat. 2021, TS no. 846, Trenwith 5224, 118 LNTS 343, 30 Martens NRG (3e sér.) 846, RGBl. 1934 II 207, 227, Verträge A 416;

Supplements no. 43; superseded by no. 154.

78. Convention for the unification of certain rules relating to international transportation by air, of Oct. 12, 1929 (effective U.S.–Germany Oct. 29, 1934):

49 Stat. 3000, TS no. 876, Trenwith 5250, 137, LNTS 11, 38 Martens NRG (3e sér.) 852, RGBl. 1933 II 1040, 1934 II 1062, 1398, Verträge A 417;

Applicable to the Federal Republic of Germany (BGBl. 1952 II 437).

79. Treaty for the limitation and reduction of naval armament, Part IV, of Apr. 22, 1930 (effective U.S.–Germany):

46 Stat. 2858, TS no. 830, Trenwith 5268, 112 LNTS 65, 23 Martens NRG (3e sér.) 645.

80. International load line convention, of July 5, 1930 (effective U.S.–Germany Dec. 6, 1933):

47 Stat. 2228, TS no. 858, Trenwith 5287, 135 LNTS 301, RGBl. 1933 II 707, Verträge A 422;

Superseded Treaty B 65. Amended by nos. 100, 240 and 243. Suspended by U.S. on Aug. 9, 1941, reinstated as of Jan. 1, 1946 (6 Fed. Reg.3999, 10 Fed.Reg.15365). Applicable to the Federal Republic of Germany as of Feb. 1, 1955 (BGBl. 1956 II 764).

Denounced by Germany, effective July 21, 1970 (BGBl. 1970 II 48, GVOBl. Berlin 1970, 668), and by the United States on July 29, 1969 (61 D.S.Bulletin 198).

81. Convention for limiting the manufacture and regulating the distribution of narcotic drugs, of July 13, 1931 (effective U.S.–Germany July 9, 1933):

    48 Stat. 1543, TS no. 863, Trenwith 5351, 139 LNTS 301, 38 Martens NRG (3e sér.) 527, RGBl. 1933 II 319;

    Supplements no. 55; amended by no. 115.

82. Standstill agreement (effective U.S.–Germany Sept. 17, 1931):

    Notice in RGBl. 1931 I 509;

    Extended by nos. 83, 85, 88, 92–94, 97, 102, 103 and Treaties B nos. 74 and 75.

83. German credit agreement 1932 (effective Mar. 1, 1932):

    DRAnz. 1932 no. 41;

    Extension of no. 82; extended by no. 85.

84. International telecommunication convention, of Dec. 9, 1932 (effective U.S.–Germany June 2, 1934):

    49 Stat. 2391, TS no. 867, Trenwith 5379, 151 LNTS 5, RGBl. 1934 II 1063, 1937 II 166;

    Supersedes no. 71: superseded in part by no. 98 and entirely by no. 126.

85. German credit agreement 1933, of Feb. 17, 1933 (effective Mar. 1, 1933):

    DRAnz. 1933 no. 56; amended no. 192;

    Extension of no. 83; extended by no. 88.

86. International sanitary convention for aerial navigation, of Apr. 12, 1933 (effective U.S.–Germany Nov. 22, 1935):

    49 Stat. 3279, TS no. 901, Trenwith 5489, 161 LNTS 65, RGBl. 1935 II 815, Verträge A 427.

87. Final Act of the wheat exporting and importing countries, of Aug. 25, 1933 (effective U.S.–Germany same day):

    141 LNTS 71, 29 Martens NRG (3e sér.) 362.

88. German credit agreement 1934, of Feb. 16, 1934 (effective U.S.–Germany Mar. 1, 1934):

    DRAnz. 1934 no. 50.

    Extension of no. 83; extended by no. 92.

89. Universal Postal Union, of Mar. 20, 1934 (effective U.S.–Germany Feb. 13, 1935):

    49 Stat. 2741, 174 LNTS 171, RGBl. 1934 II 855, 1935 II 173;

    Supersedes no. 75.

90. Convention for the protection of industrial property (revising no. 67), of June 2, 1934 (effective U.S.–Germany Aug. 1, 1938):

    53 Stat. 1748, TS no. 941, Trenwith 5516, 192 LNTS 17, RGBl. 1937 II 583, 1938 II 834, Verträge A 430;

    Replaced by no. 244.

91. Convention on the statistics of causes of death, of June 19, 1934 (effective U.S.–Germany same day):

    49 Stat. 3786, EAS no. 80, 154 LNTS 381, RMBl. 1935, 435;

    Amended by no. 101; superseded by no. 142.

92. German credit agreement 1935, of Feb. 16, 1935 (effective U.S.–Germany Mar. 1, 1935):

    DRAnz. 1935 no. 57;

    Extension of no. 88; extended by no. 93.

93. German credit agreement 1936, of Feb. 20, 1936 (effective U.S.–Germany Mar. 1, 1936):

    DRAnz. 1936 no. 61;

    Extension of no. 92; extended by no. 94.

94/95. German credit agreement 1937, of Feb. 20, 1937 (effective U.S.–Germany Mar. 1, 1937):

    DRAnz. 1937 no. 62;

    Extension of no. 93; extended by no. 97.

96. International agreement for the regulation of whaling, of June 8, 1937 (effective U.S.–Germany May 7, 1938):

    52 Stat. 1460, TS no. 933, Trenwith 5573, 190 LNTS 79, 36 Martens NRG (3e sér.) 759, RGBl. 1937 II 548, 1938 II 213;

    Amended by no. 99.

97. German credit agreement 1938, of Jan. 31, 1938 (effective U.S.–Germany Mar. 1, 1938):

    DRAnz. 1938 no. 47;

    Extension of no. 94; supplemented by no. 102 and extended by no. 103.

98. General radio regulations and final radio protocol, of April 8, 1938 (effective U.S.–Germany Aug. 25, 1939):

    54 Stat. 1417, TS no. 948, RGBl. 1939 II 421;

    Superseded by no. 126.

99. Amending protocol to the international agreement for the regulation of whaling (no. 96), of June 24, 1938 (effective U.S.–Germany Mar. 30, 1939):

    53 Stat. 1794, TS no. 944, 196 LNTS 131, 36 Martens NRG (3e sér.) 765, RGBl. 1938 II 657, 1939 II 937, Verträge A 439.

100. Amendment to the international load line convention of July 5, 1930 (no. 80), of Aug. 23, 1938 (effective U.S.–Germany same day):

    53 Stat. 1787, TS no. 942, Trenwith 5348, 193 LNTS 271, RGBl. 1938 II 907;

    Applicable to the Federal Republic of Germany as of Feb. 1, 1955 (BGBl. 1956 II 764);

    Amended by nos. 240 and 243.

101. Protocol revising the minimum nomenclature of causes of death annexed to the convention on the statistics of causes of death (no. 91), of Oct. 6, 1938 (effective U.S.–Germany Jan. 1, 1940):

    54 Stat. 2308, EAS no. 173, 200 LNTS 520;

    Superseded by no. 142.

102. Standstill agreement, of Nov. 23, 1938:

    DRAnz. 1939 no. 9 p. 2.

103. German credit agreement 1939, of May 15, 1939 (effective U.S.–Germany June 1, 1939):

DRAnz. 1939 no. 139;

Extension of no. 97, expired Sept. 3, 1939, extended by Treaty B 74.

104. Charter of the International Institute for the unification of private law, of Mar. 15, 1940 (effective U.S.–Germany Mar. 13, 1964):

15 UST 2494, TIAS no. 5743, Verträge A 441.

105. Convention on international civil aviation, of Dec. 7, 1944 (effective U.S.–Germany June 8, 1956):

61 Stat. 1180, TIAS no. 1591, 34 D.S.Bull.864 (1956), 15 UNTS 295, BGBl. 1956 II 411, 934, Verträge A 96;

Amended by nos. 206 and 271.

106. International air services transit agreement, of Dec. 7, 1944 (effective U.S.–Germany May 9, 1956):

59 Stat. 1693, EAS no. 487, 34 D.S.Bull.864 (1956), 84 UNTS 389, BGBl. 1956 II 411, 442, 934, Verträge A 97.

107. Constitution of the United Nations Food and Agricultural Organization, as amended, of Oct. 16, 1945 (effective U.S.–Germany Nov. 27, 1950):

60 Stat. 1886, TIAS no. 1554, Verträge A 5.

108. Constitution of the United Nations Educational, Scientific, and Cultural Organization, as amended, of Nov. 16, 1945 (effective U.S.–Germany July 11, 1951):

61 Stat. 2495, TIAS no. 1580, 4 UNTS 275, Verträge A 10.

109. Articles of agreement of the International Monetary Fund, of Dec. 27, 1945 (effective U.S.–Germany Aug. 14, 1952):

60 Stat. 1401, TIAS no. 1501, 2 UNTS 39, BGBl. 1952 II 637, 638, 728, 1961 II 1660, Verträge A 16, GVOBl. Berlin 1953, 199;

Amended by no. 318 A.

110. Articles of agreement of the International Bank for Reconstruction and Development, of Dec. 27, 1945 (effective U.S.–Germany Aug. 14, 1952):

60 Stat. 1440, TIAS no. 1502, 2 UNTS 134, BGBl. 1952 II 637, 664, 728, 1961 II 1660, Verträge A 17, GVOBl. Berlin 1953, 199;

Amended by no. 302.

111. Postal agreement concerning letters and cards, of Apr. 1, 1946 (effective U.S.–Germany same day):

Expired.

112. Postal agreement concerning international reply coupons (incoming to Germany only), of June 21, 1946 (effective U.S.–Germany same day):

Expired.

113. Constitution of the World Health Organization, of July 22, 1946 (effective U.S.–Germany May 29, 1951):

62 Stat. 2679, TIAS no. 1808, 14 UNTS 185, Verträge A 7;

Amended by no. 249; supplemented by nos. 142 and 172.

114. Instrument for the amendment of the constitution of the International Labor Organization (no. 58), of Oct. 9, 1946 (effective U.S.–Germany June 12, 1951):

    62 Stat. 3485, TIAS no. 1868, 15 UNTS 35, BGBl. 1952 II 607;

    Amended by nos. 198 and 280.

115. Protocol amending the agreements, conventions, and protocols on narcotic drugs concluded at the Hague on Jan. 23, 1912 (no. 55) and July 13, 1931 (no. 81), at Bangkok on Nov. 27, 1931, and at Geneva on June 26, 1936, and Annex, of Dec. 11, 1946 (effective U.S.–Germany Aug. 12, 1959):

    61 Stat. 2230, 62 Stat. 1796, TIAS nos. 1671, 1859, 41 D.S.Bull.461 (1959), 12 UNTS 179, BGBl. 1959 II 333, 1266, 1966 II 381, Verträge A 154 and A 426, GVOBl. Berlin 1959, 1181;

    Supplemented by nos. 147 and 197.

116. Telecommunication agreement concerning transit communications service, of Dec. 16, 1946 (effective U.S.–Germany same day):

    Expired.

117. Postal agreement concerning transit mail through Germany, of Jan. 1, 1947 (effective U.S.–Germany same day):

    Expired.

118. Postal agreement concerning gift parcel post service, of Jan. 15, 1947 (effective U.S.–Germany same date):

    Expired.

119. Economic Commission for Europe, Terms of reference of the Commission and its committees, of Mar. 28, 1947 (effective U.S.–Germany Feb. 21, 1956):

    BAnz. 1957 no. 150, Verträge A 89.

120. Postal agreement concerning braille matter, of May 15, 1947 (effective U.S.–Germany same day):

    Expired.

121. Postal agreement concerning illustrated postcards, of June 15, 1947 (effective U.S.–Germany same day):

    Expired.

122. Postal agreement concerning poste restante, of Aug. 1, 1947 (effective U.S.–Germany same day):

    Expired.

123. Postal agreement concerning illustrated envelopes, of Sept. 1, 1947 (effective U.S.–Germany same day):

    Expired.

124. Postal agreement concerning business mail and samples, of Sept. 15, 1947 (effective U.S.–Germany same day):

    Expired.

125. Postal agreement concerning transit parcel post through Germany, of Oct. 1, 1947 (effective U.S.–Germany same day):

    Amended by no. 146; expired.

126. International Telecommunication convention, of Oct. 2, 1947 (effective U.S.–Germany Apr. 7, 1952):

63 Stat. 1399, TIAS no. 1901, 193 UNTS 188, 194 UNTS 3, 195 UNTS 5, BGBl. 1952 II 341, 516;

Abrogates nos. 84 and 98; superseded by no. 193.

127. Convention of the World Meteorological Organization, of Oct. 11, 1947 (effective U.S.–Germany July 10, 1954):

1 UST 281, TIAS no. 2052, 31 D.S.Bull.109 (1954), 77 UNTS 143, BAnz. 1956 no. 82, Verträge A 31, GVOBl. Berlin 1956, 974;

Amended by nos. 283 and 309.

128. General agreement on tariffs and trade, with annexes and schedules, and protocol of provisional application, of Oct. 30, 1947 (effective U.S.–Germany Oct. 1, 1951):

61 Stat. parts 5 and 6, TIAS no. 1700, 55–61 UNTS, BGBl. 1951 II 173, 200 with annexes I, Verträge A 11 (vol. 1 p. 418);

Amended by nos. 135–138, 143–145, 156–161, 166, 169, 171, 176, 177, 191, 192, 201, 211, 212, 217, 219–221, 227, 238, 239, 265, 280, 282, 292, 314, 315.

129. Telecommunication agreement concerning telegraph service, of Dec. 1, 1947 (effective U.S.–Germany same day):

Expired.

130. Postal agreement concerning small packets—up to 2 kilograms, of Jan. 1, 1948 (effective U.S.–Germany same day):

Expired.

131. Postal agreement concerning registered mail, of Jan. 1, 1948 (effective U.S.–Germany same day):

Expired.

132. Agreement on freedom of the road, of Jan. 1, 1948 (effective U.S.–Germany same day):

Assumed by Federal Republic, BGBl. 1955 II 523.

133. Postal agreement concerning reply paid postcards (incoming to Germany only), of Feb. 15, 1948 (effective U.S.–Germany same day):

Expired.

134. Convention on the Intergovernmental Maritime Consultative Organization, of Mar. 6, 1948 (effective U.S.–Germany Jan. 7, 1959):

9 UST 621, TIAS no. 4044, 289 UNTS 48, BGBl. 1965 II 313, Verträge A 173, GVOBl. Berlin 1967, 440;

Amended by nos. 291 and 298.

135. Protocol of rectification to the general agreement on tariffs and trade (no. 128), of Mar. 24, 1948 (effective U.S.–Germany Oct. 1, 1951):

62 Stat. 1962, TIAS no. 1761, 62 UNTS 2, BGBl. 1951 II 173, 200 with annex II p. 1252.

136. Protocol modifying certain provisions of the general agreement on tariffs and trade (no. 128), of Mar. 24, 1948 (effective U.S.–Germany Oct. 1, 1951):

62 Stat. 1992, TIAS no. 1763, 62 UNTS 30, BGBl. 1951 II 173, 200 with annex II p. 1238.

137. Special protocol modifying article XIV of the general agreement on tariffs and trade (no. 128), of Mar. 24, 1948 (effective U.S.–Germany Oct. 1, 1951):

62 Stat. 2000, TIAS no. 1764, 62 UNTS 40, BGBl. 1951 II 173, 200 with annex II p. 1246.

138. Special protocol relating to article XXIV of the general agreement on tariffs and trade (no. 128), of Mar. 24, 1948 (effective U.S.–Germany Oct. 1, 1951):

62 Stat. 2013, TIAS no. 1765, 62 UNTS 56, BGBl. 1951 II 173, 200 with annex II p. 1241.

138 A. Protocol modifying the convention of 1928 relating to international exhibitions (no. 73 A), of May 10, 1948 (effective U.S.–Germany June 24, 1968):

19 UST 5927, TIAS no. 6548, 289 UNTS 111, BGBl. 1956 II 2087, 1957 II 252, 1969 II 1466, Verträge A 303;

Amended by no. 300 A.

139. Convention on safety of life at sea, of June 10, 1948 (effective U.S.–Germany Nov. 19, 1954):

3 UST 3450, TIAS no. 2495, 32 D.S.Bull.206 (1955), 164 UNTS 113, BGBl. 1953 II 603, 1954 II 1042, Verträge A 36;

Supersedes no. 74; superseded by no. 259.

140. Regulations for preventing collisions at sea, of June 10, 1948 (effective U.S.–Germany Jan. 22, 1954):

4 UST 2956, TIAS no. 2899, 191 UNTS 3, BGBl. 1953 II 760, 1958 II 357, Verträge A 37, GVOBl. Berlin 1954, 378;

Supersedes no. 74; superseded by no. 260.

141. Convention on the international recognition of rights in aircraft, of June 19, 1948 (effective U.S.–Germany Oct. 5, 1959):

4 UST 1830, TIAS no. 2847, 41 D.S.Bull.293 (1959), 310 UNTS 151, BGBl. 1959 II 129, 1960 II 1500, Verträge A 157, GVOBl. Berlin 1959, 625.

142. World Health Organization Regulations No. 1 regarding nomenclature (including the compilation and publication of statistics) with respect to diseases and causes of death, of July 24, 1948 (effective U.S.–Germany June 5, 1952):

7 UST 79, TIAS no. 3482, 66 UNTS 25, Verträge A 94;

Supersedes nos. 90 and 101; amended by nos. 151 and 226; supplemented by no. 172.

143. Second protocol of rectifications to the general agreement on tariffs and trade (no. 128), of Sept. 14, 1948 (effective U.S.–Germany Oct. 1, 1951):

62 Stat. 3671, TIAS no. 1888, 62 UNTS 74, BGBl. 1951 II 173, 200 with annex II p. 1282.

144. Protocol modifying Part II and article XXVI of the general agreement on tariffs and trade (no. 128), of Sept. 14, 1948 (effective U.S.–Germany Oct. 1, 1951):

62 Stat. 3679, TIAS no. 1890, 62 UNTS 80, BGBl. 1951 II 173, 200 with annex II p. 1268.

145. Protocol modifying Part I and article XXXIX of the general agreement on tariffs and trade (no. 128), of Sept. 14, 1948 (effective U.S.–Germany Oct. 1, 1951):

3 UST 5355, TIAS no. 2744, 138 UNTS 334, BGBl. 1951 II 173, 200 with annex II p. 1264.

146. Postal agreement extending transit parcel post service through Germany, of Oct. 20, 1948 (effective U.S.–Germany same day):

Amended no. 125; expired.

147. Protocol bringing under international control drugs outside the scope of the convention of July 13, 1931, for limiting the manufacture and regulating the distribution of narcotic drugs, as amended by the protocol signed on Dec. 11, 1946 (no. 115), of Nov. 19, 1948 (effective U.S.–Germany Sept. 12, 1959):

61 Stat. 2230, 2 UST 1629, TIAS no. 2308, 41 D.S.Bull.461 (1959), 44 UNTS 277, BGBl. 1959 II 333, 349, 1266, Verträge A 156, GVOBl. Berlin 1959, 1181;

Supplemented by no. 197.

148. International convention for the Northwest Atlantic fisheries, of Feb. 8, 1949 (effective U.S.–Germany June 27, 1957):

1 UST 477, TIAS no. 2089, 37 D.S.Bull.129 (1957), 157 UNTS 157, BGBl. 1957 II 265, 1356;

Amended by nos. 230, 269 A, 285, 300 B and 300 C.

149. International wheat agreement, of Mar. 23, 1949 (effective U.S.–Germany May, 1950):

63 Stat. 2173, TIAS no. 1957, 203 UNTS 179, BGBl. 1950, 131;

Abrogated by no. 195.

150. North Atlantic Treaty, of April 4, 1949 (effective U.S.–Germany May 6, 1955):

63 Stat. 2241, TIAS no. 1964, 34 UNTS 243, BGBl. 1955 II 256, 293, 630, Verträge A 70;

Amended by no. 175; supplemented by nos. 173, 174 and 218.

151. Amendment to World Health Organization Regulations No. 1 regarding nomenclature (including the compilation and publication of statistics) with respect to diseases and causes of death (no. 142), of June 30, 1949 (effective U.S.–Germany June 5, 1952):

7 UST 79, TIAS no. 3482, 66 UNTS 38, Verträge A 94;

Amended by no. 226.

152. Convention for the amelioration of the condition of the wounded and sick in armed forces in the field, of Aug. 12, 1949 (effective U.S.–Germany Feb. 2, 1956):

6 UST 3114, TIAS no. 3362, 31 D.S.Bull.283 (1954), 75 UNTS 31, BGBl. 1954 II 781, 783, 1113, 1955 II 890, Verträge A 38, GVOBl. Berlin 1954, 606;

Supersedes no. 76; supplemented by no. 153.

153. Convention for the amelioration of the condition of the wounded, sick, and shipwrecked members of armed forces at sea, of Aug. 12, 1949 (effective U.S.–Germany Feb. 2, 1956):

 6 UST 3217, TIAS no. 3363, 31 D.S.Bull.283 (1954), 75 UNTS 85, BGBl. 1954 II 781, 813, 1133, 1955 II 890, Verträge A 39, GVOBl. Berlin 1954, 606;

 Supersedes no. 76.

154. Convention relative to the treatment of prisoners of war, of Aug. 12, 1949 (effective U.S.–Germany Feb. 2, 1956):

 6 UST 3316, TIAS no. 3364, 31 D.S.Bull.283 (1954), 75 UNTS 135, BGBl. 1954 II 781, 838, 1133, 1955 II 890, Verträge A 40, GVOBl. Berlin 1954, 606;

 Supersedes no. 77.

155. Convention relative to the protection of civilian persons in time of war, of Aug. 12, 1949 (effective U.S.–Germany Feb. 2, 1956):

 6 UST 3516, TIAS no. 3365, 31 D.S.Bull.283 (1954), 75 UNTS 287, BGBl. 1954 II 781, 917, 1133, 1955 II 890, Verträge A 41, GVOBl. Berlin 1954, 606.

156. Protocol modifying article XXVI of the general agreement on tariffs and trade (no. 128), of Aug. 13, 1949 (effective U.S.–Germany Oct. 1, 1951):

 2 UST 1583, TIAS no. 2300, 62 UNTS 113, BGBl. 1951 II 173, 200 with annex II p. 1286.

157. First protocol of modification to the general agreement on tariffs and trade (no. 128), of Aug. 13, 1949 (effective U.S.–Germany Oct. 1, 1951):

 3 UST 5368, TIAS no. 2745, 138 UNTS 381, BGBl. 1951 II 173, 200 with annex II p. 1398.

158. Third protocol of rectification of the general agreement on tariffs and trade (no. 128), of Aug. 13, 1949 (effective U.S.–Germany Oct. 1, 1951):

 3 UST 57, TIAS no. 2393, 107 UNTS 311, Dt.Hand.Arch. 1951, 1443.

159. Protocol replacing Schedule I (Australia) of the general agreement on tariffs and trade (no. 128), of Aug. 13, 1949 (effective U.S.–Germany Oct. 1, 1951):

 3 UST 123, TIAS no. 2394, 107 UNTS 83, BGBl. 1951 II 173, 200 with annex II p. 1288.

160. Protocol replacing Schedule VI (Ceylon) of the general agreement on tariffs and trade (no. 128), of Aug. 13, 1949 (effective U.S.–Germany Oct. 1, 1951):

 3 UST 5383, TIAS no. 2746, 138 UNTS 346, BGBl. 1951 II 173, 200 with annex II p. 1378.

161. Annecy protocol of terms of accession to the general agreement on tariffs and trade (no. 128), of Oct. 10, 1949 (effective U.S.–Germany Oct. 1, 1951):

 64 Stat.(3) B139, TIAS no. 2100, 62 UNTS 122, and 63 and 64 UNTS, BGBl. 1951 II 173, 200 with annex p. 1427.

162. Protocol of agreements reached between the Allied High Commissioners and the Chancellor of the German Federal Republic, of Nov. 22, 1949 (effective U.S.–Germany same day):

 3 UST 2714, TIAS no. 2439, 185 UNTS 307, BAnz. 1949 no. 28.

163. Agreement concerning ECA-accounts, of Dec. 15, 1949 (effective U.S.–Germany Feb. 7, 1950):

BAnz. 1950 no. 112 p. 2;

Supplements Treaty B 87; see also *infra* no. 164.

164. Agreement concerning GARIOA-accounts, of Dec. 15, 1949 (effective U.S.–Germany Feb. 7, 1950):

BAnz 1950 no. 112 p. 4;

Supplements Treaty B 87; see also *supra* no. 163.

165. Protocol modifying the convention of July 5, 1890 relating to the creation of an International Union for the Publication of Customs Tariffs (no. 16), of Dec. 16, 1949 (effective U.S.–Germany Sept. 15, 1957):

8 UST 1669, TIAS no. 3922, 72 UNTS 3, BAnz. 1958 no. 51, Verträge A 300.

166. Fourth protocol of rectification to the general agreement on tariffs and trade (no. 128), of April 30, 1950 (effective U.S.–Germany Oct. 1, 1951):

3 UST 5399, TIAS no. 2747, 138 UNTS 398, BGBl. 1951 II 173, 200 with annex III p. 1886.

167. Agreement relating to defense materials, of Oct. 23, 1950/Mar. 6, 1951 (effective U.S.–Germany Mar. 6, 1951):

138 UNTS 67.

168. Agreement on the importation of educational, scientific and cultural materials, of Nov. 22, 1950 (effective U.S.–Germany Nov. 2, 1966):

17 UST 1835, TIAS no. 6129, 131 UNTS 25, 361, BGBl. 1957 II 170, 1467, 1960 II 2320, Verträge A 125, GVOBl. Berlin 1957, 731.

168 A. Convention establishing a Customs Cooperation Council, of Dec. 15, 1950 (effective U.S.–Germany Nov. 5, 1970):

157 UNTS 129, BGBl. 1952 II 1, 19, 1953 II 1, 1971 II 103, Verträge A 19.

168 B. Protocol concerning the European Customs Union Study Group, of Dec. 15, 1950 (effective U.S.–Germany Nov. 5, 1970):

160 UNTS 267, Dt.Hand.Arch. 1953, 529, Verträge A 6.

169. Fifth protocol of rectifications to the general agreement on tariffs and trade (no. 128), of Dec. 16, 1950 (effective U.S.–Germany Oct. 1, 1951):

4 UST 29, TIAS 2764, 167 UNTS 265, BGBl. 1951 II 173, 200 with annex III p. 1934.

170. Agreement relating to prewar external debts of the German Reich and the debt arising out of economic assistance furnished since May 8, 1945, of Mar. 6, 1951 (effective U.S.–Germany same day):

2 UST 1249, TIAS no. 2274, 106 UNTS 141, BGBl. 1953 II 331, 473, 556, Verträge A 25.

171. Torquay protocol to the general agreement on tariffs and trade (no. 128) and schedules of tariff concessions annexed thereto, of April 21, 1951 (effective U.S.–Germany Oct. 1, 1951):

3 UST 588, 1807, TIAS no. 2420, 142 UNTS 34, 143–146 UNTS, 147 UNTS 159, BGBl. 1951 II 173, 300 with annex III p. 1984, Verträge A 11, GVOBl. Berlin 1953, 1163.

172. International sanitary regulations (World Health Organization Regulation no. 2), of May 25, 1951 (effective U.S.–Germany Apr. 17, 1956):

 7 UST 2255, 2306, 2310, TIAS no. 3625, 175 UNTS 215, BGBl. 1955 II 1060, 1957 II 10, 1968 II 1129, Verträge A 95, GVOBl. Berlin 1956, 260;

 Amended by nos. 214, 228, 229, 258, 284 and 295.

173. Agreement between the parties to the North Atlantic Treaty (no. 150) regarding the status of their forces, of June 19, 1951 (effective U.S.–Germany July 1, 1963):

 4 UST 1792, TIAS no. 2846, 48 D.S.Bull.961 (1963), 199 UNTS 67, BGBl. 1961 II 1183, 1190, 1963 II 745, 1967 II 743, Verträge A 227;

 Amended by no. 179; supplemented by nos. 188A, 250, 251 and 253 as well as B 201A.

174. Agreement on the status of the North Atlantic Treaty (no. 150) Organization, national representatives, and international staff, of Sept. 20, 1951 (effective U.S.–Germany July 28, 1958):

 5 UST 1087, TIAS no. 2992, 39 D.S.Bull.296 (1958), 200 UNTS 3, BGBl. 1958 II 117, 350, Verträge A 182.

175. Protocol to the North Atlantic Treaty (no. 150) on the accession of Greece and Turkey, of Oct. 17, 1951 (effective U.S.–Germany May 6, 1955):

 3 UST 43, TIAS No. 2390, 126 UNTS 350, BGBl. 1955 II 256, 293, 630, Verträge A 70.

176. First protocol of supplementary concessions to the general agreement on tariffs and trade (no. 128) (Republic of South Africa and Federal Republic of Germany), of Oct. 27, 1951 (effective U.S.–Germany May 25, 1952):

 3 UST 3963, TIAS no. 2532, 131 UNTS 316, BGBl. 1952 II 427, 516, GVOBl. Berlin 1954, 169.

177. First protocol of rectification and modification to the texts of schedules to the general agreement on tariffs and trade (no. 128), of Oct. 27, 1951 (effective U.S.–Germany Oct. 21, 1953):

 4 UST 2313, TIAS no. 2885, 176 UNTS 2, 280, 348, BGBl. 1952 II 729, 952, GVOBl. Berlin 1953, 1163.

178. Statute of the Hague Conference on Private International Law, as amended, of Oct. 31, 1951 (effective U.S.–Germany Oct. 15, 1964):

 15 UST 2228, TIAS no. 5710, 220 UNTS 121, BGBl. 1959 II 981, 1965 II 122, Verträge A 86.

179. Agreed minute modifying the agreement of June 19, 1951 between the parties to the North Atlantic Treaty regarding the status of their forces (no. 173), of Apr. 4, 1952 (effective U.S.–Germany July 1, 1963):

 199 UNTS 109, 200 UNTS 28, BGBl. 1967 II 742.

180. Protocol for the termination of the Brussels agreement for the unification of pharmacopoeial formulas for potent drugs (no. 39), of May 20, 1952 (effective U.S.–Germany same day):

 3 UST 5067, TIAS no. 2692, 219 UNTS 55, BAnz. 1955 no. 114, Verträge A 13.

181. Convention on relations between the Three Powers and the Federal Republic of Germany, with annexes, as amended, of May 26, 1952 (effective U.S.–Germany May 5, 1955):

6 UST 4251, TIAS no. 3425, 331 UNTS 327, BGBl. 1954 II 57, 61, 1955 II 213, 218, 628, Verträge A 63;

Amended by nos. 186 and 207; supplemented by nos. 182–185.

182. Convention on the rights and obligations of foreign forces and their members in the Federal Republic of Germany, with annexes, as amended, of May 26, 1952 (effective U.S.–Germany May 5, 1955):

6 UST 4278, TIAS no. 3425, 332 UNTS 3, BGBl. 1954 II 57, 78, 1955 II 213, 224, 618, Verträge A 64;

Amended by nos. 186, 207 and 208; abrogated by no. 252.

183. Finance convention, as amended, of May 26, 1952 (effective U.S.–Germany May 5, 1955):

6 UST 4377, TIAS no. 3425, 332, UNTS 157, BGBl. 1954 II 57, 135, 1955 II 213, 227, 628, Verträge A 65;

Amended by nos. 186 and 207; abrogated by no. 252.

184. Convention on the settlement of matters arising out of the war and the occupation, with annex, as amended, of May 26, 1952 (effective U.S.–Germany May 5, 1955):

6 UST 4411, TIAS no. 3425, 332 UNTS 219, BGBl. 1954 II 57, 157, 1955 II 213, 234, 628, Verträge A 66;

Amended by nos. 186, 207 and 321; supplemented by no. 231.

185. Agreement on the tax treatment of the forces and their members, as amended, of May 26, 1952 (effective U.S.–Germany May 5, 1955):

6 UST 4370, TIAS no. 3425, 332 UNTS 387, BGBl. 1954 II 333, 1955 II 213, 241, 628, Verträge A 67;

Amended by nos. 186, 188 and 207; abrogated by no. 252.

186. Protocol to correct certain textual errors in the convention on relations between the Three Powers and the Federal Republic of Germany and the related conventions signed at Bonn May 26, 1952 (nos. 181–185), of June 27, 1952 (effective U.S.–Germany May 5, 1955):

6 UST 5381, TIAS no. 3425, BGBl. 1954 II 321.

187. Universal Postal Union, of July 11, 1952 (effective U.S.–Germany Mar. 24, 1955:

4 UST 1118, TIAS no. 2800, 169 UNTS 3, BGBl. 1954 II 1211, 1956 II 653, Verträge A 54, GVOBl. Berlin 1955, 222;

Abrogated by no 241.

188. Protocol conferring upon the Arbitration Tribunal jurisdiction over disputes arising under the agreement on the tax treatment of the forces and their members (no. 185), of July 26, 1952 (effective U.S.–Germany May 5, 1955):

6 UST 4259, 5415, TIAS no. 3425, 331 UNTS 258, 300, BGBl. 1954 II 340.

188A. Protocol on the status of international military headquarters, of Aug. 28, 1952 (effective U.S.–Germany Dec. 21, 1969):

5 UST 870, TIAS no. 2978, 200 UNTS 340, BGBl. 1969 II 1997, 1970 II 51.

189. Universal copyright convention and three protocols annexed thereto, of Sept. 6, 1952 (effective U.S.–Germany Sept. 16, 1955):

6 UST 2731, TIAS no. 3324, 216 UNTS 132, BGBl. 1955 II 101, 892, Verträge A 72, GVOBl. Berlin 1955, 222.

190. International convention to facilitate the importation of commercial samples and advertising material, of Nov. 7, 1952 (effective U.S.–Germany Oct. 17, 1957):

8 UST 1636, TIAS no. 3920, 33 D.S.Bull.549 (1955), 221 UNTS 255, BGBl. 1955 II 633, 1956 II 29, 1957 II 1688, Verträge A 81, GVOBl. Berlin 1955, 680.

191. Second protocol of rectifications and modifications to the text of the schedules to the general agreement on tariffs and trade (no. 128), of Nov. 8, 1952 (effective U.S.–Germany Feb. 2, 1959):

10 UST 1098, TIAS no. 4250, 321 UNTS 245, BGBl. 1953 II 266, 1959 II 403, GVOBl. Berlin 1953, 1163.

192. Second protocol of supplementary concessions to the general agreement on tariffs and trade (no. 128) (Austria and the Federal Republic of Germany), of Nov. 22, 1952 (effective U.S.–Germany Aug. 30, 1953):

4 UST 1631, TIAS no. 2831, 172 UNTS 340, BGBl. 1953 II 259, 526, GVOBl. Berlin 1954, 474.

193. International telecommunication convention and six annexes, and final protocol, of Dec. 22, 1952 (effective U.S.–Germany July 26, 1955):

6 UST 1213, TIAS no. 3266, BGBl. 1955 II 9, 884, Verträge A 78, GVOBl. Berlin 1955, 222;

Supersedes no. 126; supplemented by no. 215; superseded by no. 255.

194. Agreement on German external debts, of Feb. 27, 1953 (effective U.S.–Germany Sept. 16, 1953):

4 UST 443, TIAS no. 2792, 333 UNTS 3, BGBl. 1953 II 331, 556, Verträge A 25, GVOBl. Berlin 1953, 979;

Supplemented by nos. 209, 210 and Treaties B 96–101 and 128.

195. Agreement revising and renewing the international wheat agreement (no. 149), of Apr. 13, 1953 (effective U.S.–Germany July 15/Aug. 1, 1953):

4 UST 944, TIAS no. 2799, 203 UNTS 242, BGBl. 1953 II 187, 557, Verträge A 23, GVOBl. Berlin 1954, 378;

Abrogated by no. 225.

196. Agreement relating to certain libraries and properties in Italy, of Apr. 30, 1953 (effective U.S.–Germany May 1, 1953):

4 UST 376, TIAS no. 2785, 175 UNTS 89, Verträge A 21.

197. Protocol for limiting and regulating the cultivation of the poppy plant, the production of, international and whole-sale trade in, and use of opium, of June 23, 1953 (effective U.S.–Germany Mar. 8, 1963):

14 UST 10, TIAS no. 5273, 456 UNTS 3, BGBl. 1959 II 333, 358, 1966 II 385, Verträge A 216, GVOBl. Berlin 1959, 1181;

Supplements nos. 55, 81, 115 and 147.

198. Instrument for the amendment of the constitution of the International Labor Organization (no. 58), of June 25, 1953 (effective U.S.–Germany May 20, 1954):

 7 UST 245, TIAS no. 3500, 191 UNTS 143, BGBl. 1957 II 317, Verträge A 8;

 Amended by no. 280.

199. International sugar agreement, of Oct. 1, 1953 (effective U.S.–Germany Dec. 15, 1953/Jan. 1, 1954):

 6 UST 203, TIAS no. 3177, 31 D.S.Bull.218 (1954), 258 UNTS 153, BGBl. 1954 II 577, 1049, Verträge A 29, GVOBl. Berlin 1954, 606;

 Amended by no. 236; abrogated by no. 246.

200. Constitution of the Intergovernmental Committee for European Migration, of Oct. 19, 1953 (effective U.S.–Germany Nov. 30, 1954):

 6 UST 603, TIAS no. 3197, 207 UNTS 189, Verträge A 46.

201. Third protocol of rectification and modification to the texts of schedules to the general agreement on tariffs and trade (no. 128), of Oct. 24, 1953 (effective U.S.–Germany Feb. 2, 1959):

 10 UST 347, TIAS no. 4197, 31 D.S.Bull.752 (1954), 321 UNTS 266, BGBl. 1954 II 741, 1959 II 403, GVOBl. Berlin 1954, 505.

202. Agreement on North Atlantic Ocean stations, and two annexes, of Feb. 25, 1954 (effective U.S.–Germany Oct. 15, 1957):

 6 UST 515, TIAS no. 3186, 215 UNTS 245, 250, 268, BAnz. 1958 no. 55, Verträge A 131;

 Amended by no. 281 A and no. 325.

203. International convention for the prevention of pollution of the sea by oil, with annexes, of May 12, 1954 (effective U.S.–Germany Dec. 8, 1961):

 12 UST 2989, TIAS no. 4900, 327 UNTS 3, BGBl. 1956 II 379, 1957 II 1696, 1958 II 91, 1966 II 374, Verträge A 144, GVOBl. Berlin 1956, 320;

 Supplemented by no. 277.

204. Convention concerning customs facilities for touring, of June 4, 1954 (effective U.S.–Germany Dec. 15, 1957):

 8 UST 1293, TIAS no. 3879, 37 D.S.Bull.626 (1957), 276 UNTS 191, 230, 266, BGBl. 1956 II 1886, 1960 II 1511, Verträge A 128, GVOBl. Berlin 1957, 196;

 See also no. 205; amended by no. 313.

205. Customs convention on the temporary importation of private road vehicles, of June 4, 1954 (effective U.S.–Germany Dec. 15, 1957):

 8 UST 2097, TIAS no. 3943, 37 D.S.Bull.626 (1957), 282 UNTS 249, BGBl. 1956 II 1886, 1948 II 1511, Verträge A 133, GVOBl. Berlin 1957, 196;

 See also no. 204.

206. Protocol relating to certain amendments to the convention on international civil aviation (no. 105), of June 14, 1954 (effective U.S.–Germany Apr. 27, 1959):

 8 UST 179, TIAS no. 3756, 41 D.S.Bull.293 (1959), 320 UNTS 217, BGBl. 1959 II 69, 987, Verträge A 150.

207. Protocol on the termination of the occupation regime in the Federal Republic of Germany, with five schedules and related letters, of Oct. 23, 1954 (effective U.S.–Germany May 5, 1955):

6 UST 4177, TIAS no. 3425, 32 D.S.Bull.826 (1955), 331 UNTS 253, BGBl. 1955 II 213, 628, Verträge A 62;

Amends nos. 181–185.

208. Convention on the presence of foreign forces in the Federal Republic of Germany, of Oct. 23, 1954 (effective U.S.–Germany May 6, 1955):

6 UST 5689, TIAS no. 3426, 32 D.S.Bull.826 (1955), 334 UNTS 3, BGBl. 1955 II 253, 630, Verträge A 68;

Supplemented by Treaties B 142 and 143.

209. Protocol of 1954 covering German short-term indebtedness remaining after the expiry of the German credit agreement of 1952, of Nov. 19, 1954 (effective Dec. 2, 1954):

BAnz. 1954 no. 245, Verträge A 25 (vol. 3 p. 240);

Extends no. 194; extended by nos. 223, 237, 242, 247, 254 and 268.

210. Administrative agreement concerning the Arbitral Tribunal and the Mixed Commission under the external debt agreement (no. 194), with annex and exchange of letters, of Dec. 1, 1954 (effective U.S.–Germany same day):

6 UST 865, TIAS no. 3233, 210 UNTS 197, BAnz. 1955 no. 185, Verträge A 50, GVOBl. Berlin 1957, 522;

Amended by nos. 235, 262 and 322.

211. Fourth protocol of rectification and modification to the annexes to the texts of schedules to the general agreement on tariffs and trade (no. 128), of Mar. 7, 1955:

10 UST 213, TIAS no. 4186, 34 D.S.Bull.1080 (1956), 324 UNTS 300, BGBl. 1956 II 336, GVOBl. Berlin 1956, 320.

212. Protocols amending the preamble and parts II and III of the general agreement on tariffs and trade (no. 128), of Mar. 10, 1955 (effective U.S.–Germany Oct. 7, 1957):

8 UST 1767, TIAS no. 3930, 37 D.S.Bull.813 (1957), 278 UNTS 168, BGBl. 1957 II 605, 621, 1967 II 2331, GVOBl. Berlin 1957, 1335.

213. Articles of agreement of the International Finance Corporation of Apr. 11/May 25, 1955 (effective U.S.–Germany July 20, 1956):

7 UST 2197, TIAS no. 3620, 264 UNTS 117, BGBl. 1956 II 747, 901, Verträge A 105, GVOBl. Berlin 1956, 1124;

Amended by nos. 273 and 297.

214. Additional regulations amending the international sanitary regulations no. 2 (no. 172) with respect to yellow fever, of May 26, 1955 (effective U.S.–Germany Oct. 1, 1956):

13 UST 1986, TIAS no. 5156, 252 UNTS 338, BGBl. 1965 II 1413, Verträge A 112.

215. Agreement constituting an international commission for the International Tracing Service, of June 6, 1955 (effective U.S.–Germany May 5, 1955):

6 UST 6169, TIAS no. 3471, 219 UNTS 79, BAnz. 1955 no. 241 p. 3, Verträge A 73;

See also no. 216 and Treaty B 123: extended and amended by no. 261.

216. Agreement on the regulations between the international commission for the International Tracing Service and the International Committee of the Red Cross, of June 6, 1955 (effective U.S.–Germany May 5, 1955):

6 UST 6207, TIAS no. 3471, 219 UNTS 96, BAnz. 1955 no. 241 p. 5, Verträge A 73 annex A;

See also no. 215 and Treaty B 123; extended and amended by no. 259.

217. Protocol of rectification to the French text of the general agreement on tariffs and trade (no. 128), of June 15, 1955 (effective U.S.–Germany Oct. 25, 1957):

7 UST 2943, TIAS no. 3677, 38 D.S.Bull.198 (1958), 253 UNTS 316, BGBl. 1957 II 1285, 1958 II 116, GVOBl. Berlin 1957, 1791.

218. Agreement between the parties to the North Atlantic Treaty (no. 150) for cooperation regarding atomic information, of June 22, 1955 (effective U.S.–Germany Mar. 29, 1956):

7 UST 397, TIAS no. 3521, 249 UNTS 3, BAnz. 1956 no. 145, Verträge A 93;

Superseded by no. 288 B.

219. Third protocol of supplementary concessions to the general agreement on tariffs and trade (no. 128) (Denmark and the Federal Republic of Germany), of July 15, 1955 (effective U.S.–Germany Sept. 19, 1956):

7 UST 2393, TIAS no. 3629, 250 UNTS 292, BGBl. 1956 II 855, 902, GVOBl. Berlin 1956, 1124.

220. Fourth protocol of supplementary concessions to the general agreement on tariffs and trade (no. 128) (Federal Republic of Germany and Norway), of July 15, 1955 (effective U.S.–Germany Sept. 19, 1956):

7 UST 2407, TIAS no. 3630, 250 UNTS 297, BGBl. 1956 II 865, 902, GVOBl. Berlin 1956, 1124.

221. Fifth protocol of supplementary concessions to the general agreement on tariffs and trade (no. 128) (Federal Republic of Germany and Sweden), of July 15, 1955 (effective U.S.–Germany Sept. 19, 1956):

7 UST 2421, TIAS no. 3631, 250 UNTS 301, BGBl. 1956 II 873, 902, GVOBl. Berlin 1957, 196.

222. Penal administrative agreement (concerning war criminals), of Sept. 29/ Nov. 1/Dec. 20/Dec. 22, 1955 (effective U.S.–Germany May 5, 1955):

7 UST 663, TIAS no. 3549.

223. First protocol of extension of the protocol of 1954 covering German short-term indebtedness remaining after the expiry of the German credit agreement of 1952 (no. 209), of Dec. 2, 1955 (effective same day):

BAnz. 1955 no. 247, Verträge A 85;

Extended by no. 237.

224. Agreement regarding financial support of the North Atlantic ice patrol, of Jan. 4, 1956 (effective U.S.–Germany July 9, 1958):

7 UST 1969, TIAS no. 3597, 39 D.S.Bull.223 (1958), 256 UNTS 171, BAnz. 1958 no. 217, Verträge A 143.

224 A. Customs convention regarding E.C.S. carnets for commercial samples, of Mar. 1, 1956 (effective U.S.–Germany Mar. 3, 1969):

20 UST 120, TIAS no. 6632, 343 UNTS 129, BGBl. 1965 II 917, 1966 II 395, 706, 1969 II 611.

225. International wheat agreement of 1956, of Apr. 25, 1956 (effective U.S.–Germany July 16/Aug. 1, 1959):

7 UST 3275, TIAS no. 3709, 35 D.S.Bull.970 (1956), 270 UNTS 103, BGBl. 1956 II 1011, 1957 II 9, Verträge A 104, GVOBl. Berlin 1957, 196;

Supersedes no. 195; abrogated by no. 248.

225 A. Customs convention on containers, of May 18, 1956 (effective U.S.–Germany Mar. 3, 1969):

20 UST 301, TIAS no. 6634, 338 UNTS 103, BGBl. 1961 II 985, 1962 II 805, 1969 II 611, Verträge A 209.

226. Amendment to World Health Organization Regulation No. 1 regarding nomenclature (including the compilation and publication of statistics) with respect to diseases and causes of death (no. 142), of May 21, 1956 (effective U.S.–Germany Jan. 1, 1958):

11 UST 61, TIAS no. 4409.

227. Sixth protocol of supplementary concessions to the general agreement on tariffs and trade (no. 128), of May 23, 1956 (effective U.S.–Germany May 4, 1957):

7 UST 1083, TIAS no. 3591, 36 D.S.Bull.710 (1957), 244–246 UNTS, BGBl. 1956 II 1091, 1957 II 279, GVOBl. Berlin 1957, 196.

228. Additional regulations amending the international sanitary regulations no. 2 (no. 172) with respect to the form of the international certificate of vaccination or revaccination against smallpox, of May 23, 1956 (effective U.S.–Germany Apr. 14, 1966):

11 UST 133, TIAS no. 4420, BGBl. 1965 II 1413, 1423, 1966 II 888.

229. Additional regulations amending the international sanitary regulations no. 2 (no. 172) with respect to the sanitary control of pilgrim traffic, of May 23, 1956 (effective U.S.–Germany Apr. 14, 1966):

12 UST 1121, TIAS no. 4823, BGBl. 1965 II 1413, 1420, 1966 II 888.

230. Protocol to the international convention for the Northwest Atlantic fisheries of Feb. 8, 1949 (no. 148), of June 25, 1956 (effective U.S.–Germany Jan. 10, 1959):

10 UST 59, TIAS no. 4170, 331 UNTS 388, BGBl. 1957 II 265, 277, 1959 II 218, Verträge A 124, GVOBl. Berlin 1957, 731.

231. Administrative agreement concerning the Arbitration Tribunal and the Arbitral Commission on property, rights and interests in Germany, of July 13, 1956 (effective U.S.–Germany May 5, 1955):

7 UST 2129, TIAS no. 3615, 281 UNTS 3, BAnz. 1956 no. 225, Verträge A 103;

Supplements no. 184; supplemented by Treaty B 136.

231A. Supplementary convention on abolition of slavery, the slave trade and institutions and practices similar to slavery, of Sept. 7, 1956 (effective U.S.–Germany Dec. 6, 1967):

18 UST 3201, TIAS no. 6418, 266 UNTS 3, BGBl. 1958 II 203, 1959 II 407, 1968 II 786, Verträge A 148, GVOBl. Berlin 1958, 870;

Supplements no. 70.

232. Agreement on the joint financing of certain air navigation services in Iceland, of Sept. 25, 1956 (effective U.S.–Germany June 6, 1958):

9 UST 711, TIAS no. 4048, 37 D.S.Bull.906 (1957), 334 UNTS 13, BAnz. 1958 no. 155, Verträge A 179;

Amended by nos. 284 A and 305.

233. Agreement on the joint financing of certain air navigation services in Greenland and the Faroe Islands, of Sept. 25, 1956 (effective U.S.–Germany June 6, 1958):

9 UST 795, TIAS no. 4049, 37 D.S.Bull.906 (1957), 334 UNTS 89, BAnz. 1958 no. 158, Verträge A 180;

Amended by nos. 270, 282 A, 284 A and 310.

234. Statute of the International Atomic Energy Agency, of Oct. 26, 1956 (effective U.S.–Germany Oct. 1, 1957):

8 US 1093, TIAS no. 3873, 37 D.S.Bull.662 (1957), 276 UNTS 3, BGBl. 1957 II 1357, 1958 II 2, Verträge A 130, GVOBl. Berlin 1958, 301;

Amended by no. 274.

235. Amendment to the administrative agreement concerning the Arbitral Tribunal and the Mixed Commission under the external debt agreement, with annex and exchange of letters (no. 210), of Nov. 30, 1956 (effective U.S.–Germany Sept. 19, 1956):

7 UST 3442, TIAS no. 3717, 36 D.S.Bull.156 (1957), 265 UNTS 380, BAnz. 1957 no. 16, Verträge A 50, GVOBl. Berlin 1957, 522;

Amended by no. 262.

236. Protocol for the amendment of the international sugar agreement (no. 199), of Dec. 1, 1956 (effective U.S.–Germany July 24, 1958):

8 UST 1937, TIAS no. 3937, 39 D.S.Bull.636 (1958), 326 UNTS 314, BGBl. 1958 II 172, 1959 II 784, GVOBl. Berlin 1958, 871;

Abrogated by no. 246.

237. Second protocol of extension of the protocol of 1954 covering German short-term indebtedness remaining after the expiry of the German credit agreement of 1952 (no. 209), of Dec. 1, 1956 (effective U.S.–Germany Dec. 2, 1956):

7 UST 3442, TIAS no. 3717, BAnz. 1957 no. 7, Verträge A 114;

Extends no. 223; extended by no. 242.

238. Seventh protocol of supplementary concessions to the general agreement on tariffs and trade (no. 128) (Austria and the Federal Republic of Germany), of Feb. 19, 1957 (effective U.S.–Germany Aug. 21, 1959):

10 UST 1720, TIAS no. 4324, 309 UNTS 364, BGBl. 1959 II 539, 986.

239. Eighth protocol of supplementary concessions to the general agreement on tariffs and trade (no. 128) (Cuba and the United States), of June 20, 1957 (effective U.S.–Germany June 29, 1957):

8 UST 1343, TIAS no. 3882, 274 UNTS 322, BGBl. 1958 II 342, GVOBl. Berlin 1959, 420.

240. Modification of the first paragraph of Annex II of the international load line convention (no. 80), of July 13, 1957 (effective U.S.–Germany same day):

10 UST 1271, TIAS no. 4266, BGBl. 1962 II 1435.

241. Universal postal convention with final protocol, annex, regulations of execution, and provisions regarding airmail with final protocol, of Oct. 3, 1957 (effective U.S.–Germany Apr. 1, 1959):

10 UST 413, TIAS no. 4202, 42 D.S.Bull.665 (1960), 364 UNTS 3, BGBl. 1960 II 697, 1962 II 1121, Verträge A 163, GVOBl. Berlin 1960, 617;

Supersedes no. 187; abrogated by no. 289.

242. Third protocol of extension of the protocol of 1954 covering German short-term indebtedness remaining after the expiry of the German credit agreement of 1952 (no. 209), of Nov. 30, 1957 (effective U.S.–Germany Dec. 2, 1957):

BAnz. 1958 no. 4, Verträge A 132;

Extends no. 237; extended by no. 247.

243. Modification of the fifth paragraph of Annex II of the international load line convention (no. 80), of Jan. 8, 1958 (effective U.S.–Germany same day):

11 UST 1992, TIAS no. 4550, BGBl. 1959 II 22.

243A. Convention on the recognition and enforcement of foreign arbitral awards, of June 10, 1958 (effective U.S.–Germany Dec. 29, 1970):

330 UNTS 38, BGBl. 1961 II 121, 1971 II 15.

244. Convention for the protection of industrial property, of Oct. 31, 1958 (effective U.S.–Germany Jan. 4, 1962):

13 UST 1, TIAS no. 4391, BGBl. 1961 II 273, 1962 II 46, Verträge A 206, GVOBl. Berlin 1961, 703;

Supersedes no. 90; superseded in part by no. 315B.

245. Telegraph regulations (Geneva revision, 1958), annexed to the international telecommunication convention (Buenos Aires 1952) (no. 193), with appendices and final protocol, of Nov. 29, 1958 (effective U.S.–Germany Jan. 1, 1960):

10 UST 2423, TIAS no. 4390.

246. International sugar agreement of 1958, of Dec. 1, 1958 (effective U.S.–Germany Jan. 1, 1959):

10 UST 2189, TIAS no. 4389, 42 D.S.Bull.766 (1960), 385 UNTS 137, BGBl. 1960 II 1257, 1961 II 118, Verträge A 172, GVOBl. Berlin 1960, 617;

Supersedes nos. 199 and 236; amended and extended by nos. 286, 299 and 306.

247. Fourth protocol of extension of the protocol of 1954 covering German short-term indebtedness remaining after the expiry of the German credit agreement of 1952 (no. 209), of Dec. 2, 1958 (effective same day):

BAnz. 1959 no. 2, Verträge A 145;

Extends no. 242; extended by no. 254.

247A. Convention concerning the exchange of official publications and government documents between states, of Dec. 3, 1958 (effective U.S.–Germany Oct. 3, 1970):

19 UST 4467, TIAS no. 6439, 398 UNTS 9, BGBl. 1969 II 997, 1970 II 15, GVOBl. Berlin 1969, 872, 1970, 668.

247B. Convention concerning the international exchange of publications, of Dec. 5, 1958 (effective U.S.–Germany Dec. 15, 1970):

19 UST 4449, TIAS no. 6438, 416 UNTS 51, BGBl. 1969 II 1569, 1970 II 206, GVOBl. Berlin 1969, 2052, 1970, 1482.

247C. Customs convention on the international transport of goods under cover of TIR carnets with modifications of annexes, of Jan. 15, 1959, (effective U.S.–Germany Mar. 3, 1969):

20 UST 184, TIAS no. 6633, 348 UNTS 13, BGBl. 1961 II 649, 1962 II 8, 1969 II 612, Verträge A 207.

248. International wheat agreement, of Apr. 6, 1959 (effective U.S.–Germany July 16/Aug. 1, 1959):

10 UST 1477, TIAS no. 4302, 42 D.S.Bull.387 (1960), 349 UNTS 167, BGBl. 1960 II 2009, 2350, 1961 II 1630, Verträge A 178, GVOBl. Berlin 1961, 664;

Supersedes no. 225; abrogated by no. 258.

249. Amendments to articles 24 and 25 of the World Health Organization Constitution (no. 113), of May 28, 1959 (effective U.S.–Germany Oct. 25, 1960):

11 UST 2553, TIAS no. 4643, 377 UNTS 380.

250. Agreement to supplement the agreeement between the parties to the North Atlantic Treaty regarding the status of their forces (no. 173) with respect to foreign forces stationed in the Federal Republic of Germany, of Aug. 3, 1959 (effective U.S.–Germany July 1, 1963):

14 UST 531, TIAS no. 5351, 48 D.S.Bull.961 (1963), 481 UNTS 262, BGBl. 1961 II 1183, 1218, 1963 II 745, 1964 II 1231, Verträge A 228;

Supplemented by nos. 251 and 253 and by Treaties B 159–167, 198, 201 A, 208 A and 209.

251. Agreement to implement paragraph 5 of article 45 of the supplemental agreement (no. 250), of Aug. 3, 1959 (effective U.S.–Germany July 1, 1963):

14 UST 670, TIAS no. 5351, 48 D.S.Bull.961 (1963), 481 UNTS 551, BGBl. 1961 II 1183, 1355, 1963 II 745, Verträge A 230.

252. Agreement on the abrogation of the forces convention, the finance convention and the tax agreement, of Aug. 3, 1959 (effective U.S.–Germany July 1, 1963):

14 UST 686, TIAS no. 5351, 48 D.S.Bull.961 (1963), 481 UNTS 591, BGBl. 1961 II 1183, 1352, 1963 II 746, Verträge A 229;

Abrogates nos. 182, 183 and 185; supplements no. 250.

253. Administrative agreement to article 60 of the supplementary agreement (no. 250), of Aug. 3, 1959 (effective U.S.–Germany July 1, 1963):

14 UST 677, TIAS no. 5351, 48 D.S.Bull.961 (1963), 481 UNTS 565, Verträge A 232.

253A. Convention Placing the International Poplar Commission within the Framework of FAO, of Nov. 19, 1959 (effective U.S.–Germany Aug. 13, 1970):

BGBl. 1965 II 1533, 1970 II 1052.

254. Fifth protocol of extension of the protocol of 1954 covering German short-term indebtedness remaining after the expiry of the German credit agreement of 1952 (no. 209), of Dec. 2, 1959 (effective U.S.–Germany same day):

BAnz. 1960 no. 12, Verträge A 158;

Extends no. 247; extended by no. 267.

255. International telecommunication convention, of Dec. 21, 1959 (effective U.S.–Germany Dec. 28, 1962):

12 UST 1761, TIAS no. 4892, 48 D.S.Bull.418 (1963), BGBl. 1962 II 2173, 1963 II 790, 1965 II 1136, Verträge A 221, GVOBl. Berlin 1963, 79;

Supersedes no. 193; supplemented by no. 256; superseded by no. 300.

256. Radio regulations, with appendices, annexed to the international telecommunication convention, 1959 (no. 255) and additional protocol, of Dec. 21, 1959 (effective U.S.–Germany May 1, 1961):

12 UST 2377, TIAS no. 4893;

Amended by nos. 288 and 304.

257. Articles of agreement of the International Development Association, of Jan. 26, 1960 (effective U.S.–Germany Sept. 24, 1960):

11 UST 2284, TIAS no. 4607, 439 UNTS 249, BGBl. 1960 II 2137, 2363, 1961 II 1386, Verträge A 190, GVOBl. Berlin 1961, 664.

258. Additional regulations amending the international sanitary regulations no. 2 (no. 172) with respect to the health part of the aircraft general declaration, of May 19, 1960 (effective U.S.–Germany Apr. 14, 1966):

12 UST 2950, TIAS no. 4896, BGBl. 1965 II 1413, 1426, 1966 II 888, GVOBl. Berlin 1966, 161.

259. International convention on safety of life at sea, 1960, of June 17, 1960 (effective U.S.–Germany May 26, 1965):

16 UST 185, TIAS no. 5780, 536 UNTS 27, BGBl. 1965 II 465, 1966 II 33, 1472, Verträge A 267;

Supersedes no. 139.

260. Regulations for preventing collisions at sea, of June 17, 1960 (effective U.S.–Germany Sept. 1, 1965):

16 UST 794, TIAS no. 5813, BGBl. 1965 II 465, 741, 1532, 1966 II 90, Verträge A 268, GVOBl. Berlin 1965, 1825;

Supersedes no. 140.

261. Protocol renewing and amending the agreement constituting an international commission for the International Tracing Service (no. 215), of Aug. 23, 1960 (effective U.S.–Germany May 5, 1960):

12 UST 463, TIAS no. 4736, 377 UNTS 402, BAnz. 1961 no. 244, p. 2;

See also no. 264 and Treaty B 172.

262. Amendment to the administrative agreement concerning the Arbitral Tribunal and the Mixed Commission under the external debt agreement (nos. 210 and 235), of Aug. 29, 1960 (effective U.S.–Germany same day):

11 UST 2324, TIAS no. 4609, 385 UNTS 378, BAnz. 1960 no. 244, GVOBl. Berlin 1961, 670.

263. Indus Basin Development Fund Agreement, of Sept. 19, 1960 (effective U.S.–Germany Apr. 1, 1960):

12 UST 19, TIAS no. 4671, 444 UNTS 259, BGBl. 1966 II 254, 1967 II 2579, Verträge A 275;

Supplemented by no. 288 A.

264. Protocol renewing and amending the agreement on the relations between the International Commission for the International Tracing Service and the International Committee of the Red Cross (no. 216), of Sept. 30/Oct. 7, 1960 (effective U.S.–Germany May 5, 1960):

12 UST 471, TIAS no. 4736, BAnz. 1961 no. 244, p. 3;

See also no. 261.

265. Declaration giving effect to provisions of article XVI: 4 of the general agreement on tariffs and trade (no. 128), of Nov. 19, 1960 (effective U.S.–Germany Nov. 14, 1962):

13 UST 2605, TIAS no. 5227, 47 D.S.Bull.862 (1962), 445 UNTS 294, BGBl. 1964 II 716, GVOBl. Berlin 1964, 960.

266. Agreement for the mutual safeguarding of secrecy of inventions relating to defense and for which applications for patents have been made, of Sept. 21, 1960 (effective U.S.–Germany Feb. 5, 1964):

12 UST 43, TIAS no. 4672, 50 D.S.Bull.144, (1964), 394 UNTS 3, BGBl. 1964 II 772, Verträge A 242;

See also no. 276 A.

267. Sixth protocol of extension of the protocol of 1954 covering German short-term indebtedness remaining after the expiry of the German credit agreement of 1952 (no. 209), of Dec. 2, 1960 (effective same day):

BAnz. 1961 no. 16;

Extended no. 254; expired June 2, 1961.

268. Convention on the Organization for Economic Cooperation and Development and supplementary protocols nos. 1 and 2, of Dec. 14, 1960 (effective U.S.–Germany Sept. 30, 1961):

12 UST 1728, TIAS no. 4891, 45 D.S.Bull.992 (1961), BGBl. 1961 II 1150, 1663, Verträge A 195, GVOBl. Berlin 1962, 446;

Supplemented by no. 269.

269. Memorandum of understanding on the application of article 15 of the convention on the Organization for Economic Cooperation and Development (no. 268), of Dec. 14, 1960 (effective U.S.–Germany Sept. 30, 1961):

12 UST 1753, TIAS no. 4891, BGBl. 1961 II 1150, 1173, 1663, Verträge A 195 (vol. 17 p. 294);

Supplements no. 268.

269 A. Declaration of understanding regarding the international convention for the Northwest Atlantic fisheries (no. 148), of Apr. 24, 1961 (effective U.S.–Germany June 5, 1963):

14 UST 924, TIAS no. 5380, 480 UNTS 334.

269 B. Customs convention on the temporary importation of professional equipment, of June 8, 1961 (effective U.S.–Germany Oct. 11, 1969):

20 UST 33, TIAS no. 6630, 473 UNTS 153, BGBl. 1969 II 1076, 2217, GVOBl. Berlin 1969, 872, 1970, 668.

270. Amendment of article V of agreement for joint financing of certain air navigation services in Greenland and the Faroe Islands (no. 233) by increasing assessment limits, of June 9, 1961 (effective U.S.–Germany same day):

12 UST 1029, TIAS no. 4804;

Amended by no. 282 A.

271. Protocol relating to the amendment of article 50 (a) of the convention on international civil aviation (no. 105), of June 21, 1961 (effective U.S.–Germany Aug. 16, 1962):

 13 UST 2105, TIAS no. 5170, 47 D.S.Bull.754 (1962), 514 UNTS 209, BGBl. 1962 II 884, 2169.

272. Arrangements regarding international trade in cotton textiles, of July 29, 1961 (effective U.S.–Germany Oct. 13, 1961):

 45 D.S.Bull.337, 826 (1961):

 Replaced by no. 275.

273. Amendment to the articles of agreement of the International Finance Corporation (no. 213), of Sept. 1, 1961 (effective U.S.–Germany Sept. 21, 1961):

 12 UST 2945, TIAS no. 4894, 439 UNTS 318, BGBl. 1961 II 1149, 1962 II 820, 1965 II 1156.

274. Amendment of the statute of the International Atomic Energy Organization (no. 234), of Oct. 4, 1961 (effective U.S.–Germany Jan. 31, 1963):

 14 UST 135, TIAS no. 5284, 49 D.S.Bull.450 (1963), 471 UNTS 334, BGBl. 1963 II 329, 1965 II 268, BVOBl. Berlin 1963, 723.

274 A. Customs Convention on the A.T.A. carnet for the temporary admission of goods, of Dec. 6, 1961 (effective U.S.–Germany Mar. 3, 1969):

 20 UST 58, TIAS no. 6631, 473 UNTS 219, BGBl. 1965 II 948, 1966 II 52, 1969 II 848.

275. Longterm arrangement regarding international trade in cotton textiles, of Feb. 9, 1962 (effective U.S.–Germany Oct. 1, 1962):

 TIAS no. 5240, 46 D.S.Bull.431 (1962), BGBl. 1970 II 470, 988, GVOBl. Berlin 1970, 1140, 1979;

 Supersedes no. 272; extended by no. 310 A.

276. International agreement regarding the maintenance of certain lights in the Red Sea, of Feb. 20, 1962 (effective U.S.–Germany Oct. 18, 1966):

 17 UST 2145, TIAS no. 6150, 55 D.S.Bull.872 (1966) 597 UNTS 159, BGBl. 1967 II 828, Verträge A298, GVOBl. Berlin 1967, 442.

276 A. Procedure relating to the agreement for the mutual safeguarding of secrecy of inventions relating to defense and for which applications for patents have been made (no. 266), of Mar. 7, 1962, as amended Mar. 15, 1967 (effective U.S.–Germany Sept. 3, 1969):

 BAnz. 1967 no. 163, 1969 no. 194.

277. Final Act of the conference of contracting governments to the international convention for the prevention of pollution of the sea by oil, 1954 (no. 203), of April 11, 1962 (effective U.S.–Germany May 18/June 28, 1967):

 17 UST 1523, TIAS no. 6109, BGBl. 1964 II 749, 1967 II 2330, GVOBl. Berlin 1964, 1044.

278. International wheat agreement of 1962, of Apr. 19, 1962 (effective U.S.–Germany July 16/Aug. 1, 1962):

 13 UST 1571, TIAS no. 5115, 49 D.S.Bull.172 (1963), 444 UNTS 3, BGBl. 1963 II 798, 1965 II 1585, Verträge A 217, GVOBl. Berlin 1963, 916;

 Supersedes no. 248; extended by nos. 293, 303 and 312.

279. Instrument for the amendment of the constitution of the International Labor Organization (no. 58), of June 22, 1962 (effective U.S.–Germany May 22, 1963):

14 UST 1039, TIAS no. 5401, 466 UNTS 323, BGBl. 1964 II 100, Verträge A 8.

280. Final act authenticating the results of the 1960–61 tariff conference of the contracting parties to the general agreement on tariffs and trade (no. 128), of July 16, 1962 (effective U.S.–Germany Jan. 12, 1967):

13 UST 2885, TIAS no. 5253, 440, 441, UNTS, BGBl. 1967 II 1, GVOBl. Berlin 1967, 442.

281. International coffee agreement, of Sept. 28, 1962 (effective U.S.–Germany Aug. 13/Dec. 27, 1963):

14 UST 1911, TIAS no. 5505, 49 D.S.Bull.689 (1963), 469 UNTS 169, BGBl. 1963 II 915, 1964 II 1406, Verträge A 241, GVOBl. Berlin 1963, 997;

Superseded by no. 319.

281 A. Agreement amending the agreement on North Atlantic ocean stations (no. 202), of Dec. 14, 1962 (effective U.S.–Germany same day):

14 UST 133, TIAS no. 5283, BAnz. 1963 no. 220;
Amended by no. 323.

282. Tenth protocol of supplementary concessions to the general agreement on tariffs and trade (no. 128), of Jan. 28, 1963 (effective U.S.–Germany Aug. 15, 1963):

14 UST 1052, TIAS no. 5404, 476 UNTS 254, BGBl. 1966 II 306, GVOBl. Berlin 1967, 440.

282 A. Amendment of art. V of the agreement for joint financing of certain navigation services in Greenland and Faroe Islands (no. 233) by increasing assessment limits, of Apr. 10, 1963 (effective U.S.–Germany same day):

14 UST 470, TIAS no. 5343.

283. Amendments of the Convention of the World Meteorological Organization (no. 127), of Apr. 11/27, 1963 (effective U.S.–Germany same day):

16 UST 2069, TIAS no. 5947, BGBl. 1967 II 1214, GVOBl. Berlin 1967, 740.

283 A. Vienna convention on consular relations, of Apr. 24, 1963 (effective U.S.–Germany Dec. 24, 1969):

TIAS no. 6820, 596 UNTS 261, BGBl. 1969 II 1585, GVOBl. Berlin 1970, 2075, 2094.

284. Additional regulations amending the international sanitary regulations no. 2 (no. 172) in particular with respect to notifications, of May 23, 1963 (effective U.S.–Germany Apr. 14, 1966):

14 UST 1557, TIAS no. 5459, BGBl. 1965 II 1413, 1428, 1966 II 888.

284 A. Amendment of annex III of the 1956 agreements on joint financing of certain air navigation services in Greenland and the Faroe Islands (no. 233) and in Iceland (no. 232), of June 4, 1963 (effective U.S.–Germany Jan. 1, 1964):

14 UST 874, TIAS no. 5369.

285. Protocol to the international convention for the Northwest Atlantic fisheries (no. 148), of July 15, 1963 (effective U.S.–Germany Apr. 29, 1966):

17 UST 635, TIAS no. 6011, 590 UNTS 292, BGBl. 1965 II 409, 1966 II 591, Verträge A 292, GVOBl. Berlin 1965, 744.

286. Protocol for the extension to the international sugar agreement of 1958 (no. 246), of Aug. 1, 1963 (effective U.S.–Germany Feb. 27, 1964):

TIAS no. 5744, BGBl. 1965 II 398, 1966 II 32, 294, GVOBl. Berlin 1966, 760;

Expired on Dec. 31, 1965.

287. Treaty banning nuclear weapon tests in the atmosphere, in outer space and under water, of Aug. 5, 1963 (effective U.S.–Germany Dec. 1, 1964):

14 UST 1313, TIAS no. 5433, 480 UNTS 43, BGBl. 1964 II 906, 1965 II 124, Verträge A 257, GVOBl. Berlin 1964, 1044.

287A. Convention on offenses and certain other acts committed on board aircraft, of Sept. 14, 1963 (effective U.S.–Germany Mar. 16, 1970):

20 UST 2941, TIAS, no. 6768, BGBl. 1969 II 121, 1970 II 276.

288. Partial revision of the radio regulations (Geneva 1959) (no. 250), of Nov. 8, 1963 (effective U.S.–Germany Dec. 2, 1965):

15 UST 887, TIAS no. 5603.

288 A. Indus Basin Development Fund (Supplemental) Agreement, of Mar. 31, 1964 (effective U.S.–Germany Apr. 6, 1964):

15 UST 396, TIAS no. 5570, 503 UNTS 388, BGBl. 1968 II 87, Verträge A 276;

Supplements no. 263.

288 B. Agreement between the parties to the North Atlantic Treaty for cooperation regarding atomic information, of June 18, 1964 (effective U.S.–Germany Mar. 12, 1965):

16 UST 109, TIAS no. 5768, 542 UNTS 145, Verträge A 279;

Supersedes no. 218.

289. Universal Postal Union, of July 10, 1964 (effective U.S.–Germany Jan. 1, 1966):

16 UST 1291, TIAS no. 5881, BGBl. 1965 II 1633, 1966 II 937, 1967 II 822, GVOBl. Berlin 1966, 560, Verträge A 304;

Supersedes no. 241.

290. Agreement establishing interim arangements for a global commercial communications satellite system, of Aug. 20, 1964 (effective U.S.–Germany Sept. 21, 1964):

15 UST 1705, TIAS no. 5646, 514 UNTS 26, BGBl. 1965 II 1498, Verträge A 247, GVOBl. Berlin 1966, 920;

Supplemented by nos. 291 and 296.

291. Special agreement to the agreement establishing interim arrangements for a global commercial communications satellite system (no. 290), of Aug. 20, 1964 (effective U.S.–Germany Sept. 21, 1964):

15 UST 1745, TIAS no. 5646, 514 UNTS 48, BGBl. 1965 II 1498, 1511, Verträge A 247 (vol. 21 p. 454), GVOBl. Berlin 1966, 920;

Supplemented by no. 296.

291 A. Amendments of arts. 17 and 18 of the convention on the Intergovernmental Maritime Consultative Organization (no. 134), of Sept. 15, 1964 (effective U.S.–Germany Oct. 6, 1967):

18 UST 1299, TIAS no. 6285, BGBl. 1968 II 31, GVOBl. Berlin 1968, 528.

292. Protocol amending the general agreement on tariffs and trade (no. 128), to introduce a part IV on trade and development and to amend annex I, of Feb. 8, 1965 (effective U.S.–Germany Jan. 18, 1968):

17 UST 1977, TIAS no. 6139, 572 UNTS 320, BGBl. 1967 II 2005, 1968 II 1031, GVOBl. Berlin 1967, 1454, 1968, 1646.

292 A. Convention on the settlement of investment disputes between states and nationals of other states, of Mar. 18, 1965 (effective U.S.–Germany May 18, 1969):

17 UST 1270, TIAS no. 6090, 575 UNTS 159, BGBl. 1969 II 369, 1191, GVOBl. Berlin 1969, 508, 956.

293. Protocol for the extension of the international wheat agreement, 1962 (no. 278), of Mar. 22, 1965 (effective U.S.–Germany July 16/Aug. 1, 1965):

TIAS no. 5844, BGBl. 1966 II 573, 886, 1967 II 1604, GVOBl. Berlin 1966, 1498;

Extended by no. 303.

294. Convention on facilitation of international maritime traffic, of Apr. 9, 1965 (effective U.S.–Germany Sept. 24, 1967):

18 UST 411, TIAS no. 6251, 591 UNTS 265, BGBl. 1967 II 2434, GVOBl. Berlin 1968, 108.

295. Additional regulations amending the international sanitary regulations no. 2 (no. 172), in particular with respect to disinfecting of ships and aircraft and appendices 3 and 4, of May 12, 1965 (effective U.S.–Germany Jan. 5, 1967):

16 UST 1117, TIAS no. 5863, BGBl. 1966 II 802, 1967 II 2083, GVOBl. Berlin 1967, 1240.

296. Supplementary agreement on arbitration relating to the interim arrangements for a global commercial communications satellite system (no. 290), of June 4, 1965 (effective U.S.–Germany Nov. 21, 1966):

TIAS no. 5646.

297. Amendment of the articles of agreement of the International Finance Corporation (no. 213), of Sept. 1, 1965 (effective U.S.–Germany same day):

BGBl. 1965 II 1089, 1966 II 97, GVOBl. Berlin 1965, 1826.

298. Amendment to art. 28 of the convention on the Intergovernmental Maritime Consultative Organization (no. 134), of Sept. 28, 1965 (effective U.S.–Germany Nov. 3, 1968):

19 UST 4855, TIAS no. 6490, BGBl. 1968 II 1033, 1969 II 108, GVOBl. Berlin 1969, 278.

299. Protocol for the further prolongation of the international sugar agreement of 1958 (no. 246), of Nov. 1, 1965 (effective U.S.–Germany Jan. 1, 1966):

TIAS no. 5933, BGBl. 1966 II 1571, 1967 II 2084, GVOBl. Berlin 1967, 1240;

Expired Dec. 31, 1966 (BGBl. 1967 II 2341).

300. International telecommunication convention with annexes, of Nov. 12, 1965 (effective U.S.–Germany Dec. 16, 1968):

18 UST 575, TIAS no. 6267, BGBl. 1968 II 931, 1969 II 585, GVOBl. Berlin 1969, 338, 492.

300A. Protocol modifying art. 4 of the convention regarding international expositions (no. 73 A), of Nov. 17, 1965 (effective U.S.–Germany June 24, 1968):

19 UST 5974, TIAS no. 6549, BGBl. 1968 II 509, 1969 II 1467, 1970 II 470.

300B. Protocol to the international convention for the Northwest Atlantic fisheries (no. 148) relating to entry into force of proposals adopted by the Commission, of Nov. 29, 1965 (effective U.S.–Germany Dec. 19, 1969):

TIAS no. 6840, BGBl. 1969 II 745, 1970 II 189, GVOBl. Berlin 1969, 604, 1970, 668.

300C. Protocol to the international convention for the Northwest Atlantic fisheries (no. 148), relating to measures of control, of Nov. 29, 1965 (effective U.S.–Germany Dec. 19, 1969):

TIAS no. 6841, BGBl. 1969 II 745, 1970 II 189, GVOBl. Berlin 1969, 604.

301. Agreement establishing the Asian Development Bank, of Dec. 4, 1965 (effective U.S.–Germany Aug. 30, 1966):

17 UST 1418, TIAS no. 6103, 571 UNTS 123, BGBl. 1966 II 617, 1967 II 765, 1968 II 906, Verträge A 295, GVOBl. Berlin 1966, 1498;

Rectified no. 318 A.

302. Amendment to the articles of agreement for the International Bank for Reconstruction and Development (no. 110), of Dec. 16, 1965 (effective U.S.–Germany same day):

16 UST 1942, TIAS no. 5929, BGBl. 1965 II 1089, 1966 II 97.

302 A. Articles of agreement of the International Institute for Cotton, of Jan. 17, 1966 (effective U.S.–Germany Aug. 15, 1969):

17 UST 83, TIAS no. 5964, 592 UNTS 171, see BGBl. 1969 II 1525.

303. Protocol for further extension of the international wheat agreement, 1962 U.S.–Germany July 9, 1969):

17 UST 948, TIAS no. 6057, BGBl. 1967 II 1609, 1968 II 1, GVOBl. Berlin 1967, 916, 1968, 629.

303 A. International convention on load lines, 1966, of Apr. 5, 1966 (effective U.S.–Germany July 9, 1969):

18 UST 1857, TIAS no. 6331, BGBl. 1969 II 249, 1231, GVOBl. Berlin 1969, 508, 956.

304. Partial revision of the radio regulations (Geneva 1959) (no. 256), of Apr. 29, 1966:

18 UST 2091, TIAS no. 6332.

305. Amendment of article V of the agreement for the joint financing of certain air navigation services in Iceland (no. 232) by increasing assessment limits, of May 19, 1966 (effective U.S.–Germany same day):

17 UST 1521, TIAS no. 6108.

306. Protocol for the further prolongation of the international sugar agreement of 1958 (no. 246), of Nov. 14, 1966 (effective U.S.–Germany Apr. 19, 1968):
TIAS no. 6417, BGBl. 1968 II 41, 561, GVOBl. Berlin 1968, 310, 1113; Expired Dec. 31, 1968 (BGBl. 1969 II 2194, GVOBl. Berlin 1970, 692).

307. Treaty on principles governing the activities of states in the exploration and use of outer space, of Jan. 27, 1967 (effective U.S.–Germany Feb. 10, 1971):
18 UST 2410, TIAS no. 6347, 610 UNTS 267, BGBl. 1969 II 1967, 1971 II 166, GVOBl. Berlin 1969, 2549.

308. Protocol relating to the status of refugees, of Jan. 31, 1967 (effective U.S.–Germany Nov. 5, 1969):
19 UST 6223, TIAS no. 6577, 606 UNTS 267, BGBl. 1969 II 1293, 1970 II 194, GVOBl. Berlin 1969, 2052, 1970, 1482.

309. Amendments to the World Meteorological Organization Convention (no. 127), of Apr. 11/26, 1967 (effective U.S.–Germany same dates):
18 UST 2800, TIAS no. 6364, BGBl. 1970 II 18, GVOBl. Berlin 1970, 692.

310. Amendment of article V of agreement for joint financing of certain air navigation services in Greenland and the Faroe Islands (no. 233) by increasing assessment limits, of Apr. 18, 1967:
19 UST 6214, TIAS no. 6575.

310A. Protocol extending the arrangement regarding international trade in cotton textiles (no. 275), of May 1, 1967 (effective U.S.–Germany Oct. 1, 1967):
18 UST 1337, TIAS no. 6289, BGBl. 1970 II 489, 988, GVOBl. Berlin 1970, 1140, 1979.

311. Convention on the International Hydrographic Organization, of May 3, 1967 (effective U.S.–Germany Sept. 22, 1970):
BGBl. 1969 II 418, 1970 II 906, GVOBl. Berlin 1969, 372, 1970, 1914.

312. 1967 Protocol for the further extension of the international wheat agreement, 1962 (no. 278), of June 1, 1967 (effective U.S.–Germany July 16, 1967):
TIAS no. 6315, BGBl. 1968 II 787, GVOBl. Berlin 1968, 1454;
Expired July 1, 1968.

313. Amendment of the convention concerning customs facilities for touring (no. 204), of June 6, 1967 (effective U.S.–Germany same day):
19 UST 4684, TIAS no. 6461, 596 UNTS 542, BGBl. 1968 II 231.

314. Geneva (1967) protocol to the general agreement on tariffs and trade (no. 128), of June 30, 1967 (effective U.S.–Germany Dec. 31, 1968):
19 UST 1, TIAS no. 6425, 620–629 UNTS, BGBl. 1968 II 1184, 1969 II 765, GVOBl. Berlin 1969, 338, 492.

315. Agreement on implementation of art. VI of the general agreement on tariffs and trade (no. 128), of June 30, 1967 (effective U.S.–Germany Dec. 31, 1968):
19 UST 4348, TIAS no. 6431, BGBl. 1968 II 1200, 1969 II 765, GVOBl. Berlin 1969, 338, 492.

316. Convention establishing the World Intellectual Property Organization, of July 14, 1967 (effective U.S.–Germany Sept. 19, 1970):
BGBl. 1970 II 295, 1070, GVOBl. Berlin 1970, 1140, 1979.

317. Convention for the protection of industrial property, of Mar. 20, 1883, as revised July 14, 1967 (effective U.S. [only arts. 13–30]–Germany Sept. 19, 1970):

BGBl. 1970 II 391, 1073, GVOBl. Berlin 1970, 1140, 1979;

Supersedes in part no. 244.

318. International grains arrangement 1967, comprising the Wheat trade convention and the Food aid convention, of Oct. 15/Nov. 30, 1967 (effective U.S.–Germany Apr. 10, 1969):

19 UST 5499, 5772, TIAS no. 6537, BGBl. 1969 II 613, 1270, GVOBl. Berlin 1969, 604, 956.

318A. Proces-verbal of rectification of the agreement establishing the Asian Development Bank (no. 301), of Nov. 2, 1967 (effective same date):

18 UST 2935, TIAS no. 6387, BGBl. 1968 II 906.

318B. International Coffee Agreement, 1968, of Mar. 28, 1968 (effective U.S.–Germany Oct. 1, 1968):

19 UST 6333, TIAS no. 6584, BGBl. 1968 II 665, 927, 1969 II 587, GVOBl. Berlin 1968, 1454, 1640, 1969, 492;

Supersedes no. 281.

319. Amendment to the articles of agreement of the International Monetary Fund, of Apr./May 1968 (effective U.S.–Germany July 28, 1969):

TIAS no. 6748, BGBl. 1968 II 1227, 1969 II 1552, GVOBl. Berlin 1969, 338, 2556.

320. Declaration of the three Powers on the lapse of the Allied reserved powers, of May 27, 1968 (effective same date):

BGBl. 1968 I 714, 1968 II 570.

321. Letters on the termination of provisions concerning the deconcentration of the German coal and iron industry in the settlement convention (no. 184), of July 31/Sept. 17, 1968 (effective U.S.–Germany same date):

BGBl. 1969 II 607.

322. Agreement regarding the status of personnel of sending states attached to an international military headquarters of NATO in the Federal Republic of Germany, of Feb. 7, 1969 (effective U.S.–Germany Dec. 21, 1969):

TIAS no. 6792, BGBl. 1969 II 2044, 1970 II 51.

323. Agreement regarding the making available by the armed forces of the United Kingdom and of the United States of America of accommodation to international military headquarters of NATO in the Federal Republic of Germany, of Feb. 7, 1969 (effective U.S.–Germany Dec. 21, 1969):

TIAS no. 6791, BGBl. 1969 II 2048, 1970 II 51.

324. Agreement amending the administrative agreement of Dec. 1, 1954 concerning the Arbitral Tribunal and the Mixed Commission under the agreement on German external debts (no. 210), of June 26, 1969 (effective U.S.–Germany same date):

BAnz. 1969 no. 202, GVOBl. Berlin 1969, 2458.

325. Agreement amending annex II of the agreement on North Atlantic ocean stations (no. 202), of Nov. 12, 1969 (effective same day):

BAnz. 1970 no. 71.

APPENDIX IV

Abbreviations

Books Cited in Abbreviated Form:

ARNOLD/HILL/KERN, Der Freundschafts-, Handels- und Schiffahrtsvertrag zwischen der Bundesrepublik Deutschland und den Vereinigten Staaten von Amerika vom 29. Oktober 1954: Supplement to BAnz. no. 141 of July 26, 1955.

BAUMBACH/LAUTERBACH, Zivilprozessordnung (29th ed. 1966).

COHN, Manual of German Law, vol. I (2d ed. 1968).

DOCUMENTS ON GERMANY, *see*: United States Senate.

DOMKE, American–German Private Law Relations Cases 1945–1955 (1956).

EHRENZWEIG, Private International Law. General Part (1967).

Gutachten zum Internationalen und ausländischen Privatrecht 1965 und 1966 (1968), cited IPG.

HACKWORTH, Digest of International Law (8 vols. 1940–1944).

HENTRICH, Der Freundschafts-, Handels- und Schiffahrtsvertrag zwischen der Bundesrepublik Deutschland und den Vereinigten Staaten von Amerika in seiner Bedeutung für den Arbeitnehmer, BArbBl. 1956, 512–515.

KEGEL, Internationales Privatrecht (2d ed. 1964), cited as KEGEL, IPR.

KEGEL, Comments on arts. 7–31 EGBGB in SOERGEL/SIEBERT, Kommentar zum BGB, vol. V (9th ed. 1961), cited as KEGEL, Kommentar.

MANUAL OF GERMAN LAW, ed. by British Foreign Office, vol. 2 (1952).

NEUHAUS, Die Grundbegriffe des Internationalen Privatrechts (1962).

PALANDT, Bürgerliches Gesetzbuch (28th ed. 1969).

RAAPE, Internationales Privatrecht (5th ed. 1961).

RABEL, The Conflict of Laws, vol. 1 (2d ed. 1958); vol. 2 (2d ed. 1960); vol. 3 (2d ed. 1964); vol. 4 (1958).

RIEZLER, Internationales Zivilprozessrecht und prozessuales Fremdenrecht (1949).

SCHWENK, Der neue Freundschafts-, Handels- und Schiffahrtsvertrag zwischen der Bundesrepublik Deutschland und den Vereinigten Staaten von Amerika, JZ 1957, 197–204.

STAUDINGER, Kommentar zum Bürgerlichen Gesetzbuch und dem Einführungsgesetz, vol. VI/2 (9th ed. 1931) by Raape.

STEIN/JONAS/SCHÖNKE/POHLE, Kommentar zur Zivilprozessordnung (18th ed. 1953–1956); (19th ed. 1964 ss.).

United States Senate, Committee on Foreign Relations (87th Congress, 1st session), Documents on Germany 1944–1961 (1961), cited DOCUMENTS ON GERMANY.

WHITEMAN, Digest of International Law (vols. 1–5, 1963–1965; vol. 8, 1967; vols 10–11, 1968).

WIECZOREK, Zivilprozessordnung und Nebengesetze (5 parts in 8 vols. with register volume and supplement volume, 1957–1963).

WILSON, R. R., United States Commercial Treaties and International Law (New Orleans 1960).

WOLFF, Martin, Das internationale Privatrecht Deutschlands (3d ed. 1954).

Other Abbreviations:

ABl.DRPVerw.	Amtsblatt der Deutschen Reichs-Post-Verwaltung
A.D.	Annual Digest (and Reports) of Public International Law Cases
ADS	Allgemeine Deutsche Seeversicherungsbedingungen of 1919
AG	Amtsgericht
AH/RiA	Aussenhandel und innerdeutscher Handel, annex Recht im Aussenhandel
A.J.I.L.	The American Journal of International Law
AnnSächsOLG	Annalen des Sächsischen Oberlandesgerichts zu Dresden
AP	Arbeitsrechtliche Praxis. Sammlung der Entscheidungen des Bundesarbeitsgerichts, der Landesarbeitsgerichte und Arbeitsgerichte; now: Arbeitsrechtliche Praxis. Nachschlagewerk des Bundesarbeitsgerichts
ArchVR	Archiv des Völkerrechts
AWD	Aussenwirtschaftsdienst des Betriebs-Beraters
B	Beiblatt
Bad.GVOBl.	Gesetz und Verordnungsblatt für das Grossherzogtum Baden
Bad.RegBl.	Grossherzoglich Badisches Regierungsblatt
Bad.Rspr.	Annalen der Grossh. Badischen Gerichte
BAG	Bundesarbeitsgericht
BAGS	Entscheidungen des Bundesarbeitsgerichts
BAnz.	Bundesanzeiger
Bayer.RegBl.	Regierungsblatt für das Königreich Bayern
Bayer.Standesbeamter	Bayerischer Standesbeamter
BayGVBl.	Bayerisches Gesetz- und Verordnungsblatt
BayObLG	Bayerisches Oberstes Landesgericht
BayObLGZ	Entscheidungen des Bayerischen Obersten Landesgerichts in Zivilsachen
BayVerfGH	Bayerischer Verfassungsgerichtshof
BayZ	Zeitschrift für Rechtspflege in Bayern
BB	Der Betriebsberater
BEG	Bundesgesetz zur Entschädigung für Opfer der nationalsozialistischen Verfolgung (Bundesentschädigungsgesetz of June 29, 1956, BGBl. I. S. 559, 562)
BFH	Bundesfinanzhof
	Sammlung der Entscheidungen und Gutachten des Bundesfinanzhofs
BGB	Bürgerliches Gesetzbuch
BGBl.	Bundesgesetzblatt (1867–1870: des Norddeutschen Bundes from 1949: der Bundesrepublik Deutschland)
BGH	Bundesgerichtshof
BGHSt.	Entscheidungen des Bundesgerichtshofs in Strafsachen
BGHZ	Entscheidungen des Bundesgerichtshofs in Zivilsachen
Bl.f.PMZ	Blatt für Patent-, Muster- und Zeichenwesen
BlIntPr.	Blätter für internationales Privatrecht
Bolze	Die Praxis des Reichsgerichts in Zivilsachen (ed. by BOLZE)
BPatG	Bundespatentgericht
BPatGE	Entscheidungen des Bundespatentgerichts
Brem.GBl.	Gesetzblatt der Freien Hansestadt Bremen
BSG	Bundessozialgericht
BSGE	Entscheidungen des Bundessozialgerichts

BStBl.	Bundessteuerblatt
Bull.Inst.Interméd.	Bulletin de l'Institut Intermédiaire International
BVerfG	Bundesverfassungsgericht
BVerfGE	Entscheidungen des Bundesverfassungsgerichts
BVerwG	Bundesverwaltungsgericht
BVerwGE	Entscheidungen des Bundesverwaltungsgerichts
CBl.	Centralblatt für das Deutsche Reich
CCG	Control Council of Germany
Clunet	Journal du droit international privé
CoA-Rep.	United States Military Government Courts for the U.S. Area of Control in Germany/U.S. Courts of the Allied High Commission for Germany, Court of Appeals Reports
DAR	Deutsches Autorecht
DAVorm.	Der Amtsvormund
DAWRd.	Deutsche Aussenwirtschafts-Rundschau
DFG	Deutsche Freiwillige Geritchtsbarkeit
Die AG	Die Aktiengesellschaft
DJZ	Deutsche Juristenzeitung
DNotZ	Deutsche Notar-Zeitschrift
DÖV	Die öffentliche Verwaltung
DR	Deutsches Recht
DRAnz.	Deutscher Reichsanzeiger
DRiZ	Deutsche Richterzeitung
DRpfl.	Der deutsche Rechtspfleger
DRZ	Deutsche Rechts-Zeitschrift
Dt.Hand.Arch.	Deutsches Handelsarchiv
DVBl.	Deutsches Verwaltungsblatt
EGBGB	Einführungsgesetz zum Bürgerlichen Gesetzbuch of Aug. 18, 1896
EheG	Ehegesetz of July 6, 1938 (RGBl. I S. 807)
EJF	Entscheidungen aus dem Jugend- und Familienrecht
ElsLothZ	Juristische Zeitschrift für Elsass-Lothringen
EuV	Erfindungs- und Vorschlagswesen
FamRZ	Ehe und Familie im privaten und öffentlichen Recht (since 1962: Zeitschrift für das gesamte Familienrecht)
FJG	Die Entscheidungen des deutschen Reichsgerichts in völkerrechtlichen Fragen I: 1879–1929 (Fontes Juris Gentium A II 1) (Berlin 1931) II: 1929–1945 (Fontes Juris Gentium A II 2) (Berlin/Köln 1960)
Frankf.Rundsch.	Rundschau. Sammlung von Entscheidungen in Rechts- u. Verwaltungssachen aus dem Bezirke des OLG Frankfurt a. M.
Gew.Arch.	Gewerbearchiv
GewO	Gewerbeordnung
GG	Grundgesetz für die Bundesrepublik Deutschland of May 23, 1949
Gruchot	Beiträge zur Erläuterung des Deutschen Rechts (founded by GRUCHOT)
GRUR	Gewerblicher Rechtsschutz und Urheberrecht

GRUR/Ausl.	Gewerblicher Rechtsschutz und Urheberrecht, Auslands- und internationaler Teil
GS	Gesetzessammlung
GVG	Gerichtsverfassungsgesetz of Jan. 27, 1877
GVOBl.	Gesetz- und Verordnungsblatt
H	Hauptblatt
Hamb.VO	Sammlung der Verordnungen der freyen Hanse-Stadt Hamburg
Hann.GS	Gesetz-Sammlung für das Königreich Hannover
HansGZ	Hanseatische Gerichtszeitung
HansRGZ	Hanseatische Rechts- und Gerichtszeitschrift
Hess.RegBl.	Grossherzoglich Hessisches Regierungsblatt
HGB	Handelsgesetzbuch of May 10, 1897
HICOG	High Commissioner of the United States in Germany
HRR	Höchstrichterliche Rechtsprechung
ILR	International Law Reports
IPG	Gutachten zum Internationalen und ausländischen Privatrecht
IPRspr.	Die deutsche Rechtsprechung auf dem Gebiete des internationalen Privatrechts im Jahre ...
IzRspr.	Sammlung der deutschen Entscheidungen zum interzonalen Privatrecht
JFG	Jahrbuch für Entscheidungen in Angelegenheiten der freiwilligen Gerichtsbarkeit und des Grundbuchrechts
JFGErg.	Entscheidungen des Kammergerichts und des Oberlandesgerichts München in Kosten-, Straf-, Miet- und Pachtschutzsachen
JIR	Jahrbuch für internationales (und ausländisches öffentliches) Recht
JMBl.NRW	Justizministerialblatt für das Land Nordrhein-Westfalen
JR	Juristische Rundschau
JRdsch.	Juristische Rundschau
JuS	Juristische Schulung
JW	Juristische Wochenschrift
JZ	Juristenzeitung
KG	Kammergericht (Berlin)
KGBl.	Blätter für Rechtspflege im Bezirk des Kammergerichts
KGJ	Jahrbuch für Entscheidungen des Kammergerichts in Sachen der freiwilligen Gerichtsbarkeit, in Kosten-, Stempel- und Strafsachen
KO	Konkursordnung of Feb. 10, 1877 (RGBl. S. 351)
KRG	Kontrollratsgesetz
KTS	Konkurs-, Treuhand- und Schiedsgerichtwesen
LAG	Landesarbeitsgericht
LG	Landgericht
LitUrhG	Gesetz, betr. das Urheberrecht an Werken der Literatur und der Tonkunst of June 19, 1901
LM	Nachschlagewerk des Bundesgerichtshofs (edited by LINDENMAIER, MÖHRING and others)
LSG	Landessozialgericht
LZ	Leipziger Zeitschrift für Deutsches Recht

MDR	Monatsschrift für Deutsches Recht
Meck.-Schwer.GS	Gesetzsammlung für die Mecklenburg-Schwerinschen Lande
Mil.Gov.Ordinances	Ordinances of the United States Military Government in Germany
NiemZ	Zeitschrift für internationales Privat- u. Strafrecht (founded by NIEMEYER)
NJW	Neue Juristische Wochenschrift
NJW/RzW	Neue Juristische Wochenschrift/Rechtsprechung zum Wiedergutmachungsrecht
Off.Gaz.	Official Gazette
Off.Gaz.CCG	Official Gazette of the Control Council for Germany
OFH	Oberster Finanzhof
OG	Oberstes Gericht
OGH Köln	Oberster Gerichshof für die Britische Zone
OGHZ	Entscheidungen des Obersten Gerichtshofes für die Britische Zone in Zivilsachen
OGZ	Entscheidungen des Obersten Gerichts der Deutschen Demokratischen Republik in Zivilsachen
Oldenb.GBl.	Gesetzblatt für das Herzogtum Oldenburg
OLG	Oberverwaltungsgericht
	Die Rechtsprechung der Oberlandesgerichte auf dem Gebiete des Zivilrechts
OLGZ	Entscheidungen der Oberlandesgerichte in Zivilsachen einschliesslich der freiwilligen Gerichtsbarkeit
ORG	Oberstes Rückerstattungsgericht
ORGE	Entscheidungen des Obersten Rückerstattungsgerichts
OVG	Oberverwaltungsgericht
PatG	Patentgesetz of May 5, 1936 (RGBl. II S. 117), i.d.F.v. 9.5.1961 (BGBl. I S. 550)
Preuss.GS	Gesetzsammlung für die Königlich Preussischen Staaten
RabelsZ	Zeitschrift für ausländisches und internationales Privatrecht (founded by RABEL)
RAG	Reichsarbeitsgericht
RAnz.	Reichsanzeiger
RdA	Recht der Arbeit
Recht	Das Recht
RegBl.	Regierungsblatt
Rev.crit.(dip)	Revue critique de droit international privé
RFH	Reichsfinanzhof
	Sammlung der Entscheidungen und Gutachten des Reichsfinanzhofs
RG	Reichsgericht
RGBl.	Reichsgesetzblatt
RGSt.	Entscheidungen des Reichsgerichts in Strafsachen
RG Warn.	Sammlung zivilrechtlicher Entscheidungen des Reichsgerichts
RGZ	Entscheidungen des Reichsgerichts in Zivilsachen
RheinArch.	Archiv für Zivil- und Strafrecht der kgl. preuss. Rheinprovinz
RheinZ	Rheinische Zeitschrift für Zivil- und Prozessrecht

RJA	Entscheidungen in Angelegenheiten der freiwilligen Gerichtsbarkeit und Grundbuchrechts, zusammengest. im Reichjustizamt
RMBl.	Reichsministerialblatt
ROHG	Reichsoberhandelsgericht
ROHGE	Entscheidungen des Reichsoberhandelsgerichts
ROW	Recht in Ost und West
Rpfl.	Der deutsche Rechtspfleger
Rpfleger	Der deutsche Rechtspfleger
Rspr.	Rechtsprechung
RuStAG	Reichs- und Staatsangehörigkeitsgesetz July 22, 1913
RVO	Reichsversicherungsordnung of July 19, 1911, i.d.F.v. 15.12.1924
RzW	Rechtsprechung zum Wiedergutmachungsrecht
Sächs.GVOBl.	Gesetz- und Verordnungsblatt für das Königreich Sachsen
SBZ	Soviet occupation zone
SchlHA	Schleswig-Holsteinische Anzeigen
SeuffArch.	Seufferts Archiv für Entscheidungen der obersten Gerichte in den deutschen Staaten
SJZ	Süddeutsche Juristenzeitung
St.Archiv	Das Staatsarchiv (1861–1919, 1929)
StAZ	Das Standesamt
StbG	Staatsbürgerschaftsgesetz of Feb. 20, 1967
StGB	Strafgesetzbuch für das Deutsche Reich
Ufita	Archiv für Urheber-, Film- (ab 18. 1954:) Funk- und Theaterrecht
U.S.HICOG	United States High Commission for Germany
U.S.Mil.Gov.	United States Military Government (for Germany)
UWG	Gesetz gegen den unlauteren Wettbewerb of June 7, 1909
VersR	Versicherungsrecht
Verträge	Verträge der Bundesrepublik Deutschland Serie A: Multilaterale Verträge
VG	Verwaltungsgericht
VO	Verordnung(en)
VOBl.	Verordnungsblatt
Warn(Rspr.)	Rechtsprechung des Reichsgerichts, soweit sie nicht in der amtlichen Sammlung der Entscheidungen des RG abgedruckt ist (edited by WARNEYER)
WG	Wechselgesetz of June 21, 1933
WM	Wertpapier-Mitteilungen
Württ.RegBl.	Regierungsblatt für das Königreich Württemberg
WürttZ	Württembergische Zeitschrift für Rechtspflege und Verwaltung
WZG	Warenzeichengesetz of May, 1936
ZBl.	Zentralblatt für das Deutsche Reich
ZblJugR	Zentralblatt für Jugendrecht und Jugendwohlfahrt
ZPO	Zivilprozessordnung
ZZP	Zeitschrift für Zivilprozess

Table of Cases

[REFERENCES ARE TO PAGES]

I. (West-)German Cases

II. Allied Courts in West Germany

III. German Democratic Republic

IV. American Cases

V. English Cases

Index of Subjects

[references are to pages]

Bilateral Studies

In Private International Law

No. 1: American-Swiss Private International Law, New York, 1st edition 1951, 2nd edition 1958,
by Arthur Nussbaum

No. 2: American-French Private International Law, New York, 1st edition, 1953, 2nd edition 1961,
by Georges R. Delaume

No. 3: American-Dutch Private International Law, New York, 1st edition 1955, 2nd edition 1961,
by R. D. Kollewijn

No. 4: American-German Private International Law, 1st edition [American-German Private Law Relations Cases 1945–1955], New York, 1956, by Martin Domke; 2nd edition, revised and expanded, Dobbs Ferry, 1972,
by Ulrich Drobnig

No. 5: American-Colombian Private International Law, New York, 1956,
by Phanor J. Eder

No. 6: American-Greek Private International Law, New York, 1957,
by Albert A. Ehrenzweig, Charalambos Fragistas and Athanassios Yiannopoulos

No. 7: American-Danish Private International Law, New York, 1957,
by Allan Philip

No. 8: American-Australian Private International Law, New York, 1957,
by Zelman Cowen

No. 9: American-Brazilian Private International Law, New York, 1959,
by Paul Griffith Garland

No. 10: American-Chilean Private International Law, New York, 1960,
by Alfredo Etcheberry O.

No. 11: American-Austrian Private International Law, Dobbs Ferry, 1963,
by Ignaz Seidl-Hohenveldern

No. 12: American-Japanese Private International Law, Dobbs Ferry, 1964,
by Albert A. Ehrenzweig, Sueo Ikehara and Norman Jensen

No. 13: American-Swedish Private International Law, Dobbs Ferry, 1965,
by Håkan Nial

No. 14: American-Venezuelan Private International Law, Dobbs Ferry, 1965,
by Richard S. Lombard

No. 15: American-Argentine Private International Law, Dobbs Ferry, 1966,
by Werner Goldschmidt and José Rodriguez-Novás

No. 16: American-Turkish Private International Law, Dobbs Ferry, 1966,
by Tugrul Ansay

No. 17: American-Belgian Private International Law, Dobbs Ferry, 1968,
by Georges van Hecke

The publishers will be happy to place your name on standing order for future publications.